W9-AVM-248

BECOMING A LONDONER

Fiction

The Ghost of Henry James
Slides
Relatives
The Darkness of the Body
Figures in Bright Air
The Family
The Country
The Woods
The Catholic
The Native
The Accident
Annunciation
The Age of Terror
ABC

Non-fiction

Difficult Women: A Memoir of Three
American Ghosts
The Pure Lover

BECOMING A LONDONER

A Diary

DAVID PLANTE

BLOOMSBURY

NEW YORK · LONDON · NEW DELHI · SYDNEY

Published by Bloomsbury USA, New York

All papers used by Bloomsbury USA are natural, recyclable products made from
wood grown in well-managed forests. The manufacturing processes conform
to the environmental regulations of the country of origin.

LIBRARY OF CONGRESS CATALOGING–IN–PUBLICATION DATA

Plante, David.
Becoming a Londoner : a diary / David Plante. — First U.S. Edition.
pages cm
ISBN: 978-1-62040-188-0 (alk. paper)
1. Plante, David. 2. Plante, David—Friends and associates. 3. Novelists, American—20th
century—Biography. 4. London (England) —Biography. I. Title.
PS3566.L257Z46 2013
813'.54—dc23
[B]
2013018704

First U.S. Edition 2013

1 3 5 7 9 10 8 6 4 2

Typeset by Hewer Text UK Ltd, Edinburgh
Printed and bound in the U.S.A. by Thomson-Shore Inc., Dexter, Michigan

For Paul LeClerc

'You always get it wrong.'

Philip Roth to David Plante

Nikos Stangos and David Plante by Stephen Spender, San Andrea
di Rovereto di Chiavari, 1968

Author's Note

I have kept a diary for over half a century. It is many millions of words long, and is stored in the Berg Collection of the New York Public Library. This present book is just over 165,000 words, and is roughly within the scope of the first twenty or so years of my life in London, 1966 to 1986, with events from later. The book consists of selections taken from my diary, all elaborated upon by memory and, too, made informative of people and places for publication, as I find footnotes distracting, though I do sometimes introduce a name and later give the person an identifying context. It is not uncommon for me to take an entire day, or even days, to complete one diary entry. The entries are not chronological – in fact, I have eliminated all but one date with the idea of forming something of a narrative which I hope forms into a world. The narrative continues beyond this book into what may be further books, allowing me in the present book to introduce someone who will, I hope, be more fully realized in the next book. I think of the title of Stephen Spender's World within World as appropriate to what I would like to do – appropriate in many ways, as he is himself a world within the world of this book. To make a book out of the diary has meant choosing what to put in and what to leave out, and though my impulse is to put everything in as the honest way (no doubt a more honest way would be to leave everything out), the book would bulge its covers. I have had to leave out worlds of experience in Italy, in Greece, in France, in Russia, in

New York, in, oh!, Tulsa, Oklahoma, worlds which occurred within the more circumscribed London world that I have concentrated on here. And within the London world I have concentrated on people I think most representative of the culture of that world. I came as a stranger to London and here was lucky enough to form relationships with people I could not have imagined meeting before I came to London. Ideally, I would have liked to start with the very first entry of my diary, June 1959, and only after having included the entries from then arrive at June 1966, this the only date stated in this book. Within the millions of words of my diary there are worlds within worlds, but this book accounts for a span (by no means all of it) of my continuing life in London, in which world capital my life continues to expand far beyond this book.

The entries from my diary featuring Francis Bacon were collated and published in the New Yorker; the entries featuring Harold Acton were expanded from diary entries for a portrait also published in the New Yorker; as for Steven Runciman, I used a tape to record his amazing elaborations on history, especially the history of a hubble-bubble, none of which I could have remembered, the resulting portrait also published in the New Yorker. The events featuring Philip Roth were first published in the New York Times Book Review.

Spelling and usage have sometimes changed into British from American over the years, so I note that I write 'honour' but kept 'gray'. I rather like this evidence of an American becoming British while remaining American as well.

From so many years past, I feel that the events recorded in here have nothing to do with me. I have no idea whom they have to do with, this young man dazed by a world around him that in itself has gone.

As for my continuing the diary now, as a diarist I remain who I was at least in this way: possessed by a diary that is in itself possessive, always anxious that much more has been left out than got (gotten?) in.

David Plante, June 2013

London

June 1966

As I was approaching from one end of the street the house where Nikos lives, 6 Wyndham Place, I saw him approaching from the other end. He was wearing a dark business suit and carrying a briefcase, returning from the office of the press attaché at the Greek Embassy.

Meeting me, he said, 'If you'd come a minute earlier, you would have rung and no one would have answered.'

'I'd have come back,' I said.

I followed close behind him as he opened doors with keys into his flat, so close I bumped into him when he paused just inside to turn to me to ask me, his face so near mine I could have leaned just a little forward and kissed him, if I'd like to go out or stay in to eat.

'I'd prefer to stay in,' I said.

'You like staying in?'

'I do.'

'So do I,' he said.

He said he'd change, and I, in the living room, looked around for something Greek, but saw nothing.

He came from his bedroom wearing grey slacks and a darker grey cardigan, and we had drinks before, he said, he'd prepare us something to eat.

He told me how much he likes America, how much he likes Americans, who were, he believed, the only people capable of true originality.

I asked him why he was living in London.

Because, he said, living in London he was not living in Athens. His job in the office of the press attaché was the only job he had been able to get that would allow him to leave Greece.

Why?

He would tell me later.

I said, 'I have a lot to learn about Greece.'

He showed me one of his poems, written in English. It was called 'Pure Reason', and it was a love poem, addressed to 'you'. The poem read almost as if it were arguing a philosophical idea with the person addressed, the terms of the argument as abstract as any philosophical argument. The philosophical idea is reasoning at its purest. What is remarkable about the poem is that, in conveying, as it does, intellectual purity, it conveys, more, emotional purity, and it centres the purity – intellectual and emotional and moral – in the person with whom the poet is so much in love. I had never read anything like it.

When I handed the poem back to him, he asked me if I would stay the night with him.

In his bed, he said to me, 'Even if you're worried that it would hurt me, you must always tell me, honestly, what you think, because, later, your dishonesty would hurt much more.'

I said, 'I'm not certain what I think.'

'About me?'

'About everything.'

————

I am staying with Öçi in his small flat in Swiss Cottage.

He is at work, at Heathrow Airport, where he welcomes and sorts out the problems of visitors using his languages, besides English, Turkish, Greek, Hungarian, Spanish, making him linguistically the most cosmopolitan person I know.

Seven years ago, the Öçi I came to London longing to be with is no longer the Öçi I now know. I was in love with him. I don't love him as I so loved him, but he is a friend.

It seems to me that the Öçi I loved is contained within a room, a moonlit room, in Spain, in a seaside town in Spain, we both in beds across the room from each other, talking. Never mind how we found ourselves in that room, in our separate beds across the room from each other, talking, but remember the smell of suntan lotion, remember the sensation of skin slightly burnt by the sun, remember that skin seemingly made rough by sea salt, remember lying naked in the midst of a tangled sheet, the erection of a nineteen-year-old who had never had sex bouncing against his stomach. We talked, we talked, I can't remember about what – perhaps my telling him that my holiday in Spain would soon come to an end and I would go to the Catholic University of Louvain, Belgium, for the academic year, emphasizing my regret that I would be leaving Spain, which would be leaving all that was promised in my having met him – and then silence between us. He got up from his bed and, naked, went to the open window and leaned out into the moonlight and breathed the fresh pre-dawn air, from where he turned to me and I held out my arms to him. Never, never had I known such a sensation, never, and I fell in love with Öçi for the wonder of that sensation.

A sensation I had to have again and again with him, because I felt that it was only with him that such a sensation was possible.

I went to Louvain, but longed for Öçi in Spain.

When he wrote that he would be in London for the winter holidays, I, possessed by my love, came to London.

He did not love me.

Leave this, from seven years ago, but remember that moonlit room.

When I told Öçi that I had met someone named Nikos Stangos, whom I liked, he said he would find out about this Nikos Stangos through his connections. He smiled his slow, sensual, ironical smile, and said he had many connections, in Turkey, in Greece, in Spain, even in Hungary if I was interested, and, of course, in London.

Later, Öçi told me he had made contact with a Greek who had met Nikos, and, as always with his slow, sensual, ironical smile, as if this was his attitude towards all the world, he said that he had heard that Nikos, working in the Press Office of the Greek Embassy, is 'acceptable.'

I tried to smile, saying, 'That's good to know.'

———

I rang Nikos at the Press Office of the Greek Embassy. He said he had thought of going, that evening, to a cello recital by Rostropovich at the Royal Festival Hall. Would I like to go with him? During the recital I was attentive to his attention to the music. As always, I felt that he was in a slight trance; it showed in his stillness, but also in what appeared to me a presence about him, as if his calm extended around his body.

After the recital, he was silent. I didn't know why he was so silent, but I, too, remained silent. Delicate as the calm was that appeared to extend all about him, I felt, within him, a solid gravity; it was as if that gravity caused the outward, trance-like calm by its inward pull. Silent, we crossed the Thames on the walkway over Hungerford Bridge. The trains to the side of the walkway made the bridge sway. In the middle, Nikos reached into a pocket of his jacket and took out a large copper penny, which he threw down into the grey-brown, swiftly moving river far below.

'What's that for?' I asked.

'For luck,' he said.

The evening was warm and light. We walked from the Embankment at Charing Cross up to Trafalgar Square, all the while silent.

In Trafalgar Square, he suggested we sit, and we walked among the people standing in groups to the far left corner, behind a great, gushing fountain, where there was no one else and we sat on a stone bench.

We wondered who, in history, had first thought of a water-gushing fountain. In ancient Greece, Nikos said, a fountain was usually a public spigot that water flowed from to fill jugs brought by women. Perhaps the ancient Romans first thought of a gushing fountain that had no use but to look at?

After a silence, Nikos said he had thought very carefully, and he wanted me, too, to think carefully, about what he was going to say. It was very, very important that I be totally honest.

He was in a love relationship with an older Englishman, who was in fact away, and Nikos decided that on the Englishman's return he would tell him their love relationship must come to an end. He had decided this on meeting me, but I must not think that this meant I should feel I had to return the feelings Nikos had for me. I was free, and I must always know that I am free. Then he asked me if I would live with him.

I placed my hands over my face and rocked back and forth.

I moved in with him the next day.

He is twenty-eight and I am twenty-six.

———

Öçi is offended that I should have left him to move in with Nikos. He sent me a sarcastic letter, denouncing me for my 'opportunism' in my 'affiliation with Mr. Stangos,' who I must think can offer me more than he, Öçi, can as a friend. I showed the letter to Nikos; he said that he would find out about Öçi among Greeks living in London (Öçi's mother is Greek from the Pontus in Turkey, his father Hungarian, and he grew up in Turkey), and when Nikos did he said that he had passed on a message to Öçi through the network of Greek connections (a network that Nikos does everything to stay out of) that he would like to meet Öçi, that we should all meet.

———

Nikos was eager to show me something he had received from Stephen Spender, in Washington, which is on his desk in the sitting room. 'Look,' he said, 'a reproduction of Andrea del Castagno's The Youthful David.'

He said he was not sure how he would tell Spender about me when Spender returned to London.

———

We should go for the weekend to Brighton, Nikos said, to see
Francis King, who lives there. Francis has recently published a
novel, called, I think, The Man on the Rock, about an Englishman
falling in love with a Greek young man. With his pointed, pale face
and large, gold-rimmed glasses, Francis King looks like someone
who would work for the British Council, which he did do in Japan
and in Greece. He spoke a little Greek with Nikos. He arranged a
hotel for us. He said he was sorry, he had tried to put us into a
hotel for queers, but it was full up. I was relieved that Nikos and I
were not staying in a queer hotel. Our room had zebra-stripe wallpaper. We met Francis to go to a pub, and as we were entering I
realized it was for queers, and everything in me drew back from
going in with Nikos. He hung back with me and asked what was
wrong. I said, 'I don't want to go in there with you.' He asked me,
please, not to insist, and I went in.

As though he assumed Nikos would be amused, Francis
recounted how, for a pack of cigarettes, he had had sex in Greece
with a shepherd. Nikos smiled a small, tight smile, clearly holding
back from this insult to Greece.

Later, alone, he told me how the long tradition of men from
Northern Europe thinking that Greek boys were there for them to
have sex with is part of the fantasy that these men have of ancient
Greece continuing in the Greece of today, and the Greek boys are
so in need of money that they comply.

He said he was glad I hadn't wanted us to go into that pub.

Why didn't I want to go into the pub? I wanted, and want,
Nikos to have nothing to do with my past in America, in New
York, where I failed, and failed most severely in relationships that I
associate with being in the New York queer world. I want, here in
London, in England, in Great Britain, to form a new life with
Nikos, even though he is Greek and I am American, for we have
both left our countries for new lives in this country.

I want us to be, as a couple, Nikos and David, which I think we
could not be if we were Nikos and David in Athens, which city Nikos
has left, or David and Nikos in New York, which city I have left.

We went to the pier and played at the slot machines, using up many big copper pennies. A penny animated a whole landscape in a glass case: a tiny train ran about a track, children's heads popped out of flowers, and, in the midst, a large, plastic tulip opened and out of it emerged a ballerina, en pointe, who turned round in jerks and then sank back into the tulip, which closed its petals over her.

For the fun of it, Nikos and I took photographs of ourselves together in an automatic booth.

In a junk shop, as if acquiring objects that would fix us in our domestic lives, Nikos and I bought two yellow ceramic pots, an art nouveau vase with purple irises, and four blue volumes of Master-pieces of British Art with a gold art nouveau design on the covers, the objective beginnings of our shared lives.

Nikos showed me a poem which Stephen Spender, who is now resident poet at the Library of Congress in Washington, wrote for him.

> When we talk, I imagine silence
> Beyond the intervalling words: a space
> Empty of all but ourselves there, face to face,
> Away from others, alone in the intense
> Light or dark, it would not matter which.
>
> But where a room envelopes us, one heart,
> Our bodies, locked together, prove apart
> Unless we change them back again to speech.
> Close to you here, looking at you, I see
> Beyond your eyes looking back, that second you
> Of whom the outward semblance is the image –
> The inward being where the name springs true.
> Today, left only with a name, I rage,
> Willing these lines – willing a name to be
> Flesh, on the blank unanswering page.

Nikos said he loved Stephen Spender very much.

———

Why Nikos left Greece, he told me, is history – the history of his father having to leave Bulgaria, where his father's family had lived since when the town, now Sosopol, was the ancient Greek town of Apollonia; and his mother having to leave Constantinople, where her family had been since Byzantium – had to leave because Greece had invaded Bulgaria and Turkey to reclaim, after centuries, the Hellenistic empire, known as the Big Idea, but Greece had been defeated, and the agreement was, in the 1920s, an exchange of populations in which all Greeks had to leave Bulgaria and Turkey and all Bulgarians and Turks had to leave Greece. Nikos' parents were refugees in Athens, and were treated as refugees, Nikos himself always feeling that he was a foreigner in Greece, his accent not Athenian, and, his parents of the diaspora more cultured than native Greeks, more culturally and linguistically international.

He told me that if I meet Greeks who speak various languages, who are informed about art and literature and music, most likely they will have come from Constantinople or Alexandria, from both of which cities they were expelled.

The Exchange of Populations is called the Catastrophe.

'Catastrophe' is a word he often uses.

————

We are back from Yugoslavia, in 6 Wyndham Place. Coming back from our holiday together to his flat makes me feel I am no longer just staying with him, but living with him, so that his flat is my flat too.

In Venice, crossing the Piazza Grande, Nikos put his arm across my shoulders and said, 'Here in Italy, we can walk together like this.' We stayed in a cheap hotel behind the basilica.

The boat from Venice to Opatija stopped for a few hours at Pula. The little seaside town appeared to be all hard edges, with a roughness to it that was like the roughness of the khaki-green uniforms of the soldiers walking down a muddy road. Nikos and I went to the Museum of the Revolution in the ruins of the fortress on a promontory overlooking the town, a small, whitewashed museum with machine guns, yellowing posters and blown-up photographs of executions. We were the only ones there, all around us the summer sound of insects. The museum seemed to be falling apart. Nikos looked at everything carefully, even reverentially, and said, 'I feel so safe here.'

The boat took us to Rijeka, from where we took a taxi to Medveja, outside Opatija, and we found a hotel on the coast, a former mansion of Tito, where we had a small room with two very small beds. It rained a lot. Yugoslavia was not at all like Greece, as Nikos had supposed it would be, so there were no coffee houses to go to and sit out the rain. We stayed a lot in our room.

He had taken Stephen Spender's autobiography World within World for me to read. Often we read it together, both of us squeezed into one of the narrow beds.

This was a touchy period for us. We easily argued, easily became depressed about the rain or the bad food, but were also easily elated when the sun came out or when we were able to order a fresh fish for dinner. Whatever we did, whatever we said, whatever we read took on large proportions, the proportions of a relationship expanding and contracting and expanding again into some form of love. Reading passages from World within World to one another about Stephen Spender's relationship with Jimmy Younger, we were moved to tears.

And for me to read about people I had only ever fantasized about – W. H. Auden, Christopher Isherwood, and the inner world of the fantastic Bloomsbury group which included Virginia Woolf and Leonard Woolf and Vita Sackville-West and Vanessa Bell and Duncan Grant and Lytton Strachey and Lady Ottoline Morrell and T. S. Eliot and E. M. Forster, all of whom Spender in fact knew – was to open up that world, that entirely English world, in which I fantasize having a place, even if that world no longer exists in itself. It exists in the witness of Stephen Spender.

And this is my overwhelming fantasy of England: that it is a country of absolute respect for differences in each and every one, all the more so for the startling originality of each and every one, this respect made possible because they all knew one another, all of them, and they all knew that they had created in their work a new awareness that was English, whatever the Englishness of the aware-ness could be.

I fantasize myself, say, at High Table at King's College Cambridge, with Maynard Keynes presiding, I at one side of him and at the other Rupert Brooke; and after there would be wine in Maynard Keynes' rooms with Dadie Rylands and Virginia Woolf and E. M. Forster, talking about – well, talking about everyone that they knew, talking about them, however critically, with a sense that they made up a world. And they did make up a world, and they knew that the world was English. And they all slept with one another!

But, I have to remind myself, this is my overwhelming fantasy, and I have no idea if it has anything at all to do with England.

When we were lying together in the sun on the rocks by the sea, Nikos again told me that whatever happens between us depends on our being totally honest with one another. Even if I thought him ugly, I must tell him. No, I said, I didn't find him ugly.

————

Is it because I'm in Europe that I am so aware of World War II, and, behind that war, World War I, called the Great War? Our landlady, a delicate and dignified woman of extreme courtesy, on brief visits tells us of her driving a lorry during the last war, and I am aware that the wars did not take place 'over there,' but here, here, around me.

————

While alone here in our home in Wyndham Place, I filled a little notebook with what I can only think of as obscenities, all as if released from having been kept back during my life in New York, released now here in London, gross obscenities. I showed the notebook to Nikos, whose only comment was that the writing itself was good – was, because I then blackened the pages with black ink so that the text can't be read. And so, I think, I have blackened out my life in New York.

My life in London –

————

About Greece –

Nikos has a curious Greek national sense of connection with Prince Philip, whose mother Princess Alice lives in Athens, a nun. After Greek independence from the Ottoman Empire, the only person willing to take on the role of king, as at that time the titular head of any European state had to be, was a young royal from Bohemia, Otho. Princess Alice is by marriage connected to the lineage, and so, Nikos says, is Prince Philip. There are stories about her having hid Jews, and of having set up soup kitchens and having served the food to starving people, during the Nazi occupation of Athens. Apparently, she lives in a modest flat, and whether or not she has contact with her son or her daughter-in-law the Queen, very few people would know.

So I learn about Greece —

Nikos tells me there is no Greek aristocracy, which distinguishes the country from generations of European aristocracy. There are no medieval castles or Renaissance villas, for all the while Europe was evolving from the Middle Ages into the Renaissance, Greece was occupied by the Ottoman Empire. No Greek aristocracy developed around Otho or any subsequent king. The Greek royal family, Nikos said, speak German to one another.

Nikos has taught me to write the name Greece in Greek letters, which letters stand above the country's history like a temple:

ΕΛΛΑΣ

———

I haven't kept this diary in some weeks, during which I think I went through the most emotionally violent time of my life.

Nikos introduced me to acupuncture, which had been introduced to him by the painter Johnny Craxton, for Nikos' migraines; as he found it helped him, he thought the same would help me with what a doctor in New York had suggested was a duodenal ulcer, due, no doubt, to my failed life in New York, a failure that was entirely my own fault, for in New York I had behaved badly, very badly.

The acupuncturist, Indian, Singha, had his surgery in the sitting room of a semi-detached house in Hendon, and I was very skeptical the first time I went as I lay on a trolley and heard pop music from the kitchen, where I presumed his wife was. But I allowed Singha to insert fine needles between my toes and fingers, after which he left me and I had the vivid sense of falling within myself. The sessions over the weeks become confused. I remember his pressing his hands on my chest, over and over, more and more emphatically, until I was breathing in and out in spasms, and I suddenly shouted for my mother and sobbed. He covered me with a blanket and left me until I again felt as if I was falling.

On the bus back to Nikos, I sensed the darkness of my New York – say, my American darkness – open up beneath me dangerously. At home, a deep tiredness came over me after the meal Nikos prepared, as I wasn't able to move, and he helped me to bed, where I slept for over twenty-four hours. The darkness deepened. On the weekends, Nikos and I would go for a walk in Hyde Park, where it seemed to me my very body was straining to go in many different directions at once, each direction to one of the many young men in the park who attracted me, and if I hadn't been with Nikos I would have tried to go in all the directions – as I had tried to do in New York. The fact is, I had come to Europe to be promiscuous, even more promiscuous than I had been in New York, as if in my fantasy Europe offered more sexual promiscuity than America, even New York, because in Europe I would be totally free and not think of being faithful to a relationship. Nikos would say, 'Breathe in, now breathe out,' which I would do, and then – what I longed for – back home for our afternoon nap, where the greatest reassurance beyond sex was falling asleep with Nikos.

The most shocking reaction to the acupuncture didn't occur at Singha's surgery, but back home, where, again, Nikos prepared a meal after which I became immobile, he more or less carrying me to our bed where I fell and suddenly twitched violently, then more and more violently, and I began to make hissing sounds through my bared teeth and then, with clenched fist, to make stabbing gestures. Worried, Nikos rang Singha, who told him to let me be, I would be all right; and I knew I would be, as I was able to look down at myself from a distance and tell myself that I could stop the fit if I wanted to, but, here, safe with Nikos, I could let the fit take its course. It lasted the night, Nikos sitting on the side of the bed. In the morning, I found that the palms of both hands were bleeding from my fingernails. I was in bed for three days, Nikos, before work and after, having to help me to the toilet.

When, back with Singha, I recounted what had happened to me, he appeared not at all surprised, and I thought, well, perhaps it was nothing to be surprised about, but when I left him, walking along Hendon Way, the sunlight slanting through the unpainted pickets of a tall fence, I all at once knew that there was nothing to worry about, that everything would be all right, and a lightness of spirit came to me.

Strange, it is as though I didn't go through all the above, as though it happened to someone else I hardly know.

But how can I not think but that Nikos has cured me of an illness I arrived in London with?

––––––

Nikos told me he had, before he met me, invited a French boy to stay with him in his flat, Alain, and because Alain, coming to London from Paris, was counting on staying Nikos couldn't tell him no. Nikos showed me Alain's letters, in which he wrote, 'I am quite the little homosexual.' Nikos said, 'He isn't. He's joking. He wrote this, flirting, just because he wants to stay in my flat.' Now Alain is staying in the flat with Nikos and me, and he sleeps on the sofa in the sitting room while Nikos and I sleep in the bedroom. He is seventeen.

––––––

Our first drinks party together, the wine and the spirits Nikos bought cheaply from the Greek Embassy for entertaining. Because I was drunk, the only person I recall enough to distinguish him was a very tall, broad, bald-headed man, whose skull appears to be close to the skin, John Lehmann, who is a poet and who was a publisher and who worked with Virginia and Leonard Woolf at the Hogarth Press. No doubt I distinguish him because he seemed to distinguish me from the others, and, before leaving, asked me to 'swiggle' (I think that's what he said) my name and telephone number on a piece of paper. When he saw the number is the same as that of Nikos, he smiled and said, 'You live together,' and I, 'We do,' and he left.

After the drinks party, Nikos and Johnny Craxton and Alain and I went out to a restaurant, and I found I was as bored as Alain because of the talk between Nikos and Craxton about people in London we didn't know. Nikos and Craxton, smoking cigars at the end of the meal, appeared to be settled in for hours, especially when they talked to each other in Greek, and I did feel, somewhat, that I was the boyfriend, as in the periphery as Alain, both of us silent.

Johnny mentioned Lucian Freud, and I, always curious (and perhaps more than curious, possessive of a world I don't know), asked if he knew Lucian Freud, and he said, simply, that he and Lucian Freud once had studios in the same house, and I had the sense he didn't want to say more. But now I make a connection between Johnny Craxton and Lucian Freud, and I wonder what other connections are to be made. Connections criss-cross, invisibly, though the air of London.

It would be disingenuous of me to write that I am not aware of all the connections, all, I imagine, finally connecting into a London world.

Johnny has a house in Chania, Crete, and paints scenes of the Greek countryside of goats eating figs from gnarled trees and young men playing backgammon at coffee-house tables.

Stephen Spender is back in London. Nikos wanted to see him on his own before he introduces him to me. They had lunch together in a restaurant, then came to the flat, where I was waiting with Alain. Nikos came in with Spender, who seemed to pay more attention to Alain than to me. I remarked that Spender is very tall, with very large hands and feet. He made a date with Alain for tea before he left. Nikos went with him to the entry passage to the street door, from where I heard Spender say, 'He's very nice.' I supposed he was talking about me, but maybe he was talking about Alain.

Nikos asked me if I liked him, and I said yes. 'I'm glad,' Nikos said, 'I was anxious that you and he wouldn't like one another, or that Stephen would be upset by your living with me.'

Nikos took Alain and me to dinner that evening, and back at the flat Alain again slept on the sofa while Nikos and I slept together in the bedroom.

I wonder what Alain makes of us sleeping together, and, he must hear, making love together. He simply smiles a large, clear, young smile.

What worlds within worlds am I living in?

———

I didn't come directly from New York to London, but from New York went to Boston, wanting to get away from New York, but I left Boston soon after to come to London for the same reason that I had left New York: not sexual promiscuity, but sexual unfaithfulness, the two different, for sexual promiscuity is in itself irrelevant to relationships, and sexual unfaithfulness is the cause of great pain in relationships. Well, perhaps the two overlap more than not.

Helen, my faithful friend beyond sex, is visiting from Boston. We went to Hampstead Heath. After a terrible automobile accident, she limps along with a cane (in England, a stick). We walked up and down muddy paths through over-grown, wet woods, and I got lost. We wandered for over an hour, until I realized I must find the way back toward Hampstead Underground Station, as I was to have lunch with Nikos and Spender, and the time was getting late. I thought the way must be in this direction, and Helen followed me. We came out into an open space where I was able to see, in the blue, hazy distance, hills and more woods. I said, no, we must go in that direction, and we entered the woods again. Almost two hours passed. We came on no one to ask directions from. I got into a panic. I didn't want to miss Spender, and I realized just how much I wanted to see him, as though so much depended on it, as though he would think I didn't want to see him if I didn't appear and he, then, would not want to see me again. And Nikos would be worried, as he always is if I'm late. I became impatient with Helen, my old, dear friend, but the more impatient I became I suppressed the impatience with courteousness, even if this meant missing Spender. I finally found our way out, Helen more relieved than I.

When I got back to Wyndham Place, Spender was leaving, and, out of breath, I apologized. He smiled, and it occurred to me that I shouldn't have panicked, that we'd see one another again.

He seems to leave his white hair uncombed.

———

Helen and I went with the artist Patrick Procktor to Regent's Park to lie on the grass, where Patrick did a sketch of me. With a high tone that may or may not have been ironical, he said something like, 'I'm so glad Nikos now has you as his friend.' After we left him, Helen asked me, 'What did he mean by friend? Is that an English expression for something?' I, embarrassed, said, 'I haven't been in England long enough to know.' I have a life in England I wouldn't admit having in America.

Patrick as an artist seems to me to be between two totally different worlds – one of languorous and druggy young men lounging on sofas and the other of Chinese Revolutionary Guards demonstrating for the Cultural Revolution of Mao – and I can't see any meeting of the two, for I doubt that Chinese Revolutionary Guards lounge about on sofas amid flowers and smoking hashish and reading the Little Red Book in quite the same revolutionary spirit as the young people Patrick depicts in aquatints, though I suppose there is a revolution occurring in both worlds. Is Patrick being ironical, as he is about everything?

He is a friend of Nikos from before Nikos and I met, and, as with so many of Nikos' friends from before, I have no idea how they came to be friends, and I am, I admit, jealous of his relationships that had to have excluded me before I met Nikos, an impossible jealousy. So, I don't want to know what Nikos' relationships were, not even, or especially not, with Stephen Spender. I want to think Patrick's friendship with Nikos began with my friendship with Nikos, want to think that all of Nikos' past friendships in London have begun with my meeting him. Even Nikos' love for Stephen.

———

Stephen Spender telephoned. I answered. He said how happy he was that Nikos should have such a nice friend. Stuttering a little, I thanked him a little formally, though I tried not to be formal. I can't yet call him Stephen. I said I thought it was unfair that I should know so much about him from his books and he so little about me, and perhaps he could get to know me without any books. He said he would like that. After, I wondered if I had sounded presumptuous.

―――――

Öçi came for drinks, and immediately he and Nikos connected by way of the names of people they know, or know of, in Greece, or names of Greeks they know, or know of, who live in London. Öçi wore a shirt made of white, diaphanous, finely pleated material, cinched in at his waist by a heavy belt made of big blue beads. I noted how large his nose is, with large pores. Nikos wore a brown cardigan, his white shirt open at the collar. His features are refined.

―――――

Patrick, dressed in tight purple velvet trousers, a loose shirt and a silk scarf about his neck, is very tall and lanky. The different parts of his body – head, arms, long torso, pelvis, legs – appear tenuously connected, so when he moves his body moves in different, swaying directions, as if he were slowly dancing, a cigarette poised in three fingers, the little finger held out.

He lives in a walkup in Manchester Street, Marylebone, deco-rated with Oriental-like cushions and rugs, a multi-coloured glass lamp hanging down in the midst.

David Hockney is painting a portrait of Patrick in his, Patrick's, flat, which I went round with Stephen Spender to see. Stephen and I often meet as if we had all the free time in the world, though Stephen will then say he feels guilty and should be at home writing; as long as I'm with him, I feel I am learning something about London. The large Hockney painting was in Patrick's sitting room. When I said how beautifully painted the basket is, Patrick, with a laugh close to a snort, asked, 'Which basket, darling?' and I noted the bulge in the crotch of his tight trousers.

He proposed doing a watercolour of Stephen and me, on his sofa. 'Get closer, darlings,' he said, and Stephen put an arm about me and I leaned against him. The portrait of Stephen is very good, precise, and Stephen's red socks and shiny black shoes are deftly painted; I, however, have a flat, grey face and a vacuous smile and most of my body is left blank. Patrick gave the picture to me.

Stephen asked me not to let his wife Natasha know about the picture.

I said, 'How could I let her know? I've never met her.'

He looked puzzled, as if this had not occurred to him.

He said, 'It's a bore, Natasha not wanting to meet you and Nikos.'

Ah, Nikos and me, Nikos and me, known as a couple more than we would be known singly.

Are we known as a couple whom Stephen dotes on? And how is this known by Natasha? If Stephen doesn't tell her, who does?

Stephen asked Nikos and me to lunch to meet Christopher Isherwood at Chez Victor, a restaurant writers have been going to for a long while. Isherwood, with his hair cut very short at the neck so his thin nape is almost bare but kept in long bangs over his forehead, looks like an aged little boy. He and Stephen giggled a lot, often at jokes Isherwood made about Stephen, the jokes all about Stephen's boyfriends in Berlin and how one cost Stephen an expensive suit, another an expensive meal. But whereas Isherwood seemed to make fun of Stephen, which Stephen enjoyed, or appeared to enjoy, Stephen didn't make fun of Isherwood.

Isherwood didn't pay much attention to Nikos and me, though perhaps he did by thinking his making fun of Stephen would entertain us.

When he left, to go on to someone he let us know was very grand, a movie star, Stephen said that Isherwood has never been interested in his friends.

———

A lazy Sunday lunch with Patrick. He said he had seen Alain, who has returned to Paris, and Alain had told him that Stephen made a pass at him when they were together for tea.

Patrick put Alain in a painting, among many young men all standing about as in a large room.

He did pencil drawings, one of me lying on the floor and reading the Sunday newspaper.

One of Nikos and me lying on the floor together.

Stephen is angry that Patrick has been telling people that he made a pass at Alain. His large face appeared to become larger the redder it got. He said, 'I didn't.'

Nikos, too, got angry. He said, 'Of course you didn't.'

I wonder why Nikos sided so quickly with Stephen against Alain.

———

Stephen will sometimes tell an anecdote about, say, Virginia Woolf – her telling him that a writer must not publish before the age of thirty – which I had read in his World within World, and I imagine him a mediator between myself and Virginia Woolf, whose advice Stephen no doubt thinks I should take.

———

When, I wonder, will I be able to write about an English character?

What I have understood about the English I meet is their suspicion of generalizations, of abstractions, so easy for an American. The American generalization about the English being reserved I've never in fact encountered. On a bus, I sat next to an elderly lady who told me, in a very matter-of-fact way, that she had just had a hysterectomy and this was the first time since her operation that she was out. 'I'm well now,' she said, 'well and well out of it.' I said, 'Yes, I must say, you're well out of it,' and she looked at me as if pleasantly surprised by my agreeing with her and smiled.

———

Stephen often asks me if I keep a diary, and I said, yes, I do, because I feels he wants me to. Today we were wandering together through the dark, narrow stacks of the London Library, where the floors are like cast-iron grills you can see through to the floors below, he looking for a magazine he needed but which we couldn't find. Stephen said, 'You can put this in your diary.' He couldn't find the magazine, and said it didn't matter. Leaving the library, we met Henry Reed, whom Stephen introduced me to, then Ruth Fainlight, whom Stephen also introduced me to. Henry Reed, Stephen told me, is a poet whose most famous poem is 'Naming of Parts', based on instructions given to soldiers about their rifles in World War II. About Ruth Fainlight, he said she is a poet and has a brother who is a poet, Harry Fainlight. Ruth Fainlight is married to the novelist Alan Sillitoe, whose novel The Loneliness of the Long-Distance Runner I had read. And so I begin to put things together, without really knowing, now, more than the names of writers. Then we walked to Cork Street, and we looked in all the galleries at what was showing. Stephen becomes especially animated when he meets someone he knows in a gallery, and, with a long, sideways undulation of his big body, he holds out a hand to me for me to come and be introduced.

Once, we were walking along Piccadilly and Stephen, spotting someone on the other side, ran across through the traffic to speak with him, an old man with bright white hair, wearing a bright blue jacket. Stephen waved to me to come, and he introduced me to Henry Moore.

———

I had this dream – that Nikos and I were sleeping together, as we in fact were, and that I was woken by someone out in Wyndham Place, calling for help. I also heard in the dream our landlady knocking on the door of the flat and saying, 'Mr. Stangos, Mr. Stangos,' to wake him, as I, too, tried to wake him by shaking him by the shoulder. But he wouldn't wake, and all the while the voice was calling for help from the street. Then I was woken by Nikos saying, 'Yes, what is it?' and as soon as I woke I realized that the voice in my dream was me calling for help from the street, which Nikos had heard.

———

The King's Road –

Along the King's Road on Saturday afternoon, Nikos and I went from shop to shop where clothes hang on racks from high up to low down, clothes that I consider costumes and Nikos as 'inventive' (a word he likes to use, as he does 'innovative' and 'original'). He was excited by a sailor's trousers, with the buttoned panel in front rather than flies, dyed bright yellow – bright yellow and now liberated from all military discipline.

He held the waist of the trousers up to his waist so they hung down, and he laughed.

I was jealous of his excitement, which seemed to me promiscuous.

I said, 'Come on, what would you do with a pair of yellow sailor's trousers?'

He put the trousers back on a pile of old clothes that smelled as though they had been worn and he turned away.

And then I grandiloquently said I would buy him the bright yellow sailor's trousers.

'No, no,' he said.

'I want you to have them,' I said.

There, here, my proof to him that I can be more expansively liberal than he is, here I am buying him a pair of bright yellow sailor's trousers that once fit, with sensual tightness, the thighs of a fantasy sailor. How much more liberal can I be?

But since then Nikos has never worn the dyed yellow sailor's trousers. I have.

———

I should keep a diary, Stephen has told me, for the sake of my writing, which writing I have, with Nikos' insistence, been devoting myself to. Stephen said I should use my diary to write with clarity and definition. He recommended that I simply describe.

As an example, he gave me a copy of Joe Ackerley's We Think the World of You, in which Ackerley had tipped in handwritten passages that he had had to censor from the book, about a love affair between an older man and a working-class boy, whose parents say about the man, 'We think the world of you,' but don't approve of his relationship with their son. The writing is very clear.

But there is so much to describe –

Describe Patrick's flat/studio, where Nikos and I were invited to tea before the big picture of demonstrating Chinese Revolutionary Guards he is working on. We had English tea, the cucumber sandwiches cut very thin.

He told us this story: he and Ossie Clark went to Harrods to buy scarves at the counter where ladies' scarves were sold and where, prancing, they tried on different ones about their necks and looked at themselves in the mirror, and when Patrick asked the sales lady which one she thought suited him best, she said, 'The green one, it's more masculine.' Patrick laughs, in bursts, through his nose.

Then David Hockney's flat/studio in Powis Terrace to look at the etchings of naked boys he was doing to accompany poems by Cavafy translated by Nikos and Stephen, the etchings spread out on the floor with male physique magazines from California.

David gave to Nikos some etchings that he rejected from the book to be published. One etching is of a naked boy packing a suitcase and beside him another naked boy either taking off or putting on underpants. Another is of two naked boys standing side by side and looking at themselves in a mirror. Another is of what David imagines to have been Cavafy's young, plump Egyptian Ptolemy with necklace and bracelet and painted fingernails.

———

Describe Mark Lancaster's loft, where he lives and paints. Mark is suave. He goes to New York often, and has, near the Angel, a loft, like the lofts in New York converted from urban industrial buildings. He has a miniature Empire State Building. Taken as he is by American popular culture, he is doing some paintings inspired by the orange and blue of the highway restaurants Howard Johnson, but abstracted into geometrical shapes; as are his works based on the film Zapruder, an amateur film taken by a spectator of the assassination of President Kennedy, again abstracted into pale rectangles of green. There is an ineffability to his work, the abstract shapes appearing to float off the canvas. As if in passing, he mentions that he was in a film made by Andy Warhol called Couch, in which he makes love with another guy. He wants to go live in New York, and with him I wonder if it was a mistake to have left that city, if in New York the air itself is so charged with creativity just being there makes one creative, creative in the use of the colours of Howard Johnson highway restaurants.

Mark said this about a difference between New York and London – in New York if you praise a picture you've painted as great it is believed to be great and if you self-deprecate and say it's nothing really it's believed to be nothing, but in London if you say a picture you've painted is great, or even good, you're considered preten-tious and your picture not great or even good, but if you self-deprecate and say it's nothing really your painting has to be, if not great, good.

Stephen Buckley comes for drinks with his friend Bryan Ferry, both of them at art school in Newcastle. Richard Hamilton is their teacher, as he was Mark's. Hamilton is the British Pop artist, some of his works based on stills from advertisements or films which he cuts out and arranges in collages, or which he uses as the under-structure for paintings, and I prefer the paintings for the wonder of the use of the beauty of the paint, missing as I do in Pop Art just that, the wonder of the use of the medium paint – as in the paint-ing Stephen Buckley gave to Nikos and me, a finely fissured green wedge through which fissures a layer of yellow appears, the wedge upright against thickly painted brown.

He said, 'I tried to paint the ugliest painting of the twentieth century.'

Nikos and I are starting to put together a collection of pictures given to us by the artists.

Such as by Keith Milow, who gave us a work which consists of a magazine picture of a building cut up into squares and arranged on a grid, and on each square a little patch of metallic powder held in place by a clear plastic sheet, the whole in a Perspex frame.

He said he worries about his work being too elegant.

———

It comes to me: Nikos and I live together as lovers, as everyone knows, and we seem to be accepted because it's known that we are lovers.

In fact, we are, according to the law, criminals in our making love with each other, but it is as if the laws don't apply.

It is as if all the conventions of sex and clothes and art and music and drink and drugs don't apply here in London.

———

Mark came to dinner with Keith. They are having an affair that seems to be going badly, Keith saying to Mark, 'I know you don't fantasize about me when we have sex.'

How do we know so many artists?

It think it has to do with Stephen Spender's dedication to all artists, whom he introduces to us.

———

I should write that there is an essential difference between Saturday in the King's Road, which is a funfair, and Sunday on the King's Road, which is totally shut down.

In Marylebone, where we live, the very air on Sunday appears to go still and silent. There is a chemist's shop at Marble Arch that is open, but only for prescribed medications; a large grate shuts off the rest of the shop, and through the grate one sees rows of shampoo, deodorants, shaving cream, and even bags of sweets, all inaccessible. It is possible to buy lozenges for a sore throat at the counter.

Marylebone could be a provincial city within a metropolitan city. At our local greengrocer, I asked for green peppers and was told, oh, I'd have to go to Soho for that. I don't dare ask for garlic.

———

We went to Johnny Craxton's studio, the ground floor of a terrace house, the floors covered with sheets of plywood and the plywood covered with paint. Nikos told him to pay no attention to the bad reviews he was getting for a gallery exhibition of his work, too, the critics have written, picturesque. Johnny stuck out his lips so his moustache bristled.

Johnny told this story: he was spending the weekend at a country house, where the ladies left the men at the table for brandy and cigars, and where one of the men asked around, when was the last time any one of them had kissed a boy? The usual answer, at school, but Johnny, looking at his watch, said about an hour ago.

When I was alone with Nikos, he said that Greece, in the person of the Greek painter Ghika, has been a bad influence on Johnny.

Ghika is derivative of Picasso, and Johnny is derivative of Ghika. But then, Nikos said, almost all European art of Johnny's generation is derivative of Picasso.

There are the older artists whose work is derivative of Picasso and there are the younger artists whose work is derivative of Marcel Duchamp.

Nikos says that only the American Abstract Expressionists were capable of originality.

————

I saw in Oxford Street a man wearing a pinstripe suit, tight in the waist, and wearing a bowler hat and carrying a tightly furled umbrella, and I thought: but he must be in costume!

————

Patrick is one of the most intelligent people I've ever met, and also one of the people who most denies his intelligence. Listening to him talk high camp, the camp raised so high most likely by hashish, it's impossible to see him as the serious person who learned Russian in the Army, who translated hitherto untranslated Russian poets, who was among a group who walked from London to Moscow where they were allowed to demonstrate in Red Square against the atomic bomb, after which they were invited to tea with Mrs. Khrushchev. When he tells the story of the march – how the group would be picked up by a bus at night and brought to the nearest town, either back from where they'd come or forward to where they were headed, then brought back in the morning to where they had been picked up – it sounds as though no one, or at least not he, took the march seriously. As he tells the story, he plays languorously with the scarf about his neck.

His mother is often at his place, an elegant woman who, I think, runs a hotel in Brighton, and I cannot imagine what their relationship is or what she thinks of his friends, which, however, she seems to accept in an accepting English way. Is that English: not to question, but accept, the acceptance a vague cloud of unknowing that appears to float about some people's heads, their eyes unfocused?

The vague cloud of unknowing. No one seems to know, quite, what the boundaries of London are, as if London were itself within a vague cloud of unknowing. I have seen a map which left the boundaries of London open, but the metropolis centered on Hyde Park Corner, in a large black dot. When you arrive from beyond London into London, you do not arrive in any station that is iden-tified as London, but Victoria Station, Paddington Station, Liverpool Street Station. There is no 'downtown' London.

I once thought that the English were the most adroit at defining, but almost every question I ask appears met with that vague cloud of unknowing – of, say, bemusement, as if it had never occurred to the person asked that such a question need be asked. My reaction is to think: well, really, there is no need.

———

Patrick did a watercolour of Nikos and me in bed, Nikos half under the covers, I naked, bum up, on top of the covers, which Stephen commissioned from Patrick. It cost Stephen £40. Looking at it, he said he had a drawer in his desk that he kept locked and he would put it there for safe keeping.

'I have to outlive Natasha,' he said.

He never mentioned this watercolour again, and I never asked, and I wonder if he, thinking better of keeping it from Natasha, tore it up and threw it away.

———

Stephen urged me to read Joe Ackerley for clarity. Yes, but I feel Ackerley's writing lacks tension, and in my own writing I want a low level of tension which I hope to get by bringing a slight degree of self-consciousness to the sentences, perhaps the self-consciousness of a light lyricism, enough to highlight them so that they suggest a little more than what they are literally, and therefore the low level of tension between the literal and the – what? – more than literal, whatever that more than literal could be. Stephen, noting this about my writing, said he was reminded of the self-conscious writing of Julien Green, the

American writer who wrote in French, and I took this as a warning from him, but a warning I thought English, and in my writing I'm not English, but, oh, a Franco-American, whatever that means.

What it means, I suppose, is that, though French has become submerged beneath English, English nevertheless floats on that primary language, and I do write conscious that I am writing in English, and, conscious as I am, I become self-conscious, but try to use the self-consciousness to be creative in the writing, to be more than literal, to sustain the tension between the literal and that light lyricism.

———

One of David Hockney's assistants is called Mo, who does stand-up cut-outs of animals and trees and flowers in vases from plywood. Nikos has known him since before he met me, and they have a warm relationship that I am left out of. Do I mind? I mind that Mo is one of David's friends within what I think of as a magical circle and from within that circle he looks out at Nikos with fondness and not at me.

But, then, Mo was a friend of Nikos before Nikos met me, one of a number of friends of Nikos who used to meet in Nikos' flat and smoke dope and recite poems and draw pictures. Nikos told me, recounting with excitement the event from before I met him, of getting high with friends and going off with them all to the Albert Hall for a famous poetry reading, Wholly Communion. Perhaps I am, as he tells me I am, envious of that circle of friends, and, envious, instead of joining in stand apart – stand apart from it mostly by my taking a stand against dope. Dope is a great unifier of friends, and I won't be unified with Nikos' friends from before he met me. Whatever friendships Nikos had from the past that were unified by dope, he has given up, no doubt reluctantly, because I won't be unified. I have made Nikos lose friends.

David Hockney says about Mo that if he had a factory producing hundred-pound notes he'd lose money on it.

———

I am beginning to see the English as distinct from the Scots and the Welsh or even the people from Yorkshire, and certainly from the Northern Irish, and leave it – again – as a vague cloud of unknowing as to what Great Britain is. I wonder if any Brit would be able to tell me. I guess the United Kingdom has entirely to do with the Queen.

————

To be in London because I am in love – amazing!

————

David Hockney's world –

He bought a gold lamé jacket and a gold lamé shopping bag to carry his shopping from the local supermarket, and with his hair bleached and his large round black spectacles, he has become an icon of the times, with photographers flashing photographs of him on his way back from the supermarket.

He said, in his matter-of-fact Yorkshire accent, 'I know a bit of show business is important.'

Seeing the exquisitely drawn portraits David has done of Stephen Spender, W. H. Auden, Christopher Isherwood, Isaiah Berlin, Cecil Beaton, I of course wish I too were drawn by David to rise to the level of the celebrated.

And when I stand before his portrait of his friends Celia Birtwell and Ossie Clark, with their large white cat, I feel they are in a magical world that David has merely depicted them in, but which they do in fact live in. So it is a surprise to find myself, with Nikos, in the very room in which Celia and Ossie were situated to be painted and to find it as magical as it appears in the painting. David does create a magical world.

And how he believes that there is no reason why anyone else should not love life.

Interesting about David is, though he has the reputation of being something of a pop star, his tastes in literature and in music and in art are far from what the world would expect those of a pop star to be: Proust, Wagner, and I heard him say that the greatest work of art is the Fra Angelico frescos of the Annunciations in the monks' cells in San Marco in Florence.

———

In Carnaby Street, looking in shop windows at blown-up cut-outs of almost naked sexy young men among fancy clothes, I'm at first pleasantly surprised at the eroticism displayed so frankly, and then I think, But why hasn't such eroticism always been on frank display? as if any opposition to such a display of sex suddenly becomes so obsolete I can't understand why it ever was in force.

Nikos said that the Soviet ambassador approves of Carnaby Street because it is essentially inspired by the young proletariat.

———

It comes to me almost as a recollection from a long time ago because I can't recall who the girl was I was with, nor where the lawn was that we were lounging on, nor why she suggested that we drop acid. She said, 'It has to be in the country, in the midst of nature.' I said, 'Yes,' outwardly agreeing with everything in general, as Nikos tells me I do, as a way of inwardly not agreeing to anything in particular. I was alone with her. I wonder now if the appeal of the agreement with her was that it excluded Nikos, for I would never ever take drugs of any kind with him, and I wouldn't, I know, not because I would separate myself off from him but because he would separate himself off from me, and this would enrage me, as it does when, rarely, he does smoke dope. Dope may be familiar to him as a Greek, for whom the hashish dens in the port of Piraeus are a part of Greek subculture, more than as a Londoner for whom the subculture of hashish is a fashion. He has no right – I give him no right – to enter so exclusively into himself that I do not exist for him. (And yet, friends are impressed at how we, at drinks parties, each go off to speak to different people, an indication of the respect we have for the independence we have for each other; an independence we do respect even when alone together, Nikos in his study and I in mine.) Am I being introspective, which I studiously do not want to do in this? I think I'm not so much introspecting into myself as introspecting into Nikos' self, in which I imagine him wishing, at least from time to time, for total independence from me. I will not try to introspect into my noncommittal agreement to drop acid, apart from Nikos, with the girl on the lawn.

When I returned home, Nikos, preparing supper, asked me, annoyed, 'Where have you been? I was worried,' and this reassured me totally in him, a reassurance that it excluded any introspection.

I want to be free of introspection.

———

Stephen asked me to lunch with him at his club, the Garrick. I had never before been in a gentleman's club. He told me to wear a tie. I always wear a tie. In the dining room of the club, Stephen said, pointing with two fingers at a table across from us, 'There's Benjamin Britten.' Against the light from a window, I saw a man with dense curly grey hair talking with someone at his table. Stephen kept looking toward him, but Britten never looked our way. As we were leaving the club, Stephen said, having, it seemed, thought a lot about it, 'I don't think he's ever liked me.'

Later, Stephen told me he had been reprimanded by the club because I, as his guest, had stood on a rug guests are not allowed to stand on.

———

'Your life is interesting to you and to me,' Nikos said, 'but don't presume that it is interesting to anyone else.'

———

I'm told that Nikos and I live in a world beyond which we can't see the outside objections to two men in love. No doubt, but I can't imagine any reason for objecting to it. Do we ever think that the police may suddenly break into our flat and arrest us for the criminal activity of making love?

And the London world we live in is made up of many, many such criminals as we are.

We never think of the sexes of people we entertain in our flat.

———

Patrick came to dinner. I never know if he is being ironical or not, in such a grand way that he raises his chin and smiles and looks down at me from his high height with half-shut eyes, his lids fluttering, holding out the scarf from about his neck and letting it drop so it seems to float around him, and drawling, 'Darling.'

During the meal, he said something from his height that made me think that before Nikos met me he and Patrick had an affair, or something like an affair. I laughed, again not sure if Patrick was joking or not, but then I became very upset. I thought Patrick, skinny and lanky, was not attractive, and I was offended that Nikos would have found him attractive. After Patrick left, Nikos sensed I was upset, and when we were in bed together he asked me why. I couldn't tell him I was offended in my sexual pride by his having had sex with someone I thought sexually unattractive – but I said enough, finally, for him to tell me I understand nothing about sexual attraction, which is attraction, not, as he seems to think I think, towards a whole generalization of people, but towards a particular person, love making a conversation – the most intimate possible – between two people.

———

When I saw on Nikos' desk an address book, I picked it up to look through it. We are totally open to each other, so that I not only don't mind Nikos opening my post, I want him to open my post. I found that Nikos came to London with addresses and telephone numbers given to him by the Greek Surrealist poet

Nanos Valaoritis, who had lived in London and made friends among the English poets. I saw, among other names, that of Stephen Spender.

Again, I have never asked him about his first meeting with Stephen, have never asked him about his relationship with Stephen. I have simply assumed that it was a loving relationship that has developed into a loving relationship between Stephen and Nikos and me as a couple. But there is a deeper reason why I don't want to know: that Stephen is so much older than Nikos, the sex between them sex I myself would draw away from with a shudder. And Stephen is so big! I am young, and in my youth my sexual attraction is to those as young as I am. Nikos is young, and, oh yes, he is attracted to me, as I am to him, but he allows that older men are attracted to younger, and that the younger have no reason to shudder at this attraction. Does this have to do with Nikos being Greek, and I, in my not even thinking of sex with an older man, an American of – what? – puritan principles, in the sense that puritan principles are self-righteous, self-regarding, even self-loathing if they are not self-righteous and self-regarding? In no way as promiscuous as I was in New York, Nikos has revealed to me his past sexual activities in Athens, which seem to have involved more loving emotion than sexual urgency (no pornographic impulses in him); Nikos is to me free of puritan principles, but the freedom makes him very vulnerable to tender emotions. These tender emotions I have to say I had never experienced before I met Nikos, who, in the enthrallment of love, cannot be but tender.

I recall a conversation Nikos once had with another Greek: it gives so much pleasure to an older man to have the pleasure of a younger, and it requires so little effort on the part of the younger.

And this: in a just-opened so-novel sex shop in Soho with the art historian Robert Rosenblum and his wife the artist Jane Kaplowitz, Nikos picked up an enormous dildo and laughed, and Bob and Jane laughed, because, after all, the urges of sex are not to be taken seriously, and do not command sexual pride. I take

sex too seriously, and my sexual pride – that is, that I should only
be known to love someone, such as Nikos, whom the world
would admire me and even be jealous of me for – makes me a
prude about sex, and embarrassed in a way Nikos isn't, so, in the
sex shop, I had to force myself to laugh, and wished Nikos
wouldn't joke about the grotesque dildo, though I could see,
when he looked at me, that he was joking, with the slight mischie-
vousness that makes his eyes shine, because he knew his joking
embarrassed me.

When we were alone, he said, 'You didn't like my doing that.'
And I, 'What do you think I am, a prude? Of course I didn't mind.'

He said, 'You're funny about sex.'

'You're funnier,' I said.

Bob Rosenblum has given female names to all his male friends:
Nikos' name is Phaedra and mine is Faith.

––––––––

Trying to learn Greek, which becomes more and more difficult as I try, I think how strange it is that I should be so close
to someone whose native language I don't know. When I hear
him speaking over the telephone to a Greek friend, I recognize
words but not enough to know what this important conversation is about – especially the word 'catastrophi!' – important
because it is in a language I don't understand. Do I think that
he tells others in Greek what he wouldn't tell me? No, I don't,
I'm not jealous of what he keeps to himself in his language. Or
am I?

I'm very interested in reading his poems – written some in
English, which he gives to me to read and which always impress me
for the way he can make an idea appear to be as sensitive as the
touch of a fingertip, and some in Greek, which he doesn't give me
because I can't read them but which, I know, he wouldn't mind my
reading – though, finding a poem in Greek exposed on his desk
when he was out, I became determined to read it, to enter into his
language, and I stopped on:

ΩΡΑΙΟΣ ΕΦΗΒΟΣ

which words I did not understand at first reading, but which suddenly revealed themselves as:

BEAUTIFUL BOY

and, yes, for a moment I was jealous of whoever that beautiful boy was, hidden away in Nikos' poem in Greek, even if that beautiful boy existed only in the poem. I was suddenly jealous of Nikos for being Greek, for being able to claim a sensibility, a sensitivity, that allowed and still allows boys to be beautiful, that allowed and still allows the sensible, the sensitive appreciation of beauty.

There is so much to write about this: Nikos as Greek.

He smiles at my speaking whatever Greek I know, and tells me that I get the genders – of which there are three in Greek, masculine, feminine, neuter – all mixed up.

I call Nikos Αγάπη μου, my Love.

——————

I think back at my fantasies of Greece before I met Nikos, fantasies that go as far back as myself as a pubescent boy looking through the Encyclopaedia Britannica that my father, always aspiring for a higher education than his eighth-grade parochial school education, had bought from a door-to-door salesman, an encyclopedia that offered me a world view, which world view I found more arresting in the photographs than in the text, a world view that suddenly focused on photographs of ancient Greek statues when I turned the page and they appeared, statues of naked gods. (Stephen told me that as a boy his first sexual arousal came with studying, under a magnifying glass, Greek postage stamps with statues of nude gods.) I had never seen any depiction of nudity, and though I was sexually aroused, I was aroused by Greek nudity, which was the nudity of gods, which was idealized nudity, which made arousal god-like, idealized. And so, whenever I encountered, in whatever form, some reference to Greece – always ancient Greece – the reference was to the Greece of Greek gods, was an idealized Greece. Reading the orations of Pericles (one of the few books we had in our house, kept on glass-fronted shelves above a drop-leaf desk) I felt rise in me the idealizing devotion to the great patriot, the hero, the god-like. Studying photographs of Greece in a large picture book, I was, yes, aroused by the vision of asphodel in a stony field illuminated by the essential light of Greece.

And so the fantasies of an idealized Greece in all the Western world, with varying attempts to realize the idealization.

———

Leaving for New York, Mark asked us to care for his cat, a Burmese named Jasmine, which Nikos loves more than he loves me.

Johnny Craxton did a drawing of Jasmine:

The cat fixes us more than ever in our lives together: a pet to take care of.

After Mark left, I, feeling that there was more than friendship between him and Nikos, asked him if he and Mark had been lovers, and he asked, 'Would you be hurt if I said yes? He loved me.' And that Mark had loved Nikos made me think: yes, of course he did.

———

At times, usually at a meal, when Stephen and Nikos and I are together, I listen to them talk, say, about Russia and America. I note how Stephen, who so likes to speculate about international affairs and will make references to what someone told him when he was in Washington, will try to be deliberate in his speculation, and how Nikos will seem to be impatient with Stephen's deliberations and will suddenly make a statement that totally undoes those deliberations, an impertinent statement such as, 'You believe what you heard in Washington? Why not Moscow?' and Stephen will frown and blink and seem to wonder if Nikos may not be right.

Nikos once said to me, 'I should be elected President of the United States,' and when I told him he couldn't as it is in the American Constitution that all presidents must be born within the United States, he said, 'The Constitution should be changed,' and then laughed that beguiling laugh that makes me laugh.

———

Mario Dubsky, who paints large abstractions with heavy brushstrokes, gave a party for a houseful of friends on Guy Fawkes night, and in his garden set aflame odd pieces of furniture, including a bedstead, the roaring fire terrifying. Many people gathered round, illuminated by the flames they stared into, people I can now consider friends, all of us as if in flames.

I noted the painter Maggi Hambling, her necklace of brass bullets glistening in the flames, she staring out with narrowed eyes.

Also there, the artist and set and costume designer Yolanda Sonnabend, with long black hair that she keeps shaking back, and wearing large bracelets that move up and down her slender arms as she gestures. She is a close friend of Maggi, as is Antoinette Godkin, who works for an art dealer, whose beauty appears accented by a bright beauty spot on a cheek. The three seem to be the goddesses of some esoteric rite that is exclusively female, and one does not ask what goes on in the rite.

And, yes, I have to include Helen McEachrane, very beautiful and also mysterious, as I'm not sure where she is from or what she does, but, wherever she is from and whatever she does, she moves with style, always dressed as if in veils that move about her as she moves.

———

It sometimes happens that when I am speaking to Stephen over the telephone, he will suddenly ask, 'Natasha, Natasha?' and I will hear the click of a telephone receiver put down, Natasha having listened over another telephone. That Natasha, whom I have not met, should be a presence looming in my friendship with Stephen is very strange to me, and makes me wonder if Nikos and I loom in any way in her relationship with Stephen.

When I told him this, he laughed. He said that he had been talking over the telephone with his brother Humphrey, Humphrey in a telephone box from where he exclaimed that Stephen should see the beauty of a young man passing outside, and Stephen heard the telltale click of the receiver of the other telephone and knew that Natasha had been listening. Why Stephen laughed I don't know, though perhaps I do, in a way: to keep Natasha alerted to his sexuality without admitting it to her, to make her wonder. This seems to please him.

———

Now I find that Öçi is having an affair with Mario, with whom Keith had an affair. Do I, in a way, feel left out of these criss-crossing sexual affairs, which I only hear about incidentally, by living with Nikos, with whom I have more than an affair? Perhaps, at moments, I do, but only at moments, when, at a gallery opening, I talk to someone in the crowd whom I think sexy. But I know from New York about affairs, and it is always a relief to go home with Nikos and go to bed with him.

———

What is the desire – the felt need – to have lived Nikos' life with him, to have always been there with him? Is it possessiveness that makes me want to have been with him when he was eight and his father died on the day the Nazis left Athens; when, to his total bemusement, a man next to him in a cinema undid his flies and masturbated him, his first sexual experience; when he was a student at Athens College and secretly mimeographed Communist propaganda; when he was in America and for a summer worked in a meat-packing factory; when he scrubbed floors in the army; when he was rejected by a lover on holiday with him on the island of Poros? So many events, so many, and I want to have been there, just to have been there. Is this love? Is it love to want to be with him when he dies, and close his eyes?

———

When Stephen, at dinner in our flat, said he had to go to the South of France, though he didn't want to, to get trees planted in the garden of his and his wife Natasha's house there, Nikos said, 'Why don't you ask David to come with you?' This seemed to puzzle Stephen for a moment, but after that moment his face became animated and he said, his head thrust forward and his eyes wide, 'That's a brilliant idea.'

Paris

In Victoria Station, as soon as we sat in our seats on the train, Stephen jumped up and went across the aisle to speak to two men who were already seated. They were Francis Bacon and his friend George Dyer, also going to Paris. Bacon will have an opening at the Galerie Maeght, and said Stephen and I must come, which meant Stephen would have to postpone our going to the South of France to plant the trees in his and Natasha's garden, but Stephen appeared very excited, blinking his eyes a lot, and said we'd love to come to the opening. And as it turned out we were all staying at the same hotel in Paris, the Quai Voltaire, where I am now, looking out at the Seine, green-grey, as I write at a little French table sitting on a little French chair, the kind of table and chair I imagine Stephen, who is so big, would break just by writing a letter here.

Stephen asked me, at the hotel reception, if I wanted my own room, and I said no, I'd be happy to share a room with him.

I put my clothes away neatly, and he throws his all over the room.

I've spent the day alone, and will spend the evening alone, as Stephen had to go to Geneva, he didn't explain why. Francis Bacon had asked me to have dinner with him and his friends, but as it turned out plans had before that been made for him which he couldn't break. I can't see where all the horror comes from in him:

he is physically so soft, and always so polite, with strands of hair combed carefully over his forehead.

Alone this afternoon, I took a long walk. When, six or seven years ago, I lived in Paris as a student, the city was all soot black and water-streaked, and many walls were pockmarked with bullet-holes from the war. But now that it has been cleaned up it is all pink, and in the electric street lights it seems to sparkle here and there, which may simply be reflections in newly cleaned windows that are not closed by shutters. I walked around the parts of Paris that are familiar to me, and I kept wishing I could show my Paris to Nikos. My Paris? It is very strange: streets and shops and cafés here once had all kind of associations, and now I don't sense them, and I know it's because I can't associate them with him, except to wish he were here. I wore the cap Nikos gave me because he said it'd be cold in Paris.

I went to see a church that I love, Saint Severin, so old all its pillars and walls lean a little in different directions, and there I lit a candle, a big one, for Nikos. It is a Greek Orthodox church. Then I went up the Boulevard Saint Michel and down the rue des Ecoles where I lived right across from the Sorbonne, an American student imagining he could be, simply by being there, Parisian. I ate at a small Breton restaurant I used to like very much on (Stephen would say 'in') rue M. Le Prince, which has dark wood wainscoting and serves cider and crêpes. I ate potage, then veal and spinach, and drank a whole brown pitcher of cider. And I hurried to a cinema to see Ten Days that Shook the World, which I thought was the best film I have ever seen. The first scene shows an immense statue of the tsar, and suddenly hundreds of people appear with ropes to pull it down, so an arm falls off, a leg, and then suddenly all the ropes disappear, and all the people also, and the statue continues to fall apart. Then I walked back to the hotel.

I am tired, as I didn't sleep well on the train, though we had berths in a carriage that was disconnected from the rest of the train at Dover and put on the ferry and reconnected to another train at Calais.

What shall I do this evening? I hate going to a restaurant by myself. Why isn't Nikos here? Why did he insist I come without him, with Stephen? Paris is so unfriendly. The rudest city in the world is the most beautiful. On my walk, asking for directions, or in the restaurant for lunch —

Which makes me think: I once said 'lunch' to Stephen, and he corrected me by saying 'luncheon,' and I presumed that in England lunch is a verb, 'to lunch,' like 'to dine,' and 'luncheon' is a noun like 'dinner.'

— everyone was so rude, and I almost exploded with anger, as Nikos hates me to do, so, thinking of him, I remained composed.

I love him and think of him all the time. It's five o'clock here, four there. He's in his office at the Embassy, having to deal with Greek over-complications, which he can't stand. I wish he could get another job. What did he do at lunch time (which is an American way of not saying 'luncheon')? What will he do for dinner? I hope he's not frightened to stay alone in the apartment. I want to be with him and hold him and kiss him and love him —

I think the candle I lit for Nikos in Saint Severin must still be burning.

———

Stephen has come back. He came with a lot of Swiss francs, and asked me where he should hide them in the room, but I didn't say, and didn't watch where he did hide them. He's having a bath, and then we go to the Francis Bacon exhibition.

Now hours later —

About to go to sleep. Stephen already asleep in the other bed.

At Francis' exhibition, George, very drunk, took me in hand, and, all in Cockney, told me which paintings were of him, and did I recognize him? I didn't, really, but he said he saw himself in them, in the way Francis painted him. One was of him as a mutilated lump of flesh sitting on a toilet.

Stephen introduced me to many people, including Sonia Orwell, the widow of George Orwell, and the novelist Mary McCarthy and Mary McCarthy's husband and Philippe de Rothschild, and told them all, giggling, that he and I are going to the South of France to plant trees together in the garden of his and Natasha's house. He was very amused that someone named Plante would be planting trees with him.

I suddenly wondered if Natasha, whom, after all, I have never met, knew that I was going to her house with Stephen to plant trees in her garden. She gave him instructions for the planting, with a drawing, which he showed me. Where a row of cypresses are to be planted are a row of dots.

We are on a train, heading south for Avignon. It is raining, and everything is grey, dun, pale green outside – and very flat.

When I woke in our hotel room I found that Stephen had left for an early appointment. I met him at the Grand Palais. We went into the Hommage à Picasso exhibition, which was not yet put up completely, so we walked about cables and crates scattered on the floors. We saw drawings that Picasso did when he was thirteen, and from there to now masses and masses of drawings, paintings, etchings, sculpture, pottery, tiles, as if he never for a moment stopped, and, at eighty-five, has not stopped. He must be the most impatient man in the world to create, create, create as much as, or more than, anyone has ever created, and I wondered if the way he works has a lot to do with impatience. Stephen said the exhibition made him twenty years younger.

No artists we know, especially Hockney, could be painting what they paint without Picasso. Certainly Francis could not paint the way he does without Picasso having first distorted the figure, though, as David H. says, Picasso never mutilates the figure the way Francis does. Stephen said the Picasso exhibition made Francis' exhibition look pale. I said that he couldn't compare, that it was unfair to any artist since Picasso to compare that artist to him. Stephen nodded, the way he nods, blinking also, when you say something he evidently agrees with but that seems at the same time to bemuse him.

We met John Russell, the art critic, in the exhibition, and he was also enthusiastic, but I sensed in his enthusiasm the isolation, almost the loneliness, of the critic.

Stephen and I walked back to the hotel, and on the way he insisted on buying a camera to take pictures. In the hotel lobby were gathered Sonia Orwell, Mary McCarthy and her husband whose name I can't remember, the Baron de Rothschild, Francis, and John Russell. George was too drunk to come. We all went to lunch in a restaurant in Les Halles. I was wearing Nikos' cap, which, as we were taking off our coats, Sonia grabbed from my head to put on hers, laughing. She said she must buy one, and I wondered if she was implying I should give this one to her, but I didn't say anything. Nikos did tell me to be careful of her, and I was. When we all sat at the table, the cap was passed around from person to person to put it on and joke.

David in Nikos' cap

I sat next to Mary McCarthy, who was cold at first, then warmed up, I think, when, after having asked her if she thought of writing about Rome and she answered no, I asked her if she had read Eleanor

Clark's book on Rome, a great gaffe, because I suddenly realized that Eleanor Clark was married to Edmund Wilson, who of course was once married to Mary McCarthy. But, though I may have read about these relationships, I forget what I've read when I meet the person in fact, as if the person I'm meeting in fact can't really have had anything to do with the person I've read about. She didn't say she had read Eleanor Clark's book, but she laughed. When she raised her wine glass, her small finger, slightly crooked, extended in a feminine way, I was struck by how masculine her hand was.

She asked me where I'd been to college, and when I said Boston College, she said, 'You were educated by the Jesuits.' 'Yes,' I said. She said, 'I was educated by the Sisters of the Sacred Heart,' and added, as if I might not know and she wanted to make it clear that my being educated by Jesuits in no way put me at an advantage, 'the female equivalent of the Jesuits.' 'They are, yes,' I said.

Having been listening to us, Sonia, across the table, said, 'Mr. Plante, I was brought up a Catholic too.'

Philippe de Rothschild, bald and stout, was very animated. As if he were playing tricks, he parodied certain philosophers, and Mary McCarthy was the only one to become engaged in the talk. She said, 'You're an idealist,' and this made Philippe de Rothschild stop.

He asked Francis if he would design a label for a special de Rothschild wine, and Francis, with a shrugging laugh, said yes, of course.

As if, suddenly, no one knew what to talk about, Sonia brought up Stephen taking me to the South of France to plant trees, and there was some joking around the table about Mr. Plante planting trees, with advice from various people on how to plant them. Stephen seemed to like this joking.

John Russell, attentive to everyone and smiling a bright if tight smile of pleasure, again appeared to be isolated, if not lonely, in the midst of the party.

Philippe de Rothschild, who said he must go, left, but came back to tell us he had paid the bill, which, he said with great surprise, was remarkably cheap.

Before the rest of us broke up, Stephen asked Francis if he and

George would like to come stay with us in the South of France, and Francis, with that shrugging laugh he has, said yes. He won't come, I thought. I also thought: my God, I hope he doesn't come, because if he does how are Stephen and I going to find the time to plant the trees? Stephen has already told me he has great fears that Natasha will arrive next spring to find three withered trees leaning toward one another on the horizon, all he and I were able to do. He also said he was counting on me to get all the trees in the ground so that Natasha will in fact find everything she asked for done. I think Stephen imagines I'm filled with common sense and stick-to-it-iveness, more than he is, and what he is counting on is that we get the trees planted so that Natasha, if she knows about us being together, will not complain that he brought me with him just to have a good time. So I'm determined that we do get those trees planted, and I am trying to emphasize my common sense and stick-to-it-iveness. But how will we be able if we are spending our time with Francis and George, if they come?

As Francis was leaving, Mary McCarthy asked him if he would come with her to visit the studio of a friend of hers who painted owls, and Francis said of course, of course he would, there was nothing he'd like more than to see a studio filled with paintings of owls. Francis left with John Russell and Mary McCarthy's husband.

After he left, Mary McCarthy said, 'I'm interested in those owls because they look just like Edmund,' and she smiled her hard smile, all her teeth showing as in a stark rectangle.

She, Sonia, Stephen and I went to the rue de Rivoli for coffee. Sonia, maybe a little drunk, talked a lot in a high voice, to no one and to everyone, often in French. She spoke so quickly, I couldn't understand most of what she said. Mary McCarthy left. Stephen said he wanted to see Ten Days that Shook the World, which I had talked about. Sonia asked if she could come with us.

I suddenly had this feeling: that Sonia was interested in – more than interested, excited by – my friendship with Stephen.

Sonia loved the movie, and so did Stephen, who recalled having seen it in Berlin when he lived there in the thirties.

Stephen and I returned to the hotel, where we found Francis and George and others drinking in the bar. Annoying everyone, I think, Stephen insisted on taking photographs, but, as must happen with every mechanical device Stephen has ever in his life attempted to use, he couldn't get the flash to work, and then, as I'm sure always happens to Stephen, it suddenly did work.

Francis said, with a laugh, that he would never, ever design a label for Philippe de Rothschild's bottles.

I left them to go up to our room to rest. After a while, Stephen too came to rest.

At eight-thirty, a car came for us to take us to dinner at the de Rothschilds' house. The car drove through a strange quarter of Paris, among factories and what looked like warehouses, and stopped in a dismal little street. Stephen and I got out, went through an iron-grill door, then through another door, then another, as if there were deep secrecy at stake, and finally into a magnificent pavilion with an illuminated garden beyond showing through French windows.

I kept putting my hands under my arms to dry them in preparation to shake hands, as my palms were sweating.

Philippe de Rothschild told me he had just a short while before moved into this house, and when I said, 'Bonne chance,' he grabbed me by the shoulders and kicked my shins and laughed. 'I'm sorry,' I said, and said, 'Merde.' 'That's better,' he said. I had the sense from him of his being totally friendly with me because I was his guest, but that, the moment I ceased to be his guest, he wouldn't think for a moment that there was any reason to see me again.

He introduced me to his wife, the Baroness Pauline de Rothschild, tall, with a very aristocratic nose, an American who was not identifiable as an American. She was just courteous toward me.

She said she loved the new style of clothes for young people, and had been struck by a photograph she had seen in a newspaper of a group of young men wearing these clothes. She asked a footman to get it from her bedroom. He did, and she showed it to me: three or four very beautiful young men, all, as evident from the caption identifying them, from aristocratic French families. A deep sense of exclusion from their world came over me, but then I wondered if she showed me the photograph to put me at ease for the clothes I was wearing, the brown-and-white-striped Carnaby Street suit Nikos bought for me, which was inappropriate for the dinner party.

The other guests were Louis Aragon and his wife Elsa Triolet, and a Russian couple who had come recently from Moscow. Stephen explained to me later who they were: Elsa Triolet's sister Lili Brik, once the mistress of the early Soviet poet Vladimir Mayakovsky, and her husband, Osip Brik, who was one of the founders of Russian Formalism. Elsa Triolet was small and thin, her hair short and loose, and Lili Brik small and plump, wearing a stark black dress, her hair in a large, smooth chignon held by a net. We were asked into the dining room, where Pauline de Rothschild assigned me to sit at the top of the table on a grand gilt and velvet chair. Stephen was seated at the opposite end of the table. I said I was embarrassed to be given such a position, and after we were all seated Philippe de Rothschild made a face at Pauline de Rothschild, who apologized and asked me if I wouldn't mind changing. I stood. She asked the husband of Lili Brik, sitting on one of the more modest chairs along the side of the table, if he wouldn't mind changing, and he too stood. I thought she meant that he and I should change places, but footmen came and one took my grand chair away while the other took his chair away and, while we stood away, exchanged them, and I sat back where I had been but on a modest chair and he sat where he had been on the grand chair.

The de Rothschilds were trying to arrange to rent a mansion in Russia for the summer. To do this seemed to them as matter-of-fact as Lili Brick and her husband coming from Moscow to visit in Paris.

There was talk about references to the Rothschilds in literature, and I said I remembered that in Dostoyevsky's A Raw Youth the main character says his great ambition is to become as rich as a Rothschild.

In the drawing room after dinner, talk about Ezra Pound, whom Aragon said he detests. Stephen told me later Aragon detests almost everyone. He was very rude to Stephen when Stephen said, yes, Pound is horrible for being Fascist and anti-Semitic, but there is something tragic enough about him that all the horrible things he did take on the dimension of tragedy, and Stephen was drawn to the tragedy of Pound. He said the last time he had seen Pound he had found him in a grave depression, not interested in his poetry, thinking his whole life had been a waste. Aragon jingled his keys impatiently, looked at me and made a face of French intolerance.

I told Aragon how much I admired Le Paysan de Paris and asked if he minded talking about the Surrealist movement. Not at all, he said. He hated Breton. He said the movement had its value, yes, but it was never meant to wipe away the past in favor of something revolutionary. He himself had always read Hugo even when the Surrealists were disowning him. He said, rather bitterly, that the movement was dead, and he saw no point in trying to revive it, as he thought people now in the sixties were trying to do, with drugs and hallucinations.

Then, suddenly, the room was filled with rapid, crackling, flashing talk. I had come thinking I would be intimidated and unable to say anything, and I was intimidated, even frightened, but just because of this I made myself participate. And as I found I was communicating, I became excited and maybe spoke too much.

At the end of the evening, Aragon read a long poem he had written for Mayakovsky, and read it very dramatically. I was very moved, and told him so and for a moment I felt we had a contact.

He asked Stephen about me, 'Est ce qu'il a déjà publié un livre?'

'Pas encore,' Stephen answered, 'mais il en publiera.'

Aragon turned away.

Stephen and I stayed a little while with Philippe and Pauline de

Rothschild after the others left, and I felt a charm from them that, if I had counted on it, would have made me think we had become close friends.

In the car back to the hotel, I told Stephen that my fear of French cultural superiority might have something to do with my being a provincial Franco-American who grew up speaking a crude, seventeenth-century French I was aware was not, as an aunt used to refer to it, the real French French of France. But, Stephen said, he has always been frightened by French superiority, and speaking especially with André Malraux, minister of cultural affairs in France, always frightened him. Yet, he said he didn't think the French so intelligent; they're simply calculating, coldly logical, and definitive. I was sure he was thinking of Aragon.

I said, 'The relationship between the de Rothschilds and Russia must be very close for them to think of renting a mansion there.'

Stephen frowned and shook his head with disapproval. He said, 'Imagine, the de Rothschilds renting a mansion in the Soviet Union.'

The train is passing through rolling countryside, with ploughed fields.

———

We are still on the train. We left Paris at 9:15 a.m. and will arrive at Avignon at 4:30 p.m. The countryside gets more and more dramatic.

Stephen is reading, and while he's been reading I've been thinking about him and what he is doing for Nikos and me: he has opened a whole world to us. He and I were talking about Nikos, as he says we always do, and he said, 'I wish that when I was your age I had had what you have now with Nikos.' I said, 'But, Stephen, you are giving us both what you didn't have at our age.' I feel he has given Nikos and me a world in which our relationship can expand and expand, so that in discovering the world he has opened to us we are discovering one another.

But it had shocked me a little after I talked to Nikos by telephone from our Paris hotel room to feel a small flash of jealousy from Stephen, jealousy maybe not because he loves Nikos and I have him or Nikos loves me and he has me, but jealousy because we have each other. He laughs that I want to talk about Nikos so much, that I'm always writing letters to Nikos, but maybe I am exaggerating our relationship to keep him at a distance from me while I'm with him. Maybe I want to keep reminding him: I'm Nikos', and I can't be anyone else's.

The country is all round, stark hills. We'll hire a car in Avignon and drive to Stephen's house, outside Maussane. I am anxious to start digging.

When Stephen asked me if I'm writing a letter to Nikos, I said yes, and he asked if he could add to it. I gave him a blank page from the block of paper I'm writing on.

Dearest Nikos,

We are in the train on the way to Avignon, and David has been writing a letter to you. He will have told you all the news fit to print like the New York Times. David is still all in one piece and very helpful. Maybe he got a bit spoiled in Paris but that was only two days, and the digging will doubtless correct any bad results from Paris. The only qualification of this is that Francis Bacon may decide to join us. But we'd have to dig anyway. We are going to christen all the trees. Nikos will be an almond tree (or would you prefer fig?). Perhaps an oleander would be best of all. We think of you all the time and never talk of anyone or anything else. All my love always, dearest Nikos, Stephen

Mausanne

There is no electricity in the house, so Stephen and I use oil lamps.

I got up at dawn today and went out to dig. I dug two holes before breakfast. It's cold, and a strong wind is blowing. The air is brilliantly pure and, just as Van Gogh described the country to his brother in his letters, seems to magnify the colors. After breakfast, I dug thirteen holes. Workmen arrived to put up a fence, and I felt, oh, so authoritative telling them what to do.

Now I'm resting. Stephen and I share his large upstairs room, with a bed at either end. He has lent me Van Gogh's letters, so I can see Provence as Van Gogh saw it. Stephen has gone to Arles to see a lawyer, I think, on business that annoys him to have to do. As it annoys him to have to get through to Malraux in Paris to ask him to help get electricity to the house, which he said Natasha insisted he do.

Last night at dinner, Stephen and I again spoke about Nikos, and again he told me how fortunate I am. I have become close to him. I told him I'm sure I've become a different person since I met Nikos, more sure of myself, confident of things developing naturally without my having to force them. Stephen agreed that he was sure I had changed. My separation from Nikos has made me realize this very much, and it is Stephen who has given me the perspective to see Nikos and me together and how being with Nikos has changed me. What he says about us is always so right.

We talked about the stories I gave him. He said he liked them, but there are certain things I must be careful about. I must not write carelessly (which I do now and then), and I must read each story over and over, twenty and thirty times, until I have a definite sense of each one. He said he sensed a lot was in the stories, but what's in them is never fully expressed. Then he said, 'Be sane.' I was struck, and not sure I understood. He told me not to worry about making my stories imaginative as there's enough imagination in me that will come out. He said, 'Don't try to be mad, you're mad enough.' He told me not to be hysterical, because the hysteria always seems unmotivated and therefore boring. And then he said I must listen for my own voice. He asked me, 'Do you know what I mean?' 'Oh yes,' I said, 'but I wonder if my voice is locked in and I am locked in with it, and I do nothing but listen to it but can't make it heard.' 'That may be your greatest danger,' he said.

I know what we can get Stephen for Christmas: a briefcase.

––––––

I brought all three of Nikos' letters, all arrived at the same time, to Avignon and read them sitting in the square. Stephen had dropped me off for a couple of hours while he went to arrange for the delivery of the trees for which I have dug the holes. I think Nikos is lonely and depressed, and I want to go back to him. I want to tell him: you don't write rubbish in your letters, and you especially don't write anything I shouldn't, as you say, concern myself with. Your wanting to do something with your life concerns me greatly, as I assume what I do with my life concerns you. You are right to tell me you feel that I want you to remain in the position of a clerk in the Greek Embassy for my security, and you are not perverse in suspecting this in me. You will always have to fight against my wanting you to be the one with the solid job, the regular income, the one in whom I find security. You must demand security from me.

While I was in Avignon, I went to the Popes' Palace, with huge, draughty halls, great flights of stairs, narrow and high corridors, all in stone, grey, whitish, clay-color, and crumbling everywhere. After wandering around in the cold, I found the papal chapel warm with sunlight flooding through the windows. The chapel is huge and absolutely stark, and echoes in such a way that when you let out a faint shout it is like striking an immense tuning fork.

Back in the house, Stephen gave me a letter Nikos sent to him:

November 18, 1966

My dearest Stephen,

Thank you so much for taking David with you to France. I am sure that it will be very good for him for his health, and good for him to meet interesting people and to be with you in the country which I imagine being so beautiful. I wish I could have come with you but I do not resent not being able to come. On the contrary, I think that I am with you through David. You are both marvellously good to me always. Sometimes I doubt that I deserve it. I hope with all my heart that everything will go well in France and that you will love David as much as I do. I am sure that you will create a beautiful love-garden that will, perhaps, remain in history as the most beautiful love-garden in the south of France, made by the last great English romantic, the last New England idealist, both inspired by the last Greek before Greece sinks like the Atlantis.

I will be thinking of you both and imagining you planting, talking, reading, writing and being happy.

All my love,
Nikos

Reading this letter, I thought, but the garden is Natasha's!

Αγάπη μου,

We are on the train, in a compartment, Stephen, Francis, George and I, all headed back to Paris.

Though I can hardly understand what George says, I know he likes me as much as I like him, so I smile at whatever he says, and that's understanding enough between us. We will see them both in London. Francis has already suggested that we all go to a Greek restaurant together. You see, I've talked about you to them too!

They arrived Saturday afternoon, and that evening we had dinner together in the restaurant of their hotel and talked about the Picasso exhibition. Francis said he can't admire the man enough, but when I said, 'I see your work, the studies for heads, come right out of Picasso,' he looked at me with one fixed eye while the other eye seemed to drift off to the side and I felt he was, with a slight frown, thinking of how to take what I said, then he simply smiled and said nothing. I thought, though, that I should be careful of what I say to him, especially about his own work.

Francis said he had gone with Mary McCarthy to see the paintings of owls, which were dreadful, so dreadful he couldn't believe she had any appreciation of art, any at all. He laughed.

We all talked about different people, such as Sonia, but also many people in London I don't know who appear to make up a world.

George told us about his world — about being in borstal and later in prison. Everyone listened to him attentively, especially Francis, as if he had never heard George talk about his time incarcerated, and the talk appeared to excite him.

When Stephen and I got back to his house and his big room, he said to me, his hand on my head, 'I hope you won't be spoiled by all the people you're meeting.'

Feeling suddenly self-conscious, I said, 'I hope not.'

He put his hand on my head and turned it a little from side to

side to look at my face carefully, then he laughed and said, 'You look like a young French priest that older women fall in love with,' and I was relieved he was joking.

I changed into my pajamas and got into my bed at my end of the room and Stephen said to me, 'Sleep well, David.' I thought, I do love him, and how can I let him know I love him without making love with him? I fell asleep before he got into his bed.

Sunday morning, he, Francis and George and I went, Stephen driving, to Montmajour, where we took photographs.

Then we went on to Arles, where we stopped for a long time in the Roman amphitheater, Stephen and Francis talking about Shakespeare, especially Macbeth, about which Francis had strong if simple views as a tragedy, and Stephen, I noticed, agreed with everything Francis said, even, as if with excited enthusiasm, affirmed what Francis said. When Francis, as if a little impatient with Stephen's agreeing with him, said, 'But what do I know?' Stephen frowned and shut up. We took more photographs in the amphitheater.

We went to Tarascon, where we ate a bad meal. Stephen seemed embarrassed by the meal, as if he were responsible for it, but Francis and George seemed not to care, with a lightness that made me think they didn't care much about anything. Stephen whispered to me that we were lucky that Francis and George were in very good moods.

There appeared to be a lightness to Francis' very body, the way he moved in sudden, quick ways, as if he were weightless and attached to the ground by a string, and only a string, and the string jerked him into walking and sometimes gesturing, his arms held out, laughing his abrupt laugh. George, who never laughed or smiled much, always appeared very fixed to the ground.

In the evening, we had dinner in the restaurant of Francis' and George's hotel with the prefect of Maussane and his wife, whom André Malraux, an acquaintance of Stephen from a long way back, had telephoned from Paris to tell him that electricity must be brought to the Spender house. And the painters Rodrigo and Anne Moynihan, who live part of the year in the South of France, also came to the dinner.

George, who sat next to me, told me, or I think he told me, how much he loves Francis. He put his arm over my shoulder to tell me this again and again.

Alone with Stephen in the house, I felt as he walked about in the light of the oil lamps that his loneliness was as big as he is. I said goodnight and went to bed before he did.

The next morning, Monday, I dug a little until the men from whom Stephen had ordered the trees arrived and said that they would have dug the holes, and, seeing the holes I'd dug, obviously thought they'd have to improve on them.

Stephen and I picked up Francis and George at their hotel and went to Aix, where we had a great lunch, saw a little Rembrandt self-portrait Francis admired for the way the face so obviously emerges from paint.

On the way back from Aix, we passed an accident at a cross-roads where a big truck load of pigs had smashed into a tree, and the roads were littered with dead, bloody pigs. Francis, his eyes wide and head turning in all directions, got very animated by the sight as we drove past.

He said, 'It's so beautiful.'

At Maussane we again had dinner in the hotel restaurant.

Before we left Avignon this morning, we took lots and lots of photographs in an automatic booth in the train station. Francis said he uses them to paint from, especially if they're blurred or contorted in some way, so we all tried to make ourselves as blurred and contorted as possible. Francis took a bunch, Stephen did, and I have some. The best ones are of Stephen when he is not blurred or contorted. He looks marvelous, monumental, with a beauty only very few older people come into, I think.

In our compartment, which for hours we had to ourselves, the talk was very intimate, about guilt and love and sex and homosexuality.

Francis said a lesbian can pretend to be heterosexual just by lying there, but a homosexual man can't pretend to be heterosexual with a woman.

We've passed out of the sunlight of Provence into a grey fog. Stephen, Francis, George are sleeping. A Frenchman has come into our compartment, and, seeing me write this letter, has just said, 'Les lettres d'amour ne sont jamais terminées.' I wonder how he knew.

Αγάπη σου

Stephen wants to add to this letter.

Dearest Nikos,

When I first met you I couldn't have imagined that anything so wonderful would happen as you and David finding one another – still less that if it did I could be so with you both. I am very glad this has happened.

Always with my love,

Stephen

David doesn't do anything but write letters to you.

Paris

We are back in the Quai Voltaire, though we have decided to leave tonight rather than tomorrow. Mary McCarthy had invited us when we were last in Paris to dinner this evening, but when Stephen telephoned her to confirm she said something had come up and she couldn't have us. It occurred to me that she is a friend of Natasha and maybe, thinking about it, decided she shouldn't invite Stephen and me to her home. God knows what everyone thinks of my relationship with Stephen, even though he makes a point of telling everyone it is not sexual.

Last night, after we got back to Paris, Stephen, Francis, George and I had dinner in a restaurant, and for the first time I saw Francis in terms of his pictures. He got drunk, drunker and drunker, and kept repeating over and over that people are horrible, life is horrible, that everyone is scum. George, also drunk, didn't appear to be hearing. Stephen and I listened, and were defenseless. When Francis started to denounce Christianity, citing Macbeth as the most profoundly atheistic work ever, Stephen said he thought he was Christian at least in believing we must all help one another.

Francis, his lower lip stuck out and his smooth jowls bulging, fixed on him, and then he said, 'Practically, do you help others?'

'No,' Stephen said, 'I don't, and I certainly wouldn't give everything I have away to the poor, but still I believe I should.'

Francis stared at Stephen for a longer time, his lower lip stuck out more, as if, frowning deeply, he were considering deeply. He said, in a harsh voice, 'Rubbish.'

I thought, Well, of course he's right, but then I suddenly became upset, partly, I think, because he was attacking Stephen, and there was nothing I could do to stop him. I could have sided with Stephen, I guess, but I didn't, because I knew that Francis was right.

When Stephen and I got back to our hotel room, I all at once began to weep.

Stephen asked, 'Is it because of what Francis said?'

I said I didn't know.

Stephen said I should consider that Francis' paintings are just a part of life – as the war in Vietnam and all viciousness were parts of life – but that there are other parts to life, parts that Francis himself is aware of and enjoys, such as landscapes and intelligence and friendship. Hadn't I seen this side of Francis in Provence? Stephen said, 'You saw the best of Francis when he and George were with us in Provence.'

This morning, the four of us met again to go once more to the Picasso exhibition to see what we hadn't been able to see the first time, but maybe we had seen too much that first time (also Picasso, Picasso, Picasso is everywhere in Paris) because we came out feeling less than enthusiastic. Or could this have been because of Francis, who, after he started out by saying everything was marvelous, stopped saying it, but began to frown, his lower lip stuck out? Stephen has bought Nikos the catalogue as a gift.

We all had lunch with Mary McCarthy in a restaurant. Francis said he thought the paintings of the owls were marvelous. She smiled her hard smile.

Stephen and I went to look at some art galleries, then came back to the hotel to rest, and decided we would leave tonight.

So I will wake Nikos up in the morning and get into bed with him.

London

Nikos' cousin Maria is staying with us for a while before she moves into a flat in Mortlake with two other girls, all of them going to a mysterious 'school' Maria talks about cryptically. She is a dark young woman with large dark eyes made all the larger by large dark circles around them. Because she is so secretive about her school, Nikos and I wonder if it is the school of Scientology or Economic Science, which, along with schools of Indian meditation, are advertised on posters in the Underground stations. Nikos has no tolerance for such places, but he is very tolerant of Maria, who is herself so tolerant, as if some deep sadness in her has made her so deeply tolerant. Her laughter is very sad.

Like Nikos, she won't go back to live in Greece, but has decided to make England her home. In Athens, she said, she was talked badly about because she wore a skirt and blouse to a wedding. She wants to paint, to write poetry, to wear what she wants.

She says, 'I want my life to mean something.'

I am with her often, and we talk.

She is teaching me Greek.

———

Francis, with George, invited us and Stephen to dinner at the White Tower, which he chose because Nikos is Greek. I wanted so much for Nikos to like Francis and George. I am never sure that he will like the people I do. He tells me I like everybody, and expect everybody to like me. Francis was very lively, passing out pound notes to anyone who served us, even if it was just to refill our glasses with wine, and sometimes held out pound notes to people passing as if they were serving us. George smiled a contented smile, as if pleased that Francis was with people with whom he was being so spontaneously lively.

Francis said, when Stephen asked him, that he doesn't see Lucian Freud any more.

George said, 'Lucian borrowed too much money from Francis that he gambled and lost and never paid back. I told Francis, "Enough, Francis, enough of that."'

Francis laughed.

There was talk about Henry Moore, and Francis, laughing, said that Moore's drawings were knitting, just knitting. Nikos, who, I knew, could have easily disagreed with Francis in a way neither Stephen or I would dare to, said, 'That's it, they're just knitting.' After, Nikos and I walked home. He didn't say anything. I asked, 'Didn't you like Francis?' He said, 'I'm thinking.' We walked on. He said, 'He doesn't take anything for granted, anything at all. He's totally original. I think he is amazing.'

Keswick, Cumberland

I don't like being away from Nikos. I really am anxious all the while. I had thought it would be nice to get away with Maria, who said we should simply take the next train from Euston Station that was leaving after we got there, which seemed an exciting idea. But I think of Nikos all the time and want to be with him. There were moments on the train when I felt I wanted to turn right back to him. I used to enjoy travelling, but I don't now, perhaps because I feel being with Nikos is as far as I could ever hope to travel. Perhaps there's a horror in all this that I feel: we're so entangled with each other, and though the entanglement is freedom for me, I can't begin to imagine how horrible it would be if Nikos felt limited by it. I think, sometimes, I do limit Nikos, and he resents it. But I know that he frees me, in the largest sense, and I can only hope I do the same for him, in some sense.

The next train leaving Euston was to the Lake District. It took about six and a half hours, with two changes. The trip was pleasant, but towards the end when it got dark and we were told that most hotels would be closed, we had a moment of panic. But we found a hotel easily, in the center of Keswick, where I am now in bed in my room. We took a walk, but it was too dark to see anything. We talked. Nikos would not be very tolerant of our philosophical discussions about life and death, but I am enough like Maria that we get a lot from them, and sometimes she does say remarkable things.

I wish I could get the train ride in: at first leaving London, buildings grey, then green and dun-colored fields with placid cows, then it clouded over and drizzled, and as darkness came so did fog, and I felt rather sleepy so dozed a little and woke to find we were in the midst of very high, bald hills, the darkness a kind of blue-black light that made everything gleam, and then it got too dark to see anything, and going through a valley, where the train stations were illuminated by one weak lantern hung on a branch or the picket of a fence, I had the feeling that the train had left the earth and was rattling through the dark sky, and that all the very distant, very pale lights were stars in that sky. I then felt a horrible anxious-making desolation come over me. I really don't have any other stability but Nikos.

It's early, around 9:00, but we both wanted to sleep. Because of the cold damp, the bed has an electric blanket.

Bowness-on-Windermere

After breakfast, we came by bus to Friar's Crag on Derwent Water, where we are now. We're sitting, completely by ourselves, on a rock thrust out into the lake. There are dark islands, and behind them vague mountains covered in mist. In the foreground are pine branches. It is very, very quiet, the quiet that Maria calls 'silence that goes beyond silence.' But I've started to notice matchsticks and bits of paper and rubbish on the ground around us. I think we'll go.

Later. We're in Bowness-on-Windermere, in a lovely hotel right on Lake Windermere. There's a large party on downstairs, and I can hear voices and music from my room.

As we're here off-season, the rates are very reasonable, and we are indulging ourselves in ordering tea from room service and having tea together in Maria's room by the electric fire.

She says, 'It's a funny thing, this earth we walk on,' or 'It's a funny thing, hurrying and worrying about life,' or 'It's a funny thing, life,' and while she smiles, her large, dark eyes, surrounded by dark rings, are very sad.

———

Maria said she woke this morning feeling better than she has in months.

In the lounge after dinner yesterday, she told me just a little about her 'school' – or rather suggested something about it by asking me if I had ever stood up among people I didn't know and told them honestly everything I have ever done in all my life, however bad? I said no. She said, 'It's the hardest thing to do.'

London

B ack home with Nikos, who I know is the centre of my life.
He is the centre, and about him are the now many friends
we refer our lives together out to, all these friends aspects of life in
London, where we are extended into a world.

Yet, do we – no, do I, for Nikos is not interested – know
anything about what is meant to be the class system of Britain?
Here, I belong to no class, or imagine that I don't. Nor does
Nikos belong.

———

I guess the real invention in keeping a diary is the way it is written,
so allow myself to think back, inventively, at the time Nikos and I
were in Venice, our first trip abroad together after we met, on our
way to Yugoslavia. We were there for the festival of the Redentore,
and, sitting on the steps of the Salute, we watched the fireworks in
the warm, clear night, starting with a shocking bang that made the
night itself seem to shake, and then, over and over, great balls of
red, silver, gold rose into the sky and, one after another, exploded
into red, silver, gold suns that held themselves still for a moment
then, from flashing cores, were shattered into bright sparks that fell,
slowly and silently, down, down, down, and disappeared into the
darkness that appeared to be as deep as it was high. We were
witnessing the beginning and the end of the universe.

———

Stephen asked me if I would write a letter to Natasha to reassure her that she would have approved of my having gone to the South of France with Stephen, which Stephen told me she had known nothing about (and I more than suspected that Mary McCarthy, who had invited Stephen and me to dinner, cancelled after having spoken to Natasha over the telephone, Mary McCarthy referring to me and surprising Natasha that Stephen was not alone, upsetting her very much).

I wrote her this letter, hoping to humour her, hoping to impress on her that I am, oh, charmingly innocent. But I haven't sent the letter, and think I'd better not. That I started the letter addressing her as Dearest Natasha shows that I was writing to a fantasy person I've not met, and am rather frightened of meeting.

Dearest Natasha,

When Stephen said he had to go to the South of France to plant trees, I thought he'd been invited by some state cultural institution, perhaps within the realm of André Malraux as Minister of Culture, to participate in a ceremony of tree planting. He said this as if looking into the far distance at a scene of himself throwing earth into the hole around the base of a tree held by an official, and he frowned. He said, 'I'm going alone.' Nikos said, 'Why don't you have David go with you?' Stephen smiled and said he'd like that, and I had the image of myself standing behind him, feeling awkward and at the same time proud to be there, as he gave a little speech after the tree was planted.

It was only when we were on our way to Saint Rémy that I realized he was meant to plant trees – or what he called trees – in your garden. He said something like, 'My God, I forgot Natasha's plans for what we should plant where.' I was relieved that what I'd imagined a public ceremony would be private – because planting a tree must be, I felt, something of a ceremony of some kind, even if private. When we arrived at the house, Stephen, looking through folded papers that he took from all his pockets so there was a stack of them, with unused postage stamps, spectacles, pound and franc and even lire notes, and old, cancelled airplane tickets among them, he found the plans, but as clear as they were, we, not quite gardeners, prepared more for the ceremony of planting rather than the practicalities, and couldn't quite match up the sketch of the garden it would be with the garden as it was. We stood in the wind, your careful plans flapping. The light was very clear on the foothills of the Alpilles along the horizon.

Monsieur M., the French gardener, came and helped us. He wore a sagging blue overall and thick black shoes, and he listened to Stephen as if torn between his duty to do what Stephen told him what you wanted him to do and the need to tell Stephen what to do. He took the plan and turned it to the right way up, and indicated where the holes for the bushes, not trees, were to be planted in a row to form a protected walk that was to be covered in gravel. Now, the walk was uneven and weedy. Monsieur M. said he would deliver the plants.

They arrived – twigs with earth-filled pouches about the roots – and the next morning, a cold November morning, Stephen and I went out after breakfast to dig holes for them. I still felt I was about to perform a ceremony, and I thought that, as ceremonies are meant to be effortless, digging holes would be effortless. The ground was frozen, and I had to use a pick-axe to break it up, and then each time I shoved the spade into the loosened earth it struck a stone. Stephen would shovel out the earth, then I would, each in turn, and when the hole was about a foot deep Stephen would say, 'I think that's deep enough, don't you?' He or I would go for a twig, undo the pouch, and one of us would hold the plant, its roots sticking out, upright in the hole while the other replaced the earth and stones, and we'd both, each on a side, stomp. The freezing air was electric, and that electricity seemed to be the source of the constant, bright white, almost blinding light. That morning, we dug three holes and stomped three plants into them.

Monsieur M. appeared, and, examining our work, looked, again, anxious. He obviously wanted to tell us we weren't doing the work quite as it should have been done, but he was too respectful of our efforts to. His dark eyes were filmed with tears, though the tears were probably caused by the cold wind that made the twigs stomped into the earth sway.

Monsieur M. said that the earth was too frozen in fact for digging properly, and that we must not derange ourselves with trying to plant now. He would deal with that when the weather was better. Stephen and I went to lunch at a restaurant in Arles, one of those restaurants with dark wood wainscoting and where the steaming soup tureen was put on the table with an old, dented ladle. The wine was in a carafe.

I think we had some sense of celebrating our accomplishment, even though, as Stephen has told me, we planted the wrong coloured flowering bushes in the wrong place.

I haven't sent this to Natasha because, she not having met me, she most likely would think I am patronizing her, trying to make her feel that she must find Stephen's and my planting plants in her garden funny, and as funny excusable. But I like the details in the description.

―――――――

Öçi tells me that I have such interesting friends, which surprises me, as I always assumed his friends, for simply being his friends, were more interesting than any I could have.

He asks me about America, in particular about New York, where he wants to go, and where I do not want to return to.

It reassures me that Nikos reads my diary, which he says he likes to read to find out what we've been doing in this record of our lives together. I do not hold back from writing whatever I want, which allowance he not so much gives me as never questions.

This comes to me as something of a surprise: that there is no fantasy in my relationship with Nikos, in our love for each other.

———

Walking along Piccadilly, Maria and I saw on the newspapers being sold at little newspaper stands the headlines about the military coup in Greece by some colonels. She laughed both sadly and nervously.

Because I have no experience of an American national political catastrophe, I cannot imagine the effect of one, and I am unable to make the connection between Nikos and Maria, whom I know, and the catastrophe of a dictatorship in Greece, about which I know only by what I am told by Nikos. I'm unable to make a connection between him and modern Greek history, he having lived that history and I not. It is a history of many catastrophes, and therefore Nikos' so-often-used word 'catastrophe' for missing a bus, or breaking a glass, or forgetting where his spectacles were last put down. How can I know what it means to a Greek to have the country dictated to by petty colonels, and especially what it means to Nikos, working at the Greek Embassy, and, too, what it means to us together?

———

Some men, including Sonia Orwell's ex-husband Michael Pitt-Rivers, were arrested and imprisoned for homosexual activity; so many people objected to the unfairness of these convictions that the Wolfenden Committee was set up to study the law that gave rise to them, and its report recommended decriminalizing homosexual relations among consenting adults. Years after, years since the report was published, a bill has been passed in Parliament, and Nikos and I are no longer criminals. We never felt we were.

———

The military dictatorship in Greece made it politically and morally impossible for Nikos to continue to work at the Embassy, so he quit.

He had no money, but I had $3000 savings. We moved to a top-floor flat in Battersea, in Overstrand Mansions on Prince of Wales Drive, London S.W.11, overlooking the large, dense green trees of Battersea Park. The flat, with slanted ceilings because we are under the roof, has three small rooms off a corridor, which we painted all white.

Johnny Craxton gave us some furniture, some beautiful chairs and an antique chest of drawers, and the rest we bought at a huge second-hand furniture warehouse in Peckham Rye.

As Nikos says, we are creating our lives together.

My desk cost two pounds ten shillings. I've begun to write reports for different publishers, to translate technical books from French, and to write fiction.

Many of Nikos' friends from Athens have come to London in exile, and we often have them staying with us.

Through Stephen, Nikos had a few interviews with publishers. Charles Monteith at Faber & Faber told him that he should start out by getting a job in a bookshop. Nikos said, 'I didn't do all that graduate work in philosophy at Harvard in order to become a sales clerk in a bookshop.' Patrick introduced him to Anthony Blond, who was publishing guidebooks about the night life of capital cities called London Spy or Paris Spy or New York Spy and asked Nikos to do Athens Spy, but Nikos said he was not interested in the night life of Athens, where, in any case, he would not go. John Lehmann invited Nikos to lunch but had no advice.

Nikos said, 'Well, they must think I'm asking for a lot – not being English, my first language being Greek, and having no experience in publishing.'

I looked for a job teaching English to the children of families at the American army base at Ruislip, but many other young Americans wanting to live in London without work permits were also trying to get jobs there.

Then Nikos, at a drinks party, met an editor at Penguin Books, Tony Richardson, who was leaving Penguin and said there was a job going there, and why didn't Nikos apply? He went for an interview with Allen Lane, the founder of Penguin Books. The position left vacant by Tony Richardson was to be editor for poetry, art and architecture, cinema, theatre, and town planning, and Nikos got the job. He started working as an editor at Penguin Books.

He recounted to me a long walk he had with Tony Richardson, who, very ill, perhaps fatally, had to take long walks for whatever medication he was on to circulate throughout his body. He told Nikos that the only appreciation he has in art, music, literature is for the greats: Michelangelo, Rembrandt, Haydn, Mozart, Beethoven, Dickens, Dostoyevsky, Tolstoy. Recounting this to me, Nikos, as he does when he is very moved, raised his arms and lowered them, and said nothing. Tony Richardson died soon after Nikos took over his position at Penguin Books.

Nikos was granted resident status by the Home Office.

With Stephen guaranteeing me, I have also become a resident.

We see a lot of Stephen, who, when he first came to our Battersea flat for dinner, said it was just the kind of place he'd always wanted to live in.

All this is just summary, as I write only occasionally in my diary.

———

I have been reading Victor Shklovsky, who, with his friend Osip Brik, was one of the founders of Russian Formalism, and who wrote:

Sometimes books are not written; they emerge, they happen.

And suddenly, thinking of having met Osip Brik and his historical involvement with Russian Formalism, there comes to me the small shock of having met Lili Brik whose photograph by Rodchenko was used in perhaps the most famous Soviet poster, that of a woman wearing a bandana, an open hand to the side of her mouth, shouting out the good news of Communism!

And because of the way I like connecting people I've met with people they have met, as if these greater connections expand my world into that greater world, a strained sense of possessiveness comes to me with the thought that when I shook hands with the Briks I shook hands with the Russians they often had to their flat in the 1920s, including Boris Pasternak, Maxim Gorky, Vladimir Mayakovsky, Sergei M. Eisenstein, Kazimir Malevich, Alexander Rodchenko, Varvara Stepanova, Yuri Tynyanov, Vsevolod Meyerhold, and who knows how many others?

And it comes to me, belatedly because it did not come to me at the time, to wonder what Osip and Lili Brik thought of my relationship with Stephen Spender, Stephen and I perhaps to them a strange couple who, especially for Soviets, could only have come from a world so foreign to them that they must have wondered at it.

A cultural difference between Nikos and me, which difference makes him always more attractive to me. As a provincial American who grew up in a small, isolated, French-speaking parish in Yankee New England, I held and still do hold celebrated writers in some awe, and that awe is certainly a dimension in my friendship with Stephen Spender, for often I step back from our friendship and see him as a celebrated poet who is a friend. Nikos, a Greek born and brought up in a cosmopolitan family in which some of his relatives are themselves celebrated writers (among others, his aunt Tato, a novelist) and who know celebrated writers, seems to take for granted the celebrated writers in London as if he were simply transferring his familiarity with Athenian writers to familiarity with writers here. He sees Stephen as a friend who writes poetry.

And as for my awe of publishers, I once saw a commissioning editor in a publishing house as having the power to determine my life. And now Nikos is such a publisher. But, as he explains, in Athens it is no very great distinction to publish a novel or a collection of poems, as there are many publishing houses which, in the old way of publishing houses, have their own bookshops, and more often than not the writer will pay for the publishing of his or her work. Publishing a novel or collection of poems may add something to one's life, though, really, one's life is determined somewhere else, mostly by one's family, for whom publishing a novel or a collection of poems is simply a part of the family culture. Nikos is so unassuming in his position as a publisher, I sometimes wonder if he is at all aware of his power, as if to be a publisher in London were to him to have no more determining power than a publisher would have in Athens. When I visit him in the Penguin offices, I am very impressed by how matter-of-factly he appears to take to dictating to his secretary, to talking business on the telephone, to having his own personal cup for coffee on his desk.

No doubt aspiring British editors are resentful that Nikos, not British, should have such a powerful position as editor.

Nikos as poetry editor with Borges.

In Nikos' presence, though I can't recall where and to whom, I said that I don't understand how anyone can say, 'I like him' or 'I dislike her,' nor do I understand how anyone can say about a country, 'I like Italy' or 'I dislike France,' people and countries too large and complex in character to have any opinions about them. Some time later, again I can't recall where or to whom, I heard Nikos say he didn't understand how anyone can say about another, 'I like him' or 'I dislike her,' or about a country, 'I like Italy' or 'I dislike France,' and I suddenly felt in our relationship a transference that would have him repeat what I had told him as though the thought had come from him. In what other many, many ways does this transference occur, from me to him, and, more importantly to me, him to me? I find myself saying to another, 'We went to France for a weekend,' and it is with great pleasure that I hear him say to the other, 'We went to an exhibition of Courbet at the Grand Palais.'

At a dinner party, a guest said she had been to Paris for the Courbet exhibition and came away not liking Courbet. Nikos sat up straight and said, 'You can't say that, you can't say you don't like Courbet.' The guest, a woman, said, 'But I have the right to my opinion,' and placed a hand about her throat. Nikos said, 'No, you don't, you don't have the right to an opinion about Courbet.'

Nikos was among many people at a meeting in the Friends' Meeting House in Marylebone Road to speak against the dictatorship in Greece. The house was packed. He started by saying that when he was in school, at Athens College, he was threatened with expulsion for reading poems by the Greek Communist poet Ritsos and playing a Soviet oratorio by Shostakovich at an event organized by a cultural society which he was president of. He said 'ah' a lot while he spoke.

He told me that while at Athens College he had in fact been a member of the Communist Party, which was outlawed by the government. He would risk getting up during the night from his bed in the dormitory of the boarding school and go down to an office for which he, then president of the student council, had keys and where he would mimeograph propaganda, then, with the sheets hidden on him, would on a free evening go to cinemas in Athens and throw the sheets from balconies into the audience. It was dangerous to do, but he was never caught.

Nikos knows of the horrors of Communism in Soviet Russia. I would never ask him to justify his belief in Communism, the meaning of which is deep in his Greek history, but which meaning is in my American history anathema.

Stephen telephoned from Paris. He is staying in a hotel on the rue des Ecoles. He said that last night around three o'clock students overturned cars and set them on fire just outside his hotel window and bombs were thrown. He has been out on the streets himself, on the side of the students. One asked him if he was Herbert Marcuse, and he was very pleased, but had to say no. Demonstrations of students and workers go on day and night: speeches, marches, riots.

———

An uncle of Nikos, Stavros Stangos, has left Greece to live in London. He is, Nikos tells me, a well-known journalist, Leftist. He came with his wife for a meal and talked of how he used to go into the poor areas of Athens to recruit people into the Communist Party, dangerous. He talked of the defeat of the Communist Party during the Civil War, which he fought in, and which Nikos, younger, remembers. I feel that what the Greeks I have met most have to bear is the defeat of their social ideology.

Greek friends of Nikos, also having managed to get out, visit, and some stay with us for a few days until they are able to settle. Nikos and they talk in Greek, the only word comprehensible to me being 'catastrophe'.

The great Greek actress Aspasia Papathanasiou has come to London, and Nikos visits her. She is an ardent Communist. She gave a reading of Yannis Ritsos' 'Epitaphios' at a poetry reading in the Festival Hall, a lament on the death of a young Communist soldier during the Civil War, and in her declamation was the tragic voice of Greece.

W. H. Auden read on this occasion. He kept looking at his watch when other poets read. Later, he said he disapproved of Papathanasiou's recitation: one does not weep when reciting a poem.

It is strange to meet people who are exiled, people who talk of prison and torture. Though I hear about 'catastrophe' in the personal terms of people I meet through Nikos, I can't see anyone truly suffering the 'catastrophe,' certainly can't see anyone in prison and tortured, as if suffering is far beyond this or that single person but is some vastly impersonal suffering. I wonder if this has to do with the impression I retain of World War II – only an impression, because I was a little boy – of suffering on such a scale that it is difficult to reduce the suffering to someone I could possibly know, or even meet.

How my mind makes tangential connections as I write, tangents always occurring to me to draw me away from now to then, until now and then become so connected I don't make a distinction between the two. So a dinner party occurs to me, given by Nikos and me, at which Frank and Anita Kermode came with the Italian writer Luigi Meneghello and his wife Katia, on whose forearm I noted a blue, tattooed number from when she was a prisoner in Auschwitz.

Nikos told me that, after years of youthful taking for granted the Parthenon on the Acropolis, one day he looked up at the temple on the rock and the meaning came to him overwhelmingly. I can only guess what that historical meaning was – is – to him, a Greek.

―――――

A Romanian friend, Roxanne, whose aristocratic family in Romania lost everything to Communism, and who has shown us letters from her mother that have obviously been censored with faint pencil marks underlining sentences before they were allowed to be sent, admonished Nikos that he should be grateful that Greece has been kept free of Communism. Nikos closed his eyes and lowered his head.

How can I not feel in him the defeat of his ideology?

Nikos asked Roxanne if her family were Greek Phanariots from Constantinople sent to Romania by the Sultan to govern the country.

Yes, she said, four hundred years ago.

―――――

On the crowded 137 bus from Marble Arch, alone, I stood next to a young man and as the bus moved we were jostled against each other, and each time we were jostled against each other we looked at each other in the eyes. That sense came over me as of there being no two other people in the world but the two of us, we at a centre and nothing around the centre. He must have felt the same, because when I got off the bus at Prince of Wales Drive he did too, and we walked together along the drive, hardly talking, but he came with me up to the flat and we made love. I did not learn his name.

When Nikos came home I told him, and he exclaimed, 'Not in our bed!'

———

I saw Öçi alone. He said, 'I am not an envious person, but I admit to you that I'm envious of your relationship with Nikos.'

———

James Joll, historian of anarchism, and John Golding, historian of art and also a painter, live in Prince of Wales Drive. (Francis Bacon lived here once, and the woman he often paints, Henrietta Moraes, still does, the windows of her flat all year long decorated with Christmas lights.) Nikos and I were invited by John and James for a drinks party.

At the drinks party were Richard and Mary Day Wollheim. Richard is a philosopher of aesthetics, Mary Day a ceramicist of elegant pots. Richard talked of people he knows, always with a look on his face of the improbability of knowing such people, half frowning and half smiling, and making ambiguous gestures with his fingers. There was the story of the couple who, when travelling by ship from New York to Southampton, took a stateroom apart from their own for their parrot. The man will say to his wife that he cannot sit at the opera surrounded by others, so she, with the money, will buy a block of tickets, and an hour before the performance he will say he is too tired to go.

Richard and Mary Day were with Sylvia Guirey, who was once a lady friend of Richard, and is now a friend of both Richard and Mary Day.

She is in some way a descendant of Hugo von Hofmannsthal, the poet and librettist for Richard Strauss, and is more immediately connected to the American Astors. Inspired by Richard, she left her past life to lead a more imaginative, creative life in the present. She is a painter.

Because married to a Circassian prince, she is a princess. Mary Day said, 'Anyone from Circassia with a pair of boots is a prince.' Her husband the prince lives in Ireland.

From John Golding's book, Cubism, the first line: 'Cubism was perhaps the most important and certainly the most complete and radical artistic revolution since the Renaissance.'

Nikos has commissioned John Golding to write a short essay on Cubism for an anthology he is editing, Concepts of Modern Art.

———

Not I, but Nikos was invited by Stephen to the Neal Street Restaurant, a new restaurant that is meant to attract interesting people, with W. H. Auden and Cyril Connolly and Pauline de Rothschild. Nikos wore a brown overcoat and Connolly said to him, 'Brave of you to wear brown in town,' which Nikos didn't understand was not done in London, but which amused him (I would have thought, Oh, I should have known, and clearly I don't know). He said Connolly ordered a partridge, which bled when he cut into it, so he sent it back, and when the bird came back burnt black, Nikos saw Connolly staring at it with tears running down his cheeks. Stephen laughed. Pauline de Rothschild ate only one pear. W. H. Auden was silent.

———

When Nikos is with Greeks, the sexual leanings of someone not known will be questioned, and one of them, leaning his head a little to the side, will say, as if the expression has to be in French, 'Il est un peu comme ça.'

———

The Greek novelist Costas Tachtsis is staying with us. Nikos suggested to Penguin Books that the novel by Costas, The Third

Wedding, be translated into English and published, as a way of Penguin making a positive statement about Greek culture during a time when culture in Greece means nothing more than propaganda. Was Costas happy with the translation and the publication? Is Costas ever happy about anything? I arrived back home a little late to find Costas, sitting at the top of the steps to the landing outside our front door, keening, 'Ach, ach, ach!' Alarmed, I asked, 'What's wrong?' and he, throwing his arms up and raising his chin, cried out, 'My book! My book! They've destroyed my book!' He disapproved of the translation.

Praising the book, Nikos is amused by the transposition of the raving Greek female characters from raving Greek male friends.

Costas travels with a special trunk of women's clothes, not fashionable frocks, but dowdy tweed skirts and cardigans and heavy stockings, which he dresses into to – as he says – faire le trottoir along Queensway in Bayswater. He plucks his beard so he doesn't have a stubble. The men he picks up, he insists, never know that he is a man, but a woman who excuses herself from not having frontal sex because she is having her period, but is happy with backside sex. Costas earns his money, not from his books, but as a transvestite prostitute.

Johnny Craxton invited the three of us to a drinks party in the large house he lives in, Kidderpore Avenue, where, it seems, many people live and where large drinks parties are given. (Johnny's father, Harold, is famous as a coach to pianists. I once heard him say that when he was a young musician in a group of musicians, they would, when invited to play at an event at a country house, be told by the chief butler to use the servants' back entrance.) Stephen Spender was at the drinks party, and while he and I stood apart without understanding, Costas raved, as one of his female characters raves, all in Greek, which Nikos and Johnny understood and listened to without expression. Later, Nikos told me that Costas was raving about Stephen – how, in the crudest way possible in Greek, he had fucked Stephen, who, now, didn't recognize him. Knowing Costas, Nikos said, he dismissed Costas' raving against

Stephen as resentment that Stephen didn't recognize him as Greece's greatest living novelist.

I have helped Costas refine the English in his own translation of a short story, and was struck by the image of a man's large red cock as if the large red cock of a blank wall.

As for everything connecting, how can I not put in here this? Edna O'Brien invited Nikos and me to dinner with the Australian novelist Patrick White and his Greek partner Manoly Lascaris. I asked him, being Greek, if he knew of a Greek writer named Costas Tachtsis? and he, scowling, said, Yes, he once knew Tachtsis, who for a while lived in Australia. Did he? I asked. All Lascaris said was, Yes, he did, and I knew not to ask more.

———

As poetry editor, Nikos has many poets wanting his attention, poets who send him or arrange to meet him to give him the kinds of publications that originated in America, the mimeographed typed text stapled together. One is The New British Poetry. Nikos and I are archivists, and I suppose we do think that whatever is of interest now will be of even more interest in the future, including the names of the New British Poets: Allen Barry, Don Bodie, Alan Brownjohn, Jim Burns, Dave Cunliffe, Paul Evans, Roy Fisher, S. A. Gooch, Harry Guest, Lee Harwood, L. M. Herrickson, Douglas Hill, Pete Hoida, Anselm Hollo, Michael Horovitz, Alan Jackson, Peter Jay, David Kerrison, Adrian Mitchell, Tina Morris, Neil Oram, Ignu Ramus, Jeremy Robson, Michael Shayer, Steve Sneyd, Chris Torrance, Gael Turnbull, Ian Vine, Michael Wilkin, W. E. Wyatt.

Some of these poets Nikos has published: Alan Brownjohn, Harry Guest, Anselm Hollo, Michael Horovitz, Adrian Mitchell, and a poet he especially admires, Lee Harwood, whose love poetry has great tenderness, and who earns his money, Nikos said, as a bus conductor collecting fares in Brighton.

———

Asked to contribute a one-line poem to an anthology, Roy Rogers, Nikos asked me to help, and I suggested:

(   )

which Nikos submitted.

———

A group of American poets came to London to give a reading and invited Nikos, who asked me to go along with him, in a small hall, which I remember as black with a spotlight on the narrow stage. The poets were Aram Saroyan, Patti Smith, and Andrew Wylie.

GOLD

Andrew Wylie

They all appeared to form a cult, a New York esoteric club. Patti Smith had long black hair and Andrew Wylie wore a beret and dark spectacles, and Aram Saroyan appeared even weirder than they for wearing rather college-like button-down collar and chinos. They gave Nikos collections of poems in small booklets, published by Telegraph Books, one of the booklets photographs of scars instead of poems put together by Brigid Polk, one of the Andy Warhol people.

A poem by Gerard Malanga, one of the Warhol people:

> My dreams come true
> Even the bad ones

A poem by Aram Saroyan:

> HAPPY!!!
> INSTANT!

A poem by Andrew Wylie:

> I fuck
> your
> ass
>
> you suck
> my cock

To his amusement, the writer on art, Marco Livingston, told me that when Nikos visited him in Oxford to discuss a book, Nikos, noting on a shelf a long playing recording of Patti Smith singing, said he hadn't been aware that she is a singer as well as a poet. Though he couldn't see how he could publish her poems – which, come to think of it, read as if the lyrics of songs – Nikos was impressed by how original she was in herself, and he liked her.

Mark Lancaster gave to Nikos a recording of songs by Janis Joplin, and after he played one song he put the recording aside, but he kept up his interest in Janis Joplin in herself as a renegade.

Nikos likes renegades.

As for their music – as driven as it is, Nikos says there is hardly any invention in it, and invention is what Nikos is acutely attentive to in any art; their music relies on an obvious beat and does little to develop the beat, does little, if anything, to invent on the beat.

That is, when he is attentive to the music. When recorded rock music is played at a party, he likes the background beat; and though he is not at all a good dancer – at best, he sways back and forth – he likes to see me dance, which I do to the driven beat, and he stands back and smiles, and I like to think I am dancing to make him smile.

About Bach, and especially Glenn Gould playing Bach, Nikos will from time to time cry out, 'It's so inventive!' and suddenly Bach *becomes* his music, and I think of Bach, who lived within the conventions of his time, as one of the most original people who ever lived.

———

Nikos has learned that a close friend of his in Athens has been arrested, George Kavounidis.

From time to time Nikos has mentioned this George Kavounidis, who was a diplomat in some South-east Asian country from where he brought back to Athens two miniature gazelles in his diplomatic luggage, one of which died of suffocation and the other Nikos described sliding about the shiny parquet floors of Kavounidis' flat. My sense from what Nikos has said of Kavounidis is that it was through him that Nikos was able to enter into the world of diplomats and then within that world on to London, and my greater sense is that Kavounidis had an entourage of young men whom he helped, for whatever personal satisfaction. What interested me is the notion of diplomats once forming, in Greece, not only a world of people engaged in politics, but of people noted for their culture. So, the poet George Seferis used his diplomatic postings to further his career outside Greece, and so, too, Nikos, posted in London, used his post in the Press Office of the Greek Embassy to establish himself in London. About George Kavounidis – who, from what Nikos says, was a social figure in Athens – I imagined him to be in a nineteenth-century, or even traditionally older, Athenian social world in which diplomats were invited to formal occasions, and Nikos, a sortable young man as Sonia would say, was invited by Kavounidis to come with him. Nikos will say he hated such occasions in Athens, but I am struck by the formal attire he brought to London from Athens: his – as he calls it – 'smoking' (what I call tuxedo), cummerbund, shiny black pumps with little tassels, an overcoat with a velvet collar, a white silk scarf, in case his posting in London required him to attend a formal event, for if Nikos does enter into such a social event he behaves accordingly. That Kavounidis' entourage of young men was homosexual was known and, as if this was a tradition among diplomats and their entourages in that social world, accepted.

That now is past history, the colonels as dictators, Nikos said, totally uncultured, crude, stupid.

New galleries keep opening. Garage is a venue for exhibitions of art and of readings of poetry founded by Tony Stokes. Everyone is in love with Tony, including Nikos. Tony flirts with Nikos, and Nikos flirts back. Tony organized at Garage an exhibition of the works of Jennifer Bartlett and Joel Shapiro.

Tony is married to Teresa Gleadowe, who works for the Arts Council. She sometimes cares for our cats when we are away, Jasmine and, now, Mustafa. The cats are known to be very neurotic, especially the female Jasmine, who, jealous of other females, hisses at women, so Teresa had to lock her in the bathroom.

I think more of Nikos' social life in Athens, as when he told me that, to be relieved of military duty by his commanding officer on New Year's Eve, he gave him a gift of a pair of expensive leather gloves and so was free to go to an all-night party with gambling, and I wondered if such a relief by an officer of a soldier for a pair of expensive gloves was indicative of a world that has had its precedents in many many years of past military social history. I imagine that Athens, being provincial and yet, because provincial, alert to what cultured Athenians imagined to be happening in the capital cities, preserved social ways that no longer existed in Berlin, Paris, London.

———

At Garage, Nikos organized a reading by Kenward Elmslie, whose poems Nikos published, and I remember the beautiful, resonant lines:

Madonna, Madonna

read in a dry voice.

Is there in his poetry a movement away from any explicit or even implied meaning, to a lively, slap-happy activity of the mind?

> The sluggish choreography of shadows bumping,
> burping and bloating, hunching and gnarling,
> has the marijuana tempo of sex sometimes.

Kenward wears on a thin chain about his neck a locket with a black and white photograph of Joe Brainard, Kenward told me when I asked, touching the little round cut-out photograph.

Joe Brainard does drawings based on ordinary objects, a lot on comic strips, such as on the comic heroine Nancy.

IF NANCY WAS A BOY.

Joe Brainard has written a book, I Remember, which consists of one-line recollections that bring back to me so many similar recollections:

I remember my mother's sticking toothpicks into cakes to see if they were done or not.

I remember Dole pineapple rings on a bed of lettuce with cottage cheese on top and sometimes a cherry on top of that.

I remember continuing my return address on envelopes to include 'The Earth' and 'The Universe.'

———

The poet Harold Norse is in London, having come from living for some time in Athens, where there is what he calls a 'scene' despite the colonels. Nikos has published him in the series Penguin Modern Poets, along with Charles Bukowski (whose poems are brutal, filled with booze and whores and death, and who sends Nikos long, long, typed letters that read as if spilling over the edges of the pages with beer) and Philip Lamantia (the American Surrealist poet admired by André Breton who writes such wonderful lines as 'The mermaids have come to the desert'), poets Harold recommended to Nikos.

No doubt Harold brings with him a world, the, say, Beat world of America, inhabited by Allen Ginsberg and Gregory Corso and William Burroughs, but I'm not sure I'm so very interested in that world to hear about it from someone who himself inhabits it. No, I'm wrong – I do find the world fascinating, but the truth is I am so jealous of it the only way I can deal with it is to tell myself I am not interested. But I also have to admit that in the person of Harold, whom I don't in himself find very interesting, the 'scene' does contract from fantasy into the ego of a man Nikos and I find more and more difficult to indulge, as he seems to want more than we can give.

Yet, Harold's poems are so much about egolessness, expounding on mantras and karma and nirvana and the cosmos and the Hub of the Fiery Force.

I like this couplet he wrote: 'Comme c'est beau / de chier dans l'eau.'

He told us this story: having met W. H. Auden at some literary event in New York, Auden invited Harold to Saint Mark's Place, but somehow Chester Kallman thought the invitation was meant for him and he appeared first at the door of Auden, who, opening the door, said, 'Wrong blond,' for, improbable as it seems, Harold was blond, as I suppose Kallman was. Harold told this story with such animated resentment at having been outdone by Kallman, and with such insistence at getting the facts right, that I have forgotten why Kallman rang Auden's bell instead of Harold. Auden must have taken to Kallman enough because Kallman stayed on.

———

The police rang Nikos to say someone named David Gascoyne, who claimed to be a poet, had asked Nikos to be called, as David Gascoyne had been arrested for trying to get to the Queen in Buckingham Palace to inform her that her life was in danger from someone wanting to kill her. Nikos went to the police station in support of Gascoyne. Nikos believes Gascoyne to be a major poet, a true Surrealist, as the English cannot be, and a Surrealist, inspired by the French, who transformed himself into a poet of some of the most movingly vulnerable spiritual poems in modern English, which, too, put him apart from the other living English poets. From Farewell Chorus:

'The silence after the viaticum.' So silent is the ray
Of naked radiance that lights our actual scene,
Leading the gaze into those nameless and unknown
Extremes of our existence where fear's armour falls away
And lamentation and defeat and pain
Are all transfigured by acceptance; where men see
The tragic splendor of their final destiny.

This poem is dated New Year, 1940.

I also think that David Gascoyne has written the most heart-wrenching poems about World War II, as in these simple lines:

Go to sleep. Put out
That light! The War is over now. It's late.
Why don't those people go to bed?

And this makes me wonder what the generation of David Gascoyne, which of course includes Stephen Spender, for whom World War II is a lived experience, can make of England now, in which it seems that that war, or any war, is so distant in time that Joan Littlewood's Oh, What a Lovely War! comes as shock from a past that the present needs to be reminded of. Perhaps David Gascoyne, in his madness, still lives the horrors of the war.

Does Stephen? Stephen seems to live more in the present, to be amused by the style of the present, as when he showed us a new greatcoat he had had tailored especially for him by the fashionable Mr. Fish, a long, wide greatcoat with wide lapels, mauve. He laughed with pleasure when he showed it off to us.

Which reminds me – reminds me, too, of so much I don't put into this diary, as though I think of so much as insignificant, whereas it may all be wonderfully significant if this diary is ever read, as it were, historically – that Nikos bought me a greatcoat (as Stephen calls an overcoat) designed by Ossie Clark, a pink and grey tweed, which I wear with the awareness that I am wearing an Ossie Clark greatcoat that others would recognize as by Ossie Clark, making me, oh, in style!

———

How I enjoy Stephen's levity, the somewhat guilty pleasure he takes in a fancy greatcoat, in fancy restaurants, in friends, in giggling at stories he tells about himself and others – guilty because I sense in him that he feels he doesn't really deserve such pleasures but that they are generous gifts to him from a world he is bemused by – and how I am always aware of a weight in him that that levity has to sustain.

I read his poems about grief, and especially the grief of his war poems, and often enough have the sense in him of that grief when, at the news of yet another wartime horror in Vietnam, he will press his lips together and stare out and shake his head a little, and I think of his writing about:

> That wreath of incommunicable grief
> Which is all mystery or nothing.

———

It seems to me that so much history is in the 'insignificant' particulars, and that in a hundred years' time these very details will say more about the past than generalizations.

———

How did Nikos learn about contemporary British poetry? How did
he know of F. T. Prince, whom he published, and whose The Tears
of a Muse in America I read as a hymn to America. I think that if
Henry James had been a poet he would have written such a poem:

> here resolutions bristle,
> For the cause seems to shine out at me from the moment
> I grant him all the mind I can; when I in short
> Impute to him an intemperate spirit . . .
> . . . It comes to me afresh,
> There glimmers out of it upon me that I want
> Nothing of it to come at once. It glimmers,
> It glimmers from the question, of how, how shall it fall
> The moment of the simple sight?

———

Thinking of 'insignificant' details – they come to me, one after
another, and I'm not able to place them, but when each appears it
brings with it, as if momentarily filling out the darkness, a whole
world evoked by the detail. So this: hanging from a long, twisted
flex over the high headboard of a bed, a light switch which is
turned on or off by pressing a button. A tray on an unmade bed
with a small coffee pot on it and cups with the dregs of coffee and
plates with the crumbs of rolls and the unfolded wrapping of butter
and little empty jars of jam. Two towels hanging over the rim of an
old, claw-footed bathtub, the floor small black and white tiles.

When I described to Julia Hodgkin the light switch at the end
of a flex, she said, 'You've brought back my entire childhood,' and
I was amazed that a detail that meant something to me was so
meaningful to her.

———

Harry Fainlight, whose poems Nikos has been urging him to be
published, came over. Though Nikos has great patience for him,

thinking him a more than worthy poet, I find him too mentally shattered, I suppose by drugs, to make any sense of what he says. (Too, I'm
frightened of drugs – hallucinogenics – for the disarray they would
cause in what I feel my already disarrayed mind.) Harry gives Nikos
poems to be published, then takes them away, and Nikos doesn't press
him. He had come to give Nikos his poems but he left with them.

We do have a chapbook collection, Sussicran, Narcissus spelt
backwards, published by Turret Press under Ted Lucie-Smith, and
these lines from a poem about lying in bed with a stranger after sex
struck me:

> Thrown by the pattern of holes in the top
> Of an old-fashioned paraffin stove, a magic
> Cathedral window glows on the ceiling.

Nikos and I had a paraffin stove when we first moved into Over-
strand Mansions, as we couldn't afford central heating.

———

What the derivation is I don't know, but the word 'gay' has come
to mean being sexually attracted to one's own sex. Frank Kermode's
colleague at University College London, Keith Walker, said he
thought a lot about what people who are attracted to the opposite
sex should be called, and came up with 'glums.'

Stephen is teaching at the University, but feels he is doing so
badly he wants to go into the loos and write on the walls SPENDER
MUST GO!

———

Often, looking at Nikos sitting across the room from me, he reading, it comes to me, as with a little flash, to wonder what was it
like to have a German officer billeted in his family house? What
was it like to see a German soldier shoot a little boy for stealing a
potato? What was it like to hear a man with a wheelbarrow calling out, each morning, for those who died of starvation because

of the German occupation? What was it like to live in a country where torturers wiped their bloody hands on a schoolroom wall? And to live through the German occupation only to have civil war replace the occupation and having to hide under the dining-room table when the nearby airport was bombed? And to be taken out to Communist rallies by the maid, who, when no one in the family could kill a dearly bought chicken, said, 'Kill a chicken? I kill men every night'? In him, in his history, I am aware of World War II.

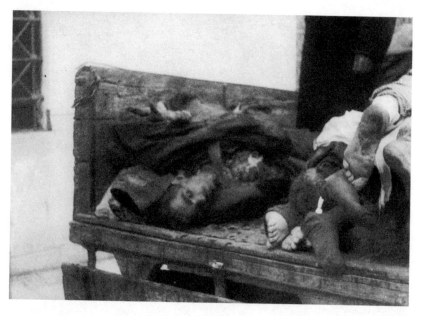

The dead, starved to death by the Nazi occupation, being taken to a mass grave outside of Athens.

––––––

Kenward Elmslie publishes a literary magazine, Z, another Z added with each magazine, and in ZZZZ is a draft of Nikos' 'Pure Reason'.

––––––

Stephen, Keith Milow, Nikos and I spent an afternoon together. Keith took photographs:

Stephen says Keith looks like a mischievous fawn.

Always in a suit and tie, his rigidly parted hair combed flat against his small, round skull with a lot of water, his slightly Asian eyes bulging behind his pink-rimmed spectacles as if to look in all directions at once (his paternal grandmother was in part Malaccan), John Pope-Hennessy's body appears too constricted to contain a soul. Too intellectually brilliant for any shadows in him, the impression he gives is of a man totally self-confident in his intelligence and knowledge and worldliness, all of which precludes any need for more than what he already has himself, and least of all any need for belief in God.

Asked at an airport check-in if he had packed his own bags, he answered, in his high pitch, 'Of course not!'

Though he always wears a tie, the collars of his shirts appear always to be wrinkled.

From time to time we meet for lunch (I imagine he would say, 'luncheon') in an Italian restaurant in Soho called Bianchi's, where on a shelf are novels written by people who frequent the restaurant, among them the novels of Iris Murdoch.

Christmas time, on my way to have lunch with him, I stopped in a shop and bought a little carved rhinoceros, Indian, for tuppence, which I gave to him. He studied it carefully, said, in his high-pitched voice that was close to being a squeal, 'Very nice,' and put it into a side pocket.

We talked about a series of books published by Penguin Books, called Style and Civilization. Nikos is the editor. Pope-Hennessy (can I possibly call him John?) said, 'I don't like the word "style."' I didn't know what he meant, and I never do dare ask him what he means – not because I think he would be offended by my asking (it is hardly possible to offend him), but because I feel that if I asked him what he means he would have had every right to ask me what I mean, and for me to try to get into such a conversation with John about style would expose my cultural limitations and pretensions. I like John, I like being with him a lot, and not only because in my defer-ence to him I would learn so much from him, but because he seems to respect my ignorance. With him, it is better to ask, 'Who was Giovanni di Paolo?' than to suggest any insights into the artist's work.

We talked about mutual friends. He was amused to hear funny stories about these friends, none art historians, anecdotes that made him laugh a high, abrupt laugh that brought his voice up to a level I had thought impossible for a human.

If he doesn't like someone, he will say, looking down, his heavily lidded eyes half closed, 'I don't like him,' and then look up and away as if the person, who seemed to have been standing before him in judgment, suddenly ceases to exist. He particularly dislikes most art historians.

———

On a Sunday afternoon, Nikos and I will amuse ourselves by lying on the floor next to each other and painting in watercol-our.

One afternoon, we amused ourselves with this:

TITLES TO ALTOGETHER DIFFERENT NOVELS

It is a truth universally acknowledged, that a single man in possession of a good fortune, must be gay.

Halfway down a by-street of one of our New England towns stands a rusty wooden house with a flat roof and a small chimney in the middle.

Call me Jezebel.

During the whole of a lively, bright and laughter-filled day in the spring of the year, I had been passing with a riotous group of joking friends, on horseback, through a colourful tract of country, and at length we found ourselves, as the sun shone at its fullest, in view of the slap-happy House of Usher.

Under certain circumstances there are few hours in life more agreeable than the afternoon hour of everyone dancing naked on the lawn.

All drinking families resemble one another, but each teetotal family is unhappy in its own way.

Longtemps je me suis couché très tard.

Once upon a time and a very bad time it was there was a lorry coming down the road and this lorry was coming down along the road and hit a nicens little boy named baby tuckoo and killed him.

Mrs Dalloway said she would buy the whip herself.

Robert Cohn was once a drag queen in a bar in New Haven.

One may as well not begin.

————

John Ashbery, in London to give a reading in his flat but somehow resonant voice, came to supper with his past lover from Paris, the poet Pierre Martory. Nikos is the first publisher to publish Ashbery's poetry in Great Britain.

John said he is working on a book to be a Henry James novel without characters or setting or plot, and this interested me, thinking everything Jamesian in the book must be all in the writing.

I never know if John is being wry or not, as when he said his mother rang him to tell him she was at an airport, and when he told her, no, she was in a home, she answered, yes, of course she knew that, she was in a home at the airport. He said he would never be explicit about sex in his poetry because his mother might be shocked, and did worry about having included in a poem something about a sexual act wiped up in a tissue and flushed down the toilet. I laugh, but he doesn't laugh, and stares at me with a slight frown.

He gave us some long-playing records of a group of comedians, called the Firesign Theatre, which he said reaches an even funnier level with a bit of smoke. After John and Pierre left, Nikos and I listened to the Firesign Theatre, but I guess with smoke they would have elicited little more than chuckles. Perhaps I do wonder if I am missing a lot missing smoke.

I once said to Stephen, 'I don't understand the poetry of John Ashbery,' and he, as he sometimes does as if to avoid making a comment, stepped sideways as if to go away, but he said, 'Neither do I.'

Stephen gave us a set of Horizon magazine, reprinted and bound in volumes – rather, he gave the set to Nikos, with a dedication thanking Nikos for allowing him to 'seduce' me by taking me to France. I look through the contents pages of the issues of Horizon and think, with the wonder of it all, so many of the people listed we've met.

There's Julia Strachey, whom we've visited in her walk-up flat in Percy Street, a small flat with slanting floors and slanting ceilings and, dominating, a large bronze bust by Stephen Tomlin. In her droll, laconic way, she complained of the rats pulling off her bedclothes, disturbing her sleep. There is a telephone service, DIAL A CHICKEN, but she prefers DIAL LIVER.

And there is Lawrence Gowing, who stutters so his saliva runs down his chin, which he wipes with his tie, a man of wonderful enthusiasms. When he became professor at the Slade, he, as an art work, had his female students outline his body as he lay naked on a sheet of plywood, spreadeagled, and, he said stuttering, 'Some-some-some-sometimes they get-get-get-get my penis pointed and some-some-some-sometimes blunt.' He and Julia Strachey were once married.

The interconnections among all the people we've met defeat me. I've read Julia Strachey's Cheerful Weather for the Wedding, laughing. Her wonderfully extravagant metaphors and similes: 'Dolly's white face, with its thick and heavily curled-back lips, above her black speckled wool frock, glimmered palely in front of the ferns, like a phosphorescent orchid blooming alone there in the twilit swamp.' It was published by the Hogarth Press by Leonard and Virginia Woolf; and then The Man on the Pier, with a jacket design by Barbara Elizabeth Hepworth, published by John Lehmann.

———

Öçi has left for New York, where he intends to make his life.

———

Nikos is very rational, so when he engages in what I think of as the irrational, I baulk – as when he has a flu and he sets up on the bedside table a glass of water, a needle, a little heap of cloves and a candle in a candlestick that he lights to perform the ritual of: inserting a clove on the needle and holding it in the candle flame and reciting, 'If David gave you the evil eye, may his eyes pop out' (he having told me that only someone with blue eyes can give the evil eye, and not intentionally but unintentionally through someone else intending evil, so it would not be my fault if the evil eye were cast on him through me), and if the clove simply sizzles I have not given him the evil eye, that burnt clove then dropped into the glass of water, and then another clove on the needle is held in the flame with the names of everyone he can think of with blue eyes; but if the clove pops when my name is pronounced, I have given him the evil eye, and the spell is broken, after which the burnt clove-flavoured water is drunk. He laughs when I say no, no, I will not assist him, but then when, his face illuminated by the candle, I see him perform the ritual, a sense comes to me of a cultural loneliness in him that may go back for centuries and still isolates him in a belief that has nothing to do with the world he lives in, and I wonder how much from his ancestry does isolate him within some form of cultural loneliness that separates him from the world he lives in.

The ritual is called Moschokarfia, and it is unique to Greeks from Asia Minor.

Does he actually believe in the ritual? I once asked him if he believes in God, and he answered, 'That is a question I never ask myself.'

He also told me that there is a special prayer, recognized by the Greek Orthodox Church, for breaking the spell of the evil eye.

———

John Ashbery has sent us a copy of the kind of publication that proliferates, mimeographed typewritten pages stapled together, this with a large black and white photograph of John on the cover, barefoot and walking near a seaside beach with bathers, the text called 'The New Spirit'.

> I thought that if I could put it all down, that would be one way. And next the thought
> came to me that to leave all out, would be another, and truer way.

Reading, I found that, though I didn't understand what the text was about, I became more and more engaged in the writing, and I was reminded of what John said when he came to supper, that he was trying to write a Jamesian text that left out everything James would have included, character, setting, plot, for the way the Jamesian prose in itself enchants. Even in reading a James novel it happens that I don't know what is going on but I am sustained by the wonderfully elaborate and always inventive prose.

I'm reminded of what Gertrude Stein wrote about Henry James in What is English Literature:

> In the meantime Henry James went on. He too needed the whole paragraph because he too was just there, but, and that is the thing to notice, his whole paragraph was detached what it said from what it did, what it was from what it held, and over it all something floated not floated away but floated, floated up there. You can see how that was not true of Swinburne and Browning and Meredith but that it was true of Henry James. And so it makes it that Henry James just went on doing what American literature has always done, the form was always the form of the contemporary English one, but the disembodied way of disconnecting something from anything and anything from something was the American way. This brought about something that made neither words exist for themselves, nor sentences, nor choosing, it created the need of paragraphing, and the whole paragraph having been being made the whole paragraph had rising from it off of it its meaning.

What rises from and floats above John's poetry, it seems to me, is some sense of meaning without my knowing what the meaning is, but the sense engages me enough to make me wonder, that wonder in itself enough to keep me reading.

My impulse is to get everything in.

Lucca

We are staying with John Fleming and Hugh Honour in their house, the Villa Marchio, in the hills outside Lucca. As they are advisory editors for Penguin art books, including the series Style and Civilization, Nikos has come to discuss work with them, and I have come along.

We were given separate bedrooms, but decided, as we were alone in a wing of the house, to sleep together in his bed. We were woken this morning by the housekeeper, Gilda, carrying in a tray with breakfast, which we didn't expect, and when she saw us both in the same bed she exclaimed, 'Ai!' and immediately withdrew. We found the tray on a table on the landing.

When I told John what had happened, he said, 'Don't worry about it.'

It is beautiful here.

The villa is eighteenth century, with mottled pink walls and green-shuttered windows and a double stone staircase up to the double doors into the main hall and wings on either side, built by local builders who perhaps didn't work from an architect's plan but their own idea of what a villa should be, and though the symmetry of the house is off it is balanced by two huge palm trees growing on either side of the double staircase. There are great terracotta pots with lemon trees leading to a loggia that overlooks a lotus pool, and the surrounding garden appears stuffed with flowers, vines, flowering trees, cypresses, all pressed together by the garden walls, in a corner of which is a chapel. There is a cantina, a long, dark-beamed hall filled with enormous tuns, demijohns, great green bottles, and very worn, wooden wine presses. John and Hugh have their own wine, olive oil, fruit, vegetables, cheese, eggs, poultry, nuts, berries. The land outside the wide gate to the garden slopes down to outbuildings and houses where peasants live and, beyond the buildings, to terraces planted partly with vines and partly with olive trees, then down steeply to dense, cool, very green woods and a small stream. All the valley is terraced with vines and olive trees, and here and there are pink stucco houses and blue-black cypress trees. Poppies are still blossoming, and yellow daisies, and lots and lots of tiny lavender flowers. John and Hugh have filled the villa itself with what they have no doubt been collecting for years: small bronzes, medallions on small round tables, huge parchment-covered books, paintings, chairs that look like large silver open shells, one shell the seat the other the back, not to be sat on, and in the sitting room there is a fresh bouquet of flowers picked by Hugh.

We were sitting under the loggia when Gilda appeared and said, sternly, 'È pronto,' meaning lunch was ready, and she served it in the dining room with a stern face. Nikos kept telling her how delicious the food was, and she did smile a little.

John and Hugh told us stories about Percy Lubbock, for whom they had been readers in his late years in Lerici when he was blind, and who, they said, would tell them stories about Henry James, one particular story about a painting that had been given to James. 'What was I to do?' Hugh said mimicking Percy Lubbock who had mimicked Henry James. 'It was of a nudity!'

This afternoon, John and Hugh took Nikos and me into Lucca to see the town, and when we came back for tea under the loggia John brought me a beautiful first edition of Italian Hours so I could read what Henry James wrote about Lucca, and reading it while he and Hugh talked to Nikos about art historians I realized what the villa had inspired in me: what I imagined a nineteenth-century

Jamesian appreciation of such a villa from all my reading of James. I know my appreciation is a fantasy, but I am possessive about the details of what I see here: the roses, the fireflies in the bushes, the smell of drying hay.

———

Hugh has a very distinct way of pronouncing various words – not 'wisteria' with the accent on the 'ster,' but 'wis-te-ri-a,' with the accent on the final 'a,' and as for place names, not 'Calay' for 'Calais' but 'Caliss,' and not 'Marsay' for 'Marseilles' but 'Marcelles,' and as for the city of Milan, he pronounces it, he said, as it scans in Shakespeare: 'Mill-an,' with an accent on the 'Mill.' And so arcane English pronunciations are preserved by an Englishman living in Italy, and who thinks of Britain, as he has said, as a small island off-shore from Continental Europe.

We slept separately last night, but this morning the breakfast tray was on the table on the landing, and we realized Gilda is allowing us to sleep however we choose.

And thinking of Jamesian fantasies –

John and Hugh took Nikos and me to meet Harold Acton in his villa just outside of and overlooking Florence, La Pietra. A cameriere in a white jacket showed us into a large, dim drawing room with sunlight showing through the closed shutters in slits onto the rich furniture and Oriental rugs. Acton, in a three-piece suit, was waiting for us, and offered us drinks, which the cameriere poured out. There was a smell of old wood smoke and parched roses. The gilt frames of the paintings glinted here and there, but the pictures themselves were shadowed. Acton seemed to be the very embodiment of the most extravagant fantasy any American could ever have of the cultured European. He was all Oriental politeness and good humor as, with a springing step, he showed us around the gardens, and at lunch in a restaurant in the country he continued to entertain, with lightly told but intimate stories about artists and writers, historians, antiquarians, about aristocrats and ambassadors and friends of de Gaulle.

He said that the damage caused by the flood in Florence is still being suffered by the working class and the peasants outside in the countryside. Shopkeepers were given money to repair their shops, money which came mostly from outside, as the Florentine upper classes did very little to help, so the shops are now bright and shiny for the tourists. But lots and lots of the money collected for the flood relief which first went to Rome remained in Rome and never got to Florence.

Back at the Villa Marchio, John and I sat together under the loggia and I listened to him talk about Acton, who, John said, has a music-hall comedian's sense of timing, making hand gestures and rolling his eyes at the most effective moments, while he also keeps a respectable exterior. He might, for example, tell an anecdote about how uncomfortable life at the Sitwells' was, as when his mother, on a visit, asked for a lavatory, and was taken down a long passage into Lady Ida's bedroom, where she was given – here Acton would pause, then say the rest quickly, with the last word as if sung out on a high note – a chamber pot!

Nikos was not impressed by Harold Acton, whom he thinks of as trying to live a fantasy he imagines is not a fantasy. Acton, in any case, does not have the socialist credentials that would make Nikos respect him. I found him fascinating, to, I think, Nikos' amusement.

I woke up from a very deep sleep, a sleep that, it seemed to me when I was fully awake, was composed of layers upon layers of impressions that have piled up over the few days we've been here, starting with leaving grey, dismal London, the plane ride to Pisa (the plane at moments seemed to stop, motionless, and float in the air), the arrival at the small airport, John and Hugh meeting us, the Italian advertising, the particular smell of an Italian farmacia we stopped in on the way to the villa, the Villa Marchio here, and especially Harold Acton's villa La Pietra and its gardens, the blurred sense of cypress alleys, complicated box hedges, wisteria-covered arbors, statues tangled in the rich vegetation, fountains at the end of sudden vistas. I woke from all this after Nikos had left me, woke to the high, large, lumpy bed I was in with a headboard of wrought iron, to the stained whitewashed walls and ceiling, the huge wardrobe, the flies droning in the hot, still air, the painted plaster Madonna's head above the bed, the open window framing palm fronds, the old tile floor, and everything appeared suddenly familiar.

Last night, as Nikos and I were making love, a firefly came in through the open window, and the dark room silently pulsed with the palest green light.

After our visit to La Pietra, John handed me Harold Acton's two autobiographical volumes, Memoirs of an Aesthete and More Memoirs of an Aesthete, and, yes, he became a fantasy figure to me, someone not only from another world but another century. My fantasy is of a world and a century of the salon, his villa itself a major salon, in which he could, just by pulling on a thread, pull together a whole tangle of interconnected aristocrats, politicians, artists and, too, homosexuals. If I were a minor Marcel Proust, what I could have made of it all!

He lived his youth, not only in terms of a villa with some sixty rooms with a grand staircase and huge tapestries and immense statues and fountains in the garden and thirty-five servants, but a style of life that allowed him to take it for granted that when he traveled he would stay in the best hotels, dine in the best restaurants, go to the best tailors. He could take it for granted that it was possible to meet anyone he wanted. When he was a boy, Serge Diaghilev and Léon Bakst, who were themselves fantasy figures to Acton, visited La Pietra. Of the older generation, he knew Bernard Berenson, Edith Wharton, Max Beerbohm, Oscar Wilde's old friend Reggie Turner, D. H. Lawrence, Norman Douglas, the Sitwells, Gertrude Stein, and of his generation pretty much everyone, Evelyn Waugh, Nancy Mitford, Diana Mosley, George Orwell, Cecil Beaton, Cyril Connolly, Henry Green, Anthony Powell, Graham Greene. He could devote his life to the purely aesthetic pleasures, such as the ballet and poetry and rococo art, and he could decide, with no worry about how he would support himself, to be a writer.

Of course I see him as a fantasy figure. He has inherited fantasy, without his having to supply one silver spoon to it, from his parents. Does Acton ever think he is living a fantasy? There have to be moments when he thought he did – as when, at Eton, he and his close friend Brian Howard, even more aesthetic than he, hired a room at the back of Dyson's, a jeweller in the town, where they played records of Russian ballet music and danced together the parts they had seen Massine and Nijinsky, Karsavina and Tchernicheva dance at performances of the Ballets Russes. Or when, later at Oxford University, he went 'tittupping' along the High Street with a gray bowler and a tightly rolled umbrella, wearing, under a long, tubular, black velvet coat, silver, mauve or pink trousers that were so wide at the knees and ankles they looked like a pleated skirt, a style he invented which was copied by many others and was finally known to the outside world as Oxford bags.

Nikos stops me from even trying to act on fantasy.

———

We went into Florence, just Nikos and I, with a guidebook. Repairs to damage caused by the flood are going on everywhere, and a lot of places are closed. And yet it is remarkable how quickly and efficiently the rebuilding was done. Along the Arno, for instance, there are photographs outside a coffee bar that show the almost irreparable damage, but the bar is now bright and new. So Harold Acton was right. You can still see the high-water marks on the buildings.

As for what we saw in Florence – I used to think that art historians might have knowledge about works of art that I didn't have, but I assumed, in my uneducated way, that if I didn't have their knowledge I had a sensitivity to art that they didn't have. I couldn't have been more wrong. In these past days, hearing John and Hugh talk about art with the greatest of outward knowledge, I realize their inward sensitivity to the art is as great. What was most wonderful in what we saw were the frescos in San Marco by Fra Angelico, but for me to try to comment on them, or to try to comment on anything else we saw, would be to presume on knowledge and sensitivity I don't have. So I'll keep my appreciation to myself, as, I realize, I already keep any appreciation of books and music that presumes on commenting on them to myself. No comments, none, on Fra Angelico or Masaccio or Ghirlandaio or Donatello or Michelangelo or Cellini or Brunelleschi or –

I tell myself: forget what you think or even feel, and simply describe.

For example, the little devil's head soldered to the barred window in Savonarola's cell, perhaps to warn him of the dangers of looking out.

I look out of the little window above the table on the landing where I'm writing and see: a rising landscape of dark and light, green and yellow, and on the top of a hill a hamlet of stone houses with red tile roofs.

––––––

At dinner, then after with coffee in the sitting room, John and Hugh often recount stories about people they've known, or about people known by people they've known, and it is as if great bubbles rise from their mouths and expand and expand with the actions, words, interrelationships of such people as Berenson and his entourage, Percy and Sybil Lubbock, George Santayana, Howard Sturgis, Logan Pearsall Smith, E. M. Forster –

About Sybil Lubbock: Percy, her third husband, had built for her a villa in the most beautiful place possible, on a promontory in Lerici overlooking the Ligurian Sea, and brought her to see it for the first time on a moonlit night, she, however, simply saying she was very tired and must go to bed. The Italian navy was practicing maneuvers off the coast, shooting cannon, which noise annoyed Sybil, so she rang the admiralty and had it stopped. Coming down to breakfast, she said she hadn't slept all night, reading Pico della Mirandola.

Hugh, who is the real raconteur, said that Percy Lubbock once told them he had told E. M. Forster, 'Morgan, one day they'll all see just how thin your books are,' to which Forster replied, 'I dare say they will.'

Lubbock's stepdaughter, Iris Origo, came to him, more or less on his death bed, to tell him he had no more money, to which he replied, 'Oh dear, I thought it would last at least another fortnight.'

I realize that here I am within a world of English expatriates (though John is Scots) who retain an Englishness that has gone in England, retained mostly in anecdotes about people once known but now dead, people who once did represent a world within the greater world of what was once the British Empire.

———

John and Hugh brought us to Pietra Santa to meet the wife of an art historian friend of theirs, the art historian Robert Goldwater, his wife Louise Bourgeois, who is a sculptor. We met her where she has her workshop – rather, a kind of open stall along a line of other stalls – and she showed us a sculpture that had just been finished, not by her but by one of the workmen, of what looked like a bunch of marble male erections stuck together, and while we all studied the sculpture I noted she seemed to study us with a wry smile. She brought us to another stall where the maquettes by Henry Moore are enlarged into monumental sculptures, and the man presiding, a large man called Agostinelli with a folded newspaper cap set firmly on his head, picked up a maquette and then showed us the monumental replica he was carving in marble. He said the final work is done in the light of a candle, which interested Hugh very much, as he said that Canova – Hugh's book on whom is his lifetime's work – did the same when refining the surface of his sculptures. Then we all went to the main piazza for coffee, and, I don't know why, I wondered about the little figure of a Hawaiian girl in a hula skirt on the side of the little cups, perhaps because the figures appeared so culturally incongruous to having coffee with Madame Bourgeois in Pietra Santa. Robert Goldwater is a scholar

on African sculptures and the director of the Museum of Primitive
Art in New York, and the talk about him among Louise Bourgeois
and John and Hugh seemed to open up another incongruous world
about us about Africa. Nikos and I, within these worlds revolving
around us in a café in Pietra Santa, were silent.

———

I asked John F. if he had asked Percy Lubbock what accent Henry
James had, and John answered, yes, as a matter of fact he had, and
Lubbock told him that James didn't have an American accent, but
neither did he have a British accent.

My fantasy of being a Jamesian character in Europe is over, and
it didn't take much, I see, to put an end to it – just being in a place
I might have once imagined where a Jamesian character would
have flourished. I realize I in fact have so little to do with being an
American Jamesian character I could have only ever had a fantasy
of what it was like to be one, because I, from a small, French-
Québécois-speaking parish in Yankee New England, am American
in a way no character in James is.

Yet, I sense some affinity with James as an American, if to be an
American is, as James wrote, to be possessed and to possess one's
possession. Ezra Pound wrote about James that he knew the world
is spherical, and his possession was to possess that spherical world,
to possess it in his books and then let it go in his books. I tell
myself: the letting it go is necessary for the world to be, on its own,
round and whole.

———

What I most like here is the little chapel in the corner of the walled-
in garden. I go in by way of the entrance at the back which opens
up from the garden. It is small, damp, crumbling, with a few very
dusty vestiges of its sanctity: grey and wet altar cloths, broken
candlesticks, a crucifix with broken arms hanging loose from the
nails in the hands, holy water fonts stuck in the wall and filled with
rags, squares on the walls where pictures had hung. There are even

two pews, with a very dusty wine bottle occupying one, having been there long enough for cobwebs to attach it to the seat. The stations of the cross – small, colored pictures in black frames – are still in place. I go in and I sit by the wine bottle and I close my eyes. Though I tell myself I am a total non-believer, with my eyes closed I know it is the religion I was born and brought up in that most deeply, most helplessly, makes me what I am, and this Henry James certainly knew nothing about.

While sitting there, a peasant woman came in from the front entrance opening from the dirt road to place a small bouquet of roses before a little shrine to the Blessed Virgin Mother.

John said the chapel is still consecrated.

San Andrea di Rovereto di Chiavari

We have come to stay in a little house on the Ligurian coast for our summer holiday. The rent is five shillings a day. The house has two rooms downstairs and two up, and is in the midst of an olive grove. The steps up to the house from the street are crowded on one side with pots and old tins of flowering plants. Hydrangeas are in bloom.

The view from the house, high on the side of the coast, is a steep descent, thick with olive trees, down to a blue-green sea. On the

right we can see all the way to the tip of Portofino and on the left to Sestri Levanti. At night fishing boats are like large lapping stars.

Nikos loves it here for its simplicity.

This occurs to me – I listen to him talk about politics, and I realize that before I met him I had none. I suppose I still have none, and have assumed his.

A few mornings ago I got up very early, went outside and sat on a step. A young woman, all round curves, passed me going down the stairs, having come from the olive grove behind, carrying a large, sloshing bucket of milk. She left a trail of splashed milk all the way down to the street.

———

After going down to the sea today by way of a narrow path through the lush vegetation, we took a nap. The room is all white, with a red tile floor, and very simple. We were covered with a stiff, almost canvas-like sheet that you get in cheap hotels in Europe, and the white afternoon light, so penetrating I imagined all the outside world was dissolved in it, burned about the edges of the closed shutter, and one long thin crack of light fell into the dim, hot, fly-buzzing room and across the sheet.

We are happy.

———

Trying to find short cuts to the sea, Nikos and I follow steep paths through olive groves, vineyards, and through woods. Just off one path we found a cement bunker from the war, like a huge, square eye closed to a slit and staring through the foliage out over the Tigullian Gulf. We found the entrance and went in. It smelled of shit. I, frightened, said we shouldn't go in, but Nikos lit a newspaper he found on the ground and we went in, crouched. There were a series of cemented caves along each side. As we went deeper into the bunker we heard voices behind us, and quickly turned back to get out and met a group of boys with a flashlight coming in. When they saw us, they, more frightened than we were, scattered.

My sexual fantasies almost cease to exist while I am with Nikos. Certainly sex doesn't obsess me as much as it did before I met him. But, then, so much in me has changed since I met him.

———

We met Stephen at the train station in Chiavari. He was wearing a shirt with the cuffs unbuttoned and dangling, and he looked very hot in the Italian heat, but we got him into a taxi and into the cool hills of San Andrea. He has come to join us for a few days. He is staying in a small hotel in the village, where he works during the day while Nikos and I go down to the beach. Every day we take the train to Chiavari, Nikos and I to shop for our meals – fish, vegetables, fruit, cheese – Stephen to buy the English newspapers, and we have meals, cooked by Nikos, in our small house. We are all three happy.

Stephen was filled with his experiences in Paris where he was during the student demonstrations. He let us read the first draft of chapters for a book, and he read out some of the students' slogans he had copied from walls in the Latin Quarter:

Prenez vos désirs pour des réalités.
    Toute vue des choses qui n'est pas étrange est fausse.
    Plus je fais l'amour plus je fais la révolution, plus je fais la révolution plus je fais l'amour.

———

Stephen and I took a walk before he left, just the two of us. We found ourselves lost on the paths through the tangled woods, then came across a disused railway track and we followed that to a small house, maybe a signaling station for the railway, the windows of which were burnt-out holes and the roof falling in. We went inside. The floor was covered with bits of plaster fallen from the walls, stones and branches and garbage, and where the walls weren't soot black from fires there were large pornographic drawings in charcoal. We went upstairs, where in one room all the walls were painted with murals, one of a woman in a green dress sitting in a chair, on either side of her a large red rooster, and near her and looking at her a smiling young man with horns and a garland of flowers about his head.

Stephen asked that his visit to us be kept a secret.

London

More and more, I wonder how it happened that Nikos and I are living together, the wonder, as wonder will do, making it all strange.

———

In homage to his beliefs, I suggested to Nikos that we go visit the tomb of Karl Marx in the Highgate Cemetery. He brought along a red rose which he placed at the foot of the huge granite plinth with the incised motto WORKERS OF ALL LANDS UNITE, the massive bronze bust above. Nikos was silent, and I sensed in him his inability to articulate why a vision that should have brought equality and justice and peace to the world went so wrong, and it seemed to me an impertinence to say to him that the vision all went wrong because of human failings, a cliché. I am always aware, against my American simplifications, of Nikos' own Greek awareness of complexities too great to react to with anything more than a pained look in his eyes, and silence.

———

A friend of Nikos, Ersi Hadgimihali, is in London from Athens, opposed to the dictatorship, but secretly.

She came to supper. A sophisticated, elderly woman, she recounted, in English, stories about escaping Nazi-occupied

Greece to go by boat to Egypt, there where the Greek royal family were in exile. Before leaving for Egypt for the long night-time crossing, Ersi had bought a watch, for which her husband commended her as keeping time was important for the crossing; but he kept complaining that he should have the watch, really it was more important for him to have a watch than for her, and she, fed up, took the watch from her wrist and threw it overboard into the sea. She writes poetry and paints very primitive paintings in bright colours. She comes from a famous family, an aunt of hers commemorated by a bust on a plinth in a square in Athens, or so Nikos told me.

Nikos seems to know a cultured class of people in Athens.

He told me that Greeks with a surname beginning with Hadgi are descended from ancestors who were baptized in the Jordan, which made me wonder what connection there could possibly be in the use of the word among Muslims who once in a lifetime go on a pilgrimage called, I think, the Haj.

To see everything, every single event, every single word, every single thing, every single person in terms of history –

———

I waited for Nikos near the Greek Embassy in Brooke Street, just behind the American Embassy in Grosvenor Square, as we had planned to meet there before joining the demonstration against the dictatorship in Greece. The only other people there on the pavement was an old woman in severe black mourning and a young man. Clearly, they wondered, as did I, where the demonstration was, and in my bad Greek I said I was waiting. The old woman asked me, in Greek, if I'm Anglos, and I answered, 'Oxi, eimai Americanos,' which made her draw back from me and spit at me, a great gob of her spit landing on one of my shoes. Never before had anyone spat on me, and that I was spat upon for being an American roused a rage in me. I wanted to tell the old woman that I was an exceptional American, not, as the Americans of the Embassy, supporting the dictatorship, but out to demonstrate against it. She, with the young man, his shoulders hunched over, left, and I, in my rage, thought of leaving also.

I walked out to Park Lane and saw the demonstration advancing, and waited until I saw Nikos in the midst, he talking animatedly with John Berger, whom he admires for his political vision, and whose book on the success and failure of Picasso Nikos had published at Penguin. I joined them, and in my continuing rage told Nikos about the insult and that I was not going to demonstrate, but would go home. He calmly said that the old woman was probably a Communist who had suffered terribly under the American Truman Doctrine which outlawed membership in the Communist Party as a capital punishment. So, I was seen as representative of the Truman Doctrine. Nikos introduced me to John Berger, and we marched on.

We passed the Greek Embassy, where Nikos had once worked and where people he had known still worked. The curtains were drawn, as if the building was abandoned, but as we passed under the windows, jeering, a hand appeared from between closed curtains to give the march the finger.

Along the way, I noted Ersi Hadgimihali appear on a side street, half hidden by the corner of a building, the collar of her coat held up to hide her face.

The march ended in Trafalgar Square. There was a huge crowd, Melina Mercouri on a platform in the midst wearing her red blouse with, it appeared, nothing underneath, so that whenever she raised her arms high to shout out against the dictators the nipples of her breasts pressed through the cloth, and the crowd roared.

I hear Greeks, having got out of Greece, talk about their recollections of the German Occupation of Athens and then the Civil War, hear them describe how during the occupation people in the streets cried, 'Pinow, pinow, pinow' ('I'm hungry, I'm hungry, I'm hungry') and died there in the streets, so others walked over their bodies; hear them describe how, during the Civil War, unspeakable atrocities were committed on both sides; hear how, now, when a group of friends go to the house of a friend for a name-day celebration and find he does not appear they know he has been arrested and interrogated and most likely tortured by having the soles of his feet beaten so no scars are left – and I react with horror, but they look at me as if I haven't in fact understood, as of course I haven't because I haven't lived through what they have. I asked Nikos' cousin Stavros, who is severe, if my expressing horror was sentimental, and I was told, severely, yes, it was.

I think of these people as having lived through brutal history, and to say to them how horrible it was makes them react, if not with a severe stare, with counter-stories of joyful times at the worst of times among families and friends, so that when there were curfews they would hold dances all night long, in which couples would meet and fall in love and eventually marry.

I asked a friend of Nikos why there is no Greek mafia, and he said because no two Greeks can agree enough to form a mafia.

Another Greek said, 'But there is a mafia – it is called Greek Government Ministers.'

———

What does Greece mean to Nikos? The country means more to him than any other, and I know that whatever he says that rejects his country is in proportion to the meaning it has for him. And I have learned this: if I say something disparaging about Greece, repeating something he has said, he will stop me with, 'What do you know about Greece?'

What does Nikos being Greek mean to me?

Do I look in him for some Greekness that antedates my knowing him, some past fantasy of Greece inspired, say, by reading Plato's Symposium, so that I fantasize his participating in that fantasy? The fantasy is there, but, in my close relationship with him, I am able to look over his shoulder at the symposium of ancient Greek literature with more of a direct view into it than ever before. Past Nikos, I see beyond Aristotle, beyond Plato, into the Pre-Socratics, who have become more and more interesting to me, as if I were seeing into them the very origins of my own thoughts and feelings, as, in essential ways, I am, and the essential way is to believe that the origin of the concept of the ONE is as central to me as it was to those ancient philosophers.

How essential to me this:

All things come out of the one, and the one out of all things.

Heraclitus

As for what Nikos reveals of Greece – within his history of living through the German Occupation and the Civil War, I think of his more personal history on the island of Poros, where he was abandoned by a lover, and where he sat on rocks by the sea, the wind-wafted scent of blossoming lemon trees from the mainland his consolation. In him, I sense the consolations of Greece are made so very poignant against the losses.

A sponsor for anti-dictatorship action in London invited Nikos to an event in someone's flat in North London to raise money, and I went along. Melina Mercouri was there, in the midst, dressed in a blouse and slacks and sitting cross-legged on the floor, her hair a mass of long dangling blonde curls. All I remember of the evening was being introduced to her and she looking up at me with large eyes and her wide smile and saying, in a low, slow, seductive voice, 'I love Americans.'

At a drinks party given by John Lehmann, I met his sister Rosamond, who, large and with bright white hair, appeared to me to be a moon goddess. When I said I'd just come back to London from Lucca, she asked, as if there could be no other place to stay there, had I stayed with John Fleming and Hugh Honour? Yes, I had. 'Then you must be very privileged,' she said, 'because I've never been invited.'

John's sister Beatrix was also there, but every time I found myself, moving among the guests, facing her, she turned away, and I wondered if she took me for a boyfriend of John whom she disapproved of, not, perhaps, because I was her brother's boyfriend, but because she assumed I was his boyfriend only for the privilege of meeting her, the actress Beatrix Lehmann, at a drinks party where she would be present.

As if to educate me about Stephen, John said to me, 'Our Stephen is very good at intuiting, and all his best writing comes from his intuition, but he's hopeless when he tries to reason a situation or problem out logically.'

I want to get this in: John once said that on a visit to Greece he had had a boy with a perfect ancient Greek profile, and I was reminded of what Nikos once said about Northern Europeans fantasizing about Greek boys.

And I'm reminded of this line from Stephen's poem 'The Funeral':

The decline of a culture
Mourned by scholars who dream of the ghosts of Greek boys.

Nikos does have one Greek friend, whom he seems more to tolerate than like – Rea Seferiadi, by marriage a (I think) sister-in-law of the poet George Seferis, shortened from Seferiadis. Nikos is not a great admirer of Seferiadis' poetry and derides him for deriding Cavafy's poetry as a pedestal without a statue. Also, Nikos thinks it morally weak of Seferis to have made, after a long period of silence, a weak statement against the dictatorship – calling it an 'anomaly' – to save his face among those opposed, especially non-Greeks outside of Greece who oppose (Greeks are more attentive to opinion from outside of Greece than from within, and wait for a writer to be praised by non-Greeks before they themselves praise him); whereas the poet Ritsos has been sent to a concentration camp on an island for being, as a Communist sympathizer, opposed to the dictatorship. But to get back to Rea, who speaks with a very upper-class English accent, and who gives the impression of knowing just what is going on in the royal family, such as the Queen will abdicate to give over her position to her son Charles, said with such authority that I thought she must know, until Nikos told me not to believe anything she says. She is a compact woman who wears plain close-fitting dresses with a pearl necklace, her hair dyed black, her large eyes black. We were invited to her flat where, in her sitting room, she made pronouncements about world news with such authority that she might have been connected at least to the ambassadors of all the most powerful countries, from whom she gets the news. Pointing to a little painting by the French painter Hélion of lips, she said, 'Those are my lips,' and this made me imagine her connections to the whole of the French art world. Her husband, whose first name I can't recall, said nothing; he works in the City, but in what capacity I don't know. Nikos makes fun of Rea, and when I asked him why he is friendly with her and her husband, he said, 'They suffered the Catastrophe,' and I had a sense of how those dispossessed people do form almost a racial group, even to intermarrying.

———

Natasha away, Stephen invited Nikos and me to a dinner party, where, Stephen told us, the other guests to arrive were Julian Huxley and his wife. Clearly, Stephen was excited to make this introduction to someone we should have known about, but whose name for me only conjured up a vague sense of a British dynastic family of many distinguished members, Aldous Huxley only one of them. Nikos of course knew who Julian Huxley is, and was able to ask him about animal charities, to which Nikos gives a lot of money, harking back to when Huxley was a zoologist and his great concern the wellbeing of animals. I had no idea what to talk about with Julian Huxley. After the dinner party, when Nikos and I helped with the washing up, as we always do, Stephen seemed annoyed with me for not having responded, as Nikos had, to meeting Julian Huxley, and all I could think of to do was shrug, which made Stephen press his lips together and turn away, and I worried that he thought I was ungrateful for the privilege when I was simply embarrassed. Yes, I should have known who Julian Huxley is – should have known his history.

The leaves are falling from the trees in Battersea Park. The sunlight is bright, the sky absolutely clear. There is a smell through the open window over my desk of burning leaves.

I can do so much. I know it, I know it.

And yet, if I were to step back into myself, which I keep myself from doing to be more outward than inward, I would ask myself, How do you know you will? and I would step back out of myself and insist, I will.

Stephen invited me to lunch at the Lyons' Corner House in Piccadilly with Elizabeth Glenconner.

With amusement, Elizabeth remembered Nikos offering her a pink gin when she came to his flat for drinks, this before Nikos and I met; the amusement was that Nikos, a Greek, should offer her a drink that was once so fashionably English, and now so out of fashion.

Stephen and Elizabeth talked about many people I don't know and couldn't place in the English world, though I listened with attention to try to make connections among them all – among all the Tennants, of which there seem to be a very complicated number, starting with Elizabeth's husband Christopher Tennant, Lord Glenconner – but the connections are too complicated for me.

When I said this to Elizabeth, she smiled and said, with a slight drawl, 'It's all very simple, really.'

They talked about someone named Anne, but I thought it would be impolite to ask who Anne was, but Stephen informed me, 'You've met Anne, Anne Wollheim, Elizabeth's sister,' which did not seem simple to me, because I have met Anne, the former wife of the philosopher Richard Wollheim, he now married to Mary Day Wollheim. Here I am, trying to interconnect people I've met. Anne Wollheim has twins, Rupert and Bruno, by Richard Wollheim, and two daughters by a former husband, Philip Toynbee, Polly and Josephine Toynbee. Josephine has a child, Pip, by a Mexican lover, a boy of great charm, who especially loves the art historian Ben Nicolson whom he greets with, 'Ben!' at a dinner party at Anne's that Nikos and I are also invited to, where Pip runs to Ben for Ben, laughing his gurgling laugh, to take him in his arms. How sort all this out in a diary? And how sort out Elizabeth's family with her husband Christopher? Leave it for now, to be sorted out later, if there is a later.

I can't recall why, but Stephen said to Elizabeth that he is 'dead middle class,' which I took him to mean that Elizabeth wasn't, and I was impressed for I had not thought of Stephen as belonging to any class, had never before heard anyone define his or her class to another.

She asked Stephen about Natasha, and I felt that for her at least there exists a world in which everyone totally, if somewhat vaguely, accepts everyone else without question, perhaps even me. Her eyes seemed to be always slightly out of focus.

She went off to a Greek lesson, as she and her husband have built a house on Corfu and will move there.

This was said with no reference to the dictatorship. When I told Nikos this, he simply said he loves Elizabeth, and I felt in that, not an excuse, but some kind of acceptance that belies Nikos' principles, which are in fact much more complicated by his history lived in the particular than I know the abstract puritan principles of my history to be.

———

Stephen asked Nikos and me to the Garrick Club for lunch with Cyril Connolly and W. H. Auden. Cyril Connolly wants one of the kittens born from Nikos' cat Jasmine, but when Nikos said they cost twelve guineas each he became thoughtful and said that a cat in his garden would upset the birds and destroy the balance of nature. Nikos spoke at length to Auden, who was very spirited and obviously liked talking with Nikos. While we others listened – and I had the impression that whenever Auden spoke Stephen and even Connolly simply listened to him – he and Nikos talked about personal happiness. Nikos wasn't going to simply listen, but had a two-way conversation with Auden, who said, when Nikos asked him, that he thought he was happy.

Part of the conversation was about the next Professor of Poetry at Oxford; Stephen, Auden, Connolly all supported Roy Fuller. At one point, Cyril Connolly asked Auden:

'Is that person who kicks over a little stone in Letter from Iceland a real person?'

'Yes.'

'May I ask who?'

'Robert Medley.'

Connolly's review in the next Observer included this information:

For sheer pleasure, the 'Letter to Lord Byron' from Letters from Iceland (1937) with its mixture of candid autobiography, journalism and genius is unbeatable – and witty as well. Who cannot thrill even now to his admission:

> One afternoon in March at half past three
> When walking in a ploughed field with a friend;
> Kicking a little stone he turned to me
> And said, 'Tell me, do you write poetry?'
> I never had, and said so, but I knew
> That very moment what I wished to do.

The friend was the painter Robert Medley.

There was speculation about the relationship between T. S. Eliot and Jean Verdenal, to whom Eliot dedicated Prufrock and Other Observations, and what the love was that Eliot had for him, Connolly quoting from the epigraph amor ch'a te mi scalda.

Coming out of the club, Auden took somebody's big black
bowler hat from a hook and put it over his head. It dropped down
over his eyes, and all one could see of his face was a great mass of
broken wrinkles, and in the midst of the wrinkles a smile.

Connolly left us, and then Nikos to go to the publishing house,
and I followed Stephen who followed Auden to the department
store Simpson's in the Strand, where in the shoe department Auden
bought a pair of carpet slippers, as, he said, his corns make wearing
shoes too painful. The salesman at first was at best deferential, but
then recognized Auden and was reverential. Auden wore the new
slippers and left the old behind, and, again, Stephen followed him,
and I followed Stephen down to the Piccadilly Underground
Station.

Auden called the round station the Fairy Circle, and when I
asked what that meant, he answered, as though a mother instructing a son in the facts of life, that this is where gentlemen pick up
young men in need of financial help. He said, 'The arrangement is
simple: you need sex and they need money,' and that, coming from
him, sounded reasonable. Stephen said nothing. A man, recognizing Auden, went to him to ask if he would sign a book, and Auden
said, 'But I don't sign books I didn't write.' I felt oh, that I belonged
to a little inner circle of people among whom one is famous, and if
anyone looked at me as belonging to the little circle he or she
might wonder who I was to belong to it.

As we were about to part to go in different directions, W. H.
Auden invited me to stay with him when I next go to New York,
and this made me think, Well, he likes me enough to invite me to
stay with him. When I told Nikos this, he said, 'You think it's
because he likes you that he invited you to stay with him?' I thought,
for a flashing moment, to be able to say I stayed with W. H. Auden
in New York might, just might, be worth whatever reason he has
for inviting me!

Later, as if to warn me, Stephen told me that Auden's house in
Saint Mark's Place in New York is as messy as the way Auden packs
a suitcase: he simply loads all the clothes he needs onto a table,

places the suitcase on the floor at the end of the table and then shoves all the clothes off the end of the table into the suitcase then closes it.

And a little revulsion at the possibility of eating there came to me when Stephen said that Auden's lover Chester Kallman makes the chocolate pudding in the bathroom washbasin.

And I'm reminded by my using 'washbasin' of the time I said 'bathroom sink' in the presence of Sonia, who stopped me with 'washbasin.'

———

In a taxi, as if being in a taxi together allowed such an intimacy, Stephen told me that when he and Natasha were in Germany after the war, on a train, she proposed that they exchange their pounds on the black market, but Stephen said, no, at the official rate; Natasha insisted, and he insisted, her insistence driven to such an extreme that she threatened to throw herself off the train if he didn't agree with her.

He said to me, 'She is that willful.'

When I asked, 'Does she do that often?' he looked out the window of the taxi and didn't answer.

———

Thomas Hardy, in Life's Little Ironies, writes about London: 'There are worlds within worlds in the great city.'

———

I sent £5 to Frank Kermode as a contribution to the memorial slab to commemorate Henry James in Poets' Corner in Westminster Abbey, and I was invited to the service. Nikos was invited by Stephen. We met by the Great West Door, where we were presented white tickets. Robert and Caroline Lowell came behind us, but because they didn't have tickets they were told to wait. Everyone was treated brusquely, which I tried to take as a formality. Nikos and I were separated, he to sit on one side of the nave, I on the other, next to Tony Tanner. The Lowells, finally admitted, sat next to me, he in rumpled suit and perhaps the last of the truly Yankee writers, and Caroline kept biting her nails. Tony and I joked, identifying people passing to go to their seats: C. P. Snow, Anthony Powell, Victor Pritchett.

The psalms from which the James took the titles The Wings of the Dove and The Golden Bowl were read, then Ralph Richardson read a passage from Portrait of a Lady, after which Tony leaned towards me and said, 'Henry James isn't getting a memorial slab in Westminster Abbey for *that*.' The dean and various prelates in red soutanes or academics in black gowns processed down the aisle, followed by Leon Edel and Stephen and a professor from the Sorbonne, and James' great-great-nephew, Alexander, carrying a laurel wreath, all wearing red carnations on their lapels. They disappeared into Poets' Corner, so we had to imagine Henry James' great-great-nephew unveiling the slab and placing the wreath. Then we heard, amplified over loudspeakers, Stephen give a short address in which he said that James was aware of the class struggle, or at least of the bankruptcy of the middle and upper classes. The Professor from the Sorbonne claimed, in French, that James was a French writer. The procession filed back down the aisle, and I heard, 'Pray for the soul of Henry James,' and for the first time I was moved. Edel started with a eulogy on the name Henry James: both given names, both democratic, and yet both the names of kings. More prayers, the organ played, and I met Nikos and we presented pink tickets to get into the Jerusalem Room for sherry. Nikos asked me, 'Weren't you moved?' I said, 'A little, but not really.' 'You weren't? Henry James means so much to you. I was. I had tears in my eyes. I couldn't keep myself from weeping when I saw Henry James' great-great-nephew, such a beautiful young man, carrying the laurel wreath down the aisle. And all the old English writers, sitting in the stalls, watching him.' 'Yes,' I said, and felt ashamed that I hadn't been more moved.

Seeing Henry James' great-great-nephew standing alone – which is an English habit I have often noted when the guest of honour is often left alone as if it would be considered a presumption to engage with him or her – Nikos and I went to speak with him, Alexander James, Jr., who was twenty-six. His charcoal-grey suit from the 1950s was, he said, borrowed, as he didn't own one. With it, he wore a white shirt with a button-down collar and a thin dark tie. His long hair was parted in the middle and combed back over his ears, and he had what I thought of as the pure features of a Yankee – a strong forehead, nose, jaw and neck – and pale but intense eyes. A great-grandson of William James, he was studying, appropriately, to become a clinical psychologist. He loved to garden. He said, quietly, 'I'm not at all used to the kind of attention I'm getting here.' Nikos stared and stared at him.

Nikos and I left with Tony Tanner to have lunch. We talked a little about British writers today. I asked, 'Is there a British writer today who is great enough to be given, after his or her death, a memorial slab in Poets' Corner?' 'No,' Tony said, 'no, no.'

I once thought that Henry James had a secret, the secret of being an American, which was to be a Yankee American, which I am not. If my sense of Henry James having a secret went, everything would go. And it did go. The straining consciousness of James – straining in the very elaboration of the writing for the totally inclusive 'everything' – seems to me the possession of a man who always feared that 'everything' was a horrifying 'nothing'.

It was in rereading a commonplace book, from those years back when I strained for the realization of 'everything' and copied down passages from Henry James' autobiographical books – not his novels, for his autobiographical books brought him closer to me as a person – A Small Boy and Others, Notes of a Son and Brother, The Middle Years – and rereading the passages revived in me a sense of – what? – a sense, of course, of 'everything.'

'. . . the wonder of consciousness in everything . . .'
'. . . It was big to me, big to me with the breath of great vague connections . . .'
'. . . an air of possibilities that were none the less vivid for being quite indefinite . . .'

'. . . my vision loses itself withal in vaster connections . . .'
'. . . who should say now what a world one mightn't read into
    it? . . .'
'. . . the far-off hum of a thousand possibilities . . .'
'. . . in the beauty of the whole thing, again, I lose myself . . .'

Reading a long, long passage of Henry James, I from time to time
forget – I am, by the elaborations detached from – what the often
repeated word 'it' refers to, so 'it' becomes 'big, big with the breath
of vast vague connections,' and 'it' becomes 'everything,' 'everything'
sensed as if as a pulse in the very consciousness of the universe. All
his life, I imagine, Henry James expected 'it' to be revealed to him.

Auden invited Nikos and me to have lunch at Chez Victor. He
held the menu wide open before him and, reading it, said, 'The
tomato soup looks good,' and Nikos and I knew we should order
the tomato soup. Then he said, 'The cold chicken and salad
looks good,' and again Nikos and I knew we must order the cold
chicken and salad. The point of the lunch was for Auden to give
Nikos a sheaf of poems by Chester Kallman for Nikos to consider
publishing.

After our luncheon, Auden looked tired, but when I said something about a nap, he said, 'Mother wouldn't allow it.'

Later, Nikos said he was very moved by Auden asking him to
consider Kallman's poems, moved and embarrassed, because he
could not see that it was possible to publish them.

Stephen rang to say that Wystan has left. He was staying at the
Spenders', and Stephen is relieved that he has left; he drinks
immense quantities, smokes so the whole house stinks, never
washes, goes to bed at 9:30. Stephen said Lizzie always wants her
bedroom fumigated after Auden has used it.

Stephen said that once, when Auden was staying at Loudon

Road, Natasha rang him up to say she would be late, and would he put the chicken in the oven? Auden did – he simply put it in the oven, didn't put it in a pan, didn't turn the heat on.

For the past weekend, Nikos has been in Manchester with Mark Lancaster and Richard Morphet, Assistant Keeper of the Modern Collection at the Tate Gallery; they were invited to judge the Northern Young Contemporaries Exhibition. So I slept alone, and slept very badly. The award went to Stephen Buckley.

Richard's enthusiasms for British art make me enthusiastic, so when he, in an excited voice, talks of an artist I've never heard of – such as the mystic Cecil Collins – I want to find out about the artist. He and his wife Sally invited us to lunch with the widow of Cecil Collins, who wore a mink hat, and talked of her life with Collins, when the kitchen was a gas ring on the landing.

Stephen has a painting by Collins, which, Stephen said, was painted to depict him, Stephen, as a holy fool, a painting especially meaningful to Stephen.

———

Mark Lancaster picked me up in his car, in a row in the back seat three sisters close together – Henrietta and Amaryllis and Fanny Garnett, all, I think, the daughters of Angelica Bell, the daughter of Vanessa Bell, the sister of Virginia Woolf, as Mark, who is inspired in his painting by Bloomsbury, had explained to me. He had also explained that Henrietta was married to Burgo Partridge, the son of Frances and Ralph Partridge, with whom – Ralph, that is – Lytton Strachey had been in love. And to complicate it all, Ralph Partridge, before Frances, had been in love with Dora Carrington, who, out of her impossible love for Lytton Strachey, killed herself. Burgo Partridge died just a few years ago. I may have got this all wrong. Mark took us all to a queer club, which, in the early afternoon, was empty except for us. Mark and I sat at a table and watched the three sisters, all in long dresses with embroidery across the bodices and even longer scarves, dance together, their clothes swinging.

Days later, Mark rang me to tell me that Amaryllis drowned herself in the Thames.

———

Stephen is finishing his book on the students, The Year of the Young Rebels. He said he is giving a lot of thought to the construction, which he thinks of as musical. 'Not that anyone will know.' We sometimes meet, after he picks up the neat chapters from his typist, at the National Gallery. He gave me two typed chapters. I found them, I'm afraid, rather dull. I said, 'I'm a little disappointed that you didn't put more of yourself in.'

'I didn't want to,' he said. 'I didn't want to make it refer to me.'

He rings up almost every morning. The conversation is something like this:

'How are you?'

'Very well. And you?'

'Oh, very well.'

'Are you working hard?'

'Yes, very hard. And you?'

'Very hard.'

'How's Lizzie?'

'How are the cats?'

He said that Natasha will be going to France for a week, which means he'll be completely free and won't have to think up excuses when he sees us. He'll come to dinner on Saturday, and we all plan on going up to Cambridge on Tuesday to see Mark, now artist in residence at King's, and, I hope, E. M. Forster.

———

Mark is fascinated by Bloomsbury and once introduced us to Angelica Garnett, who wears a colourful bandana tied tightly about her head, always appears distracted, as though by some shock. She asked us to supper. When I asked her about Amaryllis, she said she hasn't been a good mother. She seems to live within her own world, painting her charming, Bloomsbury paintings with cross-hatchings and playing her cello. She invited Nikos and me to stay at Charleston – where she more or less grew up not knowing that her father, a constant presence, was Duncan Grant – but she warned us that the roof leaked, and Nikos, as much as he likes Angelica, didn't fancy sleeping under a leaking roof. I imagine Charleston as filled with sunlight and flowers in vases and all the furniture painted in different colours, the walls painted too, always with cross-hatchings, and Vanessa Bell in one room painting, and Duncan Grant in another room painting, and Angelica, a little girl, talking with Virginia Woolf in the garden – about what?

I find I still fantasize about Bloomsbury, which fantasy I suspect will change during my life in London. But I am in the thrall of Mrs. Dalloway arranging a large bouquet of flowers in a vase; and Mrs. Ramsay reading and Lily Briscoe painting at an easel; and Percival listening to the sea waves with a shell to an ear. And characters from another writer appear. On a little pool made by rainwater, naked, splashing one another, are Mr. Beebe, George and Freddy. One of the trees is a wych-elm, and by it sits Helen Schlegel, writing a letter and hearing someone sneezing, 'a-tissue, a-tissue.' And somewhere beyond the trees, in an open space, a cricket match is being played.

It is as though I am nostalgic for a world that I in no way lived in except in the novels set in that world. Sentimental of me!

Nikos has no interest in Bloomsbury at all, and if he were to ask me what my fantasy is I wouldn't be able to say, wouldn't even be able to say what the word 'Bloomsbury' represents to me.

———

At the luncheon with Connolly and Auden, at one point everyone got involved in the discussion Nikos and Auden were having about happiness, and everyone, unable to say who was an example of a really happy person, agreed that Sonia Orwell was the unhappiest.

I saw her at an immense party (there must have been more than a thousand people) for an immense poet (Adrian Henri) at the Institute of Contemporary Arts. She grabbed me by the sleeve and

we talked, wandering through the gallery, and only half looking at
the Apollinaire exhibition, for about an hour. She is still beautiful,
though rather dry and puffy around the eyes. Stephen says she used
to be known as the most beautiful girl in London, the Venus of
Euston Road, because she posed for the painters of the Euston
Road School, which included Stephen for a short while. She laughs
hysterically, is always running her fingers through her hair and
pulling it, and she speaks so rapidly it's difficult to follow her.

(John Lehmann said, narrowing his steel-blue eyes, 'You know,
old man, everyone says that her marriage to Orwell was a mariage
blanc.')

Nikos told me of a dinner he had at Sonia's house before he met
me – she, he, Johnny Craxton, her ex-husband Michael Pitt-Rivers
from whom she had just got divorced, and Michael Pitt-Rivers'
boyfriend. Nikos said it was the most unbearable dinner party he
had ever been at. Sonia up till then had been rather seductively
interested in Nikos, but after this dinner party she simply cut him
whenever she saw him.

I recall a New Year's party at the Craxtons'. As Nikos and I
entered, Sonia rushed out from another room, kissed me and fussed
over me, speaking in very rapid French, but Nikos, standing right
beside me, she refused to see. Johnny came and tried to get her to
acknowledge Nikos, but she kept talking to me as if I were alone,
and I stupidly did nothing but smile a fixed smile at her; she grabbed
my sleeve and dragged me into the room where she had been,
saying, still in French, that I must help her, that I, knowing about
things French (which is hardly true), would understand. A young
cousin of Johnny, previously married to a queer, had been talking
all evening with a nice, very straight man who, though he showed
signs of interest, didn't seem likely to go so far as to ask her for a
date. I was to flirt with the cousin (Sonia confessed later she found
the cousin 'rather tiresome'), so that the nice straight man would,
through jealousy of me, ask her for a date. We all sat together. I
didn't say a word. Sonia spoke without stopping. She said, 'They
took away the drinking laws, everyone became an alcoholic; they

took away the gambling laws, everyone became a gambler; now they're taking away the laws against homosexuality, and everyone is becoming queer.' Then she jumped up, grabbed me by the hand and pulled me out of the room, saying, 'Did you hear? Did you hear? He made a date with her!' I hadn't heard.

Last night at the ICA she and Nikos greeted one another perfunctorily and coldly. She invited me to dinner but not Nikos, and I said I couldn't go.

Stephen said she's well known for breaking up couples, especially homosexual couples.

At the party I spoke to, it seems, hundreds of people: David Hockney, Alan Ross, Patrick Procktor, Mark Lancaster, Ted Lucie-Smith, Stephen Buckley.

Alan Ross is the editor of the London Magazine, for which he asked Nikos to write a 'Letter to Athens'. Nikos wrote of his involvement, when he lived in Athens, with an avant-garde magazine, Pali, that tried to bring new inspiration into Greek letters, badly, Nikos said, needed.

I learn from Nikos the names of Greek writers I had not known, not only contemporary, but from the past, and outstanding poets they are: Andreas Kalvos, Dionysios Solomos, Kostis Palamas, Angelos Sikelianos. And though I had read the poetry of Constantine Cavafy, it is with Nikos that I feel I am in the world of Cavafy, for the evocation of sensuality, Nikos' delicate sensuality, and the evocation of history, Nikos' Greek history. I live with Nikos in a Greek world within the outer world of London.

ΑΓΑΠΗ ΜΟΥ.

Together, we translated an erotic novella by the poet Andreas Embirikos, Voyage of a Balloon, which Alan Ross has published. It is a Surrealist novel, as there is, Nikos said, a deep Surrealist unconscious in Greeks.

———

My cousin Bryan came to stay with us. He left the States in protest against American forces fighting in Vietnam. I found out for him the address of an organization for young Americans in London who are resisting being drafted into the war. He went and when he came back said the people he spoke to were limp and altogether pathetic. He returned to the States to join the military.

Do I ever think of becoming British?

I have, in a way, a claim to be a part of British history, for my father, born in Canada, in the French-speaking village of Saint Barthélemy in the Province of Quebec, was born a subject of King George V. At the age of two he was taken in the arms of his mother across the border by train between Canada and the United States – no Ellis Island initiation into a different world, no passports, but a relocation from one part of North America into another. His father was a carpenter. They settled in a French-speaking parish in Providence, Rhode Island, where my father grew up as within a palisaded fortress against the Yankee outside world, and he lived as a subject of King George V in that palisaded fortress until, at the age of twenty-one, he and his father became citizens of the United States. I doubt his mother – my illiterate grandmother, who never left the fortress – ever did become a citizen.

I recall visiting my grandmother – whom I called Mémère – and sitting with her in her kitchen with my father and younger brother, he and I standing still on either side of our father as he spoke to his mother in French, she hardly responding, and most of the time all of us silent, as if the silence was communication enough.

We were taken to dinner by the poet Ted Lucie-Smith at an Indian restaurant. Stephen had wanted to have dinner with us that evening, and we asked Ted if he could come along. Ted said he'd be honored to have Stephen. Adrian Henri was also there.

At dinner, Ted spoke endlessly about his poetry, and though the poet Adrian Henri tried to be funny and sometimes was, the talk always came back to Ted's poetry. He sat, fat and motionless, presiding at the top of the table, his bulging eyes fixed, his smooth face fixed, and only his mouth moving. I could sense Stephen closing in more and more. He left immediately after dinner, and Nikos and I, going out to the street to say good night to him, watched him walk away, a huge figure in a raincoat, listing a little as he walked as if he were not quite sure where he was going. He rang the next morning to say he had become depressed at dinner, where he had felt too much self-importance was given to being a poet.

He came to dinner at our flat last night. He had a basket of bottles of wine and was in very good spirits. Stephen Buckley came too. Stephen B. made Stephen S. giggle, Stephen B. lightly irreverent towards Stephen S., which Stephen S. apparently enjoys.

This is totally true of Stephen S.: that he is supportive of the young.

Stephen Buckley often comes from Newcastle to stay the night in our spare room. We have just a little more money than he, as a student, has, so we find it a little presumptuous of him to say at dinner with us, 'What, liver again?' He said to us, 'I don't at all think of you as a homosexual couple, but just as Nikos and David.' As beautiful as he is, he likes, I think, to be admired by homosexuals, but has his lady friends of potent, if difficult, character. He flirts with Stephen Spender, and always makes him giggle.

Nikos and I now have a representative collection of Stephen B.'s work: heavy, the layered colours rich and sometimes brutal, the canvas often cut up into strips and interwoven to deepen the primacy of the materials, pictures that, for all the references to other artists, exist in themselves so emphatically that these non-figurative pictures are not abstractions, but have a thick, dense presence that makes the room they hang in appear abstract. They have spirited humour and, too, irony, which are Stephen's spirited humour and irony. He will say about a work, 'Oh, just torn-up bits of canvas,' and sniff, and then smile in such a way that belies what he said. He never ever talks abstractly about art, but instead will go on about the London bus routes.

A book launch for Cyril Connolly's collection of reviews, The Evening Colonnade. I wondered who arranged for Nikos and me to be invited, though Nikos said he wouldn't come – Sonia, near the entrance, who was very friendly and told me she thought I would be amused to be there. Stephen was not there. I saw Cyril Connolly talking to an elderly, refined-looking man wearing a white Stetson hat and white bandana tied about his neck, and, excited, I went to Connolly to tell him some gossip that I had had from Stephen which I assumed would impress him for my being close enough to Stephen that he would confide in me: a big row in the Spender family. Connolly simply stared at me, as did the man in the white Stetson, who, when Connolly introduced me to him – Cecil Beaton – turned away with a frown of, who is this presumptuous young man? Well, I thought, I've made a fool of myself, and so there goes Cecil Beaton.

———

Stephen gave me a first edition of E. M. Forster's The Longest Journey, published almost a hundred years ago. Stephen thinks the novel Forster's best. Reading it, I did not think so, but in it I found a vision entirely that of Forster, and whenever I came across sentences and paragraphs and passages that seemed to me original to Forster I copied them out, rearranged them and created in fragments a whole that is distinct from the novel itself as a whole. What the passages reveal is a very British – even more, Northern European – idealization of classical Greece.

> He looked at the face, which was frank, proud, and beautiful, if truth is beauty . . . Certain figures of the Greeks, to whom we continually return, suggested him a little. One expected nothing of him – no purity of phrase nor swift-edged thought. Yet the conviction grew that he had been back somewhere – back to some table of the gods, spread in a field where there was no noise, and that he belonged for ever to the guests with whom he had eaten.
>
> Ansell said, with irritation, 'But what can you expect from a person who's eternally beautiful?'
>
> Rickie thought, 'Do such things actually happen?' . . . Was Love a column of fire? Was he a torrent of song?
>
> He said again that nothing beautiful was ever to be regretted.
> 'You're cracked on beauty,' she whispered – they were still inside the church. 'Do hurry up and write something.'
> 'Something beautiful?'
> 'I believe you can. Take care that you don't waste your life.'
>
> He revisited Cambridge, and his name was a grey ghost over the door.

Ansell was at Sawston to assure himself of his friend's grave. With quiet eyes he had intended to view the sods, with unfaltering fingers to inscribe the epitaph. Love remained.

Let us love one another. Let our children, physical and spiritual, love one another. It is all that we can do. Perhaps the earth will neglect our love. Perhaps she will confirm it, and suffer some rallying point, spire, mound, for the new generation to cherish.

———

Everything David Hockney does seems an occasion for celebration, as his arrival in Victoria Station on the boat train from Southampton, where he'd arrived from New York by ship, with an American boyfriend, an art student he had met in America, Peter Schlesinger. I joined some of David's friends, including Ossie and Celia, to celebrate the arrival. David stepped off the train smiling a broad smile, and then Peter Schlesinger stepped off, as if in a daze, his blond-brown hair swinging over his forehead, walking away from us with a slow swagger to his hips and shoulders as if, curiously, he was alone. I suppose I might have gone off with them all, an animated entourage around David and Peter, but I held back, feeling that I didn't really belong among them, envious of them for a levity I wouldn't be able to sustain among them. It happens that, as much as I want to be light spirited, a sudden heaviness will come over me and lower me, and I will feel I am pretending to be light spirited, so it is better for me to withdraw.

———

We went to a poetry reading, among the poets Adrian Mitchell who seemed to sing out, as a refrain to a long poem, 'To Whom It May Concern (Tell Me Lies about Vietnam)'. There are many poetry readings in London.

I recall a poem by Spike Hawkins was read:

Pig, sit still in the strainer,
I must have my pig tea.

———

Stephen came to lunch, just the two of us. He brought a big bunch of asparagus, which he loves; I cooked it and we ate it with butter and lemon, the game pie and salad, and wine. We talked about the English class system and the American class system.

I said I didn't know if it is a matter of class, but certain English I've met seem to have the ability to loathe a person and be kind at the same time. He said that Annie Fleming, the wife of Ian Fleming and a grand hostess, would invite people to dinner whom she hated, and be very kind to them. I said I wondered if Natasha had this ability, and he responded, 'Oh no, not at all.'

He said she annoys him when she will say 'chimneypiece,' which is not of her class, instead of 'mantelpiece.'

About the American class system, he said it depended on where in America you are.

I said I know where I am there.

If to be English, or even to be British, is to be aware of where one is in a class system – a system that some people I've met say no longer exists, as does the editor Caro Hobhouse, for example, who, being a Hobhouse, should know – the system in no way exists among the people I know in London. Whatever the originating class of the people we meet at dinner parties, drinks parties, book launches, in the foyer of Covent Garden, at these occasions they appear to me so interconnected with one another that they form a class that I think of as London.

———

I met Stephen at Liverpool Street Station, and we trained up to Cambridge. On the way, he read and corrected proofs of his book about the young rebels. From the Cambridge train station, we took a taxi to King's and to Mark's rooms.

Mark had a little sherry party before lunch, and a few

undergraduates came, all with very long hair and all terrifyingly intelligent. They seemed to talk of nothing but pop music and violence. One student, with whom I sat on the floor, said he sometimes hoped the war in Vietnam would become another world war, because he believed that only violence could produce synthesis. I said I thought he was being very selfish. What an incredible level of intellectualization and inexperience they live on.

After lunch in a pub Stephen and I went to visit E. M. Forster.

When Stephen first suggested that Nikos and I meet Forster, Nikos had been against it, insisting we would be visiting a literary monument, not a person, and Nikos especially objected to my wanting to take flowers. Stephen tried to arrange a meeting with Forster through Joe Ackerley, and when Nikos saw all the wheels put into motion he said he'd come also. But then we got a letter from Forster — actually written by Joe Ackerley and signed by Forster — saying he was ill and would be going to Coventry (to his former friend's house, Stephen said, a policeman, now married), so we didn't go up to Cambridge. We had lunch with Joe Ackerley at Chez Victor. He appeared thin and wan, and as he was hard of hearing it was difficult to talk with him; in any case, he didn't seem very interested in us, even bored. He asked a waiter about a dog the restaurant used to keep as a mascot, and he was told by the waiter the dog had died. (Talking, finally, to Forster, I mentioned Joe Ackerley, and said how sad I thought it was that he should dedicate his posthumous book to his dog Tulip. Forster said, 'Oh, Joe used often to bore me with his dogs.') I sensed Ackerley had become, I thought, intentionally indifferent when Nikos and I said we wanted to meet Forster; I saw him viewing us as two crude opportunists, especially when Nikos said he had heard Forster had lots of Cavafy papers, which might have sounded as if Nikos wanted to see them. Joe said he didn't know about any Cavafy papers, and, leaving the restaurant with us, said that Forster was accessible and liked the company of young people, but he obviously left the going to us. He went to a Japanese film. Shortly after, he died. So we didn't go to King's College,

Cambridge to meet Forster, and, hearing that he had become
senile, we decided we shouldn't go.

But then Mark, as artist in residence at King's, said he saw Forster
daily, and he was very well and clear headed. Nikos couldn't come
on the day Stephen was free to go, and, in any case, wouldn't have
come, because he thought I wanted to meet Forster only to be able
to say I met him.

How did he know that for years and years I have blazoned across
my mind the admonition from Blaise Pascal, 'Curiosité n'est que
vanité le plus souvent, on ne veut savoir que pour en parler, autre-
ment on ne voyagerait pas sur la mer pour ne jamais en rien dire et
pour le seul plaisir de voir, sans espérance d'en jamais communi-
quer,' making me feel guilty of the sin of pride for voyaging on the
sea only later to write about it?

I told myself, no, I had a legitimate reason for meeting E. M.
Forster: his famous epigraph to Howards End 'Only Connect'
seemed to me more than a moral imperative, it seemed the very
reason for my wanting to see him, to, however briefly, connect
with him. So, as if justification were needed, I was justifying
meeting him by referring to one of his most famous epigrams.

I knew that Stephen had read E. M. Forster's unpublished novel
about male lovers, which I'd heard about, as literary gossip, in New
York, as if knowledge about it were knowledge about some secret
homosexual world only a few people were allowed into. On the
train, I asked Stephen, 'What is the novel like?' imagining I now
would be allowed into that closed world, as closed as the Cambridge
Apostles I'd read about. Stephen frowned and said the novel,
Maurice, didn't quite come off, and he wondered if it should ever
be published. This was the first criticism I had ever heard about
E. M. Forster, whom Stephen called Morgan, and I took it to be
the criticism, not of outside gossip, but of inside knowledge.

Stephen knocked on Forster's door and a delicate voice said
come in. He, short and bent, was in his shirtsleeves. 'I've just seen
the doctor,' he said, 'I've just seen the doctor.' 'Are you well?'
Stephen asked. 'Oh, indeed, indeed.' Stephen introduced us, and

when I shook his hand I imagined shaking hands, as if all their handshakes remained like hundreds of invisible hands about his, with Virginia Woolf, with Maynard Keynes, with Lytton Strachey, with all of Bloomsbury – and, extending even more out into the world, with Constantine Cavafy in Alexandria. He went into his bedroom to put on his jacket and on the way out shut the door of his bathroom, where I saw a long, claw-footed Victorian tub that listed. We sat before his fireplace, above which were oil paintings and, I gathered, family photographs. The furniture was all Victorian, rather old-maidenish, with knitted arm covers on the chairs. High bookcases, with big yellow and brown books, lined the walls one after another like large rectangular librarians standing at attention. I think the wallpaper was of yellow flowers. One of the oil paintings, all in vivid yellow, red, green, was of King's chapel done by an undergraduate, another a mountain scene by Roger Fry, and on a wall between the bedroom and the bathroom was a reproduction of Picasso's young man leading a horse. Forster had had painted the bottom panes of the windows so he wouldn't have to see the ugly modern building, the Keynes Building, across the way.

He paused for long periods between sentences, and seemed always to repeat what he said twice.

But when we talked about the military dictatorship in Greece – I saying I had hoped to go to Greece with my partner, Nikos, who was Greek, but as he couldn't go neither could I – he said, 'Yes, I understand. But one recalls instances in Greece that were beautiful even though the country, even then, was imbedded in muck. Somehow one's dearest memories are of events that, if one saw them in a greater context, were always imbedded in muck.'

Stephen joked about Mount Athos, the Greek peninsula of all-male monasteries where, supposedly, not even hens are allowed. Forster said he'd once been on a boat that was on an excursion to Mount Athos. 'The men got off,' he said quietly, 'but I stayed on board with the ladies.'

After a silence, we talked about Mark's paintings, which Forster said he viewed with compassion, but not much understanding.

After twenty minutes, Stephen said he had to get back to London, so we left. Mark drove us to the station, and on the way Stephen said, 'There was a lot of Forster in that remark about one's dearest memories always being imbedded in muck.' 'Oh?' I asked. 'His insistence on the muddle and confusion enclosing personal moments of vision,' Stephen said. At the station, he said there was no reason why I should go back to London with him, and Mark said I could stay with him in his rooms. I thought: Nikos won't mind. We left Stephen off and I returned to King's with Mark.

I rang Nikos, who didn't mind, but told me to spend the night.

Mark signed me in for dinner at High Table (how strange, I thought, that Forster's name should be matter-of-factly written in among the others), and we went back to Mark's rooms, where more undergraduates came in and talked about pop music, about which Mark appears to know everything. He played records.

Before dinner, he took me into the combination room for sherry. On the red walls were portraits of Bloomsbury people, such as Rupert Brooke, which I had seen in reproductions in books about Bloomsbury. The fellows appeared in their gowns hanging half off their shoulders. It was amusing to see Forster come in wearing his gown, smiling generally at everyone but not talking to anyone, and moving about quickly as he got his glass of sherry and went to the back of the room and sat in an armchair by himself. Mark introduced me to the provost, who asked me to follow him into dinner, where I sat at his left. The provost asked me what I do, and when I said I'm a novelist he said, 'Do you know we have Morgan Forster sitting at our table?' 'Oh, indeed, indeed,' I said. I saw Forster, toward the end of the table, eating with quick movements and looking up and only smiling at anyone who spoke to him. His moustache was short and stiff.

In the hall, the undergraduates, with trays, were sitting down to or getting up from their meals. The provost told me that the undergraduates had decided that they no longer wanted formal meals with the fellows, but to eat off trays. Therefore, the High Table had been moved from the far end of hall to the end near the combination room, so the fellows would no longer process through the students to the far end. And, again because of student protest, High Table was no longer on a platform, but, like all the tables the undergraduates ate at, was set on the stone floor.

After dinner, Mark said we should go back into the combination room. Forster was sitting alone, drinking coffee. Mark asked if we could sit with him, and he said, Oh, it'd be his pleasure, it'd be his pleasure. We talked about student demonstrations, about the war in Vietnam, more about the dictatorship in Greece.

And then, as if I must take advantage of this moment for some knowledge that no one would know but I because I would be the first person E. M. Forster told, I said, 'You met Cavafy,' but he only answered, 'Yes, I did, I did.'

I had to be content with the thought: though he would not remember me, I would remember him, and I had connected.

Mark asked him if he wanted to come to a Guy Fawkes party. At first he said yes, but then, as the energy visibly drained from him, he said he thought he'd perhaps better go to bed.

I left him thinking how utterly unmysterious he is. It seemed to me that he must be aware that he is the greatest living writer, and that there had to be a mystery in his being that, but he seemed not to be at all aware, and not once referred to his books. He's a few weeks away from being ninety.

The Guy Fawkes party was given in a small Victorian row house by two male friends. There were about fifty people, of all ages and, evidently, sexes. They, as mixed as they were, moved about among one another with great ease and cheerfulness. At one point the lights were extinguished, one of the hosts put on a record of the Fire Music from The Ring, drew back two curtains, opened French doors onto a balcony overlooking a back garden, and announced, 'Ladies and gentlemen, the fireworks!' From the garden, Catherine Wheels, Roman candles, flares, high-rising rockets, all in great gushes and geysers, kept people on the balcony and upstairs windows for about an hour.

Then a fire was lit in the garden, and people upstairs threw books down into the flames. Someone said, 'But you're burning Patrick White. You can't burn Patrick White.' After, there was a buffet of curry.

I fell a little bit in love with an undergraduate who kept refilling my plate.

At around one-thirty in the morning, Mark and I went back to King's and watched a bit of the American elections live on television, then went to bed, he upstairs in his bedroom, I on a sofa in the downstairs sitting room. I did think: if Nikos had once had sex with Mark, why shouldn't I? I jerked off into a handkerchief, which, in the morning, I stuffed into a pocket of my trousers. Not thinking it showed any evidence of what I'd used it for, I took it out in Mark's presence to blow my nose, and he, no doubt seeing that the handkerchief was stiff in a way it shouldn't have been, smiled, but said nothing. I've never mentioned to him his affair, however brief, with Nikos.

———

Stephen often asks me about this diary, as if he wants to be reassured I am keeping it. I feel I don't put everything in that I should or, perhaps, that he would want me to. After I came home from an afternoon with him, during which he had said something about Auden or Isherwood, I thought I ought to record his comments in my diary, but, thinking further of it, I decided it was wrong of me to record the comments, as, Stephen apart, their relevance was not to Auden or Isherwood, but to me as the diarist. For so many years before I came to London, I kept my diary recording relationships within my family and close friends, people who were relevant and important to me. But Auden, Isherwood, Forster, however often I might meet them, are not my friends, and everything I record about them can only be of an almost irrelevant literary interest – the very interest Nikos so derides and tries to break in me. But, even so, given that I am a writer, how can I not write about them? And now I regret not having recorded what Stephen told me, which I've forgotten.

As for Stephen in himself, I sometimes wonder if he wants me to write in my diary events in his life that he himself would not write in his — as his telling me, with glee in the telling, that years ago he was in Switzerland and had sex with a young man in a bush, after which he gave the young man a huge Swiss note, but the young man thought this too much, so he gave Stephen change. Stephen was bright red with laughter.

———

Some time after Nikos and I began to live together, he showed me a poem he had written before we met, called 'To a Friend Who Regretted Leaving Three Days Later,' a title that suggested more to me than I wanted to know, dedicated to someone named Toer Van Schayk.

He is, Nikos said, a Dutch ballet dancer and choreographer.

Some time later, Toer Van Schayk, in London, rang wanting to see Nikos. Nikos told me to come along, my jealousy softened by my curiosity, and we met Toer Van Schayk in a simple cafeteria. I had come thinking that if he had found Nikos attractive, he would find me attractive also. I found him attractive, a slim, elegant man, whose demeanour was self-contained and modest. He could speak Greek, which he had learned living as a local on the island of Paros, where he would enter the ancient Parian marble quarry for marble and carry out lumps to carve them into heads he would then leave about the countryside. He and Nikos spoke Greek while I listened, and the more they spoke the more stiff I became, my arms crossed, until Nikos and Toer sensed my disapproval and spoke in English, though Toer still concentrated on Nikos. He evidently did not find me attractive. My jealousy became stark, and I leaned towards them and stuck out my chin to interrupt them and said to Nikos I had to go, and if he wanted to stay that was up to him. This surprised Nikos. He knew from the past that he could, in my presence, turn his attention to someone else without intending me to feel he was being inattentive to me, he knowing that I would of course understand that he was meeting someone he hadn't seen in a long while who meant something special to him, and in the past I had understood and had deferred, especially when a Greek refugee comes to our flat for supper. But now, not looking at Toer but at Nikos, I stood, and Nikos stood, and turning away I didn't say goodbye to Toer Van Schayk.

Nikos was silent on the way home, and, at home, asked me, 'Why were you so unkind to Toer? He is a pure person, and I loved and love him.'

———

Stephen came to dinner a few nights ago with Patrick and Patrick's new, beautiful friend Gervase. Stephen spoke about his friendship with Christopher Isherwood when they were in their early twenties, when they didn't know anyone famous. He said, 'I'm sure I did more sincere work then, when I was twenty-three, when I didn't know anyone famous, than the work I did after I began to meet famous people.' We discussed successful people – that is, people who could confidently enjoy the fact that they are successes, such as E. M. Forster, Henry Moore, Francis Bacon. Patrick and Nikos said no one should allow himself to think he's a success. Stephen said, 'Well, I know I'm not a success.'

After dinner, Patrick made a reefer and passed it around. I didn't take any, nor did Gervase, who sat quietly still all evening, but Stephen and Nikos did, Nikos staring me straight in the eyes as he took deep puffs, and I went into a funk. I don't know why the very subject of hashish causes all kinds of jealousies, anxieties, depressions in me, but it does. Nikos says it is because I want to be in control, and hashish puts him beyond my control.

———

I mentioned to John Lehmann that I was looking for a job, as I'd run out of money. He asked me if I wanted to be his secretary a couple of mornings a week, sorting out papers, typing, answering business letters, and I said yes. He invited me to lunch in his flat to talk about what I would do. I went reluctantly. At lunch, he asked, slitting his eyes and leaning over the table toward me, 'Tell me, old boy, just what is your relationship with Stephen?'

When I next saw Stephen, I told him I saw John, but not why, and I said, 'He really is unpleasant, isn't he?' I said this because I knew Stephen wanted to hear me say it.

Nikos, at lunch alone with Stephen, told him that I was going to work for John, and Stephen rang me up. He said, 'Nikos told me you're going to work for John.'

I said, 'I don't really want to. What do you think?'

'Well,' Stephen said, 'I suppose it'd be silly if you turned him down.'

We talked about it for a long while, and I decided: 'I won't work for him.'

Stephen said, 'Well, perhaps I'm being unjust, but I would prefer it if you didn't. When I heard you were going to, I thought: I won't see David any longer. It's the first bad thought I've had about you.'

'I don't want you to have any bad thoughts about me,' I answered.

When, a couple of weeks later, Nikos and I saw John Lehmann again, he asked, 'When are you going to start working for me?' 'Oh,' I said, 'I don't think I'll have to now.' He said, 'I didn't think you would.'

John has the vulgar habit, on greeting Nikos and me, of kissing us on the mouth and jutting his tongue between our lips. Nikos, in front of him, wipes his mouth, but I am too intimidated by John to do anything but smile a weak smile.

———

Stephen, I think, creates guilt, both in others and in himself. We were going to the Italian Cultural Institute on Belgrave Square, as he had to copy down some Italian translations of English poems for a lecture he was to give in Rome. On the way, we passed Magoushe Gorky's house, and Stephen said, 'We mustn't let Magoushe see us. She'll tell Natasha we're together.' Magoushe is the mother-in-law-to-be of Stephen's son Matthew. After we left the Italian Institute, going back to his car, Stephen said, 'Let's go to Magoushe's and have tea.'

'But, Stephen, you didn't want her to see us together,' I said.

'Oh, it doesn't matter,' he answered. 'It's a great bore, Natasha's disapproval of you and Nikos.'

We went and had tea, and were welcomed. Magoushe and Maro, with whom Matthew has been living for years, were writing out invitations to the wedding. There was a lot of talk about who was Hon. and who not, and what titles people had. In came three women, a mother and two daughters, with the names Chloe, Clare, Chlochlo, though I was not able to sort out who was called what, all Peploes, who appeared to me to be mythological creatures. Leaving them all, Stephen paused in the street and said, 'I hope Magoushe doesn't tell Natasha we went to tea.'

———

With a single tulip, I visited David Hockney, who was surrounded by what I took to be dealers who so closed in on him all I could do was hand him the tulip and say hello. I wandered about among other visitors and noted in the middle of a room a double bed, unmade, and by the bed on the floor a large jar, the cover off, of Vaseline.

———

To my surprise, Stephen suggested we make a television script of Henry James' story 'The Author of Beltraffio,' in which a wife allows their son to die, so outraged she is by her husband having published a novel that she finds morally corrupt. That Stephen chose this story can only make me wonder what the significance of it is to him as a writer, and to him and Natasha as husband and wife. To what degree does Stephen feel that he has had to censor himself in his writing, not wanting to upset Natasha in revenge against what he would like to write? And to what degree does Stephen feel he, married to Natasha, should have the freedom to write what he wants? And write about what? Sex? I can write about sex because of the freedom the world more and more allows. Stephen is still in another, a residual world in which to write about sex is not allowed, and that other, residual world censors him, that other, residual world in which he places Natasha as a guard against the moral corruption of unlawful sex. I think: Stephen may feel that to write about sex is to break free from that other world, is to break free from Natasha as the guardian of that world. But isn't there, within their relationship as husband and wife, something more binding that holds them together, and isn't that something the source of some of Stephen's best and most moving poems, the love poems about Natasha? I am gathering together an image of Natasha that, from Stephen's telling me about her, is complex, as are his feelings towards her. It would be too easy to simplify Natasha as a willful woman who will get her way, or to simplify Stephen's relationship with her as subservient to her will, which he resents but cannot escape. Of course, I do wonder why he wants to do the adaptation of 'The Author of Beltraffio' with me. Anyway, what I cannot understand is that sex should have been, in a world not so very far removed from the world in which Nikos and I love each other, considered morally corrupting.

———

I like to think that Nikos and I together belong to three nations – both of us British, both of us Greeks, both of us Americans. What the cross-overs from country into country could mean I can only wonder.

———

I met Stephen at the Tate, where we went quickly through the de Kooning exhibition, with those large women with large staring eyes and large teeth and short legs sticking out from under voluminously painted skirts, who made Stephen giggle; then we got into a taxi as he had to go pick up plane tickets for Israel (he and Natasha are going for two weeks) and then in the same taxi went on to his publisher, Weidenfeld & Nicolson, where he was to correct the proofs of his book about the students. He wanted me to come in the taxi with him as he said that would be the only time he had to be with me.

I didn't mention that John Lehmann was coming to dinner, as I know he doesn't like Nikos or me to see John. But Stephen rang up while John was here. He rang, just before he had to get ready to leave for Israel the next morning, to give me a sentence for a blurb I'm writing for the Edward Upward novel In the Thirties. I was sure Stephen could hear John's voice and laughter, perhaps made loud because John knew Stephen was on the phone. After I wrote down the sentence, I said, 'John Lehmann is here.' I sensed Stephen's disappointment. He said, 'Well, I hope you don't prepare him as magnificent a meal as you prepare for me when I come.' 'Not nearly as magnificent,' I said, and he laughed, but I felt vaguely guilty.

I don't at all understand Stephen's relationship with John Lehmann. I sense Stephen has more resentment toward John than John toward him, if John has any resentment toward Stephen. In fact, I think John is rather large about Stephen, and though he'll say such things as 'Oh Stephen, thy name is naïveté,' there doesn't seem to be any bitterness in it. Stephen's comments about John, however, are often bitter. He thinks John mean-spirited. Stephen once gave me the plot for a story: two well-known literary figures, who look somewhat alike, are often taken for one another at parties, and act the parts of one another, while in fact they despise each other. But, as big as they both are, Stephen doesn't look at all like John. John looks sinister, his skull large and very near the surface, his eyes narrow and staring with fixed concentration, and Stephen looks the very opposite of sinister, always blinking as if innocently bemused.

John brought a bottle of Osbert Sitwell's wine when he came to dinner last night: Vini Chianti Montegufoni, proprietà Sir Barone Osbert Sitwell.

He said that if one asks for a lavatory in the castle, one is shown the way by a servant along many passageways to a room with a chamber pot – a story I have heard from someone else, but can't recall from whom.

—————

We could hardly understand Stephen when he rang for the background noise of music and talk at the wedding reception of his son Matthew and now his daughter-in-law Maro. Stephen, sentimental about how Nikos and I love each other, sounded drunk, and Nikos and I were embarrassed for him.

—————

Because Nikos couldn't come, I tried to excuse myself from going to lunch at John Lehmann's house in the country, Lake Cottage, near the town of Three Bridges, and over the telephone said I was waiting for an important call that I had to stay in London for, but he insisted: he had prepared lunch for me. The lunch consisted of a slice of meat pie with the endless egg in it, frozen peas, and a puddle of instant potatoes. John showed me a collection of photographs of young men taken just before the war, mostly in and about Vienna: blond, thin, fresh, smiling, all lovers. One was wearing the uniform of a Nazi air force man. John said, 'These aren't all of them, duckie; there were lots more.' Perhaps I'm making him sound crude. He wasn't, or if he was the crudeness is held within a tremendous, even ponderous structure of English graciousness.

He let me look through his library, all smelling of damp, of the books he published, of an extraordinary high quality. Everyone says he is a much better editor than poet.

In the entrance hall of the cottage is a large round table decorated by Denton Welch, whose delicate novels I have admired with the admiration of someone who thinks, falsely, that the admiration is unique to oneself, though in fact the admiration is of a cult. But his presence suddenly appeared unique to me, long after his death, in the solid table painted in bright red and green and yellow.

—————

The more I get to know Greeks, the more I think they are people who do not make moral judgments, but who, living the facts of history, have a very deep, unspoken, instinctive moral sense which they live by historically, and which is very accommodating of human failings. It comes to me more and more forcefully that Greece is not a country of puritan principles, unlike America, but a country deeply layered with the facts of its history that belie making judgments raised up on unaccommodating high principles.

A Greek friend of Nikos, who, as Nikos did, worked in the Greek Embassy in London but left and is now stranded because he can't return to Athens, is staying with us for a few days. He laughed saying that all Greeks are guilty, all, of complicity in deals, which are kept secret. 'Greece,' he said, 'is run on don't tell, don't tell, keep it a secret, because if you tell you bring on the evil eye.' What surprises me is that Greeks will admit this with a laugh, and then make a gesture of disgust and turn away as if from all of Greece.

But if ever I, enas xenos, a stranger, ever repeat what a Greek – even Nikos – has said to me about Greece, the look I will get – and, in the case of Nikos, the reprimand that I'm not Greek and don't know about Greece – shuts me up.

For all of that, I have fallen in love with a country I don't know.

———

Stephen came to supper, then the next day rang to say that when he arrived back to Loudon Road, where he lives, he found a taxi, its door open, waiting, and, inside, Natasha, with Sonia attending, packing to leave because she knew he had been with us. Sonia left and he calmed Natasha.

Perhaps I concentrate too closely on Stephen and Natasha in this diary, leaving other people we see outside, but it is as if I see them more and more as within a narrative that keeps me attentive because Nikos and I are in it.

We could of course tell Stephen that we think it best for Natasha and his relationship with her that we don't see him, but we won't do that.

Maro Gorky, as if to find out who Nikos and I are, came to visit, and informed me, as with delight, that Nikos is a C.I.A. agent. I thought: well, at least they – she, Matthew, Magoushe, and, too, the Peploes, Clare and Chloe and Chlochlo, all that world – are all talking about Nikos.

Nikos told me that, before he met me, the Italian writer Niccolò Tucci had stayed with him, having had to escape from the Peploes because of their pet snake. I imagine them, mother and two daughters, with names all beginning with C, in an apartment that could be anywhere in the world, in which they, in long loose frocks and barefoot, and speaking many languages, wander from room to room, with no other reason for being who they are but that they have a pet snake, which is all I know about them.

Tucci came to a meal, an elegant, multi-cultured man who seems to use three or four languages in every sentence. He has just published a novel, called Before my Time.

> I was born before my time. When my time came, the place was occupied by someone else; all the good things of life for which I was now fit had suddenly become unfit. It was always too early or too late.

When Anne Graham-Bell, who is a presence in the literary world of London and who wants to bring accord to all the world, arranged for Nikos to have lunch with her and the mistress of Allen Lane at Bianchi's restaurant, Nikos thought Tucci would charm them both and asked Anne to include him, and he did charm them both, so all Nikos needed to do was sit back. Later, Anne said to Nikos that she hoped that Tucci was discreet enough not to let on that he had had lunch with the mistress of Allen Lane, and Nikos assured her that Tucci had often had lunches and teas and drinks and dinner with the mistresses of powerful men, and knew about discretion.

San Andrea di Rovereto di Chiavari

We are again in San Andrea. Anne Graham-Bell is staying with us.

She encourages me to write. Her devotion to literature is great, and will have her pestering agents and publishers to give the writers she is most devoted to the attention she believes they deserve. There is a story that a publisher, knowing that Anne could not be stopped by his secretary from entering his office, hid away on the balcony. She writes articles warning reviewers that they must read the books they are reviewing through to the end, shocked as she is that reviewers don't read books through to the end. The shock is registered in her round staring eyes and her mouth a little agape in her long face. She will suddenly become serious about the way the standards are being lost, that look of shock leaving her bemused at how this could happen.

And of course I enjoy the connections she will refer to lightly, married to Graham-Bell who was one of the group of painters called the Euston Road School, among them Lawrence Gowing and William Coldstream and Rodrigo Moynihan and Adrian Stokes and, for a while, Stephen Spender; and, after Graham-Bell was killed in an airplane crash, Anne married Quentin Bell, the nephew of Virginia Woolf. She said about Virginia Woolf that she always appeared to be dressed in dusty curtains. Anne likes to joke that by marriage she is also related to Alexander Graham-Bell, the

inventor of the telephone. She laughs a laugh of astonishment at all
this happening to her, she, as she likes to say, a provincial girl from
South Africa.

All together, we take the bus to Chiavari to shop. In the market,
she was very keen to buy a punnet of wild strawberries, for she
must have wild strawberries, however much they cost.

More than amused by her, Nikos and I love her for her
enthusiasms.

She was with us when Stephen came to visit us, he staying in a
hotel. It embarrassed Nikos and me that Stephen paid little attention to her. We all had lunch in a restaurant in San Fruttuoso
overlooking the Ligurian Sea.

The photographs perhaps say more than I could.

Stephen and Anne have gone.

Today it is raining, so we've stayed in, reading and writing letters.
The little whitewashed house on the high steep slope of the Ligurian coast is enveloped in cloud, pouring down over the mountain
ridge above us; there is a smell of mint everywhere.

Stephen went from us to Paris to meet Natasha. His trip to Italy is a secret from her. He said, 'She's suffered so much from my friends in the past, I don't want her to suffer any more.' Another time, he said, 'Natasha despises weak people. I'm weak. I don't understand why she doesn't despise me.'

While he was here, he and I took a long walk up the mountain. Stephen was filled with anecdotes. About John Lehmann: 'Rosamond and Beatrix and John were waiting together as their mother was dying. After some time, John took out his watch and asked, "How long will this take? I have many things to do."' About Auden: 'Wystan said he would write a poem for my birthday. I thought, How nice, a poem for my birthday. Then he said, "I didn't have time to write a poem, so I sent a letter to the *Guardian*." But the letter didn't appear, and Wystan told me they must have lost it.' Talking about poetry, he said, a very revealing thing about Auden's poetry is that it completely lacks mystery. The same applies to Isherwood's prose. He thought that mystery is what his own poetry is essentially about.

The day after Stephen and Anne left seemed vacant. I said to Nikos, 'It is so mysterious when people leave: I can't really imagine

Stephen now on the same train on which we saw him off, settling into his compartment and reading his newspapers. Separation is incomprehensible.'

'I hate it,' Nikos said.

——————

We go to the beach every morning and stay until the afternoon. At lunch time, the beach becomes almost deserted, and it is hot and absolutely still. The few people remaining lie motionless on the pebbles, and waves of heat rising about them distort them.

I am never bored with Nikos. Last night, we sang songs to one another that we made up. Mine was in French:

> Sur la table,
> dans un rayon de soleil,
> se trouvent
>
> un verre d'eau
> et une pomme rouge.

His was in Italian, a tango:

> Prosciutto e melone,
> un po' di provalone . . .
> Zabaglione.

I thought, the other day, walking down the path to the beach with him: if ever I am unhappy in the future, I will have these days, these three years, with Nikos to look back to as proof that I can be happy. I'll never be able to say that I wasn't happy. I think of the change in my life from before I met him to being with him essential.

London

Back in London, where everything seems to be working for me. The short stories in Penguin Modern Stories One, with Jean Rhys, will be out soon, and two novels have been accepted by Macdonald. Of course I am pleased, and I tell everyone. But I find myself becoming depressed, and I don't know why.

Nikos says to me, 'Don't disappoint me.'

———

Nikos likes to say we are both refugees.

My father was born in Canada, in the province of Quebec, and when he was two years old was taken by his parents across the border between the United States and Canada to Providence, Rhode Island, forced out of their home because they had been reduced to poverty by the English, who dispossessed them of their inheritance, for the French were the original settlers. So, in a sense, my father's mother and father took refuge in the United States by settling anew in a Quebec French parish in Yankee New England, where the work allowed the refugees was in factories owned by the Yankees. I was born and brought up in that parish, and in all my youth I felt that we Québécois-Americans, we Franco-Americans, were a race apart.

Nikos has said he never felt he belonged in Greece, and I have never felt I belonged in the United States. To be, as I am, a

Franco-American, meaning a French-Québécois-American, is to be no one in America, because we have no identity there, none. Nikos' identity, even to his singular accent from beyond mainland Greece, was at best marginalized as a refugee.

We grew up, in our different worlds, fantasizing about a world outside which we could belong to, and that world is, if not England, and even more if not Britain, London.

I must put in that Nikos and I met the old writer Raymond Mortimer at the writer Raleigh Trevelyan's flat (and of course I'm aware of the name Trevelyan as having a long British history), and all I can recall of Raymond Mortimer is his saying he had met 'a charming blackamoor,' this said with a knowing smile, he obviously knowing that he was affecting the offensive 'blackamoor' as justified by the history of the world from centuries past.

———

Whenever Nikos and I are out in a crowded street and an old person carrying a suitcase appears, Nikos says, 'I can't bear it,' and I see tears rise into his eyes.

———

John Pope-Hennessy had a brother, an historian, known most notably for his book on the slave trade between Africa and the Americas, in which the more horrifying aspects are detailed. I visited James Pope-Hennessy in his flat above a pub in Ladbroke Grove, he thin and pale and gracious, the other guests a languid young man who never rose from the armchair under which cushion he seemed to have been born and which he did not have the strength to rise from, and a vigorous furnace stoker from the Battersea Power Station. Everyone was very friendly.

James, a masochist, was found tied up and murdered by an overly inspired sadist. John described going to the morgue to identify the corpse of his brother, his face with a dissolute, almost evil expression.

Still, John had a Roman Catholic Mass said for him. The Mass revealed to me for the first time that John himself was a Catholic, but I did not know if practicing. When I told Sonia Orwell that John Pope-Hennessy was a Catholic, she shouted, 'How can he be?' as if his being a Catholic were an outrage.

John went to Florence where an exhibition of great medieval silver chasses helped him to recover from the death of his brother.

———

Stephen invited Nikos and me to have lunch with Auden at the Garrick. Auden looks older than what I remembered, and more slovenly.

I notice, whenever I'm with Stephen and Auden, Stephen becomes very quiet and reserved, as if in recognition of Auden's superiority; he never disagrees with him, and when, a few days after our lunch at the Garrick, Auden came to dinner and Nikos argued with him about the Vietnam War (Auden is for withdrawal, but is sure this will cause chaos in South Vietnam) Stephen seemed to slip into a position that was almost reactionary in his seeming, a bit embarrassed, to support Auden.

He and Auden were coming to dinner on an evening when John Lehmann had invited Nikos and me to drinks. There didn't appear to be any reason why we shouldn't go to John's and hurry back to give Stephen and Auden dinner. An hour or two before we were to go to John's, he rang up:

'Look, old boy, Auden is coming for drinks also, but has to leave early because he and Stephen have been invited to dinner. So why don't you and Nikos come early, fifteen minutes or so, to meet him.'

I paused. 'But, John, he's having dinner with us.'

'Is he? Isn't that amusing? Stephen didn't mention a word of that.'

'Well, I wonder why.'

'You know Stephen.'

Nikos and I did go early. There were John, Robert Medley, Auden and Stephen. Auden said little. Later, in the taxi, he complained that when one's invited for drinks, there should be proper drinks, and not just champagne. Stephen had sent us a cheque to buy a big bottle of vodka for him, and when he got to our flat he made himself a huge Manhattan, took off his slippers, sat, came to the dinner table in his stocking feet, and talked the whole evening – that is, until 10:00, when, way past his bed time, he told Stephen they had to go. We'd asked John Golding and James Joll also.

Because Nikos and I are foreigners and don't really know the accords of who likes whom or the discords of who dislikes whom, and, too, because we don't think in terms of liking or disliking (or as foreigners don't have the social confidence to be able to), we're happy when, on having different people to supper, we find that among them one of them is very fond of another and both are happy to be brought together unexpectedly, or we're disconcerted when one of them very much dislikes another, and the consequences of that have led to some disastrous supper parties, as when someone was so insulting to another the only accord I could think of to bring everyone together was for everyone to sing 'Jerusalem,' after which, at 9:30, everyone left. We've been told, because our ignorance must be generally known, by a friend not to be invited with another friend, and so we learn about accords and discords, without quite knowing why so-and-so doesn't want to be invited with so-and-so.

It does surprise me when I am enthusiastic about meeting someone – and Nikos, too, who will say about someone recently met, 'She's wonderful!' – I find someone else I am also enthusiastic about knowing will say, 'I don't like her,' or even, 'How can you be friends with her?' leaving me to wonder which of the friends I should be more friendly with, and leaving Nikos to laugh a light laugh.

James and John had not met Auden, so Nikos and I thought they would be pleased.

Stephen had said, the best for Auden would be grilled chops and root vegetables, no salad, no pudding, but cheese for after. Wanting to do something special, I prepared what I found in a cookbook to be called something like Hamine Eggs, eggs boiled in onion skins for an hour or so, with mayonnaise for first, which Auden so liked he asked for the recipe and said he would tell Chester to make them.

James Joll said that he recently told the critic George Steiner that he would never speak to him again after Steiner wrote in an article what James thought unjust, but, as it was a rainy night, he offered Steiner a ride to his house, where he left him off with a final goodbye.

Auden seemed not to hear.

Auden appeared not to be interested in anyone, and I tried to rouse his interest by asking James if he had to do a lot of research as he was writing Europe since 1870. He said, 'No, I've done the research,' so the history of that period was now of an interconnected world revolving in his head, a world that to me occurs in disconnected flashes that have no chronology, none, that I can put together.

Auden did look at James for a moment, as though his attention held for a moment in which he wondered who James is, but he quickly lost interest.

Throughout the evening at supper with Stephen and Auden, John and James, it seems, said very little, but then who can say much when Auden says everything?

John Golding did say he thought that though Picasso has illustrated books he has never read a book in his life.

Stephen says Auden, in conversation, is like a great big bus with a very determined route, and either you get on and listen without talking, or you jump off. There's very little communication with him. And yet, he was very open to having anyone board him as a bus, was very relaxed, said how nice he thought our flat is, how good the food, and he was, in the way a great big red bus can be, very amiable.

I wonder if Stephen has ever admitted in print, or even in conversation, that his friend W. H. Auden is a very great poet.

Thinking about history –

History for me is always a surprise as to what happened to the past in relation to what is happening now, though I am acutely aware that what is happening now is in direct relation to what happened in long past battles, though I cannot remember dates, who fought whom, and why the battle determined the fate of the world I live in. I defer to historians for keeping the history of the world together.

But in his introduction, James does write: 'Episodes which seemed immensely important at the time sink into insignificance in the wider view. This is especially true of the history in the last twenty-five years. Since the end of World War I it is hard to decide what is important and what is ephemeral in our history. Down to the end of World War II we at least know, when writing history, what was going to happen. For the more recent past we do not know the outcome of historical events in which we are still person-ally involved.'

———

What to make of this, which I take to be entirely English only, I suppose, because it took place in England, or, more specifi-cally, in London? Nikos and I were invited by Robert Medley to a drinks party, and there he, left aged by the recent death of a lover with whom he lived and whom he cared for over many years, introduced us to a slim young man with bleached-blond hair, and we imagined him to be Robert's young lover, given the way Robert laid a loose arm about the young man's shoul-ders. There were many black people there, and the music was reggae, and the young bleached-blond man danced with a young black woman, and the way they danced, and the way they held each other even when they were not dancing, made me wonder what possible relationship Robert could have with the young man.

Maggi Hambling, whom we see from time to time, was there, standing apart, smoking a rolled-up cigarette, with narrowed eyes looking upon all the proceedings.

She said she often goes to a bar in Battersea Park Road, just behind where we live, and suggested we go with her one evening, and Nikos, who likes her a lot, said yes, yes, and so I said, yes, yes.

Stephen is away, teaching at the University of Connecticut.

John Lehmann is at the University of Texas.

At a party for the writer Jessica Mitford, I spoke to Sonia, who looked older and had put on a stone if not more, and who seemed a little cool perhaps because I hadn't seen her in a while because of her treatment of Nikos.

Sonia said, looking past me, 'There is Natasha,' and I turned and saw a tall, striking-looking woman with a broad, blonde Russian face talking to a man. I suddenly became very uncertain of myself, and squeamish. I wondered if I should go and introduce myself to her, because, after all, she would know who I was from my having gone to the South of France to help Stephen plant trees in the garden of their house, and I decided, yes, I must. The man she was talking to had hair like white plucked chicken feathers and very yellow teeth, the painter Julian Trevelyan. When I introduced myself to Natasha Spender, she appeared not to have heard of me. She talked on with Julian Trevelyan, and I just stood by, smiling stupidly, and commenting on what she said, 'How nice,' as if I were in fact participating in the talk.

The fact was that I knew about everything she mentioned: Stephen in America, the birth of Matthew and Maro's daughter Saskia, Lizzie, that the house in Loudon Road needs rewiring, that the garden of the house in the South of France is coming on, that Stephen was going to get the English Chair at University College – though, as this hasn't yet been revealed, Natasha hinted at it by saying, 'We're hoping this will be my husband's last extended trip abroad. It's time he put on his carpet slippers and settled.' She spoke with great articulation, her lips forming the words almost exaggeratedly. But I couldn't let on that I knew about Stephen getting the Chair. As friendly as I am with Stephen, with whom I talk very intimately, he as much about Natasha as I about Nikos, I am a total stranger to Natasha. I couldn't possibly say, 'Stephen rang up from Connecticut last week to say hello.'

I couldn't see myself as I listened to Natasha speak, my awareness of myself a kind of blur out at a distance from myself, that distant blur suddenly referring back to me only for a second when I raised a hand to touch my nose and realized that it was in fact my hand, but, standing before Natasha and listening to her, I thought that she saw that my hands, my face, my body were all mine, and that she must be judging me for the way she saw me. What did she see?

(I suppose the attraction of looking at photographs – or, more, of film – from a party after the event is to see oneself as others saw one, and perhaps to think: really, that's me?)

Natasha seemed not to be seeing me at all, and I turned away from her after a while and let her go on speaking to Julian Trevelyan and spoke to someone else.

Later, I talked to Sonia, who said she had wondered if Natasha and I would meet and speak to each other.

'Oh, we did,' I said.

'Yes, I saw you. You seemed to be chatting away intimately.'

'No, not at all. She talked with Julian Trevelyan, and all I said from time to time was, "How lovely."'

'Oh?'

'It's too stupid. And all for nothing. My relationship with Stephen is so innocent.'

'No,' she said, 'it isn't. It isn't innocent. Nothing involving feelings is innocent.'

'Perhaps you're right.'

I sent Sonia my novel, The Ghost of Henry James, and she sent me a sweet letter thanking me for it.

———

We went to the bar, Sporters, in Battersea Park Road with Maggi H., she dressed in khaki. There was an all-women band playing extravagantly, the drummer wearing a jacket covered in blue sequins that flashed as she swung her arms.

Maggi told us that once when she was in the bar, in came a group of men in drag as women, and some of them chatted her up and asked her if she'd like to go to a T.V. party, and Maggi, wondering what kind of party there could possibly be of men in drag watching the television, but, curious, said she'd love to go. She was taken in a lorry, the driver having to hike up his/her dress to drive, to Clapham Common, where more and more men in drag collected. Maggi asked, 'Where's the television?' and at her question the room became silent and she suddenly knew that T.V. did not mean watching television, and that the men in drag suddenly knew she was a woman, and that if she didn't get out of there as quickly as she could she'd be raped.

In the bar, Nikos appeared excited to be in an extravagant world of working-class people who, within their world, allowed themselves freedoms that were theirs entirely, a world I felt he genuinely admired, but one he could never ever be a part of.

———

To celebrate the publication of my novel, The Ghost of Henry James, Nikos invited some friends to the only truly Greek restaurant in London, in a mews off Queensway, where I drank and drank and drank and smashed the glasses on the floor. Back home, I was sick in the toilet bowl, Nikos standing above me, and between bouts of vomiting I said, 'I'm so happy, I'm so happy,' and Nikos laughed and put his hands on my shoulders.

———

Back from America, Stephen recounted how, when asked if he knew of any good new literary magazines in the States, he was amused to answer, 'Yes, Fuck You.' He laughed his high laugh, his shoulders shaking. He gave us some copies, rough paper, roughly printed, stapled, rough drawings in the Egyptian erotic style, the editorial page called EJACULATIONS FROM THE EDITOR, with exhortations IMMEDIATE GRATIFICATION, FREEDOM FOR HALLUCINOGENS, GROPE FOR PEACE,

DISOBEY!, GOD THROUGH CANNABIS, KEEP HUMP-
ING, MUSHROOMS, RESISTANCE AGAINST GOON
SQUADS, and entries by Allen Ginsberg, Frank O'Hara, Peter
Orlovsky, LeRoi Jones, Robert Duncan, William Burroughs,
Robert Creeley, Charles Olson, Gary Snyder, Gregory Corso, John
Wieners, Norman Mailer. One issue has a long poem by W. H.
Auden, 'A Platonic Blow', which, with many rhymes internal and
external admired by Nikos, such as:

> It was a spring day, a day, a day for a lay when the air
> Smelled like a locker-room, a day to blow or get blown,

describes a blow job that is not Platonic. Stephen said Auden does
not deny he wrote the poem, but is annoyed that it was stolen from
his desk.

Stephen asked for the issue with the Auden poem back.

———

Though Nikos Georgiadis and my Nikos are Greeks, I note the
difference between them when we visit Georgiadis in his flat/
studio, where, with the theatricality of a set designer, he puts on
display evidence of the different cultures within Greek history
noted by, say, Herodotus and his travels throughout the then
known world: large picture books on Palmyra, the ruins of
Carthage, Thracian gold; swaths of embroidered cloth with Eastern patterns; ancient clay vases and glass vials and alabaster cups;
and, surmounting all, the cover of an Egyptian mummy with
large staring eyes. My Nikos would consider all this as merely
picturesque, and I remark that the only Greek artifact we have in
our home is a komboloi of large blue beads given to Nikos by
someone from Greece.

We went with Nikos Georgiadis to an art film at the Curzon
Street cinema. After, in the men's room, I, turning away from the
urinal, saw Rudolf Nureyev peeing in the next urinal. Outside, I
joined both the Nikoses on the pavement, and when I mentioned

that I had just peed next to Rudolf Nureyev, Georgiadis, instead of leaving us, talked about the film until Nureyev came out and, seeing Georgiadis, joined us. Georgiadis had designed the set for the Prokofiev Romeo and Juliet in which Nureyev and Margot Fonteyn starred. He didn't introduce Nikos and me to Nureyev, and we all went our separate ways. Nikos said that Georgiadis had intentionally waited for Nureyev to come out and speak to him as a way of letting us know he knows Nureyev, and, too, that Georgiadis was letting us know that his friendship with Nureyev was exclusive of us. The next day Georgiadis rang to apologize – Nureyev had rung him to complain that he, Georgiadis, hadn't introduced us.

I thought, just as well, really, just as well, I sensing that Rudolf Nureyev could be a threat to Nikos and me.

———

Sonia's house in South Kensington has polished parquet floors and bright rugs and small, round tables with long and delicately curved legs and, always, vases of flowers on the tables, and books. There are, around the sitting room, shelves and shelves of books, for Sonia is a great reader. The fire in the fireplace might be lit. The air in her house appears filled with reflected light from polished surfaces, from crystal, from mirrors even on grim, gray days. There are drinks in the sitting room, then dinner in her basement dining room where the table is set with a starched white cloth and starched white napkins and gleaming china and glasses and silver, at the center a small bunch of pretty flowers. She wants everything to be pretty. The meals she prepares are mostly French, as are the wines she has opened and put on the buffet to breathe. A Francophile, she says the French enjoyed life more than the English, and, at the end of a meal, instead of asking everyone to go upstairs to the sitting room for coffee, she keeps her friends around the table for the coffee and more wine and talk, as she says is done in France.

She is always exhausted, as her dinner parties require of her a great effort, a duty even, and after having made the effort, performed the duty, as if to confirm that the things of this life matter because there is no other life, she hardly eats what she has prepared, but sits a little removed from the table and drinks and smokes as her friends eat, and as the evening deepens she takes a more and more commanding view of her friends, all of whom she devotes herself to. And it usually happens, when everyone is sitting about the table long past coffee but with smudged glasses of wine, that there occurs in Sonia's devotion, which is like a great cloud that envelopes everyone, a sudden shock of thunder and lightning. She attacks a friend for something he – always, as far as I knew, he – said.

At a dinner party, she suddenly attacked a friend, in the context of a conversation about the Nazi concentration camps, for the friend expressing horror at them. There was, she would insist, no expression of the horror of the camps that was equal to what they had been. She recounted having been to, I think, Belsen with her friend Marguerite Duras and her rage when Duras expressed horror, Sonia answering Duras' horror with, 'What did you imagine it would have been like? What?' To Sonia, the extermination camps were so indicative of the fact of human baseness, she took them as a given: of course people would exterminate other people, for whatever reason, of course. She even became angry at her Jewish friends for any bewilderment they might have had about why the camps: they, above all, should know why, which is the baseness of humanity. When Sonia read the unpublished memoir of a former inmate of a detention, not an extermination, camp which he was trying to get published, she said, 'He was in a very minor concen-tration camp.' Friends took this as a parody of Sonia's snobbism – and she is, she herself admits, an intellectual snob, perhaps instilled in her by the Sacred Heart nuns, also intellectual snobs: if you read about the French philosopher Jacques Lacan in the review section of newspapers, you soon met him at Sonia's house – but her denouncing the former inmate of what Sonia called a minor camp for presuming to use his experiences there to promote the publica-tion of his memoirs, which Sonia found badly written, showed the depth of her basic conviction that everyone really is vain, that vanity really is everything. Beyond stating the starkest facts, you cannot not express any feelings about horror that are not expressions of basic vanity, and the more emotional the expressed feelings the more filled with vanity.

I admire her, I admire her even when, drunk, her denunciation becomes relentless. 'How could you say that? How could you? How?' You draw back into silence, and the other guests try to change the subject, but Sonia keeps after you: 'How could you have said that?'

I never mind Sonia denouncing me at one of her dinner parties, not only because I know she will telephone the next morning to apologize and to invite me again, but because I believe that she has the right to, believe that in her rejecting a faith that tried to destroy her in the name of trying to save her she has earned the right to denounce hypocrisies, has learned that all expressions of feeling are in an essential way hypocritical. It reassures me for my hypocritical, because false, expressions of emotion to be denounced by Sonia.

Nikos is aware of these false expressions of feeling from me, but is gentler than Sonia in making me aware of them.

Francis Bacon gave Sonia a painting of a head, done in savage brushstrokes, which hangs in a gold frame to the side of Sonia's sitting-room fireplace. He is often at her dinner parties. When I, drunk, asked him, as I often asked him, if he had ever had any religious feelings, he, also drunk, said, as he always said to my question, 'Never, never, never, never, never, never, never.' But Bacon was a cynic, and Sonia not. Sonia came over to Francis and me and asked what we were talking about. Francis said to her, 'David asked me if I've ever had any religious feelings.' Sonia frowned one of her severe frowns at me and said, 'You couldn't have.' I said, trying to justify myself, which was always a mistake with Sonia, 'I just wanted to know if Francis ever in the past believed in God.' 'Don't be stupid. Of course he didn't,' Sonia, angry at me for my presumption, answered.

I had already set myself up to be denounced by Sonia that evening, so when I said, drinking more wine at the table and more drunk than before, that I wondered if, even for an irreligious writer, it was possible to write a really deep book that wasn't religious, she denounced me for not being a deep writer – she repeated, 'You can't be a deep writer if you say that. No one who says what you've said can be a deep writer' – because, she said, religion in a novel, in any work of art, made the work obvious, made the work banal and pretentious. 'I know you're right,' I said, 'I know,' and I had that curious, slightly thrilling sense of having said what I'd said just to get Sonia to react as she did. Maybe I risked bringing up religion with Sonia so she would reproach me for bringing it up. I was drawn to Sonia partly because she reassured me in my being lapsed, and I sometimes made provocative statements about religion that I knew she'd condemn me for, because her reaction, which I could count on, reassured me all the more about my being lapsed, and, more, the very attention she gave me by condemning me reassured me. I almost felt rejected by her when she desisted.

She said, 'Hrumph,' and, as if to make up for turning her attention away from me, asked me to open more bottles of wine, which were on the buffet. I did, with pleasure. Wine was essential. Food was essential. Dinner parties were essential. And in fact this evening, maybe because of Francis whom she was intimidated by, she didn't attack anyone else after she had attacked me, and certainly not Francis, and the party was altogether as pretty as the flowers at the center of the table.

She invited me to tea, maybe to reassure me after having attacked me at her dinner party. I found that when I was alone with her she would get onto a subject – almost always a friend – and talk and talk about that friend as if the talk itself would sort that person, who badly needed to be sorted, out. Most often when I tried to add to the sorting out, she would say, 'You don't understand.' This afternoon, a grim winter afternoon with her sitting room warm with a fire and bright with all the lamps lit, the person was the writer Rosamond Lehmann, whom I told Sonia I had met. I described Rosamond Lehmann, tall and big-boned with a very white face and long, white hair, as looking like a moon goddess,

which I'd thought original of me, but which made Sonia frown
severely at me as if for trying to be colourfully original. I should
have known by that frown not to continue to talk about Rosamond Lehmann, whom Sonia evidently disapproved of, but whom
she nevertheless felt compelled to sort out. I said I wondered if
what explained Rosamond Lehmann, whom I didn't know at all
well, was her belief in the ghost of her dead daughter appearing to
her, which she'd written about in her book The Swan in the
Evening. Sonia frowned even more severely.

'You read that book?'

'Yes, I did,' I answered.

'How could you have? You don't believe in ghosts, a stupid,
childish, self-indulgent belief, so why should you indulge someone
else's belief in ghosts? I don't understand.'

'I wanted to find about what she had to say.'

'About a ghost appearing to her?'

'Yes.'

'That interests you?'

'Well, yes, it interests me, in a way.'

'How could it? How could you be interested in anything so
stupid, childish, self-indulgent?'

'I guess it is stupid, childish, self-indulgent.'

Sonia lit a cigarette and shook her hair back and stared at me
with narrowed, blood-shot, angry eyes and said in a low, hard
voice, 'It is.'

While she talked, the smoke of her many cigarettes making the
air dull, I had one of those moments of wanting to die. I told
myself I must not indulge myself in it any more than Sonia would
indulge me in it. But I wasn't able to concentrate on what Sonia
said. I wanted to be as hard on myself for the longings that occurred
to me as I thought Sonia would have been had she known about
them, longings the very fact of their occurring she would have
considered only as evidence of my weakness, of my inability to
finally and forever deny them. And she would have considered any
expression of my longing to be in a world where I would no longer

have to endure the agony of the longings as nothing more than an expression of my vanity, because, again and yet again, there was no other world.

As soon as I was out in the street, I saw through the windows, over which she hadn't drawn the curtains, the lights in the sitting room go off abruptly.

———

Among the British writers whose work I read, Rosalind Belben has the most distinctive style, the writing in itself in tension with the literal, a tension that causes in the literal the sense of something much more vibrant in the literal than the literal. There are other British writers whose styles try for the more than the literal, writers whose work the writer Giles Gordon has brought together in an anthology called Beyond the Words: Anthony Burgess, Alan Burns, Elspeth Davie, Eva Figes, B. S. Johnson, Gabriel Josipovici, Robert Nye, Ann Quin, Maggie Ross, and Giles himself. And he asked me to be among them.

———

A description:

Nikos and I in Rome, where he had never been, the city, in my recollection, all flesh pinks and tans, great phalluses chalked on the walls, and the sound of water running. The presence, in museums, in public squares, in niches, of marble and of bronze, of statues glorying in their nakedness, in their sexuality, even the statues of emperors fitted with armour that, formed in the musculature of naked chests, appeared to expose their bodies beneath. The languorous nudi of Michelangelo's Sistine chapel, surrounded by phallic acorns, seeming to bulge out from the painted fresco, and the floating angels in the paintings of Caravaggio seeming ready to fall into one's arms. We stopped along the Tiber to look across at the Castel Sant'Angelo, and Nikos, pressed against a wall, said, 'I have an erection.'

———

Sonia, alone, to supper, which we ate in the kitchen. There were two bottles of wine on the table. She studied them for a while, then asked if we would mind if she paid to have a third bottle. 'Three bottles of wine are reassuring.' We didn't accept money from her, but I went out for a third bottle of what is called plonk.

———

I returned home from an evening at a dinner party Nikos had declined going to, saying he needed a quiet evening at home, but he was not at home. He came shortly after to say that Nikos Georgiadis had rung him and invited him to a party with Nureyev and Margot Fonteyn, both of whom Nikos had talked to animatedly. When Nikos told me, I became jealous of him, and he laughed.

———

The newspapers have been filled with the story that cannabis was found by the police in Francis' flat. Francis, who declares he doesn't smoke because of the asthma that he's suffered from all his life and that kept him out of the military during World War II, has accused George of planting the cannabis and alerting the police. There's been a court case, in which the police had to admit that information about the presence of the drug came from George. Francis was acquitted.

This afternoon, I was on a bus crossing Chelsea Bridge in the rain, and I saw, from an upper-deck window, George, out in the rain, walking along the pedestrian way of the bridge. The Thames was dark gray beyond him. His hands were in the pockets of his raincoat, but his head was bare and water was running off his hair.

———

Auden came to dinner with Stephen of course. We also invited Johnny Craxton and his new friend, a bricklayer who was very warm and personable, and whom I thought Wystan liked, but when I asked Stephen later if he had Stephen said he hadn't, because 'he wasn't a looker, wasn't bright, didn't have anything to make Wystan interested.' 'That's monstrous,' I said. Stephen answered, 'I think Wystan is becoming more and more of a monster.'

When he arrived, he was obviously in a sullen mood – so far to come, all the stairs up to our flat – but we gave him lots to drink (actually, Nikos made a mistake in mixing the Manhattans, putting three parts vermouth to one part vodka instead of the opposite, but Wystan didn't seem to notice this), made him the absolute center of attention, to the point where I felt we were ignoring Stephen, Johnny and the bricklayer, and gave him a very good meal, all of which revived him, and he began to tell jokes, laugh, give his calculated opinions on anything that was mentioned: cigarette lighters, cars, South Africa, recruiting students into the military on university campuses, which he approves of because that ensures educated people in the military.

He told Nikos that Greece, in all its history, was best under the Turks, because it was at its most efficient under the Turks. But Nikos told him that was ridiculous, and he smiled at Nikos for a moment as if amazed that someone was telling him he was ridiculous, then as if with the appreciation of someone telling him just that.

When Auden said that he thought Cavafy's erotic poems – not his historical poems – camp, Nikos said they have to be read in Greek, which Auden can't read.

Auden said something disparaging about Samuel Beckett getting the Nobel Prize for Literature. Nikos said, 'Who else is there?' Auden shook his head so all the sagging wrinkles shook and said, 'There's me.'

What upset me most about what he said was, in giving a sermon on hell (he said he is very fond of giving sermons, and confessed, in a game he proposed in which everyone was to say what he had most wanted to be if he hadn't been what he was now, that he had wanted to be a bishop), that each man creates the hell he deserves, so that if a drug addict can't break his addiction it's his own fault and he should use a little extra will power to get himself out of his situation.

I am making him out to be more simple-minded about this than he was, but the startling fact about him was that he did insist that everyone was always responsible for his actions. I said, 'But sometimes one simply doesn't have the will power to be responsible.' He didn't listen. To make the point, he told us of a servant he had once had, a young Spaniard, who stole some money from him, and, Wystan said, 'Of course I fired him.' I got angry, thinking, and you didn't for a moment consider that he might have needed the money, or that you had been paying him so little he had to steal?

When, at about 9:15, he said he was rather tired, he got up to leave.

It surprised me that, after Nikos had opposed him on so much, he seemed to single out Nikos for special thanks, even affectionate thanks.

As for myself, I thought, well, really, there's no reason to see him again.

I mentioned my anger at Auden to Stephen over the telephone the next day, and he said he knew exactly what I meant, and that it was highly unlikely that the servant, whom Stephen had known, had stolen the money, as Wystan often imagines things are stolen from him when in fact he has lost them.

Stephen said, 'Wystan's only interested in himself, in no one else. He doesn't listen when anyone speaks to him, and he isn't interested in any case.'

Still, Auden is a very great poet, any number of examples of his poems testament to his greatness. How moved I am every time I read 'In Praise of Limestone' for the intelligent lyricism of the flowing lines, as if the very lyrical intelligence of the poem is what makes it so very moving – and mysterious!

————

After a recital at Festival Hall of Bach by Rosalyn Tureck – a pianist Nikos admires, though he said that she did often hit the wrong note (he is much more educated in music than I am as he had wanted to be a pianist but was discouraged by his mother who even refused him piano lessons, for she had it in mind that he should be a medical doctor) – Nikos and I were invited by Rodrigo and Anne Moynihan to their large house for a post-recital party. We knew almost no one, so, unlike us, we stood together and looked about at others. I noted a little old man, with long white hair round his bald pate, and, seeing me look at him with interest, Rodrigo brought me over to meet him, Sir Francis Rose, to whom I said, to let him know that I knew, 'You were a friend of Gertrude Stein,' and he, smiling a tender smile, said, 'Yes, yes, I was,' and he seemed to wait for me to ask him questions about Gertrude Stein.

She was someone whom I used to, as a student, fantasize about, reading with wonder The Autobiography of Alice B. Toklas, writing a paper in college on Tender Buttons (not then knowing that tender buttons referred to the female anatomy and trying to make sense of a portrait of a Red Stamp as 'lilies are lily white if they exhaust noise and distance and even dust'), and, more, to playing, to the distraction of my roommate, Gertrude Stein reciting in a recording, 'Portrait of Picasso: Shutters shut and open so do queens,' as if she were opening up not just a way of writing but a way of life – the fantasy certainly an impulse to my first going to Paris and searching out 27 rue de Fleurus to stand outside and wonder at all of her world coming to visit.

But, suddenly, I had nothing to ask Sir Francis Rose about Gertrude Stein or her world, and that world vanished here in London, and I realized it was an American fantasy world, of little interest to the English, and not at all to the French.

As for the lack of interest among the English in William Faulkner, this puzzled me until it came to me that his novels are not within the narrative of English history, in which history the sale of slaves may have been a source of colonial income, but a history not wounded in the land by mass slavery, the deep and lasting wound in the land of my country.

———

Had lunch ('luncheon'?) with Stephen before he left for the South of France with Natasha. He told me to meet him at Chez Victor, where another guest – a Polish poet – was to join us. I arrived before Stephen, and taking off my coat asked for Stephen's table, and the headwaiter, big, blocking my view, turned and pointed to the table behind him where Natasha was sitting with a man I presumed was the Polish poet. We looked at one another, I, I'm sure, as expressionless as she was; then I quickly went to her, said how nice to see her, and, to my surprise as she had the last time we met ignored me, she introduced me to the Polish poet. There was another woman at the table, and when Natasha stood the other woman stood, and they both went to another table and left me sitting with the Pole.

He said that Natasha told him that she had arranged with her friend to have lunch at Chez Victor without knowing that Stephen had also arranged to have lunch there. I got up and went to Natasha and said how sorry I was we weren't all having lunch together, and suggested that Stephen had invited me because I had wanted to see Richard Wollheim, whom Stephen had invited. She smiled, and, trembling, I left her.

Stephen appeared with Richard outside, saw me through the window, which he knocked on to say hello before he came in. Natasha was in a little alcove and couldn't see him. When Stephen did come in, taking off his coat as he advanced to the table, I said, 'Natasha's here.' 'Where?' I pointed. He went to speak with her, then came back, red. All during lunch with Richard and the Polish poet, we kept looking at one another, he smiling and blushing. We finished lunch before Natasha and her friend, and, leaving, I said goodbye to her. Outside, the Polish poet left us, and Richard said something that let Stephen and me know he understood the situation.

At home, I told Nikos, and he said, 'Well, does it surprise you that Richard, that everyone, knows about Stephen and us? Thank God I wasn't there.'

Stephen, ringing that evening, said that Natasha hadn't mentioned a thing about it when she got home.

Natasha has become a big presence in Nikos' and my life, though we don't in fact see her. We dream about her, sometimes have nightmares about her. We both think she has been treated unfairly by Stephen. I think, of course: if we were really on her side we'd stop seeing Stephen, but that is impossible.

———

I have heard the curator of exhibitions and writer on art David Sylvester say that there is not a drop of English blood in him, he a Jew who dresses like a large rabbi in black with a large-brimmed black fedora, which made me wonder what it is to be English. I asked him what he considers himself, and he answered: British. The differences among the Welsh, the Scots, the Northern Irish, even, I feel, Yorkshire people as distinct from the English becomes more and more marked, and not only in my awareness but in what is called devolution. Devolution from what? From England? But what is England? I may become British one day, but I'll never be English, though I wonder who does know what it is to be English? I would say, once again, the name connotes a vagueness as vague as the boundaries of London, with, perhaps, Hyde Park Corner as the centre of the outlying vagueness. Perhaps, in my own vagueness, I can now call myself a Londoner.

———

From James Joll's The Origins of the First World War:

> Men are not motivated by a clear view of their own interests; their minds are filled with the cloudy residues of discarded beliefs; their motives are not always clear even to themselves.

I remember the end of World War II, Victory Over Japan. I was five years old. However unaware I was of the world, I, by being historically a part of the world, grew up in a world more outside me than inside me, a world that, after World War II, belies personal history for world history. As ridiculous as this may seem, given how personal my history appears, I think that really I am much more in world history than I am in my own.

It seems to me that my life occurs, in ways far beyond my interests, my motives, outside in the world, however the world outside is filled with residues of discarded beliefs, and far from any clear motives.

And Nikos is much more in world history than I am.

And think of Stephen – Stephen during the Spanish Civil War, Stephen as a Communist, Stephen during World War II, Stephen in Germany after the war, when, in Berlin, he picked up fragments from the top of Hitler's desk, for which he paid a few cigarettes to an old woman selling the fragments. Back in London, he propped the fragments on a mantelpiece until one day, studying them, he was shocked by their presence, and threw them into the rubbish.

————

We went to a party at Mark's, who had just moved into a big bright white flat near Belsize Park. We knew Stephen and Natasha were going to be there. Stephen met us at the door, smiling mischievously. Nikos asked, 'Is Natasha really here?' 'Yes,' Stephen said, 'she's in the sitting room.' Neither Nikos nor I went in for a while, then finally did. Natasha was speaking with Ted Lucie-Smith. I went up to Natasha, said hello, said hello to Ted, and went for a drink. Nikos went straight for a drink.

I was at one end of the room talking with John Russell and Nikos was at the other talking to Stephen Buckley and his new lady friend. Natasha was in the middle, on a sofa, from which she suddenly got up and went straight to Nikos and started to talk to him. Stephen B. withdrew.

Nikos told me later that they talked for about an hour, all about Nikos' upcoming operation to have a rectal polyp removed – an operation that, given the presumed nature of our sexual relationship, makes me wonder if people are somewhat amused by it, though it is hardly up to me to tell them sex is for us rather in the intercrural ancient Greek way. Natasha, Nikos said, was very concerned, advised him to have a blindfold so he would be able to sleep with the lights on, to take lots of cologne, and said that if there was anything she could do for him to let her know. Nikos said he was sweating, and the talk was very stilted, but she wouldn't stop.

Everyone was aware that they were talking. Mark came over to me and said, 'I listened in. They're talking about hospitals. It sounds rather awkward.'

Finally, Stephen went over and broke them up to go home. As he and Natasha were leaving, he turned to Nikos and said, 'We'll see you tomorrow at Richard Wollheim's.' Nikos told me that Natasha's face fell, surprised by yet another of Stephen's 'conspiracies' behind her back.

Richard and Day, having invited Nikos and me and Stephen and Natasha to dinner, wondered if they might have done the wrong thing, and Richard rang Nikos to ask him if he or I would be offended that they'd also invited Natasha. 'It's Natasha who might be offended,' Nikos said. So Richard rang up Stephen, who insisted that we should all go but that he wouldn't tell Natasha, who'd simply find Nikos and me there. But for some reason he decided to let Natasha know at Mark's party.

The next evening at Richard and Day Wollheim's, in their large studio in Pembroke Gardens, there were Stephen and Natasha. I went to Natasha immediately and began to speak to her, but she seemed to me stiff and not willing to talk. Stephen came over to us and said she had been in bed all day. Richard came over to introduce someone to Stephen and Natasha, and I left to get a glass of wine. I thought, Well, Natasha is offended.

When I turned back into the studio room, I saw her talking with Nikos, both of them with hands gesturing with great animation, their voices bright and engaged in whatever they were talking about. (Nikos said later it was all about Encounter magazine, whose chief editor, Melvin Lasky, held back from Stephen and Frank Kermode the fact that the magazine was financed by the C.I.A.-funded Congress for Cultural Freedom, a fact that, when revealed, made Stephen and Frank resign, Natasha enraged by the duplicity that Lasky forced on the unknowing Stephen and Frank.) She talked on and on.

Stephen went up to them finally and said to Nikos that he wanted to introduce him to someone else. Natasha said, 'But we're talking!' Stephen went away, then, blinking rapidly, came back a short while later and again tried to get Nikos away. Natasha got angry. Stephen left, only to go back soon after, blinking more rapidly, and almost pulled Nikos away from Natasha. I saw Nikos give Natasha a look of helplessness and shrug his shoulders. But later in the evening they were together again, Natasha now advising Nikos once again about his time in the hospital.

As she and Stephen were leaving, she came to me and said, 'You will let us know how Nikos is in hospital.'

I can't help but wonder what she wondered about in Nikos having rectal polyps.

Stephen seemed anxious to leave. They did leave, but a moment later he came back, his huge overcoat flapping, his face red, his white hair flying about, as though he had been running, only to blow very demonstrative kisses to Nikos and me, who stood and smiled back with silly smiles.

The revelation is quite simply that Stephen seems more responsible for the separation between Natasha and us than Natasha herself.

Nikos went into hospital on Monday, was operated on on Tuesday, and came home on Thursday. I went to see him twice a day, was only happy when I was on my way to see him or at the hospital bed beside him, and I hated to leave him. I minded his being there, I think, more than he did. All my hatred of hospitals came out: I resented the nurses touching him, the doctors examining him, the operation itself.

He became friendly with a Russian sailor in the ward who had had an accident on a Russian trawler off the coast of England, and had had a leg amputated, but who was very lively. He loved the care he was given in England.

While he was in hospital his cousin Maria had a total breakdown, and was in a locked ward at Friern Barnet. She finally believed she was possessed by the devil, and had to be taken away by the police in a straitjacket. When I wasn't visiting Nikos, I was visiting her.

_____

Trained in philosophy, Nikos will explain to me, say, Kant's categorical imperative, and for a second I understand, but then the second of understanding goes, and I am left, not with understanding, but a 'sense' of the concept, which 'sense' I am not able to articulate, but which appears to be a little, radiating globe in my mind.

I think I don't have ideas, am incapable of ideas, but can only have a 'sense' of meaning, the 'sense,' however, filled with more meaning than I could ever state. I have a 'sense' of meaning without knowing what the meaning is.

What is odd is that this 'sense' of meaning seems to come not from within me, but from out in the round world, for that is where the greatest meanings are.

_____

Richard Wollheim had us invited to a drinks party given by a friend of his, a large queenie man dressed in a loose white caftan, his flat as if transported from Morocco, or what a European imagines a Moroccan interior to be –

(I realize that Nikos doesn't try to transport Greece into our flat with Greek artifacts, but, as if to identify the flat as Greek more than American or English by referring to what to me is the richer world of Greece, which I, living with Nikos, make a show of belonging to, I will buy in a Greek shop a spice, machlepi, which, however, is never used, or a little coffee-making pot – briki – or backgammon – tavoli (Nikos prefers Scrabble, he always winning) – these little attempts to bring Greece into our flat amusing to Nikos)

– the lighting in the Moroccan-like flat was somber so the people appeared to move about slowly as if the air was thick, and, in the midst, a tall, wide armoire on top of which was a human skull. We were welcomed with a grand indifference by the man, as if we were there to prove ourselves before he would pay particular attention to us, and soon after Nikos suggested we leave; together, we thanked the man, who said, 'Go, go, go,' and we were being dismissed before we had the chance to say we were leaving, so we left feeling belittled, but relieved. The man, we understood, has a shop for antiques in Chelsea.

Stephen Buckley came to have lunch with the artist Jennifer Bartlett. She once had a show in Tony Stokes' gallery, Garage.

I think I amused her by reading out from Gertrude Stein's Lucy Church Amiably:

After all there are very many knives that have wooden handles.

It has been said that clouds can meet but it has not been said whether the clouds were of the same size and thickness . . .

It is always a mistake for the sun to come through the window from within to the outside.

She has an easy manner, an easy sensual manner, as if her body were one with her easy thinking and feeling, and yet, oh, there is beneath the easiness an absolute devotion to her art. She will never self-deprecate, but will say about her own work, 'It's great, isn't it,' not as a question but as an indisputable affirmation that it is great. She has a light, ironical laugh that seems to belie her seriousness, but her seriousness is absolute.

She is a friend of the artists Jan Hashey and Michael Craig-Martin from when they were all students at the Yale Art School.

After seeing the documentary by Alain Resnais, Night and Fog, about the death camps, Nikos and I were silent, and went home to a meal in silence, and after our meal Nikos said, simply, 'Let's go to bed.'

In bed, I sensed his thinking about what has no words, thinking about what is happening in the world for which there are no words. I wonder what any self-awareness in personal introspection, in therapy or analysis, can do personally to accommodate the suffering of the world; and, given such depersonalizing awareness, what any analyses of nations, of governments, of politics, of history itself, can do to make somewhat comprehensible the sufferings of the world, and, with some comprehension, accommodate the sufferings of the world.

Again, some days later, home from the publishing house, Nikos said, 'It isn't that I commission books, especially of poetry, in defiance of the horrors, because the horrors are too great to defy, but because I believe poetry is a moral and spiritual recourse for the defeated, as, I suppose, we all are.'

———

A friend came from New York to visit.

Hearing me speak – my pronunciation of certain words now deliberately British, as aluminum, vitamin, tomato – he said, severely, 'You're American, speak like an American.'

For a moment, I saw myself from his point of view as an American pretending to be British, and, more, from his point of view saw my entire life in London as pretentious, an accusation that for the moment shook me. I felt pulled back to New York, where I had felt imposed on me the condemning self-consciousness that in New York made me think that everything I did was phony. Then I thought, this is where I live, here in London.

It is because of Nikos that I began to use English expressions. Nikos is not American, and he does not have the American suspicion that Americans who speak in foreign ways must be phony (such an American expression that: phony), which suspicion Americans visiting from America have about Americans living here, perhaps because Americans have retained from

American independence a way of speaking that sets them off from the English, and, moreover, sets them off from any Americans at the time of independence who, with pretentious foppish superiority, continued to use the King's English. I know now that my self-consciousness was American enough that to shift prepositions from 'a quarter of three' to 'a quarter to three,' or from 'living on a street' to 'living in a street,' or to pronounce 'alou- mi-num' as 'al-you-minium,' or to call 'a flashlight' 'an electric torch,' was to risk being a phony. Not only is Nikos not American, his accent is not American, so he is free of any American telling him to speak like an American. He is free to choose to speak another language in any way he likes. With him I'm freed of so much of the American self-consciousness imposed on me by America that for too long has condemned me as phony. I use the English expressions he uses.

He has a delicate and precise way of speaking.

———

Sunday, and Nikos has gone to visit his cousin Maria at Friern Barnet. He has been away about two hours. I've been writing, but suddenly a feeling comes over me that he has been away for an intolerable period. I want him to be here. I feel unreserved love for him. I want to write this in here because I realize as I've never realized before how much I love him.

———

During the Nazi occupation of Athens, an aunt and uncle of Nikos hid a Jewish family in their apartment, but when the occupation ended the Jewish family refused to leave, so Nikos, visiting his aunt and uncle, would see figures passing behind semi-transparent sliding doors, the Jewish family so settled in that the aunt and uncle left the flat to them and moved elsewhere. Telling this, Nikos laughs, and my historical awareness now includes something that I would not have imagined because I was not there to have experienced the occupation and the aftermath.

And Nikos does say that he was happiest in his extended family, including the maid, when all lived together in one apartment during the Nazi occupation. He remembers bean soup, mock coffee infused from carob pods, overcoats made from blankets.

———

As if he were still a pubescent boy, Nikos has wet dreams while asleep; they wake me up but he goes on sleeping, but if he wakes he will say, sleepily, that he was dreaming of someone from his boarding school in Athens.

———

I thought of Nikos' interest in Giambattista Vico's investigation into the history of language as our richest history when I heard him discuss with his cousin, from Athens visiting London, the use of the word 'moro' in Greek – the cousin insisting it comes from the Italian 'amore,' and Nikos that the word is Turkish. This linguistic Turkish residue acknowledged by Nikos surprised me, as he always refers to Constantinople, not Istanbul, as the capital city his mother comes from.

Also, he says his knowledge of the purist language Katharevousa, which was meant to purify the Demotic Greek language of all Turkish expressions after Greek independence from Turkey, is in fact shaky, so that he had to ask his cousin to write a letter in Katharevousa for the historian Steven Runciman to send, I think, to the Patriarch in Constantinople in thanksgiving for some accolade. I rather doubt Steven, who claims to be a polyglot, knows even Demotic Greek, for when Nikos speaks to him in Greek he simply opens his hands as in a gesture of acceptance, and smiles.

But there is a big difference between speaking a language and reading it. Steven recalled his approaching the formidable historian of the ancient world, J. B. Bury, when he walked each afternoon along the bank of the Cam in Cambridge (his wife kept students away from him), and Steven revealed to him that he was interested in Byzantium, to which Bury reacted by asking Steven if he could read Russian, and, given that he could, he would be able to read Bulgarian, and should go to the library to look up a certain Bulgarian historian. Steven can read Russian, Bulgarian, Romanian, Greek, and no doubt the more esoteric languages.

About Nikos' cousin visiting from Athens – I would have thought that, under the dictatorship, Greece would be a closed country, no one allowed in and no one allowed out, but in fact there is a lot of toing and froing. Those who leave and don't return are those opposed, and I imagine those who are there and opposed hide their opposition, though Nikos tells me that many opposed are arrested and tortured. He learns about this by visiting Greeks in exile, among them the actress Aspasia Papathanaseou, in long night sessions in flats I can't picture, except as dim and filled with smoke. But he in no way disparages those people in Greece who keep their mouths shut and get on with their lives as of course has happened over and over in Greece for centuries.

I recall the wonderfully witty writer Edith Templeton saying about life in Communist Czechoslovakia, 'You keep your mouth shut and you can have a very good life,' including special retreats for writers and extra square meters of living space for their flats.

––––––

Because he knew I was interested and he wasn't, Nikos suggested that I go visit the Bloomsbury painter Duncan Grant to pick up the uncollected poetry by Paul Roche, close friend of Grant and often his model, to give to Nikos for him to consider the poetry for publication by Penguin. ('No chance,' Nikos said.) Duncan Grant, lively and sweet tempered, reminded me in his openness and matter-of-factness of his contemporary Forster. His little basement flat in Park Square West was stuffed, in an almost Oriental way, with ceramics and bits of mosaics and embroidered pillows and, of course, pictures both propped up on furniture and hanging all over the walls. As he was showing me the pictures, only a few by him, others by Vanessa Bell and minor French artists, another guest arrived, also American, and also called David. We all sat, and Paul

Roche gave me and this other David tea in two-handled cups.

I didn't like this other David. He must have known Duncan Grant well, as he called him by his first name, and, lounging back among embroidered pillows, asked Duncan Grant – no, didn't ask him, but, with what I felt an ostentatious over-familiarity, entered into Duncan Grant's life with the presumption of knowing every-thing about it all by saying something like, 'Duncan, you really were mischievous, you know, you and Virginia and Virginia's brother Adrian.' As presumptuous as I thought this, Duncan Grant responded gleefully. 'You mean,' he said, 'the Dreadnought hoax.' His lashless pink eyes blinking, he told a story, with long pauses, of a hoax that Virginia Woolf (then Stephen), her brother Adrian and others played on the British Navy: disguised as Abyssinian Princes they were welcomed aboard one of HM's ships, treated with great deference and unsuspecting interest, even when their beards began to come off in the wind. I didn't know this story, which I would have known only by having read about it, but didn't know it had been accounted for in any book, so I imagined I was hearing some-thing that could only be known uniquely from Duncan Grant, and this of course gave me a sense of privilege. But the reaction of the other David, with overly demonstrative laughter and interjections of 'Duncan, you devil you,' which Duncan Grant appeared to love, made me feel embarrassed for my sense of privilege. There was no way I could compete with this other David for the attention of Duncan Grant, and I didn't want to compete; and if I was aware of being envious of him for his flamboyant intimacy with Grant (which Paul Roche, perhaps seeing how much Duncan Grant enjoyed it, deferred to), I was more aware of myself as being all too similar to this other David and liking myself even less than I liked him. He took over, offered to heat up water for more tea, kept asking Grant to tell stories, all the while reminding Duncan Grant what a fantastic life he's led. I left.

On the tube on my way home, I thought: there is enough Bloomsbury left for someone to feel a part of it in its residue. After all, Ben Nicolson is a friend, and his Christmas dinners in a Greek restaurant in Soho, with Julia Strachey and various other Bloomsbury descendants, might have been like an occasion of fifty or sixty years ago. And Angelica Garnett is a friend. There are many people I've met who are doorways through which I could step into the company of so many more people to meet whom I have heard or even read about – such as Mary Hutchinson, born in 1889, whom I did meet with Stephen at Chez Victor, and who couldn't have more credentials for belonging to Bloomsbury, her cousin Lytton Strachey, her lover Clive Bell when he was married to Vanessa Bell, the mother of Angelica whose father was not Clive Bell but Duncan Grant, all of which Stephen told me before I met Mary Hutchinson at lunch, and, also, that Mary Hutchinson was the character in T. S. Eliot's play The Cocktail Party who keeps forgetting her umbrella – but I tell myself to stop at the doorway, because I wouldn't go in to know these people for themselves but for me to say, having entered through the open doorway and come out, oh you have to know whom I've met! I understand so clearly now what Nikos accused me of in wanting to meet E. M. Forster: I saw him as a monument I had wanted to visit to be able, after, to tell people – oh, friends in America – I have, amazingly!, met E. M. Forster. But how can I not step through the doorway opened to me and not come out and try to account for those whom I met inside, the account I of course hope to be read by someone who wasn't there at the right time at the right place at the open doorway?

When Nikos tells me I am deep down a negative person, he senses something in me that I too sense is true, but any investigation of why would be endless. Still, yes, it is true that I feel the world is one of moral and spiritual darkness, and stories of the horrors of Greece, and, too, the world wars, confirm for me that moral and spiritual darkness in the darkness of world history. It is as if the outer world darkness relieves me of any inner darkness, and, instead of indulging in personal darkness, I am indulging in the darkness of the world – for the darkness of the world is not my fault, is not darkness I have to blame myself for, but is the fault of history, and history is to be blamed.

Then Nikos tells me a funny story about how, during the German Occupation, his family kept a turkey on the balcony, but the turkey one day flapped its ineffectual wings and instead of flying fell down to the street, where a man, amazed that a turkey should fall from the sky at his feet, ran off with it. And of course I laugh, and now think that, really, I must free myself of wanting to hear the dark stories, as the bright stories do belie the dark, even in history.

———

I visited Henrietta Garnett in hospital. She told me about her attempted suicide, speaking in a low voice but enunciating every word very carefully with large, beautiful lips. Her large, wide eyes in her thin face were shining. She laughed, a slight laugh that was hardly more than a breath, from time to time. She had wanted to throw herself off from the whispering gallery in Saint Paul's Cathedral, but arrived too late, the gallery now shut. She then drove around London looking for a place high enough for her to jump from, and decided, finally, on a room high up in a hotel that she thought would do. She jumped from the window, but didn't kill herself; and though she couldn't move, she was aware of people walking past her, imagining, she thought, she was drunk. Hearing Henrietta moan, someone stopped.

———

Robert Medley came to dinner. I mentioned how sweet I thought Forster was. He said, 'Don't be fooled, my dear. He liked to give the impression that he was sweet and gentle, but he had claws tucked away in his soft paws and could and did use them. He could be a real bitch.'

Robert also said something about having been given some very early poems by Auden which always went to pieces in his pocket. I said, 'I didn't know you were an old friend of Auden.' 'You didn't? My dear, we were more than friends.' And then I recalled the reference to Robert in Letter from Iceland. But I also recalled that when I saw Wystan and Robert together at John Lehmann's, Wystan hadn't said a word to him. I mentioned this to Robert, who said, 'But Wystan's a monster. Of course he wouldn't speak to me now.'

———

Nikos has heard from his mother in Athens that Maria has died of cancer.

I went to her flat in Mortlake to sort out her belongings, but her two flatmates had already claimed most of them, one saying that Maria had promised her her record player, the other her easel and paints for painting, and both claimed her clothes. I didn't argue. When I asked about the school Maria had been to, which Nikos and I are sure was the School of Economic Science as advertised in Underground stations, they wouldn't say anything except, 'Maria had to learn to deal with her problems herself.'

———

A 'sense' of meaning – this 'sense' is in my awareness of everything, cups and plates, tables and chairs, doors and rooms, houses, trees, clouds, sky, and, oh, people and their connections one to the other, everything, somehow, connecting beyond my ability to make connections. Is the 'sense' of meaning in this: that everything, in ways beyond me, does connect?

———

A dream about my parents. They had moved to a very damp and humid country, where they lived in a huge shed built on stilts. I went to visit them. There was a bamboo screen over the entrance to the shed, wavering in a breeze, and behind the screen I could make out two people sitting motionless side by side. I knew that the two people were my mother and father and that they had committed suicide. Frightened, I raised the curtain and went into the room. On their laps were newspapers and magazines they had been reading while waiting for the poison to take effect. Their faces were hideously distended and green, already rotting. All about was great stillness and silence. Then, suddenly, my father raised his arms laboriously toward me and opened his eyes, and my mother, with great difficulty, said, 'Help us,' and I woke up.

———

We look forward to a quiet but full winter – no dinner parties, at most relaxing Sunday-afternoon teas, writing during the day, in the evenings playing Scrabble. I feel well, and everything is promised.

It seems to me that I have lived for so many years – for as far back in my life as I can remember – for the day when I would be on my own, when I would travel, when I would write. Nothing really existed in the present – not even friendship – but in terms of that very dark future. Now, for the first time, but not with complete certainty, I am living in that future, and it is not dark, but bright. I know I could never be happier with anyone else but Nikos (given our differences, our uncertainties, our anxieties), I love London, and I feel, with a fullness that is so rare I doubt it at the same time, I feel in control; the world is whole and globed.

———

It occurred to me that Nikos and I never think about 'bad sex' or 'boring sex' or whatever that we hear other couples talk about, heterosexual and homosexual. We never talk about our relationship in terms of sex, and yet I'm sure that our relationship would change if we did not make love.

———

We spent a Saturday with a young friend of Nikos, Henry, tall and good looking. They had met at a drinks party given by the Moyni-hans, and Nikos sees him from time to time for lunch. Henry grew up in Canada, on a ranch, and used to ride his horse over the Canadian countryside. He is, Nikos said, pure, as a horse is pure. He is heterosexual. The three of us walked through Hyde Park, and I noticed that Nikos was lively because Henry was with him. We went to a tea shop, where Nikos sat next to Henry on a banquette behind the small table, and Nikos sometimes reached an arm to place it along the back of the banquette, almost on Henry's shoulders. After Henry left, I told Nikos that it was evident his spirits were raised because of Henry. 'Really?' he asked. I answered, 'Come on, you know his being with you pleases you very much, enlivens you, and that's as it should be, because he's young and beautiful, and, honestly, I'm moved that you should be so responsive, and I think, yes, Nikos is alive to youth and beauty.' Nikos laughed.

More about Henry James. For so long, reading his novels in America, I imagined that his London was the true London, the London he not only accounted for in his novels but the London he dined out in, almost every evening of the year. I imagined he knew the lords and ladies, the dukes and duchesses, and, if princes and princesses, foreign ones (Italian) living in London. Certainly the London I am getting to know is not the London he knew, and his London, for so long, appeared to me the London that hovered above mine, and, up there, was inaccessible to me.

But the more I live in London the more I look at the London of Henry James as a fantasy – his fantasy! His novels are fairytales!

Andrew Lord makes ceramics, which are not to be used but are works of art, such as large, misshapen jugs with extravagant curlicue handles. I went with him to see a collection of Chinese porcelain. We were alone in a room, looking at delicate vases in an illuminated glass case, and I had such a sudden sense of Andrew's body next to me I turned and put my arms around him. He laughed, a light, shy laugh, and his body seemed, abruptly, to elude me and I dropped my arms. We continued to study the porcelain. Other people I have spoken to about Andrew are also drawn to his physical presence, solid, and at the same time elusive. He wears jeans and tee-shirts, and his hair is crew cut. As powerfully present as he is, Andrew is elusive because his center seems somewhere outside himself, and he is himself drawn to it. That center, which obsesses him, is his work in ceramics. When I am with Andrew in his studio, I imagine he has no other life but there. I are not sure where he reads and listens to music and eats and sleeps and makes love.

I was late getting home, and Nikos was obviously upset when I told him whom I'd seen. 'You can do what you want,' he said. I said, 'No, I can't, and don't want to. I don't want to hurt you, so if my seeing Andrew upsets you, I won't see him.' 'No, you must see him,' he insisted; 'it doesn't hurt me, it simply proves to me what I've always known.' 'What is that?' I asked. 'That you aren't and never were attracted to me.'

I suddenly realized this about him: that he is always looking for proof of what he thinks is the truth that I don't love him, that we are too different (he being Greek and I American) to understand each other, etc.

I said, 'You know, when you asked Stephen to take me to the South of France with him shortly after you and I met – I've often wondered why you did that. Didn't it occur to you that he might want to make love with me?'

'I was sure of it.'

'Then why did you send us off together?'

'To prove that I was right.'

'About what?'

'That you would love him more than me – or, at least, that you and he have more in common than I have with either of you.'

'But your experiment didn't work. I didn't make love with him. I've never felt I have more in common with Stephen than with you.'

'That's not true. You do – you do with all your English friends as well. It is purely a cultural thing. I don't, as a Greek, belong here, and you as an American do. I know, in fact, that when we're in company you're often embarrassed by me.'

'Embarrassed?'

'Yes.'

'Sometimes, yes, when you become needlessly difficult and argumentative, as the other night at the Stokes' when you told that woman she had no right to say she didn't like Courbet.'

'If you really loved me, you'd never be embarrassed by me. You'd agree with me that no one has a right to say he or she doesn't like Courbet. You should agree with me, because I tell the truth.'

———

I feel that Nikos and I are now within the globe of London, and within that globe are connected to friends within the globe.

Melvyn Bragg's novels about his native Cumbria are as rich as the earth he so earthily describes, such as a farmer's heavy boots of leather encased in heavy boots of mud. He is usually a reticent person, but I feel he feels close to me, and talks freely. He told me about his first wife's suicide. The last time I saw him, he said, 'I want to write about a love affair. I want it to start as a happy, a magnificent love affair, and I want it to end a happy, a magnificent love affair.'

His wife, Cate Haste, writes about how women have changed – in part have been changed and have changed themselves – since World War I, the book a testament to how World War I and World War II form a continuing consciousness for Europe.

I saw Edna O'Brien, the novelist, at a party Sonia gave for her fellow novelist Vidia Naipaul. Edna asked me to sit with her on the same small armchair. 'You won't leave me, will you?' she asked. 'No,' I said. She was wearing a fringe of jet beads across her forehead. 'I think,' she said, 'I'm going to cry – because people are so cruel to one another, so dishonest, so inhuman.' She did cry, great soft tears that dripped down her cheeks and collected under her nose.

I once asked Ben Nicolson if there is anyone he can think of in London who has a salon, and after a long pause, his fingers to his chin, he said, 'No,' then after another long pause, he said, 'Yes, Sonia Orwell.'

———

As our circle of friends grows, Nikos and I are invited for weekends – to the house, formerly an old mill, of Howard and Julia Hodgkin, in a Wiltshire valley with a stream running through the valley and grazing sheep. From our room, in bed, we hear the sound of the voices of Howard and Julia in bed in their room talking, which go on, we think, past our falling asleep. In the morning, Howard brings us large, golden cups of tea while we are still in bed. The walls of the rooms are painted a pale green, what appears to be a Hodgkin colour.

All together, we take walks in the countryside, often up to a hill where there was once a Roman villa, the tesserae of a mosaic still to be found on the ground.

Some weekends, we are invited by Joe and Jos Tilson, in Wiltshire, where a number of British artists have moved to – including Hodgkin, Peter Blake, Dick Smith – Joe and Jos in a huge old rectory with grooves in the stone floor from the tea trolley passing from the kitchen into the sitting room. Joe is making ladders – not that one can use, but inspired by – and on each rung he burns words: YEW, MOTHER, WINTER, NIGHT, SWORD, SEED. Jos spins yarn from natural wool at a spinning wheel and knits beautiful rough jumpers, scarves, caps. Joe is very generous and gives us copies of his prints.

On a weekend at the Tilsons' with Frank and Julia Auerbach – rare, as Frank hardly leaves his studio – Frank did some etchings on a press that Joe had set up, one of Julia and one of Joe. He had not done etchings in years. He gave Nikos and me etchings, one of Julia and one of Joe.

With money from an advance on a book, for £500 I bought, on Nikos' urging, an etching by Lucian Freud of his mother.

And Johnny Craxton gave us a painting of a Greek young man smoking a cigarette.

We are building up our collection.

———

Barry Flanagan, artist, will from time to time ring the bell and come up, though I'm never sure what our conversation is about. I asked him what he was doing, and he replied, 'Dentures,' paused and nodded as if to confirm what he had said, 'yes, dentures,' and I wondered if he was making dentures. 'How is that?' I asked, and he answered, 'It's like a double helix on either side of the Stone of Scone, and that's no crucifixion,' and, not ever understanding Barry, I took him literally. He gave us little pieces of stiffened burlap with what might be thin white plaster dripped on the burlap.

———

Jan Hashey and Michael Craig-Martin, who live in Greenwich, organized a picnic on the Greenwich Common. Friends invited were asked to bring picnic food, which, on the blanket, did not appear to have the congruity of a picnic. Jan and Michael's daughter Jessica, ten or so, was very impressed when David Hockney arrived with a crate of oranges. David wore a pale green suit and a red knitted tie. Barry and Sue Flanagan were there, he wearing his three-piece tweed suit and sandals without socks; when I asked him how he was, he said, 'It's all coming in through the toes,' which Sue, smiling, clearly understood, and if their young daughters Samantha and Tara didn't, they seemed to accept as a matter of fact that a father is not necessarily understood. Mark Lancaster arrived, apparently having come, as always, from an exclusive club he had access to, Stephen Buckley with him.

Thinking about works of art: Jan – who, Michael said, was at Yale when he and Jennifer Bartlett and Richard Serra were there, and who was the best of them all – does drawings of domestic objects, such as a brown bowl, on two overlapping sheets of paper, a sheet of carbon paper between, so the top drawing is in full colour and the one under is a ghost of the bowl so the bowl becomes mysterious, and yet remains the depiction of a simple bowl, implying to me a lively irony that may be an irony that Jan herself enjoys – say, in ending a meal at her and Michael's with simple frozen orange pops, which pops suggest all kinds of ironies about being original in the face of not being able to afford anything more elaborate than pops, and, too, about the pop culture we seem to live in, a culture Jan is vividly aware of. Jan certainly has style, and will appear wearing an Ossie Clark snakeskin bomber jacket or a Vidal Sassoon haircut, always appearing to be stylish within the wider awareness that style is in so many ways culture, and this makes me see Jan as more acutely aware of the culture I suppose I too live in but am in no way as aware of as she is. She makes me wish that I had more style, and that I could be as stylish as she is in serving frozen orange pops at the end of a carefully thought-out meal. And I must mention that the meal is served within, but not on, a Barry Flanagan tablecloth: a sheet of burlap from which all the rectangles at the place settings are cut out and folded back to expose the table top with the plates and glasses and knives and forks, all of which place settings would be covered if the cut-out flaps were folded down, and so the meal becomes something of a Barry Flanagan art work.

One afternoon, Michael came round to our flat to show us his latest work: little 'stories,' as he called them, written on file cards, one sentence to a card, and each story has to do with a different way in which he saw himself and how he thought others saw him.

How odd it is to see in public places works by artists one knows, or simply has met, such as the mosaics designed by Eduardo Paolozzi in the Tottenham Court tube station –

And, to see, in an exhibition, a portrait by Lucian Freud of Kitty Godley, staring out with wide eyes and apparently strangling a cat she is unaware of – Kitty, the daughter of the sculptor Jacob Epstein, married to Wynne Godley, economist, who asked me if I thought it a good idea to buy an old, semi-ruined house in Italy, which Nikos and I did and then sold to great profit, almost as though we were speculators in property, so I said yes; but Wynne and Kitty seem to lose more and more money, moving from lesser and lesser houses, until they live in a workman's cottage in the high street of a provincial town, and we have lost contact with them. I look at the portrait of Kitty with the wonder of knowing her and yet, in the portrait, of not knowing her at all, as if in the portrait Kitty has the most esoteric relationship with the Kitty we know.

———

Dinner at Anne Wollheim's, Nikos and me and Ben Nicolson.

Ben said that Virginia Woolf would make fun of him whenever he was invited, by Royal Command, to Buckingham Palace: 'Poor Ben, having to go to the Palace.' He laughed his long nasal laugh.

He told us this: as a boy he visited his grandmother who told him that his mother, Vita Sackville-West, was a raging lesbian and as for his father, Harold Nicolson, he was never out of bed with Raymond Mortimer, which information he thought about on his bicycle back to Knole, where he asked his mother if she was in fact a raging lesbian and as for his father was he never out of bed with Raymond Mortimer, to which they answered, simply, yes. Telling the story, Ben laughed a kind of deep gurgling laugh.

Anne has a constant look of bemusement and will almost always make a comment about what she has said, 'Well, I'm not sure,' and run her tongue over her lips.

She will suddenly, unexpectedly, reveal past friendships, such as Henry Green, whom she knew as Henry Yorke.

She rang me to ask if I had rosary beads, as her former husband Philip Toynbee, living in a commune with his second wife Sally, had converted, or hoped to convert, to Catholicism, and he wanted rosary beads to say his prayers on. I do have a number of rosaries, placed without my knowing in my suitcase by my mother every time I visit and found on my return, and I offered her one, to be passed on to Philip Toynbee. She invited Nikos and me to dinner and I gave her the rosary. I didn't know that Anne was brought up a Catholic, but when I expressed some hint of common interest, she laughed a light laugh and sniffed and said, 'No, no.'

After a supper party at Anne's, I spoke with Alexi Russell, a former wife of John Russell, she leaning against a door jamb as if for support and I in front of her. In a low, rather sad voice, she said, 'If you and Nikos live long enough together, you'll find that what you now think of as detracting from love – age spots, wrinkles, all of that – will make you love each other more.'

What came to me, forcefully, is this: that Nikos and I are in London loved as a loving couple.

Anne had just bought an antique rug which Nikos got down on his hands and knees to examine. He said, 'Anne, there's a defect in your rug.' She said, 'Go home, Nikos, go home.'

———

Ben Nicolson delights in telling stories, his delight making him seem to gurgle as he speaks. Here is one: J. P. Morgan had a very big nose, grotesquely big. A society lady invited him to dinner, and thought she would put her attractive daughter next to him to entertain him, but she warned her daughter not to stare at Mr. Morgan's nose and in no way refer to noses. All during the meal, the lady was apprehensive about her daughter offending Mr. Morgan by referring to noses, all too possible because she was warned not to. But all went well, the lady congratulating her daughter. In the drawing room after, the lady, serving coffee, asked, 'Mr. Morgan, how much sugar do you take in your nose?' Ben laughed, his laughter even more of a gurgle.

He said about his daughter Vanessa, 'I will accept everything about her, but if I find she is uncivil I will come down on her –' and here he slapped one palm against another hard – 'like a ton of bricks.' His wife, Luisa Vertova Nicolson, lives in Florence. What their relationship is I can only think of as incomprehensibly British.

He seems to be in love with a young beautiful man with dense black curly hair called Simon, whose interest in art history Ben encourages.

Ben's great expertise is Caravaggio and his followers the Caravaggisti.

I tell myself not to make comments, but simply describe, but how can I keep myself from noting that Ben is one of the most loveable men I have ever known?

———

Among the people we meet at Anne Wollheim's dinner parties are the art historian Francis Haskell and his Russian wife Larissa. He had been to Moscow and there visited Guy Burgess, who had escaped, or was allowed to escape, to Moscow after it was discovered he'd been a spy for the Russians. Frances said that Guy Burgess stood in the middle of his sitting room and looked up at the chandelier which he knew was bugged so everything he said would be heard, and he shouted, 'I hate Russia.'

As Francis and Larissa stay with John Fleming and Hugh Honour, Nikos and I were able to make a connection through them, even share in what it is like to stay in the Villa Marchio.

———

Sylvia Guirey does paintings of many many dots on canvas. She gave me one, of many black dots, based, she told me, on an idea I gave her, so she has dedicated the work as from me.

Nikos and I often go to her for her meals, cooked on a cooker with large iron burners in large copper pots and pans.

She gave to Nikos a delightful spoof cookbook that she wrote, called La Cuisinière Provençale, based on a recipe for cooking sausages:

She put in thyme, a bay leaf, pepper and celery salt.

Couvez et laissez cuire . . .

She found the corkscrew and opened a bottle of white wine.

She poured some into the pan, stirring as it hissed all around the sausages and smelled bright and brown.

She poured herself a glass of wine.

The man came in.

She poured him one too.

He said he would read his newspaper. He read the financial page.

She put the wine back in the refrigerator. She read the recipe again.

Sylvia has a Philip Guston abstract painting.

She likes to shop in a shop at the World's End with a large clock in the window the hands of which go backwards very quickly. The shop seems to specialize in black leather skirts and black very high stiletto-heeled shoes.

Minor, I suppose, but perhaps not, to note that when I used the word 'drapes,' Sylvia, as if she heard in that word all my American background, corrected me with 'curtains,' which I assumed to be what Americans of her background say.

———

Francis King to supper with the writer Olivia Manning.

In London, I see people in the context of their lives more than for the few hours we are together; so I see Olivia Manning within the context of her Balkan Trilogy, which I take to be autobiographical and, as autobiography, history, for in those three novels she recorded not only the displacement of the British in Romania, in Greece, in Egypt, in Palestine because of World War II, but the disassembling of the British Empire. She appears, in herself, to be displaced, dissatisfied, as though something were missing that would make her whole and that something whole, perhaps once imagined to be possible, is now known never to have been possible.

Olivia is thin, almost gaunt, and she whines, as though inside her are taut fine wires through which she speaks.

'What should I read?' she asked with a whine. 'I've read everything I want to read. I have nothing left to read.'

Perhaps, she thought, she would write a book about cats; everyone loves cats.

Francis sustained a sad smile.

I remark, in the Trilogy, someone saying about another, 'He rides the choo-choo.'

———

At Anne Wollheim's we met Ben Nicolson's wife Luisa Vertova Nicolson, whom Anne seemed uncertain about, as if Luisa might suddenly say something outrageous. She did go on about Harold Acton and how Harold will not recognize the fact that he has a half-sister in Florence, though all of Florence knows that Harold's father had a mistress with whom he had a daughter.

I like the 'all of Florence,' which seems to me a nineteenth-century term that really only applied to the English and American community there, with perhaps some Florentine aristocrats married into the community. I doubt that there was as much contact between that 'all of Florence' and the 'all of Florence' of the old Florentine families which Henry James fantasized about. There is no contact at all in the novels of E. M. Forster, his middle-class English very much a foreign community enclosed within itself in Florence, any contact with primitive sexual Italians as shocking as it is tempting, Forster's fantasy.

The fantasy of other countries!

I once read Henry James' comment: for an American all things foreign are sacred.

Luisa said that Harold's mother would not have anything to do with Florence, not after the way she was treated by the Fascists at the beginning of the war – imprisoned with prostitutes as an enemy alien – and in no way would the Uffizi get the Michelozzo painting of the Holy Family the museum wants. What Harold will do with La Pietra she didn't know, but she did know that Oxford University had turned down the offer to inherit it.

———

Nikos has translated poems by Yannis Ritsos to be published as a volume in the Penguin series of Modern European Poets. Ritsos, the winner of the Lenin Peace Prize for Literature and renowned in Russia, has been sent by the Greek dictators into internal exile, in a concentration camp on an island, where he continues to write, his poems now referring directly to ancient Greece. These poems move Nikos most:

. . . the symposia of our philosophers have all vanished . . .

Our paper and our books are burned, / the honour of our country lost.

. . . a cloud at sunset, deep, violet, moving, behind the barbed wire . . .

. . . maybe a new Kimon will arrive one day, secretly led / by the same eagle, and he'll dig and find our iron spear point, / rusty, and that too almost disintegrated, and he might go / to Athens and carry it in procession of mourning or triumph / with music and with wreaths.

Perhaps in response to the dictatorship in Greece, Nikos tells me about ancient Greek history as if he himself is renewing it, as when he told me that the leader of the Athenea, the yearly festival of Athens, was a young man especially chosen for his beauty, who for a year was not allowed to touch metal, and in a pure white robe led the procession up the massively cobbled way and up into the Acropolis and into the Parthenon.

How could I not see Nikos as the leader of the procession?

And how could this not bring tears to my eyes?

Strangely, this comes to me: that the only 'impure' part of Nikos' life I can think of, which he was forced into, was his time in the military when he had to wear a uniform and was made to shoot a rifle and use a bayonet.

———

Michael Craig-Martin has had an exhibition that consisted entirely of an ordinary glass of water on a high glass shelf, the glass itself the idea one would have of an ordinary glass. The glass of water on the glass shelf is high up on a blood-red wall, the whole length of Waddington Gallery. But, as an accompanying card informed, printed in red on white pasteboard, the glass of water is no longer a glass of water but an oak tree.

Michael was brought up a Catholic, which he has, as I have, rejected, but what else but his religion informs the miracle of the transubstantiation of the glass of water into an oak tree?

But, more than our shared Catholic pasts, I have my own view of Michael's work — which he seems to respect but not to be convinced by — in our both having been taught by Jesuits. I went to Jesuit Boston College and was taught Scholastic epistemology, which discipline has remained with me as my essential sense in my own apprehension of the world. I like to think that Michael was just long enough at the Jesuit university of Fordham to have been inspired by some idea of Scholastic epistemology, and to be intrigued by the mental process by which a specific object such as a glass of water is held in a state of momentary suspension before it is judged as this or that glass of water, so that in that state of suspension, of apprehension, the water glass becomes an oak tree.

We've become regular guests at the Queen Anne house of Adrian and Ann Stokes in Hampstead, with sherry first in the sitting room hung with a large nude by William Coldstream, and considered by Adrian a major work. Dinner downstairs in the basement, by the Aga, the table laid with Ann's pottery, with large ceramic animals as centrepieces.

Adrian especially warm towards Nikos, whom he embraces whenever we arrive, Nikos appearing to revive in Adrian a youthful erotic attraction to someone as attractive as Nikos.

As for worlds revolving around Adrian — think of Ezra Pound, think of Osbert Sitwell, think of all the Saint Ives artists including Barbara Hepworth and Ben Nicholson and Naum Gabo and . . .

And Adrian knew D. H. Lawrence, whom he visited when Lawrence lived in Italy, in the Villa Mirenda — not only knew Lawrence, but delivered Lady Chatterley's Lover to Lawrence's Italian publisher Orioli, no doubt reading that novel on the train!

Nikos is very impressed that Adrian was analyzed by Melanie Klein, and thinks that the great disappointment in Adrian's life is that analysis could not cure his daughter Ariadne of schizophrenia.

R. B. Kitaj is painting an almost life-size portrait of Nikos.

R.B. and his wife Sandra come to meals, or we go to them. At their large round dining table there are always interesting people to meet, as if R.B. (Nikos calls him Ron, but he prefers R.B. or, simply, Kitaj) sees his friends as references to the richness of culture as he sees the figures in his paintings as referring, too, to the richness of culture.

His library, with high shelves of books, forms part of his studio, there where a punching bag hangs, and I easily imagine Kitaj punching the bag when he gets frustrated at a painting not going well.

He can have a mad look.

There are so many references in his paintings. In the branches of a tree hung what looked like red ribbon, and I asked him what it referred to. He said, off-handedly, 'I just wanted a bit of red there,' which impressed me, for I sometimes think that Kitaj will sacrifice composition to the references.

At the large round table in the basement kitchen, Nikos and I have met the very old American painter Raphael Soyers and his wife. R.B. is keen on artists of the 1940s Fourteenth Street School of painters that included Reginald Marsh, Isabel Bishop, Kenneth Hayes Miller, all figurative artists, as R.B. is trying to promote figures in paintings as opposed to abstraction.

Other people we've met at their dinners:

The painter Avigdor Arikha and his wife Anne.

The film maker Kenneth Anger, whose Inauguration of the Pleasure Dome I'd seen years before. As good looking as he was, I was frightened of him because I'd heard he was under a satanic bond to kill someone.

The poet Robert Duncan, whose portrait Kitaj has drawn and who clearly has exhausted both Kitaj and Sandra by his relentlessly inventive talk, as he exhausted Nikos and me when he came to supper, theorizing about, say, Gertrude Stein in terms of the inner tensions in her work, his mind, it seems, filled with inner tensions that flash out in different directions while one tries to make the connections among all the flashes. His lover Jess Collins sat back.

Robert gave us some of his books of poems, with photomontages by Jess. So we are building up a collection of signed books given to us.

Also at Kitaj and Sandra's, we met a coroner, who said that there was nothing more beautiful than the naked chest of a dead young man.

When you meet someone at Kitaj and Sandra's, you feel the person must be rather esoteric to be of interest to them, and, in meeting this esoteric person, you hope you are rather esoteric too.

Kitaj, an American, wants to belong to what he calls the London School of Painters, wants, I think, to become as much a part of the art world of London as Whistler and Sargent were.

He is close to David Hockney, with whom he appeared on the front cover of the New Review, both of them naked, arms across shoulders.

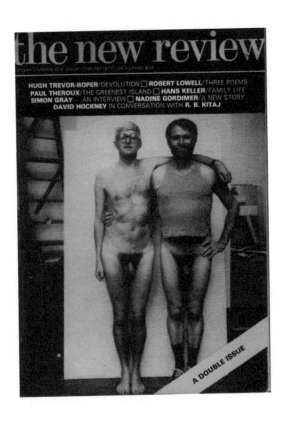

Sandra asked to paint my portrait – in the nude, if I didn't mind. I didn't mind. Then she suggested I come again and pose with another male model, very sexy, both of us nude. 'And you never know what will happen.'

She and R.B. go to Amsterdam to the live sex shows and afterwards clap.

Kitaj likes to go to the airport and take the next flight out to wherever, the last time to Athens, where he went to a whorehouse and waited until a large woman came out and, raising her arms high, shouted, 'America!' He tells this story before Sandra, who laughs, I think a strained laugh.

Their understanding is: never with friends.

Sandra is very beautiful, with a wide white smile.

––––––––––

I have no idea what it is in me that responds so with the love of details, so that, on a walk in the Wiltshire countryside, Nikos and I spending a weekend with Joe and Jos Tilson, I, after the visit and back in London, can remember almost nothing of the conversation, but remember details of the countryside, and in accounting for as many details as I can remember I feel that the visit is now fixed on a walk through an arboretum with the sunlight level through the tall, thin, straight poplar trees, the branches high up so the trunks are bare, the sunlight and shadows appearing to multiply the tree trunks, so I am in an imaginary wood; and, too, I am imagining the bracken on either side of the path, bent, bright green, thinly serrated fronds; as I am imagining the mushrooms in open spaces among the bracken, imagining a brown beer bottle, an old shoe, a tin, the details all together demanding that I make something more of them than what they are, this something more my love of them.

And at the same time I am accounting for the details as I imagine them – because, of course, they are no longer what they were – a sense of such tediousness comes over me in the effort of the accounting that I think, oh, let them all go, it would be a relief to let them all go, let my possessive love of them go. And I think of writing without any details, writing in some way that frees me of this possessiveness. Or not writing at all.

Nikos admonishes me: 'Enjoy the event in itself, don't try to possess it, because you falsify it by elaborating on it.'

And I try, I try, I do try not to try to account for all the details of a dinner party on a dining-room table – the large round pan of paella with black mussels and shrimps and red peppers imbedded in the saffron-yellow rice; try not to retain the details of a view from the window of a country pub – hollyhocks in the garden of the public house, seen through a many-paned window, bicycles leaning against a garden shed; try not to possess the details of a parade of cavalry passing – they in tight, dark blue uniforms with yellow braid and a red stripe down the side of the trousers, and dark blue casques with cockades of white plums, riding horses in parade with silver cannon on large black wheels. I try not to, as much as I honestly do find it a bore to look and then record, but I fail.

———

I've been making pottery at Ann Stokes' two afternoons a week, listening, as if in sympathy with the Greeks, to Greek bouzouki music. (Nikos is indifferent to bouzouki, as he is indifferent to anything he deems folklore. He is keen on Ann's pottery, of which he has bought stacks of plates, cups and saucers, bowls at her annual pottery sale, and she has given us vessels copied from ancient Greek types. When Ann made, in ceramics, a Free Greece medallion, and gave it to Nikos, he was very touched.) Adrian paints up at the top of the house in his studio, and comes down at tea time and we all have tea. I made a version of a Minoan storage jug, about three feet high.

Natasha saw it during one of Ann's pottery sales and wanted to buy it for the garden of their house in the South of France, to go at the end of a cypress avenue. I gave it to her. We were talking very easily with one another and tensed up, both of us, only when Stephen came to find out what we were talking about.

———

Sometimes I wonder who, really, are our close friends? and answer myself, the people I write about in my diary, and these include our friend Stephenie Bergman.

Stef lived for a while in Soho, her lover a man whose business was making pornographic films. When he died, Stef did what he had requested be done with his ashes: strew them in the gutters of Soho.

Stef is a ceramicist, and works in the pottery of Ann Stokes. We have some of her pots, collected by many people.

After one of her supper parties, she wheeled in from another room a large ceramic lorry loaded with oranges.

Her great friend is Roxy Beaujolais.

After an event in London we'd attended together, they, Stef driving, said they'd take me home. We crossed Battersea Bridge, in the middle a stand where hot dogs and drinks are sold and always surrounded by bikers in black leather jackets and their big black motorcycles. Stef said to Roxy or Roxy to Stef, 'Let's get rid of David and come back here for some fun.'

Roxy is a publican, and is the best-connected person I know in London, from politicians to City gents to artists.

She likes to wear her dress with the top slung low to expose her beautiful shoulders.

Nikos makes no generalizations about poets, but sees each in his or her self, and as an editor he remains open to whatever world they may come from. So, he has published in one volume of Penguin Modern Poets John Heath-Stubbs and F. T. Prince and Stephen Spender, and in another Geoffrey Grigson and Edwin Muir and Adrian Stokes.

He is especially moved by Adrian's poem 'Schizophrenic Girl', about his daughter Ariadne, his beautiful unbending daughter, who keeps at bay the horror of her nothingness.

At the Stokes' house, she would sometimes come into the room where I was alone working on a pot, and she would simply stand against a wall and stare. Once she undressed and stood naked, and I went on working until Ann came in and took her out. Another time she dropped a torn bit of paper on the floor near me and left and I picked up the paper and read, in upper-case letters, MUDDLE HEADED. She has been accepted into a home run by nuns, where she will spend her life.

————

I'm sometimes surprised by the independent intellectual life Nikos has. His main interest is in aesthetics, which was his graduate concentration at Harvard University. Hearing him talk to Adrian Stokes or Richard Wollheim about aesthetics, it occurs to me that they are all within a sphere of interest that is theirs, and into which I can't enter. I am always very pleased that Nikos should be within that sphere, partly because I admire his superior knowledge and intelligence, and also because, as we are a couple, his superior knowledge and intelligence reflect back on me as if I were some-one who would be equal to him in conversation with Adrian and Richard, while, on the other side of the sitting room, I am talking to Ann or Day about pottery. But I do hear enough of their conver-sation to recognize that the main topic with Adrian and Richard has to do with the psychoanalytic interpretation of aesthetics, a subject, I feel, that is very much within the circle of philosophers and psychoanalysts referred to in their conversations, such as Donald Winnicott and, most meaningfully, Melanie Klein.

Adrian had analysis with Melanie Klein.

I know of Nikos' interest, but I was surprised when, one evening on his return from work, he asked me what I thought of his starting Kleinian analysis.

I didn't know what that meant.

It was the most rigorous form of analysis, starting as far back as the good or bad breast.

This seemed to me to have nothing to do with our relationship, so I said I thought if he wanted to go into that analysis, he should. I imagined it had to do with some deep – the deepest – appreciation of the aesthetic. Nikos has collected a significant library about aesthetics, and I imagined his wanting to go under analysis was a more profound investigation into the state of mind when we think of something as beautiful. He inspired me with the acute sense of beauty – in his poetry, and also, when we were together on, say, an Underground train and he would whisper about a woman standing at the other end, 'How beautiful she is!' someone whose looks I would have not noted at all – and I believed I would, on his enhancement of his sense of the beautiful by analysis, find my sense also enhanced.

Through Richard, he was able to have a meeting with Hanna Segal, the custodian of the analytical approach of Melanie Klein. When he came back from the meeting, he told me that she had asked him basic questions – what kind of homosexual was he? promiscuous, in that he went cottaging (a term neither he nor I had heard of, but that means having sex in public loos, as Hanna Segal had had to explain to Nikos), or monogamous? He told her about us, and she said that if he were to enter into analysis he might find that his relationship with me would change fundamentally, and that he should discuss this possibility with me.

What did I think?

As he asked me this not long ago, I have to ask myself: what do

I think? I'm not sure I think anything. Is it because I feel so secure in our relationship that I don't feel any threat in his talking about our relationship with someone who sees it as if apart from us? I see our relationship from within, and to me the view is steady.

I told him to start analysis.

————

Bruce Chatwin needs to give the impression that he knows everything, needs to be able to tell you, when you stop with him at an antique-shop window off Bond Street, what factory the tea pot came from, and its date. And I'm envious of him because he does seem to know everything – my envy, again, of those who are able to make connections that I'm not able to make.

He invited me to lunch in his new flat in Belgravia. I praised it to him, but thought to myself: it is really very, very tiny. The only object he had hanging on his severe walls was a highly lacquered yin-and-yang disk from a Japanese temple. On a table he had a small collection of objects: a fragment from Persopolis, an Eskimo toggle, a pre-Colombian bit of polished black stone.

As Howard Hodgkin, one of Bruce's closest friends, says, 'Bruce is both mad and a snob about objects.'

The bathroom is very small. I said I love big bathrooms, with large baths, where I do a lot of writing in my head. 'Baths!' Bruce exclaimed. 'Oh, no, no baths! I hate bathing!' He shook his head. 'No, no.'

He placed the food we were to have on the small table – duck breasts and wild rice and a bottle of good wine – and, talking, not about baths which didn't interest him, but about writing, which did interest him, he sat and served himself first, then, still talking, touched the serving dishes with his fingertips to indicate that I should go ahead and serve myself. I was still standing.

In a high voice, speaking as if at a pitch against universal ignorance, Bruce said, 'The fact is that no one has ever understood what Hemingway was trying to do in In our Time. I ask you, has anyone ever asked why he called the vignettes that appear between the stories chapters? The book has to be seen not as a collection but as a whole, and it is, I'm convinced, a Cubist work of fiction.'

I sat and served myself and said that was fascinating.

Bruce ate quickly and went on talking, his voice rising higher and higher in excited pitch. His talk about Hemingway was fascinating.

He asked me if I'd like fresh fig, with a tone that I felt suggested he'd prefer me to say no, thank you. I said yes.

After lunch, he prepared for me a large, brown nut, a silver rim about the opening, filled with maté tea to be sipped through a silver straw with a little silver strainer at the bottom so the powdered tea wouldn't be sucked up, and then he occupied himself, it seemed to me with business: a letter he signed and folded and put into an envelope addressed, I saw because he did hold it so I could see it, to William Shawn of the New Yorker. He showed me a photograph of himself at his most stunningly beautiful, in sandals and a straw hat, and said, 'A photograph of the author.' He showed me an Italian edition of one of his books, of which he read a paragraph. It only occurred to me later that Bruce had left the letter, the photograph, the book about to impress.

When I was leaving, he gave me a copy of In our Time. He gave me a number of books, among them a collection of Ivan Bunin's short stories, and The Chinese Written Character as a Medium for Poetry by Ernest Fenollosa and edited by Ezra Pound. And when he, excited, recommended a book, I went out and found it: Xavier de Maistre's Voyage autour de ma chambre.

His excitements inspire me, but, as usual, I'm not entirely convinced by them, because they seem to me impersonal, not personal, and somewhat affected.

So, for example, Bruce will ring, and I'll ask, banally, 'How are you?', wanting to enter into some personal conversation with him, but he won't answer, and instead say, 'I think I've discovered where the socialist red flag comes from.' He thinks he's traced the flag to the bloody aprons of Argentinean butchers in an abattoir. I suggested he talk to James Joll about this, and he did, and James later told me that Bruce may have a point.

Whenever I hear that Bruce has had sex with some man, I

wonder why I do not find him sexually attractive, as beautiful as he is. He appears to me too bright to have any sexuality, too impersonally bright, as if he doesn't have a deep emotional life, or any great capacity to love. The falseness I feel about him may be the falseness of too much articulated brightness, which belies what to me is a deeper, more inarticulate sexuality. I imagine Bruce talking and talking and talking while making love, as if to make love making all articulation.

Still, I am envious of him for his ability to talk. Nikos does not at all understand this envy.

———

Nikos is disappointed that Hanna Segal will not take him on for analysis, but has recommended a Miss Richards, who has her office in a basement flat in Bayswater. Their first session, Nikos recounted a dream, and Miss Richards, he told me, said, 'You've brought me a gift.' Whatever Nikos thought, I thought this a presumption on the part of Miss Richards. Nikos tells me all his dreams.

———

Nikos is keen that I go on writing my diary, and I wonder if he thinks that I am preserving something that he wants me to preserve. As we have no secrets from each other – in fact, he reads all my post, as I read his – he will from time to time pick up the notebook in which I am currently writing and read. He says my diary makes him aware of what we are doing in a way he hadn't been aware before. And he glosses corrections in the margins.

———

The flat has been filled all day with a succession of redolent smells: the Christmas tree which I brought in this morning, bunches of hyacinths and anemones and irises Nikos brought in, then the smells of cooking cranberries and fresh bread (Nikos makes bread every week) and mincemeat pies, and finally the smell of pine bath salts which spreads out on the heat and steam from the bathroom.

All the smells combine in the awareness that this is my home.

Boxing Day

So many people over the past weekend –

Christmas Eve, Nikos and I went to church briefly, to the Brompton Oratory to light candles, then came back to the flat to have champagne and mince pies and open gifts.

Christmas Day, Richard and Mary Day Wollheim came, Adrian and Ann Stokes, Richard and Sally Morphet, Mark Lancaster, Barry and Sue Flanagan and their daughters Samantha and Tara, and Sylvia Guirey and her sons and daughter. Samantha played her viola. How did we all fit into our small flat?

Then in the evening Nikos and I went to Edna O'Brien's. Sonia and Francis Bacon were there. Francis left early. Sonia stayed and got very drunk, so I thought I should take her home. Nikos was annoyed, and I told him to stay at the party, but he said he'd come with me. (Later, he said I'm a victim of women like Sonia who have made and are responsible for their own hideous lives.) In the taxi, she babbled, in a strident, accusing voice, about how violently unhappy Francis was, George dead only six weeks.

'You don't understand – none of you understands – what desperation is. You won't help. You don't know how to help. I could kill, kill, kill, kill you all for your lack of sensitivity. Francis is suffering. Do any of you care? Do any of you ring him up? Fuck all if you do.'

Nikos got very angry, but contained his anger.

The next time I saw Francis, I said how sorry I was about the death of George, and laughing a little from the side of his mouth Francis shrugged one shoulder.

———

Nikos gave me a printing press as a gift, and the first item I set and printed out, on rough brown paper, was an invitation to be sent out:

NIKOS STANGOS

READING

FROM A WORK IN PROGRESS: PURE REASON

YANNIS RITSOS: A TRANSLATION

THE POETRY SOCIETY

21 EARLS COURT SQ.

While he read from 'Pure Reason' in his light but precise voice, I had a sense of someone near and far, someone I know and don't know, someone who loves me and someone for whom love is out there where love is a universal.

It is in being most abstract in his poems that he is most concrete, as if ideas for him have colour, shape, weight, can be seen and even smelled and touched; at the same time, they are ideas, and do not have colour, shape, weight, cannot be seen or smelled or touched. These antinomies – to use a word that Nikos likes to use himself – of the abstract and the concrete, the present and the absent, the defined and the indefinable, the invisible and the visible, create the ambiguity of both seeing and not seeing, smelling and not smelling, touching and not touching, knowing and not knowing, all at the same time.

John Golding, who came to the reading, said about Nikos' poetry that it is 'intellectually and emotionally plangent.'

———

When Steven Runciman taught at Trinity, Cambridge, his first student was Guy Burgess. In his early days, Burgess, though a bit grubby, was bright and had charm. As he got older, the charm got murkier, and after he became a Communist he never washed. 'Everyone knew he was a Communist. All the young men were Communists. They didn't sing too much about it, until the Spanish Civil War, but then people like Guy didn't go off to fight in Spain. In any case, Russia wasn't the enemy then. Russia was subversive, but Germany was the enemy. I rather mocked Guy's Communism, and, as I hated societies, mocked the Apostles, who were a supposedly secret society at the University of Cambridge devoted to high-level talk. When they got into official positions, it was thought they'd converted. I asked Guy, after he got a position with the B.B.C., "What are you doing there? Surely your Communist principles . . ." Guy said, "It is all rather different now." It was Burgess who, through machinations, got Steven his first job, in 1940, in the Ministry of Information. The Ministry needed someone to take over the section on Bulgaria, and Burgess knew that Steven read Bulgarian. Shortly afterwards, in the early summer of 1940, Steven was sent to be press attaché in Sofia. He stayed in Bulgaria until the Germans invaded, in 1941. From there to Egypt, Cairo, to organize news broadcasts in the various Balkan languages, Serbo-Croatian and Romanian, as well as Bulgarian. Then to Jerusalem, where he was a film censor for Palestine, which suited him well because there were hardly any films, so he studied religions. 'Religion is a necessary part of the human condition, even if it is a wild anti-religion. I love the study of religion.' At the time there was a détente between the Jews and the Arabs, and Steven used to invite professors of the Hebrew University to meet with Arab intellectuals, for some of the professors of the Hebrew University were deeply interested in Arabic studies. One Orientalist, Leo Mayer, was so highly respected by the Arabs that several learned Hebrew to attend his lectures. It was while he was in Jerusalem that the idea of writing the history of the Crusades came to him. 'Unfortunately – or fortunately – for me, the President of Turkey, driving around the streets of Istanbul one day, saw a building he didn't recognize, and asked what it was. Eventually, someone said he thought it was Byzantine, but no one was able to say more. He said angrily, "Do you mean to say that no one in this city knows anything about Byzantium? After all, it is a period in the history of our country." Turning to the Minister of Education, he said, "Find me a Byzantine professor at once!" The Minister of Education went to see an old friend of mine, the historian of the classical world Michael Grant, then head of the British Council in Turkey, who said they'd better get me. I received a letter from the Foreign

Office instructing me to leave my present job in Jerusalem to go to Istanbul to be a professor. I lectured in English, but the seminars and examinations were in Turkish. If you house-keep in a country, you learn the language.'

Everyone in Istanbul was praying that Anthony Eden, the British Foreign Secretary, would not succeed in bringing Turkey into the war. When the Turks did enter, on the side of the Allies, it was quite clear how the war was going to end. 'Everyone's always suspected me, I find, of being a secret agent when I was in Turkey. Not a bit of it. I was a straightforward Turkish professor. The Turkish secret service was very good at spying. At one time, when I had hepatitis and was recovering at a resort, I talked often with a charming Turk of the secret police who was there and wanted to learn English. He had been in charge of looking after foreigners in Istanbul, and the things he told me about the private lives of my English friends were absolutely amazing – things I hadn't realized. One had to be very careful. When the Italians caved in, they gave all their secret papers to the British, and in their list of British spies I was put at the top. Molto intelligente, molto pericoloso. One of my best tributes, and entirely false.' The Turks were liberal about allowing foreigners to travel as long as they kept away from the military zones, so Steven was able to do most of the Crusader journey. During his holidays, he went to Syria. Because of the appalling climate in Istanbul, he had sciatica for months on end. When the British Council asked him if he would go to Athens to direct its organization, he said he would go for two years, since Athens had a marvellous climate for rheumatism.

———

A Sunday evening, we went to the Spenders' in Loudoun Road for drinks. We were meant to give the impression, which Stephen had asked us to give, that we had never been in the house, which, however, we had been in when Natasha was away. Stephen appeared to be bigger than ever and spilled the wine as he poured it out, and he seemed very bored. Matthew and Maro and their little daughter Saskia,

who only understands Italian, were there. Also Johnny Craxton. Natasha dashed about here and there, trying to be kind to Nikos and me as
well as to the other guests, telling Stephen to refill glasses, asking
Matthew and Maro to show us some of their paintings. She asked
Nikos and me to stay on for sandwiches after everyone else had left,
and we went down to the kitchen with her to help slice the turkey,
butter the bread, get out plates. Nikos all the while, with pressing
insistence, was saying how much he liked the house and asking about
the paintings in the sitting room upstairs as if he hadn't seen them
before. Maro came down and with a kind of cackle said from the side
of her mouth, 'What's this little intimate scene all about?' Natasha,
Nikos and I laughed, but a terrible boredom descended on me
suddenly, and I knew I couldn't any longer sustain any niceness, appreciation, talk, so I became silent and wanted to leave.

But Natasha wanted to talk to me about Sonia. She said that
Sonia is helpless and hopeless, and Natasha wondered if it was part
of her own neurosis to find herself more and more involved with
people the more helpless and hopeless they become.

We were all invited to David Hockney's flat in Powis Terrace for
a late party. Stephen said he wouldn't come. Natasha drove Nikos
and me, and Johnny followed on his motorbike.

I felt old compared to everyone else at David's – all young people
bumping about – but Natasha didn't seem to be aware that she was
in any way different. While Nikos, who likes young people, bumped
among them, Natasha and I stood apart and talked more about Sonia.

Natasha said, 'Sonia has always been drawn to men who were in
one way or another inaccessible – either inaccessibly married, or
inaccessibly dying, or inaccessibly queer.'

I left Natasha to get a drink, then didn't return to her, but spoke
with Johnny, then to Mark Lancaster and to Keith Milow. I wandered
around the flat and found Natasha sitting on the floor in the bedroom
watching television. A young man was sitting on the bed, and I sat
next to him. He seemed to be a young man only because he didn't
have any breasts, though his plump face was hairless and he had shaved
his eyebrows and penciled on two long black lines and he wore mascara

on his lashes. He told me that his friends are the Queen, the Queen Mother, who likes gin and tonic, and Pablo Picasso.

He said, 'One of my closest friends is Sir Francis Rose. You know who he is, don't you? The intimate friend of Cecil Beaton, Gertrude Stein, and Hitler.'

Natasha didn't seem to pay any attention to him, but continued to watch television. After he left, she looked round at me and asked, 'Who was she?'

I said, 'It was a he.'

————

Having kept them all, an inveterate archivist, I have been going through masses of papers from as far back as my adolescence – such adolescent essays called IMPROMTUOUS (sic) THOUGHTS ON NOTHING – to insert them into the pages of a bulging notebook of my diary, as if to incorporate the long ago past into the present. My feeling is that I am taking my past before Nikos into my present time with Nikos, but he told me that I am jealous of his going into his past in his present with Miss Richards so I am bringing my past into my present.

But, wondering if Nikos talks to Miss Richards about our relationship, I was told by a friend who knows about Kleinian analysis that, as he is only months into his sessions, he has hardly approached the fact of being born.

————

On a bus home from a dinner party, Nikos said to me, 'You talked too much this evening.'

'Did I?'

'You talked to try to get people there to like you. You want everyone to like you. They think you are trying to impress them.'

'What about me am I trying to impress them with?'

'You talked to be nice, too American-nice, saying over and over, "That's so interesting, that's fascinating, that's wonderful," so no one believed you.'

'Do I do that with you?'

'I make sure you don't.'

'You don't indulge me.'

'No, I don't indulge you in that way.'

'So, I don't try to make you like me, but you do like me.'

He pressed his shoulder against mine and said, 'With some reservations.'

'Thanks.'

'Why is it that Americans so want to be liked?' he asked.

'Am I so American?'

'Aren't you?'

———

Steven Runciman came to supper, as always with six eggs from his hens wrapped in newspaper.

Steven does not keep secret his grand life as an historian. He holds honorary degrees from the four oldest English universities, Oxford, Cambridge, Durham, London, and from the two oldest Scottish universities, Saint Andrews and Glasgow, and in America his chief honour is to belong to the American Philosophical Society founded by Benjamin Franklin, and in Turkey he was President of the British Institute of Archeology in Ankara, and in Greece Foreign Fellow at the Academy of Athens, and he is an honorary member of the Academy of Palermo and a Corresponding Member of the Royal Academy of History in Madrid. He likes to say that when he is at a gala dinner, at, say, an embassy, he will, just by looking at the other guests, know where he will be seated. And he likes to refer to his 'royal' cousins on the Continent, whom he sometimes visits.

And, too, he will say he and George Orwell, then known as Eric Blair, were at Eton together, taught by Aldous Huxley.

He is not an Englishman – or, rather, Scot – who keeps to himself the people he knows and has known, but, with a display of amused wonder, his chin raised and with a vague smile, will recount how he played piano duets with the last Emperor of China, Henry Pu Yi.

Steven talking:

After he got his degree, in 1924, he stayed up in Cambridge to study with the older historian Bury, who never took on students but took on Steven because Steven was interested in Byzantium, which no proper historian at the time was interested in, assuming, as influenced by Gibbon, the one thousand years were years of Roman decadence. He came down with flu, which led to pleurisy, and he was quite ill for a time. Doctors in those times used to say, 'The boy should go on a long sea voyage.' He told his parents he would go on such a voyage if he could go to China, so he went to China. He arrived in the middle of a civil war. Though he hoped to go straight to Peking, he had a high fever, and by the time he was well again the civil war had broken off connections. This meant he was stuck in Tianjin where Feng Yuxiang, the Christian warlord, was besieging the troops of Zhang Zuolin, the Manchu warlord.

(I have to break off here to insist that as Steven talks, he remembers the names of all the historical figures, and I stop him to ask him to spell the names, which he does as if annoyed.)

He was staying with the consul-general, a cousin, at the British Consulate. Tianjin was not an exciting town, just a port town without antiquities. The Chinese Emperor, Henry Pu Yi, aged about twenty, was living there in the Japanese garrison. One day, his Australian tutor came to see the consul-general about some matter, and when the tutor met Steven he asked him if he played the piano.

'A little,' Steven replied.

'Oh, just a little is needed,' the tutor said. 'The Emperor's started having piano lessons and likes simple duets in which he plays the top part with both hands together while someone goes thump-thump on the bass.'

Would Steven come?

He went twice to the imperial residence and thump-thumped on the bass while the Emperor played nursery rhymes with both hands in unison, and when they stopped they had excellent tea and then talked a bit. He was an etiolated young man, not good-looking, with a tremendous air of aristocracy. He spoke quite good English, and told Steven that since he had the greatest admiration for the Tudors he called himself Henry. He didn't like his chief wife, whom he called Mary, after Bloody Mary, but his chief concubine was charming, and she was Elizabeth. Steven was not allowed to meet the imperial ladies.

The Emperor remained a puppet of the Japanese for years, as the Emperor of Manchukuo, until Mao conquered Manchuria. The Emperor didn't mind. If the Japanese wanted him to be an emperor he would be an emperor; if Mao wanted him to be a market gardener, he would be a market gardener. Mao liked him, and got him to write his autobiography – or, rather, sign one written for him. The last that Steven heard of him was from Queen Maria José of Italy, the daughter of the Red Queen – Queen Elisabeth of the Belgians, who always visited Communist states before anyone else did. In the early sixties, Queen Maria José went to China with her mother, and Mao provided as their dragoman the ex-Emperor – a charming gesture of Mao. 'She told me about it when she got back, and I said I wished I'd known beforehand, because I'd liked to have known how the Emperor's piano playing was getting on, though I fear it would have been discarded. He died soon after.'

Nikos told him about his beginning with analysis, and Steven, the last person to have any understanding of the value of undergoing analysis, looked at me first as with an attempt to understand what I thought, which was, really, nothing, then he said to Nikos, 'I would suggest a long sea voyage.'

———

When I stare at – stare into – this photograph of Nikos as a boy long, long before I met him, a sense of incomprehension comes to me that we did meet, in the same way that when a coincidence occurs there also occurs a strange sense that the coincidence has a meaning, but a meaning just beyond one's comprehension of it. I can name the contingencies that came together in our meeting – simply, that I was given his telephone number by a mutual friend in Boston and told to ring him when I arrived in London – but the contingencies don't add up to understanding that elusive meaning of our meeting, a meaning rather beyond the contingencies. That we did meet strikes me all the more strange, the meaning of our meeting all the more elusive, because I cannot, staring and staring into his photograph, connect with that boy, so remote from me in his different world that there is no way I could have met him; and, not having been able to connect with him then, my connecting with him now seems so strange, the meaning of our connecting so incomprehensible as to be – to use a word he uses – mysterious.

I stare more deeply into the photograph, and wish I could have known him as he was then, and, too, to have loved him then, and in my love have saved him from what he now appears to me to be in his delicate beauty: vulnerable, lonely, unhappy.

And then this happens: mysteriously connected, I see into the photograph of Nikos as a boy Nikos now, and project the loneliness, the vulnerability, the unhappiness of Nikos as a boy onto Nikos now, and I love him with the impulse to save him from the vulnerability, the loneliness, the unhappiness I see in him now.

He calls out to me, as he very often calls out to me, 'Where is the book I was reading?' and I go to try to find what he can't find and is irritated at not finding, suspecting that the cleaning lady misplaced it, or I did.

Roxy and Stef, who are something of a collective conscience to me, tell me I drop names.

In warning me that I may be basing my life too much on Stephen's, is Sonia warning me against the possible allegation that Stephen is so social his poetry is incidental to his social self? And Natasha, she claims, is as social.

How could I tell her that Stephen and Natasha impress me for their enthusiasm for going to and giving parties? Sonia would ridicule both Stephen and Natasha and me by my recounting Stephen once telling me that he and Natasha were in a quandary, as they had invited Philippe and Pauline de Rothschild to dinner but worried about what wine to serve, so Stephen rang the Wine Society to explain the problem and ask for advice. Stephen so enjoys social life, and so does Natasha. I wonder if one of the reasons why Stephen and Natasha do bond is in their attraction to going to and giving parties. Perhaps I am open to the allegation of wanting a lively social life, that I, unlike Nikos but like Stephen, so enjoy going to and giving parties.

Why will someone such as Steven Runciman be found amusing for his social life and Stephen not? Is it because they are from different classes? I came to London with the American idea that British society is structured by class, and that the classes range from the working-class navvies who work digging in the streets up to the Queen, and now I find that all this, too, becomes a cloud of unknowing. Is Steven, from a Scottish ship-owning family, upper class? I once heard Stephen Spender tells Elizabeth Glenconner that he is middle class. Perhaps it would be best not to think of classes, but of social worlds, so that Runciman belongs to a social world and Spender to another, and the navvies belong to a social world and the Queen belongs to a social world, and though the worlds overlap, they sort of float about in the cloud that is Britain.

Steven, in his world, amuses himself and amuses others, not

simply because he so enjoys it, but because of the high-pitched wit and irony in his voice which suggests that such enjoyment must not be taken seriously, must amuse; and Stephen is from a world without such irony, so his social life does not amuse. If there is irony in Stephen, it is mostly in self-deprecation; Steven's irony has a high degree of self-regard in it. Or so I sense. If I were Proust, I would develop this, especially from the point of view of Nikos and me, for though we are friends with both Stephen and Steven, they are hardly friends with each other, but seem to belong in different worlds within the world of Great Britain.

Steven has, he has said, 'endless anecdotes,' and will ask, 'Would you like to hear the story of my dancing with a lady who danced with the Prince Consort, Albert?'

Yes, we would.

'She was the daughter of the Duke of Montrose. Her mother was, I think, the Mistress of the Robes at the time that she came out, at the age of seventeen, and so a ball was given for her at Windsor, and, as it was for her, the Prince Consort danced with her. I met her when I was in my late twenties and she was in her eighties. I remember I sat next to her at lunch, and then I met her a little while later at a party where there was dancing. I very seldom dance – except in Scottish reels, at which I am quite good – but I couldn't resist when she suggested we might take a few steps together. She knew perfectly well why I was doing it, and after about three or four minutes – she really was past it, and I never really got to it – she said, "Well, now you can say you danced with someone who danced with the Prince Consort."'

He made a face as of mocking himself, drawing down the corners of his lips in the opposite of a smile, and he looked away.

———

Christopher Isherwood is staying at a friend's in South Kensington. He asked me to visit. I brought along a copy of The Ghost of Henry James and held it out to him when he opened the door, and he, seeing it, exclaimed, 'I've already read it! I love it!' and he showed me into the sitting room and pointed to a copy propped on the mantel of the fireplace.

As enthusiastic as he was, I felt something put on in the enthusiasm, as if he was trying to impress me for more than his enthusiasm about the novel, but with his own ability to enthuse exuberantly. I felt this, too, in the way he would from time to time exclaim, 'Gee!' the exclamation seemingly unrelated to whatever he was exclaiming 'gee!' about. I thanked him but kept my thanks somewhat reserved, because Nikos has told me often that I can sound affected by overstating my appreciation of another's appreciation of me, which affectation he calls the American need to be liked by everyone. Has Christopher himself become American in that way, for I so felt he wanted me to like him? I recall Stephen telling me that Auden said of Isherwood that he was 'falsch,' using the German, so perhaps Christopher has always given the impression of overstating both approval and disapproval in an over-exuberant way.

We went to a restaurant where we sat at a small square table with a votive candle between us, his gaunt but young face lit by the candle as he leaned towards me to speak. Again, I felt there was an overstatement in his telling me how happy he was that his lover, Don Bachardy, was now having sex with someone in London, Don Bachardy in bed with someone else as Christopher and I sat across from one another at the restaurant table.

He asked me if Nikos and I have an open relationship. I said, no, no, not really. Though Nikos has said that I can do whatever I want, he has also said I must not go to him after as if he were a father confessor and ask for his forgiveness. And, really, why should I have ever wanted to make love with anyone else when I have him?

Christopher smiled a rather compressed smile.

He did not ask more about Nikos, nor did he mention Stephen.

What did I feel, on my way home, about having spent the evening with someone who had been to me one of those mythological figures in a mythological world of cabaret? I felt that that world was 'falsch,' appropriately defined so in German because of

Christopher's Berlin stories, and that any attempt to hold it with nostalgia against the horrors of history – oh, to be in Weimar Berlin and indulge with wonderful freedom in sex while the Nazi troops are parading the streets! – is a very great affectation.

More and more, mythologies I once fantasized participating in fall apart when I am in contact with the people whom I once imagined mythological.

I told this to Stephen when I next saw him, and he stared at me, as if it hadn't occurred to him that I could begin to be critical of a world that I, standing outside, had no right to criticize.

Stephen once told me that his first sexual experience was with Wystan Auden when they were undergraduates at Oxford, any mythological vision of which has to be mitigated by Auden, in his rooms made dim by the curtains drawn all day, saying to Stephen, 'Now, dear, don't make a fuss,' and Stephen, always complying with a giggle to the matter-of-factness of Auden, not making a fuss.

———

After supper, sitting with Nikos on the sofa and together listening to music – Artur Schnabel playing a Beethoven sonata, the music as always chosen by Nikos, to whom I defer – I looked at him, his head lowered and his eyes closed to concentrate, and I wondered what his inner world is. Again and yet again, I imagine that inner world more historical, and as evolved from his history more cultural, than psychological. Today, he had a session with his analyst, and though he didn't talk about the session, and I did not ask him about it, I realize more than before that I'm not interested. I do not believe psychoanalysis can reveal in him what would be revealed by his history, by his culture, history and culture in one; and I think of Nikos' character, the character of his inner world, as formed by what I like to think the aristocracy of his being a Greek, of being able to claim a lineage, century upon century, through ancient Greece, through Hellenism, through Roman conquest, through Byzantium, even through the fall of Constantinople and the Ottoman occupation, through Revolution, and, as he lived it all, through Nazi occupation and through Civil War, through his education in Europe and America, through a Greece struggling to assert the ideals that Greece stands for, the surviving lineage evident, as I envisage him, in his delicate features, in the way his head is lowered and his eyes are closed as he concentrates on the music.

———

Because of the success of The Ghost of Henry James, I was asked by a producer at the BBC. if I'd be interested in doing a filmed tour of the house in Rye where he wrote his great novels.

The occupants of Lamb House are the novelist Rumer Godden and her husband. Part of the agreement in renting the house is that they would show visitors about, a duty I felt they found imposed on them a little when it came to a young American who couldn't know as much about Henry James as they did, and for whom it would have been more appropriate to give a televised tour. I did say I had read Godden's novel The River and liked it very much indeed. She gave me tea in the sitting room and informed me, as if to make her own presence more felt by me, that all the furniture in the room was hers. I recall chintz-covered armchairs and misty white curtains over the windows through which the trees outside were diffused into bright green blurs.

I had no sense of the presence of Henry James – none at all – and wondered what I had expected. In fact, according to Godden, there was very little in the house that had belonged to James, and all of what remained was in one room, just off the entry hall, which James called the telephone room as the telephone receiver was kept there. This was, if the truth be told, the only room normally open to visitors, at certain hours. I asked if I could see into it. Rumer Godden said, 'You won't see much,' and she and her husband let me go on my own.

The door to the telephone room was open. Inside, I looked at what had been recovered since the nineteen-forties, when most of James' possessions were sold at auction: his desk, some photographs, a walking stick, a cigar cutter, some books from his library. There was no telephone. Feeling low, and feeling, too, all the pretensions of my expectation, whatever my expectation had been, I left the room and closed the door. My hand on the door handle, it occurred to me that James had held the same handle and closed the same door, and a shiver passed up my arm.

When I returned to the sitting room, the tea things had been cleared, and Rumer Godden was gone. Her husband stood there, and I knew I must go. But, perhaps to make up for something, the husband, whose name I hadn't heard, told me there were still books from Henry James' library – old, uncut French novels – which I might find in secondhand bookshops in Rye, if I cared to look. He also said that James' knife boy – a boy who sharpened and cleaned the knives before stainless steel was invented and did other chores and errands – Burgess Noakes was still alive, and if I went to a certain pub I'd be bound to see him, a small, crumpled man, who would talk to me about James in exchange for a pint. Godden's husband warned me, however, that if I did speak to Noakes I'd find he remembered little about Henry James, and was not interested except for his pint.

I thought I wouldn't go to the pub, but I happened to pass it on my way down the hill on which Rye is built, and, drawn as I was to make whatever connections were available to me, I went in. The inside was musty and hardly lit with sunlight through the small windows, and there I saw a small crumpled man standing at the bar, wearing a hearing aid and blinking. I thought he must be Burgess Noakes, and I wanted to shake his hand, but he appeared too isolated to approach. I left.

Yes, gone, the ghost of Henry James.

———

While I'm making pottery with Ann, Adrian works in his study, but at tea time she asks me up to his desk and we have tea from Ann's cups.

I always bring Adrian little gifts, mostly postcards. One was of a Mughul miniature, which he liked. Another was of a Surrealist painting, and this he did not like, though his way of indicating he doesn't like something isn't to say so, but to laugh a little. Later, he told me he didn't like the Surrealists, but as an aside. My little gifts – besides postcards, a volume of three Greek poets, fancy cakes from a pastry shop in Hampstead – are offered partly with the wonder of how he will react to them.

I have no idea what Adrian's likes and dislikes are, and I realize that this both intimidates me and excites me. All I know for sure is that he has a vision, and vision excites me.

Once, having been first to Stephen Buckley's studio, I went to Church Row with a little work of Stephen's under my arm which I showed to Adrian: he looked at it for a long time on his desk, and I, standing by, wondered what he was thinking. When he said, 'Yes, I like it,' I was very pleased.

I'm always aware that his appreciation of something is, in a way, reflective, that it has to do with deciding something about the object. His appreciation is, I feel, based on the object's standing up or not to Adrian's awareness of it. I don't think: Adrian is coming to terms with the object. I think: the object is coming to terms with Adrian.

————

One afternoon, Henrietta Garnett came to visit me. She was wearing a huge ring, made, she said, from a fourteenth-century Portuguese sailor's silver buckle and an aquamarine which Ottoline Morrell (Henrietta called her 'Ot') had given to her grandmother, who had given it to her mother, who, Henrietta said, 'found it in a drawer among dirty socks, put it in an envelope which she didn't seal, misspelled my married name and got my address all wrong, and sent it off to me, and it arrived. And that is Bloomsbury.' Henrietta took the ring off and threw it across the room for me to catch.

————

Sonia invited Nikos and me for a birthday party for Francis. I sat next to Francis, and across the table was David Sylvester. I asked Francis if he ever worried about the meaning of art. 'No,' he said, and laughed.

'I just paint. I paint out of instinct. That's all.' 'Then you're very lucky others like your work,' David said. 'That's it,' Francis said. 'I'm very lucky. People, for some reason, buy my work. If they didn't, I suppose I'd have to make my living in another way.' I said, 'I'm sure people buy – or, if they can't buy, are drawn to – your work because you do paint out of instinct.' 'Perhaps it's just fashionable for people to be drawn now,' Francis said, and I said, 'No, that's not true, and you know it's not true.' He said, 'You're right. I do know. Of course I know. When I stop to wonder why I paint, I paint out of instinct.'

David looked very thoughtful. He sat away from the table, his large body a little slumped forward, his hands on his knees. Slightly wall-eyed, he stared at the table as he thought, and he finally asked Francis, very slowly, 'How does luck come into your work?'

Francis answered, 'If anything works for me in my paintings, I feel it is nothing I've made myself but something luck has given to me.'

David asked, 'Is there any way of preparing for the luck before you start working?'

'It comes by chance,' Francis said. 'It wouldn't come by will power. But it's impossible to talk about this.'

This excited me, and I immediately asked, 'Because it's a mystery?'

Francis jerked round to me, his eyes wide. He said flatly, 'I don't think one can explain it.'

I knew that I was trying to push Francis into saying something that I wanted him to say but which I also knew he disdained, as he disdained all forms of the mysterious.

Nikos warned me. 'Do you know what you're asking of Francis?'

I took the risk and asked Francis, 'Do you ever think that if one knew enough one might be able to explain the mystery of chance? And if one could explain would the mystery go and the work be destroyed?'

Francis pursed his lips. He could sometimes appear to be parodying the expression of deep thought. He asked me, 'Are you asking me if I ever think I could destroy my work by knowing too much about what makes it?'

'More than that. I wonder, have you ever wanted to explain what makes a painting work even though you knew the explanation would destroy it? I mean, do you ever worry that your work is too explicit in its meaning, not latent enough?'

Francis said, 'I can't wonder about that, because I know I would never be able to explain.' He laughed.

I take in the names – Hobhouse, Trevelyan, Huxley, Strachey – as almost words for a certain British history, and for a while I think of myself, in my name David Plante, as without history, until it comes to me to recall the Christian names of my parents – my mother Albina, my father Anaclet – or of aunts and uncles – Aldea, Cyriac, Homer, even Napoléon – or the names of nuns who taught us in my parochial school – Mère Saint Félix de Valoix – and my history takes on a deep historical depth, as far back at least to French neo-classicism if not further back, that French history transposed in name only to French Canada, but then lost in my French parish in New England when transposed from French Canada, so, really, I am disconnected from the French history in which such names had meaning, a history totally disconnected from France within the world I live in, but mine only in my fantasy history.

The only person in Britain who is aware of my being a Franco-American, and who understands historically what the names I've listed above connote, is Steven Runciman, who has said to me, his voice rising in pitch, 'North America should belong to *you*. You were dispossessed of what should be yours by the horrible William Pitt. And here you are, having made your home among the enemy.'

Thinking that we would introduce them, as if Nikos and I have taken on such a role in London that we can introduce people to one another whom we think would be of interest to one another, we invited Steven and Caro Hobhouse to dinner, and found it was as if they were relatives, knowing each other's family so familiarly they may have been distant cousins. Nikos and I simply listened.

Caro said that one of the pleasures of family gatherings, which

seem to occur with them all bouncing about together in a large
bed, is to sort out just how they are related.

And I must put this in: we thought Steven would like to meet
the writer on food Claudia Roden, whose history seems to be the
history of the whole of the Middle East. We asked them to a restaurant, and in conversation Steven said that the most noble name in
the world is Cohen, but it must be a Ha-Cohen, and Claudia,
smiling the kind of sad smile she has as if aware of all the history
from which she has emerged, said, 'My grandfather was a
Ha-Cohen.' He was, chief rabbi in Aleppo, Syria.

My second novel, Slides, published, not to good notices.

Leave out my novels.

David Hockney drew the dust jacket for Slides, back and front, of delicate drawings of slides. He said that his assistant Mo, thinking they were in fact slides, tried to pick them up. In a bookshop, I found a copy of the novel, the dust jacket evidently stolen, the novel left behind.

———

Nikos told me that Miss Richards at their last session revealed to him that she was sorry to tell him she would be leaving England to go to live in Australia. If he was upset, he didn't show it, but I was annoyed that she had – as I saw it – rejected him.

I said, 'I never understood why you should have made yourself vulnerable in wanting to have analysis.'

He shrugged.

Could it be that I do not reach into him at the depth that is in him, a depth where I feel he is defeated, at the depth of his Greek history?

If I could revive him from that defeat, if I could!

———

I thought that in ending his analysis, Nikos would resume his life as before, but suddenly, when we were together on a Sunday night in our bed, the bedside light still lit, he said, aggressively, 'You never cared about my analysis, never now care how much I suffer the end of it.'

I said, 'When I suffer anxiety, you tell me it's nonsense, that I'm being self-indulgent.'

'You are,' he said.

'I am, and you've taught me that I am.'

I could see that his eyes were open and that he was listening intently to me.

'You taught me to see that my inner darkness means nothing because it refers only to me, and I just think of what is outside me, the darkness outside me. In a way, you've made me a good Communist, more aware of historical darkness than personal darkness. And now you tell me you have this inner darkness, which is yours alone, and you expect me to cater to all the aggression that results from it just because it's yours. No, I won't. I'm entirely supportive of you—'

He stopped me. 'No,' he said, 'you're not.'

'How can you say that? I am. I know I am. I'm as supportive of you as you are of me, which is, I know, total. But to be total doesn't mean to indulge you. And you know the difference. You have made me see the difference. You have no reason to be suffering.'

He said, quietly, 'Let's go to sleep,' and he reached out to shut off the light at his side of the bed, and when the room was dark he turned to me and put an arm over me and fell asleep.

———

For the Easter Resurrection services, we went to the Russian Orthodox Cathedral in Ennismore Gardens, as we've been before. Nikos does not want to go to the Greek Orthodox Cathedral in Moscow Road, he doesn't say why, but I sense in him the resentment of someone from a refugee family who never felt at home among Athenians, and in historical fact were never made to feel at home, even to having their own cemetery, the Second Cemetery, where Nikos' father is buried, all of them remaining among themselves as refugees, Constantinopoli, who call Istanbul Constantinople.

But, if Nikos feels there is some distance kept from him as a refugee by Athenian Greeks who form the closed provincial world around the Greek Orthodox Cathedral in Moscow Road, he keeps a much greater distance because he, as a refugee, feels he is superior to them. The refugee Greeks were – they are – superior, as made evident when, at the time of the Catastrophe, they had to move from Turkey to Greece and transformed provincial Athens into a cosmopolitan city with their much more evolved culture. The Greeks of the diaspora, the 'Oriental' Greeks, have much more knowledge of bureaucracy in business transactions for having worked in the bureaucratic class of Byzantium from long before Byzantium fell to the Turks, and, after the fall, for having

Another messenger for Nikos
with love from Stephen, June 66

The Youthful David by Andrea del Castagno, sent from Stephen Spender to Nikos with the message, 'Another messenger for Nikos, with love from Stephen', June 1966. Nikos thought this 'messenger' by way of Stephen made inevitable our meeting each other.

Saturday afternoon on the King's Road, 1966: a funfair at which people dressed for a different world… I sketched three interesting characters.

Patrick Procktor's watercolour of me and Stephen Spender, 1967. Very good of Stephen.

My watercolour of Nikos, San Andrea di Rovereto di Chiavari, 1968.

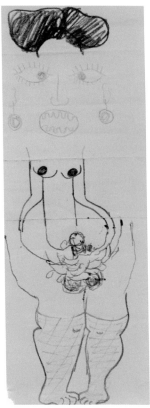

Three 'Exquisite Corpses'
from many dinner parties
Nikos and I gave for friends
during the seventies,
everyone clearly fixated on
the inventive parts.

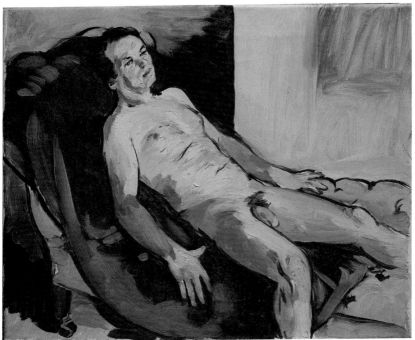

Sandra asked to paint my portrait – in the nude, if I didn't mind. I didn't mind. Then she suggested I come again and pose with another male model, very sexy, both of us nude. 'And you never know what will happen.' Dear, dear Sandra. Kitaj gave me the painting after Sandra died.

R. B. Kitaj's portrait of me, *David in Russia*. Nikos pointed out that the hands come from icons by Theophanis the Greek, mentor of Andre Rublev, the great Russian painter of icons. Kitaj didn't know this, but was very pleased, as his paintings are filled with references.

In the 1980s in London, while Keith Milow was fabricating a series of lead pieces, he heard of the death of Joseph Beuys, a mentor and an inspiration. Though the pieces were intended to be nameless memorials, as he worked on them they became charged, almost imprinted, with the presence Keith retained of having met the great man. This is one of those memorials. Lead, wood, putty, 1986.

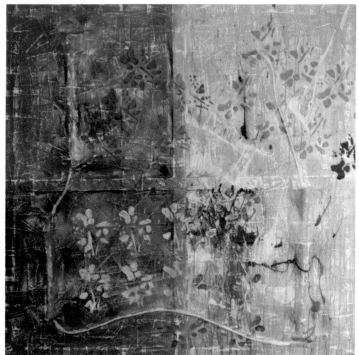

A note from Stephen Buckley: *There have been a number of paintings called FIELD over the years, none of them of a particular field, just as the flower stencil, first cut in 1963, is not of a particular flower. This flora universalis has made regular appearances over five decades in various paintings, always in colour.*

This was painted in 1972 by Adrian Stokes after an operation on his brain; he seemed to be painting on air. It is the first of eleven paintings from before he died. He gave me this, the art critic Lawrence Alloway was given the last, and the rest belong to the Tate.

functioned as tax collectors for the Sultans. This position of power and money allowed them to send their sons and daughters to be educated in Paris, Berlin, London, and so be much more in contact with Western Europe than the Athenian Greeks. Nikos tells me his mother, until she had to leave Constantinople, would never have considered even visiting the dusty, not Greek but, she said, Albanian town of Athens.

Distancing himself from the Greeks he feels superior to, Nikos for some years chose to go for the Easter Resurrection service to the Russian Cathedral. At these services, I liked carrying a lit candle and, after the archbishop shouted out, 'Christos anesti,' shouting out 'Alithos anesti' along with Nikos, those Greek words within a Russian liturgy resounding within Russian history, which multiple historical resonances I know Nikos enjoys as much as I do, perhaps he even more than I do.

(And here I make a connection with going with Nikos to the Christmas midnight Mass at the Roman Brompton Road Oratory and, standing behind a porphyry pillar because the church was too packed for us to have a view of the altar, I heard Latin being chanted, and, too, the Greek Kyrie Eleison, and with the smell of incense I felt I could be in ancient Rome. Too many connections, too many, and how can I deal with them except to let them occur?)

In the Russian Orthodox Cathedral, with our candles not yet lit for the Resurrection, we were standing near a young woman who stared up at the dome, her eyes concentrating as if at something she fixed on there, and suddenly she began to scream, a high, piercing scream, and a woman on the other side of her from us took her in her arms until she was quiet. The ceremony was being broadcast throughout the Soviet Union, so those devout there would have heard the scream and wondered what it was about. Nikos said we should leave. Back home, we set the table for the mageritza (that special Easter soup traditionally made from sheep's innards, but which Nikos, having become a vegetarian, made from vegetable stock and lots of onions and dill) and tsoureki (the Easter brioche with hard-boiled red eggs baked in it, bought the day before from a Greek bakery near the Greek Orthodox Cathedral, which we walked to, passing a house with a blue plaque on it commemorating Constantine Cavafy, who had lived there, and, and and – Where was I? Back home with Nikos for our Easter supper, the radio turned on low to a broadcast of the Mass and the chant still going on in the Russian Cathedral, and we heard the scream again and shortly after the siren of an ambulance, and Nikos turned the radio off, and we ate in silence.

———

Our rows. Almost all have to do with Nikos' need for order. I'm orderly too, but Nikos' need for order is far in excess of mine. He complains if, in the bathroom, I leave soap in the soap dish that becomes slimy, if in flossing my teeth I speckle the mirror, if I squeeze the toothpaste tube from the middle, if I do not lower the seat of the toilet bowl, if I do not hang the bath mat over the rim of the tub, if I do not turn on or off the light by the little wooden knob at the end of the cord but by the cord, if, if, if, oh, if I replace the roll of loo paper so that it rolls outwardly rather than, as he insisted, inwardly, against the wall.

Nikos listened when Steven Runciman told him that he has been in ducal houses, even princely houses, where the loo paper is always rolled outwardly, then said he always rolled the loo paper inwardly.

When I told Dee Wells, the wife of A. J. Ayer, about the rules in the bathroom, she exclaimed, 'Nikos is so anal-retentive, it's a wonder he needs a loo.'

Stephen has told us that what made it possible for us to live together domestically is that we were both orderly, which he is not, Natasha having to accept the way he simply lets his overcoat fall off from him onto the floor of the entry hall. Yes, I am orderly, but not to the extent that the socks have to be lined up in the drawer. I try to be amused by Nikos' fastidiousness, but when I shout that I will not have our lives reduced to the minutiae of order, he shouts back, 'I will not live in bedlam,' and I'm not amused.

And he never, ever apologizes, as if constitutionally incapable of apology.

———

When I arrived in Church Row, Ann told me that Adrian is dying of cancer of the brain.

I didn't make any pottery, but went directly to his study to see him. He stood, we embraced, and though he was weak he refused to sit. His skin looked gray and matt. Ann had warned me that he had very little concentration, but he seemed pleased to see me, however embarrassed he also seemed to be about his state. Finally, he sat at his desk, and for some reason laughed, in a totally expressionless way. Ann put a cup of tea on his desk, but he simply looked at it and said he wouldn't have any. He wouldn't because he couldn't lift the cup and he didn't want to ask for help. Ann held the cup up for him to drink. Again, he laughed, but again without expression. After he finished his tea, we talked a little. He said, 'I feel very calm.' Then he said he would like to be alone.

When I returned some ten days later, I found Adrian painting while Ann made a pot on her wheel. A large, loose, but finished painting was propped against the fireplace, and when I saw it I said, 'It's so beautiful.' He laughed, now expressing warmth and a curious detachment. Adrian has the ability to be both warm and detached at once, in the same way, I suppose, one can be both pleased by praise and indifferent to it. He immediately said, 'You must have it.' I said I couldn't. He said I must. I looked towards Ann, who said, yes, I must have it.

This was the first of the series he started after he was given pain-killers – pills that, he said, also made him 'very happy.'

He was, however, more confused than ever, and at moments he knew this. He said, 'I'm not really normal, you know.'

I took the painting away. It is of a cup and saucer and bottles as if almost dissolved in the loose, lyrical brushstrokes, brushstrokes so lightly applied that they appear to have been painted on air.

On my next visit, while Ann and I potted to Greek bouzouki

music Adrian painted in his studio at the top of the house. I
went up. He was hardly able to support the brush. He was painting bottles, and he wanted them arranged in a certain way, but
as he wasn't able to articulate his directives I couldn't understand how he wanted me to arrange the bottles. He'd point with
his brush and say something unintelligible, and I, feeling that I
should be able to understand, would place a bottle upright, or
on its side, but the arrangement was never what he wanted. I
said, Just say yes if I do the right thing, no if I do the wrong
thing, but this didn't work any better. He became impatient,
and said, 'It doesn't matter.' Then he seemed to become resigned.
He'd gone far from seeing objects in terms of his ideas of them;
in the last paintings – there were eleven of them – he had to take
objects as they were, beyond his control in every other way but
to paint them.

Do I understand Adrian's writing? I find it difficult to penetrate
through the dazzle of his metaphors and similes, and find I have,
not an understanding, but a 'sense' of his vision. I like to think he
uses the dazzle of his imagery, his metaphors and similes deliberately as one with the expression of his vision, not so much to
understand a work of art but to have the most vivid 'sense' of it.

No doubt I'm reading myself into Adrian's writing.

And so, too, the writing of Richard Wollheim – after reading his
Art and its Objects I look at a work of art as if it expands and
expands, not into an understanding of it, but into the 'sense' of it,
to mark a difference between understanding the meaning of something, which is difficult for me, and having a 'sense' of the meaning
of something, which is to me the most vivid appreciation of the
something I can have.

I have a 'sense' of what you mean, I say to Nikos, when he
explains a philosophical point about aesthetics, which was his
subject when he was a student at Harvard.

Why does the recollection come to me of Nikos telling me of
that time he was abandoned by a lover on the island of Poros and
he sat by the sea with the scent of lemon blossoms wafting from the

lemon groves on the distant mainland, the beauty of which was a consolation to him?

———

Nikos woke from a nightmare, shouting, and I woke. He said he dreamed that someone came into the room who was, he thought, me, and got into bed with him; he put his arms around the person and suddenly realized the person was not me, and this terrified him.

———

I recall that I was once amazed by Virginia Woolf's The Waves, and now wonder:

> The sun was sinking. The hard stone of the day was cracked and light poured through its splinters. Red and gold shot through the waves, in rapid running arrows, feathered with darkness. Erratically rays of light flashed and wandered, like signals from shrunken islands, or darts shot through laurel groves by shameless, laughing boys. But the waves, as they neared the shore, were robbed of light, and fell in one long concussion, like a wall falling, a wall of grey stone, unpierced by any chink of light.

I wrote this in response:

> She liked to use similes, and so she wrote of storm waves falling like walls, wall after wall crashing like the walls of a castle, the sunlight shot-arrows flashing through the air, and the seaweed sunken tattered robes, and the surf about the broken blocks of stone like clouds, clouds that come in to cover over the ruins and then go out to reveal the ruins, a reversed sky where the ruins float on ebbing and flowing clouds – And she paused to ask: Like and like and like and like? What is the likeness likeness likens itself to? And she put her pen down and closed her eyes.

Doubts about her use of metaphor and simile. Doubts about the use of metaphor and simile, which would never have occurred to Jane Austen as a way of enlivening writing which may otherwise be dead.

———

Stephen asked me if I would fetch the first edition of the two volumes of Du côté de chez Swann, left for him at reception at the Savoy Hotel by Pauline de Rothschild. I prepared myself to ask for a package left by 'the Baroness Pauline de Rothschild,' imagining that the receptionist would be in awe of me, he wondering who I was who was asking for a package left by the Baroness to be delivered to someone of the same world as she was. Of course he wasn't in awe, and indifferently handed me the package. Still, I was in awe of myself, and sitting in the Underground train with the package on my knees, I imagined the others in the carriage would know, simply by looking at me, that the package contained first editions of Proust from the Baroness de Rothschild which I was passing on to Stephen Spender, I participating in both their worlds by my connecting the two as a delivery boy. That I was carrying Proust, as if he himself were contained in a little coffin on my lap and his ghost hovered around it, seemed to me to expand the world outwardly into a world of literature that would be my world when I wrote it all down in my diary, creating an aura in which the entry in my diary would be read as Proustian. So here it is – my little Proustian episode.

———

A visit to Ann Stokes, she too preoccupied with Adrian to work. He will suddenly think he needs cigarettes and then goes out to buy them, Ann directly behind him; he pays for the cigarettes with a comb, and Ann, without his noticing, pays with cash, then she follows him back to the house with his cigarettes, though he does not smoke. Her face red, Ann stared at me with large eyes and I stared back.

A short time after, it seems, Ann Stokes had her annual pottery sale – her many-coloured pots and plates, and, too, ceramic birds and toads and fish spread out on tables and bookshelves and even an ironing board – and many people there, while, upstairs, Adrian was very ill in bed. Ann had arranged to have an intercom connected throughout the rooms where the sale was taking place in case Adrian should call her. Over the voices of the guests Adrian's breathing was heard, rather rough, and then, suddenly, very rough and rattling. A doctor was at the pottery sale, and he went up to Adrian and came down to say Adrian was dying. He asked Ann if she would want him taken to hospital, but Ann pleaded, no, he should die at home. Nikos and I were leaving with other guests, but Ann asked us to stay, a few close friends including Richard and Mary Day Wollheim, and Ann's sister Margaret Mellis, who was herself once married to Adrian, and Margaret's son Telfer by Adrian, and Philip, the son of Ann and Adrian, the sons both cousins and half-brothers. Ann, excited, thought we must be hungry, and over the telephone ordered tongue, and was upset that when the tongue arrived it was not salt, as she had asked for salt tongue. I felt it was very strange to be in the sitting room of the house, eating tongue and bread, while, continuing through the intercom, Adrian's always deepening rough and rattling breathing sounded loud in our silence. After a while, Nikos said we should go, and, embracing Ann and Margaret, we did. In the morning, we rang Ann, who said that Adrian died shortly after we left, and that she and her sister had spent the night together in bed speaking about their husband.

———

When I expressed to Richard Wollheim wonder at why sculptures on medieval cathedrals were placed so high no one could see them, he, atheist that I know him to be, said in a very matter-of-fact way, 'For the greater glory of God.'

———

Stephen says that to him to fall in love is to find himself hallucinated by another, and I understand this, if to be hallucinated by another is to be in a constant state of wonder about the other, to ask, over and over, who is this other? how is it that I am with this other? why am I with this other? These moments of heightened wonder occur when, lifting my eyes from a book I am reading, I see Nikos watering the plants in the sitting room, and I simply do not understand what it is in him and in me that makes me love him as I do. I feel the strain of that love as of my very heart straining to go out towards him, drawn by his presence at moments when he, as if so unaware of me he might be alone in the room, is concentrating on watering his plants. I put down my book and stare at him. This sense of hallucination in the wonder has, I think, nothing to do with any self-interested impulse, and not a sexual impulse, but is a more primitive impulse; and at these moments I am convinced by the love that religions, inspired by that primitive impulse, are meant to make central to their visions, but which love they so very, very rarely act on.

———

Through John and Hugh, who spend their winters in London as the unheated villa is too cold, we met Patrick Kinross, with whom they are guests, and he invited Nikos and me to drinks. He is known, most reputably, for his book on Atatürk, and he has also written a book on the Duke and Duchess of Windsor. He stayed with them in their house outside Paris and told this story: the Duchess called upstairs, 'David, luncheon is ready,' to which the Duke responded, 'Just a moment, darling, I have something on my mind,' which made her shout out, 'On your what?'

Among the other guests, all much older than Nikos and I, was Charlotte Bonham Carter, widow of Sir Edgar, who, blinking rapidly as she talked, mentioned T. E. Lawrence. I stopped her to ask, amazed at the possibility, if she had known Lawrence of Arabia. Blinking even more rapidly, she looked at me with a frown of annoyance and said, 'He used to come, and we'd see him; he used to go, and we didn't see him. Why do you ask?' I said, 'Well, can you imagine someone from far outside the world he inhabited excited to make contact with someone who was in contact with him?' She blinked even more rapidly and said, 'Yes, I can imagine that.'

I asked her who was the most interesting person she had met, and, blinking even more rapidly, she said, 'My dear, I think it must have been Puccini.'

Patrick Kinross told the story of visiting, as a young man, an old aunt who had been present at the assassination of President Abraham Lincoln. When he asked her, 'What was it like?' all she answered was, 'It was a great fuss.'

Some time later, I drove Charlotte Bonham Carter to the wedding of Deborah Rogers, my literary agent, and Michael Berkeley, composer, in Wales. In her old age, she has curvature of the spine, so had to lift her entire body to turn and look at me, which she did, always blinking, when she inquired, 'You're American, aren't you?' I said I was. Then she asked, rolling the R, 'Do you know the Roosevelts?' I said I didn't. 'How odd,' she said, 'I thought all Americans knew one another.'

No, I didn't know the Roosevelts, and, though it was part of my American history, I had never met anyone in America whose great-, or even great-great-aunt had been at President Lincoln's assassination. I do have friends in America, though I never think of them as all together connecting up to make a world, and I certainly never think of my family in this way. In England, it seems, if you meet one person, you find that within a short time – at a gallery opening, at a publisher's party to launch a book, at a private drinks or dinner party – you are connecting people to one another, especially in large, interconnecting families, with the deepening knowledge that they do all belong to a world that is larger than any one of them and that contains them all.

I've met Charlotte Bonham Carter any number of times (once at a lecture on stone anchors in the East Mediterranean where she sat next to me, she muttering from time to time, 'Fascinating,' and I wondering what I was doing at a lecture on stone anchors in the

East Mediterranean), but she never remembers who I am, though she always treats me matter-of-factly as someone to whom she would talk intimately about someone else whom she is intimate with, expecting me to know this person as well as she does. It hasn't taken me long to realize that the English are not reserved, but assume, even on a first meeting, the openness of telling me about a hysterectomy or about a daughter suffering from anorexia or a son who was being sent down from Cambridge for drugs. Lady Charlotte, as she is called though I learned she wasn't the daughter of a duke, a marquis, or an earl, and was perhaps called Lady Charlotte by people who didn't really know her but thought her too special to be anything but the daughter of a duke, a marquis, or an earl, whereas those who really did know her, such as John and Hugh, simply call her Charlotte, herself seems to imagine, with no sense at all of exclusiveness, that she and everyone else belongs to an England of country houses and a London of the Covent Garden Opera House, embassies, and the Royal Horticultural Hall.

Lady Charlotte is thought not to have known about the more intimate aspects of marriage on her wedding day, when she, arranging flowers on the altar, was asked who was to be married and responded, 'I am,' and when asked where she and her husband were to go on their honeymoon answered, 'I don't know about him, but I am going to Afghanistan.'

I asked her at one time about her travels, and she said, emphatically, 'I draw the line at Afghanistan.'

She sometimes visits John and Hugh in their villa outside Lucca, traveling by train and with a bag of hard-boiled eggs, sleeping in the train stations if her connections leave her in the waiting room to spend the night.

John told me that he and Hugh were in a restaurant with her, where she often made gestures to communicate with four men sitting at a table near by, and when asked who the men were she responded, 'I'm not sure, but I think the Amadeus String Quartet.'

Natasha Spender has lively stories to tell about her. Once, seeing her enter a reception and look about, Natasha, thinking she might be looking for someone she knew, went to her, and Charlotte put an index finger to her lips and said, 'Not a word, not a word, my dear, we can talk any time,' and passed her to meet people she hadn't met.

She is famous for appearing at intervals at performances, but during the performances themselves she is out at other events, even if this requires a change of clothing which she does in ladies' rooms, and at the interval of a musical evening she will say, 'Splendid, splendid, but I did think the brass was rather too loud,' to the total bemusement of the person she addresses because the performance was of a piano and violin duet.

She could only have evolved in England.

––––––––

Whenever I am in the West End, I stop to look in at the shows galleries are putting on. I stopped in the Kasmin Gallery in Bond Street and found the entire large clear white space filled with one work by Anthony Caro, Prairie, a vast bright yellow sheet of metal supported as if magically at one corner so the vast bright yellow sheet of metal appeared to float. I was struck: this is a great work of art. This is sublime!

––––––––

John Russell lives with Suzi Gablik. They give drinks parties where Nikos and I have met, oh, so many. Francis almost always comes. Suzi said that expecting nothing from Francis is a condition of one's friendship with him. At one drinks party, I found Francis standing by himself and went to speak to him. He was wearing tight gray trousers, a black turtleneck pullover, and another turtleneck pullover on top of this, but this one white. I imagined his body as having very thin legs and a bulging belly. The sleeves of both pullovers were pushed up, showing his powerful forearms and red hands.

I knew it was risky – but I liked taking such risks with Francis

– but I tried to start a conversation by saying that the writer Jean Rhys had told me that she had flashes of religion. 'Does she, now?' Francis asked. Drunk myself, I asked him if he ever did. He laughed. 'Never, never never never never never.' I had heard him say this before, but, as before, I wanted to know what he was vulnerable to, and I asked him if he had any addiction. He didn't have any, he said. I said mine is sleep. 'Sleep?' he asked. 'Really?' I asked him, 'How much do you sleep?' He said, 'I get up every morning at seven o'clock.' 'I wish I could do that,' I said. He asked me, 'But don't you like consciousness, David? I love conscious life. I love being conscious.' He stuttered, but he didn't laugh.

———

We went to the opening of the Cecil Beaton show at the National Portrait Gallery, curated by Roy Strong, the director of the museum.

At the entrance was a photograph of a totally naked young man and woman, which announced that the National Portrait Gallery had opened itself up to the times, and there was an excitement in the dense gathering of the opening – yet, as if assumed among everyone that the opening had always been there privately but never quite announced publicly, as if the openness to sexual frankness had been a given among everyone there and only required an exhibition to make the inward given an outward given. So, no sense of shock, but of: yes, of course, of course. Yet, a sense of liberation in the of course.

Sitting on the top step of the flight just outside the exhibition was the most beautiful person I had ever seen, a young man wearing a silk bomber jacket embroidered on the back with a Japanese roaring lion, and standing around him, looking down at him, was a circle of admirers. Among them I saw Peter Schlesinger. I asked him, 'Who is that?' Peter whispered, 'His name is Eric Boman. He was a friend of Salvador Dalí and Marilyn Monroe.' I stared at this Eric Boman, who kept his eyes fixed on the steps below him.

———

For Easter we went for the Resurrection services at the Cypriot Orthodox church with Julia Hodgkin. She was amused that while the priest was at the altar a man was leaning on it as if they were having a business talk while the priest was officiating. There I saw Öçi's mother Mrs. Ullmann and his brother Tony, but I knew from the past that she was suspicious of me for my relationship with Öçi, so I stayed away even from asking how Öçi was in New York.

———

Ann Stokes, to supper, asked us what we thought of her joining a circus, as she had always longed to ride into a circus ring on the head of an elephant.

———

Having commissioned the historian Roy Strong to write a monograph on the paintings of Charles I on horseback by Van Dyck, Nikos went to Brighton where Roy Strong lives to talk about the book, and I went along with Nikos. We walked along the seafront. Roy was wearing knickerbockers with, I felt, the same aplomb with which, in the age of Charles I, he would have worn a wide-brimmed slouch hat, a lace collar, knee-breeches and silk stockings and shoes with pompoms. Roy appears to assume that all of British history is his, and he can, rightly, inhabit whatever period he chooses, and though I imagine him at ease in Elizabethan London, the elegance of early seventeenth-century British court life under Charles I would do, with poems, medals, eulogies, music, and such grand masques as Britannia Triumphans, all to end in the execution of Charles I by Oliver Cromwell.

Roy said he thinks of me as a Henry James character.

Nikos and I often have dinner parties in our small flat in Battersea, and often enough Francis Bacon comes. More often, Francis invites us out to restaurants, sometimes with as many as ten or twelve people around tables pushed together. At a restaurant, we met Francis' friends Dicky Chopping and Denis Wirth–Miller, both artists. Francis at restaurants is always as attentive to the waiters as he is to his friends, and whenever a waiter puts a bottle of wine on the table Francis hands him a pound note. I once saw him put a pound note in a bread basket that was being passed around by the people at the table. After, Nikos and I would drive Francis home to his studio flat in Reece Mews, in South Kensington, and wait for him to open his narrow door among the wide doors of the mews garages and climb his steep flight of stairs, sometimes stumbling and falling to his knees as he went up.

And we see him at drinks parties. At one party, he was introduced to Lee Miller, then Francis came to where Nikos and I were standing with Stephen and Natasha and said to us, laughing dryly, 'You mean, that's the Lee Miller whose photograph was taken by

Man Ray? I would have thought her beauty would have remained, but nothing of it has, has it?' We also laughed, too intimidated by Francis to stand up to him.

He had arrived drunk, and he was almost incomprehensible when he spoke. After Nikos had left our group because he wanted to but wouldn't stand up to Francis, Francis said to Stephen and Natasha and me – in reference to what, I didn't know, but I wondered if he was thinking of George – 'In every relationship there's always a cherished and a cherisher, always a cherished and a cherisher.' I said, 'I wonder if that's true. In my case – or, rather, in Nikos' and my case – I don't know who is the cherisher and who is the cherished.' 'Oh yes, you know,' Francis said, 'oh yes, and don't deny it. Don't deny being cherished. Don't deny it. Take it. Let yourself be cherished. You're the cherished one. And don't deny yourself being cherished.' Natasha said, 'But you don't understand, Francis. David is the cherisher.' Stephen said nothing. Francis lurched away with a jerk of his whole body, as if someone had suddenly called him away, and staggered from person to person.

Natasha left Stephen and me to talk with others, and Francis staggered back to us. Stephen asked him if he was working on something new, and Francis, loosely nodding his head, said, 'Yes. I'm doing paintings of two bodies locked together. Locked. Locked together.' He lost his balance whenever he paused to talk, but each time he regained his balance he repeated, 'Locked together, two bodies.' I said, 'Then they'll be love paintings.' He leaned towards me and almost fell onto me, his wine splashing from his glass. 'Yes,' he said, 'yes.' Then he stumbled backwards, his head up, and there suddenly came to his face a look of such terror that I laughed. I then realized that he was about to fall backwards, but before I could reach out to grab him he regained his balance and turned towards the wall and went to stand with his back against it. He mistook a door for the wall, however, and when he leaned against the door ajar it gave way, but, again, he righted himself just as I rushed to him to stop him from falling. Leaning now against the solid wall, he said, 'I want real tragedy.'

———

I am always aware of, even always in a daze of wonder about, the world I'm in. When Nikos and I were at the house of Patrick Kinross, I wondered why he, showing us into his sitting room – what I guess he calls his drawing room – stopped to stand still to admire, as he finally said, the proportions of the room, as if he had suddenly become aware of the proportions, which I too admired with the wonder of the room that appeared to float within its white proportions, the furniture and pictures suspended within the space.

And how could I not wonder, the other guests at dinner John Fleming and Hugh Honour, why the roast chicken, which Patrick had prepared, had so many feathers left on it, which, however, he seemed not at all to be aware of, nor John and Hugh, but which Nikos and I smiled about across the elegantly laid table?

Patrick seems always to be in a vague state of suspension.

———

Sorting out papers, as I often do, because Nikos and I keep everything from postcards and invitations to exhibitions to letters and drafts of fiction, I came across a story that Jean Rhys and I wrote together after the incident in which, both of us drunk in her hotel room, I used the lavatory then she, and –

He heard, 'Maurice!'

He went to the lavatory door and leaned close.

'Maurice!'

'Yes?'

'Help me, please.'

His hand on the door handle, he hesitated. He opened slowly but quickly closed the door when he saw Lucy Nicholson holding her frock over her raised knees, her feet off the floor, her large, loose knickers about her ankles, leaning sideways, stuck in the toilet.

He had forgot to put the toilet seat down.

Jean told me that if I ever found myself again in such a situation with a lady, I should place a glass of water and an aspirin beside her bed and leave quietly, and on telling the story later I must make it funny. As we did writing this story, giggling.

Dear Jean, now dead and cremated and ashes.

She once said to me: all of literature is a great lake, and there are rivers that feed the lake, such as Dostoyevsky and Tolstoy and Dickens and Balzac, and there are trickles such as Jean Rhys, but however little one must always believe in feeding the lake.

———

Peter Schlesinger has left David Hockney for Eric Boman, and David is very upset. The many people around David comfort him, and, slumped over, he puts a hand to his chin and sticks out his lower lip then says, 'Oh, I don't know.'

———

Jean Rhys once told me that she writes to let everything go, and I do often think, Let it go, let it all go, though I'm not sure what the 'all' is that I want to let go of.

———

We are often invited by Eva Neurath, the head of the publishing house Thames & Hudson, to drinks parties, to dinner parties, to the opera or to recitals.

She is not Jewish, but in Nazi Berlin she identified with Jewish students, and when they were expelled she herself left school. She was fourteen years old. She educated herself. She married a Jew and with him and a son left Germany. She speaks about the horrors both with gravity and – not a contradiction – almost a lightness of tone, sometimes with a delicate snort of laughter. She would never, she says, have become what she became if it hadn't been for that 'chap' in Germany, meaning Hitler.

Often interrupting her talk with a nasal 'Hum?' which, it seems, is a way of making sure one is keeping up with her, Eva recounts stories from her past life. If we are having a meal with her in her home, just the three of us in the basement, her stories will include her asking us to go to the wine cellar for another bottle of wine, and I think this is not as a sudden request but yet another turn in the multi-cornered story. When the story all comes together, it is like a whole world and she is aware of all the details of its history: from her childhood in Berlin, the detail of being accidentally stuck in the eye with the nib of a pen, the detail of listening to her older sister play the piano in another room for Eva to guess which notes she was striking, the detail of her mother coming into her room to say goodnight before going off for the evening.

When she and her husband first arrived in London, Eva and her son lived in dim rooms, and she worked as a domestic; her husband was interned as an enemy alien on the Isle of Man. In the camp he became friendly with a German Jewish inmate, Walter Neurath, who had been living in England for some time. Working for the book 'packager' Adprint, Neurath had been responsible for a series, Britain in Pictures, which was seen as proof of his loyalty to Britain, and he was released. He was asked by Eva's husband, who remained interned, to help his wife and son, and Walter Neurath not only found Eva a job at Adprint, but started, in 1949, the publishing house Thames & Hudson with her. They married.

Eva is open with us, and she expects us to be open with her. She often asks Nikos and me about our relationship as lovers. 'I don't mean your sexual relationship. I mean your night-time relationship.' This amazed me until I knew that Eva is very attracted to Jungian analysis.

Nikos and I might be with her in the foyer of Covent Garden during an interval, all of us talking about the opera performance, when, suddenly, she will, with a quick, elegant movement of her wrist, grasp one's chin and, smiling, kiss one on the lips.

At an elaborate dinner party she gave, with many tables set in her dining room and sitting room, my place card had me sitting next to

Hattie (I think the spelling) Waugh, the daughter of Evelyn Waugh. She said to me, 'I hope I don't like you, as I have too many friends as it is,' which only someone brought up in a certain British culture could say, she not only not being offensive, but with a wit that I like to think I am British enough to be amused by.

———

Catharine Carver would want to be left out of this diary, but I can't leave her out. Editor at Chatto & Windus, she asked to read a novel I'd written in America, but was sorry to say it is unpublishable. Still, she takes an interest and reads what I've written and advises. A scout for Viking, Gwenda David, is waspish about Catharine liking her hot-water boiler to break down so she must bathe in cold water, but she did tell me that Catharine was/is the editor for writers such as Saul Bellow, John Berryman, e. e. cummings, Bernard Malamud, Elizabeth Bishop, Lionel Trilling, Katherine Anne Porter, Hannah Arendt, Flannery O'Connor. I know she is working closely with Leon Edel on a one-volume edition of his biography of Henry James. A while ago, Catharine rang me to say she would like to burn all the letters she had from whomever, and would I drive her out into the country to a field where she could make a pile and set it aflame? I answered that we would be arrested. I imagined the letters she wanted to burn would be from the writers whose work she had edited, and hoped that her not being able to make a pyre of them would deter her from destroying them in any less dramatic way. But she rang me a few days later to tell me she had thrown them all out into the rubbish.

Before she left America, she traveled to every state, then she left New York, where she was a publisher, to come to London, never to return to America.

All she ever said about her youth in America, without saying where in America, was that as a girl she once threw herself down a flight of stairs.

Nikos and I had a drinks party with an odd mixture, I suppose, but we like odd mixtures – including Catharine and Patrick Kinross, who sat side by side on a sofa, she small and grey and he large and red, Patrick smoking a cigar from which he flicked ashes onto Catharine's head. Leaving, she asked, 'Who is that wonderful man?' I now always think of Catharine as having ashes flicked on her head and finding the abasement – wonderful!

———

And I must include Joe McCrindle – stocky Joe, American living in London, rich, owns the Transatlantic Review, in which a short story of mine was published, my first time published. Joe also published in the Transatlantic Review the poem, 'Present Absent,' that Stephen wrote when I was staying with him at Saint Jérôme.

Heathcote Williams is the editor. He intimidates me, if not frightens me, for his startling good looks and startling bad behaviour, justified to himself, I think, as a Rimbaud qui essaie de dérégler ses sens. In a way, I envy him.

In the basement flat that is the office of the Transatlantic Review, I met B. S. Johnson, who appeared to me large and dark. He had a novel he had just published, the pages unbound so they could be arranged in different ways, the pages held in a box. It is called The Unfortunates. Adamant, Johnson said he was not interested in the creative imagination, no, but in describing a football match in itself, for itself; or the work of fishermen in itself for itself. He said he hated fiction. In his large dark presence I felt such a force of resentment towards the world for not recognizing his large dark presence.

When I heard he had killed himself in part for not being recognized, I thanked God that Nikos has always warned me about resenting the world at large for non-recognition, has told me that even the expectation of recognition is an egotistical self-indulgence. What did B. S. Johnson expect from the world?

Many of the walls of Joe's large flat are hung, it seems from ceiling to floor, with red-chalk drawings of male nudes.

He has massive drinks parties. If books do make a room, people who are celebrated make a party, though they do not in London. Once, I was surprised to see at one of Joe's drinks parties

Christopher Isherwood, standing alone with a drink, and I went to him. We talked about the revelation that Encounter magazine, of which Stephen was co-founder and editor, had recently been revealed as being financed by the American C.I.A. Christopher Isherwood said he wondered why there was such an objection to the C.I.A. financing the magazine, as it was in fact a very good magazine. This, I think, would have made Stephen pause, but would have enraged Natasha, who took the betrayal of Stephen as personal, it seemed, to herself. To account for all of this episode would so overweigh this diary that it would fall flat, and, in any case, however much I try simply to account, the matter has been looked at by people involved, which I was not. Natasha has written, for the record, her account, as though she were the commanding conscience of Stephen.

It happens often enough at drinks parties in London that I remark it: the most 'celebrated' guest is left alone. I recall one book-launch party for Toni Morrison at which she seemed to be left by herself in the midst of other people talking, she standing with a warm glass of white wine, and I, thinking this was impolite, went to speak to her. Is it because the Brits think it would be a presumption to speak to the 'celebrated,' and, not wanting to risk that grave social sin, ignore the very person the party is given for? I feel embarrassed for the Brits that that person does seem to be ignored, so, not being a Brit (yet), I do presume. I saw, at one of Joe's drinks parties, L. P. Hartley, standing alone and looking about, and I thought, But it's socially wrong to leave him alone! so introduced myself and said I hoped to live long enough to see my past as another country, and this seemed to please him, and it pleased me to be able to speak to L. P. Hartley shortly before he died.

Joe's parties appear to fluster him terribly.

———

I see less and less of Rachel Ingalls, which I'm sorry for, but she seems not to want to see me. Both of us American, we have known each other since before we published, when we saw a lot of each other. We talked about writers and writing, especially about Ernest Hemingway.

Her first book, Theft, is a passionate retelling of the death of Jesus Christ, a great lament. In the novel, she reduced the settings to timeless images, such as rocks, prison bars, cups.

Whereas I am eager to meet critics who may, just by getting to know me, write in my favour, Rachel will not meet any, as she thinks that would be opportunistic and falsify her as a writer true to the writing.

Whatever the weather, Rachel always appears – or so I think of her – wearing gloves with buttons at the wrists and carrying a fold-up umbrella.

She has never invited me to where she lives, which I assume is one room, with a telephone in a passage outside. She requests that I do not ring her whenever, but send her a postcard to let her know just when I'll ring, and she sends back a postcard to confirm or not that she will answer. She may not be able to because she is writing or washing her hair.

Her style is of great clarity, and her subjects have become more and more strange, such as a young couple in a car lost in the countryside, the car attacked by a mass of man-eating frogs. It is the remarkable clarity of the writing that raises the dark subject to works of high literature.

I introduced her to Sonia Orwell, who invited us to tea and, as Sonia can do with flashing spontaneity, she took from a wall a painting that William Coldstream had done of her and gave it to Rachel.

She does not respond to my cards or, even, letters asking if I have offended her. Uncompromising as she is about standards, perhaps Rachel thinks that I have let go of standards.

––––––

As I read more of Victor Shklovsky I find more in his books that is meaningful to me, not only in the way I think of writing, but in my constant awareness of connections, for he was in love with Elsa Triolet.

And of course I am charmed by him into imagining Lili Brik:

Lili Brik loved things – earrings in the shape of golden flies and antique Russian earrings. She had a rope of pearls and was full of lovely nonsense, very old and very familiar to mankind. She knew how to be sad, feminine, capricious, proud, shallow, fickle, in love, clever in any way you like.

———

There are times while writing when I stop at a word and the word appears suddenly strange, an apparently simple word such as struggle, and I wonder not only about the origin of the word, if it is possible to think back at a time when the word was first used, but how the word has changed meaning over the centuries, accruing many different meanings. Such words are so one with their historically multiple etymologies that they appear, paradoxically, to be outside of time, timeless in time.

Idioms to me refer too much to the time in which they have appeared, so I don't use idioms.

This may have to do with Nikos' English, which is without contemporary idiom, is in a way purist for not being colloquial, and, of course, grammatically correct. I once asked him, 'Who do you love?' and he corrected me, 'Whom do you love?' And he seemed puzzled when I said that sounded pretentious, as if for him grammatical structure, as logic to thinking, is what language is essentially about.

He would never say, 'Someone has left their book on a chair.'

Nor would he ever say, 'Hopefully, the letter will arrive tomorrow,' or, 'He's too judgmental.'

Steven Runciman does not say 'healthy food,' which gives to food its own awareness about its health, but, instead, 'healthful' food.

———

At a gallery opening, I saw Ossie Clark, wearing, as he always seems to wear, a tight, sleeveless jersey knitted with many colours in a jigsaw pattern. He looked at me as if wondering if I recognized him enough for him to say hello, which surprised me as I had always felt he hardly recognized me and never made an effort to say hello. I noted how his long hair was greasy, his face pale and narrow and creased. I'd heard that he'd separated from Celia and that the business, badly mismanaged, had filed for bankruptcy. I'd also heard that he was deeply into hard drugs. He appeared isolated, perhaps even ashamed to be among people who had once gathered round him but who now left him alone, the past designer of frocks that appeared to float about the thin, long-legged models like large, light, fluttering wings.

———

At a dinner party of a rich Greek Nikos and I were invited to, he having reluctantly accepted because I said I wanted to find out about rich Greeks, I sat next to a woman who asked me if Nikos always takes off his shoes on entering our flat, and on my saying yes, he does, she simply smiled as if knowingly, she having put Nikos into a world she, a thoroughly Anglicized Greek, was ironically aware of; and the habit of Nikos taking off his shoes and putting on slippers before entering our flat (which he never insisted I do, but which habit I took on) became, to me, not a personal habit but a habit identifying the history of a culture. How could I have ever thought of wearing in our flat shoes that I had worn in the dirty street?

———

Anne Graham-Bell invited us to a dinner party. When I stepped out of the Underground train, I saw Nikos waiting for me on the platform. He was laughing. He had been in the same carriage as I, but at a far end, and, somewhat myopic, concentrated on someone at the other end he thought sexy – me!

———

Through Sonia, who told us how to answer a formal invitation, we were invited by the French ambassador to meet the writer Nathalie Sarraute, Sonia herself not attending. I arrived before Nikos, and found Marina Warner was seated next to me, and, as happens when I meet someone I know from a different context, I wondered through what connections she was there. I know her more from her novels than I know her in person, so I see her within the context of her novel The Skating Party rather than her lived life, always a strange way to see writers. As we were in the French Embassy, it seemed right that we should speak in French. The ambassador's wife came to me to ask when Mr. Stangos was to arrive, and I noted an empty place at the ambassador's table. I apologized, something must have delayed him, but, please, the luncheon must not be delayed. Across the table was, I recognized, Lee Miller, whom I'd seen at a drinks party at Suzi and John's flat. I kept hoping Nikos would arrive, but the chair at the ambassador's table remained empty. The dessert was a high, tapering configuration of profiteroles down which caramel dripped. After the meal, Marina introduced me to Lee Miller, who spoke to me as if she had always known me, which I imagined she did with everyone she met. She said she had to go to a department store to buy a clothes hamper, and would I like to go with her? I said I would, and thought it strange, very, to be in a department store with Lee Miller looking for a clothes hamper, she who had been photographed in Hitler's bathtub after the war, who had, a fashion photographer, gone into the death camps and taken photographs of the horrors, after which she stopped taking fashion photographs of bottles of perfume, who had been in the film Le Sang d'un poète by Jean Cocteau, had been painted by Picasso, had been married to Man Ray and an inspiration to the Surrealists, and was now married to Roland Penrose and devoted to cooking. At home, I rang Nikos, who said he really hadn't wanted to go to the luncheon, and would write a note of apology. I thought, well, we won't be invited again. I hadn't met Nathalie Sarraute, whose nouveaux romans Nikos admires more than I, for he is always keen on what he calls 'innovation,' and he will exclaim 'how innovative!'

about books, paintings, music, his exclamation not restricted to the contemporary, for he'll become even more excited in his appreciation of how 'innovative' Bach's music is.

———

For a week or so I've had the flu.

Nikos said he likes me to be a little ill so he can take care of me. But when he is ill, he doesn't want any care; he becomes impatient, and won't even stay in bed.

Stephen came to visit with a Picasso etching from the Vollard Suite, a monstrous, stony Minotaur raping (?) a delicately outlined woman, which he said he wanted me to have. As I have nothing, he said laughing, I should have this in case Nikos threw me out. He had taken it from the wall in his study where I had seen it in Loudoun Road.

Nikos said, 'But what if Natasha asks where it is? She'd be furious to find out we have it here, and rightly so.'

'She won't find out,' Stephen said. 'She knows I'm always turning in pictures to sell them to buy others. But there'll be hell to pay if she does find out. If she ever comes here, make sure you hide it.'

I thought, he obviously likes the possibility of her finding out.

I wonder if Stephen would become bored with us if we really became friendly with Natasha.

———

All that is left in my memory of a drinks party, as if I have reduced it in my memory to what most struck me in it, was seeing Christopher Isherwood among a number of people, and as I went towards him he, I thought, came towards me, but he didn't stop, he went on past me, all the while humming, his eyes staring out from beneath hanging lids and long drooping eyebrows.

Providence, Rhode Island

I am staying with my parents in my old parish home. While they are asleep, I look through the desk in the living room, through the pigeonholes where papers are kept, among them envelopes with clippings from the first haircuts of all my parents' seven sons, each envelope with the names of my brothers and me written on it by my mother in pencil. I also found many bits of paper on which my mother wrote in pencil sayings and fragments of poems that struck her while reading magazines and newspapers. This most struck me:

The realm of silence is large enough beyond the grave.

The winter afternoon is waning.

———

In London, I am constantly threatened by American darkness, which at moments comes over me portentously – comes over me, I feel, from outside, as if the vastest generalizations in America do exist outside, and the most vast is the darkness of 'everything' failing, of 'everything' just about to give way to 'nothing,' of 'everything' coming to an end. How dark American literature is, how fatalistic that America will fail, and the 'everything' promised will become nothing, that the end is always nigh.

When back in London, I will see through the surrounding large dark globe of America, see through it to the particulars of the London world about me, but there are those unaccountable moments when the globe becomes opaque and closes in on me, with both a sense of threat of its portent and a sense of the sublimity of its portent. The English live without it, and it is a relief to me to be among them; but, lacking that fatalistic, sublime dark, the English to me lack – what? – the spiritual, lack souls.

A difference between America and Britain: in New York, I would see people carrying placards warning against Armageddon, and in London I sometimes see a small man walking up and down Oxford Street carrying a placard warning the world against SITTING.

The constant impending threat in America of failing the written Constitution.

In Great Britain, no written constitution.

London

When I met the Briks in Paris, I wondered how they, Soviets, were able to visit Paris, as I thought Soviets were not given exit visas easily.

Recently, I've read that Osip Brik worked for Cheka. Boris Pasternak, who often visited the Briks, said he was terrified by Lili telling him to wait on dinner because Osja had not yet come back from the Cheka. Did he wear the long black leather overcoats and black leather cap? Did he participate in interrogations, in torture, in condemnations to death he knew were falsified? Did he believe that terror was the best way to govern?

And I think: there I was, in Paris, invited to dinner by the de Rothschilds, where I sat at the same table as Osip Brik, and even had my grand chair exchanged for his lesser chair in deference to him. Was it known that he worked for Cheka? Of course it was known, if not, as I believe, by Stephen, by the de Rothschilds.

In the same way that it is unbearable to be with a person who has been tattooed on entering a death camp and yet survived because her experience, as that of Katia Meneghello, is unbearable to any sane imagination, it is unbearable that I sat with a member of Cheka, because I cannot sanely imagine that Osip Brik's experience was the experience of a sane man. And yet, there he was, a man who seemed to me rather mild, perhaps, unlike his wife, shy.

I think this: that you have had to live through an experience, even the historical ones about which everything seems to have been exposed, to know what the experience in fact was to live through.

I asked Nikos what he thought, and he raised his arms high and dropped them, and turned away.

———

We are invited more and more by Natasha to dinner parties at Loudoun Road.

She always has an anecdote to tell, and she tells each rounded out with all the articulation her mouth and tongue allow, often with glee in the telling. She had a career as a pianist until a double mastectomy ended it. When she played at Wigmore Hall she, at the keyboard, would from time to time look up to the apse over the stage where a Dantesque figure writes on a long, flowing scroll, the figure, Natasha thought, marking down every one of her missed notes. She laughed. When she laughs, hardly more than opening her mouth so the muscles of her cheeks rise, she also appears to be thoughtful, frowning a little, as if wondering why she is laughing.

She laughs at Stephen's anecdotes, méchant of him, she says, to tell, but without that slight frown and thoughtfulness, she clearly amused by him by the way her eyes shine looking at him. Somewhere in their relationship is, I think, his joking and her appreciation of his joking, however méchant he is. She may exclaim, 'Oh, Stephen, really!' but with delight as he laughs, delighted by his joke.

For one dinner party, Sonia came early to help Natasha with making a coulibiac, and from the kitchen, where they both were, I heard from the dining table where I was sitting Sonia contesting something that Natasha had done to undo her, Sonia's, work on the coulibiac. I rang Natasha the next morning to thank her, and she asked if I had noted Sonia's contention about the coulibiac, and I said, well, yes, I had, and I felt that I was taken into Natasha's confidence about her strained relationship with Sonia, which made me feel confident in my relationship with Natasha. Whoever was most responsible for the coulibiac, it was very good.

Nikos did not like the way Penguin Books was going after the death of the founder, Allen Lane; he thought the emphasis was on being commercial not on upholding the standards.

He has gone to the privately owned Thames & Hudson, whose chairman – as she insists on being called – is Eva Neurath.

Nikos was invited to her house in Highgate for an interview before he was hired, and he came home to say they had had tea, beautifully laid among her beautiful Biedermeier furniture, on a table by her chair the poems of Heine, in German of course. She didn't talk with him about publishing, but the late quartets of Beethoven. Nikos was hired as a director.

At Thames & Hudson, Nikos's first impulse was to publish all the works of Adrian Stokes in three large volumes.

He has plans for books on David Hockney, Francis Bacon, Lucian Freud, Howard Hodgkin, Frank Auerbach . . . And he has contacted art historians to write books, among them the great expert on Cézanne, John Rewald, who is meant to be very, very difficult, but whom Nikos has charmed. Rewald has invited Nikos to stay with him in his castle in France. The castle, he told Nikos, has runnels over the main gate from which flaming oil was poured when in the Middle Ages an invading army tried to break through the closed gates; Rewald has kept them in case the self-justifying connoisseur of art Douglas Cooper ever dares to cross the drawbridge to try and enter before the doors close on him. Nikos does not like being a guest except with close friends.

The Mother of Feminist Art History, Linda Nochlin, greets Nikos with embraces and kisses, and has introduced to him her feminist disciple art historian Tamar Garb; together they gave Nikos a white yarmulke embroidered in silver, making him an honorary Jew as well as a feminist. Nikos has said that Jews, of all the other people in the world, just may be superior to the Greeks.

He will publish David Sylvester's interviews with Francis Bacon.

It is no surprise to Nikos that all the poets who were once keen to meet him when he was poetry editor at Penguin Books no longer have a vested interest. In fact, he took this as an of-course, perhaps a relief.

———

Somewhere in the writing of William James – whom I read as if to remain in contact with the American spirit that is everywhere in his writing (if in his writing the spirit isn't German!), for I am after all American – I came across an abstraction made concrete by his use of an example something like: when Peter and Paul are asleep together, Peter becomes Paul and Paul becomes Peter. I thought of Nikos and me, for whom sleeping together is perhaps where we are most attractive to each other, and where, after a row, everything that was contentious between us is resolved. What is that attraction?

Before we fall asleep together, he says a little prayer in Greek and makes the sign of the cross on me, and then he, as if this is his role, switches off the lamp on his side of the bed.

———

Stephen and I were on the crowded pavement among people coming out of the Aldwych Theatre after the performance of a play by Shakespeare (Henry V), and a man behind him in the crowd tapped his shoulder so Stephen turned round to the man and, beside him, a short, almost diminutive man with a long grey beard to whom the man introduced Stephen. As if lost in the crowd, Stephen simply reached out a hand to shake the hand of the short, almost diminutive man with the long grey beard, then Stephen turned away. I said, 'Stephen, that was Solzhenitsyn you shook hands with,' and Stephen frowned. 'Was it?' 'Yes.' He frowned more, with the expression of bemusement I've become familiar with, as though he couldn't quite believe that he had just shaken hands with someone who could only have existed on the world stage.

Because he had not seen his mother in Athens in years, and because the dictatorship is weakening, Nikos did go to visit his mother. While in Athens, he saw Chester Kallman at a kafenion where Chester spends most of the day, drinking, every day, bottles of ouzo, in the company of young men. Nikos said the young men were suspicious of him for what he might be after from Chester, whom they appeared to treat with protective affection. Nikos was expected to pay the bill.

Back from Athens, Nikos brought with him little tins – like paint tins – of gliko koutaliou, small oranges or strawberries or even rose petals preserved in a thick syrup which are meant to be eaten with a spoon, a specialty of the island of Chios. He also brought back a jar of almost solid but ductile white paste made from sugar and mastic, also from Chios, the basis of something of a ritual: a spoonful is plunged into a glass of cold water and left for a little to flavour the water, the spoonful of mastic is then licked or pulled out with one's teeth, and the water then drunk, called ypovrihio.

So I learn something about the past daily life of Nikos in Greece. As if nostalgic, he told me his aunt always set out on the dining-room table a starched white cloth and starched white napkins and small coffee cups and little crystal dishes with silver spoons and a crystal bowl of gliko koutaliou, all prepared for him on waking from his afternoon sleep, he to take a spoonful of gliko (strawberry, made by his mother once a year, the only time she goes into the kitchen), she then making coffee in a little pot, called a briki, over a burner, heavy rather bitter coffee to shock him awake. Perhaps it was I who felt the nostalgia, if it is possible to have nostalgia for a world never lived.

No doubt I romanticize Nikos' Greek life with these effects, but how can I not? And, yes, I romanticize Nikos' history, which is the history of gliko koutaliou from Chios, mastic from Chios, which island became famous and rich for sweets and gum from mastic trees in the Middle Ages, if not earlier.

And how much refers to the past life of his family in Constantinople? As a treat for me, he will prepare Kidonato, lamb with quince, which he says is Anatolian, or Chounkiar beyendi, lamb in a tomato sauce with a puré of aubergines made from the vegetable reduced outwardly to charcoal under a grill, the innards scooped out and squeezed and then cooked with milk and butter. And he talks of a pudding called Taouk kioktsou, chicken breasts pounded into a paste and boiled with milk and sugar. Surely, these, which may be merely picturesque to me, refer in him to a past deeper than his past, to layers and layers of civilization, if not civilizations.

He tells me that Turkish cuisine is really Byzantine.

And I see in his very features, which have an Oriental cast about his eyes, a past from so long past yet present in him that I imagine he in his very body dates back to a Mongol in a Byzantine Emperor's court and a lady in waiting to the Empress.

———

Separate from Nikos who was to come on his own from the publishing house, I went on my own to an opening of an exhibition at the Hayward Gallery, and, entering, I saw, standing facing me and talking to others, Pauline de Rothschild. I approached her to say hello and she turned her back to me. I thought she hadn't recognized me, or had had her attention taken away by someone behind her who had called her name and to whom she had turned. Her hair was in a long thin plait that fell between the delicate shoulderblades that jutted out through the thin black material of her dress. I went round to her side, where I spoke to people I knew to let her know, I supposed, that I privileged to be invited to the opening was able to engage familiarly with other privileged people also invited (this entirely because of Nikos, for he is invited as a publisher of books on art, and I as his partner), and, there at the side of Pauline de Rothschild, I positioned myself so that if she glanced to her side she would see me. She did glance and she turned away again. And again, I thought, if I were to retain her attention even for a second she would recognize me and engage in talk, and I would remember with her that time in Paris when she entertained Louis Aragon and Elsa Triolet and Osip and Lili Brik, to relive a little an evening that had meant so much to me that I wrote it all down in my diary, amusing her with an anecdote or two. (I think I am getting rather good at telling anecdotes – never, however, as well as Natasha, who will tell one after the other in a vivid and well-rounded way, even though she, laughing, told me that a friend of hers driving with her to the South of France begged her, please, no more anecdotes.) I stepped round the group of people Pauline de Rothschild was among, now no longer talking to anyone, and I faced her, and she for a moment faced me and I nodded and she nodded, and she turned away, and I knew she did not want to engage in any way with me. Still, someone I knew standing by me asked, 'Who is that?' and I said, 'The Baroness Pauline de Rothschild,' as if I had just had an intimate conversation with her that ended with her inviting me to the Château Mouton. That she kept turning her back on me didn't offend me, and it didn't because I saw the scene – rather, see it now as I write about it – as literature, as Proustian literature, which surrounds the event with literary charm, for it was literature to me. Yet, why had she turned her back on me? What was there about me she didn't like? That there are people who don't like me does, I suppose, offend me, but, again, not much, no, not much.

When I was in Providence, I went one afternoon to the Rhode Island School of Design Museum to look at the classical torso there that I used to go study as a teenager and, within a world so far removed from Greece that Greece was certainly not aware of, revered Greece for having meaning in all the world.

About classical Greece, a Greek friend said, 'Modern Greece has nothing, but nothing, to do with classical Greece.'

Still, when Nikos props on his desk a postcard of the bronze charioteer from Delphi, standing still in his long chiton, his eyes staring far out, the horse reins a suspended tangle in his hands, I feel that the classical love of the beauty and the virtue and the honour made evident in this statue remains vitally meaningful, and, because Nikos has propped the postcard on his desk with special veneration, I feel that the statue is especially meaningful because Nikos is Greek. Nikos may be within a myth, a myth more meaningful to him than it is to me, for he is Greek, but in him the myth has to me, non-Greek, a great meaning.

Empedocles:

Don't try to see love, don't try to hear love, for love is a sphere of joy all about us, is all harmony inspiring harmony in the world, in which we do see, in which we do hear, in which all our senses are harmonious, and our deeds too.

———

Frank Kermode often stays with Nikos and me when he is in London for meetings, as he is now at King's College, Cambridge.

He got up before Nikos and me and went down to the kitchen to make coffee. I heard a big bang, and got up and went down to see Frank, staring out of the kitchen window, coffee grounds splattered everywhere and the Italian coffee pot exploded into two. He said, 'My father told me I would never be capable.'

He suggested to me that we write together a book to be called CONNECTIONS, which would connect all the characters of recorded history to one another, but the accounts had to be first-person accounts, forming, Frank thought, a daisy chain.

We have got this far:

CONNECTIONS:

King George III and Dr. Johnson Dr. Johnson and Boswell
and Boswell and Rousseau and Boswell met Voltaire and
Rousseau met Napoleon and Chateaubriand met Napoleon
and Chateaubriand also met Louis XVI and Chateaubriand
writes of meeting Washington in his memoirs and Lafayette
writes of meeting Washington in his memoir and Mrs Catherine Macaulay met Washington and Washington left no
account of meeting anyone . . . Napoleon met Goethe and
Goethe and Beethoven met and Napoleon and Stendhal
conversed outside the gates of Moscow and Goethe and Crabb
Robinson met and Crabb Robinson Blake and Blake and
Voltaire and Voltaire and Frederick the Great and Frederick
the Great and Haydn and Frederick the Great and Casanova
and Haydn and Mozart met Haydn and Beethoven and Haydn
and Scarlatti and Beckford was taught the harpsichord by
Mozart and Mozart and Maria Theresa met and Mozart met
Fanny Burney, who met George III.

If I were knowledgeable enough, I would write a book about
connections among writers that cross the borders of nations and
their national identities and languages in order to see the more
international influences of writers among themselves, such as Dickens on Dostoyevsky, Ruskin on Proust, Edgar Allen Poe on
Baudelaire, Honoré de Balzac on Henry James, Gustave Flaubert
on Franz Kafka, etc, etc, etc . . .

———

Waking and rising from bed before me, Nikos opened the
curtains and said, 'Snow!' and I saw thin English snow falling,
and I lay back in bed while he, as he likes, spent the morning
alone, shaving, bathing, having his coffee and breakfast. Snow
continued into the waning of the winter day, and I, at my

desk, felt just enough of the effects of the winter afternoon to remember heavy, snow-bound New England winter afternoons – those paradoxically stark but deep afternoons that waned both outside and inside the house, in which details I fixed on as I walked restlessly from room to room appeared to take on a vividness and even a portentousness: the open book on an armchair, the tea mug on the kitchen table, the fluted, fringed lampshade of a floor lamp. I wonder if the deep but stark winter afternoons I remembered from when I was a boy make up the dimension of my awareness, the awareness in which details do become vivid and portentous, the awareness that so fixes my concentration on the details that they become, oh, meaningful! And so, away from my native New England, in England, in France, in Italy, in Greece, even there, I fix on details as if my awareness of them remains my native awareness, that deep but stark, stark but deep winter awareness that, in fact, defies any meaning, or, perhaps, any more meaning than the meaning of a winter afternoon.

This comes to me: that we are not only formed by our history but by our geography, and both history and geography together.

And this comes to me: the objects of my family house which I grew up with, objects that predated my birth, objects that had their presence in the house before I was present, objects that had, and in my memory have, more presence than I did, and do, objects that make me aware of how little actual presence I had, and have.

———

Sonia is not rich, but she often gives to friends who can't afford them gifts to help those friends live their lives as well as possible. When her friend the writer and very much bon vivant Cyril Connolly died, he left huge debts, and Sonia helped with letters of appeal to all her friends to raise money for his widow, Deirdre.

On the verso, Sonia wrote:

I've been so involved in this horror that I haven't been able to ring you. The point is do you know anyone I could usefully send this to??? Any ideas would be marvellous. Please suggest as it is desperate. Love, S.

Nikos did send some suggestions, and, too, some money.

To the rumor after that Deirdre Connolly was using some of the money to buy champagne Sonia replied, in a rage, 'Of course she bought champagne.'

———

Some of Frank's anecdotes he loves to tell:

At a reception, Oscar Browning, the Cambridge don, accosted Tennyson and announced, 'I'm Browning.' Tennyson peered myopically at him for a while, then said, 'No, you're not,' and walked away.

Maupassant, on his only visit to London, was entertained by Henry James. According to an anecdote by Oscar Wilde, Maupassant, dining in a restaurant with James, pointed to a woman sitting at a nearby table and asked Henry to go over and bring her back to their table. James carefully explained that in England there was the matter of being properly introduced. Maupassant tried again. Pointing to another woman, he said, 'Surely you know her at least? Ah, if I could only speak English!' When James had refused, with full explanation, for about the fifth time, Maupassant was said to have remarked irritably, 'Really, you don't seem to know anyone in London.'

When Picasso came to London for the first time, he was invited by Roland Penrose, who, unable to meet him at Victoria Station, sent Victor Pasmore. Pasmore could not speak French, and Picasso no English. In Pasmore's car, they were silent for a long while, then Pasmore said, 'Je suis peintre.' Picasso paused, then said, 'Moi aussi.'

Frank laughs – his laugh always subdued – when asking the riddle of the weasel and the stoat: how can you tell the difference between a weasel and a stoat? The one is weasily distinguished and the other is stoatally different.

––––––

In the past, the classics scholar Peter Levi would sometimes stay with Stephen and Natasha, then Stephen found that Levi, having the Oxbridge power, voted against him getting the Oxford Chair of Poetry, which he may have rightly believed Stephen didn't deserve, but, I think, he shouldn't have also presumed on a friendship with Stephen. A moral judgment which I shouldn't make, but this turned me against him. He writes poetry himself – Pancakes for the Queen of Babylon – copies of which he once gave to both Nikos and me, perhaps hoping that Nikos would publish other poems, but Nikos did not, which he told Stephen. Peter is good-looking, quick, decisive, knowing, always distracted so that I feel he is attentive to me only in passing, as when he said to me, 'You are too pretty to be taken seriously,' then hurried away, as he always seems to be in a hurry. A Jew who converted to the Roman Church and became a Jesuit, he left the Order to marry the widow of Cyril Connolly, Deirdre.

Which does make me wonder what is, or was, done with the money Sonia raised to pay off Cyril Connolly's debts, apart from his widow buying champagne. Nikos and I contributed some small amount. I think Anne and Rodrigo contributed substantially.

––––––

Nikos and I were in a taxi with Suzi and John, and as the taxi went round Hyde Park Corner, John said, forming the words with his entire mouth to stop from stuttering, his eyes bright in his red face, 'A man shouldn't live with a woman for more than seven years.' I asked, 'How long have you been with Suzi?' John did stutter when he answered, 'Seven years.' Suzi smiled a wide smile, clearly thinking that John was talking in a general way that didn't apply to her. But she rang the next morning to say that John is leaving her to move to New York, where he will be art critic on the New York Times. Suzi depends on the I CHING for advice as to what to do now.

She makes collages made of images she cuts out of glossy picture books of jungles or rocky bare landscapes or animals or the natives of primitive tribes, dense collages that conjure up an alternate, magical world.

She so believes that art has lost the essential enchantment art must have, and talks of the re-enchantment of art.

Suzi lived for a while with René Magritte and his wife, during which time she gathered together her book on Magritte, the best book, John Golding has said, on the artist. Magritte gave Suzi a drawing of flying nib pens pursuing a man running down a street and Suzi gave the drawing to Jasper Johns in exchange for a small encaustic of the American flag in which Suzi's picture is imbedded. Suzi crosses many borders in the art world and at the crossroads is making a life of her own.

Lockerbie, Scotland

Nikos commissioned Steven Runciman to write a book on Mistra, the Byzantine capital in the Peloponnese. Steven asked him to stay in his castle in Scotland, Elshieshields, and I was asked along. We arrived in darkness at the Lockerbie train station, from which a driver took us into deeper darkness to what Steven called his house. There had been no restaurant car on the train, so we arrived hungry, and Steven served up plates of ham and salad in his study. 'I'm not going to give you water in your malt whiskey,' he said.

He showed us to our rooms, mine hung with paintings by his mid-eighteenth-century Scottish relatives John and Alexander Runciman – among those in the family who had 'gone in reck-lessly for the arts.'

There was no question that Nikos and I would share a room.

After breakfast – prepared by Steven, who walked up and down alongside the sideboard on which were a silver tea pot, a silver coffee pot, a silver water jug, silver toast-racks, and porcelain egg-coddlers – Nikos and I took a walk on flat country roads. We were late for elevenses. Steven had already had his coffee. He looked at us sternly, but he made another pot for us, waited for us to drink, then left us to go to his study.

Nikos joined me in my room, where we tried to read, but the cold was numbing, and not relieved by the electric fire on the hearth. From the windows was a view of high Scottish firs, in which rooks cawed: 'Car-car, car-car.'

Unable to bear the cold, Nikos said he would go out to look for a warm room, and returned after fifteen minutes, laughing. He had found a room with a fire, but shortly after he sat down before it, a door opened at the back of the room, a door made up of the spines of books to blend in with the shelves of books on either side, and Steven entered and said, seeing Nikos, 'You're not allowed in here.' This amused Nikos.

We were on time for luncheon. The paper napkins were printed with poems by Burns. Steven had prepared curried chicken livers. I salted the liver before tasting, and Steven leaned over the table towards me, as he does when he has something that you take to be personally addressed to you, and said, 'I don't invite guests who salt my food before tasting it to come back.'

'I'll try to be better behaved,' I said.

'It will help to know you'll try,' he said.

On the wood-panelled dining-room walls were large paintings by John and Alexander Runciman.

Nikos and Steven discussed the lack of interest that the West had had in Byzantium until, really, Steven inspired attention to those 1000 years of civilization.

Nikos suggested that the Phanariots kept Byzantium alive.

I had to ask who the Phanariots were.

'Are,' Nikos said.

Steven explained –

They are the Greeks of Constantinople who remained after the city fell to the Turks in 1453. By the sixteenth century, they were rich and influential, and even more so in the seventeenth century. They were called Phanariots because they lived in the Phanar, the Greek quarter of the city, a self-contained group, intermarrying and inter-quarrelling. The Ottoman Sultans appointed them Princes of Walachia and Moldavia in Romania, and from there they dominated Greek civilization from the late seventeenth century through the eighteenth, and maintained the great

Hellenic-Byzantine tradition. They had printing presses in Bucharest, discouraged in Constantinople.

Smiling, Nikos listened as Steven went on to me, 'They maintained the now defunct Big Idea to resuscitate Byzantium.'

'Resuscitate?' Nikos asked, offended.

'I am sorry,' Steven apologized to him. 'Their Big Idea was to get hold of the Ottoman Empire from within. The Phanariots existed as the aristocracy of Romania until the last world war.'

Nikos said, 'They've never been very welcome in Greece itself.'

'Because they were thought to be too grand and too pleased with themselves.'

'Koraïs disapproved of them.'

'That monster Koraïs.'

And so more explanation for me:

Adamantios Koraïs, a European Greek of the late eighteenth and early nineteenth century, was one of the instigators of Greek liberation from the Turks. 'Doing it safely from a flat in Paris,' Steven said. 'He was totally Westernized, and had hardly ever been to Greece. He visited once or twice Chios, where his family were from. Like all Europeans of the time, he saw Greece purely in classical terms. After all, the Turks had occupied what we now know as Greece for four hundred years. The Greeks there hadn't thought of classical times at least for that long. It was the Orthodox Church that kept everyone aware of Byzantium during the Ottoman Occupation, because the Church was functioning all during that time. Koraïs disapproved of Byzantium, disapproved of the Orthodox Church, disapproved of Greeks of his day. He disapproved because of Gibbon. Gibbon thought the whole of Byzantium decadent. And Gibbon was the god of Koraïs. He thought all Greeks should be like the classical heroes. I can't think why people praise him, except that he did leave a very good library on Chios. About the only good thing he did. He was basically responsible for Katharevousa. Just think of all that poetry written in a language now disclaimed. It's the great disaster of Greek literature written in Katharevousa.'

'Oh, I know,' Nikos said.

'Of course, Koraïs was European, and no European of that time thought of Greece as anything but classical. Think of Byron.'

'And Greeks welcomed the myth of ancient Greece imposed on them by Europe. They wanted to be European too.'

'Would you say that is still true?'

'Greece wanting to be European? Yes.'

'They repudiated Byzantium, these Europeanized Greeks. Koraïs disapproved, and they, ashamed, disapproved.'

'But so much of the recent – well, recent in your lifetime – revival of Byzantium is due to you.'

'I hope I played a little part. I think I made Greeks a little more aware of Byzantium than they had been. When I first started, and even after the last world war, when I was living in Greece, it was thought somewhat odd to be interested in Byzantium. It was certainly not fashionable.'

'It became fashionable among Greeks because a foreigner took it up,' Nikos said.

'How the Greeks explained the survival of Hellenism when they took out pretty much all of the Byzantine centuries, and took out entirely the Turkish domination – well, how they did it was not historical. My book The Great Church in Captivity was one of the first to deal with Greece under the Turks – a very necessary link in Greek history.'

Nikos simply nodded, as he was not going to disagree with Steven.

'In some ways I regret the passing of the Ottoman Empire,' Steven said.

I asked, 'Why is that?'

'Because I'm the Grand Orator of the Great Church of Constantinople, which in Ottoman times would have entitled me to be a prince. Alas, the Ottoman Empire has fallen.'

Steven stuck out his lower lip and made a face as of someone looking down at another from a great height.

Maussane

We are in Provence staying with Stephen and Natasha.
It was six years ago that I was last here, alone with Stephen, which I found out later upset Natasha very much. Now she asks me if I saw this or that when I was here.

She has been tremendously hospitable. Today she drove Stephen, Nikos and me up to the Ardèche Gorge, a very long way, for a picnic, prepared and packed by Natasha in a basket with plates and knives and forks and napkins. We've just got back, and it's late, but while Nikos sleeps I, in the bed next to him in the guest room, want to describe the day, which was so much like a dream I want to get it down before, like a dream, it fades.

The mistral is blowing outside.

We stopped at various belvederes on the way for views of the gorge, the river flat and black and shining far below between the steep white rocky banks. From one belvedere, Nikos spotted some bathers far below in the river, and we decided to go down to the river bank to have our picnic lunch. We walked down and down a path, through woods still filled at this late date with purple wild flowers, Stephen's untied shoelaces getting tangled in the branches of small bushes, then down rocky places, all of us laughing, until we came to the broad flat stone bank of the river, like a number of smooth stone platforms that seemed to float in strata one above the other by the side of the river, green and flowing over and around boulders out in the current. Some people were swimming in the river, some canoeing. I put down the basket I was carrying and Nikos the rug he was carrying, and the four of us went to look out at the river, and just then there swam toward us three youths, their bodies green in the green water, who rose up onto a stone platform below us, naked. Their hair was long and wet. Touching their genitals, they stood in the sunlight to dry themselves, then sat on the rock.

Natasha turned away to go back to the picnic basket and unpack it, and I quickly followed her to help. Nikos came, too, to spread out the rug. Only Stephen remained where he'd been, and sat on the edge of the platform and took out his spectacles from his shirt pocket and put them on to stare down at the boys.

Natasha called Stephen to eat, and all the while we had the picnic the boys remained on the rock below us. Natasha and Nikos and I pretended that they were not there and didn't look toward them, but Stephen kept his spectacles on and didn't stop looking at them, smiling. I heard them speaking German, and I thought that they had put a spell over us and were tempting us to acknowledge them, and, in acknowledging them, something would happen to us that Natasha and Nikos and I must not acknowledge. And yet I was, as much as I pretended not to be, always aware of them while Natasha and Nikos and I talked and laughed about anything but where we were. I didn't even focus on them closely enough to find out if they were in fact attractive, but just my awareness of them naked and near us gave to that river, to the rocks, the trees, the entire gorge a sense of sexual potency that was all the more potent to me for being unfocused. Stephen alone acknowledged them. The spell they cast lasted long after we had finished our picnic and walked back up the path to the car.

I told myself I knew what Nikos' and my reactions to the boys were, and there was no doubt about Stephen's reaction, but I had no idea what Natasha's reaction was.

She drove very fast, often all of us in silence, but she stopped again at different spots so we could get out to see the gorge, which had now become enchanted.

Then Natasha drove through beautiful countryside, past beautiful little villages on the sides of green hills, to Orgnac, where we
stopped to see the grotto. Natasha stayed in the car to rest while
Stephen, Nikos and I went down, giggling and now able to talk
freely about the German boys, into an enormous space of stalactites
and stalagmites, the air damp and feverishly cold. We were with a
group, and before the tour the group's photograph was taken, then
we went down deeper and deeper, down long flights of cement
stairs, into a surreal world. Stephen and Nikos, however, were
bored, and Stephen said, 'I always feel that what I imagine these
places to be like is always better than what they in fact are.' Perhaps
he was right, but it was strange enough that when we came out
into the sunlight and flat ground I had the strong feeling that I had
just woken up from a dream. Stephen had bought and given to us
a copy of the group photograph.

And then I felt I went right back into the dream as Natasha
drove us on, through Barjac, through small towns like Tharaux and
Rochegude, and by the time we got to Uzès it was dark. We had
dinner there, and on the way back to Maussane we saw, the moon
shining through one arch, the Pont du Gard, seeming to float like
a dream image in vast blackness. We saw the castle at Beaucaire, the
medieval dungeon at Tarascon, the Roman triumphal arch and
mausoleum at Saint Rémy.

Now I will go to sleep.

When I got up, Stephen was having breakfast and I joined him.
Natasha and Nikos were out in the garden, working. The mistral
was still blowing, and from the breakfast table we could see them,
through the French doors, their clothes and hair blown out.

I said to Stephen, 'Those boys we saw yesterday in the Ardèche
River, they were Rhine Maidens.'

I had thought this would be our joke, which we might share
with Nikos later, but keep from Natasha because she would not
find it amusing, but Stephen, excited, said, 'That's wonderful!' and

he immediately got up and went out into the garden and called, 'Natasha! Natasha!' She and Nikos stopped working, and 'Yes?' she called back. Stephen shouted in the wind, 'Those boys we saw in the river, David says they were the Rhine Maidens.' I saw Natasha laugh and say something to Nikos, who smiled, and I thought that the spell the boys had cast on us all was broken.

Natasha, Nikos and I walked through the valley of the Alpilles to pick blackberries. The mistral was blowing harder than ever, and sometimes pushed us forward, sometimes drew us backward. Tree branches and cane thrashed. The light was bright and pure, as were the smells: smells of lavender and rosemary and mint and thyme and fennel and juniper, bits of which we picked off as we walked along. The smell of lavender or rosemary or any other wild herb seemed, as I breathed it in deeply, to hollow out, as penetratingly as the smell of ammonia, a great dark space behind my sinuses and the space filled up with the scent, so pungent that I'm able to recall the smell long after having dropped the twig of lavender or rosemary.

It was very curious, the three of us walking along. I kept wondering what our relationships were, Natasha's to Nikos and me, ours to her, and, even, Nikos' to me and mine to him. What, I wondered, did we really think of one another as we walked along together? Nikos picked almonds and broke them open on the paved road with a stone, Natasha picked thyme, I found a snake's shed skin tangled in grass – little events which themselves seemed very strange to me.

When, later, I was alone with Natasha in the house, both Stephen and Nikos in their rooms reading, she told me about her childhood: that she was an illegitimate baby, her mother an actress, her father a Welshman, brought up by a working-class foster mother, finally taken back by her own mother.

After dinner, which Nikos prepared, the four of us worked in the garden. The moonlight was bright, the stars dense, the Milky Way showing like a thin, luminous mist, the mistral still blowing strong, and the rocky hills of the Alpilles beyond the garden looked to be wild and to be moving. We transplanted irises. Stephen would simply dig a hole and stuff in all the irises he could fit in, then stomp the earth in around them. His white hair flying about, he would then ask, 'Is that all right, Natasha?' She would answer, 'It's perfect, darling,' and when he'd go for more irises she'd smile at Nikos and me.

I think he was worried about having Nikos and me here before we arrived, but he has relaxed. However, he still seems particularly to want Natasha to like Nikos, because whenever Nikos does anything or even says anything, Stephen draws Natasha's attention to it as if hoping to make her see how helpful or how intelligent he is. Natasha is always appreciative.

He has three kittens he has become very attached to. He feeds them over and over all day and keeps trying to pet them, but they run away.

London

Nikos keeps adding to the poem he showed me when we first met, 'Pure Reason.' I have never asked him whom the poem was initially meant for, someone he loved and someone whom I don't want to know about, because I want that someone to be a vague presence that Nikos is filling out, perhaps, after all, with me. The additional layers consist of an investigation into what love means, and Nikos has looked into our love for each other with a critical eye, at times severe:

Disjunction has triumphed. Now each on our own, we muse about our pure craving . . . We have failed. Each of us keeps to himself.

Reading this, I'm shocked, and wonder what happened between us to make him write this.

Then, after many considerations, many of them when he is alone, the revelation comes to him: love is a category of the mind, an absolute.

Once the centre is fixed we can allow the antinomies to revolve around it, to resolve themselves as if by magic, and fabulous marriages will take place among them.

———

Conversations with Frank (his heavy-framed spectacles too big for his pale face, his longish hair in wisps, preoccupied with keeping his pipe lit) seem to be incidental. It is as if he, well known among his friends to be self-deprecating, wants at best to keep his comments light-spirited, yet he touches lightly on some of the major issues of literature. He never in these conversations refers to any of his books, but it is in his books that the issues, these too seemingly incidental to him, are made so vital. And the one that strikes me personally as being most vital is The Genesis of Secrecy.

> If there is one belief (however the facts resist it) that unites us all . . . it is the conviction that somehow, in some occult fashion, if we could only detect it, everything will be found to hang together.

(What a Jamesian expression that: to hang together!)

How might this be done? By halting the movement of the senses, or by trying to – which I take to mean: by fixing on what Frank calls an immediate interpretation to focus in the blur of sense for one central sense about which the infinite chaos of objects will come together as a temporary whole.

> . . . the shrine of the single sense.

(This is Wallace Stevens.)

I remark: Frank does not use the word idea, but 'sense'.

The very last sentence of the final chapter ends: 'our sole hope and pleasure is in the perception of a momentary radiance, before the door of disappointment is finally shut on us.'

As for what the book reveals about Frank himself – he never assumes it would be possible for him to be a 'spiritual insider,' and yet remaining a 'carnal outsider' doesn't give him a 'hold' to see 'inside.' He is a 'carnal' working-class man from the Island of Man, an outsider to the rest of the world, but being such a 'carnal outsider' doesn't give him an identity enough, a 'hold' enough, to reject the

identity in order to free himself and find his way among the 'spiritual insiders,' where, however, he wants to be. So he is neither
outside nor inside.

Anita told me that Frank deliberately changed his Manx accent
into what he thinks a more conventional English accent. She also
told me that, having been rejected by Oxbridge and so educated at
Leeds instead, he always felt like an outsider, but an outsider who
wanted to get inside, which outside was, for him the one most
open to him, that of literature. As much of a 'spiritual insider' as
Frank is, and he is considered to be very much one, he himself does
not consider himself to be one, not really. He does not feel entitled.

What does Frank want?

Frank is in 'love' with literature, in which he finds his greatest
fulfillment, but the moments of fulfillment are only held for as long
as the radiance lasts against the overwhelming threat of the unfulfilled. The spiritual is too inconstant to be anything but a
disappointment.

I honestly feel there is a lot of Frank as a person in this. I remember what the moral philosopher Bernard Williams once said about
him: that Frank can't bear too much feeling, and shuts the door on
it when it threatens him.

Only once did he tell me he had an experience that had a 'sense
of meaning': he was in Japan, and was asked to place a branch on
an altar, and as he did that 'sense' came to him. He told me this
simply, and then went silent. He remembered the 'sense,' was even
able to refer to the 'sense,' but it passed.

In his dedication to Nikos and me on the flyleaf of The Genesis
of Secrecy, Frank wrote, 'Keep the carnal outsiders outside . . .'

———

Alone, Suzi continues to give drinks parties, and Francis, faithful to
Suzi, comes. After one party, when most people had gone, Francis
said to me, 'Let's go to dinner – you, Nikos, Suzi, me, we'll go to
dinner.'

At the restaurant, Greek, Nikos said, reading the menu, 'They have grilled gray mullet. That's what I'll have.' Francis said, 'That's what I'll have, too. Grilled gray mullet. I love that. I'm a simple person. Aren't I a simple person? Aren't I, Suzi?' Suzi smiled and reached across the table and squeezed one of his hands. Nikos asked him, 'What do you mean by simple?' He answered, 'I'm direct and I'm obvious. I've had an appalling life. I've had a very unhappy life. I don't think about it. There it is. That's simple.'

Suzi asked him, 'You've never been happy?'

'Once or twice,' he said. 'When I was young, in moments of ecstasy. Now I'm too old. I don't think about it, about happiness. There are many things I don't think about. I've done horrible things in my life, horrible. There they are. I don't think about them. I'm too old.'

His dyed hair, with, it appeared, a hair cream to make it smooth and keep it starkly in place, was combed against his head, with some stiff strands carefully arranged down over his forehead. He said, 'I've had a horrible life, a tragic life.' He picked up a small pickle from a white plate and ate it, picked up another one, a large one, ate it, picked up another one, a large one, ate it, picked up another and put it into his mouth, and as if the taste had only now occurred to him, he said, 'These pickles are horribly sour.' He didn't laugh but everyone else did. He said, 'I'm a very simple person who's had an appalling and tragic life.'

Nikos said, 'What's been so appalling? You've never been seriously ill, you've never had to worry about money.'

Francis said, 'You're right. I was pretty when I was young. Old men liked me. One old man, an old Greek — I even remember his name — fell in love with me, gave me money, and I used the money to paint. I lived off old men. I always had a clear idea of what I wanted to do. I wanted to be exceptional. I wanted to do exceptional work. I just took money. I was an old whore. I still am. An older whore. A lucky old whore.'

A strange sensation passed through me. I sat back and tears came into my eyes.

A waiter put a gray mullet in front of Francis and he asked, 'What's this?' 'Your grilled gray mullet,' Nikos said. 'I hate this,' Francis said, 'I can't eat it. I couldn't get a forkful down me (sic) throat.'

Nikos asked Francis, 'What makes your life tragic?'

'I've been in love, and love is tragic.'

'Love can make you happy,' Nikos said.

Francis said, 'I was in love with someone who killed himself. That made our love tragic.'

———

When I told Sonia about the deaths of my parents, she didn't react, just stared at me, her eyes, within puffy lids, hard. Then, after a moment she said, still staring hard at me with bloodshot eyes, 'Now there is nothing between you and eternity.'

———

In what way am I essentially American? Though I have dismissed Henry James as a fairytale European, I go back to him as an American, and I go back to him for what I believe an essentially American awareness that has survived in me for the simple fact that I was born and brought up in America –

I counted the use of the word 'everything' over eighty-five times in The Wings of the Dove, which I have recently reread after many years. For example:

'I want everything at once and together –'

'There was more to come – everything.'

'I want the whole thing.'

'It gains you time.' / 'Time for what?' / 'For everything.'

'It makes everything fit.' / 'Everything.' / The word, for a little, held the air, and he might have seemed the while to be looking, by no means dimly now, at all it stood for.

'But a denial, when it comes to that – confound the whole thing, don't you see! – of exactly what?' It was as if he were hoping she would narrow; but she in fact enlarged. 'Of everything.'

Everything had never yet seemed to him so incalculably much. 'Oh!' he simply moaned into the gloom.

'He has done everything.' / 'Oh, everything! Everything's nothing.'

The word, repeated so often and in so many contexts, appeared to me to attract the whole novel into itself. Was 'everything' money? Was 'everything' life? Was 'everything' a horror? Was 'everything' a great and final fulfillment? What was 'everything' in itself? (As Ezra Pound wrote: 'Henry James was aware of the spherical form of the planet . . .') The awareness of 'everything,' the possession to connect 'everything' into a whole, the need to have everything – isn't that essentially American, and isn't my essential, impulsive American awareness to sustain that 'everything' within one spherical globe?

When I recall myself, a college student in Boston, walking around Louisburg Square, the Hub of the Hub of the Yankee Transcendentalist Universe, I, in my Ivy League suit, desiring 'everything . . .'

In London, this desire is mitigated by the particulars that life here is essentially made of, particulars so particular they belie the desire for 'everything,' which is, of course, a spiritual desire, but in London to be kept to myself, my secret.

Nikos, from whom I have no secrets, is aware in me of that desire.

———

Suzi gave a dinner party for Sonia, Francis, Nikos and me. Francis didn't drink, and put his hand over his glass whenever Suzi was about to pour wine into it. He didn't say much all evening. He looked sad – polite and attentive but making an effort to be so.

We talked about people becoming dependent on others, and Francis said, 'George became dependent on me. If he hadn't, he'd probably be alive now. He was a thief, an inept thief, always getting caught, when I met him. He'd probably be in jail and alive now if he hadn't met me. But he did, he drank himself into a mad state and, because of me, killed himself.'

Sonia said, aggressively, 'He didn't kill himself. I read to you the medical report, in English. His death was accidental.'

'He did,' Francis said, 'he killed himself.'

I thought of Frank Kermode when I read the following:

> We count and name whatever lies upon the special lines we
> trace, whilst the other things and the untraced lines are neither
> named nor counted. There are in reality infinitely more things
> 'unadapted' to each other in this world than there are things
> 'adapted'; infinitely more things with irregular relations than
> with regular relations between them. But we look for the
> regular kind of thing exclusively, and ingeniously discover and
> preserve it in our memory. It accumulates with other regular
> kinds, until the collection of them fills our encyclopedias. Yet
> all the while between and around them is an infinite anony-
> mous chaos of objects that no one ever thought of together,
> of relations that never yet attracted our attention.
>
>   William James, The Varieties of Religious Experience

When I quoted this to Anita, she sat back, as though a revelation
had occurred to her, and she told me that when Frank sets himself
to read a novelist it is to discern the untraced lines, the connections
that the text makes but that haven't yet been made by another
critic. He uses the word 'occult' a lot, trying to trace lines that form
a pattern in the details. It is natural that Frank should turn to the
Bible, that most occult of texts. What he longs to do is write a
book about religious heresies.

Interesting, Anita's telling me that Frank has lost interest in the
poetry of W. B. Yeats for being too obvious, and has instead taken
on the more occult poetry of Wallace Stevens.

The title, The Genesis of Secrecy, was Anita's idea.

It is odd to go to her for an elucidation of Frank's work, which
he would never elucidate.

Often, when we have dinner parties for friends, we play the game of Exquisite Corpses – that is, a sheet of paper is folded into four or five parts, one person draws a head and folds it over so the next person can't see it and this person draws the shoulders and torso, which is folded over so as not to be seen, and the next person draws the thighs and genitals, and on and on until a whole figure is drawn, which is then revealed when the folded sheet of paper is unfolded. There have been evenings when we were howling with laughter.

So far, these are the friends who have played the game with Nikos and me:

Mark Lancaster, Andrew Lord, Keith Milow, Stephen Spender, Suzi Gablik, Stephen Buckley, James Joll, Tony Stokes, Teresa Gleadowe, Stephenie Bergman, Gregory Evans, David Hockney, Barry Flanagan, Sue Flanagan, Jan Hashey, Anne Wollheim, John Golding, Frank Kermode, Keith Walker, Michael Craig-Martin, Antoinette Godkin, Maggi Hambling.

———

About Patrick Kinross – he goes to North Africa for paid sex with young men (which Nikos seems to accept as what is done between older and younger men, and he laughs), and, after a recent tryst there, in London became afflicted with a disease that can't be diagnosed that wastes him away, so he is becoming thinner and thinner.

I suddenly recall Patrick opening the door to Nikos and me and, as I saw, noting that I had a small wound on my forehead, and this made him smile in a way I thought knowing, as if the small wound, which was caused by my bumping my forehead against a low lintel, signaled to him an activity, shared by Nikos, which he indulged in and that involved wounding.

From time to time, hinted at and then withdrawn, a suggestion opens up of a world Nikos and I know nothing about, that of sado-masochism, a world that seems as closed as the world of homosexuality once was, but, as once happened among homosexuals, hinted at and the hint withdrawn if the hint is not taken up. My impression is that the world includes all sexes, as if sado-masochism is a sex in itself, in which wounding and being wounded identifies the sex. I find myself wondering about so-and-so or so-and-so if he or she is of that sex, which keeps itself closed, but the members of which may be among my close friends. And I find myself not expressing horror at one person inflicting pain on another for pleasure, in case someone who is a friend is far from horrified – as, I suppose, a heterosexual may hold back from saying anything against homosexuality which he suspects in a friend he loves.

———

More and more, Nikos' memories become mine. I feel I was with him when he was a child and his family during the summer they moved from Athens to what was then the countryside in Kifisia and he was allowed one white balloon to play with. I think his memories have become more important to me than my own because I imagine I can possess them in a way I can't possess my own, he someone I view from the outside, and so, outside of me, viewed by me as more contained in himself than the uncontainable thoughts and feelings that I have inside of me. Yes, I would have to be him to make all the connections among the memories he recalls for them to be mine, all his memories beyond me. Still I go on to record his memories, and perhaps one day the complex context of all my own massively posses-sive feelings and thoughts about him will go and he will remain, himself, apart from me in this writing, on his own.

———

Stephen gave me a copy of his short stories and novella, The Burn-ing Cactus, which he asked me to 'edit.' I took him at his word, and did just that, limiting myself to one story, 'The Dead Island,' in which I crossed out lines and whole paragraphs to tighten the text, and what I mostly crossed out were metaphors and similes:

The sea was silent and brittle like smashed glass. The water looked so clear that it seemed like varnish adding colour and translucency to shoals of darting fish . . . She paused in her walk and listened closely to the birds' song bursting from the packed bushes, like white satin streamers against the cork-screwing cypresses . . .

It seems to me that Stephen relies on metaphors and similes to nail down impressions he is otherwise unsure of nailing, as if the simple The sea was silent . . . or She saw through the clear sea water shoals of darting fish . . . or She paused in her walk and listened to the birds' song in the cypresses . . . do not flash in the mind with the vividness metaphors and similes should give them. I want to say to him that it is not that I don't believe in the vivifying effects of metaphors and similes, but that I believe they are such mysterious workings of the imagination that they are miracles, and so should be used with all the respect miracles demand, perhaps one a book, and used as the key to unlock and reveal the meaning of the book. (As Frank does when he uses 'a ghost of a cup of tea' to unlock and reveal an inner meaning of Conrad's Under Western Eyes, and I wonder if this image of a 'ghost of a cup of tea' is what Frank would consider a 'shrine of the single sense' in which an 'immediate interpretation' is sustained for as long as any interpretation can be sustained.) I didn't go on about the deepening doubt I have that literature is too dependent on metaphor and simile, as if uncertain about anything but the use of imagery to sustain itself. I gave the book to Stephen and he thanked me, but he has not mentioned it to me. He did, however, tell Nikos that he was impressed by what I had done, and Nikos passed this on to me, and, oddly, I was embarrassed and would have preferred Stephen not telling Nikos, who he knew would tell me. But perhaps Stephen, too, was embarrassed that I should edit his stories.

———

I recall David Sylvester coming to dinner, where, as usual, he pushed back his chair to think about something that had been said, to think a long while. He said, 'I'm trying to think . . .' and everyone else at the table stopped to listen, and after a very long pause David said, 'I'm trying to think why . . .' and there was another long pause before David said, 'I'm trying to think why Cimabue is a greater artist than Fragonard.'

———

Nikos is more interested in writing poetry than being an editor, which poetry he allows only me to read. In his poetry the most abstract ideas are plangent, as in this, in which not one image occurs, but which expands into a sensitive plangent sense within the idea:

THE DEFINITION OF GOOD

Stripped finally of the 'bare essentials'
he had achieved a 'luminous simplicity'.
Removing one by one the layers of all that was 'superfluous',
down to the 'hard core',
divested of all 'attributes',
aspiring to a 'simple idea',
he strived to 're-define reality'.

Simplification, his aim, was a mere pose, we said.
Therefore, we concluded, he lied.
And yet, to him his pose was how he saw himself.
This was how he was . . .
He saw himself engrossed in, obsessed even
by the 'process of simplification', or 'self-simplification'.
What did this 'mean'? What did it mean to him, to us?
To him it meant arriving, through this process,
at some simple 'truth', a 'unit'
that could not possibly be simplified any further.
But this was vague – or so it seemed to us.
To us, 'simplification' meant, really, a dangerous, a suspect
obsessive drive to 'reduce' things, himself,
to what we called, in a derogatory sense, 'over-
simplification'.

That is, to us it meant, again, lying of sorts. To him?
The fact is he believed in this 'good', whereas we didn't.
We neither 'believed' nor understood what 'good' means.

———

Though it is impossible to ring Lucian Freud – contact with him
can only be made through his solicitor – he often rings Nikos at
home, at any hour, to insist, say, that there be no page numbers
wherever a reproduction of his work appears. Nikos asks how a
reference could then be made to a specific work, but Freud
remains adamant, so there are no page numbers where his works
are reproduced.

Stephen Spender calls Freud evil, and recounts the story of a book
dummy that they once did together, Stephen writing and Freud
drawing, which Stephen had but which Freud stole. He is also
known to lie, and worse. Does he think that after his death none of
this will be revealed? Better, I think, to reveal all when alive.

———

Costas Tachtsis, Nikos has heard, was murdered in Athens, where
he had had more of a money-making career among certain men
than he did as a writer among readers. Fed up with how little his
novel The Third Wedding was selling, he went out into the street
and sold copies as a hawker. It was known that he kept a diary,
recording the names of the men who came to his flat, but the only
object stolen from his flat was the diary. The rumour, Nikos was
told, is that his murderer has found pre-planned refuge in a monastery on Mount Athos, the Greek peninsula of monasteries where
no women are allowed. Eulogizing him on his death, Melina
Mercouri, now minister for culture, made a statement about Costas,
that he was the best Greek novelist after Kazantzakis.

———

No doubt partly to get into her good graces, which I am eager to do, and also because I find her fascinating, I offered Natasha to help her in her garden in Loudon Road, which help she accepted. But first lunch, where she told me a lot about her youth, much of which she had told me when we were in the South of France. Her mother, Ray Litvin, is alive still, and I gather lives in a flat whose rent is paid for by Stephen. I may get the sequence somewhat wrong, but the episodes from Natasha's life stand out. She had told me that she was illegitimate, the daughter of a music critic. She was sent as a baby to a home where she was restricted to a high chair, and all she could say when her mother visited her with a friend was 'Gwen, down, down,' referring to herself as Gwen; this alarmed her mother's friend, who suggested that Natasha be put in fostering care in a working-class family, where the mother, however strict, used to hold Natasha on her lap and close to her, the only reason, Natasha said with a short laugh, she is in any way sane. There was no recrimination in what she recounted, but everything sustained on a level of fact, and I wondered why she was telling me such intimate facts. Unknown to her, her father did arrange for Natasha to have what she called her other family, upper-middle class and wealthy, where she would spend periods and where she was encouraged in her gift of playing the piano. Her mother, an actress, became deaf, and blamed Natasha, whom she brought home – I think to a flat in Primrose Hill – and at eleven years old her mother instructed her to take a number such and such a bus and get off at such and such a stop and ring the bell at such and such an address, and the man who would answer would be her father, from whom she must ask for £15. Natasha did, and her father almost immediately engaged her in talk about music, which led to Natasha playing the piano for him. Whether or not she was given £15, I'm not sure Natasha said. Living with her mother, with no money, Natasha would sometimes go out on a walk for hours, distracted, then would look about with the realization that she had no idea where she was, but would then have to walk back. (This distraction, a sudden blankness, often comes over Natasha's face, even while she is talking, as if a sudden shock occurs to her.) She managed to continue with her piano, and at sixteen won a scholarship to the Royal College of Music. Years later, she found herself in a train compartment with Sybil Thorndike, and mentioned that her birth had caused her mother to go deaf and therefore ruin her career as an actress, and Sybil Thorndike said, 'But, Natasha, your mother was always deaf.'

In her late age, Natasha's mother has taken to painting, as instructed by Maggi Hambling; the garden shed is filled with her paintings.

Stephen, it seems, just about tolerates her.

Out in the front garden, I mostly dug and pulled up long tangled roots, while Natasha appeared not quite to know why she was there, but watched me.

She said, suddenly: when she opens a drawer and finds a photograph of a young man she does not know, obviously taken by Stephen, her heart crashes to her feet; but then she closes the drawer, thinking, he is not doing it to hurt her.

About W. H. Auden, Natasha told me she once confronted him with the moral problem of his sexuality and his calling himself an Anglican, to which he replied, 'I sin. There it is, I'm a sinner.'

———

A description:

Nikos and I on the Spanish island of Minorca for a summer holiday – the sun so bright it appeared to be black, but bright black as in a bright night, and the moonlit night appeared to shine with the blue light of day, and there was a sense of such freedom in the strangeness of it all.

Dry stalks of plants were covered with snails, and the stone walls along burnt-out fields looked like walls of skulls, and in the burnt-out fields were rough cactus.

Nikos took a film of me standing naked in the landscape.

———

What could be more relevant to today than this?

> Do we learn with one part of us, feel angry with another, and desire the pleasures of eating and sex with another? Or do we employ our mind as a whole when our energies are employed in any of these ways?
>
> Plato

———

Sebastian Walker (Sebbie), who has begun publishing pre-literate books for children (I asked him, 'Have you become a millionaire, Sebbie?' to which he replied with half-closed bulging eyes, 'Multi'), sponsored an evening of piano played by Alfred Brendel in the Middle Temple.

Nikos declined the invitation.

I went with Julia Hodgkin, she in a simple black evening frock and carrying a small black reticule covered with black sequins and

I in black tie. The taxi driver, leaving us off, asked, 'Important do this evening?'

The Middle Temple has stone-paved passages with polished wood-paneled walls and portraits of men in old frames. Just within the entrance was a round table with cards with names written on them arranged in circles to indicate at what tables and in what rooms people would sit for supper, then down a wooden staircase with a thick wooden banister and a red runner patterned with large blue flowers out into a garden where men and women in evening dress were gathered along a stone parapet, a wide, deep lawn extending beyond the parapet. A waiter came to offer us flutes of champagne from a silver tray.

I heard someone near by say, 'Really, Sebbie only gives a do like this to be able to invite the royals.'

'We'd better go up to the recital hall,' Julia said. 'The seats are unreserved.'

The hall is large, with a groined ceiling and high, wood-paneled walls. Along a high shelf all round the hall are placed breastplates and helmets, and painted on every wooden panel is a coat of arms.

Julia and I sat behind Stephen and Natasha Spender. I leaned forward to say hello to him, and he turned to me as if with a shock and asked, 'What are you doing here?'

I smiled.

He said, 'You're wearing a clip-on bow tie.'

I put a hand over my tie.

Natasha didn't turn to me.

Alfred Brendel came in, sat at the grand piano, adjusted the height of the stool by turning knobs on either end, and then held his fingers over the keys for a moment before he struck the first chord. All the while he played, people in the audience coughed.

Julia and I sat at a table among barristers and their wives. Napkins falling to the floor from laps, everyone rose when the royals, the Duke and Duchess of York, she at one table and he at another, got up. The Duchess, her eyes wide and staring apparently at nothing, walked through the standing guests, and, still apparently without seeing anything as she stared out, stopped for a second before a woman and smiled a smile that seemed to float out from her face and have nothing to do with her. The woman curtsied. Then, as soon as the royals had left, the guests dispersed, as if in a hurry to get away.

I heard this conversation:

'I was a long way from being seated at the best table.'

'What was the best?'

'With the Duchess.'

'And the second best?'

'With the Duke.'

'I would put our table at, say, fifth best.'

'Not too bad.'

I did not see Stephen and Natasha leaving.

Vera Russell asked Nikos to choose poems by Auden to be included in a large book of etchings by Henry Moore, and Vera arranged for Nikos to accompany Auden to Henry Moore's estate. Entering, all Auden said was, 'You must be a millionaire,' and lit up a cigarette, then, as if to himself, wondered why poets are not millionaires, and then consoled himself with the thought that when an artist does go into a slump he never rises from the slump, as though poets never go into slumps from which they never rise. What this had to do with Henry Moore, who clearly is not in a slump, Nikos had no idea, nor, he thought, did Henry Moore, who simply stared at Auden smoking his cigarette, his large, deeply wrinkled jaw thrust out, the bangs of his hair falling over his deeply wrinkled forehead. He showed no interest in Henry Moore's work, nor in the book. He was mostly silent at the meal of ribs of beef, which he ate, grease dripping down his chin, 'ravenously' Nikos said, after which he said, 'Well, I prefer mutton.' Nikos was very amused by this, and admiring of the total self-containment of Auden, as total as a monument so aware of its own monumentality that it is indifferent to spectators. Yet, perhaps because he was somewhat aware of his duties as a guest, he did talk, in his monotoned, gravelly voice, not so much to communicate as to express his many opinions about his many subjects, everyone else simply listening, as of course one does simply listen when a monument speaks.

Nikos told me he recounted to Stephen the visit and Auden's behavior, and Stephen, opening and closing his lips as if to suppress a smile and frowning a little, appeared to be thinking, More evidence of the personal monstrousness of Auden.

————

Marina Warner is often a guest at Sebbie's. She is an editor for Vogue magazine, or so I imagine, as her elegance makes her appear to be familiar with that world; but, too, when I hear her talking so knowledgeably with Dawn Ades about art history, also at Sebbie's, I imagine that the academic world is where she most fits in. Perhaps she lives one world within the other. She wears her spectacles at the tip of her nose.

Nikos was the first to publish Dawn, her book Photomontage.

————

We see a lot of Francis, who invited us to the Colony Room, which he calls Muriel's because it is run by Muriel Belcher, a close friend whom he paints. Up a flight of old stairs, the walls painted dark green where the plaster hasn't fallen away, we went into a small room with a filthy gray carpet, dirty pale-green walls, empty bottles under the chairs, and on the floor a large tin tub filled with ice and green bottles. The first time we went there, a mirrored door at the other side of the room opened and in came a man with loosely curled hair, spectacles, and a black-and-gold scarf about his neck. He was supporting an old woman in a lank gray dress. The man helped the woman to a stool at the end of the bar, near the entrance, and Francis introduced Nikos and me to her, Muriel, and to the man, Ian Board. Muriel's hair was long and thin and pulled tight over her skull so her scalp showed. Her face was long, wrinkled, slack; her mouth was always open, and her teeth made me think of her skull. Her gums were bleeding so she held a handkerchief to her mouth. She didn't look at us so much as tilt her head and throw an approximate glance at us. Francis said, 'Isn't she beautiful?' We said yes. Francis ordered champagne from the barman, whom he introduced us to. His name was David. Then Francis introduced us to the pianist, a young handsome man named Felicity, then Francis ordered a brandy-and-soda for Felicity from David. Francis, Muriel, Ian, Nikos and I talked about sex. Francis said, 'I hate sex in the morning.' 'When do you like it?' I asked. He said, 'Between three and four in the afternoon, with sunlight blazing through the windows.' I said, 'Nikos and I like it any time.' Muriel tapped me across the cheek with the back of a twisted hand and said, 'You old cunt.' Nikos said, 'You tell him.' Ian said to Nikos and me, 'You should come often, darlings.'

———

David Hockney comes to our flat, lounges on a chaise longue and answers questions Nikos asks him, which answers are recorded; Nikos has the tapes typed out then cuts himself out and arranges the text so it forms a narrative for a book. David has lively anecdotes to tell: how, on his first trip to Switzerland, he had looked forward to seeing the mountains, wanting to make a painting of them in 'Gothic gloom,' which he loves as much as Mediterranean or Californian; but, unfortunately, he didn't see the mountains as he was in the back of a little van and thought it polite not to ask to sit in the front as this was the first time his friend had been to Europe, a shame, as he had so wanted to paint the mountains; yet, when he returned to London he did do a painting with made-up mountains, called Flight into Italy – Swiss Landscape. He laughs a high bright laugh when he tells such anecdotes, and I hear them wishing I too had been in the back of a van unable to see the mountains and then be able to tell an anecdote about being in the back of a van and unable to see mountains.

———

We asked Stephen and Francis to dinner. As if he had all the time in the world, Francis arrived before Stephen. In the living room, I asked him to sit, but he said, 'No, I'll stand. I like being uncomfortable.'

At our small, oval dining table in a bedroom, Stephen asked Francis, 'How old are you?' Francis said, 'I was born October 28, 1909, so I'm sixty-eight.' 'And I was born February 28, 1909,' Stephen said. 'So I'm six months older than you,' Francis said. 'Six months younger,' Stephen said. Francis looked puzzled. 'Oh yes,' he said. Stephen said, 'And you were in Berlin while I was there. I wonder why we didn't meet.' 'We probably went to different places,' Francis said; 'I used to be in the clubs all the time.' 'So was I,' Stephen said. 'Then we were probably in the same club at the same time,' Francis said.

'How did you get to Berlin?' I asked Francis.

He seemed to like being asked questions about his life. 'Oh,' he said, 'my father found me wearing my mother's underclothes, and to put me right he sent me to a friend – like my father, a horse trainer. This was in Ireland. I left home to go with my father's friend, who took me to Berlin. He was very rich and we stayed in a grand hotel. That was the first time I had sex with anyone. From there, I went to Paris. My mother sent me three pounds a week. I never really went back to Ireland.'

―――――

Natasha's mother has died. She spent her last days in Loudoun Road. After she died, Natasha was very apprehensive about reading her letters to her mother, worried that they would be filled with reproaches; but she found reading them that they were written with tenderness and love, and this came to her as a great moral relief.

I recall Stephen once telling me that he and Natasha were in Germany just after the war, on a train; Natasha insisted that they change their pounds on the black market, and Stephen said, no, he'd rather the official rate, which made Natasha react by threatening to throw herself off the train and kill herself if he didn't agree with her. I wonder if she does sometimes assert her will by threatening to kill herself. But how could I imagine this to be heroic, which I do? Leave aside whether or not Stephen was more admirable than Natasha in wanting to exchange pounds at the official rate (it is very much in Stephen to want to do this), I see her threat to kill herself as a way to assert her will within the whole of her past life, a past life she had to will herself to survive, and which she continues to will herself to survive.

I've heard people say about Natasha that the best they can do is tolerate her because of Stephen, who suffers her will. These people, I feel, don't see what an heroic struggle it is for Natasha simply to will herself to live, helpless as she is against a past life that she could easily have not survived.

I once asked her if she was happy, and she said, 'That is something I never consider.'

She told me that there was a trying time when, inspired by the Farm Street Jesuit Martin D'Arcy, she thought of converting to the Roman Catholic Church, and read a good deal of theology about relinquishing one's will to the will of God.

———

After the death of W. H. Auden, whose funeral service she went to in Kirchstetten in the countryside of Austria, Sonia seems to have taken on caring for Chester Kallman, whom she invited Nikos and me to meet at a dinner party. He appears to have become Auden, in manners and speech, his features as pendulous as Auden's.

He lives in Athens, no doubt at Auden's expense, and while Sonia was downstairs in the kitchen preparing a meal he told us that what he likes to do with Greek boys is have bubble baths with them, and I had the horrific vision of him, hump-backed and hump-stomached, in a large bath of three or more boys cavorting among foam and rising bubbles.

A few days later he sent us a poem he had written on the death of a young Greek lover, a tender poem:

How, darling, this innocent grief
Must irk you, more
Even than those outraged, mute
Or pleading jealousies, though now
This you are too pitiless to refute,
Making me all you disapprove:
Selfishly sodden, selfless, dirtier, a prodigal
Discredit to our renewed belief in love:
And addressing the dead! You'd laugh.
Yet I can't imagine you dead
As I know you are and somehow
Hold this one indulgence you allow,
You who allowed me so much life.

This was translated into Greek by Costas Tachtsis. I didn't know that he and Chester Kallman knew each other, but more and more I expect people I meet to have themselves met one another.

———

The time came for Nikos and me to move from Battersea into central London, partly because he had a long way to go to his office at Thames & Hudson, and partly because we had enough money now to move to a bigger flat in what I at least thought a nicer area of London. Nikos liked Battersea, liked the working-class shops and, too, the park just across Prince of Wales Drive, where we had picnics with friends. And, too, he said it was there that we created our lives together, painted the walls, bought furniture (some given to us by Johnny Craxton), hung our pictures, sewed curtains, and where, in our small sitting room we had so many drinks parties, and where in our smaller dining room we had so many dinner parties.

Between the time we sold the flat in Battersea and were able to move into the one in Montagu Square, more or less around the corner from where we had met in Wyndham Place, we stayed in the pied-à-terre of Nikos' cousin in Ovington Square, which to Nikos was like being homeless. This panicked him.

He is always anticipating a catastrophe.

He asks, Does he have cancer? No, I answer.

Does he have a bad heart? No, I answer.

Will he lose his job? No, I answer.

Will the flat we're supposed to move into be taken away from us? No.

Will his kitties die? No.

(He now has two cats, Jasmine and an offspring called Mustafa.)

His uncertainty, often parodied by himself and made into a joke, fills me with affection for him and the desire to reassure him.

But to truly reassure him would be to go back into his past and relieve him of the fear of belonging to a refugee family; his uncertainty, his sense of impending catastrophe, are in his history. I would like to undo his history, but cannot.

In Montagu Square, we now live in a Georgian house, the top maisonette, overlooking a garden in the square. We have a key to the garden. The area of the house has black iron railings about it, and the front door, wide and shiny black, has a bright brass knob. We have had our furniture removed from Battersea, hung our pictures, organized books in especially built bookshelves, and each of us has a study. We have our bed from Battersea, the bed that means so much to Nikos, as if that, where we sleep night after night together, where we make love, is where our lives together are most our lives together.

I sometimes dare to think Nikos is happy.

He longs, he says, to stay in – no drinks parties, no dinner parties, neither ones we give nor ones we are invited out to.

He says, 'Please, no socializing.'

I should put in that since we last lived in Wyndham Place, the neighbourhood has changed, and where there was once a greengrocer where you could not buy green peppers because such a vegetable was too foreign, there is now a Lebanese grocery where vegetables and fruit are on sale that are totally foreign to us (thinking they were bananas, Nikos bought plantains), and where Nikos can buy Greek pasturma, halumi, feta cheese. The grocery is open on Sunday, as are all the grand department stores in Oxford Street.

I forgot to put in that we now lived next to where Trollope lived and died.

The story is: he was working on a novel but was so disturbed by a man playing hurdy-gurdy in the square, he raised the sash, leaned out, shouted that that abomination must stop, and had an apoplexy and died.

———

A Sunday afternoon, Nikos and I walked about Hyde Park, and I was reminded of the times we used to walk there when we lived in Wyndham Place. I remembered how anxious I was, and how Nikos would say, 'Now breathe in deeply, and look closely at what's around you.' The flowers in the parterres we walked along appeared to me dead. Now, walking along the same parterres, the flowers appeared brightly alive. I wondered about the difference between then and now. Perhaps we were closer then, not despite, but because of my mental illness, for it was an illness, and Nikos cured me.

———

It is only at odd moments that I feel this flat is home. Nikos said he feels the same, that he imagines he is a guest in someone else's flat. Then he said something that struck me as being true for myself as well as for him: that he doesn't feel he belongs in such a posh, upper-middle-class neighbourhood. I can understand why I feel this, but he, used to his own upper-middle-class culture, should feel comfortable here, if somewhat disdainful. When we lived in Battersea and came into more central London on walks and passed through the kind of neighbourhood we now live in, Nikos, looking through the windows of elegant houses, would ask, 'Why can't we live in such a place?' as if it were not simply a question of money but that we were not allowed. Again, I understand this in myself, but in Nikos I can only think his having felt more comfortable in working-class Battersea (where he liked to go to Clapham Junction to the working-class department store Arding & Hobbs for his socks and underwear), was because he felt he was not entitled to live in what friends now say is a 'posh' place, his sense of class in fact weak from coming from a refugee family who, though upper-middle class from Constantinople, were not accepted into middle-class Athens, so Nikos grew up feeling déclassé.

We keep saying we want to be quiet in our new flat, but we see many, many people.

I repeat once again the observation I have made over and over about our similarities and differences. If I am discontent, I blame myself (at a drinks party, I drank too much so have a hangover), whereas Nikos, discontent, blames the world (if people did not invite him out to a drinks party he wouldn't drink so wouldn't suffer a hangover, and he thereby puts the blame, not on himself, but on others inviting him out!).

———

Sue Flanagan came to tea. She talked about herself and Barry. Barry, living away, wants a divorce, Sue doesn't. I asked, 'How can you know what Barry wants, given how convoluted his talk is?' Sue said, 'That's because he didn't learn to speak until he was eight or nine, but I understood him, he wants a divorce.' 'Why?' 'He says he is in love with someone else.' 'Are you sure that's what he said?' Sue did laugh a quiet laugh. I told Sue that in fact I had met the woman, Ann, some time before at a drinks party, and she had said that she understands Barry and that with her he is perfectly clear when he talks, which she thought had to be a sign that something was going well between them. Sue said, 'She's a liar. I do understand Barry, I do.' And I wondered about two women contesting their love for a man because they understood, one better than the other, what Barry meant by – as I recall him saying to me – 'It's a melon thrown at me from a truck driving at a hundred miles an hour.'

———

That Nikos and I arrange books together, that we shop together, go to a recital together, makes these banal activities aspects of our relationship, imbues these activities with the multi-dimensional and in doing so imbues our relationship with the multi-dimensional. Our relationship needs these activities, I realize, in that the degree that they come alive in our performing them together is the degree that our relationship comes alive.

Nikos has gone to bed. Now I'll go to bed.

I said to him today, 'I really love this flat,' and he said, 'I do too.'

———

I am alone in our flat, and I try not to think of anything but what is immediately about me, as I feel anxious in his absence and don't want the anxiety to take hold of me, which it so easily can do when I am alone.

I love London. In the morning, I went out to walk about the neighborhood, and everything appeared so vivid, as if I were seeing everything for the first time. The weather was gray and wet, and I loved this, too.

New Year's Eve, Roxy and I gave a party.

Roxy: 'I awoke one morning with the horrors, you know them, having an unstructured life, no job, just the round of parties, openings and movies, and realizing I'm not in love with the boyfriend, nor he with me, quel sadness, so I went back to bed for the rest of the day, sleeping heavily and now, a week later, I still feel dozy. But we shall have a wonderful party on New Year's Eve. Do you think sandwiches and Christmas cake and tequila, or something more traditional like blinis and glasses of stout? Mr. Keogh from Dublin says the best poured glass of stout in London is to be had at the Catholic Martyrs Club in Aldgate.'

Frank and Anita, that day back from Jerusalem, came to the party. Natasha, who had been so adamant on saving Frank's first marriage to Maureen and so alienated herself from Anita, came, and was, as she would have said, on her 'best behavior' with Anita, and was affectionate towards me. Stephen is in New York. The poet Al Alvarez and the child psychiatrist Anne Alvarez came. Suzi. Sue Flanagan (she has split up from Barry). Joe and Jos Tilson. Old friends, old friends! In the Greek manner, I opened the windows at midnight, as we all drank sparkling wine, to let the old year out and the new year in.

The day after, to Sylvia's for supper. She said, 'You're in a very lively state. I wonder if, however much you love it, London will pull you down.'

'But I'm in a lively state because I am in London,' I said.

I feel loving towards everyone.

———

John Fleming, staying with us in Montagu Square, told us this, which we hadn't known: one of the previous occupants of the house, married and with children and living in the country, would come up to London from time to time to stay in the flat and from there go to Piccadilly Circus and the arcade of flashing pinball machines and pick up boys and bring them back, one time a boy scout who went to the police, so the man was arrested. Charlotte Bonham Carter, hearing of this, shouted, 'Those terrible, terrible boy scouts, they should be disbanded.'

———

In what he calls the bottomless pit in the basement of Loudoun Road, where years of accumulations are stored, Stephen found an envelope with old photograph negatives which he had printed and which, to his surprise, revealed in black and white people he had known in Berlin. They include Stephen (taken by his brother Humphrey) and Christopher and his boyfriend and the original Sally Bowles, in fact Jean Ross, she standing full square in a loose smock and loose slacks and ballet slippers, a beret tipped to one side on her head, and she looking out at the camera with large dark eyes. Stephen gave us a set. The photographs taken in Weimar Berlin appeared to me to be representative of all of Weimar Berlin, as if all of that period of history was consciously being lived by

those photographed – whereas, as I heard Christopher once say to
Stephen, the boy in the photograph is not thinking of history but
of a suit he hopes Stephen will give him, while Stephen is worried
that he won't have the money to buy the suit. Really, photographs,
if seen as taken, not within history, but within the moment, demythologize history, and there is every reason to demythologize
history when it is as romanticized as Weimar Germany.

———

We were, Nikos and I, collating the dates in our agendas, which we
do every Sunday as it sometimes happens that he has written in a
date when I haven't, or vice versa, and we double date. I saw that
he had written down, for lunch, Paul.

I asked, 'Paul who?'

He laughed. He said, 'My old friend Paul.'

'You didn't tell me you were having lunch with him.'

'If I didn't, it was because I didn't think it was important
enough to.'

'Of course it's important. He loved you and you made love
together. Of course it's important. And you were keeping it
from me.'

'I wasn't.'

'It doesn't matter.'

'You don't believe me.'

'No, but it doesn't matter. It's not important.'

'Of course it's important that you should believe me.'

This went on for a while, then I came up to my study and my
desk to work, and he came in.

He said, 'You've got to trust me.'

'I don't, not entirely. You've destroyed letters in the past then
conveniently forgotten what was in them so I wouldn't know. Of
course you've hidden things from me. But I have to recognize that
you did this just so I wouldn't be hurt. I accept that.'

'You've got to trust me. I do tell you the truth.'

'I don't quite believe you.'

He went out.

Later, I went downstairs to find out what he was doing. We are always checking on what each other is doing, as out of curiosity. I found him in the kitchen preparing supper for John G. and James J. We hugged each other, then laughed. I left him, as he wanted to prepare the supper, and I went back to my desk, thinking, It doesn't matter.

———

Our downstairs neighbours in 38 Montagu Square are Joseph and Ruth Bromberg.

Joseph is originally from Russia, from a family of furriers; he grew up in Berlin. As a boy, he was taught tennis by Vladimir Nabokov, a relative through marriage to his wife Vera. Joseph said that, really, Nabokov would let him and his brother play in whatever way while he sat on a bench on the side of the court and read. Ruth was from Nuremberg, where Jews were allowed to own land, she from a family of gentlemen farmers, her father even calling himself, as a descendant, the Third, which is not Jewish. He and his family escaped by way of Cuba, she by way of going east, to Japan, to San Francisco, to New York. They met in New York.

She stayed with an aunt who did not like her, and restricted even her food, so that Ruth with all of ten cents bought apples which she had to hide in her room until her aunt, coming in, sniffed and said, 'I smell apples,' and Ruth had to give them up.

Ruth remembers walking down Broadway with her bobby socks and pleated skirt and hearing a man call out, 'There goes an American girl!'

After they married, Ruth's aunt said to her, 'So you've married a kike.' He was from Russia and she from Germany.

From Milan, where they lived for thirty years, Joseph working his way up to head of a furrier company, they moved to London, where their son Michael, after unsuccessful treatment for leukemia, died, a young man. His absence is also his presence in their flat.

Ruth is completely autodidact, especially in old master prints.

She completed the catalogue raisonné of Canaletto prints, and is now working on the catalogue raisonné of Walter Sickert prints, of which they buy as many as they can for her to study them closely. Nikos and I proofread her entries.

She says we are all family.

They invite Nikos and me to grand restaurants, and we invite them to less grand. Or they invite us to dinner parties, catered, with other guests from the world of art historians and museum curators, as the Brombergs have endowed a fellowship in their son's name for research in prints, and, too, they often donate money and works to the Print Department of the British Museum.

Ruth sits to Frank Auerbach every Wednesday. Every Tuesday, she has her hair done at a hairdresser in preparation. From time to time, Frank, as a gesture of thanks, gives Ruth a portrait he has painted of her. Each time a new one is given, all the pictures have to be rearranged, and, when Nikos and I visit, Ruth looks down at us from many different angles with contorted faces, but always with a rather comic smile applied, it appears, almost as an afterthought with a quick stroke of the brush.

Because he hardly ever goes out, very occasionally Frank and his wife Julia come to dinner at the Brombergs', and Nikos and I are invited.

This amazed me:

Joseph said that the most powerful image in the Western world is the image of Jesus Christ crucified on the cross. I still hear him saying, as if in awe, 'He gave up his life for the salvation of human-kind.' He asked Frank what he thought, and Frank, in a low voice, said, yes, there is no more powerful image in the Western world.

Sometimes, when I am alone with Joseph, he will tell me stories that he does not want Ruth to hear, they would upset her; and I weep.

———

We commissioned Keith to do a work for us, one to fit into a narrow space in our new flat, but, Keith being Keith, he brought to the flat a work so large it has to take up an entire alcove where there was once a fireplace. It dominates the room, and it dominates with grandeur: it is made out of sheets of lead folded over wooden frames so that each frame is the size of a building block, the lead blocks layered to form a wide, high, semi-circular wall, rather like the stone wall within a medieval tower, between the blocks non-drying putty that drips oil onto the lead. The whole is majestic and has the quality that Keith says he wants in his work: classical.

A comment about Keith's work –

He uses raw, perhaps what he considers essential, materials – lead, resin, cement, plywood, copper, sheets of plastic – and with them structures works that themselves stand for essentials in, say, the essential shapes of tondo, cross, cenotaph, different stylized architectural forms, all essentially timeless, majestic, classical, and all with an intellectual 'edge' to them that defines them with clarity.

We also have a large cross by Keith, made of cement and resin, one vertical half of the cross flat and the other vertical half at a slant, the whole giving the impression of a Greek kouros with one leg rigidly straight and the other taking a step forward, and, again, there is classical grandness to it.

And we have other works by Keith, some we have bought, some he has given to us.

One of our pleasures is to acquire a work of art and then spend all weekend rearranging the hanging of all the pictures.

What we have: paintings by Adrian Stokes, paintings by Stephen Buckley, a painting and prints by Mark Lancaster, two etchings by Frank Auerbach, a cut-out tin piece by Julian Opie, a painting by Lisa Milroy, prints by Joe Tilson, prints and a small painting of me by R. B. Kitaj, an etching by Lucian Freud, etchings and drawings and a small painting by David Hockney, a drawing by Sandra Fisher, drawings and a sculpture by Barry Flanagan, a pastel by John Golding, drawings by Michael Craig-Martin, drawings and a water-color by Patrick Procktor, a stone tondo by Stephen Cox, a large pastel by Jan Hashey, a print by Howard Hodgkin –

———

David Sylvester will ring up to ask if a sentence he has written sounds right, and, with long pauses, he will be on the telephone for hours, getting the sentence right. The people he rings talk among themselves, perhaps with a degree of complaint, about those long conversations, but no one would want to be left out. And it is certainly a sign of belonging to a circle to be invited to dinner by David to his house (bought by his selling a painting that Francis Bacon gave him, which Francis did not seem to mind), the house like a private museum, all dominated, it seems, by an immense sandstone Egyptian pharaoh standing within a bay of windows, outside the windows a screen of high reeds. You ask if you may look about the house, and David, not saying anything, stares so intensely at you that you wonder if you shouldn't have asked, but that's the way with David, he doesn't say yes or no, he simply stares. The house has bare wooden floors painted a carefully chosen slightly mottled, pale grey-blue, with only fragments of rugs here and there, and from room to room, each object given space to set it off, you see a Kerala canoe, battered Roman busts on marble columns, an African Nupe stool, a Neolithic pottery jar, a drawing by Joan Miró, a Regency card table, a lute, a large painting by William Turnbull, an Indian sandstone female torso, etchings by Picasso, an Italian walnut wardrobe, drawings by Giacometti. You say, 'David, this is all wonderful,' and again David stares at you, then finally says, 'But I don't have one major work,' and you feel a little badly for him that he doesn't.

The evening will have been as carefully arranged as the furniture and pictures and antiquities in his house, and you always have the sense of the privilege of being invited, though, at the glass-topped table, David will listen with acute attention to what you say, staring at you, one eye drifting off to the side as if with the strain of his attention, and after saying what you think of as at best incidental, if not stupid, David will seem to think a long while about it, then say, portentously, 'That is very profound.'

Nikos and I were invited to a dinner party at his house, Marina Warner also invited, and Sarah Whitfield, from the house next door, a partner to David, who in fact prepared the meal, the menu chosen by David. Suddenly, David got up from the dining table and went out then came back with a picture which he handed to me across the table, saying, 'The only gift worth giving is a gift it hurts to give,' and I reached out for a colourful drawing by Stephen Tennant of an ancient Greek goddess among white roses, a fantasy cover for a book of poems by Stephen Spender. It was as though David were giving me a world of associations, and I realized that David himself lived in that world, was himself a world of associations.

During a weekend when I was away, Nikos saw Dawn Ades, and, he told me when I returned, they had asked each other whom they would like to sleep with, just lay next to and sleep, and Nikos said, 'David Sylvester,' and Dawn said to Nikos, 'You!'

———

Pleading with me when I feel I have failed as a writer, Nikos asks me, 'Isn't my love for you enough?' and I become weak and want to fall on the floor.

———

A sun-filled Saturday, edged with blossoming daffodils. Suzi came to lunch, then we sat in the sun on the roof, Nikos repotting some plants there. After Suzi left, Nikos and I had a nap. We will have drinks with the Brombergs, then all go together to our local church – Saint Mary's – to hear Bach's Saint Matthew Passion.

If no one had ever conceived of eternity, of timelessness, which we long for, especially on a day like this, perhaps we wouldn't mind the day passing because we would not imagine anything different. But the fact is we do imagine. As we'll never realize what we imagine, I wonder if imagination is our greatest curse.

———

When I rang Stephen and Natasha to invite them to dinner, they both answered on separate telephones, as they often do, so there is a three-way conversation. Stephen said, alas, they couldn't come because they were to take an American professor to the theatre, as he'd entertained them when they were in Nashville, Tennessee. Natasha asked Stephen, 'Where will we take him to dinner after the theatre?' and she and Stephen had a little discussion as to what restaurant they'd go to while I listened in, then Stephen said to me, 'I have an idea – if I buy some meat pies and wine, can we come to you and Nikos after the theater?' and I, feeling small because I hadn't suggested this first, said, 'Of course you must come here, and don't bring anything, as I'll make a stew of some kind that will keep,' and they were filled with thanks. Natasha said, 'Thank you v. v. v. much.'

Nikos was pleased.

The next day, Stephen rang and said, 'Honestly, Natasha shouldn't have agreed to your offer to entertain us all. I feel she takes advantage of her friends.' I thought back at our conversation, wondering if I had remembered correctly, but was pretty sure I had: Stephen had proposed coming to us.

I also asked Melvyn Bragg and Cate Haste, to whom I'd explained that Stephen and Natasha would come late; they arrived about 10.00, and they and Nikos and I drank wine and talked, I wondering when Stephen and Natasha would come.

They arrived late, about 11.30. Stephen had a basket of three bottles of good wine. We sat around the sitting room and ate off our laps as there was not enough room at our dining table. The professor hardly spoke, hardly ate the food I served him. We others talked about the campaign to retake the Falkland Islands, which everyone agreed was a mistake. It was, as Natasha would say, a jolly good evening, or so I thought; she was especially lively and talkative. Then everyone got up to leave, and as Melvyn and Cate were saying goodbye, I saw Natasha looking at a picture in the sitting room, and I suddenly thought: My God, the Picasso etching!

I've mentioned the etching in here: Stephen gave it to me in case Nikos threw me out, so I'd have something to rely on. At that time, he also gave one to David Hockney as a gesture of thanks for all the drawings and etchings David has given to him. Shortly after, he and Natasha were at David's studio, and Natasha, seeing the Picasso, said, 'Oh, we have one just like that,' and David said, 'Stephen gave it to me.'

There are many stories of Stephen giving precious possessions away without telling Natasha, the most dramatic story being: Stephen gave to Natasha as a wedding gift a special bound copy of World within World, his autobiography, which some years later Cyril Connolly saw in their house and asked for, and Stephen simply gave to Cyril what he had given to Natasha as a wedding gift; when Natasha, perhaps one day looking for it and not finding it, asked Stephen where it was, he told her he had given it to Cyril, and she went into a state; Stephen asked Cyril, explaining the situation to him, if he'd give the book back and Cyril said no, and from then on Natasha wouldn't speak to him.

When Natasha was told by David H. that Stephen had given the Picasso etching to him, she went into a state – at home, of course, alone with Stephen. Stephen had told me this story and admonished me, 'For God's sake, don't let Natasha know you have that Picasso. It's an atomic bomb!' How he explained its disappearance from the house I didn't know. Each time Natasha came to the house, I had to remember to take down the etching and replace it with something innocuous, say a drawing by Johnny Craxton. Sometimes I remembered to change it only minutes before she arrived. This evening, I forgot.

When I saw her studying the etching, I quickly went to her, not knowing what to say. She said, 'That's nice,' and I said, 'But that's yours.' 'Oh,' she said, 'is it?' I said, 'We have many pictures that belong to you.' 'Oh yes?' she said. I didn't know what else to say, and looked across the room towards Stephen, who gave me one of his looks of combined anger and defeat. They left with the American professor, Natasha hardly saying goodnight.

Nikos said, 'Well, you'll simply return the etching.'

It took me a long time to fall asleep.

As I'd anticipated, Stephen rang me in the morning. I

apologized for what had happened, and he said, 'No, don't worry. Natasha didn't mention a thing about it.' We talked more, and I heard the second receiver being lifted and Natasha listened for a moment before Stephen asked, 'Natasha?' and she said, 'Oh, I'm sorry,' and hung up. I said to Stephen, 'I feel awful about that Picasso. Supposing I had given one that Nikos and I owned to a young man without telling him and he found out, of course he'd be angry. I'm amazed that Natasha isn't. You must have it back.' He said, 'Well, if she asks for it, perhaps. But no one is going to sell it. There it is. Why shouldn't you be enjoying it?' 'No,' I insisted, 'Nikos says I must give it back.'

———

Vera Russell is writing her memoirs. In conversation, she will say, 'Henry told me . . .' and one has to know this is Henry Moore, or 'Sam told me . . .' and this is Samuel Beckett, or 'Joyce once told me . . .' and you think this must be James Joyce, or 'Igor . . .' and who else could this be but Igor Stravinsky, or 'Serge . . .' and, yes, Serge Diaghilev, and 'Valéry' had to be none other than Paul Valéry, but when she mentioned that 'Albert once said . . .' I was hard put to know that this was her friend Albert Schweitzer. As she has no money, she rang the dealer in books and papers George Lawson to ask him to come round to see the letters she'd saved and to give an estimate of their value. George came back saying, 'It's absolutely true – Vera has known everybody.' Her memoirs, which require the help of a research assistant, are already four volumes long. We had lunch in a restaurant in Hyde Park, where she said, 'I'll have a big steak. I need strength.'

She said to me, 'Henry told me that he believes the word is more powerful than the image. Writing matters more than painting or sculpture.'

'That's reassuring to me,' I said.

'I have known Henry for fifty years,' she said, 'and worked with him for twenty-five.'

The impression (and I rely on the word: impression) is that Henry could not have achieved what he did without her.

'When I was placing Henry's —' and here she identified a huge sculpture — 'in the landscape of Yorkshire —' and I imagined Vera hefting the huge piece and placing it on a hill, or in a dale.

I shouldn't be making fun of her.

She showed me her essay on Henry Moore. 'I wrote this five times. I wanted to write something about him that hasn't been written before.' The essay is filled with wonderful non-sequiturs. 'Because I am a revolution baby' (she was born during the Russian Revolution in Moscow and can remember, she says, looking out the window and seeing the Revolution happening) 'I understand Henry Moore's art —' No, this isn't right. I am making fun of her.

Once, she showed me a reproduction of a painting by Francis of a grotesque figure with a leg in a large plaster cast, and Vera said, 'That's me.'

————

Francis invited Nikos and me and Stephen to meet his new friend, Bill. We hadn't known he had a friend since George. Bill is an electrician. Sonia says telephone engineer. He is a broad, very handsome man who wants to become a policeman in New York but who is intelligent enough to know that he really only wants to satisfy a fantasy he has about New York cops. His life, it seems, is devoted to satisfying his sexual fantasies. He's been all over the United States, and Canada too, and he can tell you where the best bars are, and where men like one thing or another. Because of his looks, he said that every time he goes into a queer club in America the bouncer will say to him, 'You do realize, sir, that this is a club for homosexuals?' He loves asking policemen in the street for the way to bars and clubs that, he said smiling, they of course know are queer. Bill's smile is wide and clean and very white.

After dinner at Langan's Brasserie, for which Francis insisted on paying, we all got into a taxi to go to a club in Leicester Square called Adam's. The taxi stopped and started, stopped and started in the Friday late-night traffic in the West End. Once we got to

Leicester Square, Stephen said he thought he'd go home – it was still early enough to catch the tube.

Adam's is a large, crowded club with gold chandeliers and gold-framed mirrors, and is so dark and filled with smoke we could hardly see. Francis, Bill, Nikos and I stood by the bar. Francis kept giving Bill twenty-pound notes to buy bottles of champagne. We talked a lot about sex. Bill said he liked to be fucked, fist-fucked, and he also liked, from time to time, 'G.B.H.' Nikos asked, 'What's that?' 'Grievous bodily harm,' Bill said, and smiled his bright smile. 'And you've had it?' Francis asked him. 'Only a couple of times,' Bill answered. 'Real welts and wheals?' Francis asked. 'Oh yes,' Bill answered; 'I enjoy it but it has to be done by someone you like. And there's always the danger that they won't be able to stop when you want them to.' 'Well,' Francis said, 'I like G.B.H. now and then. I had a friend – he finally killed himself – who had a collection of whips he kept at my place. A while ago, I took someone there who said he was interested in whips, and I showed him the collection.' Francis laughed. 'Well, I undressed and got on my fish-net stockings –' 'Black?' Nikos asked. 'Of course black, stupid,' Francis said. 'And he started to beat me. But he got carried away. He wouldn't stop. I'm a total coward. In nothing but my black fish-net stockings, I ran out into Reece Mews.' He laughed a loud laugh.

A tall, blond man came up to us and asked, 'Who are you all? You all look so interesting, so glum.' Not even Francis spoke to him. He asked Nikos and me, 'Do you two live together?' 'Why do you think that?' I asked. 'I can tell,' he said. A friend behind him said, 'Come on, let's go, they look creepy.'

We were in the club until three-thirty. Nikos and I left only when Francis said he'd leave. Bill remained with a fellow who looked like a bearded Greek priest.

Outside, Francis said, 'Bill and I spent four days together and discovered we're incompatible because we both like the same thing. But we've remained friends.'

I ran around the square trying to find a taxi, but none would stop for me though their lights were lit. Francis, who hadn't moved,

simply put up a hand and a limousine, not a taxi, stopped in front
of him. A young man rolled down the window and said, 'You look
like three cold gentlemen. I'll drive you wherever you want to go.'
Francis got in beside him, Nikos and I in the back. The driver
asked, 'Now, what have you been doing up at this hour when all
honest people are in bed?' Francis answered, with that short, shrugging laugh he has, 'Not being honest.' He asked the driver his
name. 'George,' the driver said; 'and what's your name?' 'Francis.' 'Is
that Mr. Francis?' 'Mr., Mrs., Miss – however you like it,' Francis
said. The driver left Nikos and me off first.

I asked R. B. Kitaj what he thinks of Francis' painting, and he wrote
me, on many postcards, his favourite form of communicating:

> For me, Bacon is not a great painter like Matisse or Picasso.
> He is a narrower talent, and he seems to have refused to draw,
> but from my perspective he is the best, most original and
> engaging painter . . . I cherish unusual paintings and, boy oh
> boy, are they rare and hard to achieve! Bacon keeps doing
> them . . . Of course it's all a matter of taste, so I don't wish to
> argue Bacon with those who are turned off by him, including
> brilliant friends of mine . . . But I do think he sings the song
> of himself. His pictures are every bit as elegant as the high
> American abstraction, but he engages his urbane nihilism to
> one's one neurotic unease and achieved a psychological bloody
> pitch which almost always holds my attention.

A conversation with David Sylvester. He wondered if Yeats, great a
poet as he was, failed to be the greatest because he lacked 'helplessness.' Nikos said that Yeats is limited because he is, however subtle,
rhetorical – his poetry is constrained by its complicated intentions.

I said I wonder if this applied to Francis' paintings, but with an
essential difference: he himself is aware of the constraint of

intention and tries, with more than will power, with passion, to go beyond intention and give his work 'helplessness.' I wondered if Francis in fact succeeds, if there is too much intention in his attempt to give himself up to the unintentional, even by throwing paint on the canvas then to work it into a figure. Nikos smiled and said nothing, but, as he always does, David looked at me for a very long time, and after a very long time he slowly, carefully said, 'That is very interesting,' as if he himself had not thought, among many, of such an obvious comment about the works of Francis Bacon.

When I think of 'helplessness' in writing, I think of Victor Shklovsky, who started out a novel with an intention but at the end he found he had written a novel completely different from what he had intended it to be, a novel that had occurred and expanded beyond his intention; so, when he started a new novel, he gave in helplessly to whatever novel would occur, that novel expanding as if on its own intentions beyond his, and he did this by writing whatever came to him, however seemingly disconnected, taking it on faith that everything in the end would connect, but not as he had thought. The unintended is truer than what is intended, because – and this I wonder at – what can't be helped is truer than what can be helped, what is allowed to happen is truer than what one tries to make happen, what one gives in to is truer than what one imposes oneself upon.

But what is the unintended that expands on its own, to which the writer and the artist give themselves up helplessly? What expands beyond intention? What is it that we can only ever have a 'sense' of, can never give a rhetorical name to? What? We can't say, but it is in us – it strains in us, it strains with a longing in us – to want to say what it is, to release it, to see it formed out there around us into – what? – a bright globe of everything, everything, everything all together held in that one great globe, is that all I can imagine of what it is?

————

Paul Levy (writer on all forms of culture, including cuisine) and Penny Marcus (editor) give large parties in and outside their large stone house in Oxfordshire, parties during which the guests seem to fall in love, sometimes in the barn in the straw, or guests fall out of love, in no place in particular. Usually, the party takes place in the garden, as if in the midst of greenery diffused into the green air, where there is a site-specific rock sculpture by Barry Flanagan. And there is a long table covered with a white cloth and food and bottles, though the guests more often than not wander about, attaching and detaching, and so I attached myself to Beryl Bainbridge (novelist) and asked her if Maggie Drabble (novelist) and Michael Holroyd (biographer) – standing side by side near a brick wall against which was an espalier apple tree, he a tall man slightly stooped and she, shorter, her shoulders thrown back and her chin, as if she were at attention, held in – are a couple, to which Beryl, at first testing the elasticity of her mouth by twisting it about so her nose swerved, answered, confidentially, 'If I tell you nothing,' which left me to go to Maggie and Michael to ask them nothing but say how lovely to see them, they both nodding and smiling.

Maggie said, 'Come to me for lunch, then we'll go to Michael's later for tea.'

In Paul and Penny's sitting room, over the mantelpiece, is a painting of Paul by Howard Hodgkin, which does look like Paul, round and multi-coloured. During the party, he, his hands out and twiddling his fingers, goes from guest to guest, while Penny sits still.

In China, Paul, who is what is called a 'foodie,' that is someone who is interested in and writes about even the most exotic cuisines, went to the market where caged dogs are sold for their meat, but the cages were empty. He was told that though the Chinese eat dog, they do have pet dogs they love.

Dinner at the Glenconners', in London from Corfu for the winter. Vidia Naipaul and his wife Pat were there.

The Naipauls have, for twelve years, lived in the gatehouse of the house Christopher's brother Stephen inhabits in Wiltshire. They have never seen him but once, when, across a lawn, they gently waved to one another.

Stephen Tennant stays in bed all day, all winter, spring, autumn. His bed is covered with objects, mostly dolls, so he can't move. Only in the summer does he get out of bed to go down to the west lawn to sit for an hour. He wears jewelry and make-up. And from time to time he does drawings, of flowers and French sailors.

Christopher said, 'It is wonderful that he's never bored.'

When he's in London, Christopher goes to Wiltshire to see him. He spends twenty minutes by his brother's bed, then his brother says, 'I'm really rather tired,' and Christopher goes down to the kitchen to have a meal with the housekeeper and her husband, whose company he loves, then he returns to London. He never spends the night; the beds are too damp. Clearly, Christopher is supporting his brother Stephen and would never pass a judgment on him, but say, 'He's wonderful.'

Christopher said, 'Nothing really matters, you see. I'm not a believer, really, but I'm sure the workings of the universe are on such a grand scale that what we consider important isn't. There is no reason to be upset by anything. I'm a very happy man.'

———

I asked John Golding if his being an historian in any way influenced him, or, perhaps, hindered him for the self-consciousness that history might have imposed on him, and he said, No, not at all, he was able to work in direct contact with the painting. Yet, John, in writing, say, about Malevich (in an essay contained in a book that Nikos was responsible for Thames & Hudson publishing, Paths to the Absolute), will include an appreciation of art by Hegel that he supposes was an appreciation of art by Malevich: 'Hegel's view of evolution, as propounded in the 1820s, is that in which spirit detaches itself from nature and achieves total freedom, thus becoming "pure universal form . . . in which the spiritual essence attains the consciousness and feeling of itself." It was this state of advanced spirituality that Malevich felt had at last been brought to a conclusion by himself.' Malevich's work became 'frankly mystical.' There is not a hint of irony in John's attributing the spiritual, the mystical, to Malevich, none. But he would not, ever, attribute the same words to his own work, which, in conversation, he described as being influenced by Adrian Stokes' view of the body, as in Adrian's essay 'Reflections on the Body.' (I once told Adrian how wonderful I thought that title, which made him look at me with bemusement, for I had seen in the title a wet body on which light was reflected.) I said to John, 'I don't at all see the body in your paintings,' which consist of very abstract planes of colour that, on looking for a long while at them, appear to take on dimensions, one plane receding and another plane coming forward, and he said, after a long pause, 'Well, the spirit,' and I pointed at him and said, 'I've got you,' and laughed, and he laughed a little, grudgingly.

There is a divide between the appreciation of art allowed by a critic, which appreciation can make use of transcendent words, and the view an artist (most of the artists of today, who seem to deny the transcendent, or at least refuse to admit it) has of his/her own work.

I think of the white-on-white paintings of Robert Ryman, about which he will only say that they are white-on-white paintings, as if to deny he has any intention in painting them than that they should consist of white-on-white paint, so that everything unintended beyond his intention is left to the art critic to admire – which admiration, however, I can only think Ryman reads with the thought, yes, yes, that's what my work is all about, but I would never say so. At the exhibition of his work at the Tate, I thought: But he's wrong not to admit that his paintings have transcendence, because they do have transcendence. I asked him to sign the catalogue, which he did reluctantly, as if that would be to give too much of himself away.

After I've been to a dinner party where I've heard a remarkable story – one of those stories that belies the reserve of the English – I,

at my desk, write out the story with the idea of using it as the basis
of fiction. I wrote out the following some time ago, long enough
that I forget (just as well) who gave the dinner party and whom
(better) the story was about.

> She went to Ghana where she fell in love with an African,
> became pregnant, came back to England, near Salisbury, went
> into a wood, nine months pregnant, and tried to kill herself
> by slitting her wrists, made a mess of it, woke up covered in
> blood, staggered out to a road, was picked up by a farmer who
> took her to hospital where her baby was born, took baby to
> Ghana, a boy, drowned it and gave the dead body to the father,
> a tribal chief who in his grief went off into the jungle, but
> came back to try to help his imprisoned, mad wife, swearing
> to a judge that the baby had died a cot death, so she, free,
> returned to England, her mother bought her a slum house in
> Brixton, where she now lives alone, and where her husband
> comes from Ghana once a year to visit her.

Coming across this, I thought, but there is no way I can turn it into
fiction, and put it into my diary as a story in the history, not only
of this woman, but of Great Britain – of colonial Great Britain,
about which I know so little, my ignorance very much a gap in my
ever becoming British.

I think of John Osborne's play at the Royal Court Theatre,
West of Suez, and a scene in which all the actors sit on canvas
lawn chairs in a circle and announce where each was born, not
one in Great Britain, and I felt a circle of loneliness among them,
all of them displaced, dissatisfied, even defeated, and yet nostalgic for a lost world. What I don't understand is the residue of
colonial times, in which, it seems to me, the above tragedy
occurred, as if the nostalgic were deep in the post-colonial
conscience, but not the tragic. For all that I recall, the above
story might have been recounted with irony, a British affectation
I often find difficult to appreciate when I hear someone British

dealing with tragedy, and which Nikos disdains. I remember the story above was told with amusement, and, yes, it was told by someone of the upper classes, among whom I can hear the dictum: we do not take ourselves seriously.

———

Harold Acton rang. He had got, he said, our number from Eva Neurath, whom he sees in Florence. Nikos is not interested, but indulges my interest – my fascination! I invited him to supper. How could I not be fascinated by Acton for the worlds he is connected to? Nikos suggested we invite Howard Hodgkin. Acton arrived in a three-piece grey suit, elegant, and he was all elegant declamations about our flat, our food, ourselves, with something of a Chinese elegance. He and Howard had more connections to make than Nikos and I with him, for Howard is well connected. In our flat, I saw, as if visible about Acton, his villa and gardens, and what amused me was his complaining about the responsibilities of the villa and garden. 'Oh, it is a prison, a prison. I hardly dare leave it for what may happen while I'm away, the staff not to be trusted, no, not to be trusted. And how can I afford to keep the staff?' He made elegant gestures with his hands and said, 'There should be a charity for destitute millionaires,' and smiled. After he left, Nikos asked, 'Why did he want to see us?' I said, 'I have no idea.' Howard stayed on and we talked about the artists we know, he praising the work of Stephen Buckley.

A few days later, a thank-you letter: 'Much love to you both, Yours ever, Harold, hoping to see you in Florence.'

How can I not be impressed by this? – though I admire Nikos, keeping an ideological distance, for not being impressed, though he was very courteous towards Acton.

———

Strange, violent dreams about Nikos. Here is one: he, in the centre of a room, is fashioning a work of art out of variously shaped blocks of wood, and pays no attention to me, so I, angry, throw things at him and his work of art; he remains indifferent, his indifference calculated; he is resentful of me, will have nothing to do with me, though I have no idea why he is resentful, why he won't have anything to do with me, and my anger turns to rage. What I wonder is: who is this Nikos in my dreams, a Nikos who reoccurs in my dreams, and who is completely unlike the Nikos I know and love? In life, Nikos is never indifferent to me, never even suggests rejecting me. Why, in my dreams, does he reject me so often?

———

I am always, if less and less, surprised by the way the sexualities of people in London appear to be incidental to friendship. So, I think of Stephen Buckley, who has all the seductive good looks of a young man who rather enjoys the friendships of other young men – in particular, Mark Lancaster – who are seduced by his good looks. That Stephen has girlfriends – in particular, Stevie – in no way diminishes his friendship with those others who have flirtatious feelings for him. Stevie became pregnant by Stephen, and gave birth to a daughter. I went to visit her in hospital with a large pot of blue hydrangeas, but I couldn't recall her maiden name, which, as she and Stephen were not yet married, she still went by, so I had to go along the beds looking for Stevie, who waved to me. They married some time after.

With pleasure, I thought this was rather bohemian of them.

———

If I were to try to create a British character, how would I characterize him/her? Would I centre on someone I know somewhat – say, A. J. Ayer who represents Logical Positivism as a thoroughly British mode of thinking? I see him from time to time at the Spenders', and once had an amusing talk with him about the Assumption of the Blessed Virgin Mother, trying to establish the date of her bodily assumption and the speed at which she was assumed into heaven, whereby we would be able to calculate where in the universe she is, and, if she had reached heaven, where in the universe heaven is. His wife Dee said he visits the Jesuits in Farm Street to talk about Scholastic philosophy, which talk I would very much like to hear, Ayer against Aquinas! Dee told me that e. e. cummings, a friend, described Ayer as having a stainless-steel mind. How would I be able to give a character based on Ayer a soul? And by soul I mean: what can't be made logically positivist, what is beyond intention. Would such a character in a novel be interesting? Doesn't Ayer's Logical Positivism reduce the novel to, at best, social life? Could I possibly create a British character with a soul, a soul in an agony that embarrasses him for being an agony, so a soul he must deny as an indulgence for not being positively logical? And whom would that be based upon?

Could it be Stephen Spender?

I would never try to engage Freddie Ayer in a conversation that had any hint of being serious, but I would like to ask him, in a joking way, if what is called an idea is no more logically positive than a vague 'sense' of having something to think about, in which vagueness we imagine we think logically, especially when we think we are thinking logically? The joke would be that, as I am not good at logic, better do away with it all as illogical. The closest to making a reference to his own philosophy – if it can be called that – is my hearing Ayer say, with a gesture as of cancelling it out of the air, that the end of Wittgenstein's Tractatus, when Wittgenstein states that the mystical shows itself, is rubbish. It is just this affirmation of the mystical that appeals to me in Wittgenstein, but I laughed at Ayer's affirmation that it is rubbish, thinking to myself: yes, it is rubbish, and everything that has its appeal for being imagined mystical is rubbish. This reassurance lasted only as long as I was with Ayer.

To listen to Dee talk about her past is to be entertained by a whole life, at least in her telling, of entertainment. Just this: when young, living in Paris, she became infatuated with a man from Oklahoma, a man whom she was warned against because he lived in a hotel known for – a nod of the head – men like that. Queer?

Impossible! No man from Oklahoma could be queer! She invited him for supper, calculated the drink to get him drunk but not too drunk, but drunk enough that – oh dear! – he missed the last Métro back to his hotel, so he'd have to spend the night.

———

A long walk with Anthony Page through Hyde Park, he telling me about directing in the presence of Samuel Beckett at the Royal Court Theatre in Sloane Square. About directing, Anthony told me this:

'The first thing is to know the text of the author you're directing as well as you can. What the conscious structure of the piece is, how thoughts and lines connect with each other.

'My ideal is that the actors should come knowing their lines when we start rehearsing. They will make any excuse to avoid this but it gives you the equivalent of at least ten days' extra rehearsal when you have a month.

'Noël Coward and my teacher Sandy Meisner both felt very strongly indeed about this. Meisner said that rehearsing without knowing your lines was like acting with a grand piano on your back and for me from the very beginning of rehearsal the actors should start working on their relationships with the other characters, their objectives and so forth. Very difficult if you're reading or feeling for lines.

'The director is largely responsible for the atmosphere at rehearsals and he needs daring actors who are in touch with their instincts. He needs to keep the objective balance and structure of the play in his mind, at the same time encouraging fun and freedom and improvisation. Unintellectual instincts are often what make the most magical side of a production. This freedom should be retained right through the run of the play.

'I hate productions which are too choreographed, self-conscious – too obviously directed. Better by far if the direction is invisible, unnoticed – and if the action seems every time to be happening for the first time ever before the audience's eyes.

'If a play has been rehearsed and its foundations laid in this way it can continue to develop and to grow in truth and strength for the whole run. Once it's in front of an audience, who reveal new things to the actors, the job of the director is rather like gardening. New growths spring up – often by instinct – and may need to be watered – by making the actors aware of them. Also inevitably there are weeds, temptations to cheapen, which must be got rid of.

'Ideally a director should visit a production – at least for part of the performance – every two weeks or so. And give notes to the cast. Probably written down. Actors often aren't too happy with notes once a play has opened and if they can read them it gives them a chance to ponder, and try them out and not to forget them, if they agree with them.'

———

Nikos and I have seen such extraordinary productions in the theatre, most notably the plays of D. H. Lawrence, and among these the Widowing of Mrs. Holroyd, with its scene of the widow washing the dead body of her husband, killed in a mine, and keening over his body. I thought: yes, for all that D. H. Lawrence intended too much in his writing – what his friend Bertrand Russell condemned as a philosophy of 'blood-consciousness' that led straight to Auschwitz, and that Virginia Woolf derided, too, as philosophy, which she did not want in a novel (she wanted 'no preaching: things in themselves: the sentence in itself beautiful . . .') – for all that D. H. Lawrence intended in his writing, the unintended, beyond his philosophy, has more of a soul than any of his contemporaries, especially the Bloomsbury writers, and especially Virginia Woolf, could ever have been capable of expanding upon in their writing.

———

To Stephen and Stevie Buckley to supper at the long, wide refectory table from King's College, Cambridge, from when Stephen was artist in residence there. The architect Max Gordon was at the table, and Stephenie and Roxy, and Suzi. Nikos talked of some good reviews I've had. I said, 'Nikos tells me I have become terribly immodest.' No one said anything, not even Nikos. I said, 'Well, I see no one is denying that I am.' They all laughed. Stephen said, 'You can always count on your friends.'

Suzi sat next to me at the end of the table. She asked me, 'Do you believe in God?' 'No,' I said. She said, 'I find it difficult to understand how anyone cannot believe in God.' I said, 'I find it difficult to believe how anyone can.'

A little while later, Stephen described how he, as a student, was visited regularly by a ghost which stood silently by his bed.

Suzi asked, 'How did it manifest itself?'

'By its silent presence.'

'Was it a man or a woman?'

Stephen said, 'I couldn't tell.'

I am amazed when I find close friends believe in what I find unbelievable. It makes those friends, whom I consider familiar, to be totally unfamiliar, and more interesting than before.

We drove Max to his flat in Mayfair.

He talked about Jennifer Bartlett. 'She's really a dumb artist. She knows nothing about technique. In fact, she's an appalling technician. When she succeeds technically, it's by sheer accident. But she has something that goes beyond technique, and when she's able to realize that her work is sensational.'

———

From the time I last saw them until recently, Maggie D. and Michael H. have married, but they still live separately.

The sitting room of Maggie's terrace house in Hampstead has large, deep armchairs and a sofa, and the wallpaper is a dark red William Morris pattern with simplified, overlapping leaves or feathers, I can't recall which, though I do like to get the details right. At the other end of the room was a guitar on the floor leaning against a wall, and a black, perhaps lacquered grand piano painted with Chinese scenes about its curved body, a glass of bluebells on it, and beyond it glass doors out to what looked an overgrown garden whose large-leafed plants pressed against the lower panes. On a wall across from the piano are bookshelves, floor to ceiling, but books were strewn about everywhere. Once again, I try to see such details as referring to something more.

We talked about London.

I said I never feel that, in the multi-roomed houses of London, I understand what all the furniture, the pictures, the books, the bibelots, the teapot and cups and saucers mean. My incomprehension makes me feel I'm not in London.

Maggie said, 'But I don't feel I'm inside either. I'm not from London, I'm from Yorkshire, and that makes me a foreigner in London. I didn't know anyone here until I came, after I graduated from Cambridge. I certainly didn't know any writers. I was the first writer I'd ever met.' She spoke calmly, sitting straight, her hands, palms down, on her knees, her fingers straight. She asked Michael, 'You don't feel you're a part of London, either, do you?'

Rising from a slouch, he said, 'No, no. I'm hardly English. My father was half Irish and my mother Swedish. And I grew up everywhere. I recall a time when I was a boy waking up in a wet, cold place, and not knowing where I was, and being told I was in Vienna.'

'Why Vienna?' I asked.

'I'm not sure why. My parents divorced and remarried again and again, and I'd spend time with my father and my stepmothers and with my mother and stepfathers in different places. One stepfather was Hungarian, another French. I was all over the place. The closest I got to proper English life was when I stayed with my grandparents, my father's parents, in the country here. When I came to London, finally, I felt I didn't know anyone. I still feel I don't, really.'

Brushing her bobbed hair back over an ear, Maggie said quietly, 'Your childhood was a muddle.'

'Yes, a muddle.'

Michael's face looks as if he usually wears spectacles that he at some point in contemplating the world he took off, and he wonders where he has put them. 'It may have been Venice,' he said, 'the cold, wet place I woke up in.'

I said, 'I'm very surprised. I thought you'd both feel very much at home in London.'

'No, no,' Maggie said.

And I said, 'Well, if you two don't feel at home in London, what can I feel?'

While Maggie prepared a hollandaise sauce in the kitchen, Michael and I had gin and tonics in the sitting room.

He said, 'They're very demanding, the people I write biographies about.'

'Because they demand you get in the whole world each one lived in?'

'The whole world.'

'But writing biography is like writing fiction, isn't it?' I asked. 'Trying to realize characters, trying to realize the worlds of the characters, which, after all, exist in the writing.'

'If only one didn't have to verify all the facts,' Michael answered.

In a shiny apron, Maggie appeared to say lunch (or did she say 'luncheon'?) was ready – steamed salmon and boiled potatoes and the bright hollandaise sauce. Michael opened a bottle of white wine. The table was set near windows, the outside plants pressing against the panes.

Again, we talked about London, or I wanted to talk about London, as I always do. We talked mainly about writers from the past, and the talk gave way to Bloomsbury and the survivors, such as Henrietta Garnett, the grandniece of Virginia Woolf, who had just published a novel – which, in fact, Henrietta had shown me and which she wanted to call Catherine's Bidet, but published is called, I think, Family Skeletons, and this made me feel I may be a little more involved in London than Maggie and Michael.

Then talk about recycling of rubbish, which we were all for, and as anyone with any common sense would be for. I suddenly looked at Maggie and, as if an insight had come to me about her, I said,

'You appear to be, but you're not at all commonsensical, are you?' She has a way of jerking back her head so her hair, with long bangs, swings forward about her cheeks. She said, 'No, I'm not. How did you guess?'

As we were leaving to go to Michael's apartment, he and Maggie with bags and books, she asked him, 'Do you have chapter sixteen?' He opened his red plastic carrier bag and answered, 'Yes.' 'Whose chapter sixteen?' I asked. 'Michael's,' Maggie said. 'He keeps a copy of everything he writes on top of my wardrobe for safekeeping. I don't keep a copy of what I write, the typescript is all it is.'

Michael's apartment is in Ladbroke Grove, where, Maggie said, the air is less salubrious than in Hampstead. She said this in such a careful way, her chin jutted out, I thought she was being ironical, but wasn't sure.

Michael's wide sitting room is muted yellow, and three busts – of Augustus John, Lytton Strachey, and Bernard Shaw – all larger than life, keep strange company with one another, all looking away from one another. Everything neat, the books if not placed in their proper places on shelves stacked in piles.

When I thought of asking them why they live separately, I thought, no, don't, and I felt I had been long enough in London to know what to ask and what not to ask. Asking would have been like asking them to justify their marital relationship, and to ask anyone to justify his or her life is never, ever done. But I did say that, given all relationships are necessary but impossible, it is a very sensible arrangement, thinking to myself at the same time that, as the English would of course say to themselves about the arrangement, it was really too peculiar.

Maggie smiled, and with a fine irony said, 'Very sensible.'

Tea in Michael's garden, and talk about Margaret Thatcher and the threat to freedom of expression, which should be considered violations of human rights. And the absurdity of her claiming that Socialism is dead! Maggie said this is her basic belief: that the State is responsible for the ill, the old, the out of work and poor, and students, and, yes, we pay our taxes for this responsibility of the

State. But Thatcherite Britain couldn't last, Michael said, which he thought is already beginning to crack. Looking at the ground, Maggie said, 'I'm not so sure.' Michael raised his hands and said, 'Of course, I don't know.'

Maggie, in a canvas chair, dropped her wooden clogs and folded her legs under her, and the long afternoon light shone on her smooth face. Contradicting what they had said when I first came about not feeling they are part of London, we talked of people we know, people we meet over and over again in different contexts, at concerts or plays or openings of exhibitions or book-launch parties or dinner or drinks parties, and I felt that particular charm of being with friends with whom idle talk about other friends, or even talk about flowers, can seem the most intimate talk you've ever known.

Michael told a story about being driven by Charlotte Bonham Carter in her motor car, she often swerving to drive on the left side of the road.

———

I recognize this about Nikos: though he is constitutionally incapable of apologizing, as if it is a deep Greek trait never to blame oneself but always another, when he knows he has been unfair to me by blaming me for, oh, never mind what, he will press his forehead against mine for a long while and smile, and I always smile in return.

———

Stephen Buckley's wife, Stevie, was among a number to hold a jumble sale of whatever they no longer wanted but thought could be interesting to others – old tea caddies, stoneware bottles, crocheted antimacassars – the sale organized in the loft-like post-industrial space overlooking the Thames, near Tower Bridge, where some artists have their studios. We added to Stevie's stall whatever we no longer wanted, whatever was now irrelevant to our lives together, and among these were the sailor's trousers dyed bright yellow that I once bought for Nikos on a Saturday afternoon on the King's Road, then when the King's Road was as if a road into a world in which people dressed for a different world and, too, fell in love and had sex in a different world. Though I had bought the trousers for Nikos, he'd never worn them. In the loft saw a boy, the son of an artist and his wife, study the yellow trousers with an attentiveness that could only have been inspired by fantasy, though his fantasy was all his. I said to Nikos, 'Give him the trousers, just give them to him,' and Nikos was amused to give them to the boy, who took them away to wear in whatever he fancied his world to be.

Francis told us he has a new friend he wants us to meet. His name is John, John Edwards, and he runs a pub in the East End. On a Sunday morning, Nikos and I drove Francis there. John has black curly hair and wore a smart grey-flannel suit. Nikos and I were in jeans. We had drinks in the saloon, where young men were playing snooker. John's boyfriend Philip was among them. A pretty, blond young man with pimples along his jaw, he couldn't go more than a mile from the pub, as he'd been convicted of a crime and was awaiting sentencing. After some drinks, we all went to another pub, which closed while we were there, but we stayed on behind the locked doors and met a number of middle-aged Cockney queens and their boyfriends. They and John and Philip and Francis and Nikos and I, about twelve of us, went out for late lunch at a Chinese restaurant, all of us about a large round table. One bleached-blond queen said to Francis, 'So you paint pictures, do you, Francis? Excuse my ignorance, but what kind of pictures do you paint?' This was all said in East End Cockney. Francis said, 'Well, it's difficult to say.' 'Like, do you paint landscapes or people?' 'Sometimes landscapes, sometimes people.' 'Do you paint pictures of dogs, Francis?' someone else asked; 'I like pictures of dogs myself.' 'I used to paint dogs years ago. I don't any more.' 'What do you do with your paintings, then? Do you show them on the railings along the park in Bayswater? I seen paintings, on a Sunday, all along the railings.' Francis, laughing, said, 'I haven't come to that yet. I might soon.' John said, 'His paintings are fucking awful. He can't even draw as

good as that Piss-casso, and fucking awful he was, too.' 'Right,'
Francis said, 'I can't.' John said, 'Ask him to paint a picture of you,
it don't look anything like you, all a mess.' 'That's right,' Francis said,
'I couldn't do a portrait that looks like anyone to save my life.'

In the car, riding back through the East End, Francis said, 'I feel
an idiot among them. I feel they know so much more than I do.'

'What?' Nikos asked.

'I don't know,' Francis answered.

———

Nikos, not feeling well – which is rare of him – stayed home from
work. In the afternoon I asked him if he was better, and he said,
'Yes, because you've taken care of me.' This surprised and pleased
me because he usually doesn't like being cared for

———

After her death, Francis wanted to talk to me about Sonia. I went
to his mews flat in Reece Mews about midday. He said he wasn't
working for a few days. We drank three or four of what he called
Dead Dogs, I think. I asked him if Sonia had ever attacked him, as
she had attacked almost everyone. He thought for a long time.
There is something comical about him when he is thoughtful: his
expression is almost a parody of thoughtfulness, one eye low, the
other high. He is looking more and more like one of his paintings.

He said, 'I don't know, really. I think it may be because I was
introduced to Sonia by the art collector Peter Watson, whom she
was desperately in love with. Of course, he was queer. He was a
marvelously good-looking man, and intelligent, and rich. He had
all the qualities Sonia needed in a man to fall in love with him,
especially his being queer.' Francis said this with a barking laugh.
'Perhaps she never attacked me because she associated me with
Peter in some way, and she would never attack Peter.'

'I wonder,' I said; 'I suspect she never attacked you because she
was frightened of you.'

'Frightened of me? Why?'

'Because Sonia was frightened of people – or at least was in awe of people – whom she thought had succeeded totally in their creativity. She believed you have.'

Now he shrugged and again laughed, now a high laugh. 'Did she? I can't see why she should have believed that. I'm not a success.'

I said, 'Sonia had a great deal of respect for creativity.'

'I think she did,' Francis said; 'I think she wanted very much to be creative, and even tried, but she failed. You know, she was sent by the Observer's editor David Astor to Israel to interview General Dayan, and she went with great enthusiasm, but when she got back her piece on Dayan was found to be unpublishable. She simply didn't have the talent.'

'I wonder if her realization that she had no talent changed her. I've often wondered what changed her from the charming, bright, young woman everyone thought she was to the dark woman I knew her to be.'

Francis said, 'Drink.'

'Yes, but why did she drink?'

'I think you're right – one of the reasons, perhaps the central reason, was that she wanted to be creative, and knew she couldn't be. And once she knew she couldn't, once she denied it totally in herself, she was in awe of it in others.'

Odd, I thought, that Francis could take what I had said and repeat it in a way that seemed to be original with him.

I repeated, 'Only those others she thought had really succeeded in realizing their creativity, which were not many.'

'Not that she knew much about books or paintings or music. She read a lot, but, as far as I heard when she spoke about the arts, all her ideas were received.'

'About books, I think her enthusiasm was great, and her enthusiasm about certain writers – I remember her praising Victor Hugo – was inspiring – she made me want to read Victor Hugo. But she didn't know much about painting and music.'

'Nothing.'

'And yet, and yet,' I said, drunk enough to repeat myself, 'she had this tremendous respect for all creativity. She thought it was what she most wanted but didn't have. She wanted to possess it in others, but couldn't. At times, she imagined that if she couldn't be creative herself she could understand creativity, especially writing. I remember her once talking to Jean Rhys and me about a writer's intention, and Jean and I both said, "No, it's not that way," meaning there is much more to writing than what the writer intends, much more, much much more, and Sonia looked very puzzled – puzzled and hurt – and said, "Tiens, that goes to show I know nothing about writing."'

Francis said, 'Nothing about what happens.'

I asked, 'Do you think she was a pessimistic person?'

Francis answered, 'Totally, totally pessimistic. You see, I am at least optimistic in the moment –'

'When you're painting?'

'When I'm painting.'

'Because to create is to be optimistic. Sonia didn't have that. At least that's what I imagine.'

'As much as one can be right in anything one imagines,' Francis said, 'I think you're right. I think you are.'

We were sitting at the bare table before the windows at the end of the long narrow room which is his living room and bedroom; bare bulbs hung from the ceiling, and though the electric fire was lit, there was a chill.

John Edwards came. We went out for lunch. We drank three bottles of wine. I was very drunk. After, we got into a taxi to go to the Colony, where Francis ordered a bottle of champagne. I can't recall what the three of us talked about. For a while, we talked to a short, dark, bull-like man who spends four months working in an Arab country running a power station, then four weeks in London, over and over; he has done this for fifteen years. Very friendly, he invited us all to Sunday lunch: roast lamb. Francis said, 'We'll come. That'll be lovely. We love roast lamb.' The man left. I asked Francis, 'Where are we supposed to meet him?' 'I have no idea,' Francis said, and laughed. He ordered another bottle of champagne.

One glass more, and I knew I was going to be sick. I said I had to go. Francis helped me down to the street, asking if I'd be all right. Yes, I said, but I would be all right only if I kept moving, so crossed streets if the little man was red. In the bathroom, I lay on the floor, naked, and from time to time vomited into the toilet.

When Nikos returned from his office he found me on the floor. He had planned on taking me and Stephen out to dinner. I said, 'I can't go out.' Stephen arrived. I fell asleep on the bathroom floor. Whenever I woke, I heard Nikos and Stephen downstairs talking while they ate an improvised meal Nikos prepared.

It took me a couple of days to recover.

———

I have never asked Francis what he thinks of Minimalist Art, that of Robert Ryman, Agnes Martin, Donald Judd, Dan Flavin, Richard Serra, which Nikos and I have seen most prominently displayed in the privately owned Saatchi Gallery in Boundary Road. (I have to interject here that when I told Stephen S. about the Boundary Road Gallery, he frowned as if what I knew, which he had not heard about from more authoritative sources, could not really be serious. I resented this a little, and told Nikos as much; Nikos, unabashed, then told Stephen, who told Nikos that, yes, he could only take seriously people of his own generation, and found it difficult to take seriously younger people.) No doubt Francis would stick out his lower lip and say, as he says about the Abstract Sublime (a term David Sylvester prefers to the Abstract Expressionists), that it is all wallpaper. Sometimes, studying a painting by Francis, I eliminate with a hand the figure if I can, and see in itself the space in which the figure appears, space delineated by lines that stand out from the flat backgrounds, space that seems to me the essence of his pictures, the figures the accidents. But this is getting too close to opinion, which I won't allow myself. To go back to the Boundary Road Gallery. The Saatchis never appear at the openings of the exhibitions there, so, at those amazing openings, those invited are aware of them with more amazement at what they have accomplished than if they were there. I've met them, Charles and Doris, at Stephen and Stevie Buckley's house, and, talking to Doris, I had more than an impression that it was she who determines the exhibitions in their gallery, especially the works of the American Minimalists, against whose works I see her, her very pale hair half covering a pale, delicately angular face, precise, her demeanour itself apparently minimalist.

The photograph of her by Robert Mapplethorpe shows this.

Doris Saatchi, 1983 Copyright © The Robert Mapplethorpe Foundation. Courtesy Art + Commerce

About Robert Mapplethorpe, Doris said he is a very gentle man.

The Boundary Road Gallery was designed by Max Gordon.

Max gives the impression of not only knowing everyone intimately but of being an influence in their lives, such as his promoting the work of Lisa Milroy to the Saatchis, Max particularly keen on Lisa's paintings of piles of folded shirts, for Max collects shirts which he keeps in piles in drawers. His flat, designed by himself to be all white space, appears meant to be a space for the art he collects. It amuses him to point to the floor at a very tiny house in bronze, or perhaps iron, by Joel Shapiro, the size of it made all the more meaningful spatially in the space of the room. Max is very much in contact with New York artists such as Joel Shapiro and Ellen Phelan and Jennifer Bartlett. Max also collects narrow boxes that tubes of toothpaste are sold in, his prize a box with the brand name Craig-Martin.

He urged Jennifer Bartlett to give the name Rhapsody to a large work of art, many white enamel plates covered with different-coloured dots and dashes that cover whole walls, which the Metropolitan Museum of Art in New York have bought.

Learning to be English –

I received a notice from H.M. Inland Revenue to inform me that I had overpaid my tax for two years and I would soon be getting a 'check' (American) to the amount of £1,517.08. I have learned that in England such things take a long time. I waited a few months, then thought I would notify the Inland Revenue that I hadn't got it, as I had asked at my bank if it had been deposited.

A handwritten note came back a couple of weeks later expressing surprise. The cheque (British) should have been sent. The note was signed by a Mr. Ridge, with his telephone number and extension.

A soft-voiced man, he said he didn't at all mind my ringing him. I gave him my reference number. 'That's just what I wanted,' he said, then added, 'Now let me see if I can find your file.' He came back and said he was terribly sorry, he couldn't find my file, but they did have a system whereby lost files were eventually 'kicked up.' I asked him if he minded my ringing him again in a week's time, and he said not at all.

My file still hadn't been kicked up by the time I rang again.

Mr. Ridge said, 'You can't imagine the confusion here.'

I said I would ring again in a week, and by then my file was found. Mr. Ridge had placed it on his desk in anticipation of my ringing him. The problem seemed to be what had happened to the cheque. He couldn't issue a new one without finding out what happened to the old. Had it been cashed? And if it had, who had cashed it? This he couldn't find out himself, but would have to alert the Computer Centre in Worthing to do so. He would write to them that very day.

He hadn't heard from Worthing when I rang him a week later. He couldn't understand why. Never for a moment did I doubt that Mr. Ridge had in fact written. We decided between us that we would give them another week. We did, and they still hadn't responded. Mr. Ridge would write to them again, and he would mark his letter urgent.

When I rang a week later, as usual on a Wednesday, I was told that Mr. Ridge was on sick leave for two days. I said I'd ring again on Friday, and the receptionist said I would have a much better chance of getting Mr. Ridge on Monday.

Monday morning, Mr. Ridge, recovered, was back at his desk, but he hadn't yet sorted out the morning's post, so he wouldn't be able to tell me till the afternoon if Worthing had responded, though, as far as he knew, Worthing hadn't responded to his letter marked urgent while he was on sick leave.

I rang him at 3.00, but Mr. Ridge was still out to lunch. I rang at 4.00 and found that Mr. Ridge had gone home.

I rang the next morning. He explained that, as he hadn't had any word from Worthing, he hadn't wanted to disturb me, but, perhaps, today there would be a notice from Worthing. I asked him what was a good time to ring him in the afternoon, and he said 3.30. But Worthing hadn't sent him the information he had so urgently requested.

He said, 'You could threaten to write to your M.P. That always gets them going.'

'I hadn't thought of that,' I said, not wanting him to know that, as a non-voting foreigner, I didn't have a Member of Parliament to whom I could threaten to write. 'But I wonder if, in the meantime, we might give Worthing another chance by in fact telephoning them and speaking to them directly.'

'That is a possibility,' he said.

He rang me that afternoon to tell me he'd spoken with Worthing. I would appreciate that they were in the process of transferring one tax district from another (indeed, I had had a notice about a year before that my tax district had been changed to Willesden from I can't recall what previous district) and the information I requested was not yet on the computer. He suggested I ring in two weeks.

I'd be happy to know, he told me when I next spoke to him, that the information was on the computer, but the computer would take forty-eight hours to come up with it. This was Friday, and he wasn't sure the computer worked over the weekend.

Each time I spoke with him, he reiterated the problem: he could not issue a new cheque until it was clear that the previous one hadn't been cashed. He said, 'There is a possibility, you see, that you might have cashed it.'

I had a moment of English doubt. Had I, without remembering, cashed it? But for the first time I became irritated, angry even, that he should be making me doubt myself.

I said, 'Of course I didn't cash it.'

'Of course you didn't,' he said.

When I next rang him, the computer still hadn't come up with the information. Mr. Ridge had done everything he could, and was going on holiday for three weeks.

I said, 'This has to be settled before you go.'

He would do everything he possibly could, but if he couldn't bring the business to a satisfactory conclusion before he left, he would leave it in the hands of Miss June, his colleague, to whom he would explain the situation.

Miss June startled me by saying she had not yet 'gotten' information from Worthing, and I was worried that that Americanism

(however old English it is meant to be) indicated American infiltra-
tion into the Inland Revenue. She was understanding, and said she
would keep ringing Worthing until she had the reply she wanted.
We spoke every day, I often ringing her, she sometimes ringing me.
Whispering, she told me, just between us, that Worthing was in a
terrible state, but she would keep trying.

I did get the cheque (British).

———

Thinking about Sonia –

Sonia rejected God, any God, with a force that would have
destroyed God had God existed. A cigarette in one hand and a glass
of wine in the other, her ash blonde and grey hair shaking as she,
frowning deeply, shook her head from side to side, she would rage,
rage, not only against any belief in God, which she found totally
uninteresting, but against God Himself for ever having supposed
He existed, for ever having supposed He was of any interest to
anyone. He had never existed, and he was of no, but absolutely no,
interest.

I knew that if I asked Sonia if anything at all was left of her once
having believed in God, she would have answered, 'Don't be so
stupid. Of course not.' But Sonia remained a passionately negative
Catholic, a kind of passionately negative Catholic missionary to
friends who doubted: there is no transcendence, no redemption,
no realization of any promises made by Catholicism or any other
religion. She considered herself a realist. And she was, and the
greatest expression of her realism was her pretty dining-room table.

Sonia said to me, 'Our both being Catholic is our secret.'

———

There was a time in my life when I believed the Roman Catholic
Church, under the absolute dictatorship of the Vatican that I was
brought up not to question, portraits of Pope Pius XII hanging in
our church and school rooms as the supreme authority over moral-
ity, dictated to me whom I could love, and what the expression of

that love could be. Imagine. The residue of that belief has gone, gone, gone, and so dated it is not of any interest to me. What the residue of my religion that remains is – oh!

———

If she is to be away, Natasha will ring us and ask us, please, to take care of Stephen. Often, we will be just the three of us for a meal, and I will mentally draw back from the conversation and look at Stephen and wonder how it happened that he is with us, this person who connects us to people from the past who survive in cultural history, this witness to so much history, our closest friend. How can we not be attentive when he recounts bringing T. S. Eliot and Igor Stravinsky together, Eliot complaining that his blood was too thin and Stravinsky bragging that his blood was thick enough to form rubies? And his laugh, his high, bright laugh when he tells a story that Natasha calls méchant, his face beaming red, how can we not be as amused as he is? And how he turns self-deprecation into something to laugh at, as when he told us he had been to a dinner party in some Mid-Western American city where he sat next to a woman who asked his name, she reacting dismissively when he told her with: the only Stephen Spender she had heard about, a poet, was dead. At moments, his large body appears to be too large for him to support it, and he slumps a little, as he appears, too, to slump in spirit, but only for a moment, because he would say he has had a good life, a very good life. He may hint that it is only because of his connections that he has had the recognition he has had as a poet, but he goes on writing his poems, and from time to time shows us a draft – rather, shows it to Nikos, and if Nikos suggests a change in one line Stephen will rewrite the entire poem.

———

Max Gordon invited Nikos and me to the Albert Hall for a performance of music by John Cage. After, he said we should go backstage, and Nikos and I, assuming that Max was friendly with Cage, went with him to the entrance to the backstage, where, however, a guard stopped us and said we were not allowed in. Max simply walked past him. Nikos and I held back. The guard, who was stunned by Max simply walking past him, stepped aside, and Max, beyond him, gestured us to follow him. We did, into a wide, curving corridor with many closed doors along it. Max opened door after door, until he opened a door onto a room where, it appeared to me, at a far distance were John Cage and the pianist and composer David Tudor and others, who stared at us clearly without knowing who Max was and who we were. Again, Max told us to follow him in, but Nikos and I held back and said we'd rather not, and left. The next day Max rang to say we should have stayed on, he had joined the group and with them gone to a restaurant for a meal.

I have been reading the diary of Virginia Woolf. As fascinated as I was by the people who I imagined would appear in the diary before I started to read, I find that as I read my fascination diminishes and I see, not a world, but a room with blank windowless walls and a low ceiling, Virginia's own room where she is locked in, locked in with people whom she gives no space to move about, to talk to one another, to be themselves; and she won't let them escape her severe judgments of them. I think: I would not have wanted to be locked in that room.

Steven Runciman at dinner:

'Here is an anecdote for you from my stay in Jerusalem in 1913. I was staying at Government House, where my fellow guest was the late Lord Athlone and his wife, the late Princess Alice – Victoria's last-surviving granddaughter. There was a British regiment in Jerusalem, and the colonel of the regiment, a certain Colonel Montgomery, used to come to dine at Government House. He lectured us on our unnecessary luxuries. He was priggish, and we all loathed him. It so happened that at one of the ceremonies of the Church of the Holy Sepulcher, I was next to Princess Alice in the gallery; we looked down, and there was Colonel Montgomery's bald patch just below, which prompted Princess Alice to say, "See if we can hit him with some wax," so I tilted my candle, as she did, and she was a better marksman than I . . . She wrote later in her memoirs about being in disgrace with the future Lord Montgomery for accidentally dropping wax on him. I reproved her, and she said, "I know, my dear, but I didn't think it would do to say I did it deliberately." "You've been a coward," I said, "you've put history wrong." She giggled. I met her after the war, and she said to me, "Do you remember when we dropped wax on Field Marshal Montgomery?" And that was the first time I realized that the odious colonel was the odious field marshal.'

———

Mary McCarthy wanted to have, not a service, but a gathering at which friends would speak about Sonia. The writer Francis Wyndham rang to ask me if I would be the compere, as he did not want to be, and I agreed – agreed, no doubt, because the position gave me some prominence in London. The gathering was in a stark hall with rows of folding chairs and a simple table. A song was sung to a guitar, a poem was recited, and I read from my diary an account of Sonia staying with me in Italy. Nikos told me later that the critic and editor John Gross, in the audience, seemed to be scowling at my presuming to speak about Sonia. Then Mary McCarthy spoke, her rectangular smile held rectangular and exposing her teeth as she spoke, and what she said about Sonia didn't seem complimentary, except her comparing Sonia's pure English looks to a portrait painting by Reynolds. I'm very pleased that, a few days later, I had a postcard from Miriam Gross, John's journalist wife: 'I thought your diary was marvellous – it evoked Sonia with terrific accuracy and vividness.' This makes me feel I in some way belong in London.

———

I asked Gregory Evans, David Hockney's assistant, how often it happens that he and David don't know all the people they are entertaining in a restaurant, and Gregory said, 'Oh, all the time.' Among the people at a table in a restaurant, David presiding (and as always paying in the end), was a delicate youth with golden eyelashes and golden hair. I later asked David who he was, and David said, 'Ian Falconer,' and David said, 'He's in love with me. He wants to come to California to stay with me and study art with me. But I'm intimidated by him because he's so beautiful. I'm always intimidated by beautiful boys, and can hardly speak to them.' I said, 'I used to feel that way. Since I've been with Nikos, I don't any longer.'

Some days later, Nikos and I went to the Mughul Exhibition at the Victoria and Albert Museum, where we met, by arrangement, Ian, and the three of us stood together in the wonderfully decorated tent of panels of Indian chintz, the panels decorated with small vases at the bottom from which expand and expand and expand flowers that cover the panels, and on the tent's roof more flowers, so we were in a bower of flowers. After an hour, we went together to David H.'s studio. David, with so many demands made on him, had to leave, and Nikos and I stayed on with Ian, whom Nikos flirted with. Later, Nikos said, laughing, 'I wouldn't mind making love with Ian.' Well, he is very beautiful. I said, 'Nor would I.'

───

It used to be that when Nikos and I had a row, I would say, 'We've got to talk about this,' to which he'd respond, 'No, we're not, I'm not going to indulge you in your American introspection.' We would be silent towards each other for a while, then I'd think, Well, I know he loves me, and conversation would be resumed.

I don't introspect in my diary. Nor, I hope, do I express opinions.

As an aside: Steven Runciman recounted his having invited the Queen Mother to his club, the Athenaeum, when she asked him what men did in their clubs. He booked a room and invited what he called other queens, as the Queen Mother likes queens. After their meal, he showed her about, and noted, as they entered the large common room, men in their deep armchairs lower their newspapers and frown at the sight of a woman, until, that is, they recognized who she was, and, my God, they stood to attention! I asked him, 'What is she like?' to which he answered, 'She is not introspective.'

I think I am not, after all, an introspective person, and it's because I'm not that I so easily accept that Nikos will not talk about our rows. Perhaps I feel that our love for each other is in some way objective, and contains us as a great globe, and has love's own will.

———

From Frank's An Appetite for Poetry, this:

We understand a whole by means of its parts, and the parts by means of the whole. But this 'circle' seems to imply that we can understand nothing – the whole is made of parts we cannot understand until it exists, and we cannot see the whole without understanding the parts. Something, therefore, must happen, some intuition by which we break out of the situation – a leap, a divination . . . whereby we are enabled to understand both part and whole.

———

A novel, The Family, has been published. I call it a novel, but it is entirely autobiographical, and a lot of it comes directly from my diary.

The residue of my religion – what is left is not belief, no, but a constant awareness of a way of thinking and feeling. What awareness? It is the awareness inculcated in me by my religion, the essential teaching of which was: the reason why we are on this earth is to suffer in order to earn our places in heaven to be with God for all eternity.

As a boy, I had no choice but to believe. Again and again, I recall how, in my parochial primary school, I and all the first-grade students standing by our scratched and ink-stained desks were taught by a nun to make the sign of the cross. The nun, rigid in her black robes, faced the class and, slowly repeating the gestures over and over, demonstrated on her body the sign that the students were to repeat on their bodies. But I couldn't do it. I was so aware of myself in the glaring ring of my concentration I became uncoordinated and wasn't able to tell my right from my left, my forehead from my chest. The nun had to take my right hand and guide the tips of the fingers first to my forehead, then to the middle of my chest, then to the left shoulder and across to the right. The nun nailed to my small body the sign of the suffering of my Savior, the Savior whose suffering gave meaning to my suffering, to all the world's suffering, because it was by suffering that I and the world would be raised into heaven to be with God eternally. Our deepest love was for God in eternity, and our deepest longing was to be with God in eternity.

No, I do not believe in God, but the love and the longing remain – remain, however, love and longing that cannot be fulfilled, because there is no God in eternity.

Sometimes I feel that everything I see, hear, smell, taste, touch I do in that awareness, so that even the sight of a glass of water on a sunlit windowsill will fill me with the awareness of something promised in the glass of water on the sunlit windowsill, something that I sense so profoundly is there to be fulfilled, but can't be fulfilled.

Walking along Oxford Street among the crowds, that awareness comes over me about everyone I walk along with or pass, that awareness of so many of us aware of what we love and long for, but what we can't have, because it is beyond having.

When I am with Stephen Spender, I may suddenly see in him a large, awkward man who wants to fulfill so much more than he knows he can fulfill, and a feeling of tenderness comes to me for him.

Even with Nikos – say, sitting next to him at the Wigmore Hall for a recital of Bach's Well-Tempered Clavier, he so attentive to the music and I trying to be attentive – a loneliness will occur to me that isolates me, a feeling that as much as I love him and long to be with him, the love and the longing will never be fulfilled, not fully, because it can't be.

That awareness is the dimension in which I wrote the novel, The Family. The awareness I retain most of my family is the love and the longing that surrounded us all – the love and the longing inculcated in all of us, mother and father and seven sons, by the enclosing religion of a small, working-class, French-speaking parish in Yankee New England, a parish that might have been enclosed by a palisade – and within that surrounding awareness the memory of my father coming home to say he had been fired from the factory, the memory of my mother in a daze after shock treatment, the memory of my hysterical self shouting that I'll kill myself, memory after memory after memory, and all, again, within a surrounding awareness that made us helpless, and because helpless innocent, and because innocent vulnerable to a world promised to us in our suffering, suffering that would earn us our places with God in eternity.

It ends with a prayer.

Pray to God the Father
    To the Holy Spirit
    To the Son
    To the Virgin Mother
    To all those, in their strange high country, in their large bright house, pray for the small dark house in this low country.

Catharine Carver worked closely on editing the novel, but did not want any acknowledgment.

Stephen is enthusiastic about the novel, as if for him I have finally situated the characters in the world.

It especially pleases me that Sonia Orwell said, 'Enfin, you've written a novel I can take seriously.'

Frank Kermode gave it a nice quote.

Nikos said, 'The suffering of your family.'

Jennifer Bartlett is in London to design the dining room, in tiles she paints, for Doris and Charles Saatchi. We went together to the Saatchi house, which is attached to another house used for their collection of modern art, including a huge John Chamberlain crushed-automobile sculpture standing alone in one room. Doris prepared tea for us while Charles, hardly greeting us, played backgammon with his brother Maurice, of Saatchi & Saatchi, meant to be responsible for Margaret Thatcher being elected as Prime Minister with the slogan: Labour isn't working. Doris moves slowly, with the grace of a ballet dancer, and as carefully.

Left alone, Jennifer and I lay on a bed and talked and talked, often shifting positions. She prefers lying down to standing.

———

Invited by Tony Stokes, Jennifer gave a reading at Garage from her book, The History of the Universe, in which she recounts, in a flat tone, recollections from her life:

> I went to swimming lessons at the bay. The lifeguard wore red trunks, the water was blue, the sky was blue.

In that same flat tone, she recounted very intimate facts about her life.

In the book are written portraits of her friends, including Jan Hashey, her pseudonym Meredith Ridge Slade-Ryan, and Michael Craig-Martin, his pseudonym Robin Slade-Ryan ('In Corsham, Wiltshire, England, Robin and Meredith fell in love with the same student, Brian, a young boy committed to an extreme evangelical faith which involved speaking in tongues and being moved by the spirit'); also of Keith Milow as Gavin Frazer; then there is the woman Maggi Hambling ('He lived for some time with a woman who became a lesbian'), and I, Daniel Francoeur, the name I use for myself in The Family ('During college Daniel woke up, looked out the window and even if the day was fine thought of suicide. In London, Daniel was cured of an ulcer by acupuncture. During the course of the cure he went mad, beat his hands against the head-board of the bed, wept, screamed, shook, shouted. Since then he hasn't been seriously depressed. Andreas, who is a poet and works in a publishing house, took care of him').

The epigraph of the book is from Gertrude Stein: 'She was more interested in birds than flowers although she wasn't really interested in birds.'

Jennifer would like to meet Francis Bacon, but I'm not sure Francis would get on with her.

Needless to say, Nikos has no interest in all of this, but allows me my interest and, yes, amusement, and, yes, more than amusement in the charm I feel when I am with Jennifer.

© Eric Boman

Nikos has made me aware of the critical works of the French decon-structuralists, Piaget, Foucault, Lacan, Derrida, and especially of Roland Barthes whose books take up a length of shelf space in his library. I pick up a book, read here and there, and pick out a word that seems charged with meaning for me, then I close the book. Such a word is 'syncretistic.' Out of its original context, I use the word 'syncretistic' in conversation with Nikos, and he asks me what I mean, and I suggest the meaning is in connections that all come together in a way that Frank means by 'divination,' and Nikos, smiling, asks me, a little devilishly, what I mean by divination, and I try to give 'divination' a definition that I trust Nikos will understand in the way he understands me, and I answer, 'That there is an impulse in the mind to make everything connect,' and he smiles more and looks at me as if I were a student whose naïveté he is touched by.

———

The BBC producer and interviewer and critic Julian Jebb asked me to drinks, or so I thought, and as I was sure he wouldn't mind – also, to show her off to him and a friend of mine he would not have suspected I had so he would have been surprised and intrigued – I brought along Jennifer. Julian welcomed us as if he had been expecting us. Jennifer and I joked lightly with each other more, I felt, than we talked to Julian, she and I as though lolling together in the talk. In fact, Jennifer does have a way of lolling, even when sitting on a chair, and often she will slip off the chair and loll on the floor, her head propped up by her elbow against the floor and her hand to her cheek, and then, that too taxing, she will lie flat on the floor, but go on talking. I felt Julian liked her, but was bemused, and all the more bemused when I said we had to go, for he said I had been invited to dinner with Vidia and Pat Naipaul. Apologies, of course embarrassed apologies, but Julian insisted, all was prepared. Jennifer sat back on the chair when the bell rang and Julian went to open to the Naipauls.

I wanted them all to wonder what I was doing with her and what she was doing with me as a couple, which I wasn't sure of myself.

Julian said he had to go to court for not having paid his bills, but he couldn't, he simply couldn't, open brown envelopes with narrow windows in them that show his name and address.

———

I should write about our evening out with Francis and Stephen. I should, and yet I don't want to. Why? When Nikos and I were driving Stephen back to Loudoun Road after, Stephen asked, 'Will you write about this evening in your diary? It was very strange.' 'Yes,' I said, 'of course I will.' The evening was strange, but I think the strangeness can't be accounted for.

As usual, we all met at Francis' flat in Reece Mews. John Edwards was there (his friend Philip is still in prison for raping a woman at knifepoint, and John misses him terribly) and a young, thin, beautiful man named Roc. Whereas John, who is working class from the East End, was dressed in a smart gray suit with a white shirt and a dark silk tie and smelled cleanly of cologne, Roc, who is upper class and from a very rich family, was dressed in a black motorcycle jacket too big for him, shabby, tight corduroy trousers, and old, narrow and pointed black suede shoes, and he did not give the impression that he was altogether clean. It took me a while to recall that I had met Roc before at a big party given by Rodrigo and Anne Moynihan, and that he is Roc Sandford, the son of the writer Nell Dunn. In Francis' narrow sitting room–bedroom with the large, smashed mirror held together with duct tape, in front of which, Francis likes to say, someone tried to kill him by throwing an ashtray at him that missed, we drank champagne. Francis showed us the only work of art by another artist he owns: done by a Royal College of Art student, a girl, a sewn portrait of her mother, so the nose, made out of canvas, was sewn on, and the open mouth and tongue and teeth, and eyes and eyelashes, and even the hair, were all sewn onto the canvas, the hair, Francis said, the hair of the artist's mother. He said it was the only good work of art he had seen by a living artist in a long while, and he had bought it. After he showed it to us, he propped it against a wall, in a corner. We all said it was extraordinary; we didn't know what else to say about it. We drank two bottles of champagne and then went to an Italian restaurant round the corner, a basement restaurant, where we all sat at a long table. I sat across from Roc. I realized I had as much difficulty understanding Roc's upper-class accent as I did John's Cockney. I asked him what he did, and it seemed to me improbable that he does what he said he does: runs a large farm, a family farm, on Majorca. He flies between Majorca and London often, but he isn't happy in Majorca and wants to stay in London, though he doesn't know what he'll do here. He looked at me deeply in the eyes, then, suddenly, he slumped back and put his hands over his eyes, and I wondered if he had passed out or had a fit of depression. No one took any notice of him, and I joined the conversation of the others, which was about John's friend in prison and how cruel it was to keep him in prison for so long. Francis said, 'It's criminal.' Roc appeared to revive, and drank more, and when the waiters came he asked for all the food to be heaped on his plate, so he had a mixture of pasta, beans, boiled potatoes, roast potatoes, cannelloni, and on top a big gob of mustard. While he ate, the rest of us talked, then, again suddenly, he slumped back and put his hands over his eyes, and when he lowered his hands he smiled at me and said he'd just had a little sleep.

When we got out of the restaurant, Roc invited us all to his flat in Soho for vodka. Francis said he'd go home, and the rest of us, Stephen (who appeared bigger and less coordinated than ever), John, Nikos and I, and Roc, left Francis in the street and went by Nikos' and my car to Roc's flat in Brewer Street. The flat is the top floor in a building among porno film houses, the lights of which flashed through the curtainless windows. The flat appeared to be in the process of being torn apart, with exposed wall struts, and rubbish. One room, the bedroom only because there was a mattress on the floor and clothes thrown about, though there was also a mattress on the floor of the sitting room, the sitting room only because of some broken chairs and a big record player.

I sat with John by a wood fire, the only light in the room – Roc appeared to be burning bits of table he'd smashed – and we talked, though I wasn't sure I understood, about Francis. He loves Francis, and Francis is helping him to buy a pub, but their relationship is non-sexual; he feels he can do Francis a favour, however, by making sure his friends don't nick him, so at least Francis is safe in a world of thieves.

On the mattress on the floor were Stephen, Nikos and Roc, reclining and laughing. John asked me if I thought Stephen would write a poem for Philip to give to him in prison – John can't write at all – to tell Philip how much he loves him, and I said I'd ask Stephen, and did, but Stephen appeared very puzzled, as if he didn't understand the request, or perhaps he didn't want to write the poem. He said to John, 'I'd love to, I really would, but it takes a very long time to write a poem.' 'I understand,' John said.

Then a door opened and a girl came in. Her hair was bunched up at the top of her head and fell in front of her face; her black eyes, through the hair, appeared startled. Seeing her, Stephen said, 'I must go.'

John, Nikos, Roc, I pulled him up onto his feet; he was unsteady, and I worried that he might fall back. Roc showed us all out. On the street, Stephen asked, 'Who was that ugly girl? She ruined everything.' Nikos said, 'Pity her if she's Roc's girlfriend.' John kissed us, over and over, and left us to go to clubs.

On our way to Loudoun Road to leave Stephen off, we were stopped in Portland Place by a policeman who held out a hand. There were many policemen about. The one who stopped us looked in, then waved us on, and I said, 'I guess we look proper.' I imagined the policeman thought Stephen looked like a minister of some kind. Stephen kept repeating, 'How strange it's been. How strange.'

———

Another Easter, and we wondered where we would go for the service, and decided on the Ethiopian Orthodox Church, Saint Mary of Debre Tsion in Battersea, where we went with Doris Saatchi, now divorced from Charles Saatchi. We had to take off our shoes and place them in large pigeonholes, and as the nave was filled we climbed up to a gallery to look down at the service of priests in white and gold robes chanting and acolytes beating drums, one acolyte carrying a large white umbrella with a long fringe about the edge. The congregation, almost all in white,

stood to pray with their hands held out. First the men advanced
for communion, each given a little cloth with which to wipe his
mouth and then throw onto a growing pile; then the women.
Near us in the gallery was a man, who appeared to be English,
dressed as a woman in a long, sleeveless shift and golden bracelets on his bare arms, he talking animatedly with Ethiopians
around him. Nikos was disappointed because there was no
moment of resurrection, which we had all imagined would
happen with the loud beating of drums but didn't, and people
began to leave before the Mass finished, and we left too. The
three of us went to our flat for the traditional Greek Easter
supper, which, however, was out of the cultural context that
used to give it meaning.

What was most strange about the service was that it did not seem
strange at all, not even the presence in the church of the man
dressed as a woman.

───

More and more, I like to think that keeping a diary has to do, not
with the writer, but within the historical time that the diary is
written. And if there should be any deep structure to that time, the
structure would be in the diary. A diary, which is supposed to be
the most personal of all forms of literary expression, really is the
most impersonal, having to do not so much with the writer but the
times in which the writer lives.

───

In London and staying with us, John and Hugh invited us to meet
Douglas Cooper. John likes to give us a little biography of people
he thinks we'd find interesting, or, perhaps, who'd find us interesting, and told us that Douglas Cooper is a close friend of Picasso and
a collector of his works which hang in his grand chateau in France,
and who, during the war, was particularly adept at interrogating
young German soldiers, terrifying them with his command of
German, so that Nikos and I were prepared for the entrance of a

large man with a large-brimmed Texan hat coming towards the restaurant table and more or less shouting, in what sounded like a Texan accent, that paintings by Picasso had been stolen from his chateau, but had been found in Switzerland.

He took no interest at all in Nikos and me, which we thought just as well.

Nikos did not mention that he publishes the books of John Rewald.

After Cooper left, John and Hugh said there was some suspicion that the paintings were not stolen but spirited away to get them into Switzerland and out from under a French ruling that they must remain in France.

———

We had not seen Patrick Procktor for a while, then, out doing Saturday shopping, came across him in carpet slippers walking his dachshund and looking very thin and wan. He asked us to join him in a pub, and though Nikos was reluctant I agreed and at the pub realized that Patrick was already drunk. He spoke nasally, sometimes snorting with brief snorts of laughter, his head held high enough to look down at us.

He seemed to sum up his life by recounting the meals he and his son Christopher have every day, grilled sausages, and I saw a grill dripping with grease. When I asked him what he is working on, he raised his head even higher and swung it away and looked into the distance, and I knew he has stopped painting. Nikos wanted to leave, and I thought that this would most likely be the last time we saw Patrick.

———

Steven Runciman to supper, always with eggs from his hens from his castle in Scotland, and always with amazing anecdotes.

I can't resist including some of his anecdotes:

'Virginia Woolf never forgave Ottoline Morrell for not introducing her to her half-brother the Duke of Portland, because

Virginia aspired to know the royals. Virginia Woolf dressed out of the acting box.'

'My father was a friend of Maynard Keynes, who introduced me into the fringes of Bloomsbury. Lytton Strachey, of whom I was very fond, was very kind and very entertaining to the callow undergraduate I then was, at Trinity, though I knew more people at King's. I met Lady Ottoline Morrell when we were doing a cure together for rheumatism at Tunbridge Wells. She had her Thursday-afternoon tea parties to which guests had to be specially invited, but I could come any Thursday as long as I let her know beforehand. This was in case she was away, or in case something else had come up, and that was fair enough, I thought. At her tea parties, one met every sort of person. There I met and disliked Yeats. Ottoline thought it would be lovely for the poet of Byzantium to talk to the student of Byzantium, but Yeats didn't think that was at all lovely. He didn't want to talk to anyone who knew about Byzantium. Sturge Moore, one of whose poems, "The Gazelles," appears often in anthologies, haunted Ottoline's. He was a brother of G. E. Moore, the philosopher, but, unlike his brother, had a slightly common voice. He was terribly jealous of Yeats, because he knew he would never achieve his eminence. Sitting next to me at Ottoline's, he kept saying to me, "That man Yeats, why does he put so much gold in his poetry? You can't read a line of Yeats without there being gold in it. You go and ask him why he puts so much gold in his poetry." I was nagged into moving over to Yeats and getting the conversation around to gold. Yeats looked at me coldly and said, "Gold is beauty."'

Lockerbie, Scotland

But how can I leave Steven with so little to account for such a presence in our lives? Again and again, I'm overwhelmed in this diary with what I want to account for and what it would take me volumes and volumes to account for.

Steven has allowed me to write a profile of him for the New Yorker, and I've stayed at Elshieshields for some days. When I was not recording him with a microphone, I would, each evening, write out what I remembered of our conversations.

Steven does not allow anyone into his kitchen but himself, not even his staff to do the washing-up, as he thought anyone but himself would chip his china. He does the cooking while I wait in the dining room, in the basement of the castle. The plate before me was illustrated, in sepia, with a scene of a Jesuit in a canoe, two Indians paddling him through rapids. I didn't presume to go for the bowls of soup that appeared on the shelf of the hatch to the kitchen, not sure what was right and what not, but waited until Steven came out of the kitchen and himself brought the bowls of soup to the table. Before placing the bowl on the plate set before me, Steven said, 'I chose that with its scene specifically to refer to your ancestry.'

He said, 'I have told you that you are, in Britain, among the enemy. You are aware, are you not, that you will join the enemy by becoming British? Do think carefully before you do.'

'That has occurred to me.'

'On several counts – the British enemy for dispossessing you of La Nouvelle France, which in war they won, and for going to war with your American colonials to stop the American Revolution, which war they lost. But, being French of a long and, I dare say, distinguished American history, perhaps you don't quite think of the British colonials as your ancestors.'

'No, I never did quite think of the colonials as my ancestors. In my French-Canadian-American parochial school in New England, an attempt was made to integrate us into Yankee America by emphasizing the role played by Lafayette in the American Revolution, but I was never really proud of Lafayette as one of us, representing us. He was an honorary Yankee.'

'Whom do you honour in your history?'

'No one, no one I can think of.'

'Would your parents have had a sense of their history? Would they have known about the defeat of the French on the Plains of Abraham in Quebec by the British, a turning-point in North American history? If the French under Montcalm had succeeded in repulsing the British under Wolfe, the British colonials would not have assumed the security they needed to expand into French territory, and La Nouvelle France would still claim most of the continent. I do enjoy speculating about what would have happened in history if wars had been won by the opposing forces. Alas, I must stick to the facts.'

'My parents wouldn't have known about the Plains of Abraham. Their sense of history was very limited, and perhaps went no further back than to their own parents and their emigration from farms in French Canada to work in the textile mills of Yankee New England.'

'They wouldn't have known about the Jesuits and the Indians?'

'Only in that my father was a quarter-breed Blackfoot Indian, his grandmother lost, as it were, in the forests of North America along with the Jesuits who braved rapids to reach them to convert them. I was brought up with almost no sense of my own native history.'

Steven suddenly said, 'I see you eyeing the bottle of wine.'

'I did happen to glance at it.'

'Wine is not drunk with the soup.'

'I admit that I do have a lot to learn.'

'If you were familiar to the household, you would be allowed to add a dash of sherry to your soup, but I think that would be too familiar of you as a guest.'

'I wouldn't dare.'

Steven took the soup bowls into the kitchen, and I waited, studying the scene on the plate of my ancestry, and a deep loneliness in my isolation surrounded me like the shadows that encircled the dimly lit room.

The panel to the hatch rose, and there appeared on the shelf an elaborate tureen.

'What,' Steven asked, lifting the cover of the tureen to reveal kedgeree, 'do you know of the battle of Ain Jalud?'

'I wouldn't try to fake even guessing.'

'The most important battle in the Western world, and you know nothing of it?'

'You won't tell me?'

'I am ashamed of you for not knowing, but you must learn, as you say. The battle of Ain Jalud occurred September 2, 1260, between the Muslim Marmelukes of Egypt and the Mongols under the Christian general Kitbuqa. Had the Mongols won, Islam might have crumbled in the whole Turkish Crescent and possibly the Turks might have become Christian. As it was, the Muslims won and punished the native Christians for their friendship with the Mongols. And the Mongols in the Near East eventually turned Muslim.'

'I didn't know.'

'Again, my failing as a proper historian – I speculate too much on what might have happened if, the if always suggesting a fantasy of an entirely different world.'

'You fantasize about history?'

'About a world that might have been, yes, I do.'

'A better world?'

'A different world.'

'Different in what way? More to your liking?'

'As much as I must stick to the facts, I am all too human in wanting a world more to my liking.'

'Which would be?'

'Dear boy, you do have an American way of asking questions that are too personal. If you are to become truly British, you must understand that we British do not indulge in the personal, which is of little interest even to oneself. What is of interest I leave for you to find out.'

'Manners?' I asked.

'Well, you are astute.'

'I can claim to have been brought up to be polite, to hold the door open for women, to stand when a woman enters the room, to walk along the outside of the pavement if I am escorting a woman. But this is rudimentary.'

'You have been brought up well, and have the basics. As for British manners, you have more to learn. Where, for example, would you place the pudding – "pudding" being an acceptable term except for fruit salad – fork and spoon?'

'At the sides, always at the sides,' I said, seeing where they were placed at either side of his plate.

'What about fish knives and forks?'

'You tell me.'

'I was once in Bucharest with my mother at the Jockey Club there – we were on a cruise in the family yacht – and we heard a woman at the other side of the dining room shout out, "Take this fish knife and fork away. What do you think I am?" We never had them at home. In later life, I was given a set as a gift, and gave them away, but, on reconsidering, I thought that after all they are rather useful, so I bought a set. One must adapt to the changes – we are no longer in an era when knife boys must clean the knives of those who could not afford silver, distinguishing, all too undemocrati- cally, the lower classes from the upper. Fish knives and forks are a sign of a democratic spirit, in a rather conservative way.'

'What about placement cards?'

'Perfectly acceptable, but the full title must be written, and they must never be the vulgar stand-up kind, but must lie flat on the plate.'

'Finger bowls?'

'Also perfectly acceptable, except when you have royalty.'

'Why?'

'The royal would be offended if someone passed a glass over the fingerbowl, reminding him or her of Bonnie Prince Charlie having to cross the water to escape death. I must say, I was once derided by Lady Holmes for being such a stickler about not having finger bowls when royals come to a meal, she insisting that it would do simply to put one's hand over the bowl when raising one's glass.'

'I'll remember that.'

Steven thought. 'Odd, I must say, that the British should have put up a statue of George Washington in Trafalgar Square – a traitor.'

———

The next day, in his drawing room, I recorded Steven talking.

Propped in a corner were a Regency table harp, a Javanese one-stringed instrument, and a nose flute from Borneo, and a hubble-bubble, a water pipe of green glass with simple flowers painted on it.

I asked Steven about the hubble-bubble.

'Do you really want to hear?' He seemed a little annoyed.

'Please.'

The September sunlight on the lawn, seen through glass doors, was low and long. Steven sat at the edge of his chair, his thin legs turned to the side, as if the room did not have enough space for him. He didn't look at me, but at the walls of the room, and he smoked a cigarillo.

He started with a faint growl.

From the recording:

'When I was in Istanbul, in 1942, to teach Byzantine history at the university, I was allotted a handsome young lady to be my translator and assistant. Her family, the Karaçalaris, had been old-established tobacco magnates in Kavala when it was Turkish. She was related, in the female line, to the founder of the line of the Egyptian khedives. Some generations before, a husband and wife – ancestors of those tobacco people in Kavala – had an only daughter, admirably well endowed financially but not physically, and when she was married off to the son of a neighboring tobacco king and he unveiled her he couldn't face it, so an Albanian adventurer, having heard the story, went to the father and said, "It's a good dowry, I'll take her on," and he did, and they were the parents of Muhammad Ali, the first khedive of Egypt. For a time, the Egyptian government kept up the house where he was born in Kavala. Kavala, as you must know, was transferred earlier from the Turks to the Greeks, and all the Turks had to leave. The Karaçalaris family in Kavala had always rather despised their relatives in Egypt. Muhammad Ali had assigned them large lands in Egypt, but they had never bothered to go to Egypt or do anything about the land. It was only at the exchange of populations between Turkey and Greece, in 1922, that the Kavala cousins remembered their rich cousins in Egypt. But it was too late. Everything had gone by default. They had to go to Istanbul.'

I tried to keep my mind fixed on Steven's words, which rose in pitch, so at sudden moments I heard only the rising pitch, and I must fix my mind on the words.

'My assistant's uncle was a great friend of Atatürk. Atatürk came to the house once while she was studying, and he asked her what she was studying, and she said, "Old Hittite." Atatürk wanted to prove the Turks Hittites. He said, "It's just like old Turkish, isn't it?" She said, "No, it's more like old Armenian." The family were aghast. Atatürk giggled and said, "You know, sometimes I think I'll have to prove the Armenians Turkish." She was a bright girl. She was married to His Highness the Çelebi Effendi. Of course, he wasn't allowed to use his title in Turkey, but he was the hereditary head of the whirling dervishes – the Mevlevi dervishes – descended in a direct male line from the founder, the great philosopher Jalal ad-Din ar-Rumi. Before the sultanate was abolished, in 1922, the whirling dervishes had a great many establishments all over Turkey, and, indeed, the hereditary head was one of the chief people in the Ottoman regime. He had to gird the Sultan with the sword of Islam, even though the Mevlevi dervishes were considered a little heretical, a little bit too tolerant, by strict Islamic standards. Then, with the revolution, Atatürk secularized and annexed all the Mevlevi establishments in Turkey and banned the use of titles. So the Çelebi Effendi moved to Syria and settled in Aleppo, where he still had his tekke, or monastery. Just before the Second World War, the Turks managed to force the French, who were then in charge of Syria, to yield the province around Antioch to Turkey. The Syrians were furious, and turned out all Turkish citizens living in Syria, including the Çelebi Effendi. He had to go back to Turkey and live there as a private citizen. He was out of touch with all his remaining establishments in Syria and Aleppo, and, of course, the war made him even more out of touch.'

Steven's voice reached such a pitch it became song, and he seemed, for all the dense interconnected detail of his account, to go into a trance, as if such dense interconnections always put him into a trance.

'As he was the husband of my assistant, I saw the Çelebi Effendi often. The first time I dined with them, he said that if I could smoke a hubble-bubble without being sick he'd give it to me. And there it is. Not a very beautiful one, as hubble-bubbles go. One day, he died, quite suddenly, leaving by an earlier marriage a son of sixteen, who was the heir. This was towards the end of the war, the beginning of 1944. The boy, in order to be accepted as head of the Mevlevi, had to go round the various establishments and have his knee kissed. That was the proper ceremony. But how could a boy of sixteen, in war conditions, get a visa to Syria? The Free French were in occupation, and I had a friend among them,

Count Stanislas Ostrorόg, who was of a Polish family that, in the eighteen-forties, had fled Russia to settle in Istanbul. They had one of the most beautiful houses on the Bosporus, where Stanislas' elder brother lives, married to a daughter of Sir Basil Zaharoff, the arms magnate.'

Steven stopped, closed his eyes for a moment as though to contemplate the circumference of his trance, then, opening his eyes wide, said quietly, 'Sorry for all these details,' and closed his eyes to continue, with a slight swaying of his shoulders, within his ever widening trance. 'I had stayed with Stanislas in Damascus before the war, when he was Résident there, and I knew he would understand, because he was interested in such things as the whirling dervishes. I wrote to him. The immediate result: a huge envelope came back to the boy, addressed – never before had he been addressed like this – to "Son Altesse le Çelebi Effendi," with the visa and everything needed for his trip to have his knee kissed. So off he was able to go to Syria, blessing me. And when I followed, on leave, a month or so later, at every station a delegation of whirling dervishes came to greet me. They asked me if I would like them to dance for me, and I made them dance at Aleppo and Homs. I thought that perhaps twice was enough. Anyhow, they all said, "You see, you're one of us."'

Steven now looked at me and, back to a low, growling voice, said, 'In Istanbul, they were started up as a tourist attraction, which is really monstrous. We real ones consider this indecent. We don't approve. But we are in a very bad way, because the Syrians decided to close the tekke in Syria. One had a wonderful international situation – the Turkish government suing the Syrian for annexing the property of Turkish citizens, though they'd done it themselves several years before. Practically no tekke is dancing still. I'm not sure the one in Cyprus dances.'

I was, in my own way, in a trance, assuming as I did that Steven's ability to make connections could go on and on, connecting all the stars, making of them all one great story. He did tell a story, the suspense sustained not just because of the unexpected events but the unexpected connections. I had asked myself if the young Çelebi Effendi would be able to get out of Turkey to have his knee kissed and save the Mevlevi. The answer was yes, made possible by the unexpected connection in Istanbul between a Polish count from Russia and a Scottish historian. And all along there were unexpected connections made – Turkish, Greek, Egyptian, Albanian, Hittite, Armenian, French, Syrian, Polish, Russian – so I was drawn into the story with expectations of the even more unexpected, which was the interconnection of everything. I understood so little, but I thought that there was no way, ever, for me to understand everything, and that was the great mystery of history: to understand everything. I imagine Steven does.

A spoon, a button, a coin could be the center of world history, so complex, however, that the history could never for me be known.

And, in a sense, I imagine my diary as historical, recording what may appear to be incidentals, spoons, buttons, coins, arcane table manners, but about these incidentals expands more than I could ever possibly account for, expanding into history.

I think I am in one place at one time, but really I'm in many places and at many times, too many for me to make the connections that Steven is capable of making.

Steven Runciman on history:

'From my earliest childhood, I've liked history. I wasn't drawn to it by a scientific desire for knowledge. Oh, no. I was drawn by romantic imaginings. I've always liked stories. I've always liked people, and I've always liked trying to understand the great stories of the past. As romantic as my imaginings are, I have always wanted my stories to be based on truth. Because of this, I have never got much pleasure out of reading ghost stories that are fiction. I like my ghost stories, too, to be real. I prefer history to fiction – though, like all historians, I would like to write an historical novel. It would be so marvellous to be able to put down what you're quite sure did happen but you can't prove it. It's a wicked temptation, however, and I must stick to the sterner discipline.

'The Crusades was one of the big stories of history, and, as it hadn't been told recently, I wanted to tell it. I suppose I'm considered a rather old-fashioned historian. What the Namier historians of the new French style think of me I can only too easily imagine. They concentrate on details, and I – well, I know I'm terribly in disgrace with the Crusading historians because I'm not interested in things like the detailed legal arrangements, although I know roughly what they were. These historians are very recondite, I think, and have a snobbish and undemocratic view of history. I, in my old-fashioned way, am much more democratic. I want to know what made the whole story happen. They forget that the word history means story.'

I said I would like to know how he writes history.

He sat at the very edge of his armchair, with a pile of newspapers and magazines behind him.

'Well, one starts with the sources. Published sources proliferate. If Gibbon, who when he wrote the Decline and Fall had consulted practically all the printed sources available to him in his day, were to write the same book today, he'd have about three times as much to consult. Then, there are the unpublished sources – the material in archives, often ill catalogued, and sometimes not catalogued, or even arranged in any order. Then, there is always the possibility of something hitherto unknown being discovered – the life of a saint in a monastic library, or a batch of letters, or a forgotten character. But in classical and medieval history such finds are very rare, and most primary material has been published. Occasionally, one thinks as one goes through catalogues of collections, oh, this would be interesting. Then one finds it has been published in slightly different form or under a different heading elsewhere. I've never found, myself, any new manuscript of any value. In fact, I'm not very good at reading manuscripts. And I can't bear reading on microfilm. I've got a rather fitful memory. When I go into a library and don't happen to have a notebook on me and I see somewhere in a book something that is of great interest, I think that I shall certainly remember it. I remember exactly what it looked like on the page, but I can't remember which book it is in. In the end, I'll locate it.'

Steven was not looking at me but over my head.

'With so much to consult, a historian, not unnaturally, does tend to take refuge in details, a detailed discussion of some small point. What he produces is very useful, but he is not really writing history; he is providing another secondary source. To write history, he has to bring the details together into a significant whole.'

(How can I, in recording this talk, not stop on the words 'a significant whole,' which suddenly appeared to centre my whole life in a vision?)

'There are some historians who begin with the significant whole – before they have mastered the details. The trouble is that to explain the course of all history you should be acquainted with all history – and it would be hard to find such a polymath. I rather like the idea of writing a story. The idea is to find some well-rounded theme – without being afraid of the large theme – that makes a story of its own. But it must fit into the stream of history, and the historian must be conscious of its causes in the past and its influences in the future. All the reading takes time, but during that time you're thinking about the work, consciously and often subconsciously. Much of your best thinking is done, say, on a country walk or when you're working in the garden. It's helpful to have a garden.'

History to Steven is world history.

London

I don't know why, but when people insult me I take the insult as a joke.

I was invited to a conference at Assumption College in Worcester, Massachusetts, on Franco-American literature, I suppose because I have written in The Family about the Franco-American world, the world of my family.

At the conference, someone approached me and asked, 'Est-ce que vous connaissez Paul Theroux (the The- pronounced as Té-)?'

I answered that I had met him.

Why, I was asked, had Paul Theroux, a Franco, not written about us, Franco-Americans?

I didn't know.

Back in London, at a book-launch party, I saw Paul and went to him, and, hardly saying hello to me, he spoke about himself so rapidly it was as though he was stopping me from talking about myself. I tugged at the lapels of his jacket and said, 'Paul, it's about you that I came over to talk to you.' He waited, and I told him what I had been asked by someone at the conference: why doesn't he write about Francos, as he is one? He jabbed a finger at my chest and said, 'Because you do.'

Then I said, 'Il m'a demandé si je te connais.'

'Et tu as répondu?'

'Oui.'

He looked up and away and said, 'Si quelq'un me demanderait

si je connais David Plante, qu'est-ce que je lui dirais?' He looked down at me and said, 'Non.'

He turned away and I did laugh.

It is innate among Franco-Americans, our truly lost tribe, that not one of them wants to know, much less help, another one, and how very few we are.

I would never expect from Paul Theroux any recognition of any kind.

———

John Fleming has written that Patrick Kinross is dead. The illness that killed him was never diagnosed. He was reduced to a skeleton.

Thinking about him, I think of how, the more I live in London the more, yes, I am fascinated by connections that take me back into history, and, yes, people I have met in London have taken me far back into history, far back, linking me to history, which I think of as the most formative evolution of anyone's life; and the connection with one person in the past brings more than that person into the present, the connection brings into the present past époques.

So when I, turning the pages of a biography, came across a photograph taken in the 1920s of Patrick Kinross dressed for a fancy ball in eighteenth-century court dress complete with wig, he among others also in fancy dress, leaning over a pit in which roughly clothed navvies are digging, one of them with a pneumatic drill, Patrick and his company presumably in conversation with the navvies, I reacted with a mixture of revulsion at the class divide (as would Nikos) and fascination (as would I). The fascination is, I like to think, justified by my seeing the scene historically representative of past ages, for Patrick in his court dress does appear to have come directly from the eighteenth century and to have found himself in a London where, curiously, men were digging a pit with a strange, stuttering instrument that he must stop and ask about. But, yes, I am glad that the époque of Patrick in fancy court dress divided by class from the navvy in overalls with his pneumatic drill is past, however fascinating I find it, because, if I had been born and raised in working-class

England as I was in working-class America, I would have been the navvy in the pit looked down upon by the baron.

Still, Patrick did make even details historical, as when he said that, before attending the coronation of Queen Elizabeth in his robes, he was warned to pee, because the ceremony would be interminable, and I took this as a detail that was a warning to everyone in the deep past who attended royal ceremonies, a detail that gives historical particularity to the historically grand event. I do like details.

And no doubt the Queen sustains the details of history.

Roy Strong told me that he loves being High Bailiff and Searcher of the Sanctuary at Westminster Abbey, an honorary role which includes attendance at all great state occasions in the building, which duty allows him to wear a ruff.

———

An image often comes to me – as do many many many images – from when I first came to Europe in 1959, when I was nineteen and in Barcelona in a barber's chair from which I saw reflected in the mirror before me a door behind open and a man's hand appear holding the edge of the door, the nail of his little finger long and pointed, and a shudder passed through me at what I had never seen affected by a man, and what I later learned was his way of demonstrating that he was not a manual worker, and this made me wonder at the long history of keeping the nail of one's baby finger long and pointed. And so, over and over again, I find myself wondering about such small details for having long histories. And it was in Spain that I met a Spaniard who, shaking my hand, scratched my palm with his index finger, I wondering what this meant and only after realizing that it was a sexual message, a message, I imagined, that had its long history within Spanish sexual signaling. It is always a pleasure to me to try to decode these coded messages, which make me so aware of what I like to think of as an occult foreign world.

And so the occult world of London.

And, more, Nikos' occult Greek world.

———

More about Patrick Kinross.

After Oscar Wilde, whose trial and imprisonment did cause such contemporaries as Arthur Symons anguish by suppressing their sexuality, and did ruin the lives of such men as Simeon Solomon arrested for importuning –

(though I do wonder if, for queer men of this past generation, the law did not discriminate unless some more serious crime was committed to which sex was incidental, but which, in the process of the trial, became more and more the issue, for, surely, there must have been male brothels the police knew about as they also knew about those men who frequented the brothels, both tolerated by the police) –

but which trial and imprisonment of Oscar Wilde seems not to have caused queers of the generation of Patrick Kinross, not so far removed in time from the trial and imprisonment, to suppress knowledge of their sexuality, and not even to stop them from acting on their sexuality. The trial and imprisonment seem, instead of leaving a legacy of harsh suppression and harsher trial and imprisonment, to have brought out the sexuality of the generation of Patrick into common knowledge. They, the queer men of Patrick's world, must have assumed the law that condemned Wilde didn't apply to them, for why should any disposition as common as homosexuality be criminal? And all their friends, of whatever sexuality, assumed the same about them. Everyone must have known that when Patrick married he was queer, and that he divorced because he was queer, and I dare say he remained friends with those who knew he was queer, such as Charlotte Bonham Carter. All this, perhaps, among the upper-middle into the upper classes. But this is only guessing about a world I know nothing about, and dangerously near the speculation I avoid.

Still, it comes to me: we of course take an outstanding event from the past, as the trial and imprisonment of Oscar Wilde, to speak not only for the whole past but the whole present, and this is what causes are based on.

Chartres

Nikos and I went to Chartres to visit the cathedral.

I had been before, when I was a student at the Catholic University of Louvain, Belgium, where theology was a living discipline with essential problems to be discussed: how can the immutable and eternal God, the Uncaused Causer, change enough in time to have caused the universe and the world, to have created Adam and Eve, to have condemned them for their sin, then to have changed again in time from condemning them to forgiving them? As I no longer believe in God, these problems are mere curiosities. But I had believed when I first visited the cathedral.

From the car, we saw the spires of the cathedral rise from the flat, pale green fields of spring wheat. I pulled over to the side of the road, not far from a ditch along which were pollarded willow trees, and I stopped the car. This view couldn't have changed in twenty-five years.

There was heavy traffic in what was no longer the town I'd known, but a city. The buildings were new and had wide, stark windows, and the traffic was dense. Nikos and I had a row. With difficulty, we found in a hotel a room with a view of a darkening back yard.

As if our being late was my fault, Nikos said resentfully, 'We'll unpack later. We'd better get to the cathedral before it closes.'

He was always the one who was late and whom I had to hurry along.

With a map, we found our way to the vieille ville, which had been, I recalled, all the ville when I'd been there, and I thought I should be able to find my way in the vieille ville to the cathedral. Nikos asked, Was I sure? Yes, I was sure. But I lost the way. Finally there, a guard said the cathedral was closing.

I told Nikos I was sure I could find a restaurant from years before. I was sure it was on a street very near the cathedral. It had white curtains on a brass rod over the lower part of the many-paned window, and through the top you saw inside to the dark wood wainscoting. I walked up and down the streets.

'I guess it's gone,' I said.

He found a restaurant in the nouvelle ville.

While we were eating, I said, 'I really am sorry that restaurant is gone. It was run by an old woman, I remember. The floor was flagged with stone, and the restaurant smelled like a stone cellar. I remember the old woman, without being asked, bringing glasses and a carafe of wine, then soup bowls, those heavy, deep, white soup bowls, and a metal tureen of potage which she carried by its handles with a dish towel and placed on the table, where it steamed in the chilly air. We served ourselves. The big ladle was dented.'

'We should have looked more carefully,' he said.

'This place is fine.'

'But I want everything to be the way you remember it.'

'Maybe it's just as well it isn't.'

In our hotel room, we undressed silently.

We lay flat on our backs in bed, our heads on the long bolster. We didn't sleep well.

In the morning, I got up before Nikos and sat in a chair before the window that looked out onto the back yard, where a young man was holding the front wheel of a bicycle off the ground and rotating it, so its small, rapid clicks became a whir. A woman came into the yard pushing a bicycle. By the time Nikos got up there were ten people with bicycles in the back yard; they spun their wheels and talked quietly.

I don't know why, but these details are important to me,

perhaps because our visit to Chartres was in every way important to me.

I said I'd go now to the cathedral, but he said he'd want breakfast first. Would he mind if I didn't join him, but went off to the cathedral? He looked hurt, but he said, 'Go, of course go,' and offered me the map as he knew I wouldn't be able to find my way on my own.

I didn't take the map, but after a few wrong turns I came to the cathedral. A great cloud was passing high above the spires, and, as though my senses were caught off balance, it appeared to me that the spires were moving, the cloud was still.

I hesitated before I pushed open the frayed, padded door, and blinked in the inside dimness. From what seemed to me far below, I saw high pillars, and I walked among them. I came upon an altar, before which, stuck on rows of spikes on wrought-iron racks, were hundreds of burning tapers leaning towards one another and melting in the heat. The wax dripped onto iron sheets below the racks. I looked at the burning tapers and the flames reflected in hundreds of golden hearts hanging around them.

I leaned my forehead against a pillar and wept, but turned when I felt a hand on my shoulder to see Nikos standing by me.

He said, 'Give in, give in.'

I asked, 'To what?'

Greece

I finally got my driving license, and in a car Nikos is allowed as director of Thames & Hudson, I drove us – I'm tempted to use the old British expression, 'we motored,' which doesn't indicate who drove, as if the motor car could motor itself – down through France and Italy on our way to Greece, and on the way stopped to stay with Elizabeth and Christopher Glenconner on Corfu.

As a car can't reach the house, Christopher met us in a little boat, and then a walk along a path through pines, he, perhaps not knowing quite who we were, but, as guests of Elizabeth, his guests, and he laughed with the pleasure of having to meet us in a boat and the walk through the pines.

We arrived in time for drinks, Christopher taking charge, though I noted that he stared at the bottles for a long while to figure out what was what, but, as always, he laughed lightly as with the pleasure of preparing drinks. And Elizabeth looks on him with what I can only think of as a slightly unfocused, but, for all that, total love.

He told us about his exploits in the navy during the war.

Nikos said later that Christopher is a hero in the cause of liberating Greece from the Nazis.

Christopher has taken to painting, his favourite view that of the small bay below their house, down a rocky cliff.

Stephen and Natasha have stayed, and so has Steven Runciman, who gave to Christopher and Elizabeth an icon to keep the house blessedly safe.

And now in Nikos' occult world, and I in it as if a Frank Kermode trying to find in it the occult meanings –

In Athens, where there are graffiti on walls from the years of the dictatorship, stenciled images of the phoenix rising from flames. Here and there, in scruffy plots of red earth, small playgrounds for children, I suppose to show off the concern the colonels had for the very young. And, given the colonels' lack of zoning – thinking there should be freedom to exploit wherever exploitation was feasible – apartment buildings encroaching on the holy hill of Lycabettus, the least of exploitations. On a long walk, we passed an abandoned building where, Nikos said, prisoners of the colonels were tortured. Once again, when I hear about torture I can't particularize any one person being tortured, and, much less, any one person applying the torture, as if this last can't be attributable to a human being.

The flat of Nikos' mother, in Tsoha Street, has green mottled marble floors in the entrance and parquet elsewhere, and there is a sense of white space in the rooms.

Here I am, where Nikos' world is most emblematic in objects that he tells me about, and that I am possessive of, as if possessive of his world.

The silver dish is from Constantinople, taken with whatever the family could take, at the time of the exchange of populations in the 1920s.

On the dining-room table is a green bowl on three pedestals, a great chip broken from it, the result of a bomb meant for the airport near where Nikos' family lived in Elliniko but exploding in and destroying the house next door, the shockwaves causing a fragment of the ceiling of the dining room in the family house to fall and break the bowl on the dining-room table. The shockwaves also caused the locks in the house to jam. This was when Nikos and his mother and aunt Fula were hiding under the dining-room table, the live-in maid with them, all crowded together.

In the living room, furniture designed by Nikos' father, an architect who designed the neo-classical Athens College, where Nikos spent ten years of his life as a boarder.

Also in the living room, small chairs with carved wood frames and string mesh for the seats, from, Nikos said, an island, though he wasn't sure what island, as his family do not come from an island about which they can say, 'Our island,' and return there for holidays. His mother has no interest in the Greek islands.

In fact, his mother had no interest in Athens, having lived in Constantinople, to her Athens a dusty provincial town, the Greeks there not Greeks but Albanians.

The rugs, which Fula identified, also brought from Constantinople.

Nikos told me that she still has her dowry, gold sovereigns, which she keeps in secret places but she forgets where. When she forgets, she blames the maid for stealing the coins. She came out of the kitchen with a tea caddy – only, Nikos said, for fascomilo tea, mountain tea, drunk only when not feeling well – and from it took

out a little bag with a draw string and from the bag a gold sovereign
which she gave to Nikos. He showed it to me: a small coin minted
with the profile of EDWARDVS VII D: G: BRITT: OMN: REX
F: D: IND: IMP. To read in Athens on a gold coin minted in Great
Britain an honorific in Latin – to account for the history of these
conjunctions would, I thought, require a study in Western history,
and here it was in the palm of my hand. Nikos said that these gold
sovereigns are still the basis of calculating, say, the price of a house
in a contract. As for aunt Fula's dowry – her prika – it was never
used, for her role was set for her to take care of her older sisters, she
the cook, the over-looker of the maid, the factotum.

Once I said to her that Nikos is a complainer, which she took in
with her jaw stuck out and her lips pressed tightly together. Nikos
told me that she then went to him to inform him not to trust me,
as I speak behind his back. So I am warned.

In the kitchen, even there I look for totems of a world that I want
to be mine, and note the large tin of olive oil beneath the sink, the
bottle of ouzo on the marble counter, and in a cup a thin gelatin made,
as Nikos explained, by the seeds of quince – kidonia – in water,
prepared by Fula for her to drink, Nikos wasn't sure for what reason.

And then, oh yes, there is the ceremony of the gliko koutaliou and
cold water and coffee, all prepared by Fula for when Nikos and I wake
up from our naps, those deep, deep naps that seem to come with an
Oriental stupor in the afternoon, a stupor which needs the shock of
the sweet and the cold water and the coffee to wake one from.

And the walks about Athens, Nikos' Athens, the Athens of his
youth – such as the nineteenth-century apartment building behind
the cathedral where his extended family lived during World War II,
when, he said, family life was a circle of devotion. He pointed out
to me the balcony where his family kept the turkey that flew down
to the street and was grabbed by an amazed passer-by.

And in the entrance hall of the apartment building, the floor,
Nikos showed me, is paved with white and black squares of marble,
which often come into his dreams. And so, I am able to participate
in his dream imagery.

We went to neo-classical Athens College, designed by his architect father. There, Nikos spent eight years of his youth, and, from outside, he pointed out the window of the dormitory room where he slept.

He showed me the cinema, Rex, where he was awakened to sex by a man sitting next to him who unzipped him and masturbated him, Nikos so amazed that he got up and left the cinema with his penis exposed.

And we stopped outside the basement garçonière (I noting the use of French) which he had rented to get away from home, acceptable among Greeks of his world, though assumed without it being said, for the sexual life of a young man that he cannot have at home; and I did have more than a twinge of jealousy for the past Athenian sexual life of Nikos, as I fantasized it, there in the basement of an apartment building, a sexual life that of course left me out, but in which I should have been the partner.

As we passed a low, abandoned building somewhere up the hill from the American Embassy, and not far from the American ambassador's residence, Nikos said that here people were tortured during the dictatorship, the building spiritually and morally and, I felt, physically contaminated, now left to decay.

Nikos' mother, Natalia, is a delicate woman, in no way the prototype of a Greek mother.

Sustaining a fashion that has long gone out of fashion where it originated in Paris and London, Nikos' mother has at-homes every Wednesday. When Nikos was living at home, he used to like to shock the friends his mother received by revealing family secrets, as he cannot abide by the secrecy that seems to be the way all of Greece works: don't tell, don't tell, keep it a secret. In Constantinople, an impoverished member of the extended family went to the opposite side of the city to work as a seamstress to keep the humiliation a deep secret, or, again in Constantinople, an impoverished family would take out their best china and silver and clink the silver against the empty china, the windows open, so that neighbours would think they were having a feast. Never mind, Nikos said, what the government ministers are keeping secret, to which his mother quietly demurred, but she then did say, 'You see, we were so long under the Ottoman Empire, and had to keep our secrets.'

Mrs Stangos – or I like to address her in the Greek Kiria Stangou, which seems to me to add a linguistic dimension to her name – speaks perfect English, with the soft accent Nikos has. She also speaks French and German and Russian, but only kitchen Turkish, though born and brought up in Istanbul. She winces at the Greek pronunciation tri-buison for the French tire-bouchon, and in English will use French expressions such as vernissage, which Nikos used to use until, in London, he changed to 'gallery opening.' I note that, in Athens, he uses English expressions that he has taken on, I think, intentionally, such as 'that's rich,' or 'that's rum,' or 'stuff and nonsense,' as if to claim his foreignness in a country where he has always felt a foreigner.

Fula, not the mother, answered the door when Nikos rang, I behind him, and Nikos and Fula embraced warmly. His mother, in granny shoes, came and held Nikos lightly. They spoke in English, I thought because of me, and she greeted me in English. She had been a teacher of English at Athens College. I noted that her most overt sign of affection towards Nikos is to tap him on the arm and smile at him, somewhat sadly, and he smiles back somewhat sadly. A refined woman, of a deep culture that evolved over more years than her age, she wears her hair in braids curled in spirals that cover her ears.

We went to visit his aunt Tato. He had talked to me of her, a formidable woman whose formidability was rounded out by history that made her presence historical. She is, as I learned to distinguish, from other Greeks, Cosmopoliti, those Greeks from Constantinople a class apart, in fact more cosmopolitan than Athenian Greeks.

She was dressed in black, her grey hair pulled back in a small chignon, and I immediately felt that I was in her good graces when Nikos introduced me as a young writer, which to her meant that I was of course a cultured person. Nikos had told me one of her novels was based on a very intense relationship, a loving relationship, between two girls, equal, he thinks, to anything written by

Colette. We spoke in French. A maid served us ouzakia – the glasses and bowl of pistachios served on a round tray covered in a cloth embroidered in gold, details that I am always attentive to – while Tato spoke with the kind of authority that can only come from having lived through what many others were defeated by, with no nonsense. There were piles of books everywhere, books with paper covers as is the way in Greece, and among them Nikos pointed out a collection of American Black poetry translated into Greek by Tato's husband, now dead. He and she had monumental rows, monumental. She told me she would very much like to go to America to see the Mississippi River.

As we walked about Athens, Nikos stopped at the bust on a plinth of Ersi Hadgimihali's aunt, which I remembered Nikos mentioning when Ersi visited us in London, Ersi now dead.

In Ermou Street, we saw a man goading a dancing bear to keep on dancing, stepping from side to side, the bear with an iron collar with a chain that the man held in one hand as he goaded the bear with the other. And we saw beggars exposing their stumps of legs and arms. And there was a barrel-organ player, turning the handle to play folk tunes.

From time to time in London, Nikos has severe migraines, so severe one of his eyes becomes bloodshot and weeps. Here in Athens, his migraines are frequent. Though it is not done to close a door – I closed the door to our room where I withdrew to lie down but Nikos' mother opened it, asking didn't I prefer to have the door open for the air to circulate? to which I demurred – when Nikos feels a migraine come on he asks me to come into our room with him and, he sitting on the edge of his bed and I standing before him, he presses his forehead into my abdomen. This fills me with feelings too strange to sort out, from an erotic charge to the greater charge of such love for him in his helplessness that I would like to stay forever with him there, he in unendurable pain pressing his forehead into my abdomen.

His mother does not open the door.

She treats me with delicate affection.

Nikos had warned me not, in Athens, to call him Agapi mou, allowed only between lovers.

Nikos has shown me photographs from his past:

Nikos orating before a class at Athens College.

Nikos with mates from Athens College in a taverna. He is on the extreme right.

Nikos with someone he said he would rather forget, on an excursion to an island.

And then Nikos showed me documents from the German Occupation:

On the back is written, in cursive Latin letters, 'Stangos', and in English, 'He will help you unload things give him a tip I will pay the five hundred,' signed illegibly, and also in English, 'Received with thanks,' and signed in cursive Latin, 'Adamantiadis,' Nikos' uncle.

And this, with stamps costing 2,000,000,000 drachmas each:

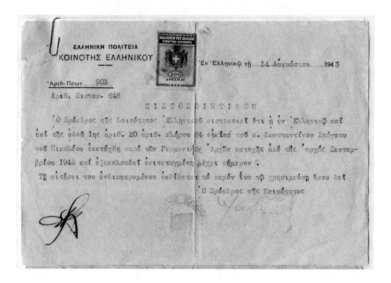

From a more remote past, this photograph, taken in 1913 by Nikos' mother of a friend in Constantinople, the friend dressed as an ancient Greek.

How can I get all of Nikos' past life in here, as I want to, as I am possessed to do?

I went with him and his mother to the cemetery, the Second Cemetery where refugees are buried, to wash the family tomb, where his father is buried, and stood to the side when Nikos asked a priest to come and say a prayer before the tomb, he in his long black robe and high black conical hat, rocking back and forth, chanting the prayer, for which Nikos gave him a coin. Nikos' mother appeared hardly able to endure being there, as if it was all Nikos' desire to be there, to wash the tomb, to have a prayer said, his desire a stubborn need for ritual.

This need in him occurred to me as if for the first time, for observing Christmas and the New Year and Easter, and, especially, birthday celebrations, he insists on, as a matter of principle that he – yes, stubbornly – must not give up on, as if against a fate that threatens to defeat all such rituals. He will say he doesn't want to socialize, but he will be the one to insist on having many friends round for a holiday celebration, for which we spend a lot of time preparing.

London

Nikos came home with a copy of Ezra Pound's Cantos, published by Faber & Faber in what Nikos complains of as a shoddy publication of a great work. This comes to me: Nikos' admiration of Pound goes beyond the amazing use of images, as amazing as any images in all of literature, but for an ideology that is in fact opposed to Nikos' ideology, as opposed as Communism is to Fascism; for, though Nikos is in his very instincts opposed to the imposition of any ideological dogma, he has a vital sense of the importance of ideology as inspiration, and has the deepest appreciation of someone whose vision is of 'un paradiso terreste,' as was Pound's. But, deeper than that appreciation of a vision of a 'paradiso terreste,' as different as they are in their visions, what they share, as I sense Nikos senses in Pound, is that in their visions of a 'paradiso terreste' both are defeated. I may think to myself, thank God both visions are defeated, but I can feel that the defeat of an ideology aspired to is tragic.

In the poetry of Pound, the following moves Nikos to a state in which he is speechless for what it expresses beyond words, so that he simply closes his eyes and shakes his head:

I have brought the great ball of crystal.

What daring to write that in all its sublimity.

Ah, to rise in a diary to the level of

> A little light, like a rushlight
> To lead back to splendour.

But something more comes to me thinking of Nikos and Ezra Pound: that in the way Pound was essentially intellectually and culturally and ideologically centered in the world of the ancient Mediterranean, so is Nikos, and so in Nikos am I.

Ἠγάπησεν πολύ

And this comes to me: hang it all, Pound, your Sargasso or my Sargasso, your Sargasso your Cantos, my Sargasso my diary.

And in my diary to sustain the belief in the divination, in the faith: it coheres all right, even if my notes do not cohere –

––––––––

Julian Jebb has killed himself. He was someone who could only have evolved in England, as, say, the Samuri evolved in Edo Japan. Julian was known to be elfin, with tight trousers and a polo-neck jersey, his gestures quick and fluid, his effeminacy such that if he had been an American no American would possibly have taken him seriously as an interviewer, critic, man of intelligence and culture. How far I have come from America to have appreciated Julian for what he was as English, for I was always aware that he was English. Even in his suicide, I think, he was English, in that I imagine him saying to himself as he swallowed pill after pill with water, as I suppose, 'Now don't be histrionic about this, just get on with it.' (Which makes me think of someone else whom I consider to have evolved in England and in no other country, the costume and set designer David Walker, elfin too, with tight trousers and a tightly fitting shirt often printed with little flowers and buttoned at the neck, his wig very carefully calculated to blend in with whatever hair he has, whom I see from time to time and who once told me that a friend of his, a young woman, had confided in him that she couldn't bear living any longer and longed to do herself in, to which David advised, 'Then do it, darling, but don't make a fuss of it.' I asked, 'Did she do it?' and David, extending his neck and thrusting out his jaw and looking at me expressionlessly, said starkly, 'Yes, she did.') I am incapable of that utter distancing of feeling from death, even from grief, which I think of as English (or whatever small enclave of the British I know), and will never be able to reconcile myself to it. So, what do I remember Julian for and hope to appreciate in him? For his own appreciation of intelligent wit, that appreciation so marked in his interview with Evelyn Waugh (in which Harold Acton is mentioned) for the Paris Review, as when he asked Waugh if he found any professional criticism of his work helpful and mentioned Edmund Wilson, about whom Waugh asked, 'Is he an American?' and went on, after Julian said yes, 'I don't think what they have to say is of much interest, do you?' And I can hear Julian's delight. What am I to feel about his suicide? Germaine Greer, who is not English, published a severe letter addressed to him in which she condemned him for the act.

———————

In what other world than the world Nikos and I live in could this have been written by one man about another?

From 'Pure Reason', Nikos' additions from since we met:

> I pray for you in a way you never suspect except perhaps intuitively when we touch in sleep. I pray for you without knowing I pray, for when, asleep myself, I hold you at night something like prayer flows from me, surrounds you, enters you through your skin.

Perhaps, without our being aware at all of this in our love for each other, we are ourselves living a cause. I say this, because we in fact do not participate in the gay movement, would not, for example, go to a reading of gay poets because they are gay to support them for being gay. Our failing.

———

At dinner at Ann Stokes', one of the guests, a lively friend of Ann's, told me I was wrong to assume Edward VIII abdicated for political reasons: 'Not at all, I know exactly why he abdicated. My mother told me, and she was very much a part of that world, so would have known. He abdicated because he had no testicles. There was no way he could have had children. He had to step down.'

———

At times, Nikos will say something that strikes me as odd coming from someone I know to be intelligent and original but who seems not to be aware that what he says is a sentimental cliché – such as his describing someone having skin like jasmine petals and eyes like sapphire, or, to express regret, that we long for what we can no longer have, too late now – and then it comes to me that Nikos could be quoting from poems by Constantine Cavafy. In fact, such sentimental clichés are expressed in Cavafy's poems and are accepted by Nikos not only because within the poetry of Cavafy but within a tradition in which Cavafy wrote his poetry, a tradition in which Nikos, too, finds his expressions. If I were a social anthropologist – and living with Nikos makes me aware of culture as I never had been before – I would try to investigate the derivations of these sentiments, which I think refer to layers and layers of culture that make up Greek culture, and I would guess that one of these layers is, say, French literature of the Belle Epoque, and, of course, Baudelaire, all evident in the more recherché poems of Cavafy.

I'm reminded of Nikos talking, with amusement, of an uncle who in his youth was known as the Oscar Wilde of Constantinople, which suggests a quite dazzling layer of the culture of one country becoming the cultural history of another, very different country.

———

Steven Runciman has sent me this limerick:

> The stories I tell David Plante
> Soon acquire a curious slant.
> His fertile invention
> Twists all that I mention.
> I could tell him more,
> But I shan't.

Paris

I'm in Paris, on my own, to see Kitaj and Sandra, who have been living here for some months. They told me to meet them at a brasserie in rue des Ecoles for dinner, where they were sitting by the window at a table covered with a stiff white cloth, the napkins stiff and white, too. We embraced over the table.

They said they see few people and work, and I had the sense, all the more vivid for seeing them out of London context, of their exclusivity, which makes seeing them something of a privilege. And, looking at them, I had the momentary flash that they were strange, and I noticed things about them that I hadn't before, or had lost sight of. Sandra sits upright, looking right at you, smiling with her American red lips open, her eyes American bright, her long black American hair loose about her shoulders. It is as if to be attentive is to her to smile. Kitaj's deafness is worse, so he has to lean close, his elbows on the table, his left or right ear turned towards you as he tries to look at you at the same time, but as he can't quite manage this he keeps turning his head in different directions. His way of being attentive is to frown and press his lips together. His beard is almost all white.

We seemed to be reflected on all sides by mirrors.

We ordered. The waiter said something in French to Kitaj which he clearly didn't understand, but as he didn't want to let on that he doesn't know French, all he said was, 'Bien, très bien,' and with a gesture dismissed the waiter, who appeared puzzled.

Sandra defers to Kitaj. He said he first came to Paris when he was nineteen, in 1952. With the hesitant way he speaks, often clearing his throat and hitching up a shoulder as if to put a muscle back in place, he told me he had wanted to come to Europe because of the writers he'd read who had found Europe a revelation of creativity, and one of those writers was of course Hemingway. He knew that a great creative flowering, equal to that of fifth-century Greece or Renaissance Florence, had occurred in Paris over a period of, say, a hundred years, when so many of his American compatriots had gone and themselves produced amazing works. But when he got to Paris he found something different: Paris only seven years removed from German occupation. 'And imagine what it felt like,' he said, 'to walk down a street and know that people there had been pulled out by the Gestapo and sent off to concentration camps. It was, really, my first awareness of being a Jew. At home, I was brought up with little awareness of being Jewish. In my high school, before a game, I'd make the sign of the cross and say a prayer. Europe made me aware of something I hadn't expected.'

He spent only a few days in Paris, then he took the Orient Express to Vienna, and there it was as if the war had ended the day before he arrived. He saw American jeeps being driven around, and in the jeeps soldiers from each of the Four Powers. His grandmother, who was born in Vienna but went to America, had inherited a chemist's shop in Vienna that had been taken over by the Nazis; the reparation money Kitaj himself collected from a lawyer representing his grandmother, just enough money to live on while he studied at the academy in Vienna. The lawyer lived in a medieval courtyard. Once a week, Kitaj would go to his flat for the money. The flat was over a Soviet barracks, and after lights out the lawyer and Kitaj would go into the bathroom to listen to the soldiers singing in the darkness. People wore the same clothes they had worn during the war. He remembers people in the streets grovelling for food, and the great number of beggars.

I said that, when I first came to Paris in 1959, I came expecting the Paris of Gertrude Stein and Ernest Hemingway and Ezra Pound, came expecting that that world, which seemed to me a secret world within the larger secret of Paris, was there to be discovered, found that my attention walking down a street was not on the architecture but on the bullet-strafed walls. The real secret of Paris was the war.

Kitaj said, 'You talk about the secrets of Paris.' He put his hands behind his head and raised his elbows, and as he did he spoke from the side of his mouth, his eye narrowed. 'Perhaps there are no longer the secrets we fantasized were here, but I make it my business to invent a secret Paris, even if it doesn't exist, or only partially. I have two secret cities here.' He leaned forward and put his elbows on the table edge, and continued to speak from the side of his mouth, often stretching his neck as if he was wearing a tight collar, or hitching a shoulder as if to ease a suspender strap. The collar of his shirt was open, and his jacket was unbuttoned. 'The first secret,' he said, 'has to do with sex. I first visited the red-light district along the rue Saint Denis about thirty years ago, and it hasn't changed much, or at least I tell myself it hasn't. A few of the women there are beautiful.' He stretched his neck and laughed. 'They renew themselves like sperm all up and down the mile-long street. I find places where I can lose myself in forgetfulness. I usually go to bed early, but a couple of nights during the month I'll disappear into Saint Denis. Sandra knows about it. I have no secrets from her.' Sandra smiled. 'In Saint Denis I can create my own Paris, and savour the sexual flavour of the place. I go to restaurants, bars, among whores and pimps, and I write or sketch. One reason why I came to Paris is to enjoy the myths. Sex is a myth.'

'And the other secret Paris,' he said, now sitting back in his chair, but with his hands on the table, 'is what is left of Jewish Paris. In the Marais, deep in the Marais, is the Pletzel, the area where the Jews still have their separate culture, and Sandra and I will have a meal, once a week, in a kosher restaurant there. What is it called?'

'Joe Goldenberg,' Sandra said.

'We don't have many friends here except for Avigdor Arika and his wife Anne, he a Jew who was in a concentration camp, she an American Jew who only heard about the camps. With Anne I went to Drancy, once a concentration camp for Jews outside of Paris where they were sent before being sent off to the death camps. Avigdor didn't want to go. Drancy is a Communist working-class area. The buildings of the camp, originally thirties buildings, are now council flats. There is a monument to the Jews, an eleventh-rate sculpture. That's all. There's no coincidence between good art and such—' He stopped, both his eyes blinking, not both together, but one after the other. He appeared to have suddenly forgotten what he was talking about. He looked out.

I asked Sandra when she first came to Europe.

'In 1969,' she said.

I asked, 'Why did you come?'

She clapped her hands together and then pressed them into her lap so her shoulders were raised, and she leaned her elongated body to the side. As if worried about what she would say, she smiled at me.

'I guess it's an impossible question,' I said.

She said, 'In Los Angeles, I painted in the morning before going to work. I dreamed of coming to Europe to become a painter.'

'Did you have an image of Paris before you came?'

'From pictures and from what I'd read. I don't feel sentimental about some lost European culture, but I sense that here there are so many references to the past that are still alive. A plate of oysters and a glass of white wine are reinforced by paintings, by literature.'

After dinner, Kitaj and Sandra and I walked to their apartment, near the Seine, in what Kitaj said is one of the oldest streets in Paris, the rue Galande. His studio is the largest room in the apartment, and has stone walls and a well, as in a medieval courtyard. By the well is an easel. Paved with lithograph stone, the floor has large sheets of paper strewn over it. Kitaj picked up the sheets, one at a time, to show me soft-ground etchings and people he knows, and drawings of himself with twisted expressions.

I asked him if there were any exhibitions of art that I should see.

He said, 'Not that I know of. It pleases me that there's no

noteworthy painting going on. There is only Avigdor. He's the greatest artist-scholar alive, and he is my mentor here. I see him every other day.'

Kitaj has a way of making such a statement, this about Avigdor, sound portentous.

I said, 'For myself, it isn't what is going on in the world of European writing that I live in Europe. My writing isn't at all connected to anything happening here. Not that I think it is connected to what is happening in America.'

'What's that?'

'Oh, what are called the Fabulists.'

Kitaj grunted.

He said, 'If what you're talking about is what's finished for you in Europe, what's finished for me is my affair with Mediterranean-centred European culture. That's all gone for me.'

'Ezra Pound.'

'My favourite anti-Semite.'

And yet, I said, European culture does exist. Living in Europe, have we just become so used to the culture that we don't see it any longer, in the way we saw it as Americans before we even came to Europe? We're no longer self-conscious about being Americans in Europe.

'Are we used to it?' Kitaj asked. 'No, I don't think so. I think it was never ours for the having. It was and is an alien culture in which I had and have no business. Were Hemingway and all kidding themselves in their love affair with Europe? I don't know.'

'Then why do you stay?'

'Habit,' Kitaj said. 'And habits are not simple. They're as complex as love affairs.'

As he was showing me out, Kitaj said, 'Did I tell you I discovered that we're living over a medieval Jewish cemetery? Right under our feet are Jewish bones.'

He smiled his large rectangular smile, his white clenched teeth showing in his white beard.

I'm writing this in my hotel room.

London

L unch with Caroline Lowell. She appeared to age in the few hours we were together, she drinking vodka after vodka. We talked about the Falkland Islands crisis, about which she was witty, scathing, and utterly pessimistic. Britain in the person of Margaret Thatcher is trying to flex muscles, and in showing off is revealing just how flaccid the flexed biceps of the country are. In going to war to keep the tiny, insignificant Falkland Islands British, what Britain is demonstrating to the world is how tiny and insignificant the country is. Even if it recovers the islands from Argentinian occupation, the country has lost, and won't regain, what remained, in myth, of its prestige as a nation. Caroline rings up her friends in New York for the real news, as the British news fabricates in favour of a petty war. She can laugh and groan at the same time, a dry laugh and a dry groan. Her large green eyes are as they appear in the painting of her by Lucian Freud, and when I look into them I see the painting, not in terms of art, but of personal relationships that come before art.

———

Nikos' mother has died, and he went to Athens for the funeral and burial. In the cemetery, his mother in a coffin in a room where the coffins were kept for burial, he insisted on having the cover removed to see her. He said he touched her and felt she was still warm, and believed that she was alive, and was horrified that she would be buried alive.

Stephen has given me a copy of E. M. Forster's Commonplace Book, just published. He said he didn't want it in the house in case Natasha picked it up and read what Forster wrote about him, as it would upset her. How could it not upset Stephen? 'Stephen Spender loses honour constantly through an interminable diarrhoea composed not entirely of words.' Is this what Forster thought of Stephen when we visited him?

And there is an entry about Natasha and Stephen's former lover from before he married Natasha, Tony Hyndman, who visited Forster: 'Tony Hyndman has been in, recovering from shock also, administered electrically at the Fulbourne mental . . . Natasha Spender has come out well. I did not suspect such generosity and responsibility. I saw only the climber, who is always with the most interesting people.'

Forster was right about Natasha's generosity and responsibility, which Nikos and I have experienced in her inviting us into her life with Stephen.

Often I do think that I don't care at all about keeping a diary, have no interest at all in keeping a diary, so must stop.

Not less and less as time separates us from the past, but more and more, a photograph of bombed-out buildings in a magazine will make me aware that Nikos and I, he ominously, are of the after-war generation. I believe that we have inherited the consciousness of, even the conscience of, the total incomprehensibility of World War I and World War II, the history of those wars dumb-making, blind-making wars that leave one asking, What were they about? What? What? Was it something more primitive than the justification of war in defense of an ideology, so primitive it stands apart from any ideology, more powerful in its destructive domination of the world than any ideology, even an ideology intent on dominating the world, with its own overwhelming intentions far, far beyond the intentions of any ideology? What, what was the instinct that left churches bombed-out ruins? When looking at images of the devastation, the reaction is, with a helpless loosening of all one's mind, Unbelievable, unbelievable, unbelievable.

Ossie Clark was found dead in bed, murdered, it's reported, by a boy he picked up for sex.

Nikos has written a letter to Anthony Blunt to express his sympathy for the pain his having been exposed as a spy for the U.S.S.R. must have caused him. We have at times met Anthony – at the flat of John and James, or at the flat of the art historian John White and his Alexandrian wife Xenia, and once were invited for lunch in the flat he and his partner John Gaskill had in rooms above the Courtauld Institute in Portman Square, in an Adam-designed house. As Anthony was the Keeper of the Queen's Pictures, she would have lunch with them in their flat, and John, the cook, would simply set an extra place for her at the table. After the revelation, they moved to a high-rise off the Edgware Road. John and James asked Nikos and me if we would collect Anthony and John and drive them for lunch to their house – now in the curiously named Ashchurch Park Villas, where they've moved to, and where they had given Anthony refuge. I parked the car before the high-rise apartment block and Nikos went in to let Anthony and John know we were waiting, which, as he said once they were in the car, surprised John, as others would park blocks away and ring from a distance. I suppose I anticipated Anthony saying something extraordinary, as if to have him in the car, he now notorious, was to anticipate the extraordinary, but he said nothing. His face was gaunt and his lips very thin, the upper part of his body apparently twisted in one way at the waist and his head turned the other way, and his arms twisted in different ways. John looked old and worn, unshaven. Talk at lunch – which consisted of a pie made with boiled eggs and wild rice and wild mushrooms – had mainly to do with the world of art historians, as if Anthony were still an active part of that world. He said a young man had, a few weeks back, read to him a paper about Lukács, but Anthony didn't know who Lukács was. This was extraordinary, that Anthony Blunt hadn't heard of the greatest Marxist critic.

———

Steven Runciman, at supper, mentioned that in 1963, when King Paul and Queen Fredericka of Greece made a state visit to London, he was in Fredericka's entourage in the foyer of the Covent Garden Opera House when someone shouted an insult at her, 'Boo, bourgeois', so Steven stood up in her defence and retorted with, 'No, upper class'. I think Steven toned down the insult.

Then Nikos revealed that he had been in the large company of the King and Queen when they'd made that controversial state visit to London, their train met at Victoria Station by Queen Elizabeth and Prince Philip; he had even attended a reception at Buckingham Palace.

Did I think Nikos hypocritical for having been ancillary to that state visit? No, because Nikos has his own reasons, which I never judge.

What, I asked Steven, is to him bourgeois?

'I think Beethoven the beginning of the end. Beethoven is where the bourgeoisie come in. And, as for Wagner, that's the bourgeoisie pushed all the way to fascism. I detest Wagner, but I love Verdi.'

———

Richard Wollheim arranged for us to be invited to a drinks party given by friends of his, psychoanalysts, who have a flat on Primrose Hill overlooking the zoo, from which they can hear the cries of the animals at night. I'm sure we were both invited because of Nikos, who is publishing Richard's books, the last called Painting as an Art. In the crush of many people, I was introduced to Hanna

Segal, and I, with a sudden audacity and also thinking that she as an analyst would indulge my audacity, told her that my partner Nikos Stangos had gone to see her for possible analysis, and that she had told him that analysis would change our relationship in an unpredictable way, but that, when Nikos reported that to me, I was so sure of our relationship I was willing to accept the unpredictability of his analysis. I also said that Nikos was disappointed that she hadn't taken him on but had passed him onto a Miss Richards, who had left him to go to Australia. 'Where is Nikos?' Hanna Segal asked. 'I want to speak to him.' I went into the crowd to find him, but when I did and with him returned to find Hanna Segal, she was gone.

———

At lunch with Stephen and Natasha, Nikos proposed that he and I give Stephen a party for his birthday. I recall Stephen once saying that he has sacrificed his poetry to his friendships, which he considered much more important. He knows he is social, sees an amused and amusing right to drop names, and is excited by parties. But, at the lunch with him and Natasha, when we asked whom he'd like to have to his birthday party, he said, 'I have no friends.' Natasha said, 'Oh come now, you have so many friends.' He insisted, 'No, I don't. Who are my close friends?' Natasha went silent.

Nikos tells me I have no friends.

Nikos did most of the cooking for the party: lentils, rice, a chicken stew, salad. We bought a huge vulgar cake. And there were many bottles of wine.

Stephen had asked us to invite: Stephen and Stevie Buckley, Frank Kermode, Francis Bacon (who came with John), and, somehow, Caroline Lowell came. On our own, we invited Suzi Gablik and Germaine Greer. Then Matthew Spender and Maro Gorky, who were staying with Stephen and Natasha, came too.

I was, throughout, anxious that the people would not get on, that one of them might have said something that was not, say, in the spirit of the party. The fact is, I am not, basically, a social person, if to be social is to feel at ease among people. I kept filling glasses with wine and talking, talking, talking, and whenever there was a moment of silence I talked as though to talk for everyone all together. Nikos was at ease, but not I, and I wished, by 9:30, that everyone would go, but everyone stayed on till late, and I, drunk, had to let go of my attempt to keep all the connections vital and let whatever happened happen. And the connections did in themselves seem to sustain vitality without me straining to sustain them.

After everyone left and I hardly had enough energy to do the clearing and washing up, Nikos said, 'Well, that was a nice party.'

What people talked about, and which person to which other person, I can't at all recall. Did Suzi have anything to say to Germaine, Germaine to Maro? Did Frank and Francis speak to each other, and if so, about what? And whom did Stephen B. joke with apart from Stephen who likes Stephen B.'s quick wit? And Natasha, whom did she talk with? All I can recall of any talk was that of Caroline Lowell, who is finishing a book about the Duchess of Windsor that is so libelous it can't be published as it is, and who said, 'As a matter of fact, Edward abdicated for the reason everyone believes he did abdicate for: because he loved Wally and wanted to marry her, and he couldn't have as king. He really was in love with her.'

———

Do I have a vision? Yes, I do – and the more I consider it the more it rounds out simply in the vision of all things coming together to form a whole globe, but coming together somewhere beyond my intending the coming together, it all happening of itself and suddenly occurring, and I as suddenly recognizing that it has all come together, and thinking: the joy of it, the joy of it!

———

I think of Richard Hamilton as a political artist.

I once told him that I believe his painting of the Northern Irish H Block prisoner, The Citizen, is equal in its power to

Jacques-Louis David's The Death of Marat; he looked at me, I guess, with appreciation, but also as if I didn't quite understand.

He has long narrow teeth – teeth so long and narrow he seems to talk through them – and small eyes set high in his face, always wearing a denim jacket and a denim cap.

And it seems to me that the work of Rita Donagh, the partner and later wife of Richard Hamilton, that concentrates on the H Block makes her a political artist. Her subtle work of delicate lines and passages sensitizes that place of brutality, giving the brutality the sensitive dimensions of tragedy.

David Hockney rang from California, grumbling that no one in London was reacting against Margaret Thatcher's Clause 28, which makes it possible for anyone to object to an exhibition or drama or book that favours homosexuality and that is supported by local government funds. It's true that Nikos and I are not very active in promoting homosexual rights – not, say, in the way the artist Derek Jarman is – but we took up the cause and sent a letter to a number of people asking for them to sign a petition in protest. We asked R. B. Kitaj to be the recipient of the letters in response, thinking that he, unambiguously heterosexual, would make the claim more – what? – unbiased. A trick was to include in our letter the list of people to whom it was sent, so that each person would know what company he or she was signing up with it. Nikos was the one who was most responsible for the letter and the list.

I remember being with Kitaj and Sandra and Nikos in the basement of the Marlborough Gallery, waiting for a telephone call from the Sunday Times, a long time in coming, Kitaj, pacing, more and more impatient, his impatience rising to anger. Whoever the editor was should have known that R. B. Kitaj wanted to speak. The call came and Kitaj spoke in a severe tone. He was promised that our letter to the Sunday Times and the list of protestors would be published. It was, more or less as a footnote in the back pages.

As I think of my diary as a repository of what one day will be considered more than a personal diary, but an account of a certain time, I include the letter and the names of the people who signed, who in themselves represent much of what was happening during that certain time:

Fighting censorship tooth and clause.

Your editorial on clause 28 expressed the hope that the clause 28, now clause 29, 'will prove to be unworkable as its critics predicted . . . that having been put on the statute books it will now be forgotten'.

Though we appreciate the stand taken by those against the clause, we think it must not be forgotten. The House of Commons did confirm it, and anyone who wishes to invoke it may do so if she or he feels that a local council contravenes it. Contravention of the clause is open to interpretation, both arbitrary and subjective. The mere possibility that anyone may now initiate what are in effect procedures of censorship will also result in self-censorship by libraries, galleries, theatres, and so on funded by local councils. In a country without a declaration of human rights [I must say, I wanted this in], this clause is a real threat to civil liberties.

David Hockney is not alone in perceiving the pernicious implications of clause 29. Any person who is concerned about the erosion of civil liberties in this country must agree that clause 29 constitutes a grave danger, not just to arts, but to the future of our society.

Roger de Grey PRA, Sir Alan Bowness, Neil MacGregor, Sir Hugh Casson PPRA, Sir Michael Levey, Nicholas Serota, Sir Norman Reid, The Duke of Beaufort, Francis Bacon, Frank Auerbach, Howard Hodgkin, R. B. Kitaj, Leon Kossoff, Michael Andrews, Richard Hamilton, John Piper CH, Sir Laurence Gowing, Dame Elisabeth Frink RA, Dawn Ades, Eileen Agar, Craigie Aitchison RA, Gillian Ayres, Barry Barker, Nancy Balfour, Glen Baxter, Adrian Berg, Tony Bevan, Sandra Blow

RA, Lewis Biggs, Peter Blake RA, Stephen Buckley, Robert Buhler RA, H. T. Cadbury-Brown RA, Jeffery Camp RA, Fabian Carlsson, Richard Cork, Michael Craig-Martin, Trevor Dannatt RA, Richard Deacon, Jennifer Dixon RA, Anthony d'Offay, Rita Donagh, Peter de Francia, Robyn Denny, Joanna Drew, David Elliot, Anthony Eyton RA, William Feaver, Stephen Finer, Sandra Fisher, Angela Flowers, Barry Flanagan, Terry Frost, Hamish Fulton, Frederick Gore RA, Anthony Green RA, Janet Green, John Golding, Patrick George, Andy Goldsworthy, Alex Gregory-Hood, Nigel Greenwood, Tim Head, Maggi Hambling, Colin Hayes RA, Gerard Hemsworth, Patrick Heron, Paul Huxley, Timothy Hyman, Nicola Jacobs, Bernard Jacobson, Bill Jacklin, Tess Jaray, Derek Jarman, Allen Jones RA, Anish Kapoor, John Kasmin, Philip King, James Kirkman, Mark Lancaster, Catherine Lampert, Christopher LeBrun, Lillian Lijn, Kim Lim, Marco Livingston, Gilbert Lloyd, Richard Long, Peter Logan, Leonard McComb, Bruce McLean, James Mayor, Dhruva Mistry, Robert Medley RA, Lisa Milroy, Richard Morphet, Julian Opie, Maureen Paley, Myfanwy Piper, Jacqui Poncelet, Nicholas Pope, Patrick Procktor, Deanna Petherbridge, Piers Rodgers, Norman Rosenthal, Leonard Rosoman RA, Vera Russell, John Russell Taylor, Michael Sandle, Richard Shone, Karsten Schubert, Anne Seymour, Yolanda Sonnabend, Frances Spalding, Julian Spalding, Ruskin Spear RA, Jenny Stein, David Sylvester, John Titchell, Joe Tilson, Peter Townsend, Julian Trevelyan, William Turnbull, Euan Uglow, Lady Vaizey, Hester van Royen, Leslie Waddington, Richard Wentworth, Bill Woodrow, Jack Wendler, Carel Weight RA, Richard Wollheim.

Some days later, at a gallery opening, I heard David Sylvester shout at Anthony Caro, 'Why didn't you sign that letter?' to which Caro replied, 'I only sign letters I've written.'

———

I met John Gaskill in a supermarket in the Edgware Road and asked him to come to tea. He looked as if he could hardly bear the weight of his short, square body. At tea, he told me that he had had no idea, none, about Anthony being a spy, which had shocked him. Shortly after the revelation, Anthony suggested they go to Florence, which John thought would be a relief, but wondered where they would stay in Florence. Anthony said, with the British consul. John replied that they couldn't. And Anthony asked, why not? 'He never took in what he had done,' John said, and shrugged and sighed. He regretted leaving after an hour, and I felt sorry to let him go.

John Golding, in charge of Anthony's memoir, which Anthony wrote while staying with John and James, said that he has given it to the British Library with an injunction of some years. Laughing, John said that the big secret of the memoir is how boring it is.

———

Francis rang and asked Nikos and me and Stephen to dinner in a restaurant. I drove us to Reece Mews, and, crossing the cobbles to where he lives over a garage, I saw him look out of a window. He met us at the top of the steep stairs and kissed us all on the cheeks.

He said, 'John wanted to come, too, but he's too drunk,' and he laughed his rough laugh that dismisses everything as: well, of course.

In his narrow sitting-room–bedroom, at one end with a large oval bed covered with a multi-coloured spread and a bookcase and a table by the bed piled with books, we sat at the near end on sofas and drank champagne, and we talked about drawing, and what really is drawing. While I wasn't talking myself – and Nikos tells me I talk too much – I told myself to pay attention to the conversation of the others, which was extraordinary, and remember it all, Nikos' incisive remarks, Stephen's impressionist remarks, and Francis' authoritative ones, but I've forgotten, but how alive the remarks were, and how alive I felt.

Stephen was very attentive to Francis, was, as I once noted he was with Auden, deferential to him. To whatever Francis said, Stephen responded with, 'Yes, you're right,' to which Francis responded with, 'Well, perhaps I'm not at all right. I don't know how to draw, really.'

Like a son who, at a certain age, sees a weakness in his father, I saw a weakness in Stephen, and I quite consciously decided that I would not defer to Francis, but disagree with him. I no doubt said some silly things about drawing, but I had said them and I wouldn't give them up when others — especially Francis — didn't agree, or didn't see my point. I thought Stephen became a little annoyed with me because I didn't defer to Francis but was expressing something that I presumed was of interest to him. I know that Stephen can't take seriously what I say, and is puzzled by my — what he himself would say about himself — near success as a writer. That I should take myself seriously talking to Francis (whom Stephen considers a genius) Stephen, I feel, takes as an impertinence. Maybe I'm imagining this — imagining his disapproval of me — but his look, his eyes half lidded and his jaw set, seemed meant to stop me from talking, and I wouldn't be stopped. Nikos didn't stop me. At times, Francis would say, 'David has made an interesting point,' and only then would Stephen nod and say, 'Yes.' Then I thought that Stephen resented that I was paying more attention to Francis than to him, so I tried to pay as much attention to him as I did to Francis, asking Stephen questions. This is all very silly. We drank three bottles of champagne.

Then, at the restaurant, more lively talk, now about intention in art. As this interests me a lot, I, again, said what I had to say, and Francis pushed what I said as far as it could be pushed by saying, 'I have no intentions. I don't know what I'm doing, not at all. I have a critical sense, developed over the years, and I rely on that, a purely instinctive critical sense, but beyond that I have no idea what I'm doing.' I said, 'Do you count on anyone — say, some really informed critic — to say what you might be doing?' 'No,' Francis said, 'I don't.'

I recalled seeing, on the big, plain table under the window of the sitting-room area, books by Michael Leris, the French philosopher who has written extensively on Francis.

Francis talked about Van Gogh and intention or the opposite of intention, and once again I concentrated, thinking, I must remember this, but I've forgotten.

Stephen said, 'I like to think that if I'd been around when Van Gogh was painting, I'd have been one of the few to recognize his genius, but, in fact, I think that I, like most people, would have considered him an impossible mad man, and wouldn't have wanted to have anything to do with him.'

'I should think definitely not,' Francis said; 'he was mad.'

Then we talked about health, I don't know why. Stephen keeps going to doctors for tests, though he says he is in perfect health, really. He said, 'Somehow I'm not frightened of death. I think I was brought up not to be frightened of it, but to consider it as something that would inevitably come and not to be made a fuss over. I suppose I don't think myself important enough to make a fuss about dying.'

Francis said, 'I'm frightened of death. I'm very frightened of it.' He laughed. 'Of course, I may die tomorrow. I'm seventy-three – just your age, Stephen.'

Stephen said, 'How is it, then, that my hair is white and yours not?'

'Because I dye it,' Francis said. 'You should try it.' He named the dye and how to use it.

I asked Francis, 'Why are you frightened of dying?'

He said, 'Because I love life. It's all I have, and I don't want to lose it. I love it.'

'So do I,' Stephen said.

'David doesn't,' Nikos said.

'You don't?' Francis asked me.

'I love Nikos,' I said.

A waiter came to Francis and whispered something into his ear, then left. 'It's John,' Francis said to us. 'He's out in the street, drunk. I'd better go get him.' He left, and in a little while came back with John, who did not appear to be drunk.

He had not been able to get the fancier pub he'd been negotiating for, and we were sorry for him; but he didn't seem to mind, and said, 'It don't matter.' He told us about his trip to America, to Atlantic City, with his brother, with whom he's going into business buying and selling old furniture. Francis said, 'Really a load of old junk.' I wondered how much old furniture they could buy and sell in Atlantic City, the gambling capital of America, and thought that couldn't be their business.

Then he took out a photograph of himself and his boyfriend Philip, who had been allowed out of prison on a three-day pass. John wanted to give the photograph to Francis, and asked Nikos, sitting next to him, if Nikos would spell out his dictation, so that he, John, could write it, as he couldn't spell words but he could write letters. As Nikos dictated the letters, John wrote: FOR MY FRANCIS WITH MY LOVE JOHN.

John leaned over the table towards Francis and said, 'I want to tell you something,' and Francis leaned forward so John could whisper into his ear. Francis sat back suddenly and said, in a loud voice, 'That's ridiculous. I'm not going to listen to it. That you want to die is ridiculous. I'm not going to listen.' John smiled. He held out his hand to Francis and Francis took it. John said, 'I love you.' Francis said, 'And I love you, and because I do I'm not going to listen to you talk nonsense.' John turned to us. He said, 'I love Francis. I love my friend in prison, and I love Francis, though, you know, with Francis I have a non-sexual relationship.' And we all nodded.

John told us he has a new house, a big house in the country, with outbuildings and two acres of farmland, where he would live with his boyfriend. They've been together for fourteen years, and they make love every day, sometimes twice a day, except when Philip is in prison. 'I'm real horny,' John said. He'd decided to live in the country because if he and Philip continued to live in London they'd end up killing themselves with drink or get some terrible sexually transmitted disease. About the house, he said, 'Of course Francis helped me.' About the house in the country, John said he had had one of the outbuildings done up into a cottage for Francis to stay when he visited. Francis raised his shoulders and let them drop and said, 'I loathe the country.' John said, 'The cottage has a nice view.' 'I loathe views,' Francis said. They both laughed, John very amused by Francis. John invited Nikos and me to the house in the country for Easter Sunday lunch.

It was midnight, and Stephen said he had to go. Nikos and I left with him. I had drunk very little to be able to drive. On the way to his house, Stephen said, 'All night, whenever Francis said something extraordinary, I'd tell myself, this is something I'll never forget, and I've forgotten everything. I must try to remember it all for my diary.'

We talked about the relationship between Francis and John. Stephen said, 'Of course, anyone who has a relationship with a genius will end up wanting to kill himself out of a sheer sense of inadequacy.'

We left Stephen off a block away from his house. He said Natasha didn't know he was having dinner out with Francis and us, and might get upset if she saw us leave him off; she'd think we were conspiring to keep her out.

Back home, Nikos and I talked about Francis. 'He's wonderful,' Nikos said; 'he's totally without pretensions. Totally. I've never known a man to be so totally unpretentious.'

Often, over the evening, I'd look at Nikos and think: how beautiful he is. A great refinement has come to his face. I'd think, And he's my love! with surprise at the fact.

The next time Stephen came to us, I noted that he had brightened his hair with a blue rinse.

An observation – though there are multiple connections among people in London, there are, too, many intended disconnections, for Steven Runciman may know Stephen Spender, but does not like him, and does not connect with him.

An example of Steven's irony, this about the ritual of the ceremony of fire in the Church of the Holy Sepulcher in Jerusalem.

The sepulcher itself is held by the Greek Orthodox Church, and every Easter appoints a priest, frisked first so it is sure that he doesn't carry matches or anything that will ignite a fire, to enter into the sepulcher, which is then sealed until the priest knocks to be released, always, unfailingly, carrying a candle lit miraculously in the sepulcher, from which all the candles in the church are lit. Having told the story, Steven will stick out his lower lip and raise his chin as if in defiance of anyone contradicting him and his implied belief that of course the candle was lit miraculously. As amused as he is by telling such a story, the irony is that you are left thinking he may in fact believe in the entertaining miracle.

Stephen is incapable of such subtle irony, and would frown with disapproval that anyone should be so ridiculous. This is not to say that Stephen doesn't have any respect for belief, but, unlike Steven, he takes such belief seriously, for, as I've written before, Stephen is not good at irony.

Nor am I good at irony. I sometimes write prayers, one of which I gave to Stephen, who, I saw, was moved by it. I would never give a prayer to Steven, who, claiming as he does that he is a warlock and can cause someone to break his leg, would take the prayer to be at the same level of entertaining magic.

This comes to me as a little revelation, though I don't at all know what it means: that Nikos and I know people who may have met one another, but who would have no interest in, or would even withdraw from, knowing one another. So, I can't imagine Steven Runciman and Francis Bacon spending an evening together, or Stephen Spender and Patrick Kinross, or . . .

———

While Nikos was at work —

I rang Germaine Greer to ask her to lunch. I thought I'd invite Stephen too, and rang him, and then asked if Natasha would like to come, so they both came: game pie and salad and cheese and grapes, with wine.

Germaine was animated. At moments, she stopped talking, put

her hands across her bosom and made a moue of her lips as if in astonishment, then suddenly laughed as if at herself. She made the luncheon party.

Talk about the war in the Falklands, everyone horrified by Thatcher's grandstand gesture.

After lunch, Stephen asked me if I'd written in my diary about our dinner with Francis the other night, and I wanted to say, 'But you said I mustn't mention that in front of Natasha.' I said, 'Yes,' and offered to read out the entry, which, with coffee, I did – leaving out the reference to Natasha. Now, at least, Natasha and Germaine know I keep a diary, and what it is like. I could have said I've stopped keeping it, leaving it to be read after everyone, including myself, is dead; but then I thought that would be a lie, so why not let everyone know what I write while we're alive?

I said, 'In my diary, I never try to account for others' opinions, always too complicated, too subtle, for me to account for them in a sentence or two.'

Stephen said, 'You try to be descriptive.'

'I try,' I said. 'I would never try to account for Germaine's opinion about abortion.'

'No,' she said, 'you don't do that. But you sin by omission. You use the glass-pane technique, which is just to record what you see. You may think that's truthful, but it can be a total distortion of the truth. If you see someone washing his face in vodka, and record that, you give the impression that the man is a mad alcoholic; it may be that he's cut himself and is using the vodka as an antiseptic.'

Natasha said nothing.

I did think that if I saw a man washing his face in vodka, I would wonder if he was simply bonkers.

Nikos returned early from his office and I recounted the luncheon party to him, not sure he was interested.

———

Should I wonder that most of the people we see are that much older than we are – old enough to be of another generation? The

attraction is simple: we have so much to learn from them historically, as they do represent history. What they have to learn from us
I have no idea.

But then there are friends of our generation whom we see often:
Stephen Buckley, Keith Milow, Mark Lancaster when he's in
London, Richard and Sally Morphet, Julia and Howard Hodgkin,
Joe and Jos Tilson, Kitaj and Sandra, all in the art world. Do we
have any close friends among writers of our generation?

———

The Falkland Islands have been freed of Argentinian occupation,
and Britain shows off to the world that there is still a British Empire.

———

Nikos and I received invitations to the opening of Francis'
grand retrospective at the Tate Gallery. There were long tables
covered with white cloths and waiters standing behind the
tables serving champagne and cooks serving portions from
whole salmons.

John was as excited as if a party was being given for him. He was
wearing a beautiful suit. He told Nikos and me he was very angry,
as one of Francis' old cronies from the Colony Room had, on this
most important occasion, asked Francis for fifty pounds, and John
had insisted Francis not give the money. John said to me, 'I was
having a nice time until this happened. Francis has given him
hundreds of pounds, more than hundreds, and he never pays back.
If you borrow, you pay back. Fuck it.'

Francis' friend Dicky Chopping came to us and said, 'Francis is
going round to look at his pictures. Why don't you join us?' We
followed Francis from picture to picture – Study for Portrait of Van
Gogh II, Lying Figure with Hypodermic Syringe, Crucifixion
1965 – and standing for a moment at each one he would laugh and
say, 'Isn't it loathsome? I loathe it. I really loathe it.'

I went off on my own to study the great Triptych May–June
1973, the one depicting the death of George Dyer in the hotel in

Paris when Francis was having his grand retrospective show in the Grand Palais. George is doubled up on a toilet in the left-hand panel; in the right one he is vomiting into a washbasin; and in the central panel he is half dissolved in blackness that pours out through an open doorway. I saw how essentially, how passionately, how heartbreakingly this triptych depicted Francis' reaction to the horror of the death of someone he had loved.

From this I went to the pastel, almost sentimental portraits of John, filled with – what can I write? – tenderness.

Dawn Ades, who wrote an essay for the catalogue, said she thought the colours were 'breathed on to the canvas,' and she held her palm before her mouth and breathed onto it.

––––––––

What would I most like to write? I would most like to write a short book called The Spiritual in Literature, something like Kandinsky's Concerning the Spiritual in Art.

––––––––

To tea at Kitaj and Sandra's. I mentioned that Avigdor Arika had given to Nikos an etching of himself, perhaps in recognition that Nikos had included him in the Dictionary of Art and Artists, which Nikos is editing and in which he does include Keith Milow and Stephen Buckley, but Kitaj looked away, and Sandra said, 'We don't see Avigdor any more,' and I was left wondering what had happened, but wouldn't ask.

Then, as if by looking in the distance is the dimension in which Kitaj thinks, he turned to me and said he had recently seen Francis Bacon in the street, Francis wearing red basketball shoes, and Francis asked him, 'Do you ever have days when everything goes wrong?' Now Kitaj laughed his shrugging, masculine laugh, his eyes bright. I wonder about Kitaj's obsession with being Jewish, for though his stepmother was Jewish, I think, from what I've heard him say, that his biological mother and father were not, and, if so, he was brought up so far removed from Jewishness that, and this he did once tell me, when he was in high school he used to pray a Hail Mary and make the sign of the cross before engaging in a baseball game. He is taking instruction from a rabbi before marrying Sandra, who is Jewish, but he baulks at the problem of how God could allow so much suffering to his people. Kitaj listened to me when I said I object to the word 'Holocaust' to define the horrors of Jewish suffering, as that means a burnt offering to God, and what God would accept such an offering, and to what end? I prefer to use 'Shoa,' which, incidentally, the Vatican uses, understanding the meaning of 'holocaust.' Kitaj said nothing, and I worried if I had offended him, so went on to say that I believe his painting If Not, Not, which has been made into a tapestry that hangs in the foyer of the British Library, is a masterpiece, no greater indictment of the horrors of the twentieth century, more potent than Eliot's The Waste Land, than that painting, with the façade of the entrance building of Auschwitz commanding the landscape of civilization in ruins.

———

Sylvia Guirey asked me to come to her studio to show me her latest paintings, all dots, and to talk to me about her relationship with Richard and Mary Day. Mary Day has accepted Richard back on the condition that he does not see Sylvia. Sylvia is bewildered by the whole situation and doesn't know what to do.

I listened, but didn't understand; when friends confide in me, which they seem to do, they confide generally, leaving the details out, so that when, later, another friend tells me the details, I'm amazed, even at times shocked. I had no idea why Sylvia wanted to talk to me.

I walked home through South Kensington, through Kensington Gardens and Hyde Park; the chestnut trees and hawthorn are in full bloom, and the grass is thick and fresh.

Nikos had some Greek friends for drinks. As I came in, he said, 'Your editor at the New Yorker, Dan Menaker, just rang to say they've taken your latest story.' I had drinks with his Greek friends, who stayed for supper.

———

Could it be that the images we witness of World War I and World War II have more power now than they would have had at the times of the wars, and form in us the consciousness, the conscience, of a world united in suffering – suffering, once seen as localized among certain people, now made global as the images expand beyond the local into the world, and, if it can be said that the wars had any positive legacy, expanding into the consciousness, the conscience, of a whole world that has, all together, to guard against such suffering?

The nuclear bombs, impelled by the wars, make us think of the whole round world.

Certainly, it is unthinkable that Germany and Britain could possibly be at war with each other, which occurred in my lifetime, and which I believe must now bring Britain and Germany, and all of Europe, close together, that consciousness, that conscience, formed by the suffering of the wars that divided the countries now uniting them.

And so I believe in and take joy in the possibility of a United States of Europe, and, with even more extended belief and joy, in a United States of the World.

This vision of the whole world has evolved, if in part as an intention, mostly unintentionally, historically.

———

Nikos and I to supper at John Golding and James Joll's, who have been painted as a couple by R. B. Kitaj. Mario Dubsky there, and, however much I should by now assume it as common, I was surprised by the appearance of someone in a social situation I know from another social situation, for I didn't know that John and James know Mario. Conversation about the art world.

I said I would like to write a frivolous novel about a young man who cannot see the causal relationship between work and money, and imagines they have nothing to do with each other. John said, 'No one has ever assumed for a minute that you imagine they have anything to do with each other.' Nikos smiled, and, I don't know why, I felt the attention paid me was in itself an affectionate compliment.

Florence

After the death of John Pope-Hennessy –
Some years after he had retired from his curatorial positions at the Victoria and Albert, the British Museum, and the Metropolitan Museum in New York, and moved to Florence, I would visit him from Lucca, where Nikos and I have a small flat in a duecento tenement building, up seventy-three steps. John did once visit us there, and, looking about, again as if in all directions at once, squealed, 'Very enviable.' In Florence, I climbed the wide stone stairs within the courtyard of the palazzo to the doors of the apartment on a landing and rang the bell at the side of the thick glass doors with heavy metal grill, forged into decorative curves, over the glass. The door was opened by a maid in a black dress and white apron (as his maids were dressed in London and New York), and I was shown into the sitting room to wait. There, in a corner, stood a Venetian cabinet of curiosities, and I stopped to look through the glass – the original glass, John later told me – which made the objets de vertu inside appear to waver as I studied them, and among them was my little carved wooden rhinoceros I had given to him in London. (The meaning of objets de vertu intrigues me – were precious objects seen as inspiring virtue?) When, moving as always briskly, John entered, I thanked him for keeping that little memento, but he didn't respond. He had just bought a painting of the Assumption of the Holy Virgin Mother by Pietro de Francesco

degli Orioli, and together we looked at it.

After he died, the contents of this flat were auctioned by Christie's in New York, and I saw in the catalogue the furniture, the bronzes, the pictures I had seen in the flat. When I had visited him, the rooms, especially a round, rotunda-like dining room with a round cherrywood table in the center, the walls, as I recall, pale yellow, with vitrines on three sides filled with objects as in a museum, made the objects contained in them appear so carefully and knowledgeably chosen that I felt whatever small items of little worth I had were collected haphazardly and without any overriding historical knowledge to make them a coherent collection. In no way could I have identified a Giorgio d'Alemagna miniature, a red-chalk drawing by Ventura Salimbeni, a painting of the Baptism of Christ of Pier Francesco Mola and more, and all privileged by the knowledge of Pope-Hennessy. But, again, seeing them separated out in the catalogue, they lost that privilege. He had often said he had no money, and, studying the objects in reproduction, I realized that, of course, he had had money, but not enough that individual works, taken out of the context of the flat in Via de' Bardi, retained the uniqueness they appeared to have there. I was told that there was a blizzard at the time of the auction, and the sale was not as had been hoped. Among the items of furniture auctioned was the Venetian lacca povera corner cabinet, decorated with commedia dell'arte figures, in which my little carved rhinoceros had been displayed, but that object clearly not auctioned.

John liked, he said, to show friends off on trains, and from the other side of the Arno he would accompany me across the Ponte Vecchio, walking more vividly than I, past the Giotto Tower and Baptistry and the Duomo and all the tourists and to the train station at Santa Maria Novella. The whole of Florence seemed to be his privilege, his way through the city le droit du seigneur.

When with others, he went first through a doorway or up a flight of stairs; he took it for granted that his position in a car was next to the driver. A mutual friend said about him, 'It's not as though he has bad manners, it's that he has no manners at all.'

And yet, in his apparent total, authoritative self-confidence, he was a man without conceit, without pretensions.

I always felt totally intimidated by him, and never understood why we were friends.

One hot evening we arrived too late at the station for the train to Lucca, and he matter-of-factly announced, 'You'll have to spend the night.' Back in his apartment, he asked his assistant to show me to a bedroom, and I was given toiletries, pajamas and a change of underclothes for the morning by his assistant, Michael Mallon. I did not sleep well.

At breakfast, Michael Mallon, as if this needed a reminder, said that the day was Epiphany, and Pope-Hennessy (or, as he was called, the Pope) was almost operatically high-pitched when he exclaimed, 'Off to Mass!' and he and the assistant left me to go for their missals, I now at the front door waiting for them. They were off to Mass in a church, S.S. Annunziata of the Servite Friars, whose devotion was (is) to the Mother of God, especially as La Mater Dolorosa. By special dispensation from the Vatican Pope, the old Tridentine Mass of 1570 was celebrated, the Mass, I said, of my youth, long before the Second Vatican Council of the early 1960s changed the Latin Mass to the vernacular. I asked if I could join them, and was not refused.

But we were early, and went into the Ospedale degli Innocenti across the Piazza Annunziata to look specifically at a painting of The Adoration of the Magi by Domenico Ghirlandaio, a strange painting, for behind the scene of the Magi bringing gifts to the infant Jesus and his parents was the gory scene of the Massacre of the Innocents, perhaps an ironical reference to the Ospedale degli Innocenti which was established to save orphans from death. No one said a word, but simply studied the painting for a long while, long enough to take in all its details, especially the Massacre of the Innocents enacted in a bloody landscape behind the manger, which I so wondered at, but which I felt I must not ask about. No doubt my silence was guarding my ignorance, but I also sensed too great a reverence in the silence of Pope-Hennessy and his assistant to break it.

The Mass was very much the Mass of my youth. John and Michael followed the ceremony in their missals, which I vividly remembered doing when I was at Mass in my parish. The priest, in a green chasuble and carrying the chalice under a green veil, one hand flat on the square purse on top and the other holding the chalice beneath the veil, came down the aisle of the small white church. Two servers in surplices were with him, one carrying a smoking censer by its chains and the other a little silver boat of incense. The choir in the loft at the back of the church sang. The priest climbed the steps to the altar and placed the veiled chalice on it before the tabernacle and descended the steps, made the sign of the cross then turned to the congregation and held out his arms and intoned, 'Introibo ad altare Dei,' and the servers on either side of him responded, 'Ad Deum qui laetificat juventutem meam,' and I felt a strange movement in me at those words invoking God the joy of my youth.

In the church of S.S. Annunziata in Florence, memory brought back Sunday after Sunday in my parish church. I remembered the Latin. I remembered the times to stand, to kneel, to sit. I remembered the way the wide, stiff chasuble of the priest moved with the movement of his shoulders when, his back to the congregation, he moved his shoulders with the movements made in the ritual. I remembered the Bible on its stand being changed by the server from one side of the altar to the other.

I watched the priest lift the purse from the veil and remove from it the corporal, the white linen, handkerchief-like cloth, which he spread on the altar; watched him remove the veil from the chalice placed on the corporal, still covered by the pall and the purifier. I remembered all the names. And I remembered the moment of the elevation and consecration of the host, announced by the delicate chiming of bells rung by a server, and the bowing of the congregation in adoration of that high white host which was no longer a wafer but was transubstantiated into the body of Christ.

A feeling started up in me that I felt sway back and forth in me, like keening. John and his assistant went to the rail for communion, but I, more than ever, could not. The choir in the organ loft sang.

After the Mass, out on the pavement, Pope-Hennessy intro-duced me to a number of people, one of whom a countess who, in refined appreciation of the chant, commented that the Gloria was pre-Gregorian.

I left John Pope-Hennessy for the train station and on the train to Lucca I looked out at the grey and dun-brown Tuscan winter countryside, where, here and there, bare persimmon trees were hung heavily with bright orange fruit, and I calmed down.

A mutual friend who lived in Florence, Thekla Clark, rang me out of interest to tell me that John Pope-Hennessy had told her that I was praticante. I said, no, no, I was not praticante. She asked, 'You're an agnostic?' and I answered, 'I'm an atheist.' She repeated, 'Not an agnostic?' And I repeated, 'No, an atheist.'

Some time later, another mutual friend, John Fleming, with whom the Pope often stayed, rang me to inform me: my visit with the Pope had not been a 'success.' Oh? I had gone to Mass as a non-believer. This shocked me. The Pope objected to my going to Mass for the aesthetics of the ceremony. This shocked me more. I protested: I had gone because the Tridentine Mass was the Mass of my youth and as such had a very deep meaning to me, whatever that meaning was. Well, I might write a postcard to the Pope to explain. I was on the verge of being excommunicated. I did write a postcard, and I did see Pope-Hennessy again, this time as guests of John Fleming and Hugh Honour outside Lucca, and no mention was made of my heresy.

As if to get back into his good graces, I mentioned that I had been very impressed by an essay he had written on Michelangelo, which ended with something like: 'Michelangelo prayed for the angels to descend to help him, and the angels did.' On that high note that was always near a delicate screech, he turned away and said, 'I don't remember,' and my attempt to be blessed was dismissed. Michael Mallon was able to name the essay with which the lines concluded.

We were, with drinks before lunch, beneath a loggia by a lotus pool. John didn't refer to my postcard or his having objected to my going to Mass as a non-believer, and I knew not to refer to either myself. As he had dismissed my reference to angels in his essay on Michelangelo, I thought I would be clever by saying how marvelous the footnotes are in Gibbon's The Decline and Fall of the Roman Empire, in particular the footnote about the prophet Iamblichus who miraculously evoked two fountains to rise from the desert from which the gods of love, Eros and Anteros, emerged, fondly embraced him, and at his command stepped back into the fountains which would then sink back into the earth.

Self-consciously laughing, I said, 'If only that were possible.'

John did laugh, and I thought I had at least amused him. Then he asked, 'You don't believe in miracles, David?'

'No,' I said somewhat apologetically.

'You don't believe that the natural order can be suspended and what was thought to be impossible becomes possible?'

'I'd like very much to believe that,' I said, 'but I don't.'

He said, 'I believe all the miracles depicted in predelle.'

John laughed his high, abrupt laugh and turned away, but I felt that what he had said was not a joke. It was as though he, with the absoluteness of his self-confidence, had never questioned his belief in miracles, had not even considered that some people do not believe. I couldn't see John Pope-Hennessy as helpless in any way, couldn't see him giving in to longing, or, more, passion, but I saw him encircled by absolute belief, and this precluded any questions. Did he know theology as thoroughly as he knew the history of art? He would have thought it impudent of me to question not only his absolutism but the absolutism of Roman theology. I could no more have questioned him about his beliefs than I could have asked him why he had kept that little wooden rhinoceros in a cabinet in his sitting room.

And yet, the questions remain.

If he hated aesthetics, hated style, what was his vision of art?

What, I wonder, did he see in the Domenico Ghirlandaio painting of The Adoration of the Magi in the Ospedale degli Innocenti with the Massacre of the Innocents as background?

London

Dinner at Germaine's (individual soufflés, boiled mutton with a caper sauce, rhubarb sponge, all prepared on an enormous cooker with many ovens and hobs, and the wines very good, as if Germaine has all the time in the world and all the money in the world for such a meal) in honour of the writer David Malouf, an Australian compatriot of Germaine. She invited Stephen and Natasha, Stephen often laughing at her inventive use of expletives, Natasha wide-eyed with amazement so that, as she told me later, she kept thinking her eyebrows would fall off. Germaine, like an Italian peasant woman, never sat with us, but prepared the courses while we ate, and the food appeared and disappeared and appeared on the table.

She kept apologizing about the food, and treated it, in serving it, as if she was embarrassed that it wasn't good enough and shouldn't be given the attention it in fact deserved.

Feeling at home with her, Nikos carved the mutton joint; I helped with wine, coffee.

I had the vivid sense of a woman entertaining completely on her own who was frantic that she wasn't up to the entertainment. All the while we ate, the telephone kept ringing and other people, among them Melvyn Bragg, kept arriving.

An insight into Germaine, or so I like to think: she has a huge chest of drawers inlaid with mother of pearl, as extravagant as I imagine Germaine to be, but when I commented on it she told me she didn't like it, and if I wanted it to take it away. So I see in her an attraction to the extravagant and, at the same time, indifference to that extravagance, she herself as if between extravagant statements and at the same time willing to let the statements go.

Her palms pressed to her bosom to make the enthusiasm heartfelt, she so enthused over a poster by David Hockney he had given to us that we gave it to her.

She can be so intimate, taking one's chin in her hand and staring into one's eyes as if one were the only person in the world, and then she turns away and she sees something altogether unrelated to one that leaves one totally apart, leaving one to wonder what that intimacy was all about.

A memory: John Byrne – who, I must say, has all too meaning a name as he was severely burned when a boy, dancing in a hula skirt too close to an electric fire in his mother's sitting room – is a close friend of Germaine, and he invited her and Nikos and me to a fish and chip restaurant, which John, not the richest young man in the world as a dealer in rare books and manuscripts with Bertram Rota, could afford, and there, all of us in a booth, Germaine held John's chin tightly and kissed him on the lips, the expression on John's scared face one of joy, an expression of unrestrained affection on Germaine's part that was for the moment, after which she looked with a frown at the menu, as if in Germaine there is no continuity between a moment of almost sexual affection and what to order on the fish and chip menu.

Nikos thinks Germaine amazing, as he says when he meets someone who is totally original – that is, she takes nothing for granted, but will, after having made a statement for which she in the public is known, overturn the statement and make a contradictory statement, such as her finding Muslim women in an Arab country perfectly content to be in purdah.

Steven Runciman sent me this limerick about Germaine, whom he met at supper at our flat:

They told me to stay clear
Of the formidable doctor Greer,
But, in spite of her learning,
For all my discerning,
I find her rather a dear.

———

John Gaskill has killed himself.

The art historian Michael Jaffe told me that when he was showing the Queen round the Fitzwilliam Museum, she paused at the painting by Poussin she recognized from when she had had lunch with Anthony, and all she said was, 'Poor Anthony.'

———

Nikos, always enthusiastic about works he calls 'innovative,' took on at Thames & Hudson a book called Current Trends in British Art, among the young artists in the book Liam Gillick, Grenville Davey, Damien Hirst, Gary Hume, Michael Landy, Sarah Lucas, Lisa Milroy, Julian Opie, Rachel Whiteread. Many of these were students of Michael Craig-Martin at Goldsmiths' College. Looking through the book, it is very difficult to generalize about the works as representative of a generation, given that some seem to be contained within flat rectangles while others are as free of the containment as glass milk bottles and stacks of chairs, or the list of bids at the auction of a Stradivarius violin, or photographs of the artist in a morgue among the dead, the faces and bodies of the dead blocked out. I defer to Nikos, he who will say with excitement about Titian, Vermeer, Chardin, 'How innovative!'

———

To Loudoun Road, the blue and white house set among dark green bushes, for tea with Stephen, Natasha out. We sat in Stephen's study, the tall, glassed-in bookcase with a classical bust in plaster on top, all around loose papers, letters, books and paddy bags, crumpled newspapers, he in an armchair and I on a chair. I said never mind the tea, as Stephen, in his deep armchair, appeared so deep in it I thought it would be difficult to rise, and there he appeared to be settled deeply into his life.

He spoke of people whom I knew of from his autobiography, World within World: of the family cook and housekeeper, Bertha and Ella, who were called, together, Berthella. Berthella didn't approve of having bells rung for them by the family and served meals only when they were ready to. Stephen spoke lightly in a dry voice of his older brother Michael, a young man who insisted that even the beauty of the music he played so well on the piano could be explained scientifically; his sister Christine, who, receiving instruction to become a Catholic, refused to believe dead unbaptized children go to Limbo. He laughed lightly, as if he, in his advanced years, was seeing his early years with humor. But when he remembered his father saying, 'May God, for as long as possible, preserve my son in his innocence,' he became silent and I sensed him withdraw into himself in a way he almost never allows, and from which he suddenly sat up a little and said that perhaps we should have tea. I said I'd prepare the tea, and he thanked me and sat back into his armchair.

After our cups of tea, Stephen did heft himself up and out from the armchair to go out, and, alone, I stood and turned to the glass-fronted bookshelves in which the room was dimly reflected, so that, my back to the room, I saw the reflection as another room, and between the two rooms were shelves of books as if suspended in space. Leaning close, I saw some of my own novels were there on a shelf, and it came to me that years have passed since I first came to London and met Nikos, met Stephen, met so many people that do make up a world.

When Stephen returned, he suggested we listen to some of Tristan and Isolde, and again we sat in our deep armchairs, he so deeply that I rose to change the records. Hours later, during the Liebestod, Natasha appeared at the doorway and, seeing Stephen and me in a state of stupefying enthrallment, smiled and left us.

———

Nikos and I went to a recital at the Institute of Contemporary Arts of one of John Cage's chance pieces for piano. He had taken a blank score sheet and placed over it a map of the stars, and wherever there was a star he pushed a pin through to the blank score sheet below, which pin pricks became notes, notes played on a piano by an intense-looking woman with thin grey hair, each note, it sounded to me, a non-resounding plunk. After the recital a brief talk given by David Tudor, John Cage standing by, and after the lecture questions from the audience. I raised my hand and, standing, I asked, If there is, as there seems to be according to research into linguistics, a deep generative grammar that makes sounds into words and sentences, couldn't there possibly be a deep generative grammar to sounds that makes sounds comprehensible as music, so that random sounds aren't comprehensible as music is? David Tudor said something, but John Cage nothing.

Later, I talked about this with Nikos. He said, yes, I may be right about that deep generative sense of music, but perhaps what seems superficial chance in the music of Cage and Tudor is in tension with that essential sense, and, simply by our paying attention to their music, that essential sense makes sense of the superficial chance, and it may even be that the essential sense rises up and makes of the superficial chance a composition that is not intended by the composers but that occurs beyond their intentions.

Yes, I said, yes, of course, but I do sometimes want some intention to contain, to proportion and balance the unintended. I wonder if too much is left to chance in all the art forms and not enough is brought up of the essentials to the surface.

It is as though the essentials are not for us to determine, but must assert themselves against our inability to determine them, or, even, against our doubt that they exist, so we rely on chance with a strange faith that the essentials will determine themselves, or even show that they exist.

I would like to write an essay on how, in literature, the reliance on imagery, on description, has become the only way a writer – who cannot allow himself to determine the essentials because he doesn't know what the essentials are, or if there are any essentials – has of allowing the essentials to show themselves, as if faith in the image is for the writer the only chance he has for something more to occur in his writing than what he can make occur. More and more, I think this reliance on the image is limiting, and imposes itself on literature in a way that flattens out the deeper, generative grammar of essential human values in justice, in love, in grief, and, too, beauty, which values are as deep in us as language. I wonder if style has been subjected to the use of superficial imagery to the detriment of style, and so I read Jane Austen for a style that, not dependent on the image, brings the essentials somewhat closer to the surface with a greater depth of deep, generative grammar than the image can. But this is a huge subject.

John Edwards' house is in Suffolk. It is a brick house, and its outbuildings are behind a brick wall, in very flat green countryside over which the wind blew hard when Nikos and I were there. About twenty cars were parked in a field outside the brick wall. Within the gate we saw no one, and the place appeared deserted. It was only when we approached the house that I saw, through a window, Francis sitting at a table, talking to someone and smiling, not country people, but city people who preferred to stay inside.

Some sixty people were inside the house, most of them John's family and friends from the East End, and some queens from the Colony Room. I met John's mother and father, he a retired publican, and the rest of the family. They were all talkative and friendly and called me Dave. 'Whenever you'd like to come to my house in Portugal, Dave, you let me know,' one of John's brothers said, and I said I'd like that.

I wandered about the house, which is furnished with over-sized Victorian-Italian-Renaissance pieces, the mantelpieces elaborate. On the walls are many framed reproductions of Francis' paintings, among them paintings of John. In one room, Philip, sunk into an armchair, was smoking pot.

In yet another room, I found Nikos listening to Ian, the man who runs the Colony Room, shouting at Denis Wirth-Miller, 'You're a fake. A total fake. You're a terrible painter. The only person who would buy one of your paintings is the Queen Mother.' Denis, who at around seventy years old looks like a withered boy, simply smiled. His friend Dicky Chopping was also standing in the room, but looking away. I stood by Nikos and listened to Ian, who continued to shout at Denis, and Francis, wavering as he walked, came into the room and he, too, stood and listened with his head lowered, looking like a priest listening to a confession. When Ian paused, Francis raised his head and said calmly, 'It's absolutely true, Denis is a fake. That's what he is, a genuine fake.' Denis went on smirking, his teeth showing. I left.

I went to look at the outbuildings, one of them the cottage done up for Francis. The interior of one long outbuilding was converted into a snooker room with a fringed, green lamp hanging low over the snooker table. At the end of the room were floor-to-ceiling mirrors and a bar, and over a beam of what must have been a barn roof dangled a pair of boxing gloves. Some men were playing snooker.

I returned to the house to find Nikos, who said, 'You shouldn't have left. In a strange way, those men were showing affection for one another.'

We went to the snooker room, where Francis was watching the men playing. Francis said, 'I loathe parties. I simply loathe them.' Then John came into the room with friends and Francis said to him, with a wide smile, 'What a lovely party, John. Such a lovely party.'

Nikos and I had to leave. Francis walked us to our car. Outside the brick wall in the field, we stood in the wind and talked about John.

Nikos said, 'He's very special.'

'He's very special,' Francis said.

'He is,' I said.

'He can't read or write,' Francis said, 'but, you know, there really is something very special about him. You see, John is an innocent.'

In the car, Nikos and I waved at Francis who was still standing in the field. He was wearing a suit and tie. His thin dyed hair was blowing in the wind. He smiled and waved. The green field behind him was flat and gave way to equally flat green-gray countryside.

Why is it that the words I want to use, but which I am too intimidated to use because I'm told that they do not convince in the age I live in, are convincing in song, in, especially, Schubert, in Wolf, in Strauss? – in Wagner? I don't believe that such singing refers so much to the historical age in which the songs were composed that I can respond to them only as some residue of that past historical age, for when I hear the singing something rises in me, in this historical age I live in, that strains for an expression that I feel so passionately it has to be rising from deep within the age I live in. What is it that strains so for expression that I sense so deeply is in this age, but for which this age can't find the expression? The inner straining – yes, the longing – for the moment when everything does come together into a whole globe, and then the expression of it . . . ?

Nikos and I to Loudoun Road for lunch.

We talked about the bad reception I am getting for my book Difficult Women, about my relationships with Jean Rhys, Sonia Orwell, Germaine Greer, all taken from my diary.

I said, 'I don't understand what, in England, is private and what is public, what you can say "in the club," and what you can't say outside it.'

Nikos said, 'I don't know if I see the difference between what is known about me by a few people and by many people.'

'But there is an enormous difference, Nikos!' Natasha said.

Stephen sat back and looked worried, then he said, 'It shocked me when people objected so much to my portrait of Ottoline Morrell in my autobiography that they wouldn't speak to me – and all I'd said was that she dropped an earring in her cup of tea and, moving, disarranged her clothes so a breast was exposed – and yet these same people would, among themselves, say much more objectionable things about Ottoline.'

'I suppose I should worry that I have written objectionably about Jean and Sonia and Germaine,' I said.

'You perhaps should worry,' Natasha said.

'Nonsense,' Stephen exclaimed. 'You should write exactly what you want. For forty years I haven't written anything because I've been made to feel I'd offend if I wrote what I've wanted to write.'

'Oh,' Natasha exclaimed even more, 'that's not true!'

'It is,' he said.

'Well,' Nikos said, 'it is obviously a very complex moral problem.'

'Yes,' Natasha agreed; 'and I think writers shouldn't write auto-biography, but fiction, because, even though we may all know who's being written about, the public don't. Fiction is a mask.'

We talked on, Nikos often saying, 'It is a complex moral problem.'

After lunch, Nikos and I worked in the garden with Natasha for an hour while Stephen, in his study, worked on a book that Nikos had commissioned: a book about China, where Stephen had gone with David Hockney and Gregory Evans, Stephen to write the text, David to do the drawings, Gregory to organize them.

Perhaps Stephen is truly anti-class when he says, 'Write anything you want.' But, then, he doesn't do it. I do.

———

Vera R. to tea. She asked me, 'Tell me, David, are you, as I am, high-born?'

'No,' I said. 'I'm working class.'

'Oh, that doesn't matter. Henry –' I understood her to mean Henry Moore – 'is working class. I'm talking about something of the spirit. You've a high-born spirit.'

'Maybe that's my French-Canadian blood,' I said, and wondered if she knew I was joking.

She said, 'Yes, you have a high-born spirit, and, like me, are attracted, as high-born people are, to common people – you to common women, I to common men.'

'I never thought that,' I said. 'I'll have to give it a lot of thought.'
'Do think about it.'

———

I saw Stephen and Natasha, who had seen Germaine, I think at a reception. She had told them, as Stephen recounted, that I am a 'creepy crawler,' which made Stephen laugh his shaking laugh and made Natasha look at him with that somewhat suppressed delight she has in his being méchant.

———

A weekend with Frank and Anita K. in Cambridge, Nikos and I and Michael Craig-Martin. Michael helped Anita design the layout of her flowerbeds, which she can now consider works of art. While they worked, Frank and Nikos and I read the Sunday papers. Then lunch, and help laying the table while Anita cooked, she keen on using exotic spices. A sense among us of containment, yet, at the same time, of dimensions around us of the outer world of art and literature which we referred to as we ate. Stephen is right: we do live worlds within worlds. Also, extending in unknown dimensions all about us, were our different lives when we are not together. I know about Nikos' and my lives together, but of Frank's and Anita's only what they reveal by their easy reactions to each other on a charming weekend with friends, and Michael, who is wonderfully knowledgeable and articulate about what is going on in the art world, reveals nothing about his life.

Then there are unexpected dimensions. Tony Tanner told me something that revealed, in the Kermodes' relationship, a passion and turbulence that I had not been aware of.

I sense none of that passion in Frank as he calmly smokes his pipe, which keeps going out and which he keeps relighting.

But some time later Anita told me this story from early on in her relationship with Frank:

She and Frank, having left their families and pasts to be together, were living in a rented flat across from the British Museum. There, all of Anita's inherited jewelry was stolen, along with the food – including a duck and the wine and cheese and even a cauliflower – meant for a dinner she was going to prepare before she and Frank were to leave for France. They did leave at the end of the rental period, and had no place to return to. The idea was that they would drive, in a rented car, to the South of France. In Angoulême they quarreled. The reason for the quarrel was incidental to the way Anita felt defeated by Frank's vicious use of words, leaving her deprived of any language at all and helpless. The quarrel was so fierce that they stopped at the first hotel in the town they came to and Anita got out with her suitcase and Frank drove off to another hotel. It was a Friday evening in the town, which was deserted, but in the morning the square outside the hotel was filled with market stalls, parked cars, a crowd of people. Anita waited but Frank did not show up. She waited for hours, and he didn't appear. She felt shocked and abandoned. After more hours, she thought that Frank may have driven off to Stephen and Natasha's house, Saint-Jérôme, in the Apilles. She decided to chance taking a train to Maussane, the nearest town to Saint-Jérôme, and there she found a hotel and asked the proprietor to phone the Spenders, but no one was there. Clearly, she had no idea where Frank had gone.

Several days went by. Then a dream she had about being alone on a Russian seashore after World War III made her feel she was alone in the universe, but that it was all right. On long walks in the countryside she tried and failed to understand what had happened. On the fifth day she thought to telephone a mutual friend in London, and he told her that Frank was there, staying with him. In Angoulême, market day, Frank hadn't been able to find the car he had parked the day before in the town square; when he had found the car, he couldn't remember what hotel he'd left Anita off at, and went from hotel to hotel, but she was in none. He thought she must have returned to London, so in his rented car drove back there, where, with no other place to stay, he was staying with their mutual friend. Though Frank had very little money, as did Anita, he flew back to France and from the airport, rented a car and drove to Maussane where he and Anita put their quarrel to bed. The mix-up in Angoulême, Frank tried to explain, was typical of the utterly absurd situations he tended to find himself in.

Hearing Anita tell this story, I, forgiving myself, laughed, but she laughed too. She said, 'It is all one with the passionate madness of our relationship.'

———

Do I dare put this in, which may smack of just what Nikos has told me I must not do, justify myself? I had from Philip Roth, living in London with Claire Bloom, a letter praising Difficult Women and asking if we could meet. Well, yes, we could, and we did, and we meet often for lunch in a restaurant in Notting Hill, where he has a studio. He told me he had had a long row with Harold Pinter about the book which may have ended their friendship.

As I was entering a drinks party, I saw, across the room, Vidia Naipaul, who with both arms raised beckoned me to him. On the way, I did stop to have a word with one or two friends and when I got to Vidia he said, with a smile, 'David, you have become so grand you didn't come immediately.' He put his hands on my shoulders and said that he had read my book about the women, his only criticism being that I was too kind, and that, because of the book, he had decided to stop writing fiction and from now on would write only non-fiction.

Philip said to me, 'You're a tough person. An enigmatic and tough person. Perhaps there's a note of masochistic self-exposure about the book, but you do stand out as tough.'

———

I collected John Lehmann in my car to take him to Stephen's for luncheon. John is as feeble as he is big; he walked very slowly and unsteadily with a stick to the car and got into the seat with great difficulty; he smelled of whiskey and uncleanliness.

He said, 'I may have to leave Stephen's rather early, dear boy.'

John Golding and James Joll were also there, and the Australian poet Peter Porter. Natasha is in the South of France, and Nikos at the publishing house.

Stephen told me to sit at the opposite end of the table from him – he giggled – 'As the wife.'

He had prepared a huge roast, but the roast potatoes that went with the meat were inedible.

He seemed hardly to speak to John, on his right, and often Stephen got up to serve more beef, but not the potatoes.

From time to time, John would ask, 'How are your legs, Stephen?' or 'What did you think of the reviews of your last book, Stephen?'

After dinner we all went upstairs to the sitting room, the talk inconsequential, and shortly after John asked if I'd take him home.

In the car he was silent for a long while, then he said, 'I suppose I must accept the fact that Stephen and I, after all these years, can't be friends. I can't help but feel he's suspicious of me.'

'What do you mean?' I asked.

'I'm not sure what I mean, dear boy.'

'It's very interesting, and you should think about it.'

'It is interesting.'

'Oh yes.'

He said, 'I keep hoping that a true affection will flow between us but it never does.'

I let him off in front of his door.

The next morning I spoke to Stephen over the telephone, and recounted what John had told me, hoping that Stephen might be touched by John's wanting affection to flow between them.

Stephen said, 'Suspicious! Of course I am. Did you hear those catty questions he kept asking me? Still, perhaps I didn't pay him much attention during the evening –'

Stephen has said, with a laugh, that it's assumed he and John once had an affair because they are both so big; then Stephen frowned and, with sudden anger, insisted, 'We did not!'

———

Nikos is in Russia, commissioning books.

While he is away, Roxy and I went to Paddington Station to meet Joe and Jos Tilson, up from Wiltshire, to join a huge CND demonstration against the proliferation of nuclear bombs. Many special trains were arriving at the station, which was crowded with demonstrators who stood on the platform with their banners, waiting for the organizers with megaphones to tell them what to do. Some young punks, with red and blue hair and ⌾ painted on their cheeks, were passing out placards on sticks; we each took a placard and by tube went to Notting Hill, where, at Ladbroke Grove, a third of the demonstration (the Western contingent) was forming into a long, wide march. On the pavements, West Indians were beating bongo drums. Young people wearing fall-out cover-ups, white with zippers up the front, passed along the crowd with plastic buckets, asking for donations, and people threw in loose change. We stood for a while on a pavement by the bongo players and watched the march go by, wanting to choose which banner, held by the leading representatives of each contingent, and when a beautiful purple banner with silver fringe approached we all said, 'That's lovely! That's the one!' but when we saw emblazoned on the banner FEMINIST LESBIANS AGAINST DEATH we decided to wait, given that we were not lesbians. There were banners for doctors, scientists, musicians, trades unions, and mostly for towns and cities from all over Great Britain. There came along a small wood of large, paper oak leaves carried on sticks, and on the leaves was SAVE NATURE, and Joe thought we should join this contingent, which reminded him of his art, and so we did, and behind the wood we marched down Ladbroke Grove, up Notting Hill, down Kensington Church Street.

At one point in Kensington Church Street we stepped out of the march to go into a pub for beers, and through the high windows of the pub we could see the banners go by. It was a bright, hot day.

We rejoined the march, which turned into Kensington Gardens and from there into Hyde Park, where we marched along curving paths, and at the curves were able to see, ahead and behind, the marchers with their banners, and the march appeared endless; it was as though we were looking at a distant march under the great green plane trees, and it was with a sense of wonderful unity that I realized that we were in a long, long march of demonstrators that reached so far ahead there was no seeing to the beginning and so far behind that there was no seeing to the end.

Demonstrators were also coming into the park from Hyde Park Corner and from Oxford Street. Our Western contingent along with the converging Northern and Southern contingents advanced towards a massive crowd in the middle of the park, all gathered about a platform and a number of huge megaphones high on a derrick. We didn't stay for the speeches.

A youth was arrested for igniting a smoke bomb, a harmless bomb that released a cloud of bright orange smoke. Five policemen took him away, two grasping his arms, all of them smiling. The boy, half the size of the smallest constable, looked down, frowning.

I thought, as we marched: this demonstration would not be allowed in Russia.

There were about a quarter of a million people.

Joe and Jos and Roxy came to the flat for lunch.

———

I drove Stephen and Natasha (just back from the South of France) to dinner at the Glenconners'. I sat between Natasha and Lord Esher, with whom I had a very interesting talk about 'half-truths' in writing and autobiography. He was wearing an ugly, green and red knit tie (a New Yorker, a stickler for what is and what is not done, once told me that one never wears a knitted tie in the evening, a fact of sartorial knowledge that the American would assume an Englishman must of course be fully aware of); and it came to me that he was not so much wearing that tie as wearing a tie, and it didn't matter what it looked like.

While he has been away, I've had disturbing dreams of Nikos abandoning me.

———

Stephen, laughing as he spoke, said he is very keen on hearing what Nikos has to say about Russia. 'We should devise a chart,' he said, 'with on one side the insights into Russia by Thatcher, Reagan, Brezhnev and on the other side Nikos' insights, and then calculate which side wins.'

———

Nikos has come back from Russia with many Communist badges on his lapels.

James Joll told him that he is the last of the Romantic Communists.

Nikos retorted: James did not understand what Communism meant in Greece after the defeat of the ideology in the Civil War, for Communism meant equality and justice for all people, meant the fulfillment of a promised Republic.

James nodded.

Nikos and I talked about the U.S.S.R. and the U.S., I complaining that, whereas he protests violently against the U.S. suppressions in the world he doesn't about the suppressions of the U.S.S.R.

He said, 'The two cases are utterly different.'

'They may be. I'm talking about what you feel towards Russia and America.'

He said, 'I loathe Russian suppression – of course I do – and you know that I love America. But I'll tell you: in my heart I believe that Russia is on the side of life and America is on the side of death.'

I sat back, silent, and I suddenly thought: is he right?

———

Getting into bed with Nikos, I said to him, 'You know, I don't believe I give you any joy.'

'Sachlamares!' he said, meaning, 'What rubbish!'

———

Both Stephen and I were surprised when, at supper, Nikos said about Russia: 'No one calls Leningrad Leningrad, but Saint Petersburg. The country is ready for another revolution.'

––––––

I always feel, in a social situation with Natasha, that she thinks my presence is a presumption on my part, as though I have somehow ingratiated myself into a world in which I do not belong. Stephen has told me that the only reason why Natasha has accepted us is because so many people she knows have accepted us. Elizabeth Glenconner, he says, particularly loves Nikos, doesn't stop talking of Nikos before Natasha, as if to let Natasha know that if she, Natasha, can't ever feel close to him, she, Elizabeth, does, and what else can Natasha do but sit at the same table with Nikos – and, by extension, with me? If I were a different kind of writer, I'd have presented to me the makings of a comedy of manners.

––––––

Stephen rang me to say he'd written a long account in his diary about a luncheon he'd recently had with John Lehmann; he wanted me to read it and invited me to lunch to do so. It is very funny and, I hope, indicative of the diary Stephen says he has been keeping religiously. What he wrote about John Lehmann has the quality of humor Stephen has in conversation but not in his writing, the quality in which resides, W. H. Auden said, Stephen's genius.

––––––

At the opening of an exhibition of Adrian Stokes' paintings at the Serpentine Gallery, I met Natasha, and together we walked to the Royal College of Art, where she teaches, I think, aspects of music. She said, 'Let's sit on a bench for a while and have a little gossip,' so we sat by a group of school children playing ball in Hyde Park, and chatted.

––––––

As we were standing together on a corner in Notting Hill Gate by a red postbox, Philip Roth and I were talking when an Englishman

I knew came towards us in the crowd, and I wanted him to see me talking with Philip Roth, but he didn't see us, and walked past.

When Philip is keen on whatever he is talking about, his nostrils contract. He stops talking, and his eyebrows, too, contract. I always take the first step to get us walking again. As we walk, he talks, and often stops, and he talks much more than I do, and much more intensely.

The last time we met at the restaurant, he talked of 'real stuff' in writing, and gave me this, written on a torn sheet of paper, to think about:

You must so change that in broad daylight you could crouch down in the middle of the street and, without embarrassment, undo your trousers, and evacuate.

I forget where the quotation comes from – I think from some nineteenth-century author.

Philip added: 'The emphasis is on the word could. Not that you would, because you wouldn't, but you should be capable of doing it.'

We went to his studio, a simple room in a white stucco town house, with a large electric typewriter on a desk and a huge waste-paper basket on the floor by the desk, the basket filled with discarded pages.

Philip said, 'Updike and Bellow hold their flashlights out into the world, reveal the real world as it is now. I dig a hole and shine my flashlight into the hole. You do the same.'

I said that I want to write about the moment I'm living in, as I do in my diary. In my fiction, I'm still an adolescent, learning about a world that's now no longer the world I live in.

We went on to a nearby restaurant, Monsieur Thompson's, with white tablecloths and white napkins peaked on white plates.

Philip asked me if I often think of death.

'For some reason,' I said, 'I'm reassured by death. I guess the reason is that death can't be faked.'

This startled him. 'Oh no,' he said, 'you can't be reassured by that.'

'I shouldn't be.'

His hand to his chin, he appeared to study me for a long while, then, with a quiet seriousness I have got used to in him, he said, 'Yet I'm sure of the final doom. The nuclear holocaust is well on its way.'

'And that reassures my dark soul.'

He dropped his hand from his chin as if with impatience with me, and brusquely asked, 'What is your dark soul?'

'Of course it must never happen, but that it could happen reassures me in my sense that what is true is that everything is fated for destruction and that there is nothing we can do about it all happening.'

Again, he stared at me. 'There is a devil, isn't there?' he said.

I laughed.

'Now I've become rather dark myself,' he said.

'I'm sorry.'

'Can you write when you're in a dark state?'

'Yes, I can.'

'I can't. I have to be in a lively state.'

We mixed up sexual obsession in our talk about doom. I said I am less and less obsessed, and this is a relief. He said, 'I'll be as obsessed when I'm eighty exactly as I was when I was eighteen.'

———

I visited Tony Tanner in his rooms at King's Cambridge. He asked me to attend a seminar he was to give on George Santayana. The Last Puritan meant a lot to me when I read it as a teenager, so I felt drawn to a seminar about his work, but, at the seminar table with the graduates, I realized that what I knew about Santayana (that he was homosexual, that he died cared for by Blue Nuns in Rome during the time of Mussolini, that he was Spanish but never repudiated Franco) would be irrelevant to the more elevated vision of the philosophy of Santayana that was the subject of the seminar. The moment I try to expound upon a philosophy, I'm lost, and in no coherent way can I articulate the vision. (Nikos can.) So I have to bring myself down from the high level of philosophy to the low level of sex, place, nationality, politics. I resent this deeply, because, oh, what I long to write is PHILOSOPHY. I said nothing during the seminar.

Back in Tony's room, he told me that he had tried to kill himself. He had made a terrible mistake leaving King's to go to Johns Hopkins in Baltimore and King's had him back. Drink ruined his nervous system so he walked with two sticks. But he always appears dapper, usually with a black polo shirt and a tweed jacket, and he was, as always, affable.

'Read this,' he said, and handed me, open to the page, Winnie-the-Pooh, and after I read about Eeyore's gratitude at being given a deflated balloon, Tony asked me, 'Whom does that remind you of?' and I said immediately, 'Frank!' and we doubled up with laughter. 'Of course,' he said, 'we love Frank,' and I said, 'Of course,' but we couldn't stop laughing.

Paris

We are in Paris, Hotel de Suède, with Julia. We've come to see the Chardin exhibition in the Grand Palais. The walls of the hotel room are pale grey, and the carpet is soft, pale grey. I am lying on one of the two single beds, the silky spread rumpled at the foot, and I am covered by a loose blanket and a sheet. When I lie back fully my head lolls on the bolster and the large, square pillow and I look through the net curtains of the double windows at the soft, grey rain falling. Lolling, I am attentive to all the most delicate details in the room.

From down a passage beyond the other bed comes the sound of splashing water. Those sounds of Nikos splashing water against himself in the bath fills me with great contentment.

Later —

Nikos came in from the bath and sat next to me on the edge of my bed, so I moved to let him lean back against the same pillow and bolster I rested on, and he looked with me out of the window where the rain was falling more fully.

I said, 'What a dreary morning.'

'Is it?' he asked.

'Isn't it?'

'You mean, outside?'

'I mean outside.'

'It's not so bad inside.'

And one of those times occurred as if different from anything else we'd ever known, together or apart.

Heavy rain was hitting the windows, and through it the light from outside became stippled with fine shadows in the room, and gently swaying vertical stripes appeared on the grey walls.

I ordered two cafés complets, and, each of us in a bathrobe, we sat on delicate chairs with rattan seats and backs at a delicate table with a marble top.

'Give me your cup,' he said. I did, and he poured into it steaming coffee from a tall white porcelain pot with a little bouquet of flowers on its side. The white cup, so fine the coffee showed through, was also decorated by a tiny bouquet of flowers. I took the cup back from him and added, from a heavy silvery jug, a dollop of milk that almost remained intact until, with a silvery spoon, he stirred it round and the black coffee turned dark brown. I said, 'I think I'll take sugar,' and Nikos handed me the two-handled basin, also heavy and silvery, from which I lifted a cube with the small tongs and dropped it, with a splash, into my cup, and then, saying, 'I'll take two,' I dropped in another cube and stirred the coffee and milk and dissolving sugar into a liquor that became rich enough to ripple thickly about the spoon, and, sipping it, I said, 'Oh yes,' and Nikos smiled.

There were croissants, warm and wrapped in a large, bright white napkin in a silver basket, and rolls of butter on crushed ice and little jars of jam, each one of which Nikos picked up to study – fraises, abricots, myrtilles – choosing, finally, the strawberry. I watched Nikos put the napkin, pleated and standing upright on his plate, to the side and pick up a croissant and pull it apart, the thin, flaky, tawny crust separating to reveal a pale, elastic interior, and, placing one-half of the croissant on his plate, he used the butter knife to take up a whole roll of butter, scored and dotted with water, to transfer it to the edge of the white plate, and then, with his shining knife, he spread the butter onto half the warm croissant, after which he used the tip of his knife to scoop up one whole but almost liquid strawberry to smear it into the melting butter. As he brought the confection to his open mouth, he looked up at me smiling at him.

When we met Julia in the foyer to go to the exhibition, she said that in the morning she had looked out of her window into the rain and seen a body in a body bag being taken out of the hotel into a waiting van, the back doors open.

———

Philip said to me, 'You're not taking care of yourself, David. You should join a club and go every morning for an hour's exercise. You're too young and good looking not to take care of yourself. And you should go to a hair clinic to get some treatment to keep your hair from falling out. It's too late for me, but not for you.' He went on and on. I said, 'All right, all right,' thinking that of course I wouldn't do anything of the sort.

———

Nikos' interest in aesthetics makes me interested, so I find myself wondering, Well, what does constitute a work of art? Self-containment, and within the self-containment proportion and balance?

We went to Paris for a grand exhibition of the paintings of Chardin. How beautiful the still lifes, in which the perspectives are all at different angles, and the whole so proportioned and balanced.

Even though John Golding claims Cubism to be a radical shift from Renaissance perspective, studying an Analytic Cubist painting by Picasso, I see it as self-contained, proportion and balance delicately, exquisitely sustained.

And then, at an exhibition of the works of Marcel Duchamp at the Tate, I stare at a miscellany of odd objects in a glass case, and I think, Well, out go self-containment, balance and proportion.

Michael Craig-Martin, teaching at Goldsmiths, told me that he had a Japanese student whose work consisted of his burning lumps of Styrofoam with a hot poker, and when Michael, not knowing what else to say, commented, 'It's very ugly,' the student responded, 'Yes, yes, very ugly,' and Michael went on to the next student.

He says there is no definition, none, to what is or is not art.

Perhaps there is an aesthetic for the unformed in art rather than the formed.

Karsten Schubert, gallery owner, says there is no way that one can relate the work of Andy Warhol to that of, say, Chardin, no way.

————

Lunch with Philip at Monsieur Thompson's. I had given him my story, 'Paris, 1959,' published in the New Yorker, to read and, if he wished, to comment on. He said it's the best writing I've done and he also said, 'You're an odd bird, Plante, a really odd bird. I'm not saying you write oddly, I'm saying you're odd, and that's why your writing is odd.'

I said, 'Your praising my writing terrifies me.'

'Why? Because you feel you've got to start taking yourself seriously as a writer?'

'If, five years ago, I fantasized about a respected writer praising my writing, I can't imagine I would have considered you as a possibility. Our writing is so essentially different from each other.'

'It is,' he said. 'But whereas you think you're a dreamy writer and I'm a realistic writer concerned with the hard facts of life, the opposite is true: I'm the dreamy writer who's always trying to invent a world in which all my dreams will be fulfilled. My writing doesn't come from my life. I make up everything.'

'And I'm a realist?'

'Yes, you are. Goddamn it, you are. You're tougher than I am.'

We talked about many subjects, always autobiographically.

He said, 'To be an American simply requires one to be obsessed with finding out what an American is,' and he described how he, from his childhood, felt he was a foreigner in America wondering what America was, and then he realized that this very condition made him an American.

I told him that Antonia Fraser once told me that she plays a game to herself whenever she is with you and her husband Harold

Pinter: she tries to guess which of the men will be the first to use the word 'Jew,' and within how many minutes of their meeting.

Philip asked me, 'How long do you give me?'

'Before you say anything else when we meet, even hello, you say, "Jew."'

He tilted his head back and laughed.

I said, 'You can question what it is to be an American Jew because there are enough American Jews to give you an American identity. Try questioning yourself as a Franco-American. We have no American identity at all. How many Franco-Americans do you know, and what do you imagine can be their identity in America?'

'I don't know any,' he said.

We walked together to a bookshop in Notting Hill, and he told me about Claire and how he loves her. He is quite sure he is keeping her from suicide. In the bookshop, he looked around for a short while as if generally, then left, and I stayed an hour.

———

At supper, Nikos told me that when he came to London from Athens, he was filled with ambitions. He had had a list of people he wanted to meet, and he has met them all. He said, 'I was going to take London by storm.'

'And do you feel you've fulfilled your ambitions?'

He smiled. 'Some,' he said.

'Which?' I asked.

'My biggest ambition was that I would meet someone and fall in love and live with him.'

'And was that ambition fulfilled?'

His smile deepened. 'Somewhat.'

Florence

In Florence, I rang Harold Acton. As there is only one telephone in the villa, I had to wait until he came to it, no doubt handed to him by the butler who had answered. He is well over eighty, and he seemed not to have changed since his sixties. He greeted me in the drawing room and made Oriental gestures of welcome, leaning forward a little and rolling his hands on his wrists. His skin appeared tight on his long face and bald head, his nose thin with high, arched nostrils. He started almost every sentence with 'Ooooh' and spoke with an accent that put the emphasis, often on one syllable of a word, at odd places in the sentences. 'Ooooh, you will tell me about people in London.'

He asked me, as he always did, if I would like to see the garden, and as we walked about the statues among the cypresses he told me, as he always did, how the cocks of the statues had been knocked off. Someone had suggested that Acton kept the statues as mutilated as they were to be able to talk about his 'problem' – should he replace the 'appendages,' or, instead, attach fig leaves which would, by the bulge in them, suggest 'something substantial underneath?' He retained his curious, lightly jerking walk.

His Tuscan kitchen would, he said as we walked back to the villa, produce a very modest meal, not up to the culinary delights he was sure I was used to. We had spaghetti to start, then slices of beef and peas served by the white-haired butler, Dino, in the high,

vaulted dining room, among polychrome wooden statues of saints
on chests.

Acton said he could hardly leave his house now – only for brief
periods – for fear of its being broken into. It had already been
broken into eight times. A painting by Daddi was taken off a wall
and never recovered. He couldn't trust anyone, not even his staff.
(About a new cameriere, he said, 'His room, into which I happened
to step to enquire about some small matter, is a great mess, filled
with cigarette butts –' he used the American expression – 'and
reeking of cigarette smoke.') His staff didn't do their jobs properly,
were in fact quite useless, but what was one to do today when help
simply could not be found and no one was to be trusted? He delicately shrugged his broad shoulders and pressed his thin lips
together. How he envied people who weren't dependent on staff,
how he wished he weren't dependent, but what could one do? To
give up his staff would be to give up La Pietra.

'How times have changed,' he said. 'When my parents were alive,
they had a staff of thirty-five. I have only a staff of twelve, and I
don't dare ask them for anything.'

When he started to talk about a recently published novel which
he thought terrible, he became violently angry. He called the
writer, a woman, a bitch, a slut, a third-rate whore – Barbara
Skelton – and I had no idea why he should rage so against her, but
thought it must be for personal reasons. He said, 'Yes, art excuses
all. With art one can write about anything, anything. But that
novel is too bad even to say about it that it was written.' He was
raging.

To get him down to a subject that would make him less aggressive,
I asked him what his favorite work of his own was. He raised his
hands and said he always reread his work with great embarrassment.

I said, 'All writers do that. The fact is, we don't really know if
what we write is good or bad.'

He bowed his head and said, 'Ooooh, that is true.'

And then he became light spirited, and began to gossip. He said,
'Count Morra, whom I used to visit in his peculiar villa outside

Cortona, used to be somewhat to the Left, you know, somewhat to the Left. I often wondered if this had something to do with his liking for Blacks.'

He became even more light spirited talking about sex, about, ooooh, lovely cocks.

After lunch, Acton asked me if I'd like a nap, as the train I was to take to London was to leave in the evening. He asked a maid to prepare the blue room, la camera blu, which I followed him upstairs to. It was a huge, high-ceilinged room, with a great bed and tapestries and paintings on the walls, and a view of the cypress avenue to the gates from the high windows. He left me with the maid, whom I helped put linen sheets on the bed. She also brought in an old electric heater because Acton said the room was cold. I undressed and got into bed and looked at the room beyond the gilded, spiraling columns at the corners of my bed, and I thought: Well, here I am.

He was waiting for me in the drawing room for tea before I left, and here he continued to gossip about people in London, mostly homosexual men, with lightness and charm.

He was as he had once been, when his talk was all lightness and charm, with pauses that suspended you in the wonder of what the point of a sentence was going to be.

He said, 'I am preparing for my departure –' he paused and smiled a little '– to Switzerland.'

After tea, I walked along the cypress avenue to the gate and got onto a crowded bus into the center of Florence.

London

Walking alone along Wigmore Street, I heard my dead mother call out my name.

———

Like Stephen (and he has noted this, joking that we are both Piscean, whereas Nikos is Scorpion), I do not have an analytical mind, and whenever I try to be 'philosophical,' whenever I try to 'intend' an explanation of a 'philosophical' vision, I make a mess of it. Still, I know that I am as if within the circle of a vision that is greater than myself.

It happens from time to time that I read something which sets off in me an illuminating awareness of the vision. (Nikos tells me that almost everything I read I read as if included in and expanding on the vision.) I think that what Frank wrote in The Genesis of Secrecy illuminates the vision. And recently I read in William James' lecture 'Philosophical Conceptions' this:

> A collection is one, though the things that compose it are many. Now, can we practically 'collect' the universe? Physically, of course we cannot. And mentally we cannot, if we take it concretely in its details. But if we take it summarily and abstractly, then we collect it mentally whenever we refer to it, even as I do now when I fling the term 'universe' at it, and so seem to leave a mental ring around it.

Oh, I think, yes, yes, that's the vision I have which is the mental ring about everything I think and feel, and certainly everything I write, even in this diary.

———

I'm at my desk in my study. Nikos just came in from his study, where, when we have a rare evening at home, he works on his poetry. He said, 'You're writing in your diary.' 'Yes,' I said. He said, 'I've stopped reading your diary.' 'I know,' I said, 'but why?' He said, 'You've been writing things against me, which I don't want to read.' I didn't think there was anything in my diary against him, though it is in him, as a Greek, to imagine even me writing things against him. He would never stop me from writing anything I want.

———

Stephen and Natasha came to dinner.

Stephen was very excited about the bitchy remarks about him in the latest volume of Virginia Woolf's diary to be published; he laughed a lot, quoting them.

Spender has the makings of a long-winded bore –

Natasha said, 'You'd think that Stephen would at least have been told by the editors, if not given the choice as to whether the remarks should be published or not.'

She spoke in an emphatically rotund way.

Stephen seemed to enjoy the notoriety of Woolf's remarks, if that's the word.

He went on to talk about Auden: 'He never wanted to drive a car. He always imagined himself, never a car, but a train, for which all the lights would automatically be changed to green.'

Someone is writing his biography, which Stephen is not enthusiastic about. As excited as he seems to be by Virginia Woolf mentioning him in her diary, he does not want a biography. This occurs to me: he is excited – excited and amused – by the Woolf comments because they're unsympathetic, because they don't take him seriously. Stephen can't bear to be taken seriously, not really, as he feels anyone taking him seriously would soon reveal the pretensions of the seriousness of, as Woolf wrote, 'his muddled theories.' He reads the Woolf comments as lively jokes, and he loves jokes, especially about himself. He told me that his favourite work of literature is The Importance of Being Earnest, and he adores reading parodies, especially Beerbohm's, which have become his preferred reading. As Auden once said, I recall, Stephen's genius is all in his sense of humour, and he has never used that in his writing.

Natasha has obviously read the first draft of the biography, because she said, 'I've got the writer to limit the use of "homoerotic" to once per page, so the second draft won't be as bad as the first.'

After dinner, we played Scrabble (Natasha of course won – she always wins – and there is among the other players a deference to her true intelligence) and then we listened to music. Again, within a private circle, Natasha is loving. Nikos and I knew that she and Stephen were both pleased to have spent the evening with us, and there were kisses all round with the goodnight.

Mind you, Stephen may be deeply hurt by the comments made about him by Virginia Woolf, whom I do not think of as a nice woman.

But many think of me as not a nice man.

Stephen said, 'I told Natasha that when I die I don't want any services of any kind, especially no memorial service. I made her promise that.'

Natasha appeared distracted, as she often does appear, and in her distraction a blankness comes to her face.

When this happens, Stephen tries to bring her into the conversation, which, however, she seems not to have heard.

She asks, 'Yes, darling?'

He presses his lips together.

Then he will tell another anecdote, slightly irreverent, laughing brightly. And Natasha, looking at him, smiles. She calls him 'méchant.'

The next day, Saturday, Nikos and I arranged books, went grocery shopping, had our usual afternoon nap, and in the evening went to a recital at the Wigmore Hall.

———

To dinner, Nikos and I, at Loudoun Road, the other guests Elizabeth and Christopher Glenconner and Anne Wollheim and Valerie Eliot.

It comes to me that dining tables are very often the settings of diary entries, and this is because dining tables are where people most often gather. Valerie Eliot was very amusing, her skin smooth and clear and bright. (Stephen says she has marzipan hair.) There were times when I thought she had all the gusto of a young working-class man in drag affecting seriousness and class, and then suddenly the seriousness and class would collapse and she'd laugh. I'd thought she'd be reserved about talking about her husband, but no, not at all – 'Tom did this, Tom did that.'

We were sitting together on a sofa before going down to the dining room to dinner. She told me how when she and Tom were in America newspapermen invaded their privacy all the time, even to hiding tape recorders behind sofas. I said, 'It's dreadful, the way they have no respect for privacy.' 'Yes,' she said, 'dreadful.' Then she asked what I do and pretended to have heard of me when I told her. She asked what my last book was, and I said, 'Oh, I think you'll disapprove of it. It's an invasion of the privacy of three friends.' 'Oh?' she asked, and her eyes widened. 'Yes,' I said, 'I've written of my rather personal relationships with Jean Rhys, Sonia Orwell, and Germaine Greer.' She rubbed her hands together, threw her shoulders back, and, her face bright red, she exclaimed, 'But that sounds like great fun!' and it was as though she was prepared for a good old gossip. But Natasha, hearing us, came over and changed the subject; Valerie Eliot, however, wouldn't change, and told me stories about the writer Djuna Barnes and what a difficult woman she was! Again, it was as though she had dropped all the affected disapproval of a middle-class woman to become suddenly a drag queen eager for a gossip and loving it, even parodying it with slight exaggerations of her hands and voice. I was sorry when we had to go down to eat, where we were separated. I sat between Natasha, who never sits at the other end of the table from Stephen, and Anne.

I heard Valerie Eliot talking with Christopher. She said something about 'Tom,' and he asked, 'Who's Tom?' She answered, 'Oh, my late husband, who was Tom Eliot.' 'And what did he do?' Christopher asked. 'He was a poet,' she said. 'Oh, isn't that lovely,' Christopher said; 'a poet! What fun to be a poet!'

Christopher never remembers who Nikos and I are, but is as gracious to us as if we just might be old friends. He never quite knows where he is, but acts as if wherever he is is familiar to him. He laughs and claps his hands and says, 'How lovely! How lovely!' He probably doesn't recognize Stephen and Natasha.

She prepared a wonderful meal: onion soufflé, then poached salmon with boiled potatoes and cooked cucumber and home-made mayonnaise, then a pudding of sliced apples cooked in butter. Champagne and very good wines.

As Nikos and I were leaving, Stephen, laughing, said, 'I know I'm getting old. You may be alarmed by it, but for a moment this evening, when you both came in, I didn't know who you were.' Nikos and I laughed with him.

———

Could T. S. Eliot have been a human being, married, in love with Valerie? Could he have been more than a disembodied spirit?

I did once see him. He came to Boston College, when I was a freshman, to give a reading of his poetry, and I sat marginally on the stage while he, centered at a podium, read in a low cadence, the cadence often the meaning of the poem whose meaning was higher than my understanding. And now I think the meaning was higher, too, than his own understanding.

I used to think he knew exactly what was meant by the lady and the three white leopards under a juniper tree, but I think now he wrote somewhere between intention and the unintentional, and often the unintentional rose higher than the intended, and he let this occur, let this occur especially in the music, so the music filled his low dry voice with the resonance of what his poetry tried to say but, on his own admission, could only fail saying.

I do go to Four Quartets for spiritual recourse.

But I think

> In the room the women come and go
> Talking of Michelangelo

the silliest couplet in the English language, 'go' and 'Michelangelo' occurring suddenly to Eliot, who liked silly rhymes, his only way of using it seriously in a serious poem, however, to condemn it as silly, so it is not he who is being silly but the women coming and going in the room. And the exegeses on such silliness.

In fact, I often go to Four Quartets for spiritual recourse, as this, written with such conviction:

> And all shall be well and
> All manner of thing shall be well
> By the purification of the motive
> In the ground of our beseeching.

– the word 'beseeching' stirring in me the residue of a religion in which to beseech was, perhaps still is, the impulse, though to whom it may still be the impulse I have no idea.

What a relief it would be to think and feel within the defining intentions of a religion, which I imagine T. S. Eliot finally did.

I recall from the church services of my youth: pray for the intention of . . .

The unintentional and the intentional – what Nikos would call the antinomies, arguments contradictory but equally reasonable.

Florence

Harold Acton is dead. I spoke at length about Acton and La Pietra with Giuseppe Chigiotti, a young, close friend of Acton, particularly in his last years.

He told me the funeral in the church of San Marco in Florence was very solemn, with carabinieri in full-dress uniform flanking the coffin. John Pope-Hennessy was the first to arrive, then Joan Haslip, the historian of European royalty, looking rather like a widow. (Joan Haslip had hoped to be left something by Acton, but she got nothing.) The butler, the cook, the head gardener (who, alone of all the domestics, was left five million lire, about three thousand dollars) were present, and a few people from the Florentine aristocracy. Florence was represented by many officials, and the British ambassador gave a reading. A young, distant kinsman of Acton appeared, wearing a hat with a feather, and was shown to the front of the church, the only self-proclaimed kinsman of Acton to attend. But there seemed to be no representatives of the royals, whom he had entertained at La Pietra, not even an equerry. The Mass was said by the Jesuit priest who had administered Extreme Unction to Acton.

Was, I asked, Acton religious? No, Chigiotti said, religion for him didn't exist. He was, however, superstitious, and kept chestnuts on his desk and medals in his pocket. Though he didn't have anything to do with religion, the formalities of the Catholic Church were very important to him. He was, to the world, a man of great formality, a formality he felt was in keeping with La Pietra.

After the Mass, people were invited to the villa for breakfast, during which Chigiotti saw that some objects were missing from the rooms. There was, he found, no proper inventory of the contents, and the disappearance of items went unexplained. Chigiotti wondered if the key to the La Pietra safe was still under the wooden Buddha in the library where it had been kept when Acton was alive.

The day after the funeral, New York University held a luncheon party at the villa to inaugurate its activities. La Pietra, Chigiotti said, was supplied with an avalanche of silverware, but the silver was gone. And never would Acton have had a marquee put up on the grounds, but there it was, huge. And never would he have walked with people about the garden with drinks (he always accompanied guests about the garden, didn't leave them to wander on their own), but there hundreds of people were wandering in the garden with glasses. And many of the people invited to this luncheon Acton, who was very open about inviting people, would never have invited to his home – people he didn't like, people who simply wanted to see where the royals had stayed, small functionaries from Florence.

Giuseppe Chigiotti, an attractive, clear-faced man with delicate eyelashes, held up his hands and shrugged.

Could he tell me why Acton left nothing to Florence, which had made him an honorary citizen shortly before he died? Chigiotti said that Acton's relationship with Florence was 'un po' complicato.' Certainly Florence had hoped to get something. The Uffizi was hoping they would get the Vasari, and the Bargello one or two statues.

But Acton knew that the Bardini collection, which had been given to the city, was destroyed by being dispersed, and he did not want La Pietra to be destroyed in the same way. It would be better to give La Pietra to an English or American university, with Harvard's commitment to Bernard Berenson's I Tatti as a good example of what an English or American university could do. La

Pietra was offered first to Acton's college at Oxford, Christ Church, who turned it down, then to New York University, who accepted.

However, there were other reasons why Acton didn't leave anything to Florence that went back to his parents and the way the Italian Fascists had treated his mother. Mrs Acton refused to have anything to do, not only with Florentines who had been Fascists, but with all Italians, and spent most of her time in the villa, dressed in Chinese Mandarin clothes, drinking. Acton's mother so repudiated Italy, she would go, once a month, all the way to Switzerland to have her hair done. And Joan Haslip said to me, 'Because of the way his mother had been treated by the Fascists, Harold would never have dreamed of turning La Pietra over to the Italians.'

But Florence had never taken much interest in the Actons, as it had never taken much real interest in Berenson and his circle. As provincial snobs, the Florentine aristocracy had few relations with foreigners, and most of these few were entirely sexual, not social. Acton's father had affairs with Florentines with whom he had illegitimate children, but there was the question of his own legitimacy (Arthur Acton, whose name does not appear in Burke's Peerage, may have been illegitimate, and all the information Harold Acton gives about his father's past in More Memoirs of an Aesthete is: 'as an orphan he had been brought up by priests . . .'), which itself would have made him not quite respectable.

Though Harold Acton, after his mother's death, did entertain Italians, including some members of the Florentine nobility such as the Frescobaldis, Florentines on the whole, if they thought of him at all, thought of him as too worldly for them. When he was knighted, Florentines were not impressed – they had thought Acton was a baron, which was in fact a title given to him by his domestics.

But by the time Acton did impress Florence by having the royals stay, particularly Prince Charles and Princess Diana, Acton lost interest in the city. He was invited everywhere, and, out of as much curiosity as a sense of duty, he went (though before he went to certain houses, where he knew he would be served only a scrawny battery chicken, he asked for sandwiches to be made at La Pietra for his return), and he was more and more disappointed. He had thought the city had something for him, had thought he would discover a Florence of interesting people, as interesting as Florence was in the twenties and thirties, when Orioli was publishing sexually explicit books that couldn't be published elsewhere and there was an Italian avant-garde. He didn't find it.

Florence, Chigiotti said, drained Acton. Even the British Institute, which his father had helped found and which he was for a while governor of, and where he was treated as a royal himself with an armchair in the first row for any lecture he attended, in the end disappointed him. It was for his services to the Institute – and not, he would say with a wry smile, for his writing – that he was knighted, but he argued with the director, his old friend Ian Greenlees, about Greenlees' boyfriend, who behaved badly and insulted people and was simply not sortable (passed the jug of cream, he would, after pouring some onto his pudding, lick the spout before passing it on) but who was made by Greenlees the Institute's librarian, and Acton distanced himself.

Though he didn't think his life's work was to be the custodian, the vestale, of La Pietra, what else was there for him to be? Because of La Pietra, Acton became worldly in a way he did not want to be. He became something of a tourist attraction in Florence, showing around strangers from England and America who had heard about La Pietra.

He became, Giuseppe Chigiotti said, a prisoner, not only of his duties toward La Pietra, but of his own illusions about his fame. Every time he walked down the main street of Florence, the Via Tornabuoni, he imagined people recognized him. Chigiotti would tell Acton about places he'd been to for a bit of amusement, and Acton, who was always very curious, especially about anything that had to do with sex, would say, Oooh, he wished he could go, but how could he, with La Pietra on his shoulders? Though he was not a puritan about sex, his grand sense of ufficialità would not allow him to be public about what he in private had no reservations about admitting, with a warble of pleasure. And he became especially concerned about his reputation when the royals began to visit, as he would have worried very much about his causing, as their host, any sexual scandal that might reflect on them as guests.

However, Acton learned to use La Pietra. The young friends of older friends were always welcome, and no doubt a handsome young man of twenty to twenty-five would be very impressed by Acton, as polite and deferential as a Chinese aristocrat, inviting him into his humble house.

In the end, he had lived in five rooms — his small study, the library, but only to pass through it to go to his study, the drawing room, the dining room, and his bedroom — and all the rest of the rooms were eternally closed.

Soon I will be in Lucca, in a flat Nikos and I bought for holidays, and here I find myself within yet another world among the many worlds I appear to live in.

Every year, for the past 1,168 years, a procession takes place in Lucca in honour of the Volto Santo, or Holy Face, a dark, wooden, Byzantine-like, life-sized figure of Christ which is supposed to have been carved by a disciple, Nicodemus, and which mysteriously reached the Ligurian shores in a boat pushed off from the coast of ancient Palestine, a long and circuitous way. Both the Pisans and the Lucchese claimed the Volto Santo, their dispute resolved when the statue was place in a cart with two white oxen on a road that diverged at one point toward Lucca and at another point toward Pisa, and the oxen took the road to Lucca. The Volto Santo became one of the most revered icons of the Middle Ages, and it is seriously revered, as everything in Lucca is. It is a conservative town, and when it celebrates the festival of the Volto Santo, called La Luminara, it does so with a certain calm, even grim, devotion. There is something even a little severe about the procession, with drums beating a slow, heavy march, and long periods when it progresses in total silence.

I was invited by a Lucchese woman to view the procession from the open windows of her palace. Along the old stone sill, held by rusted iron rings long ago inserted into the stone, was a row of flickering white votive candles in clear glasses. Across the square the palaces were all outlined, along window sills, around the architraves of doorways, along the lengths of façades, with flickering candles, so that the buildings appeared to disappear and Lucca, all other illumination turned off, became a transparent town made up entirely of candle flames. And when I leaned out the window, I saw the long line of the procession, the people in it carrying candles, enter a cathedral of light, the bell tower illuminated at each arched Gothic level with fire. The last people of the procession to enter the cathedral were dressed as they would have been dressed centuries ago, the men in doublets and the women in gowns with long, loose sleeves, their waists cinched in tightly.

The party I was invited to was held in an apartment with high, high-beamed ceilings and dull red-tile floors without rugs, and large paintings of mythological figures and tarnished mirrors in Venetian frames tilting out from the walls, where a *cameriere*, wearing a white, high-collared jacket, circulated among the guests, the women wearing pearl necklaces and the men somber ties, the *cameriere* offering glasses of red or white wine or orange juice. And at the end of the procession, the *cameriere* came in with a large steaming tureen of pasta. I was not only in a different world, I was in a different age.

I spoke with a woman who is the minister of culture of the town. She is, she said, worried about mass tourism, bus loads of tourists who wander the narrow, traffic-free, medieval streets in large groups. Lucca doesn't need tourism, she said; Lucca is a rich place. Smiling a little, I suggested shutting the town gates, those enormous, wooden, spike-studded doors, some quite rotted, which perhaps haven't been shut since they were opened for Napoleon.

I left the party about eleven o'clock to go into the cathedral, all the high pillars draped in red damask, and to see, in a separate little temple behind a grill, the Volto Santo, wearing a golden crown, a golden apron and golden shoes which are for the rest of the year preserved in the cathedral museum.

And then I wandered, alone, around Lucca. Off the main streets
– the principal one being the Fillungo, paved in endless semi-circles
of small paving stones – I found myself completely alone, though
the votive candles were still flickering along the outlines of the
buildings. I felt, alone, not only safe, but secreted away in the town,
and because secreted away in possession of the town. As I crossed a
narrow side-street, I saw, where it ended at the town walls, fireworks exploding on the walls, and I stood and watched them, then
walked on, and saw no one else, no one else at all, until I reached
the medieval building where Nikos and I have an apartment. But I
stood outside in the street for a while longer, amazed, I suppose, by
the sense of everyone in the town behind locked doors and closed
shutters, while their streets were still blazing with candles.

I heard, in the far distance, an odd sound. The sound became
louder and louder until I saw, coming toward me, a woman on a
bicycle. As she passed me, saying 'Buona sera,' I noticed the chain
of her bicycle was hitting the mud guard and making the noise, that
tiny noise echoing throughout the silent town. Then there was the
deep, deep silence again.

I went to have a look around La Pietra, invited by Alexander
Zielcke, a painter and photographer, and Acton's companion for
some thirty years. It was raining. Inside the gates of the grounds,
the taxi passed, on the right of the avenue up to the villa, an olive
grove with high, uncut grass. In the wild-looking olive grove was
a very well-maintained, small garden and in that garden well-
restored buildings identified by a sign as offices of OLIVETTI,
who had the buildings on a lease from the estate. Just as the taxi
left the olive grove a statue on a pedestal appeared, its forearm
broken off, a rusted iron rod sticking out from an elbow.

The taxi circled a great stone tub in the midst of clipped hedges
and stopped at large, nail-studded, double doors, shut. A woman,
in a pink and white striped smock and a blue and white striped
apron, was standing at a smaller door to the left. As I got out of the
taxi, she said that she was the cook, Vanna, and that all the other
servants had gone, and, also, that there was no one guarding the

villa. She spoke in a high voice, as if I were very far away, and she apologized that she couldn't show me in through the main entrance but must ask me to come in through this side entrance. This led into the chapel of the villa, grey and white, with tall candlesticks and two bottles of champagne on the altar. In the holy water font just to the side of the entrance were, I noted, some rags. The chapel looked dusty. When I asked if it had ever been used, Vanna said no, no, as if it had never occurred to her that it could have been used. It led into an anteroom with a telephone, and from this room I went into the main entrance hall of the villa.

The rotunda, built into what was originally the fifteenth-century central courtyard, had a fountain in the middle, a huge stone goblet with goldfish. A circular flight of stairs, with tapestries hanging on the curved walls, went up to the next floor.

The rotunda was where Harold Acton had been laid in state for three days.

Vanna took me beyond into the drawing room, il soggiorno, to show me the chair where il Barone always sat, a red, wing-back armchair among other armchairs and a red sofa. The upholstery of the chairs looked stained and threadbare.

From there, we went through a doorway at the side of a huge fireplace into the vaulted library, with medieval wooden poly-chrome statues of saints on top of the Renaissance shelves. Hanging over the long table in the center of the room from chains were three lights, the red, fringed shades shredded and decomposing. In a corner was a large Buddha.

The study, like the library, was vaulted and had Renaissance bookshelves, but as narrow as a passageway. The shelves were sagging under sets of books such as The World's Best Literature, The Encyclopaedia Britannica, La stirpe de' Medici di Cafaggiolo. Acton's desk was a big table, narrow like the room, on which were piles of papers that looked as if they had been there years and years, untouched, and in the midst of the papers a framed, black and white photograph of a thin, elegant woman which appeared to have been taken in the thirties.

I said to Vanna that must be Acton's mother.

Vanna sighed and said yes, a beautiful woman. He loved her very much.

On the desk was a silver pen holder which had in it, along with old pens and pencils and stamps and paperclips, chestnuts. Touching them, Vanna said il Barone thought they brought luck.

He was a Catholic, wasn't he? I asked.

Oh yes, Vanna said, il Barone was religious. He kept in the breast pocket of his jacket silver medals and crosses. No, he didn't go to church, but he believed. He received Extreme Unction and Communion before he died.

Vanna bit her lips, as if hesitant, then said that three days before il Barone died he called for her to come to his room. He was suffering so much. He asked her to put her hand on his back, and she did, and that helped him. He thanked her sincerely. Tears rose into Vanna's eyes. Il Barone was a very special person, she said, unique, a gentleman who even when he was in carpet slippers always wore a suit with a vest. She missed him very, very much. Would she stay on when the villa was taken over by the University? She looked around and more tears rose to her eyes, and wiping them away, said she didn't know, but she was very attached to the villa. 'Sono molto attaccata alla villa.'

At the rear of the study were closed double doors, and when I wondered what was behind them, Vanna opened them into what she thought was a sala d'attesa, a waiting room. On first view, the room, Venetian-like, with delicately painted walls and sconces with porcelain statuettes, gilded armchairs upholstered in yellow silk, a birdcage on a scagliola-topped table, appeared grand, but the more I looked the more I saw flaking, nicks, worn patches, a fine greyness over everything, and I thought no one had sat in one of the chairs for ninety years, which was since Acton's father, Arthur Acton, had bought the fifteenth-century villa and had it redone.

Vanna asked if I wanted anything to drink, and I said, yes please, a glass of mineral water. Because I wanted to see as much of the villa as I could, I followed her down a passage into a large, vaulted anteroom to the kitchen, with glass-fronted cupboards all round the walls filled with piles of plates and wine glasses, and silver salvers and silver platters with covers. On the walls over the cupboards were pock-marked frescos of landscapes in tromp l'oeil. Vanna took a glass from a cupboard and a silver salver from another and placed the glass on the tray, and I followed her into the kitchen proper where there were plastic bottles of mineral water on a table.

The kitchen was stark, with two large working tables in the middle, a stainless-steel sink, and a gas stove which Vanna said was getting too old to cook on, and was no longer good for the soufflés il Barone had liked so much.

She told me how every Monday the maggiordomo, the butler, came and told her he was in his armchair in the soggiorno ready to talk to her, and how il Barone would, gentilemente, tell her to sit by him, and they would go through the guest list of the week, arranging menus according to who was coming. When the Prince and Princess of Wales had stayed, they'd eaten her food, though they ate little.

Then, as if she couldn't not tell me and had been waiting for the moment, she told me, breathlessly, that she had seen il Barone, he had appeared to her, but, looking around to make sure we were alone, she said people would think her mad for saying this. 'Io sono molto sensibile,' she said. She sensed presences. She was sweating, and said there were presences around which were making her sweat. Then she began to weep more.

From another part of the villa, someone called, 'Vanna, Vanna,' and she, anxious, ran, I behind her, to the room with the telephone, where Alexander Zielcke, a large, pale, middle-aged German with grey, longish hair combed smoothly back and leaving his ears exposed, was waiting. In a slightly false voice, Vanna told him that she had been telling me how il Barone and she used to discuss the week's menu.

Zielcke, impatient with her, said, No, il Barone never was so concerned about the week's menu.

He was, Vanna insisted.

'No, no,' Zielcke said, turning away abruptly. Then he turned back and asked Vanna for coffee to be brought up to the office and she went back to the kitchen. Zielcke left me to wander alone, which I could not have done while Acton was alive.

I went up the circular stairs in the rotunda to the next floor. The shutters couldn't be opened because of the alarm system, so there was electric lighting in the corridors. I wandered down a long corridor, with double doors along it which I opened into dim, shuttered bedrooms, the bedclothes heaped up on the beds, and bathrooms with enormous tubs behind screens, and chaises longues and tables covered with objects.

I passed an internal window, and through it saw the pink-orange plaster falling away from a wall.

The master bedroom, called la camera della Baronessa, which had been the bedroom of Acton's mother and which had been used for royal visits by the Prince and Princess of Wales, by Princess Margaret, by the Queen Mother, had a large Renaissance bed, covered with a red silk counterpane, with gilded columns at its corners, and over the grand fireplace the most valuable painting in the villa, a Madonna and Child with Saint John the Baptist by Vasari, still in its original frame. The fringe hanging from the bottoms of the chairs was in places coming off, the gilt on the slightly tilting columns at the corners of the bed was worn, and the counterpane looked as if it had not been cleaned since the Renaissance.

From this bedroom I went into a bathroom, where a man in jeans and a tee-shirt was measuring a wall from a corner to the edge of the deep embrasure of a window. He was taking measurements of all the rooms. Beyond the bathroom was a low, very narrow room with a new toilet, perhaps put in especially for the royals.

When I came back along the corridor, I found Alexander Zielcke and the lawyer in charge of the will and the secretary in the office, all gathered about a sheaf of papers held by the lawyer. I nodded at them and continued down another corridor.

In a huge, dim room, many eighteenth-century chairs were

lined up along the walls. I was in the ballroom. From there, I opened double doors onto another room, so dark all I could see were points of dim light and shapes of furniture, and I didn't search for a light switch. I shut the doors and returned to the office.

Before I left, Zielcke said he would walk around the grounds with me. With an umbrella, we went into the walled-in garden to the side of the villa, where vegetables and flowers for the house were grown. There were many lemon trees in pots which would, during the winter, go into the immense limonaia, a vast building with a dirt floor and huge beams along one side of the garden. Then we wandered about the formal garden at the back of the villa.

Zielcke said he had been having some of the box hedges replanted. He couldn't have done this while Sir Harold, as Zielcke called Acton, was alive. Sir Harold, who didn't notice how the garden was going in places, would have been worried by someone replacing old, dying hedges with new ones. He had thought every-thing was in perfect order. The garden, designed in 1904 by Sir Harold's father after a Renaissance garden, was as old as Sir Harold himself. I noted, as we walked about the garden, that the statues were crumbling, as were the architectural follies. A stone bench in front of cypress trees was broken in two. The steps of pebbles imbedded in cement were covered with moss and the kerb stones cracked. Sections of hedge were missing, and sections so overgrown I could see through the dark green leaves to the grey twisted branches.

I am, I know, indulging somewhat in the decay of the villa, and, with the villa, the, to me, fantasy life lived there. Perhaps I am jealous, perhaps, and want it all to decay. I do realize, more than ever, just how much Harold Acton was a fantasy figure to me, and, yes, the fantasy does – no, did – hold me. Trying to be as sincere as I possibly can be, I also realize that the fantasy no longer does hold. Nikos is right to have derided me for my fantasy figures. The sense of possibility I had in knowing Acton – the possibility of entering a world that should have been the realization of a young man's most colorful vision of an artistic, a social, and, especially, a sexual world – seems to me exposed as having in fact little possibility in it, and, in fact, to be abandoned by the world for some other world that Nikos would approve of. The world of Harold Acton is in no way in my world to revive it in my memory, but I have the deep sense that it has little inner value in the memory of the outside world, which outside world Nikos has always been more aware of than I have.

If I were to tell Nikos this, he would simply smile, not quite believing me.

London

Of course, I think of writing novels and short stories, which require forms of art, as being superior to writing a diary.

Where else but in fiction can such moments occur as – ?

When, in Pride and Prejudice, Darcy lets go and admits to Elizabeth: 'I love you.'

When, at the end of Dostoyevsky's The Idiot, Prince Myshkin weeps over the body of the murderer Rogozhin, so his tears drip on the face of Rogozhin.

When, in Conrad's Heart of Darkness, we hear out of the darkness, 'Mr Kurtz, he dead.'

When, in Hardy's Jude the Obscure, we read the note, 'Done because we are too menny.'

When, in Waugh's Brideshead Revisited (and this is the only novel by Waugh that rises to the pitch), Lord Marchmain makes the sign of the cross before dying.

———

When I tell myself, everything is too much, I can't bear it, what, I ask myself further, is that everything that is too much and that I can't bear?

If too much, let go of everything, let go for –

What?

———

When I saw Nikos silently lower a book he had been reading –
Chekhov stories, and I knew in particular 'Ward Number 6'
– now in tears, this came to me: that Nikos feels he is a defeated
person.

In him the sense of the unbearable is not merely aesthetic, but
moral, spiritual, because it comes to him with such an acute awareness of all that is unbearable in the world.

This came to me: that I need him to give authority to an authentic moral and spiritual awareness of the world, he so much more a
witness than I.

Then this came to me: that as I do need him for the authenticity
of a feeling I have in me, the feeling has to be in me, has to be in
me and has to be crying out to him to make it relevant to a world
I hardly belong to, a world in whose history I have so little a part,
but a world that I feel is the world at its most authentic, which is
Nikos' world.

Does he know this about me, that I need this in him because it
is a need in me? A strange need. I think he does know, for, his book
lowered, he stares at me staring at him, and he smiles a little, and
what happens? – I feel roused in me an almost sexual desire to go
to him to be held by him.

About Chekhov: how can any reaction to his work be anything
but moral, spiritual?

———

As the birthdays of our neighbor Joseph Bromberg and of Frank
coincide, Nikos and I offered to give them a joint birthday party.
In the dining and sitting room, we arranged card tables covered
with white cloths, and bought folding chairs, enough places for
some fifteen or more people. Anita helped to serve the Kidonato
– lamb and quince – that Nikos had prepared. And there were
many bottles of wine. Most of the guests were friends of Frank and
Anita: Al and Anne Alvarez, Jonathan (writer and director of plays
and operas) and Rachel (medical doctor) Miller, Luigi (novelist)
and Katia Meneghello, and our mutual friends Richard and Mary

Day Wollheim, and Nikos' and my friend from Greece, Fani-Maria Tsigakou. And, Philip Roth being away from London, Claire Bloom on her own. The Brombergs supplied the dessert, a confection of ice-cream in a bowl made of ice.

Nikos presenting the ice-cream to Claire, Joseph looking on, and hidden behind Claire Ruth, a hand held out.

It is very strange to meet someone who is as famous as Claire Bloom, so that when I am with her I am with Charlie Chaplin in Lime Light, with Laurence Olivier in Richard III (which I saw when the film was shown on black and white television in the living room of my family home when in 1955 I was fifteen, an event of very high culture), with Richard Burton in The Spy Who Came in from the Cold. Claire's refined beauty appears to be one with the refinement of a culture she represents as an actress, and even when we are talking about, say, the weather, I hear in her voice the voice I have heard declaiming Shakespeare. In person she seems shy, and often pulls back her hair as if suddenly not sure of herself, and then a look of sadness comes to her eyes.

About Chekhov, Claire Bloom made this remarkable connection – when she was in Hollywood preparing for her part as The Brothers Kavamazov with Yul Brynner to play Vronsky, he suggested they have a Russian coach, Michael Chekhov, the great-nephew of Anton Chekhov.

———

Fani-Maria is staying with us. She is a curator at the Benaki Museum in Athens. Thames & Hudson published her book The Rediscovery of Greece, which expands on what Nikos has told me about Europeans and Europeanized Greeks wanting in A.D. 1830 to reclaim 500 B.C. Greece from the defeated Ottoman Empire.

Fani-Maria explained how the myth of ancient Greece has been such an influence in Greek history.

During the four hundred years of Ottoman Occupation and continuing after Greek independence from the Occupation, the myth of Hellenic Greece – that is, the myth of a unified Greece that in reality hardly ever existed in ancient history – was kept alive as a way of 'determining the ideological and cultural identity of an independent nation in the collective memory of Greeks.'

This myth has had some bad consequences.

'Hellas' became the rallying cry in the early nineteenth century for Greece to invade Turkey to win back the Empire of the Hellenes, but Greece lost, and the result was the Catastrophe.

'Hellas' also became the rallying cry of the colonel dictators, who used the age of Pericles as their dictating mythological vision of Greece.

That myth of ancient Greece in Greek education is still seen as a source of enlightenment dating from the ancient illustrious ancestors, but also resented because it is a myth. The Greek political Right emphasize that ancestry, which the Greek political Left keep challenging as nationalistic.

And yet, the myth is there, informing Greeks that they have a past that dates back to Plato and Aristotle, Solon and Pericles, Aeschylus, Sophocles, Euripides, Aristophanes, Phidias and Praxiteles, Ictinus and Callicrates, for the reality of the myth is that the greatest philosophers to define all the philosophy of the Western world remain Plato and Aristotle, the statesmen who defined Western democracy were Solon and Pericles, the greatest playwrights ever are Aeschylus, Sophocles, Euripides, Aristophanes, the greatest artists are Phidias and Praxiteles, the greatest architects are Ictinus and Callicrates, and all were Greek. There is a degree of indulgence for a Greek in – and here Fani-Maria stopped for a moment as if not sure she should use the word, but then she did – 'narcissistic' feelings for being poised between the myth and the reality of Greece's classical past, with an emphasis on the myth.

Well, what is the reality? There is no doubt that there exists one unbroken and living bequest from the classical past: the Greek language.

Fani-Maria said she becomes both furious and sad that not just foreigners but Greeks are unaware that, however altered grammatically and syntactically, modern Greek is in an unbroken line from ancient Greek, the vocabulary of which can be traced back to Homer.

I said I recalled from when Nikos and I, on the island of Paros, were walking along a field where farmers were working, and a woman raised her arm at us and called, '*Xairete*,' and Nikos told me that that is an ancient Greek expression of welcome.

'There, you hear?' Fani-Maria exclaimed.

When I asked what remains in Greece of the four hundred years of Ottoman Empire, which most Greeks I know do not quite recognize as a determining part of the reality of Greek history, she listened but she didn't respond.

As I want to get world events into this diary, I should put in that, after a referendum in Greece, the young King Constantine, heir to the Greek throne, lost, and now lives as ex-King with his family in London.

Stephen told me that his daughter Lizzie, who had been on holiday in Greece where, with friends, she more or less lived and slept on a beach, back in London was invited to an event where she knew the ex-King Constantine would be, and she brought along photographs of Greece to show him, he filled with nostalgia for a country he cannot return to.

Nikos said that the ex-King has enough money in Switzerland that he doesn't have to be nostalgic for Greece, which, given his non-Greek ancestry, was never his native country.

———

Philip telephoned to say he is back in London after the funeral and burial of his mother. He said he couldn't look at her body. He didn't want that meaningful image to obliterate all the images that matter.

During the two weeks he spent with his father he took notes about the funeral and burial. He is still taking notes.

I asked, 'What kind of people are we that we don't even stop taking notes about the funeral of a mother?'

'Good enough,' he answered.

'Are we?'

———

At an Italian restaurant with John Lehmann and his young nephew or cousin. John moves with great difficulty because of his hip. He is hard of hearing. His hands shake badly, so when he pours out wine the bottle shakes against the glass and wine spills over. His false teeth keep falling out; he smiles a tight, sinister smile to keep them in. So few people like John. Do I like John? Like or dislike, such unimportant opinions; I neither like nor dislike John, for there he is, and I am interested in him for what he is. His nephew or cousin and I did most of the talking while John smiled at us.

His nephew or cousin is an historian. I said, 'I know so little history, but would you consider me justified to think that historians have tried for too long, and with too limited a vision, to identify nations and national politics and sciences and arts, whereas, really, they should pay much more attention to international politics, to the international influences on the sciences and the arts? I think history should refer outwardly to relating and integrating the whole world in every historical event. Steven Runciman, I believe, does this.' He said, 'Yes, you're right, history should do what you say, as expansive a task as that would be. But I don't like the history of Steven Runciman so very much; his writing is dull.'

As I do, and I'm ashamed that I do, I assumed to know better by knowing Steven Runciman, and I said, 'I once asked Steven if his style of writing was influenced by any other writer, and he answered, immediately, yes, Defoe.'

This made John's relative jut out his chin.

———

When I mentioned to Caro Hobhouse that Sybille Bedford was to me a mythological figure, a writer whose work I think of as itself having a mythological aura about it, especially The Legacy, Caro said, 'But Sybille Bedford is not at all a mythological figure,' and she arranged a dinner party for me to meet her. I arrived early, and Caro asked me to stir a special sauce she was cooking and not stop stirring until she told me to, and I felt at ease, as I felt at ease with Sybille Bedford, the talk about the table mostly about haute cuisine. Sybille Bedford appeared to me a dry but sharp woman, her face pale and her long thin hair pulled back severely except for strands. I knew that she knew Bruce Chatwin, and she said how much she did admire his writing and took it seriously, if – and here she smiled a tight smile – she found him in himself perhaps a little too glamorous to be taken with total seriousness, and, as circumlocutious as this was, I sensed it was a dry, sharp judgment. I felt I should be wary of her for her judgments on any form of pretension, but I wanted her to like me. I offered to drive her home, which she accepted, and outside where she lived we sat together in the car for a little while and she thanked me for admiring her work, which, however, was earning her so little she was not sure what she would do, and I felt she was making herself vulnerable to me, and, by making herself vulnerable to me, I thought that she must like me. I asked if I could see her again, and she said it would be a pleasure.

A week or so later I invited her to a restaurant not far from her in Kensington Church Street, collected her, and hoped the restaurant, though simple, would be to her liking, which it was as she asked for a card and even the number of the table we sat at so that she would be able to reserve it. I asked her to choose the wine, which she did carefully, clearly aware that I was being extravagant by inviting her. She said sharing a meal is a ceremony, and I did imagine we were engaged together in a ceremony of getting to know each other.

She talked about Brian Howard, whom she knew: a failed poet, an exquisite man who, having found his wallet and all his clothes stolen from him in a male brothel in Paris, borrowed an apron from a maid and went out into the street to hire a taxi to take him to his hotel; he was very courageous during World War II, acting in the resistance to save people's lives at the risk of his own life, a soldier at the landing of Dunkirk, an agent for MI5.

Now a connection occurs from outside: Keith Walker rang the day after he came to a supper party at our flat to say that he had had an adventure back at his flat during the night: wanting to pee, he, still drunk and stark naked, went out of his flat onto the landing looking for the loo, and the door shut behind him; he waited until dawn and rang the bell of his neighbour to ask for a blanket, and, wrapped in the blanket, he went out into the street to hail a taxi to bring him to his office at University College where he had extra keys to his flat and money.

Keith thinks that the recently discovered long poem by Byron about his love affair with a boy in Athens is genuine.

Back to Brian Howard, with another connection to the side: Stephen told me that Howard once complained to Auden that he, Auden, didn't have enough imagery in his poetry, so Auden wrote 'The Fall of Rome' (dedicated to Cyril Connolly, but I'm sure there is a poem by Auden dedicated to Howard), which has the most haunting last image of any imagery I know of:

> Herds of reindeer move across
> Miles and miles of golden moss,
> Silently and very vast.

Stephen – who, I think, is not within the world of Harold Acton, nor Christopher Isherwood nor W. H. Auden – told me that Blanche, of Brideshead Revisited, is partly based on Brian Howard, Stephen referring to a world that he seems to look at from a distance.

I know that whenever I mention Steven Runciman, Stephen frowns with disapproval.

Yet another aside: when referring to W. H. Auden to Nikos and me, Stephen never calls him Wystan, even when in his presence, but always as 'Auden,' as if Stephen is shy of presuming on familiarity with Auden.

My mind is always making connections, now so many that I do begin to think that they refer to one another more than they refer to me, so that I have begun to assume that everyone I meet knows everyone else, and all of them with their own interconnections too complicated for me to sort out.

Sybille Bedford had heard of Nikos, and asked about him – and how long had we been together, where did we live, did we have pets? Then, leaning towards me over the table, she said, 'You must always hope to outlive Nikos to save him the pain of grief,' and for a moment we looked steadily into each other's eyes. She did not talk of herself, and I knew I shouldn't ask her. When she stood to leave, she put her hands into the pockets of her trousers with something of a masculine gesture, and she appeared about to fall over but she righted herself and walked to the restaurant door, as if leaving alone.

———

Something I've been wanting to write about – I rang Claire to invite her and Philip to dinner, but they couldn't make it. I emphasized how much I want to see them, and sent her love, etc. After I hung up, Nikos admonished me, 'You were totally false. Utterly insincere.' I groaned. 'I know, I know,' I said. 'I thought you had outgrown your falseness, your insincerity. Your niceness towards Claire was completely unconvincing. I really thought you had reached a point in your development where you were no longer like that.' I groaned more. 'What shall I do?' I asked. He said, 'Be aware. The fact is, you're intimidated by Claire and Philip, that's why you are the way you are with them. I thought you were no longer intimidated by people you think grander than you are. I thought you'd even become bold.' 'You're right,' I said, 'I am intimidated by them. I've ceased to be intimidated by most people. But I am by them.' 'Why?' he asked. And I thought: He isn't intimidated, so can't understand being intimidated by people I believe to be on a level of having something I do not have.

Later, this occurred to me: that, yes, I have ceased to be intimidated by certain people because I do not want anything from them, whereas I remain intimidated by people from whom I want something they have, which, in the case of Claire and Philip, is their fame. This is difficult to admit.

———

When Nikos came home from work, he, cold, got into a hot bath and while he soaked I sat on the edge of the bathtub and we talked. I left him to go down to the kitchen to prepare hors d'oeuvres

– mussels and bits of lobster and spring onions and thin slices of toast – and drinks, for when he came down, and we talked more. For supper we had a gray mullet baked with dill and lemon, and we talked more. Nikos said, 'How lucky we are to have what we have,' and then he added, 'Spit three times because we may lose it all,' and I said, 'We won't lose it.'

———

A party at Claire and Philip's house in Fulham. At 10:30, I said to Philip, 'I must get home and write in my diary for an hour. I don't want to experience any more today, I've got all I can manage to get in. So no more stories from you.' He said, 'I'll write my stories down for you and you can simply paste them in.' Nikos and I came home and, very tired from seeing so many people, went to bed. I had had no intention of writing in my diary, and I wonder if I'm at the point of giving it up, as I so often want to do.

———

Stephen rang to say that he'd woken that morning at three o'clock and couldn't go back to sleep. I asked him why. 'I have so much work,' he said. He is working on publishing his journal, on a new Collected Poems, on his translation of the Oedipus plays. Stephen is the least self-indulgent person I know towards critical reception of his work – that is, outwardly – and he expects others to be the same. He was annoyed with me for being upset about the bad press I had for Difficult Women. I feel he is now upset by his bad press which has continued since the publication of his last book of poetry, The Generous Days, but he would never admit this. As Auden used to say, 'Mother wouldn't allow it,' I think Stephen says to himself, 'Wystan wouldn't allow it.' I wonder if the reason why he can't sleep is that he is in fact worried what the reaction will be to his journal, his Collected Poems, his translation – all of which he must feel his final work.

I've sensed in the past his hidden upset as a tremendous inability to concentrate on what I'd been saying to him, as if he couldn't help thinking of something he at the same time told himself he must not think about. He frowns. Perhaps because he is such a big person, all of this seems to happen on a massive scale. Then, suddenly, he does rise above his upset, and I tell him something that makes him giggle.

Because Nikos was too tired and needed to be alone for a while – he worries about losing his soul by socializing – I went alone to Loudoun Road for dinner with Stephen and Natasha and Lizzie, en famille. It was a deeply pleasant evening. 'Cozy,' Natasha called it. I left feeling I love them, their lives, their house, the objects in their house –

The next day Natasha was off to the South of France, to Saint Jérôme, to pick olives. Stephen rang. Often, speaking to one or the other of us, he'll say, if me, 'I'd like to ask David –' and if to Nikos, 'Would you and Nikos like to –' as though he displaces one of us for the other. He didn't have anything to do that evening, and wanted to invite Nikos and me to dine at the Savile Club with him. I told him to come have supper with us at home. Julia Hodgkin coming.

Nikos and I prepared risotto, mussels, salad and cheese, tangerines, marrons glacés and coffee, and of course wine. Stephen and Julia kept saying, 'A feast!'

Stephen said, 'Wystan always thought that if he got a bad review it was because the reviewer wanted to go to bed with him. He never cared about reviews. Now, what do we think about them?'

Quietly, Julia said, 'We don't think about them.'

Stephen said, 'Yes, quite,' and he sat back.

Julia then said, 'Of course I'm not the one to say, as I don't get reviewed.'

I wondered if Stephen was referring to the mixed reviews his latest volume of poems has had, The Generous Days.

He had given copies to Nikos and me, each one of us, a deluxe edition. In the one he gave Nikos he inscribed, 'see page 9,' on which page is his poem to Nikos, now a 'Fifteen Line Sonnet in Four Parts.' In the copy he gave me he inscribed, 'see page 16,' and there I found this poem:

PRESENT ABSENCE

You slept so quiet at your end of the room, you seemed
A memory, your absence.
I worked well, rising early, while you dreamed.
I thought your going would only make this difference –
A memory, your presence.
But now I am alone I know a silence
That howls. Here solitude begins.

This poem refers to that time when Stephen and I were at Saint
Jérôme, supposedly working in the garden planting trees but tour-
ing about with Francis and George. Stephen and I shared a large
room, he sleeping at one end and I at the other, I sleeping deeply
and, yes, dreaming. When I read the poem, I think: does he love
me so? Does he love Nikos so? In whatever way, he loves us, I feel,
as a couple, even more than he loves us individually, and his love is
a world about our world.

I also feel that London loves us as a couple more than we are
loved individually, and I owe London that love.

———

How often lines from Stephen's poems come to me, as:

My love and my pity shall not cease . . .

Or:

Was so much expenditure justified
On the death of one so young and so silly
Lying under the olive trees, O world, O death?

And I try to see these thoughts and feelings as having come from
Stephen when I see him. They move me as if distanced from him,
and often enough lines move me more than entire poems (which
happens to almost all poems I read), but do I read them as having

been written by Stephen, he at our dining-room table for a supper of cottage pie, which he likes? And yet, he wrote the lines, and I am aware that somewhere in his spirited talk is a deeper spirit, that of love, of pity, of grief, the deeper spirit which in love, in pity, in grief calls out, O world, O death!

And how beautiful and mysterious the lines:

> The outward figure of delight
> Creates your image that's no image
> Dark in my dark language.

———

Philip belongs to a club in Pall Mall, the Royal Automobile Club, where we from time to time have lunch, he always ordering chicken sandwiches without mayonnaise, as he is very conscious of his diet for reasons of health. His health is a big preoccupation. About the club, he of course joked about being a Jew who finagled to get in. The last time we met, he told me he has decided to move back to New York. Claire will go with him. He needs the vulgarity of New York against the politeness of London, the hypocritical politeness. He needs someone in a traffic jam to roll down his window and shout at him, 'Asshole,' which would make him relax and with a deep sigh of relief feel he was back at home.

He told me he had taught Claire to use the word FUCK, and had had printed as the headlines of a fake newspaper something like SHE HAS USED THE WORD! and presented it to Claire, who was amused and touched.

———

Of course, once again, I ask myself why I keep a diary, why I have kept it for years, day after day after day, trying to include everything that I can possibly include. Is it, as Nikos tells me, because I am so possessive that I must get everything in? The only other way, I think, is to leave everything out, and not account for anything.

I think that in the end, whatever the end may be, my diary will have nothing at all to do with me, but on its own bulge with such a vast roundness that it will go on turning of itself, and I will no longer command a diary but the diary will command me. My diary is in itself more possessive than I am, possessed by the concept of everything, and impelled by the possession. I have tried, over and over, to stop writing my diary, but my diary won't allow me to stop. My diary is a vast jealous One who will have everything, and won't listen to me insisting that that can't be, that my diary can have this or that or the other, but cannot have everything, which is impossible; no, the One will. This is a One beyond believing in One or not, a One with the One's own all-commanding will to have everything in one great round world.

─────────

I've lived long enough in London to have memories of my life here – as when Nikos and I were with Francis in the Colony Club, where the barman – not Ian, but a young man with tight black curly hair who was very very good looking – flirted with Nikos, who responded with a shy smile. I had never seen Nikos respond to someone flirting with him, nor would I have thought he would have responded by smiling a shy smile, because I don't think of Nikos as shy. My reaction was to wonder: why wasn't the barman flirting with me?

─────────

Evening after evening alone together at home, Nikos and I. We are very close – closer, I think, than ever before. He has come round to loving our flat here at 38 Montagu Square, as I do: our home.

We listen to music, Nikos and I, always his choosing, as he has much more understanding of music than I do, and I defer. My ear concentrates on the moment, on, say, a passage, while

Nikos hears the development of a passage into a whole, as in a fugue.

We were sitting side by side on the sofa, listening to Artur Schnabel play a Beethoven sonata, and it occurred to me to wonder again:

What is that too much when, listening to music, you feel that the music is too much, is beyond all my feeling and thinking too, and you tell yourself, I can't bear this?

Frowning as he listened, Nikos' eyes were closed.

Will whoever reads this indulge me for claiming that this is what I feel, this is what I think, when I look at Nikos and tell myself I can't bear my love for him?

He seems to me to be content.

As I write this, I hear him come in downstairs and call me –

———

Some time after Francis Bacon died, Nikos, looking through the catalogue of a posthumous exhibition, came upon a photograph and stopped and, calling me over to the desk, pointed to it and said, 'That's you!' Among the mess of rubbish left on the floor of his studio, piece by piece catalogued and sent to a reproduction of Francis' studio in a museum in Dublin, was this:

I recognized the photographs from when, in the train station at Avignon, Francis, George, Stephen and I had taken photographs of ourselves in an automatic photographing box. From the number Francis had taken away with him, he later pasted three strips on the back of an old cover of a book. In the caption under the reproduction in the catalogue I was not identified. I rang Miss Beston at Marlborough Gallery, who took care of Francis – if he wanted £10,000 in cash, she had it sent to him – and I identified myself, and she sent me the above. My wonder is: why did Francis paste me alongside himself and George?

———

Both Nikos (he at a weekend conference in the country) and Natasha (she in the South of France) away, Stephen invited me to dinner with Julian Trevelyan and his wife Mary Fedden. I did not know his paintings, but looked them up, and wondered if Surrealism was ever really possible in Britain, as Surrealism requires deep shadows and I have no sense of these deep shadows in the British, considered by the British as negatively unBritish as Logical Positivism is British. It seems to me axiomatic that for a Brit, if it can't be articulated, it is of no interest. Yet there is a primitive charm to his work. As there is to hers, based on, say, the simplicity of fruit and flowers.

Julian talked of having been the head of the Etching Department at the Royal College of Art, where one of his students was David Hockney, and he praised David's line.

Stephen had prepared, or bought, kipper pâté, then a risotto which I helped him with. His shirt tails were out and he was in his stocking feet.

During supper, he said, 'I sometimes think that the most important relationships are invisible relationships. Matthew is my son, but, really, I think of him as a brother, and our being brothers is an invisible relationship that is stronger than the visible. I think I have invisible relationships with David and Nikos in which they are my sons. All these relationships are so much more real than the visible.'

I was very moved by this, and, walking home, I thought of all my invisible relationships, invisible even to me but important to me, and I thought: they are your reason for being alive and loving life, those invisible relationships all around you right now, as you walk home.

I slept alone.

I'm reminded of the fragment from Sappho that Nikos used in 'Pure Reason': ἐγω δε μόνα κατεύδω . . . I sleep alone.

———

I often think of how I almost didn't meet Nikos. I was given his name and telephone number by a mutual friend in New York and I rang him on my arrival in London and he invited me to tea on a

Sunday afternoon, but when I at four o'clock rang his doorbell at 6 Wyndham Place he didn't answer. I thought he had meant five o'clock, so wandered about Hyde Park for an hour, among people lounging on the grass in the sunlight, then returned and rang his doorbell, and he answered, and I, oh yes, went into a trance that has lasted all these years since. He told me later that he, standing at the window of his flat, had seen me ring a bell but his bell inside hadn't rung. When he saw me leave he went out to test his bell and found it didn't work. He unscrewed it, attached some wires that had become detached, and thought, that was that, assuming I would not return, as he would not have returned if someone who had invited him wasn't there to welcome him. If he had not lived on the ground floor and had not been standing at the window to see me, and if he had not wondered if I was the one he had expected and, after my leaving, had not gone out to check his bell and repaired it, and if I had not returned, I would not have met him. But I did return.

———

Here are some photographs taken at a book launch given by Thames & Hudson, photographs I found in a drawer that bring back memories of the world Nikos and I have lived in:. Sonia and me, behind us Frank Auerbach:

Nikos:

The back of Big Suzi, on either side Francis Bacon and Stephen Spender:

Robert Medley and John Russell and Frank Auerbach, Francis in the left-hand corner:

Freda Berkeley and Lucian Freud in the distance (and next to him, I think, the head of Marlborough Gallery, Harry Fischer) and the eye surgeon Patrick Trevor-Roper:

And so we have lived long enough in London to look back at events fixed in photographs.

———

How little I account for in my diary, how very very little.

Some Thirty Years Later

I remain an American citizen, and I am also, officially, a British citizen, with my United Kingdom passport in which I am inscribed as a citizen, an anomaly, certainly, as the United Kingdom is not a republic.

So many of my early fantasies about living in England did come true. As writer in residence at King's College, Cambridge, I did sit at High Table wearing an academy gown. I sat across from the Lord Kahn who, I was told, had given to Maynard Keynes all his ideas about economics. I had pre-prandial sherry in the combination room with the Bloomsbury paintings hanging on red walls, and I went to the College Feasts when all the silver was brought out from the vault. I had drinks in the rooms of Dadie Rylands, there where, on a window seat, Virginia Woolf had thought of writing A Room of One's Own, Dadie's rooms decorated by Dora Carrington, and on the wall a portrait of Lytton Strachey. In a cupboard I found the pictures that had hung in E. M. Forster's set, the one I most remembered of a boy leading a horse by Picasso. I went every evening to Evensong, especially during Lent when the chapel was almost empty but for the dean, the lay dean, the choir and the choirmaster, the boys singing plainchant and the flames of the candles in their glass chimneys shaking in the cold drafts.

But so much of the London I knew in the first formative years of my life here has gone.

W. H. Auden is dead, Sonia Orwell is dead, Mary McCarthy is dead, Philippe and Pauline de Rothschild are dead, Francis Bacon is dead, Stephen Spender is dead, Natasha Spender is dead, John Lehmann is dead, Adrian Stokes is dead, Patrick Procktor is dead, Johnny Craxton is dead, Lucian Freud is dead, James Joll is dead, Frank Kermode is dead, Richard Wollheim is dead, Catharine Carver is dead, Patrick Kinross is dead, Christopher Glenconner is dead, Tony Tanner is dead, Anne Wollheim is dead, Sylvia Guirey is dead, David Sylvester is dead, Joe McCrindle is dead, Eva Neurath is dead, Robert Medley is dead, Anne Graham-Bell is dead, Keith Walker is dead, Bruce Chatwin is dead, Vera Russell is dead, Öçi Ullmann is dead, John Fleming is dead, Ben Nicolson is dead, John Russell is dead, Nikos Georgiadis is dead, A. J. and Dee Ayer are dead, R. B. Kitaj and Sandra are dead, John Edwards is dead, Barry and Sue Flanagan are dead, Francis King is dead, Olivia Manning is dead, Max Gordon is dead, Sybille Bedford is dead, Mario Dubsky is dead, Joseph and Ruth Bromberg are dead, Sebbie Walker is dead, John Golding is dead, Angelica Garnett is dead, Valerie Eliot is dead –

And, oh, my great love Nikos is dead.

Julia Hodgkin, our pal when Nikos was alive, the primary witness to our ups and downs and always reminding us of the ups, came to his burial in Athens and she held me as I sobbed in her arms.

I went with her to visit the cathedral at Durham, which I had for years wanted to do with Nikos, and which Julia proposed we do shortly after his death.

When we entered the great Norman cathedral, I had the vast sense, a sense held down by the grand pillars, of vast associations that I would not have felt had I not been British, a sense that I was now within my history. That the history of the cathedral is Norman, a history imposed on Anglo-Saxon history, made me aware of layers of history, layers and layers, and all together British history.

And, too, I had the more personal sense that I have my own British history. I came to London from New York in 1966 with a sense of total failure – failure in my vocation as a writer and failure in relationships. In London with Nikos I began a positive life, and to have lived for forty years in a relationship sustained by love, and, too, to have achieved some realization of a vision as a writer, can only be to have grown from the immaturity of previous years into years of maturity in London. Yes, that's it: I grew up in London, the most important years of my life those early years in that world – early years that developed into later and later years, all those forty years during which Nikos' and my inward world extended into an outer world. Nikos and I had – and I still have – our deep London past, and by extension beyond London into Wiltshire and Devon and Yorkshire and Cambridgeshire and Oxfordshire and Somerset and Cornwall and Cumbria and Wales and Scotland our British past, our past of friends and events, of worlds within worlds which I felt revolving around me in the cathedral.

Julia and I stayed in the cathedral for a long while, the sunlight through the high windows slowly fading. The hour for Evensong was approaching, and as if in inverse order to the central service of the cathedral tourists left rather than gathered. Julia and I sat at the very front row of chairs to watch the procession, the verger leading, carrying a great silver mace over a shoulder, followed by other members of the clergy and the choir into the choir stalls. A member took hold of the thick, multi-coloured pull attached to a rope that, beyond view, was attached to the bells, and the sound of the bells was so distant the resonance was all we heard. And the choir sang.

At the same time, in all the cathedral towns of the realm, choirs were singing, as they have for centuries.

Whatever 'British' means to me, at that moment the meaning was filled out, rounded out, with love.

Acknowledgements

Bloomsbury has opened up a world to me, and for that I thank Alexandra Pringle, Michael Fishwick, Anna Simpson, Phillip Beresford, Oliver Holden-Rea, David Mann, Paul Nash, Tess Viljoen and Ellen Williams; Nancy Miller and Sara Mercurio at Bloomsbury in New York; and Peter James, Sarah-Jane Forder and Geraldine Beare.

Index

INTRODUCTION

I have always felt that a poet participates in the management of the estate of poetry, of that in his own language and also that of world poetry. Thinking about that estate, such as it is at the present moment, I decided I could contribute to its possessions provided, however, that instead of theory, I brought to it something of practice.

Poetry in this century is alive, and I value many poets, some of whom I have translated into Polish, beginning with T. S. Eliot's *Waste Land* and *Burnt Norton*. Yet no poem by T. S. Eliot is included in this book, and this fact elucidates my purpose. I rejected in advance the idea of doing justice to the canon of today's American and World poetry. Many poems that I like or admire are not in this anthology because they do not correspond to my criteria of size and accessibility to the reader. I leave to others the exploration of the whole territory of poetry in its richness and variety. I, instead, carve from it a province of my own.

For many decades I have been an observer of and a participant in revolts, movements, schools, whatever their names, in the literature of the twentieth century. Here, I try to forget about those trends. My proposition consists in presenting poems, whether contemporary or a thousand years old, that are, with few exceptions, short, clear, readable and, to use a compromised term, realist, that is, loyal toward reality and attempting to describe it as concisely as possible. Thus they undermine the widely held opinion that poetry is a misty domain eluding understanding. I act like an art collector who, to spite the devotees of abstract art, arranges an exhibition of figurative painting, putting together canvases from various epochs to prove, since those from the past and from the

present meet in an unexpected way, that certain lines of development, different from those now universally accepted, can be traced.

My intention is not so much to defend poetry in general, but, rather, to remind readers that for some very good reasons it may be of importance today. These reasons have to do with our troubles in the present phase of our civilization.

It has happened that we have been afflicted with a basic *deprivation*, to such an extent that we seem to be missing some vital organs, even as we try to survive somehow. Theology, science, philosophy, though they attempt to provide cures, are not very effective "In that dark world where gods have lost their way" (Roethke). They are able at best to confirm that our affliction is not invented. I have written elsewhere of this deprivation as one of the consequences brought about by science and technology that pollutes not only the natural environment but also the human imagination. The world deprived of clear-cut outlines, of the up and the down, of good and evil, succumbs to a peculiar nihilization, that is, it loses its colors, so that grayness covers not only things of this earth and of space, but also the very flow of time, its minutes, days, and years. Abstract considerations will be of little help, even if they are intended to bring relief. Poetry is quite different. By its very nature it says: All those theories are untrue. Since poetry deals with the singular, not the general, it cannot— if it is good poetry—look at things of this earth other than as colorful, variegated, and exciting, and so, it cannot reduce life, with all its pain, horror, suffering, and ecstasy, to a unified tonality of boredom or complaint. By necessity poetry is therefore on the side of being and against nothingness.

The place where I gathered my hoard is not without significance. To some degree it explains the contents. Berkeley has, probably, the best bookstores in America, and also good libraries, including the libraries of theological schools of various denominations. Its university constantly reminds one that California faces the Pacific, something to which the number of students from Chinese, Japanese, or Vietnamese families testifies. To this should be

added the role of Buddhism in the somewhat too syncretic mosaic of religions. Besides, Berkeley possesses a quite high density of poets per square mile. As a consequence of all this, its bookstores afford a good opportunity to browse in poetry. I have found there also many translations of Asian poets, who have sympathetic readers here. Those volumes distinguish themselves favorably upon the background of poetry written in our epoch. Old Chinese and Japanese poetry has exerted an influence upon American poetry since the beginning of this century, and became a field of competition for ambitious translators, among whom the best known are an Englishman, Sir Arthur Waley, and the California poet Kenneth Rexroth.

What do we, shaped by a civilization so different, find in those masters, what attracts us to them in particular? Undoubtedly, what accounts for much is the very discovery that we can understand them, that through their lips eternal man speaks, that love, transience, death were the same then as now. Yet what is also valuable for us in them is the reminder that man may relate to the world not just through confrontation. Perhaps Taoism and Buddhism, with their contemplative leanings, enabled poets to look at a thing and identify with it, strengthening in that way its being. The very reminder of it directs our attention toward similar attitudes within our civilization—and they are not rare, either in poetry or in painting.

Paul Cézanne is considered a forerunner of twentieth-century painting. It is probable, though, that he, since he was inclined to outbursts of anger, would horribly abuse his successors for their betrayal of nature, his venerated mistress. He invoked Boileau and recited: *Rien n'est beau que le vrai, le vrai seul est aimable* (Beauty is only in the true, only the true is lovable). "My method, my code," he declared, "is realism." And against disintegration of the object into fragments in consequence of the discoveries of science, he would probably allow me to quote his opinion: "After all, am I not man? Whatever I do, I have the notion that this tree is a tree, this rock a rock, this dog a dog." Or: "Nature is not on the surface, it is inside. Colors, on the surface, show that inside. They show the

roots of the world." And again this: "Right now a moment of time is fleeting by. Capture its reality in paint! To do that we must put all else out of our minds. We must become that moment, make ourselves a sensitive recording plate . . . give the image of what we actually see, forgetting everything that has been before our time" (in Joachim Gasquet, *Cézanne*). If readers find in my book poems fulfilling Cézanne's advice, I will be pleased. What surprises me in his pronouncement is the stress laid on the moment—by a painter. Time thus appears to be composed of moments—things, or things-moments. And the artist in his work has to capture and to preserve one moment, which becomes, indeed, eternal. In that way time is valorized; its every small part deserves an alert noting down of its shape and color.

In my essays on the beginning of the nineteenth century I stand for "classicism" against "romanticism." And this authorizes me to quote the praise of objective art pronounced then by Goethe in his conversations with Ackerman: "We are bid to study the ancients; yet what does that avail us, if it does not teach us to study the real world, and reproduce that?—for there was the source of the power of the ancients." "I will now tell you something, of which I think you will find frequent confirmation in your experience. When eras are on the decline, all tendencies are subjective; but, on the other hand, when matters are ripening for a new epoch, all tendencies are objective. Our present time is retrograde, therefore subjective; we see this now more clearly in poetry than in painting, and other ways. Each manly effort, on the contrary, turns its force from the inward to the outward world. In important eras, those who have striven and acted most manfully were all objective in their nature" (translated by Margaret Fuller, 1852). It is difficult to dismiss lightly that affirmation, especially if one thinks—as I do—that the end of the "objective" order in music occurred precisely at the time of Goethe.

Another name I may invoke is Schopenhauer. How could I not acknowledge his influence if I looked to him (in this I was not alone) for praise of art as a remedy against the cruelty of life? We are today skeptical of "systems," but his vision of the universe as

Will was born in the mind of a man particularly sensitive to pain and suffering as the universal law. The famous pessimism of Schopenhauer comes from a compassionate observation of live beings crushed and crushing each other because of the Will seated in them; in other words, "the instinct of self-preservation," "the struggle for life," and so on. Schopenhauer is our contemporary, for he was the first to draw conclusions from the biological sciences (a Darwinist before Darwin). At the same time he was the first European philosopher open to the religions of India, and his theory of art is somewhat similar to the saving message of Prince Siddhartha called Buddha, who offered to humans liberation from suffering by stepping beyond the infernal circle of fears and desires. Artists, according to Schopenhauer, are committed to a completely "unpractical" activity. In order to attain beauty they rid themselves for a moment of those urges to which as human beings they are all subject. Art liberates and purifies, and its tokens are those short moments when we look at a beautiful landscape forgetting about ourselves, when everything that concerns us disappears, is dissolved, and it does not matter whether the eye that looks is that of a beggar or a king.

Among works of painting, Schopenhauer assigned the highest place to Dutch *still life*: "Inward disposition, the predominance of knowing over willing, can produce this state under any circumstances. This is shown by those admirable Dutch artists who directed this purely objective perception to the most insignificant objects, and established a lasting monument of their objectivity and spiritual peace in their pictures of *still life*, which the aesthetic beholder does not look on without emotion; for they present to him the peaceful, still frame of mind of the artists, free from will, which was needed to contemplate such insignificant things so objectively, to observe them so attentively, and to repeat this perception so intelligently."

The secret of all art, also of poetry, is, thus, distance. Thanks to distance the past preserved in our memory is purified and embellished. When what we remember was occurring, reality was considerably less enticing, for we were tossed, as usual, by anxieties,

desires, and apprehensions that colored everything, people, institutions, landscapes. Remembering, we move to that land of past time, yet now without our former passions: we do not strive for anything, we are not afraid of anything, we become an eye which perceives and finds details that had escaped our attention.

I do not pretend, though, that in selecting poems for this book I constantly kept in mind Schopenhauer's principles, because many texts included depart from those principles.

The word "objective" repeated in the quotations from both Goethe and Schopenhauer is, I suspect, used for lack of a better term, though we understand, more or less, what those authors wanted to say. In the nineteen-twenties a group of "objectivists" was active in New York, with a program advocating attention to objects that surround us (note the famous "Red Wheelbarrow" of William Carlos Williams), but this proves only how various can be the uses of the word "object." Though some poems of "objectivists" are included in my selection, I do not have any intention of subsuming the whole under any all-embracing category, of objective, antisubjective poetry, or something of the kind. Yet, since I am obviously interested in the visible world, again and again unveiling itself and offering itself to the eye, I would have nothing against calling my anthology a book of enchantments.

Epiphany

Epiphany is an unveiling of reality. What in Greek was called *epiphaneia* meant the appearance, the arrival, of a divinity among mortals or its recognition under a familiar shape of man or woman. Epiphany thus interrupts the everyday flow of time and enters as one privileged moment when we intuitively grasp a deeper, more essential reality hidden in things or persons. A poem-epiphany tells about one moment-event and this imposes a certain form.

A polytheistic antiquity saw epiphanies at every step, for streams and woods were inhabited by dryads and nymphs, while the commanding gods looked and behaved like humans, were endowed with speech, could, though with difficulty, be distinguished from mortals, and often walked the earth. Not rarely, they would visit households and were recognized by hosts. The Book of Genesis tells about a visit paid by God to Abraham, in the guise of three travellers. Later on, the epiphany as appearance, the arrival of Christ, occupies an important place in the New Testament.

D. H. Lawrence in his "Maximus" returns to the polytheistic world, and the poem is so effective that we feel a shock of recognition, as if we ourselves were visited by the god Hermes. Maximus is the name of a philosopher who was a teacher of the emperor Julian, called the Apostate because he tried to restore paganism.

Epiphany may also mean a privileged moment in our life among the things of this world, in which they suddenly reveal something we have not noticed until now; and that something is like an intimation of their mysterious, hidden side. In a way, poetry is an attempt to break through the density of reality into a zone where the simplest things are again as fresh as if they were being seen by a child.

This anthology is full of epiphanies. I decided to place some of them in a separate first chapter to highlight this aspect of poetry. These particular poems are a distillation of my major theme.

MAXIMUS

God is older than the sun and moon
and the eye cannot behold him
nor voice describe him.

But a naked man, a stranger, leaned on the gate
with his cloak over his arm, waiting to be asked in.
So I called him: Come in, if you will!—
He came in slowly, and sat down by the hearth.
I said to him: And what is your name?—
He looked at me without answer, but such a loveliness
entered me, I smiled to myself, saying: He is God!
So he said: *Hermes!*

God is older than the sun and moon
and the eye cannot behold him
nor the voice describe him:
and still, this is the God Hermes, sitting by my hearth.

KIKAKU
1661—1707

In Japanese haiku there are often flashes, or glimpses, and things appear like lightning, or as if in the light of a flare: epiphanies of a landscape.

Above the boat,
bellies
of wild geese.

Translated from the Japanese by Lucien Stryk and Takashi Ikemoto

ISSA
1763—1827

From the bough
floating down river,
insect song.

Translated from the Japanese by Lucien Stryk and Takashi Ikemoto

JEAN FOLLAIN

1903—1971

It seems nothing peculiar happens when somebody walks on a road and kicks an empty can. But here, in French poet Jean Follain, this movement, like an immobilized frame of a film, suddenly opens into the cold of the cosmos. Because it is winter, the road is frozen, the keys are iron, the shoe is pointed, and the can itself is cold, empty.

MUSIC OF SPHERES

He was walking a frozen road
in his pocket iron keys were jingling
and with his pointed shoe absent-mindedly
he kicked the cylinder
of an old can
which for a few seconds rolled its cold emptiness
wobbled for a while and stopped
under a sky studded with stars.

Translated from the French by Czeslaw Milosz and Robert Hass

CARLOS DRUMMOND DE ANDRADE
1902—1987

This poem is like a joke and we are inclined, first, to smile, yet a moment of thought suffices to restore a serious meaning to such an encounter. It is enough to live truly intensely our meeting with a thing to preserve it forever in our memory.

IN THE MIDDLE OF THE ROAD

In the middle of the road there was a stone
there was a stone in the middle of the road
there was a stone
in the middle of the road there was a stone.

Never should I forget this event
in the life of my fatigued retinas.
Never should I forget that in the middle of the road
there was a stone
there was a stone in the middle of the road
in the middle of the road there was a stone.

Translated from the Portuguese by Elizabeth Bishop

Nature

Our attitude towards nature is not the same as that of our ancestors. The Book of Genesis authorizes man "to have dominion over the fish of the sea, and over the fowl of the air, and over the cattle, and over the earth, and over every creeping thing that prospereth upon the earth." The line separating man from the rest of living creatures remained firm for centuries, and as late as the seventeenth century Descartes considered animals to be living machines. With the progress of life sciences this line has become blurred. Man now realizes that our species shares with animals their physiology and their basic drives. Nature, as we approach it, has grown much more enigmatic: our feeling of kinship engenders both empathy and guilt. At the same time, Nature stands before us as the great Other, deprived of any notion of good and evil, and therefore perfectly innocent, even if it is *Natura Devorans* and *Natura Devorata,* the devouring and the devoured. We are akin to it and yet we are alienated by our consciousness—our curse and our blessing. And precisely this ambiguity in our relationship, marked by the warmth of closeness and by the cold of detached observation, transpires in many poems.

DAVID WAGONER
1926—

Alexander Wilson (1766–1813), who appears in this poem by David Wagoner, left Scotland, where in his youth he acquired popularity as a folk poet, for political reasons, and moved to America, where he dedicated himself to observing nature, particularly birds. His American Ornithology, *with hand-colored woodcuts, appeared in 1808. He was the first great ornithologist to follow Audubon. The first half of the nineteenth century was, in Europe, as well, a time of beautiful atlases of nature, hand-colored. The poem in fact deals with the impossibility of mutual understanding between man and nature. The hunter-artist believes that the woodpecker should be killed so that it may exist in books. This would not be well received by the bird, who could have answered that his only, individual life is taken from him so that paper may preserve a portrait, not of himself, but of his species. The artist, as an observing mind, participates in the misfortune of the bird, though at the same time he is a hot-blooded being, bound to the woodpecker by some kind of fraternity.*

THE AUTHOR OF *AMERICAN ORNITHOLOGY* SKETCHES A BIRD, NOW EXTINCT

(*Alexander Wilson, Wilmington, N.C. 1809*)

When he walked through town, the wing-shot bird he'd hidden
Inside his coat began to cry like a baby,
High and plaintive and loud as the calls he'd heard
While hunting it in the woods, and goodwives stared
And scurried indoors to guard their own from harm.

And the innkeeper and the goodmen in the tavern
Asked him whether his child was sick, then laughed.
Slapped knees, and laughed as he unswaddled his prize,
His pride and burden: an ivory-billed woodpecker
As big as a crow, still wailing and squealing.

Upstairs, when he let it go in his workroom,
It fell silent at last. He told at dinner
How devoted masters of birds drawn from the life
Must gather their flocks around them with a rifle
And make them live forever inside books.

Later, he found his bedspread covered with plaster
And the bird clinging beside a hole in the wall
Clear through to already-splintered weatherboards
And the sky beyond. While he tied one of its legs
To a table leg, it started wailing again.

And went on wailing as if toward cypress groves
While the artist drew and tinted on fine vellum
Its red cockade, gray claws, and sepia eyes
From which a white edge flowed to the lame wing
Like light flying and ended there in blackness.

He drew and studied for days, eating and dreaming
Fitfully through the dancing and loud drumming
Of an ivory bill that refused pecans and beetles,
Chestnuts and sweet-sour fruit of magnolias,
Riddling his table, slashing his fingers, wailing.

He watched it die, he said, with great regret.

David Wagoner seems to be seized by a passion for drawing birds in his verse, and reading him I think of my friend, a Swiss painter, Robert Hainard, who chose as his profession wandering with a notebook in the Alps to sleuth birds and animals, or my high-school classmate Leopold Pac-Pomarnacki, hunter and sketch artist, at one time a prisoner of the Soviet gulags, a soldier of the Polish army in Italy, and finally a forester in Poland. In a way, a poem is in one respect superior to a drawing, because it may follow a sequence of movements. The Northwest of the United States is the territory of Wagoner's observations: the love display of certain waterfowl, particularly interesting in grebes and loons—the latter a permanent part of the misty lakes of the north.

LOONS MATING

Their necks and their dark heads lifted into a dawn
Blurred smooth by mist, the loons
Beside each other are swimming slowly
In charmed circles, their bodies stretched under water
Through ripples quivering and sweeping apart
The gray sky now held close by the lake's mercurial threshold
Whose face and underface they share
In wheeling and diving tandem, rising together
To swell their breasts like swans, to go breasting forward
With beaks turned down and in, near shore,
Out of sight behind a windbreak of birch and alder,
And now the haunted uprisen wailing call,
And again, and now the beautiful sane laughter.

JEAN FOLLAIN
1903—1971

In French poet Jean Follain a kinship of man and bird is shown in the reverse order. The shapes and colors of singing birds lead to a reflection on the strangeness of the body of his lover. Besides, in poetry and folk songs a girl often appears as a bird—a nightingale (Philomela in Ovid), a turtledove, even a sparrow.

A TAXIDERMIST

A taxidermist is sitting
before the russet breasts
green and purple wings
of his song-birds
dreaming about his lover
with a body so different
yet so close sometimes
to the body of the birds
that it seemed to him
very strange
in its curves and its volumes
in its colors and its finery
and its shades . . .

Translated from the French by Czeslaw Milosz and Robert Hass

LI-YOUNG LEE

1957—

Li-Young Lee is an immigrant from China but he writes in English. Yet perhaps in his work there is a strong current of Asian poetry.

IRISES

1.

In the night, in the wind, at the edge of the rain,
I find five irises, and call them lovely.
As if a woman, once, lay by them awhile,
then woke, rose, went, the memory of hair
lingers on their sweet tongues.

I'd like to tear these petals with my teeth.
I'd like to investigate these hairy selves,
their beauty and indifference. They hold
their breath all their lives
and open, open.

2.

We are not lovers, not brother and sister,
though we drift hand in hand through a hall
thrilling and burning as thought and desire
expire, and, over this dream of life,
this life of sleep, we waken dying—
violet becoming blue, growing
black, black—all that
an iris ever prays,
when it prays,
to be.

ROBERT CREELEY
1926—

*Man confronting nature fears his foreignness and is ashamed of his intrusion. He
would like to return to the earthly paradise before Adam's sin. This seems to be
a very American dream, and Robert Creeley's poem pays tribute to that tradition.*

LIKE THEY SAY

Underneath the tree on some
soft grass I sat, I

watched two happy
woodpeckers be dis-

turbed by my presence. And
why not, I thought to

myself, why
not.

ADAM ZAGAJEWSKI
1945—

We're separated from nature as if by a glass wall—and this is the subject of this Polish poet. Poets have always been fascinated by the incomprehensible behavior of some creatures, for instance, the moth, which strives toward light and burns itself in the flame of a candle or kerosene lamp. Thence come comparisons: Love, as a fire which lures the lovers to their destruction. Yet moths, because they come from darkness into our circle of light, are, at the same time, messengers of that which is the most other. In this poem, people have their small security in a lighted house, but beyond the window, immeasurable spaces of the cosmos stretch, and the moths are like visitors from other galaxies.

MOTHS

Moths watched us through
the window. Seated at the table,
we were skewered by their lambent gazes,
harder than their shattering wings.

You'll always be outside,
past the pane. And we'll be here within,
more and more in. Moths watched us
through the window, in August.

Translated from the Polish by Renata Gorczynski, Benjamin Ivry, and C. K. Williams

MARY OLIVER
1935—

*Nature is perfect, that is, perfectly functional and deserving admiration, "so long
as you don't mind a little dying." Not a little, indeed, but only our consciousness
knows that what a kingfisher knows is its only truth—hunger. Faced with a self-
functioning order in which one creature serves as food to another, our consciousness
renounces judgment. "I don't say he's right. Neither do I say he's wrong." Yet no
action of ours is as efficient as the kingfisher's skill, submitted to instinct.*

THE KINGFISHER

The kingfisher rises out of the black wave
like a blue flower, in his beak
he carries a silver leaf. I think this is
the prettiest world—so long as you don't mind
a little dying, how could there be a day in your whole life
that doesn't have its splash of happiness?
There are more fish than there are leaves
on a thousand trees, and anyway the kingfisher
wasn't born to think about it, or anything else.
When the wave snaps shut over his blue head, the water
remains water—hunger is the only story
he has ever heard in his life that he could believe.
I don't say he's right. Neither
do I say he's wrong. Religiously he swallows the silver leaf
with its broken red river, and with a rough and easy cry
I couldn't rouse out of my thoughtful body
if my life depended on it, he swings back
over the bright sea to do the same thing, to do it
(as I long to do something, anything) perfectly.

WISLAWA SZYMBORSKA
1923—

We were taught that only man has an immortal soul. If today we speak differently
of a line separating us from the rest of living beings, does it mean that this line,
for us, doesn't exist? We feel it exists, and, using an old-fashioned expression, it
is due to the consciousness and free will of man. In other words, only we know
guilt, amidst the universal innocence of nature. And this is the subject of Wislawa
Szymborska's poem.

IN PRAISE OF SELF-DEPRECATION

The buzzard has nothing to fault himself with.
Scruples are alien to the black panther.
Piranhas do not doubt the rightness of their actions.
The rattlesnake approves of himself without reservations.

The self-critical jackal does not exist.
The locust, alligator, trichina, horsefly
live as they live and are glad of it.

The killer-whale's heart weighs one hundred kilos
but in other respects it is light.

There is nothing more animal-like
than a clear conscience
on the third planet of the Sun.

Translated from the Polish by Magnus J. Krynski and Robert A. Maguire

A similar theme is treated in this poem: the self-torment afflicting us in the early morning.

FOUR IN THE MORNING

The hour from night to day.
The hour from side to side.
The hour for those past thirty.

The hour swept clean to the crowing of cocks.
The hour when earth betrays us.
The hour when wind blows from extinguished stars.
The hour of and-what-if-nothing-remains-after-us.

The hollow hour.
Blank, empty.
The very pit of all other hours.

No one feels good at four in the morning.
If ants feel good at four in the morning
—three cheers for the ants. And let five o'clock come
if we're to go on living.

Translated from the Polish by Magnus J. Krynski and Robert A. Maguire

THEODORE ROETHKE
1908—1963

Ecological poems began being written toward the end of this century, though the idea of protecting nature is much older. In the 1920s, as a twelve-year-old, I drew the map of my kingdom. It had only forests, no fields, and the only means of transportation allowed was canoes. The only inhabitants of my kingdom were lovers of nature with proper diplomas.

We are sensitive today to the destruction brought by man to nature. A poem by Theodore Roethke tries to capture the vague feeling of shame that probably has more than once visited the destroyers. Roethke was the son of a gardener, an owner of large greenhouses, and he often returns in his poetry to the country of his childhood.

MOSS-GATHERING

To loosen with all ten fingers held wide and limber
And lift up a patch, dark-green, the kind for lining cemetery
    baskets,
Thick and cushiony, like an old-fashioned doormat,
The crumbling small hollow sticks on the underside mixed with
    roots,
And wintergreen berries and leaves still stuck to the top,—
That was moss-gathering.
But something always went out of me when I dug loose those
    carpets
Of green, or plunged to my elbow in the spongy yellowish moss of
    the marshes:
And afterwards I always felt mean, jogging back over the logging
    road,
As if I had broken the natural order of things in that swampland;
Disturbed some rhythm, old and of vast importance,
By pulling off flesh from the living planet;
As if I had committed, against the whole scheme of life, a
    desecration.

DENISE LEVERTOV

1923—

On our planet, the presence of nature, the enchantment of being, and the feeling of transience all go together. Every day is precious because this earth goes through its seasons, and every season might be our last; every moment of meeting an earthly creature is unique, unrepeatable. As here, the frailty of a salamander reminds one of the frailty of our lives.

LIVING

The fire in leaf and grass
so green it seems
each summer the last summer.

The wind blowing, the leaves
shivering in the sun,
each day the last day.

A red salamander
so cold and so
easy to catch, dreamily

moves his delicate feet
and long tail. I hold
my hand open for him to go.

Each minute the last minute.

ROBERT FRANCIS
1901—1987

*And if nature asks us to treat it with humor? If Winnie the Pooh, Piglet, and
Rabbit and his friends-and-relations, if all that humanization is precisely what
nature expects from us? In other words, perhaps we are unable to say—to tell
her—anything, except ascribing to her sadness, smiles, ominousness, serenity? It is
just or not, but we like some species and don't like others. And Robert Francis
likes waxwings so well that he decided to become one in order to attain wisdom.*

WAXWINGS

Four Tao philosophers as cedar waxwings
chat on a February berrybush
in sun, and I am one.

Such merriment and such sobriety—
the small wild fruit on the tall stalk—
was this not always my true style?

Above an elegance of snow, beneath
a silk-blue sky a brotherhood of four
birds. Can you mistake us?

To sun, to feast, and to converse
and all together—for this I have abandoned
all my other lives.

PHILIP LEVINE

1928—

I like Philip Levine's work, but I chose a poem which is not typical. And it seems to me I recognize here his garden in Fresno, California, where he has been a college professor for many years.

A SLEEPLESS NIGHT

April, and the last of the plum blossoms
scatters on the black grass
before dawn. The sycamore, the lime,
the struck pine inhale
the first pale hints of sky.
               An iron day,
I think, yet it will come
dazzling, the light
rise from the belly of leaves and pour
burning from the cups
of poppies.
           The mockingbird squawks
from his perch, fidgets,
and settles back. The snail, awake
for good, trembles from his shell
and sets sail for China. My hand dances
in the memory of a million vanished stars.

A man has every place to lay his head.

ROBERT HASS
1941—

Is this a poem about nature? Yes, because it deals with the change of seasons. It's not difficult to place the countryside near San Francisco. Hass, co-translator of my poetry into English, is an essentially Californian poet. Here he was born, and here he works as a professor at Berkeley.

LATE SPRING

And then in mid-May the first morning of steady heat,

the morning, Leif says, when you wake up, put on shorts, and that's it for the day,

when you pour coffee and walk outside, blinking in the sun.

Strawberries have appeared in the markets, and peaches will soon;

squid is so cheap in the fishstores you begin to consult Japanese and Italian cookbooks for the various and ingenious ways of preparing *ika* and *calamari*;

and because the light will enlarge your days, your dreams at night will be as strange as the jars of octopus you saw once in a fisherman's boat under the summer moon;

and after swimming, white wine; and the sharing of stories before dinner is prolonged because the relations of the children in the neighborhood have acquired village intensity and the stories take longer telling;

and there are the nights when the fog rolls in that nobody likes— hey, fog, the Miwok sang, who lived here first, you better go home, pelican is beating your wife—

and after dark in the first cool hour, your children sleep so heavily in their beds exhausted from play, it is a pleasure to watch them,

Leif does not move a muscle as he lies there; no, wait; it is Luke who lies there in his eight-year-old body,

Leif is taller than you are and he isn't home; when he is, his feet will extend past the end of the mattress, and Kristin is at the corner in the dark, talking to neighborhood boys;

things change; there is no need for this dream-compelled narration; the rhythm will keep me awake, changing.

ZBIGNIEW MACHEJ
1958 —

I know a poem of a young Polish poet on summer, on wanderings of water from the depths of the earth upwards into the leaves and roots of fruit trees, and still further and higher, into the fluid of a cloud.

ORCHARDS IN JULY

Waters from cold springs
and glittering minerals
tirelessly wander.
Patient, unceasing,
they overcome granite, layers
of hungry gravel, iridescent
precincts of clay. If they abandon
themselves to the black
roots it's only to go
up, as high as possible
through wells hidden
under the bark of fruit trees. Through
the green touched with gray, of leaves,
fallen petals of white
flowers with rosy edges,
apples heavy with sweet redness
and their bitterish seeds.
O, waters from cold
springs and glittering
minerals! You are awaited
by a cirrus with a fluid,
sunny outline
and by an abyss of blue
which has been rinsed
in the just wind.

Translated by Czeslaw Milosz and Robert Hass

W. S. MERWIN

1927 —

I don't know whether this fine poem expresses more than the inadequacy of our language before sunrises and sunsets. Perhaps we cannot do much without personifying. The sun behaves as a live being does, even a human being; its sunset is melancholy, "in the cold without friends," though without regrets because it worked well all the day long for people. Yet it believes "in nothing," which may mean too that it doesn't believe in its resurrection after the night. Why a stream? . . . Pursuing the light, the stream also is alive; it splashes on the stones, and this is its flute-playing. It will run all night long, till dawn. And so, as we try to describe the most ordinary dusk, the mythological transformation of phenomena into persons occurs. And it's no wonder that many people have given to planets, to the sea, to the rivers, to the streams, faces of smaller or bigger deities.

DUSK IN WINTER

The sun sets in the cold without friends
Without reproaches after all it has done for us
It goes down believing in nothing
When it is gone I hear the stream running after it
It has brought its flute it is a long way

D. H. LAWRENCE

1885—1930

D. H. Lawrence, in all his philosophy, turned against inhibitions invented by civilization to bind people and not to allow them to live in agreement with their inborn instincts. Thence such an importance is given to sex in his writing, because by getting rid of his inhibitions in this respect, "natural man" appears in all his nakedness. In the America of the 1960s, not without referring to that current of thought, a very amusing series of cartoons appeared with a hero by name Mr. Natural. Yet this poem of Lawrence's speaks, on the contrary, about the difficulty of merging with nature. A warm garden is like the garden of Eden, but in it Adam, looking at the butterfly, realizes that he cannot establish contact with it, and cannot warn it not to fly away to its perdition. Compared with the butterfly, he is nearly omniscient.

BUTTERFLY

Butterfly, the wind blows sea-ward, strong beyond the garden wall!
Butterfly, why do you settle on my shoe, and sip the dirt on my shoe,
Lifting your veined wings, lifting them? big white butterfly!

Already it is October, and the wind blows strong to the sea
from the hills where snow must have fallen, the wind is polished
      with snow.
Here in the garden, with red geraniums, it is warm, it is warm
but the wind blows strong to sea-ward, white butterfly, content on
      my shoe!

Will you go, will you go from my warm house?
Will you climb on your big soft wings, black-dotted,
as up an invisible rainbow, an arch
till the wind slides you sheer from the arch-crest
and in a strange level fluttering you go out to sea-ward, white speck!

Farewell, farewell, lost soul!
you have melted in the crystalline distance,
it is enough! I saw you vanish into air.

GARY SNYDER
1930 —

My guess is that inspirations from Zen Buddhism in Gary Snyder explain his gift of attention. Much empathic attention is needed to meditate upon the fate of one small living creature.

DRAGONFLY

Dragonfly
Dead on the snow
How did you come so high
Did you leave your seed child
In a mountain pool
Before you died

Evolution Basin IX 69

THEODORE ROETHKE

1908—1963

To describe a bird, an animal, a plant is difficult, because they elude that imperfect instrument which is our language. A pedantic description in textbooks of zoology or botany does not attempt to capture the very essence of a given species, but a poet likes to nail down something which is proper only to a given thing, be it "wolfishness," "elephantineness," "mapleness," or "carnationness." He makes use of comparisons: carnations have leaves like "Corinthian scrolls," and the chilly air is "hyacinthine." Though we are not sure that he succeeds, because a carnation does not mean the same thing to each one of us.

CARNATIONS

Pale blossoms, each balanced on a single jointed stem,
And leaves curled back in elaborate Corinthian scrolls;
And the air cool, as if drifting down from wet hemlocks,
Or rising out of ferns not far from water,
A crisp hyacinthine coolness,
Like that clear autumnal weather of eternity,
The windless perpetual morning above a September cloud.

ROBINSON JEFFERS
1887—1962

*A foundation of admirers of Robinson Jeffers preserves as a relic his home in
Carmel on the shores of the Pacific. When Jeffers and his wife, Una Custer, after
the dramatic procedures of her divorce, first came to Carmel in 1914, it was a little
village in the pine forests. Jeffers bought land and built their house by the sea from
granite boulders, which he called Tor House. They lived there together until her
death, and then he lived there until his death in 1962. Today the shore is completely
built up, fortunately with one-family homes rather than high-rise buildings such as
one finds on the shores of the Mediterranean in France and Spain. In this poem,
Jeffers gives a short presentation of his philosophy, which he called "inhumanism."
It advises inhumanization, that is, getting rid of human measurements, which deceive
us because everything then refers to man, without whom the universe can perfectly
exist. According to his philosophy, the human species, that destructive plasm on the
surface of the globe, will disappear, and then everything will once again be perfectly
beautiful.*

CARMEL POINT

The extraordinary patience of things!
This beautiful place defaced with a crop of suburban houses—
How beautiful when we first beheld it,
Unbroken field of poppy and lupin walled with clean cliffs;
No instrusion but two or three horses pasturing,
Or a few milch cows rubbing their flanks on the outcrop rockheads—
Now the spoiler has come: does it care?
Not faintly. It has all time. It knows the people are a tide
That swells and in time will ebb, and all
Their works dissolve. Meanwhile the image of the pristine beauty
Lives in the very grain of the granite,
Safe as the endless ocean that climbs our cliff. — As for us:
We must uncenter our minds from ourselves;
We must unhumanize our views a little, and become confident
As the rock and ocean that we were made from.

GALWAY KINNELL
1927—

Perhaps poets of the twentieth century are busy making a catalog of all existing things. Here they have a good patron and predecessor, the omnivorous Walt Whitman. But it is interesting to note that in the very beginning of our century Rainer Maria Rilke—a poet, it would seem, of inner experiences—tried to describe things of the visible world in such poems as "The Panther," "Blue Hortense," "Archaic Torso of Apollo," "Persian Heliotrope," "Mountain," and "The Ball."

DAYBREAK

On the tidal mud, just before sunset,
dozens of starfishes
were creeping. It was
as though the mud were a sky
and enormous, imperfect stars
moved across it slowly
as the actual stars cross heaven.
All at once they stopped,
and as if they had simply
increased their receptivity
to gravity they sank down
into the mud; they faded down
into it and lay still; and by the time
pink of sunset broke across them
they were as invisible
as the true stars at daybreak.

MYSTIC

They call all experience of the senses *mystic,* when the experience
    is considered.
So an apple becomes *mystic* when I taste in it
the summer and the snows, the wild welter of earth
and the insistence of the sun.

All of which things I can surely taste in a good apple.
Though some apples taste preponderantly of water, wet and sour
and some of too much sun, brackish sweet
like lagoon-water, that has been too much sunned.

If I say I taste these things in an apple, I am called *mystic,* which
    means a liar.
The only way to eat an apple is to hog it down like a pig
and taste nothing
that is *real.*

But if I eat an apple, I like to eat it with all my senses awake.
Hogging it down like a pig I call the feeding of corpses.

ROBERT MORGAN

1944—

Some poets, concentrating their attention on the object, renounce the privileges of their "I," approaching the object cautiously, and even ascetically. Robert Morgan writes about things known to him in his childhood in a rural region of America. "Honey" is not unlike practical advice for a beekeeper.

HONEY

Only calmness will reassure
the bees to let you rob their hoard.
Any sweat of fear provokes them.
Approach with confidence, and from
the side, not shading their entrance.
And hush smoke gently from the spout
of the pot of rags, for sparks will
anger them. If you go near bees
every day they will know you.
And never jerk or turn so quick
you excite them. If weeds are trimmed
around the hive they have access
and feel free. When they taste your smoke
they fill themselves with honey and
are laden and lazy as you
lift the lid to let in daylight.
No bee full of sweetness wants to
sting. Resist greed. With the top off
you touch the fat gold frames, each cell
a hex perfect as a snowflake,
a sealed relic of sun and time
and roots of many acres fixed
in crystal-tight arrays, in rows
and lattices of sweeter latin
from scattered prose of meadow, woods.

JOANNE KYGER
1934—

A few words on a king. He doesn't know that he's a king; he's taciturn and a hermit. But the human imagination has adorned him with features proper to a monarch. He is also a sage, though he doesn't speak at all. He appears in innumerable fairy tales and legends. The bear doesn't visit European poetry anymore, but he quite often does American poetry, as in California poet Joanne Kyger. She belongs to the movement of the Beat Generation, studied at the University of California at Santa Barbara, practiced Zen, lived a couple of years in Japan, and now lives in Bolinas, California.

DESTRUCTION

First of all do you remember the way a bear goes through
a cabin when nobody is home? He goes through
the front door. I mean he really goes *through* it. Then
he takes the cupboard off the wall and eats a can of lard.

He eats all the apples, limes, dates, bottled decaffeinated
coffee, and 35 pounds of granola. The asparagus soup cans
fall to the floor. Yum! He chomps up Norwegian crackers
stashed for the winter. And the bouillon, salt, pepper,
paprika, garlic, onions, potatoes.

         He rips the Green Tara
poster from the wall. Tries the Coleman Mustard. Spills
the ink, tracks in the flour. Goes up stairs and takes
a shit. Rips open the water bed, eats the incense and
drinks the perfume. Knocks over the Japanese tansu
and the Persian miniature of a man on horseback watching
a woman bathing.

        Knocks *Shelter, Whole Earth Catalogue,*
Planet Drum, Northern Mists, Truck Tracks, and
Women's Sports into the oozing water bed mess.

                                                    He goes
down stairs and out the back wall. He keeps on going
for a long way and finds a good cave to sleep it all off.
Luckily he ate the whole medicine cabinet, including stash
of LSD, Peyote, Psilocybin, Amanita, Benzedrine, Valium
and aspirin.

MARY OLIVER
1935—

In view of the great number of nihilizing experiences in literature of the twentieth century, one should appreciate wisdom drawn by people from their contact with nature. Those experiences cannot be rationally defined. But perhaps most essential is the feeling of a universal rhythmn of which we are a part simply thanks to the circulation of our blood. In this poem of Mary Oliver's, good and evil, guilt and despair, are proper to the human world, but beyond there is a larger world and its very existence calls us to transcend our human worries.

WILD GEESE

You do not have to be good.
You do not have to walk on your knees
for a hundred miles through the desert, repenting.
You only have to let the soft animal of your body
    love what it loves.
Tell me about despair, yours, and I will tell you mine.
Meanwhile the world goes on.
Meanwhile the sun and the clear pebbles of the rain
are moving across the landscapes,
over the prairies and the deep trees,
the mountains and the rivers.
Meanwhile the wild geese, high in the clean blue air,
are heading home again.
Whoever you are, no matter how lonely,
the world offers itself to your imagination,
calls to you like the wild geese, harsh and exciting—
over and over announcing your place
in the family of things.

WISLAWA SZYMBORSKA

1923 —

Szymborska's poetry is strongly influenced by modern science. She assumes that the borderline between us and the rest of nature is tenuous. On the other hand, she knows that our inveterate habits incline us to look at animals and insects with a feeling of our special privilege. Thence her ironic poem.

SEEN FROM ABOVE

On a dirt road lies a dead beetle.
Three little pairs of legs carefully folded on his belly.
Instead of death's chaos—neatness and order.
The horror of this sight is mitigated,
the range strictly local, from witchgrass to spearmint.
Sadness is not contagious.
The sky is blue.

For our peace of mind, their death seemingly shallower,
animals do not pass away, but simply die,
losing—we wish to believe—less of awareness and the world,
leaving—it seems to us—a stage less tragic.
Their humble little souls do not haunt our dreams,
they keep their distance,
know their place.

So here lies the dead beetle on the road,
glistens unlamented when the sun hits.
A glance at him is as good as a thought:
he looks as though nothing important had befallen him.
What's important is valid supposedly for us.
For just our life, for just our death,
a death that enjoys an extorted primacy.

Translated from the Polish by Magnus J. Krynski and Robert A. Maguire

JANE HIRSHFIELD
1953—

Young Prince Siddhartha, carefully protected by his parents from the knowledge that there exist illness and death, once escaped from his palace and in the streets of the city discovered suffering as the law of the world. A great compassion for all living creatures forced him to look for a means to liberate them. After years of ascetic contemplation he became a Buddha and gave rise to one of the great religions of humanity. This poem about a mother who would like to protect her child from unavoidable knowledge was written by a California poet, a Buddhist, and, besides, a person whom I number among my friends.

A STORY

A woman tells me
the story of a small wild bird,
beautiful on her window sill, dead three days.
How her daughter came suddenly running,
"It's moving, Mommy, he's alive."
And when she went, it was.
The emerald wing-feathers stirred, the throat
seemed to beat again with pulse.
Closer then, she saw how the true life lifted
under the wings. Turned her face
so her daughter would not see, though she would see.

JEAN FOLLAIN
1903—1971

FACE THE ANIMAL

It's not always easy
to face the animal
even if it looks at you
without fear or hate
it does so fixedly
and seems to disdain
the subtle secret it carries
it seems better to feel
the obviousness of the world
that noisily day and night
drills and damages
the silence of the soul.

Tanslated from the French by Heather McHugh

JORGE GUILLÉN
1893—1984

Incarnating oneself in a bird: how many associations with mythology in the history
of poetry? Not only incarnation, but also feeling what a bird feels, an imagination
allowing us to do that. This poem by the Spanish poet Jorge Guillén has as its
subject the delight of existing, which we guess to be in all living beings because,
since it is not refused to us, it must be all the stronger when it is more spontaneous
and further from thinking.

FLIGHT

Through summer air
The ascending gull
Dominates the expanse, the sea, the world
Under the blue, under clouds
Like the whitest wool-tufts,
And supreme, regal,
It soars.

All of space is a wave transfixed.

White and black feathers
Slow the ascent,
Suddenly slipping on the air,
On the vast light.

It buoys up the whiteness of the void.

And suspended, its wings abandon themselves
To clarity, to the transparent depths
Where flight, with stilled wings,
Subsists,
Gives itself entirely to its own delight, its falling,
And plunges into its own passing—
A pure instant of life.

Translated from the Spanish by Reginald Gibbons

EMILY DICKINSON
1830—1886

A NARROW FELLOW IN THE GRASS

A narrow Fellow in the Grass
Occasionally rides—
You may have met Him—did you not
His notice sudden is—

the Grass divides as with a Comb—
A spotted shaft is seen—
And then it closes at your feet
And opens further on—

He likes a Boggy Acre
A Floor too cool for Corn—
Yet when a Boy, and Barefoot—
I more than once at Noon
Have passed, I thought, a Whip lash
Unbraiding in the Sun
When stooping to secure it
It wrinkled, and was gone—

Several of Nature's People
I know, and they know me—
I feel for them a transport
Of cordiality—

But never met this Fellow
Attended, or alone
Without a tighter breathing
And Zero at the Bone—

ROBERT FROST
1874—1963

THE MOST OF IT

He thought he kept the universe alone;
For all the voice in answer he could wake
Was but the mocking echo of his own
From some tree-hidden cliff across the lake.
Some morning from the boulder-broken beach
He would cry out on life, that what it wants
Is not its own love back in copy speech,
But counter-love, original response.
And nothing ever came of what he cried
Unless it was the embodiment that crashed
In the cliff's talus on the other side,
And then in the far-distant water splashed,
But after time allowed for it to swim,
Instead of proving human when it neared
And someone else additional to him,
As a great buck it powerfully appeared,
Pushing the crumpled water up ahead,
And landed pouring like a waterfall,
And stumbled through the rocks with horny tread,
And forced the underbrush—and that was all.

ANNA SWIR
1909—1984

THE SEA AND THE MAN

You will not tame this sea
either by humility or rapture.
But you can laugh
in its face.

Laughter
was invented by those
who live briefly
as a burst of laughter.

The eternal sea
will never learn to laugh.

Translated from the Polish by Czeslaw Milosz and Leonard Nathan

The Secret of a Thing

Poetry has always described things surrounding us, but as if inadvertently, swerving for a moment from the main topic, for instance, from the military action in the *Iliad*, to present in detail Achilles' shield. In European painting, an originally supplementary detail eventually becomes autonomous: the landscape, at first used as a background, became a *paysage;* dishes, meats, fruit, all that accompanies people, filling their tables, changed into "still lifes," a genre which attained its highest achievements probably in the seventeenth century by Dutch masters, in the eighteenth century by Chardin, and in the twentieth century by Cézanne.

In modernism there is much fascination with the object, and our changing attitude toward poets of the past seems to be connected with a shifting focus of attention. It is possible that the influence of the poets of old China and old Japan has contributed to the new awareness. That influence is already visible by the beginning of this century, in American imagism.

The modern poet has discovered how difficult it is to describe a thing, giving it center stage, withdrawing himself or herself, "objectivizing," for every one of us is bound to it by emotional ties inherited together with the language; our very vocabulary resists a detached contemplation. When the Japanese poet Bashō advised a poet describing a pine to learn from the pine, he wanted to say that contemplation of a thing—a reverent and pious approach to it—is a prerequisite of true art.

WALT WHITMAN
1819—1892

The strong presence of a thing described means that the poet believes in its real existence. That is the meaning of a programmatic and unfinished poem by Walt Whitman, "I Am the Poet," which rehabilitates a "naive" approach and rejects philosophy's unfavorable opinion on the direct testimony of our senses.

I AM THE POET

I am the poet of reality
I say the earth is not an echo
Nor man an apparition;
But that all the things seen are real,
The witness and albic dawn of things equally real
I have split the earth and the hard coal and rocks and the solid bed
    of the sea
And went down to reconnoitre there a long time,
And bring back a report,
And I understand that those are positive and dense every one
And that what they seem to the child they are
[And that the world is not joke,
Nor any part of it a sham].

WILLIAM BLAKE

1757—1827

William Blake had not, whatever his critics might have said, the mentality of a medieval peasant. He quarreled with his contemporaries, extolling the value of direct, naive perceptions, as opposed to images suggested by scientific theory. In defending the flat earth, he wanted to say that its image is better adapted to human needs than the image of an earth-ball, one of the planetary bodies.

FROM "MILTON"

And every Space that a Man views around his dwelling-place
Standing on his own roof or in his garden on a mount
Of twenty-five cubits in height, such space is his Universe:
And on its verge the Sun rises & sets, the Clouds bow
To meet the flat Earth & the Sea in such an order'd Space:
The Starry heavens reach no further, but here bend and set
On all sides, & the two Poles turn on their valves of gold;
And if he move his dwelling-place, his heavens also move
Where'er he goes, & all his neighbourhood bewail his loss.
Such are the Spaces called Earth & such its dimension.
As to that false appearance which appears to the reasoner
As of a Globe rolling thro' Voidness, it is a delusion of Ulro.

WALT WHITMAN
1819—1892

THE RUNNER

On a flat road runs the well-train'd runner,
He is lean and sinewy with muscular legs,
He is thinly clothed, he leans forward as he runs,
With lightly closed fists and arms partially rais'd.

A FARM PICTURE

Through the ample open door of the peaceful country barn,
A sunlit pasture filled with cattle and horses feeding,
And haze and vista, and the far horizon fading away.

SU TUNG P'O

1036—1101

The affinity between painting and poetry was strongly stressed in ancient Chinese poetry, and often a poet and a painter filled a scroll of paper together. But in the Western world also, poetry was early compared to painting, and Horace said "Ut pictura poesis" (In poetry, as in painting).

ON A PAINTING BY WANG THE CLERK OF YEN LING

The slender bamboo is like a hermit.
The simple flower is like a maiden.
The sparrow tilts on the branch.
A gust of rain sprinkles the flowers.
He spreads his wings to fly
And shakes all the leaves.
The bees gathering honey
Are trapped in the nectar.
What a wonderful talent
That can create an entire Spring
With a brush and a sheet of paper.
If he would try poetry
I know he would be a master of words.

Translated from the Chinese by Kenneth Rexroth

ROBERT MORGAN

1944—

Robert Morgan's ambition is to describe objects in a matter-of-fact manner. And he finds his material in the countryside and small towns of the Midwest.

BELLROPE

The line through the hold in the dank
vestibule ceiling ended in
a powerful knot worn slick, swinging
in the breeze from those passing. Half
an hour before service Uncle
Allen pulled the call to worship,
hauling down the rope like the starting
cord of a motor, and the tower
answered and answered, fading
as the clapper lolled aside. I watched
him before Sunday school heave on
the line as on a wellrope. And
the wheel creaked up there as heavy
buckets emptied out their startle
and spread a cold splash to farthest
coves and hollows, then sucked the rope
back into the loft, leaving just
the knot within reach, trembling
with its high connections.

JUDAH AL-HARIZI
c.1170—1235

But let us move back to the middle ages. In Spain, Toledo was, at that time, a
known center of writing in Hebrew, and there was born the poet Al-Harizi, author
of the slightly jocular quatrains that I include here.

THE LIGHTNING

And the lightning laughs at the clouds,
like a warrior who runs without growing weary or faint.

Or like a night watchman who dozes off,
then opens one eye for an instant, and shuts it.

Translated from the Hebrew by T. Carmi

THE SUN

Look: the sun has spread its wings
over the earth to dispel the darkness.

Like a great tree, with its roots in heaven,
and its branches reaching down to the earth.

Translated from the Hebrew by T. Carmi

THE LUTE

Look: the lute sounds in the girl's arms,
delighting the heart with its beautiful voice.

Like a baby crying in his mother's arms,
while she sings and laughs as he cries.

Translated from the Hebrew by T. Carmi

Poems, as realistically descriptive as possible, occasionally engage in polemics with those who might question the choice of topic, as, for instance, in this poem of Robinson Jeffers.

BOATS IN FOG

Sports and gallantries, the stage, the arts, the antics of dancers,
The exuberant voices of music,
Have charm for children but lack nobility; it is bitter
    earnestness
That makes beauty; the mind
Knows, grown adult.
                  A sudden fog-drift muffled the ocean,
A throbbing of engines moved in it,
At length, a stone's throw out, between the rocks and the
    vapor,
One by one moved shadows
Out of the mystery, shadows, fishing-boats, trailing each other
Following the cliff for guidance,
Holding a difficult path between the peril of the sea-fog
And the foam on the shore granite.
One by one, trailing their leader, six crept by me,
Out of the vapor and into it,
The throb of their engines subdued by the fog, patient and
    cautious,
Coasting all round the peninsula
Back to the buoys in Monterey harbor. A flight of pelicans
Is nothing lovelier to look at;
The flight of the planets is nothing nobler; all the arts lose
    virtue
Against the essential reality
Of creatures going about their business among the equally
Earnest elements of nature.

EVENING EBB

The ocean has not been so quiet for a long while; five night-
    herons
Fly shorelong voiceless in the hush of the air
Over the calm of an ebb that almost mirrors their wings.
The sun has gone down, and the water has gone down
From the weed-clad rock, but the distant cloud-wall rises. The ebb
    whispers.
Great cloud-shadows float in the opal water.
Through rifts in the screen of the world pale gold gleams, and the
    evening
Star suddenly glides like a flying torch.
As if we had not been meant to see her; rehearsing behind
The screen of the world for another audience.

ROBERT HASS

1941 —

Robert Hass, like Jeffers, is a California poet. In this poem, an object (clay figurine) and a typical California landscape are given simultaneously.

THE IMAGE

The child brought blue clay from the creek
and the woman made two figures: a lady and a deer.
At that season deer came down from the mountain
and fed quietly in the redwood canyons.
The woman and the child regarded the figure of the lady,
the crude roundnesses, the grace, the coloring like shadow.
They were not sure where she came from,
except the child's fetching and the woman's hands
and the lead-blue clay of the creek
where the deer sometimes showed themselves at sundown.

ROLF JACOBSEN
1907 —

Colors are the most essential qualities of things, not lines. Since Cézanne so believed,
he admired the Renaissance painting of Venice, because of its luxuriance of color.
In Norwegian poet Rolf Jacobsen, colors—as they are of feminine gender—are
a feminine part of nature, and are treated as women. For him, Crimson is "she,"
and Cobalt, too, is "she."

COBALT

Colors are words' little sisters. They can't become soldiers.
I've loved them secretly for a long time.
They have to stay home and hang up the sheer curtains
in our ordinary bedroom, kitchen and alcove.

I'm very close to young Crimson, and brown Sienna
but even closer to thoughtful Cobalt with her distant eyes and
        untrampled spirit.
We walk in dew.
The night sky and the southern oceans
are her possessions
and a tear-shaped pendant on her forehead:
the pearls of Cassiopeia.
We walk in dew on late nights.

But the others.
Meet them on a June morning at four o'clock
when they come rushing toward you,
on your way to a morning swim in the green cove's spray.
Then you can sunbathe with them on the smooth rocks.
        —Which one will you make yours?

Translated from the Norwegian by Roger Greenwald

WALLACE STEVENS
1879—1955

Wallace Stevens was under the spell of science and scientific methods. An analytical tendency is visible in his poems on reality, and this is just opposite to the advice of Zen poet Bashō, who wanted to capture the thing in a single stroke. When Stevens tries to describe two pears, as if for an inhabitant of another planet, he enumerates one after another their chief qualities, making his analysis akin to a Cubist painting. But pears prove to be impossible to describe.

STUDY OF TWO PEARS

I

Opusculum paedagogum.
The pears are not viols,
Nudes or bottles.
They resemble nothing else.

2

They are yellow forms
Composed of curves
Bulging toward the base.
They are touched red.

3

They are not flat surfaces
Having curved outlines.
They are round
Tapering toward the top.

4

In the way they are modelled
There are bits of blue.
A hard dry leaf hangs
From the stem.

5

The yellow glistens.
It glistens with various yellows,
Citrons, oranges and greens
Flowering over the skin.

6

The shadows of the pears
Are blobs on the green cloth.
The pears are not seen
As the observer wills.

WILLIAM CARLOS WILLIAMS
1883—1963

The Objectivists, active in New York in the 1920s, left a durable trace on American poetry; the poem "The Red Wheelbarrow" by William Carlos Williams, who for a time was one of them, is a classic that must not be omitted from my collection. Maybe in this poem all his warmth and compassion are hardly signalled, but the poem is important.

THE RED WHEELBARROW

So much depends
upon

a red wheel
barrow

glazed with rain
water

beside the white
chickens.

WISLAWA SZYMBORSKA

1923—

*Poetry in the twentieth century has been moving, in at least one of its branches,
toward the philosophical essay, and this has gone along with a certain blurring of
borderlines between literary genres. If abstraction is dangerous to poetry, this tendency nevertheless contributes to its ability to ask some basic questions about the
structure of the universe. A poem by Wislawa Szymborska opposes the human (i.e.,
language) to the inanimate world and shows that our understanding of it is illusory.
Personally, I think that she is too scientific and that we are not so separated from
things.*

VIEW WITH A GRAIN OF SAND

We call it a grain of sand
but it calls itself neither grain nor sand.
It does just fine without a name,
whether general, particular,
permanent, passing,
incorrect or apt.

Our glance, our touch mean nothing to it.
It doesn't feel itself seen and touched.
And that it fell on the windowsill
is only our experience, not its.
For it it's no different than falling on anything else
with no assurance that it's finished falling
or that it's falling still.

The window has a wonderful view of a lake
but the view doesn't view itself.
It exists in this world
colorless, shapeless,
soundless, odorless, and painless.

The lake's floor exists floorlessly
and its shore exists shorelessly.

Its water feels itself neither wet nor dry
and its waves to themselves are neither singular nor plural.
They splash deaf to their own noise
on pebbles neither large nor small.

And all this beneath a sky by nature skyless
in which the sun sets without setting at all
and hides without hiding behind an unminding cloud.
The wind ruffles it, its only reason being
that it blows.

A second passes.
A second second.
A third.
But they're three seconds only for us.

Time has passed like a courier with urgent news.
But that's just our simile.
The character's invented, his haste is make-believe,
his news inhuman.

Translated from the Polish by Stanisław Barańczak and Clara Cavanagh

FRANCIS PONGE
1899—1988

*Francis Ponge, a rationalist in the Cartesian tradition, wrote "objeu" (objet-jeu—
object-play) poems, in which things provided him an opportunity for linguistic games.
I suspect he wrote less about visible phenomena than about their adventures within
the dictionary of the French language.*

THE FROG

When little matchsticks of rain bounce off drenched fields, an
amphibian dwarf, a maimed Ophelia, barely the size of a fist, sometimes hops under the poet's feet and flings herself into the next pond.

Let the nervous little thing run away. She has lovely legs. Her
whole body is sheathed in waterproof skin. Hardly meat, her long
muscles have an elegance neither fish nor fowl. But to escape one's
fingers, the virtue of fluidity joins forces with her struggle for life.
Goitrous, she starts panting. . . . And that pounding heart, those
wrinkled eyelids, that drooping mouth, move me to let her go.

Translated from the French by Beth Archer

ALEKSANDER WAT
1900—1967

*Looking at a painting is like second-degree contemplation, entering into cooperation
with the painter who had seen and admired the colors of the object.*

FACING BONNARD

Blond light blew away grayness, shadows, mists,
from a body that left the bathtub and does not yet go to the
    coffin.
The body is tawny, flame-spotted, and the bathtub, rosy,
    flesh-colored.
And the coffin? As usual with a coffin: dimly purple.
(Besides, the coffin's not visible: its colors suffice).

That translation from our world, don't ask whether faithful,
gives pleasure to the eye. The other senses are mum.
But to the eye it gives pleasure. That's enough. Quite.
Be patient. Wait. You will see how that pleasure
opens up as an egg of dream-meditation.
Our artist enclosed in it a ballet of possibilities
where he himself—and you—are both an observer and an author,
a corps de ballet, surely, but also a true soloist.

Translated from the Polish by Czeslaw Milosz and Leonard Nathan

MUSO SOSEKI

1275—1351

It is amazing to what extent the mountain appears and reappears in poetry of various languages, beginning of course with the Bible, as a sacred presence to be contemplated. Often its autonomous existence is opposed to the passing states of mind and feelings of a human being.

MAGNIFICENT PEAK

By its own nature
   it towers above
      the tangle of rivers
Don't say
   it's a lot of dirt
      piled high
Without end the mist of dawn
   the evening cloud
      draw their shadows across it
From the four directions
   you can look up and see it
      green and steep and wild.

Translated from the Japanese by W. S. Merwin

DENISE LEVERTOV
1923—

WITNESS

Sometimes the mountain
is hidden from me in veils
of cloud, sometimes
I am hidden from the mountain
in veils of inattention, apathy, fatigue,
when I forget or refuse to go
down to the shore or a few yards
up the road, on a clear day,
to reconfirm
that witnessing presence.

Travel

In old Arabic poetry love, song, blood, and travel appear as four basic desires of the human heart and the only effective means against our fear of death. Thus travel is elevated to the dignity of the elementary needs of humankind. "To sail is necessary, to live is not" *(Navigare est necesse, vivere non est necesse)*—these words were, according to Plutarch, pronounced by a Roman before the departure of a ship in tempestuous weather. Whatever practical reasons push people out of their homes to seek adventure, travel undoubtedly removes us from familiar sights and from everyday routine. It offers to us a pristine world seen for the first time and is a powerful means of inducing wonder. And since poetry is an expression of wondering at things, landscapes, people, their habits and mores, poetry and travel are allied.

Man has always travelled, yet the great mass of humanity remained sedentary, and only since the beginning of the twentieth century have we witnessed the new phenomenon: tourism. Fast international express trains and transatlantic steamers were greeted by poets as the implementation of modernity and of a new cosmopolitan spirit. The buoyant mood of the period just preceding World War I, called in France "La Belle Epoque," is present in French poets such as Valery Larbaud and Blaise Cendrars. Larbaud invented a figure of an international traveller, a millionaire, Barnabooth, and published his presumed poems in 1908. Cendrars (in reality a Swiss, born Ferdinand Sauser) drew the images of his largely descriptive poems from both America and Russia. In 1912 he published his famous poem "Easter in New York," as important for modern poetry as is "Zone," by his friend Guillaume Apollinaire. In 1913 he wrote his long poem entitled "Prose of the

Transsiberian Railway and of little Jeanne of France." His postwar poems were snapshots from different continents, often collages.

Travel provided one of the main topics for old Chinese poetry, but it was not international. The huge size of the Empire gave much opportunity to discover the unfamiliar and the exotic within its borders. These were journeys by land, often to remote provinces.

I have selected several poems about the train, because it has stirred the imagination of poets (beginning with Walt Whitman's in "To a Locomotive in Winter"). The train means a deployment of sights and people beyond the window, but often acquires sinister traits.

Of course, I could not omit poems dealing with the most ancient way of travelling—by foot.

IMAGES

1

One day in a popular quarter of Kharkov,
(O that southern Russia where all the women
With white-shawled heads look so like Madonnas!)
I saw a young woman returning from the fountain,
Bearing, Russian-style, as Roman women did in the time of Ovid,
Two pails suspended from the ends of a wooden
Yoke balanced on neck and shoulders.
And I saw a child in rags approach and speak to her.
Then, bending her body lovingly to the right,
She moved so the pail of pure water touched the cobblestone
Level with the lips of the child who had kneeled to drink.

2

One morning, in Rotterdam, on Boompjes quai
(It was September 18, 1900, around eight o'clock),
I observed two young ladies on their way to work;
Opposite one of the great iron bridges, they said farewell,
Their paths diverging.
Tenderly they embraced; their trembling hands
Wanted, but did not want, to part; their mouths
Withdrew sadly and came together again soon again
While they gazed fixedly into each other's eyes . . .
They stood thus for a long moment side by side,
Straight and still amid the busy throng,
While the tugboats rumbled by on the river,
And the whistling trains maneuvered on the iron bridges.

3

Between Cordova and Seville
Is a little station where the South Express,
For no apparent reason, always stops.

In vain the traveler looks for a village
Beyond the station asleep under the eucalyptus:
He sees but the Andalusian countryside: green and golden.
But across the way, on the other side of the track,
Is a hut made of black boughs and clay,
From which, at the sound of the rain, ragged children swarm forth,
The eldest sister, leading them, comes forward on the platform
And, smiling, without uttering a word,
Dances for pennies.
Her feet in the heavy dust look black;
Her dark, filthy face is devoid of beauty;
She dances, and through the large holes of her ash-gray skirt,
One can see the agitation of her thin, naked thighs,
And the roll of her little yellow belly;
At the sight of which a few gentlemen,
Amid an aroma of cigars, chuckle obscenely in the dining car.

Post-Scriptum

O Lord, will it never be possible for me
To know the sweet woman, there in Southern Russia,
And those two young friends in Rotterdam,
And the young Andalusian beggar
And join with them
In an indissoluble friendship?
(Alas, they will not read these poems,
They will know neither my name, nor the feeling in my heart;
And yet they exist; they live now).
Will it never be possible for me to experience the great joy
Of knowing them?
For some strange reason, Lord, I feel that with those four
I should conquer a whole world!

Translated from the French by William Jay Smith

BLAISE CENDRARS
1887–1961

ALEUTIAN ISLANDS

I

High Cliffs lashed by icy polar winds
In the center of lush meadows
Reindeer elks musk-oxen
The Arctic foxes the beavers
Brooks swarming with fish
A low beach has been prepared to breed fur seals
On top of the cliff are collected the eider's nests
Its feathers are worth a real fortune.

2

Large and sturdy buildings which shelter a
    considerable number of traders
All around a small garden where all vegetation
    able to withstand the severe climate has
    been brought together
mountain ash pine trees Arctic willows
Bed of heather and Alpine plants

3

Bay spiked with rocky islets
In groups of five or six the seals bask in the sun
Or stretching out on the sand
They play together howling in that kind of hoarse tone
    that sounds like a dog's bark
Next to the Eskimos' hut is a shed where
    the skins are treated

Translated from the French by Monique Chefdor

FISH COVE

The water is so clear and so calm
Deep at the bottom you can see the white bushes
    of coral
The prismatic sway of hanging jellyfish
The yellow pink lilac fish taking flight
And at the foot of the wavy seaweeds the azure
    sea cucumbers and the urchins green and purple

Translated from the French by Monique Chefdor

HARVEST

A six-cylinder car and two Fords in the middle of
    the fields
In every direction as far as the horizon the slightly
    slanting swaths crisscross in a wavering
    diamond-shaped checkerboard pattern
Not a tree
From the North comes down the rumble and rattle of the
    automotive thrasher and forage wagon
And from the south come twelve empty trains to
    pick up the wheat

Translated from the French by Monique Chefdor

SOUTH

1. Tampa
The train has just come to a stop
Only two travelers get off on this scorching
    late summer morning
Both wear khaki suits and cork helmets
Both are followed by a black servant
    who carries their luggage
Both glance in the same casual way at the houses
    that are too white at the sky that is too blue
You can see the wind raise whirls of dust and the flies
    buzzing around the two mules of the only cab
The cabman is asleep the mouth wide open

Translated from the French by Monique Chefdor

FRISCO-CITY

It is an antique carcass eaten up by rust
The engine repaired twenty times does not make
   more than 7 to 8 knots
Besides to save expenses cinders and coal waste
   are its only fuel
Makeshift sails are hoisted whenever there is
   a fair wind
With his ruddy face his bushy eyebrows his pimply nose
   Master Hopkins is a true sailor
Small silver rings hang from his pierced ears
The ship's cargo is exclusively coffins of Chinese
   who died in America and wished to be buried
   in their homeland
Oblong boxes painted red or light blue or covered
   with golden characters
Just the type of merchandise it is illegal to ship

Translated from the French by Monique Chefdor

LI PO
701—762

Sometimes it is enough to climb a nearby mountain to see all human affairs literally from above, as is done by this great poet of the T'ang Dynasty, the Golden Age of Chinese poetry.

ANCIENT AIR

Climbed high, to gaze upon the sea,
Heaven and Earth, so vast, so vast.
Frost clothes all things in Autumn,
Winds waft, the broad wastes cold.
Glory, splendor; eastward flowing stream,
This world's affairs, just waves.
White sun covered, its dying rays,
The floating clouds, no resting place.
In lofty Wu-t'ung trees nest lowly finches.
Down among the thorny brush the Phoenix perches.
All that's left, to go home again,
Hand on my sword I sing, "The Going's Hard."

Translated from the Chinese by J. P. Seaton

CHANG CHI
768–830

When traveling, looking for a place to spend the night, we sometimes arrive at a spot we wouldn't otherwise ever have seen, as in the following poem by a Chinese poet.

COMING AT NIGHT TO A FISHERMAN'S HUT

Fisherman's hut, by the mouth of the river,
Water of the lake to his brushwood gate.
The traveler would beg night's lodging,
But the master's not yet home.
The bamboo thick, the village far.
Moon rises, fishing boats are few.
There! far off, along the sandy shore
The spring breeze moving his cloak of straw.

Translated from the Chinese by J. P. Seaton

PO CHÜ-I
772—846

And here travel at night, before dawn, in a horse carriage, obviously only one stretch of a longer journey—it associates in my mind with similar travels in my childhood when automobiles in my remote corner of Europe were few. I love Po Chü-I for the extraordinary vividness of his images.

STARTING EARLY

Washed by the rain, dust and grime are laid;
Skirting the river, the road's course is flat.
The moon has risen on the last remnants of night;
The travellers' speed profits by the early cold.
In the great silence I whisper a faint song;
In the black darkness are bred somber thoughts.
On the lotus-bank hovers a dewy breeze;
Through the rice furrows trickles a singing stream.
At the noise of our bells a sleeping dog stirs;
At the sight of our torches a roosting bird wakes.
Dawn glimmers through the shapes of misty trees . . .
For ten miles, till day at last breaks.

Translated from the Chinese by Arthur Waley

Po Chü-I is also the author of a poem of another kind of travel—travel in dreams.

A DREAM OF MOUNTAINEERING

At night, in my dream, I stoutly climbed a mountain,
Going out alone with my staff of holly-wood.
A thousand crags, a hundred hundred valleys—
In my dream-journey none were unexplored
And all the while my feet never grew tired
And my step was as strong as in my young days.
Can it be that when the mind travels backward
The body also returns to its old state?
And can it be, as between body and soul,
That the body may languish, while the soul is still strong?
Soul and body—both are vanities;
Dreaming and waking—both alike unreal.
In the day my feet are palsied and tottering;
In the night my steps go striding over the hills.
As day and night are divided in equal parts—
Between the two, I *get* as much as I *lose*.

Translated from the Chinese by Arthur Waley

LI PO
701—762

It is somewhat surprising that this dramatic poem is the work of a Chinese poet. In Western poetry, dreams of ascending are quite common because they refer to the vertical structure of the Western religious world. No wonder that Dante ascends to Paradise. But here we have a flight upward, following a goddess in a multicolored robe, and, in contrast, the sudden sight of the earth below, the poor earth of misfortune, after an invasion.

ANCIENT AIR

Westward over Lotus Mountain
Afar, far off: Bright Star!
Hibiscus blooms in her white hand,
With airy step she climbs Great Purity.
Rainbow robes, trailing a broad sash,
Floating she brushes the heavenly stairs,
And invites me to mount the Cloud Terrace,
There to salute the immortal Wei Shu-ch'ing.
Ravished, mad, I go with her,
Upon a swan to reach the Purple Vault.
There I looked down, on Loyang's waters:
Vast sea of barbarian soldiers marching,
Fresh blood spattered on the grasses of the wilds.
Wolves, with men's hats on their heads.

Translated from the Chinese by J. P. Seaton

War against peoples pressing out from the center of the Asiatic continent fills a considerable part of Chinese history. The travels of soldiers or officials sent to the "outskirts" are the frequent subject of poems. A whole cycle of such travel poems was written by a famous painter and poet, Wang Wei. He was a poet of Taoist and Buddhist inspiration, but he pursued the career of an official as well, albeit somewhat unwillingly, travelling through the vast spaces of the borderland territory.

SONG OF MARCHING WITH THE ARMY

Horns blow the travelers into movement.
Noisily they get under way with the sad sound
of reed pipes and chaos of neighing horses
as everyone struggles to ford Gold River.
The border sun settles in the desert
while sounds of war rise in smoke and dust.
We'll bind the neck of every chieftain
and bring them as presents for the emperor.

Translated from the Chinese by Tony and Willis Barnstone and Xu Haixin

As far as I know, among the translators of this poem there is a controversy as to the name of the bird shot by the hunter's arrow. Some opt for the vulture and some for the eagle. Apparently, in Chinese the same word is used for both. Of course I am not competent to take a position.

WATCHING THE HUNT

Strong wind. The horn-bow sings.
The generals are hunting in Wei Cheng.

In withered grass, the falcon's eye is sharper.
In melting snow, horse hooves are light.

They've just passed New Harvest Market
yet are already home at Willow Branch.

They look back. They shot the vulture
in a thousand miles of twilight clouds.

Translated from the Chinese by Tony and Willis Barnstone and Xu Haixin

CHANG YANG-HAO

1269—1329

Several centuries have passed since Wang Wei was writing his poems. We are now in a different period of Chinese history, and the reflection on time's passing makes an integral part of this poem—a poem like the Bible's vanity of vanities, with two magnificent concluding lines.

RECALLING THE PAST AT T'UNG PASS

As if gathered together,
　　　　　　　the peaks of the ranges.
As if raging,
　　　　the waves on these banks.
Winding along
　　　　　these mountains & rivers,
the road to the T'ung Pass.
I look west
　　　　& hesitant I lament
here where
　　　　　opposing armies passed through.
Palaces
　　of countless rulers
　　now but dust.
Empires rise:
　　　　people suffer.
Empires fall:
　　　　people suffer.

"Made new" by C. H. Knock and G. G. Gach

ROLF JACOBSEN
1907—

There is no reason to stay with Chinese poetry, so I return to the twentieth century and to train travel. Very often, the train is presented as the site of observation by a person who travels. Beyond, out the window, there are towns, cities, and in this case a Norwegian landscape of villages, provoking a philosophical reflection on the life of their inhabitants, life deprived of love, unfulfilled, with an enormous potential which waits for liberation.

EXPRESS TRAIN

Express train 1256 races alongside hidden, remote villages. House after house wanders by, pale gray, shivering. Rail fences, rocks and lakes, and the closed gates.

Then I have to think in the morning twilight: What would happen if someone could release the loneliness of those hearts? People live there, no one can see them, they walk across rooms, in behind the doors, the need, blank-eyed, hardened by love they cannot give and no one gets a chance to give them. What would rise higher here than the mountains—the Skarvang Hills—what flame, what force, what storms of steady light?

Express train 1256, eight soot-black cars, turns toward new, endlessly unknown villages. Springs of light behind the panes, unseen wells of power along the mountains—these we travel past, hurry past, only four minutes late for Marnardal.

Translated from the Norwegian by Roger Greenwald

A train compartment, not necessarily what is seen moving beyond the window, may appear as the background, with fellow passengers as the object of attention, and speculation about their internal world—thoughts, dreams. Nevertheless, the duality of motion internal and external seems to be important. Antonio Machado places his characters in a night train; the visibility of what's outside is limited. "A traveler mad with grief" and the narrator both are busy with their reminiscences. Unexpectedly, the end is like an epiphany.

RAINBOW AT NIGHT

for Don Ramón del Valle-Inclán

The train moves through the Guadarrama
one night on the way to Madrid.
The moon and the fog create
high up a rainbow.
Oh April moon, so calm,
driving up the white clouds!

The mother holds her boy
sleeping on her lap.
The boy sleeps, and nevertheless
sees the green fields outside,
and trees lit up by sun,
and the golden butterflies.

The mother, her forehead dark
between a day gone and a day to come,
sees a fire nearly out
and an oven with spiders.

There's a traveler mad with grief,
no doubt seeing odd things;
he talks to himself, and when he looks
wipes us out with his look.

I remember fields under snow,
and pine trees of other mountains.

And you, Lord, through whom we all
have eyes, and who sees souls,
tell us if we all one
day will see your face.

Translated from the Spanish by Robert Bly

WILLIAM STAFFORD
1914—1993

Until recently, the train symbolized any travel, and that's why poets wrote so much about it. They were fascinated by landscapes, scenes moving beyond the window— mysterious because seen only for an instant. And so for William Stafford, a group of Indians out the window of the dining car reveals itself as the Other, with its own sequence of events (a funeral), which, for a short time only, crosses the sequence inside.

VACATION

One scene as I bow to pour her coffee:—

> Three Indians in the scouring drouth
> huddle at the grave scooped in the gravel,
> lean to the wind as our train goes by.
> Someone is gone.
> There is dust on everything in Nevada.

I pour the cream.

JOHN HAINES

1924 —

Here again a window, and the filling of the immensity of space, mostly deserted, as a typical feature of the American continent. It is the north we nearly see, the stern and miserly light above a certain geographical latitude. The settlement is really a camp by a mine, and there is the hint of a complete barrier between the white observer and the Indian tribe.

THE TRAIN STOPS AT HEALY FORK

We pressed our faces
against the freezing glass,
saw the red soil
mixed with snow,
and a strand of barbed wire.

A line of boxcars
stood open on a siding,
their doorways
briefly afire in the sunset.

We saw the scattered iron
and timber of the campsite,
the coal seam
in the river bluff,
the twilight green of the icefall.

But the coppery tribesmen
we looked for had vanished,
the children of wind and shadow,
gone off with their rags
and hunger
to the blue edge of night.

Our train began to move,
bearing north,
sounding its hoarse whistle
in the starry gloom of the canyon.

BRONISLAW MAJ
1953—

A very different landscape makes its appearance beyond the window in a poem by
Bronislaw Maj: autumn countryside in Poland (mist, newly plowed earth, women
in dark shawls), but here too the Other calls for reconstructing some common story,
and for retaining it in memory because this image is given only once.

SEEN FLEETINGLY, FROM A TRAIN

Seen fleetingly, from a train:
a foggy evening, strands of smoke
hanging immobile over fields,
the humid blackness of earth, the sun
almost set—against its fading shield,
far away, two dots: women in dark wraps
coming back from church perhaps, perhaps
one tells something to another, some common story,
of sinful lives perhaps—her words
distinct and simple but out of them
one could create everything
again. Keep it in memory, forever:
the sun, ploughed earth, women,
love, evening, those few words
good for the beginning, keep it all—
perhaps tomorrow we will be
somewhere else, altogether.

Translated from the Polish by Czeslaw Milosz and Robert Hass

EDWARD FIELD

1924—

Travel by a suburban train may sometimes be an entire odyssey, if we consider the intensity of feelings in the person travelling. Such is the case in this poem by Edward Field. We don't know the reasons for the enormous internal tension in this man; we know only that he experiences a breakthrough in the flowing sequence of joy, fear, and weeping. But the last station means the resolution of his tension, and radiance.

A JOURNEY

When he got up that morning everything was different:
He enjoyed the bright spring day
But he did not realize it exactly, he just enjoyed it.

And walking down the street to the railroad station
Past magnolia trees with dying flowers like old socks
It was a long time since he had breathed so simply.

Tears filled his eyes and it felt good
But he held them back
Because men didn't walk around crying in that town.

Waiting on the platform at the station
The fear came over him of something terrible about to happen:
The train was late and he recited the alphabet to keep hold.

And in its time it came screeching in
And as it went on making its usual stops,
People coming and going, telephone poles passing,

He hid his head behind a newspaper
No longer able to hold back the sobs, and willed his eyes
To follow the rational weavings of the seat fabric.

He didn't do anything violent as he had imagined.
He cried for a long time, but when he finally quieted down
A place in him that had been closed like a fist was open,

And at the end of the ride he stood up and got off that train:
And through the streets and in all the places he lived in later on
He walked, himself at last, a man among men,
With such radiance that everyone looked up and wondered.

CH'IN KUAN
1049—1101

Travel by water is older than other kinds of travel, and sailing has its honorable place in poetry—in China, too, testifying to the importance of rivers and canals in that country.

ALONG THE GRAND CANAL

Hoar frost has congealed
On the deck
Of my little boat.
The water
Is clear and still.
Cold stars beyond counting
Swim alongside.
Thick reeds hide the shore.
You'd think you'd left the earth.
Suddenly there breaks in
Laughter and song.

Translated from the Chinese by Kenneth Rexroth

WANG WEI
701—761

And here is a charming poem about a marvel of a city to which we arrive by water for the first time. I, too, lived through a similar experience, in which three of us, twenty years old, approached the embankment of the city of Constance in southern Germany by canoe, A.D. 1931. I should add that if Wang Wei was not a very willing sailor, he was at least a curious one. He was forced by the duties of his office to travel, but he longed for a Buddhist detachment, which, in his verse, is always symbolized by white clouds.

MORNING, SAILING INTO XINYANG

As my boat sails into Xingze Lake
I am stunned by this glorious city!
A canal meanders by narrow courtyard doors.
Fires and cooking smoke crowd the water.
In these people I see strange customs
and the dialect here is obscure.
In late autumn, fields are abundant.
Morning light. Noise wakes at the city wells.
Fish merchants float on the waves.
Chickens and dogs. Villages on either bank.
I'm heading away from white clouds.
What will become of my solitary sail?

Translated from the Chinese by Tony and Willis Barnstone and Xu Haixin

JOHN HAINES
1924—

Anybody who has wandered in the mountains will recognize the precision of description in this poem by John Haines.

ON THE MOUNTAIN

We climbed out of timber,
bending on the steep meadow
to look for berries,
then still in the reddening sunlight
went on up the windy shoulder.

A shadow followed us up the mountain
like a black moon rising.
Minute by minute the autumn lamps
on the slope burned out.

Around us the air and the rocks
whispered of night . . .

A great cloud blew from the north,
and the mountain vanished
in the rain and stormlit darkness.

JAAN KAPLINSKI
1941—

Whoever wants to combine looking and reflection should walk. In this poem a father and his son walk along a river, in the spring, it seems—which in their country, Estonia, comes late and has recurrences of frost. The conversation with the son about the moon is not lacking a curious contradiction: in the Baltic countries, celestial bodies were once worshipped as divinities, and so one should know how to address the moon. But, at the same time, the father provides the son with some scientific information.

WE STARTED HOME, MY SON AND I

We started home, my son and I.
Twilight already. The young moon
stood in the western sky and beside it
a single star. I showed them to my son
and explained how the moon should be greeted
and that this star is the moon's servant.
As we neared home, he said
that the moon is far, as far
as that place where we went.
I told him the moon is much, much farther
and reckoned: if one were to walk
ten kilometers each day, it would take
almost a hundred years to reach the moon.
But this was not what he wanted to hear.
The road was already almost dry.
The river was spread on the marsh; ducks and other waterfowl
crowed the beginning of night. The snow's crust
crackled underfoot—it must
have been freezing again. All the houses' windows
were dark. Only in our kitchen
a light shone. Beside our chimney, the shining moon,
and beside the moon, a single star.

Translated from the Estonian by Jaan Kaplinski with Sam Hamill and Riina Tamm

Places

We visit various places in travelling. Yet travel has always had something mysterious in it, because it is an expectation of the not-yet-known. Perhaps this is a sufficient reason for introducing a separate chapter of poems that deal with places. Yes, we arrive somewhere from our home in another town, city, or village, but not necessarily romanticizing the new, for often we are compelled by circumstances: our employment, our studies, or exile. A given place becomes our temporary home, and yet we preserve a sufficient distance to feel its strangeness, not perceived by those who live there permanently.

WANG CHIEN
736—835

The ancient empire of China was an entire world for its inhabitants. Its remote provinces seemed to be exotic countries distinct by their geography and their people's way of life, such as, for instance, the South, largely identical with the territory of present-day Vietnam.

THE SOUTH

In the southern land many birds sing;
Of towns and cities half are unwalled.
The country markets are thronged by wild tribes;
The mountain-villages bear river-names.
Poisonous mists rise from the damp sands;
Strange fires gleam through the night-rain.
And none passes but the lonely seeker of pearls
Year by year on his way to the South Sea.

Translated from the Chinese by Arthur Waley

TU FU
713—770

A journey to the North of China in autumn, when one could feel in the air the approaching frosts and snows, didn't incline this poet to optimism—who, as we can easily guess, took part in an expedition because of his office.

TRAVELLING NORTHWARD

Screech owls moan in the yellowing
Mulberry trees. Field mice scurry,
Preparing their holes for winter.
Midnight, we cross an old battlefield.
The moonlight shines cold on white bones.

Translated from the Chinese by Kenneth Rexroth

PO CHÜ-I
772—846

The vast network of the state administration employed well-educated men, many of them poets, as was the case for practically all the most eminent literati at the time of the T'ang Dynasty. Disgrace and assignment to a post in a distant province were quite common; thence exile as a topic of poetry. There were also journeys on official missions, escapes from rebellions, service with armies, or just searches for a peaceful retreat in a bucolic setting far from the court and the market. All such situations would give occasion for poems.

AFTER COLLECTING THE AUTUMN TAXES

From these high walls I look at the town below
Where the natives of Pa cluster like a swarm of flies.
How can I govern these people and lead them aright?
I cannot even understand what they say.
But at least I am glad, now that the taxes are in,
To learn that in my province there is no discontent.
I fear its prosperity is not due to me
And was only caused by the year's abundant crops.
The papers I have to deal with are simple and few;
My arbour by the lake is leisurely and still.
In the autumn rain the berries fall from the eaves;
At the evening bell the birds return to the wood.
A broken sunlight quavers over the southern porch
Where I lie on my couch abandoned to idleness.

Translated from the Chinese by Arthur Waley

RAIN

Since I lived a stranger in the City of Hsün-yang
Hour by hour bitter rain has poured.
On few days has the dark sky cleared;
In listless sleep I have spent much time.
The lake has widened till it almost joins the sky;
The clouds sink till they touch the water's face.
Beyond my hedge I hear the boatman's talk;
At the street-end I hear the fisher's song.
Misty birds are lost in yellow air;
Windy sails kick the white waves.
In front of my gate the horse and carriage-way
In a single night has turned into a river-bed.

Translated from the Chinese by Arthur Waley

TU FU
713—770

ANOTHER SPRING

White birds over the grey river.
Scarlet flowers on the green hills.
I watch the Spring go by and wonder
If I shall ever return home.

Translated from the Chinese by Kenneth Rexroth

SU MAN SHU
[dates unknown]

*Sometimes the place of exile was farther than the poet's own continent—here,
within the continent, it was in Japan.*

EXILE IN JAPAN

On the balcony of the tower
I play my flute and watch
The Spring rain.
I wonder
If I ever
Will go home and see
The tide bore
In Chekiang River again.
Straw sandals, an old
Begging bowl, nobody
Knows me. On how many
Bridges have I trampled
The fallen cherry blossoms?

Translated from the Chinese by Kenneth Rexroth

JOSEPH BRODSKY
1940—1996

For a newly arrived immigrant, Russian poet Joseph Brodsky, the American Midwest was a completely exotic land. He introduced young Americans to the arcana of poetry at the University of Michigan in Ann Arbor.

IN THE LAKE DISTRICT

In those days, in a place where dentists thrive
(their daughters order fancy clothes from London;
their painted forceps hold aloft on signboards
a common and abstracted Wisdom Tooth),
there I—whose mouth held ruins more abject
than any Parthenon—a spy, a spearhead
for some fifth column of a rotting culture
(my cover was a lit. professorship),
was living at a college near the most
renowned of the fresh-water lakes; the function
to which I'd been appointed was to wear out
the patience of the ingenuous local youth.

Whatever I wrote then was incomplete:
my lines expired in strings of dots. Collapsing,
I dropped, still fully dressed, upon my bed.
At night I stared up at the darkened ceiling
until I saw a shooting star, which then, conforming to the laws of
    self-combustion,
would flash—before I'd even made a wish—
across my cheek and down onto my pillow.

Translated from the Russian by George L. Kline

ODYSSEUS TO TELEMACHUS

My dear Telemachus,
           The Trojan War
is over now; I don't recall who won it.
The Greeks, no doubt, for only they would leave
so many dead so far from their own homeland.
But still, my homeward way has proved too long.
While we were wasting time there, old Poseidon,
it almost seems, stretched and extended space.

I don't know where I am or what this place
can be. It would appear some filthy island,
with bushes, buildings, and great grunting pigs.
A garden choked with weeds; some queen or other.
Grass and huge stones . . . Telemachus, my son!
To a wanderer the faces of all islands
resemble one another. And the mind
trips, numbering waves; eyes, sore from sea horizons,
run; and the flesh of water stuffs the ears.
I can't remember how the war came out;
even how old you are—I can't remember.

Grow up, then, my Telemachus, grow strong.
Only the gods know if we'll see each other
again. You've long since ceased to be that babe
before whom I reined in the plowing bullocks.
Had it not been for Palamedes' trick
we two would still be living in one household.
But maybe he was right; away from me
you are quite safe from all Oedipal passions,
and your dreams, my Telemachus, are blameless.

Translated from the Russian by George L. Kline

LOUIS SIMPSON
1923—

America, even for an American, may present itself in quite an alien manner, and the streets of big cities at night seem to contain the essence of alienation, which is faithfully conveyed by Louis Simpson's poem.

AFTER MIDNIGHT

The dark streets are deserted,
With only a drugstore glowing
Softly, like a sleeping body;

With one white, naked bulb
In the back, that shines
On suicides and abortions.

Who lives in these dark houses?
I am suddenly aware
I might live here myself.

The garage man returns
And puts the change in my hand,
Counting the singles carefully.

ALLEN GINSBERG
1926—

Fortunately, America is, for the most part, not all big cities—but often little towns and villages. Allen Ginsberg, though a native of New York, lived in his youth in Berkeley and San Francisco, and from that time comes the following poem.

A STRANGE NEW COTTAGE IN BERKELEY

All afternoon cutting bramble blackberries off a tottering
brown fence
    under a low branch with its rotten old apricots miscellaneous
under the leaves,
    fixing the drip in the intricate gut machinery of a new toilet;
    found a good coffee pot in the vines by the porch, rolled a
big tire out of the scarlet bushes, hid my marijuana;
    wet the flowers, playing the sunlit water each to each,
returning for godly extra drops for the stringbeans and daisies;
    three times walked round the grass and sighed absently:
    my reward, when the garden fed me its plums from the
form of a small tree in the corner,
    an angel thoughtful of my stomach, and my dry and love-
lorn tongue.

JAMES APPLEWHITE
1935—

The province and the big metropolis—in America, above all, Babylon: i.e., New York. But for the inhabitants of the southern states—such as, here, North Carolina—there is a latent dislike of the Yankees, going back to the Civil War. James Applewhite, a poet from the South, sends his son on his first trip to Babylon with a blessing but also with a warning.

PRAYER FOR MY SON

The low river flows like smoked glass.
Small bass guard their nest. Next
To our house, the cardinals in their
Crabapple feed two open mouths.
Parents and offspring, we flex
And swing in this future's coming,
Mirror we look into only darkly.
My youngest is boarding an airplane
To a New York he's never seen.
Raised in such slumberous innocence
Of Bible schools and lemonade,
I adjust poorly to this thirst for
Fame, this electronic buzz prizing
Brilliance and murderers. Oh son,
Know that the psyche has its own
Fame, whether known or not, that
Soul can flame like feathers of a bird.
Grow into your own plumage, brightly,
So that any tree is a marvelous city.
I wave from here by this Indian Eno,
Whose lonely name I make known.

PO CHÜ-I

772—846

There are many varieties of coping with life in exile and Chinese poets are very skillful at them—like this poet, my favorite realist, Po Chü-I. He came up with a good approach to exile.

MADLY SINGING IN THE MOUNTAINS

There is no one among men that has not a special failing;
And my failing consists in writing verses.
I have broken away from the thousand ties of life;
But this infirmity still remains behind.
Each time that I look at a fine landscape,
Each time that I meet a loved friend,
I raise my voice and recite a stanza of poetry
And marvel as though a God had crossed my path.
Ever since the day I was banished to Hsün-yang
Half my time I have lived among the hills.
And often, when I have finished a new poem,
Alone I climb the road to the Eastern Rock.
I lean my body on the banks of white Stone;
I pull down with my hands a green cassia branch.
My mad singing startles the valleys and hills;
The apes and birds all come to peep.
Fearing to become a laughing-stock to the world,
I choose a place that is unfrequented by men.

Translated from the Chinese by Arthur Waley

ELIZABETH BISHOP
1911—1979

Trying to show how poets of various languages and epochs describe things and places, I move among many lives, faces, dresses, each time identifying myself with one character; and I jump in time and geography. It's far from China to Brazil such as it was when it didn't have that name, when the first whites landed on its shores, and a clash occurred between Roman Catholic civilization and Nature, with its demonic and innocent sensuality, and with the people there, "savages," "children of nature." Or perhaps that clash is such as we represent it—we and Elizabeth Bishop, who, besides, lived a long time in Brazil and describes a landscape well known to her.

BRAZIL, JANUARY 1, 1502

. . . embroidered nature . . . tapestried landscape.

——SIR KENNETH CLARK
Landscape into Art

Januaries, Nature greets our eyes
exactly as she must have greeted theirs:
every square inch filling in with foliage—
big leaves, little leaves, and giant leaves,
blue, blue-green, and olive,
with occasional lighter veins and edges,
or a satin underleaf turned over;
monster ferns
in silver-gray relief,
and flowers, too, like giant water lilies
up in the air—up, rather, in the leaves—
purple, yellow, two yellows, pink,
rust red and greenish white;
solid but airy; fresh as if just finished
and taken off the frame.

A blue-white sky, a simple web,
backing for feathery detail:
brief arcs, a pale-green broken wheel,
a few palms, swarthy, squat, but delicate;
and perching there in profile, beaks agape,
the big symbolic birds keep quiet,
each showing only half his puffed and padded,
pure-colored or spotted breast.
Still in the foreground there is Sin:
five sooty dragons near some massy rocks.
The rocks are worked with lichens, gray moonbursts
splattered and overlapping,
threatened from underneath by moss
in lovely hell-green flames,
attacked above
by scaling-ladder vines, oblique and neat,
"one leaf yes and one leaf no"; (in Portuguese).
The lizards scarcely breathe; all eyes
are on the smaller, female one, back-to,
her wicked tail straight up and over,
red as a red-hot wire.

Just so the Christians, hard as nails,
tiny as nails, and glinting,
in creaking armor, came and found it all,
not unfamiliar:
no lovers' walks, no bowers,
no cherries to be picked, no lute music,
but corresponding, nevertheless,
to an old dream of wealth and luxury
already out of style when they left home—
wealth, plus a brand-new pleasure.
Directly after Mass, humming perhaps
L'Homme armé or some such tune,

they ripped away into the hanging fabric,
each out to catch an Indian for himself—
those maddening little women who kept calling,
calling to each other (or had the birds waked up?)
and retreating, always retreating, behind it.

ROLF JACOBSEN
1907 —

The goal of European travels, beginning with the Renaissance, was to gain an acquaintance with the marvels of architecture and art left by the past. The privileged place was Italy, and wanderers and pilgrims from Northern Europe would go there. That custom didn't disappear completely, though "cultural tourism" became but a part of the general rush to visit places in the search for new impressions. Rolf Jacobsen, as we see, travelled from his native Norway to Italy not in search of the sun only.

THE CATACOMBS IN SAN CALLISTO

A city in death with the streets caved in and the traffic lights
    still.

A city seen in a broken mirror we have to rub the darkness
    from with our hands.

Beneath the stars and beneath the earth, a city like a laugh
    behind a closed door.

A Venice of night, bridges reflected in dust.

The world's pride, a city with its forehead split and its face
    overgrown with slime.

Thin shreds of roots like fingers and feet, hands and shoulder
    blades of skeletons.

Roots and branches of roots, dead that bend their fingers
    around the dark as around a stone.

A tree up from our broken reality, with its root planted in
    humiliation.

A tree that stretches out over the earth and
    reaches almost to the stars, Arcturus, Capella.

A tree from the earth's heart. Wondrous. Keeping faith.

Translated from the Norwegian by Roger Greenwald

GUNNAR EKËLOF
1907—1968

Another Scandinavian, Swedish poet Gunnar Ekëlof, looked for Greece not among
the vestiges of antiquity but in a pastoral mountain landscape.

GREECE

  O whitewashed chapel
with icons worn out by kisses!
Your door is shut
only with a spike and a twist of wool
such as one gathers among thistles
and twines around the finger
The oil cruse stands ready
and the greasy lamp, and the plate
for him who has a penny
for him who has matches
Old and new icons
a gift of mothers
—occasions have not been wanting—
for him who was left in the pass
for him who was taken as a janissary
for him whose eyesight was emptied
for him who was lost with Markos—
cheap prints under glass
Big as a sheepcote:
Your bells the sheepbells
tinkling somewhere up in the mountains
chapel whose lock is wool.

TOMAS TRANSTRÖMER
1931–

Here, the Greece of islands and ports gives occasion to Swedish poet Tomas Tranströmer for a descriptive poem which changes into a moral parable.

SYROS

In Syros' harbor abandoned merchant ships lay idle.
Stem by stem by stem. Moored for many years:
CAPE RION, Monrovia.
KRITOS, Andros.
SCOTIA, Panama.

Dark paintings on the water, they have been hung aside.

Like playthings from our childhood, grown gigantic,
that remind us
of what we never became.

XELATROS, Piraeus.
CASSIOPEIA, Monrovia.
The ocean scans them no more.

But when we first came to Syros, it was at night,
we saw stem by stem by stem in moonlight and thought:
what a powerful fleet, what splendid connections!

Translated from the Swedish by May Swenson and Leif Sjöberg

LINDA GREGG
1942—

Once again Greece, this time seen with the eyes of an American woman, and, to the credit of the poet, we should acknowledge that she was aware of the tragic modern Greece.

NIGHT MUSIC

She sits on the mountain that is her home
and the landscapes slide away. One goes down
and then up to the monastery. One drops away
to a winnowing ring and a farmhouse where a girl
and her mother are hanging the laundry.
There's a tiny port in the distance where
the shore reaches the water. She is numb
and clear because of the grieving in that world.
She thinks of the bandits and soldiers who
return to the places they have destroyed.
Who plant trees and build walls and play music
in the village square evening after evening,
believing the mothers of the boys they killed
and the women they raped will eventually come
out of the white houses in their black dresses
to sit with their children and the old.
Will listen to the music with unreadable eyes.

ADAM ZAGAJEWSKI
1945—

What follows is probably the shortest poem on the twentieth-century mania of visiting places, all over the earth, as tourists.

AUTO MIRROR

In the rear-view mirror suddenly
I saw the bulk of the Beauvais Cathedral;
great things dwell in small ones
for a moment.

Translated from the Polish by Czeslaw Milosz and Robert Hass

SANDOR WEORES

1913—1989

The Hungarian pushta, *a limitless plain, is the subject of this poem by Sandor Weores. This poem surprises me somewhat because Weores was considered a difficult, very avant-garde poet, whereas here he is a painter of the landscape, much in the nineteenth-century tradition.*

THE PLAIN

A muddy-wheeled cart goes lurching
between the poplar trees' wide rows
just where the narrow track
cuts from the main road.

Crops, naked fields, horizon
and sky surround the single horse
and driver in a wide frame,
hiding them in fixity that never alters.

The distant here seems very near
and what's near seems far away:
all sing together as one—
everywhere furrows, lumps of clay—

horse, driver and small cart
rolling the working hours away
through slow centuries,
and buried by the nights and days.

Translated from the Hungarian by J. Kessler

TOMAS TRANSTRÖMER
1931—

A transformation of the landscape, and awareness of the alienation of man in new surroundings, transpire in this poem by Tranströmer.

OUTSKIRTS

Men in overalls the same color as earth rise from a ditch.
It's a transitional place, in stalemate, neither country nor city.
Construction cranes on the horizon want to take the big leap, but
    the clocks are against it.
Concrete piping scattered around laps at the light with cold
    tongues.
Auto-body shops occupy old barns.
Stones throw shadows as sharp as objects on the moon surface.
And these sites keep on getting bigger
like the land bought with Judas' silver: "a potter's field for burying
    strangers."

Translated from the Swedish by Robert Bly

DAVID KIRBY

[date unknown]

A poem on an American student in Paris is a good example of familiarity seasoned with a feeling of not-quite-belonging. Something of the sort may also be found in poems on modern tourism. Neither a short visit nor a longer stay reveals things completely new to the citizen of the global village, yet a certain distance favors observation of the detail.

TO A FRENCH STRUCTURALIST

There's no modesty, Todorov,
in the park where I read:
the young mothers and working girls
raise their skirts and open their blouses
to the sun while the children play,
the old men doze, and I wrestle
with your *Poetics*. When I look again,
perhaps they'll all be naked;
they'll make for the seesaw and jungle gym,
bosoms swinging and long legs flashing
in the midday light. Ah, that clerk
at the Préfecture de Police
looked at me with such disdain
when he asked what I was doing in Paris!
It was a lie, Todorov,
when I shrugged and said, "Nothing."

ANTONIO MACHADO
1895 — 1939

Willis Barnstone, translator of Wang Wei, considers Antonio Machado to be the most Chinese of Spanish poets and he sees in the following poem an "uncanny closeness" to the Chinese poet he translates.

SUMMER NIGHT

A beautiful summer night.
The tall houses leave
their balcony shutters open
to the wide plaza of the old village.
In the large deserted square,
stone benches, burning bush and acacias
trace their black shadows
symmetrically on the white sand.
In its zenith, the moon; in the tower,
the clock's illuminated globe.
I walk through this ancient village,
alone, like a ghost.

Translated from the Spanish by Willis Barnstone

WANG WEI
701—761

*In the nineteenth century people visited certain wonders of nature, for instance, the
waterfall of Schaffhausen in Europe, and, in America, Niagara Falls. It seems that
in old China, similar wonders also attracted visitors.*

A WHITE TURTLE UNDER A WATERFALL

The waterfall on South Mountain hits the rocks,
tosses back its foam with terrifying thunder,
blotting out even face-to-face talk.
Collapsing water and bouncing foam soak blue moss,
old moss so thick
it drowns the spring grass.
Animals are hushed.
Birds fly but don't sing
yet a white turtle plays on the pool's sand floor
    under riotous spray,
sliding about with the torrents.
The people of the land are benevolent.
No angling or net fishing.
The white turtle lives out its life, naturally.

Translated from the Chinese by Tony and Willis Barnstone and Xu Haixin

OU YANG HSIU

1007—1072

There's a considerable number of Chinese poems in this book, for a simple reason: the pictorial qualities of that poetry, expressed in close cooperation with a calligrapher and an artist. "Fisherman" is really like a painting. And in fact the poem has been "translated" into an image by the brush of a painter, many times imitated and often reproduced in books on Chinese art. Drizzle and mist form an obstacle to seeing clearly, and this reminds us that a seeing person—an observer—exists.

FISHERMAN

The wind blows the line out from his fishing pole.
In a straw hat and grass cape the fisherman
Is invisible in the long reeds.
In the fine spring rain it is impossible to see very far
And the mist rising from the water has hidden the hills.

Translated from the Chinese by Kenneth Rexroth

LIU TSUNG-YÜAN
773—819

A fisherman in the landscape was a beloved subject of poets and painters. This poem, however, seems to me quite complicated, in spite of its apparent simplicity. For here there is action, and the fisherman himself appears only toward the end, as somebody who rows somewhere far.

OLD FISHERMAN

Old fisherman spends his night beneath the western cliffs.
At dawn, he boils Hsiang's waters, burns bamboo of Ch'u.
When the mist's burned off, and the sun's come out, he's gone.
The slap of the oars: the mountain waters green.
Turn and look, at heaven's edge, he's moving with the flow.
Above the cliffs the aimless clouds go too.

Translated from the Chinese by J. P. Seaton

And now a short, economic (in movements of word and brush) poem by Wang Wei.

MAGNOLIA BASIN

On branch tips the hibiscus bloom.
The mountains show off red calices.
Nobody. A silent cottage in the valley.
One by one flowers open, then fall.

Translated from the Chinese by Tony and Willis Barnstone and Xu Haixin

The Moment

Poetry feeds on the remembrance of our perceptions that are no more, since they belong to a moment in the past. That past may be of a year or of a minute; we do not write of what is presently happening, but always of something at a remove, albeit even the shortest. Remembrance of the things that are past allows for a dispassionate description: "Distance is the soul of beauty" (Simone Weil).

A moment is like a frame of film. Some poems attempt to catch and fix a moment, and thus to stop the film of time, to glance attentively at one of its frames. Probably modern poetry has been influenced by film in this respect. After all, a frame is a unit of space-time; i.e., a moment is not an abstraction, but is filled with what is seen by the eye. Time is not "an element" stretching infinitely, in a linear way, backwards and forwards; it always offers itself to the eye as saturated with a fragment of space, as in a film frame. This has been expressed in a famous passage of St. Augustine's *Confessions*: "So what is time? If no one asks me, I know: if I want to explain it to a person who asks, I do not know anymore and yet I affirm with certainty that, had nothing passed, there would not be past time—had nothing happened there would not be future time, had nothing existed, there would not be present time."

Some poems describe a moment placed far back in time; some create an illusion of the present—for instance, Walt Whitman's short poems, scenes of the Civil War, that resemble illustrations drawn for a magazine. When one approaches a poem it is interesting to ask where—how far away in time—a described moment resides. It makes a reader more attentive—and reading a poem is, after all, always an exercise in attention.

WALT WHITMAN
1819—1892

CAVALRY CROSSING A FORD

A line in long array where they wind betwixt green islands,
They take a serpentine course, their arms flash in the sun—
  hark to the musical clank,
Behold the silvery river, in it the splashing horses loitering
  stop to drink,
Behold the brown-faced men, each group, each person a
  picture, the negligent rest on the saddles,
Some emerge on the opposite bank, others are just entering
  the ford—while,
Scarlet and blue and snowy white,
The guidon flags flutter gayly in the wind.

ALOYSIUS BERTRAND

1 8 0 7 — 1 8 4 1

This poem in prose by French poet Aloysius Bertrand is somewhat similar to a painting. It describes what a mason, Knupfer, sees while standing high on a scaffolding above a city. Yet there are, here, two moments, and between them, duration, because Knupfer, after his day's work, notices something else in the evening—the fire in a village situated not far from the city. This is a fine poem, but a bit too literary. It looks as if the author, influenced by his reading, decided to give a synthetic drawing of a city with a cathedral in the middle.

THE MASON

The Master Mason. —Look at these bastions, these buttresses; one would say they were built for eternity.

SCHILLER,
William Tell

The mason Abraham Knupfer is singing, trowel in hand, scaffolded so high in the air that, reading the Gothic verses on the great bell, he puts his feet on a level with both the church with thirty buttresses and the town with thirty churches.

He sees the stone monsters vomit the water from the slates into the confused abyss of galleries, windows, pendentives, bell-towers, turrets, roofs, and timber work, which the slanting motionless wing of the falcon marks with a grey spot.

He sees the fortifications outlined in a star, the citadel cocking itself up like a hen in a pie, the palace courtyards where the sun dries up the fountains and the monastery cloisters where the shadow turns around the pillars.

The imperial troops are quartered in the suburb. There is a horseman beating a drum down there. Abraham Knupfer makes out his tricorn hat, his shoulder-knots of red wool, his cockade crossed with a gimp, and his pigtail knotted with a ribbon.

He sees more: there are old soldiers who, in the park adorned

with huge leafy branches, on broad emerald lawns, riddle with arquebus shots a wooden bird fixed to the top of a maypole.

And in the evening, when the melodious nave of the cathedral went to sleep lying with its arms in a cross, he saw from his ladder on the horizon, a village, set on fire by soldiers, flaming like a comet in the blue sky.

Translated from the French by E. D. Hartley

KENNETH REXROTH
1905—1982

To sojourn in the now. *Kenneth Rexroth, whom I knew personally, was a kind of father of the Beat movement in poetry, which was born in San Francisco and Berkeley. At that time Rexroth was already considered the most eminent poet in California, in those circles which took an interest in poetry. Sympathetic toward the young, and close to them in his anarchist convictions, he backed the doings of disheveled and savage youngsters who, however, were better educated than one might guess from their subversive syntax. An excellent translator of Chinese and Japanese poets; cosmopolitan, because he passed some time in France (he published a volume of Oscar Milosz's poems in his translation) and in Japan; he entered into the spirit of Buddhism, of which some of his poems remind us, resembling the poetry of Asia. Of course he was also a reader of Christian mystics, such as Jacob Boehme, a German cobbler of the seventeenth century, author of spiritual works.*

SIGNATURE OF ALL THINGS
Part I

My head and shoulders, and my book
In the cool shade, and my body
Stretched bathing in the sun, I lie
Reading beside the waterfall—
Boehme's "Signature of All Things."
Through the deep July day the leaves
Of the laurel, all the colors
Of gold, spin down through the moving
Deep laurel shade all day. They float
On the mirrored sky and forest
For a while, and then, still slowly
Spinning, sink through the crystal deep
Of the pool to its leaf gold floor.
The saint saw the world as streaming
In the electrolysis of love.
I put him by and gaze through shade

Folded into shade of slender
Laurel trunks and leaves filled with sun.
The wren broods in her moss domed nest.
A newt struggles with a white moth
Drowning in the pool. The hawks scream,
Playing together on the ceiling
Of heaven. The long hours go by.
I think of those who have loved me,
Of all the mountains I have climbed,
Of all the seas I have swum in.
The evil of the world sinks.
My own sin and trouble fall away
Like Christian's bundle, and I watch
My forty summers fall like falling
Leaves and falling water held
Eternally in summer air.

Another poem of Rexroth's is a description of what happened to him on a certain summer night, yet in order to render the experience in all its intensity he has to speak of it in the present tense. Let us imagine the effect were we to introduce the past tense. "I took a telescope, I looked, my eyes and brain were not asleep, I didn't know where I began or ended." Instead of immediate experience, we would introduce remembrance, whereas in the poem perception is given directly.

THE HEART OF HERAKLES

Lying under the stars,
In the summer night,
Late, while the autumn
Constellations climb the sky,
As the Cluster of Hercules
Falls down the west
I put the telescope by
And watch Deneb
Move towards the zenith.
My body is asleep. Only
My eyes and brain are awake.
The stars stand around me
Like gold eyes. I can no longer
Tell where I begin and leave off.
The faint breeze in the dark pines,
And the invisible grass,
The tipping earth, swarming stars
Have an eye that sees itself.

TU FU

713—770

Rexroth translated much Tu Fu, the leading poet of the T'ung Dynasty. As far as I know, he was helped by French translations. Nevertheless, comparing his versions with others, I admire his conciseness and choices of image. In "Sunset" Tu Fu enumerates actions of nature and of people at dusk-time (a series of moments). Mention of the "thousand cares" at the end of the poem introduces duration, and thus the poem, though it praises the very capturing of a moment, also expresses joy at the wine's ability to liberate us from the burden of the past.

SUNSET

Sunset glitters on the beads
Of the curtains. Spring flowers
Bloom in the valley. The gardens
Along the river are filled
With perfume. Smoke of cooking
Fires drifts over the slow barges.
Sparrows hop and tumble in
The branches. Whirling insects
Swarm in the air. Who discovered
That one cup of thick wine
Will dispel a thousand cares?

Translated from the Chinese by Kenneth Rexroth

What attracts me to the Chinese poets most is their ability to draw with a few dashes a certain situation, for instance, in this poem by Tu Fu, the hour before dawn, after an entire night of carousing with friends.

WINTER DAWN

The men and beasts of the zodiac
Have marched over us once more.
Green wine bottles and red lobster shells,
Both emptied, litter the table.
"Should auld acquaintance be forgot?" Each
Sits listening to his own thoughts,
And the sound of cars starting outside.
The birds in the eaves are restless,
Because of the noise and light. Soon now
In the winter dawn I will face
My fortieth year. Borne headlong
Towards the long shadows of sunset
By the headstrong, stubborn moments,
Life whirls past like drunken wildfire.

Translated from the Chinese by Kenneth Rexroth

Is this Tu Fu poem also about a moment? It enumerates the most common features of springtime, so perhaps this is just a poem about that season. But a man who writes clearly places himself in the now, and the word "now" could really precede every sentence.

SOUTH WIND

The days grow long, the mountains
Beautiful. The south wind blows
Over blossoming meadows.
Newly arrived swallows dart
Over the streaming marshes.
Ducks in pairs drowse on the warm sand.

Translated from the Chinese by Kenneth Rexroth

One more by Tu Fu: the moment immediately after rain. "Ten thousand miles" means simply a great distance, and not a precise measure. "West wind" simply blows from far away, over the continent.

CLEAR AFTER RAIN

Autumn, cloud blades on the horizon.
The west wind blows from ten thousand miles.
Dawn, in the clear morning air,
Farmers busy after long rain.
The desert trees shed their few green leaves.
The mountain pears are tiny but ripe.
A Tartar flute plays by the city gate.
A single wild goose climbs into the void.

Translated from the Chinese by Kenneth Rexroth

GARY SNYDER
1930—

This poem by Gary Snyder is like noting down what, precisely, happens; in other words, the time between seeing and noting is very short. The snowpeak changes color, shadows gather in the gorge, as if the writer sitting by the fire had an open notebook and tried to fix what he saw and what he, himself, was doing. Of course, the poem might not have been written at that moment in that landscape, but, rather, uses this device.

LATE OCTOBER CAMPING IN THE SAWTOOTHS

Sunlight climbs the snowpeak
    glowing pale red
Cold sinks into the gorge
    shadows merge.
Building a fire of pine twigs
    at the foot of a cliff,
Drinking hot tea from a tin cup
    in the chill air—
Pull on a sweater and roll a smoke.
    a leaf
    beyond fire
Sparkles with nightfall frost.

KEITH WILSON
1927 —

In this poem by Keith Wilson the description of the twilight is, again, in the present tense. There is a defined place from which the observer looks at the changes in the falling night. He stands in the yard and watches the walls and windows of his house. He notices a candle in his daughter's hand, her lit face; he hears pecans falling from the tree, which means that the tree rises above the roof of the house; he is aware of the moon rising and of its light, like platinum. And so there is a convention of simultaneity between observation and recording.

DUSK IN MY BACKYARD
San Miguel, N.M.

The long black night
moves over my walls:
inside a candle is lighted
by one of my daughters.

Even from here I can see
the illuminated eyes, bright
face of the child before flame.

It's nearly time to go in.
The wind is cooler now,
pecans drop, rattle down—

the tin roof of our house
rivers to platinum in the early moon.
Dogs bark & in the house, wine, laughter.

TED KOOSER

1939—

This poem, on a little town in Minnesota, is a synthetic image or even a collage.
There is no single observer. First, we see the last car of a moving train, then we
receive information about two lights in the darkness, one a bulb in the prison, the
other a flashlight handled by an old woman going downstairs to the bathroom. And
so altogether a province. The prison is an important building; an old house with
cats belongs to a lone woman (the husband dead, children somewhere far away).
Simultaneous images—moments are recaptured.

LATE LIGHTS IN MINNESOTA

At the end of a freight train rolling away,
a hand swinging a lantern.
The only lights left behind in the town
are a bulb burning cold in the jail,
and high in one house,
a five-battery flashlight
pulling an old woman downstairs to the toilet
among the red eyes of her cats.

TOMAS TRANSTRÖMER

1931 —

This poem by Tranströmer is the most literally spoken in the now, and it's so impressive that we forget to ask when—how long ago—the observer lived through it. It's like a snapshot, though enriched by things known from the past, in a dream or during illness.

TRACKS

Night, two o'clock: moonlight. The train has stopped
in the middle of the plain. Distant bright points of a town
twinkle cold on the horizon.

As when someone has gone into a dream so far
that he'll never remember he was there
when he comes back to his room.

And as when someone goes into a sickness so deep
that all his former days become twinkling points, a swarm,
cold and feeble on the horizon.

The train stands perfectly still.
Two o'clock: full moonlight, few stars.

Translated from the Swedish by Robert Bly

ROLF JACOBSEN
1907—

This poem by an eminent Norwegian poet, Rolf Jacobsen, notes down a moment at dawn and concentrates attention on the traces left by tires, then changes its perspective to that of an ant inside the letter "G," which for an ant is a tremendous obstacle.

RUBBER

One pale morning in June at four o'clock
when the country roads were still gray and wet
in their endless tunnels of forest,
a car had passed over the clay
just where the ant came out busily with its pine needle now
and kept wandering around in the big G of "Goodyear"
that was imprinted in the sand of country roads
for a hundred and twenty kilometers.
Pine needles are heavy.
Time after time it slid back down with its tottering load
and worked its way up again
and slipped back again.
Outward bound across the great, cloud-illuminated Sahara.

Translated from the Norwegian by Roger Greenwald

AL ZOLYNAS
1945—

*In the life of California poet Al Zolynas, a moment of activity, namely, washing
dishes, and the moment of the poem itself are not separated, and we can even
imagine that he talks to himself washing dishes and that a tape has recorded his
words. This would be a new kind of coping with time, though we know that
composition is an integral part of poetry, and that direct reaction to events is rather
rare. We are rather inclined to consider this poem a composition on the subject of
washing dishes, with a consciously maintained illusion of the present tense.*

ZEN OF HOUSEWORK

I look over my own shoulder
down my arms
to where they disappear under water
into hands inside pink rubber gloves
moiling among dinner dishes.

My hands lift a wine glass,
holding it by the stem and under the bowl.
It breaks the surface
like a chalice
rising from a medieval lake.

Full of the grey wine
of domesticity, the glass floats
to the level of my eyes.
Behind it, through the window
above the sink, the sun, among
a ceremony of sparrows and bare branches
is setting in Western America.

I can see thousands of droplets
of steam—each a tiny spectrum—rising
from my goblet of grey wine.

They sway, changing directions
constantly—like a school of playful fish,
or like the sheer curtain
on the window to another world.

Ah, grey sacrament of the mundane!

BRONISLAW MAJ
1953—

This poem by Bronislaw Maj tells about a moment lived long ago, when he was
four. The intensity of perception was so great that it remains fixed in memory as
forever present, as if it had just taken place. He uses the present tense, and perhaps
for the best, because the past tense might be somewhat sentimental.

AN AUGUST AFTERNOON

An August afternoon. Even here is heard
the rush of the glittering Raba.
We look at the mountains,
my mother and I. How clear the air is:
every dark spruce on Mount Lubon
is seen distinctly as if it grew in our garden.
An astonishing phenomenon—it astonishes my mother
and me. I am four and do not know
what it means *to be four.* I am
happy: I do not know what *to be* means
or *happiness.* I know my mother
sees and feels what I do. And I know
that as always in the evening
we will take a walk
far, up to the woods, already before
long.

Translated from the Polish by Czeslaw Milosz and Robert Hass

RAYMOND CARVER

1938—1988

*Just before daybreak, when it is still dark, an electrical blackout causes the speaker
to look outside at the landscape, which appears extraordinarily calm. The speaker
feels pure inside at that moment. Later the same morning, electricity is restored
and "things stood as they had before."*

THE WINDOW

A storm blew in last night and knocked out
the electricity. When I looked
through the window, the trees were translucent.
Bent and covered with rime. A vast calm
lay over the countryside.
I knew better. But at that moment
I felt I'd never in my life made any
false promises, nor committed
so much as one indecent act. My thoughts
were virtuous. Later on that morning,
of course, electricity was restored.
The sun moved from behind the clouds,
melting the hoarfrost.
And things stood as they had before.

JEAN FOLLAIN
1903—1971

An opposition between once in the past and now, in this poem by French poet Jean Follain, begins with a thought about a woman who buys an elixir in a city hundreds or thousands of years ago. The word "elixir" is important because it has magical connotations. What if she were buying cabbage? We don't know anything about this woman; we receive no image of her, and yet our awareness that she lived, existed, liberates in us a feeling of closeness to her, in her flesh. A woman who died long ago becomes like our contemporary women. The poem conveys a very complex set of feelings about the frailty and transience of the body, which is precisely what makes our life "vertiginous."

BUYING

She was buying an elixir
in a city
of bygone times
yet we should think of her
now when shoulders are as white
and wrists as fine
flesh as sweet
Oh, vertiginous life!

Translated from the French by Heather McHugh

I have doubts about some of Follain's poems. Since my ideal is simplicity, a work that pushes conciseness beyond a certain limit seems to me too literary, or too sophisticated, which are often equated. "Black Meat" expects the reader to guess that primitive cave dwellers are involved, for whom precious stones would have no value, and we don't know why those stones are there, where hunters used to carve their game.

BLACK MEAT

Around stones called precious
which only their own
dust can wear down
the eaters of venison
carve in silence
their black meat
the trees on the horizon
imitate in outline
a giant sentence.

Translated from the French by W. S. Merwin

Frankly, the modernist technique consisting of unexpected associations is not to my liking, as at the end of this poem, in which drops of blood fall upon a road. In order to understand this, we must presume that there are hunters in the neighborhood, that they shot a bird, and that a wounded bird flies over the road.

SCHOOL AND NATURE

Drawn on the blackboard
in the classroom in a town
a circle remained intact
and the teacher's chair was deserted
and the students had gone
one sailing on the flood
another plowing alone
and the road went winding
a bird letting fall
the dark drops of its blood.

Translated from the French by W. S. Merwin

LINDA GREGG

1942 —

This poem of Linda Gregg's is maintained entirely in the convention of narrating in the now. The narrator, as we guess, sits before a house in a Greek town and what she sees and hears makes the content of the poem. And thus we are close to the technique of communicating immediately one's perceptions. Yet even if one can command: "Oh, Moment, stop, you are beautiful," it is not a landscape completely free from anxiety. "The dark thing," the sea seen through the leaves, acquires in one's consciousness the symbolical meaning of danger, and in that manner "now" is entangled in the past and the future.

A DARK THING INSIDE THE DAY

So many want to be lifted by song and dancing,
and this morning it is easy to understand.
I write in the sound of chirping birds hidden
in the almond trees, the almonds still green
and thriving in the foliage. Up the street,
a man is hammering to make a new house as doves
continue their cooing forever. Bees humming
and high above that a brilliant clear sky.
The roses are blooming and I smell the sweetness.
Everything desirable is here already in abundance.
And the sea. The dark thing is hardly visible
in the leaves, under the sheen. We sleep easily.
So I bring no sad stories to warn the heart.
All the flowers are adult this year. The good
world gives and the white doves praise all of it.

ALEKSANDER WAT
1900—1967

This poem by Aleksander Wat is interesting for me because I know the place from which he looks down on the landscape of Provence. And that is La Messuguière, the retreat for writers, near Cabris. "How hot it is." This reminder is here to create the impression that this scenery is observed at that particular moment. The description of what one sees from above is precise, the comparisons—hand as wing, women as olives, little church as cypress and shepherd—introduce reflection, as does the mention of the youth of the world. The conclusion is unexpected. The landscape is dramatized by the personal situation of the onlooker, as he realizes his situation in a life of exile, far from the country where he was born, Poland.

FROM ''SONGS OF A WANDERER''

*It is the nature of the highest objective art to be clean.
The Muses are maidens.*

A. LANG
Homer and Anthropology

So beautiful the lungs
are breathless. The hand remembers:
I was a wing.
Blue. The peaks in ruddy
gold. Women of that land—
small olives. On a spacious saucer
wisps of smoke, houses, pastures, roads.
Interlacing of roads, o holy diligence
of man. How hot it is! The miracle
of shade returns. A shepherd, sheep, a dog, a ram
all in gilded bells. Olive trees
in twisted benevolence. A cypress—their lone shepherd. A village
on a Cabris cliff, protected
by its tiled roofs. And a church its cypress and shepherd.
Young day, young times, young world.

Birds listen, intently silent. Only a rooster crowing
from below in the hamlet of Spéracèdes. How
hot it is. It's bitter to die on foreign soil.
It's sweet to live in France.

Translated from the Polish by Czeslaw Milosz and Leonard Nathan

OSCAR V. DE L. MILOSZ
1877—1939

This French poet of Lithuanian origin, Oscar V. de L. Milosz, my relative, has found fine translators in English, beginning with Ezra Pound, and followed by Kenneth Rexroth, David Gascoyne. His poetry is steeped in the aura of the epoch of symbolism.

THE BRIDGE

Dead leaves are falling in the dormant air.
Look, my dear, what autumn did to our dear isle!
How pale it is!
What an orphan it is, so humble and docile!
Bells ring and ring at Saint-Louis-en-Isle
For a dead fuchsia of the bargemaster's wife.
Heads low, two horses, obedient, sleepy, take their last bath.
A big black dog barks and threatens from afar.
On the bridge only I and my child:
Her faded dress, frail shoulders, face white,
Flowers in her hands.
Oh my child! What will the coming time bring!
To them! To us! Oh my child! What will the coming time bring!

Translated from the French by Czeslaw Milosz and Robert Hass

JAAN KAPLINSKI
1941—

This is a perfect remembrance of things past. The narrator knows his botany well. He is able to name, in Latin, some ordinary plants beneath his feet, and one of those plants, Potentilla Anserina, goose tansy, suddenly opens the memory of childhood.

MY WIFE AND CHILDREN

My wife and children were waiting for ice cream.
For a while, I had nothing else to do
but stand, looking underfoot:
Festuca, Poa, Trifolium repens, Taraxacum vulgare
and just on the edge of the sidewalk, where people
often pass hurrying from the market hall to the bus station,
it's you, Potentilla Anserina, an old acquaintance
from Tartumaa and Võrumaa farmyards
we can never forget as we cannot also forget
gooseshit I so often stepped in
and that stuck between my toes.

Translated from the Estonian by Jaan Kaplinski with Sam Hamill and Riina Tamm

WALT WHITMAN
1819—1892

A moment and remembrance, this time in Walt Whitman, though here only a campfire and darkness with army tents are concrete, while the subject of the narrator's thoughts is "solemn and sweet and slow."

BY THE BIVOUAC'S FITFUL FLAME

By the bivouac's fitful flame,
A procession winding around me, solemn and sweet and
slow—but first I note,
The tents of the sleeping army, the fields' and woods' dim outline,
The darkness lit by spots of kindled fire, the silence,
Like a phantom far or near an occasional figure moving,
The shrubs and trees, (as I lift my eyes they seem to be
stealthily watching me,)
While wind in procession thoughts, O tender and wondrous
    thoughts,
Of life and death, of home and the past and loved, and of
those that are far away;
A solemn and slow procession there as I sit on the ground,
By the bivouac's fitful flame.

EAMON GRENNAN

1941 —

Human windows and everything that occurs behind them. The curiosity of a passerby,
but also a voyeur, or a poet, a fairy-tale teller, a novelist, composing all biography
and tales from a detail seen through a window. It may last just an instant, but
sometimes, as in this poem by an Irish poet, probably a little longer.

WOMAN AT LIT WINDOW

Perhaps if she stood for an hour like that
and I could stand to stand in the dark
just looking, I might get it right, every
fine line in place: the veins of the hand
reaching up to the blind-cord, etch
of the neck in profile, the white
and violet shell of the ear
in its whorl of light, that neatly
circled strain against a black
cotton sweater. For a few seconds

she is staring through me
where I stand wondering what I'll do
if she starts
on that stage of light
taking her clothes off. But she only
frowns out at nothing or herself
in the glass, and I think I could,
if we stood for an hour like this,
get some of the real details down. But
already, even as she lowers the blind,
she's turning away, leaving a blank
ivory square of brightness
to float alone in the dark, the faint
grey outline of the house
around it. Newly risen, the half moon casts

my shadow on the path
skinned with grainy radiance
as I make my way back
to my own place
among the trees, a host of fireflies
in fragrant silence and native ease
pricking the dark around me
with their pulse of light.

CHARLES SIMIC
1938—

*A dream may transform a moment lived once, at one time, and change it into part
of a nightmare. Charles Simic, an American poet born in Serbia, remembers the
time of the German occupation in his country. This scene from childhood is put in
relief as the present which is no more, but which now, when the poet writes,
constantly returns in dreams. In other words, it has its own present, of a new kind,
on the first page of a diary of dreams.*

EMPIRE OF DREAMS

On the first page of my dreambook
It's always evening
In an occupied country.
Hour before the curfew.
A small provincial city.
The houses all dark.
The store-fronts gutted.

I am on a street corner
Where I shouldn't be.
Alone and coatless
I have gone out to look
For a black dog who answers to my whistle.
I have a kind of halloween mask
Which I am afraid to put on.

PO CHÜ-I

772—846

*And here a true study of the moment, and of the relationship between dreams and
reality, by Po Chü-I.*

SLEEPING ON HORSEBACK

We had ridden long and were still far from the inn;
My eyes grew dim; for a moment I fell asleep.
Under my right arm the whip still dangled;
In my left hand the reins for an instant slackened.
Suddenly I woke and turned to question my groom.
"We have gone a hundred paces since you fell asleep."
Body and spirit for a while had changed place;
Swift and slow had turned to their contraries.
For these few steps that my horse had carried me
Had taken in my dream countless aeons of time!
True indeed is that saying of Wise Men
"A hundred years are but a moment of sleep."

Translated from the Chinese by Arthur Waley

WAYNE DODD
1930—

Rain doesn't appear often in poetry but it has its right of citizenship, and usually induces a mood because certain states of withdrawal and meditation are associated with rain.

OF RAIN AND AIR

All day I have been closed up
inside rooms, speaking of trivial
matters. Now at last I have come out
into the night, myself a center

of darkness.
Beneath the clouds the low sky glows
with scattered light. I can hardly think
this is happening. Here in this bright absence

of day, I feel myself opening out
with contentment.
All around me the soft rain is whispering
of thousands of feet of air

invisible above us.

SANDOR WEORES

1913—1989

This poem by a Hungarian, Sandor Weores, builds upon the symbolic value of rain, which, after all, is water, abundance, a giver of the green, of growth, of crops. In Weores, the desire to become rain is his longing for the descent of grace into human life. For rain is also often the symbol of grace falling from above, a magnanimous gift, of liquid penetration, and the poem praises liberation from inhibitions that hamper our love for the human tribe.

RAIN

The rain's pounding away
    at the rusty eaves.
Twirling, sliding bubbling foam—
    well, that's rain.

You too, and I should walk now
    as free as that
on cloud, on air, the meadow
    and the vapor roads.

Move around up there and here below
    like this liquid thing,
flowing into human life on rooftops
    and on shoes.

Translated from the Hungarian by J. Kessler

People Among People

People observe and describe people, people pronounce their opinions on people, but, above all else, people are bound to people by feelings of love, hate, compassion, fear, admiration, loathing. It is not certain whether good poetry can arise from hatred. My anthology shows that I select mostly poems that express warm feelings. At the risk of being pedantic, it is worthwhile to invoke here three Greek words denoting kinds of love. *Eros* is sexual love, but not only such, because it is "an intermediary between gods and humans," an unlimited desire, a true motoric force of creativity in art and science. *Agape* is love of our fellow men, love-empathy, allowing us to see in another human being a creature as frail and as easily hurt as we are ourselves: that is the same as Latin *caritas*, charity. A third Greek word, *storge,* denotes a tender care, affection uniting parents and children. Perhaps some teachers feel such a love for their pupils. It is also not impossible that *storge* may be applied to the relationship between a poet and generations of readers to come: underneath the ambition to perfect one's art without hope of being rewarded by contemporaries lurks a magnanimity of gift-offering to posterity.

WANG WEI

701–761

I will begin with a poem of observation, which would be less interesting had our contemporaries been involved. But if we think about these characters, that they lived some twelve hundred years ago, then their faults and sins, so arch-human, incline us to indulgence and even sympathy.

SONG ABOUT XI SHI

Her beauty casts a spell on everyone.
How could Xi Shi stay poor so long?
In the morning she was washing clothes in the Yue
    River,
In the evening she was a concubine in the palace
    of Wu.
When she was poor, was she out of the ordinary?
Now rich, she is rare.
Her attendants apply her powders and rouge,
others dress her in silks.
The king favors her and it fans her arrogance.
She can do no wrong.
Of her old friends who washed silks with her,
none share her carriage.
In her village her best friend is ugly. It's hopeless
to imitate Lady Xi Shi's cunning frowns.

Translated from the Chinese by Tony and Willis Barnstone and Xu Haixin

The next poem is an observation-portrait, and the poor scholar who appears here is familiar; he may even provoke warm feelings in his successors, struggling against poverty in societies addicted to the cult of money.

DANCING WOMAN, COCKFIGHTER HUSBAND, AND THE IMPOVERISHED SAGE

The woman from Zhao sings dirty songs
and does dances of Handan
while her husband knocks about, puts on cockfights
for the king of Qi.
With yellow gold he buys songs and laughter from
    a whore.
He never counts his coins.

Xu and Shi, relatives of the Emperor, often come
    to his house.
Their high gates are crowded with four-horse carriages.
A scholar lives in their guest house,
bragging about his rich patron, Zou Lu.
For thirty years his meals are the books he eagerly
    consumes
but his waist belt has no money in it.
His is the way of scholars, of the sage.
All his life he is poor.

Translated from the Chinese by Tony and Willis Barnstone and Xu Haixin

TU FU

713—770

Tu Fu is probably the biggest name in old Chinese poetry. His complaint about the lack of recognition in his lifetime brings to mind the fate of eminent artists of the nineteenth and twentieth centuries, who acquired fame only after their deaths; had they obtained but a small fraction from the sale of their books and paintings, it would have been very useful to them. Reading this poem I reflect upon the obstinacy of artists. Whence comes our passion, our zeal, in working at the risk of possible loss? Is this only ambition, or a bond with people who might come after us, some kind of love?

TO PI SSU YAO

We have talent. People call us
The leading poets of our day.
Too bad, our homes are humble,
Our recognition trivial.
Hungry, ill clothed, servants treat
Us with contempt. In the prime
Of life, our faces are wrinkled.
Who cares about either of us,
Or our troubles? We are our own
Audience. We appreciate
Each other's literary
Merits. Our poems will be handed
Down along with great dead poets'.
We can console each other.
At least we shall have descendants.

Translated from the Chinese by Kenneth Rexroth

MEI YAO CH'EN

1002—1060

*Now a true love poem about the love of man and woman, husband and wife, but,
above all, about mutual tenderness.*

A DREAM AT NIGHT

In broad daylight I dream I
Am with her. At night I dream
She is still at my side. She
Carries her kit of colored
Threads. I see her image bent
Over her bag of silks. She
Mends and alters my clothes and
Worries for fear I might look
Worn and ragged. Dead, she watches
Over my life. Her constant
Memory draws me towards death.

Translated from the Chinese by Kenneth Rexroth

SEAMUS HEANEY
1939—

All poetry of Seamus Heaney is rooted in his native Ireland, in his country childhood, country labors, and Catholic rites. This reticent and modestly entitled poem is in Fact, as biographers of the poet know, a farewell to his mother.

FROM "CLEARANCES," IN MEMORIAM M.K.H. (1911–1984)

When all the others were away at Mass
I was all hers as we peeled potatoes.
They broke the silence, let fall one by one
Like solder weeping off the soldering iron:
Cold comforts set between us, things to share
Gleaming in a bucket of clean water.
And again let fall. Little pleasant splashes
From each other's work would bring us to our senses.

So while the parish priest at her bedside
Went hammer and tongs at the prayers for the dying
And some were responding and some crying
I remembered her head bent towards my head,
Her breath in mine, our fluent dipping knives—
Never closer the whole rest of our lives.

CONSTANTINE CAVAFY

1863 — 1933

Cavafy has written one short poem about a mother's love. As usual in his work,
he takes Greece as a background, its islands, its sailors, and its religion, here
Christian in its Orthodox variety.

SUPPLICATION

The sea took a sailor to its deep. —
His mother, unsuspecting, goes to light

a tall candle before the Virgin Mary
for his speedy return and for fine weather —

and always she cocks her ear to windward.
But while she prays and implores,

the icon listens, solemn and sad, knowing well
that the son she expects will no longer return.

Translated from the Greek by Rae Dalven

WALT WHITMAN
1819—1892

Walt Whitman had avid eyes. He wanted to see everything, to memorize everything, and to enclose it all in his poems. But he remains for us primarily a poet of great heart, of all-embracing love, which fuses its varieties into one love, erotic, but also compassionate, protective, and marvelling at everything great and magnificent in man. This aspect of his poetry prompted me to place several fragments of his oeuvre in this chapter.

FROM "I SING THE BODY ELECTRIC"

I knew a man, a common farmer, the father of five sons,
And in them the fathers of sons, and in them the fathers of sons.

This man was of wonderful vigor, calmness, beauty of person,
The shape of his head, the pale yellow and white of his hair and
    beard, the immeasurable meaning of his black eyes, the
    richness and breadth of his manners.
These I used to go and visit him to see, he was wise also,
He was six feet tall, he was over eighty years old, his sons were
    massive, clean, bearded, tan-faced, handsome,
They and his daughters loved him, all who saw him loved him,
They did not love him by allowance, they loved him with personal
    love,
He drank water only, the blood show'd like scarlet through the
    clear-brown skin of his face,
He was a frequent gunner and fisher, he sail'd his boat himself,
    he had a fine one presented to him by a ship-joiner,
    he had fowling-pieces presented to him by men that loved him,
When he went with his five sons and many grand-sons to hunt or
    fish, you would pick him out as the most beautiful and
    vigorous of the gang,
You would wish long and long to be with him, you would wish to
    sit by him in the boat that you and he might touch each
    other.

Some Civil War poems of Whitman's should be placed here, because they are the most direct in invoking the dead of that war.

AS TOILSOME I WANDER'D VIRGINIA'S WOODS

As toilsome I wander'd Virginia's woods,
To the music of rustling leaves kick'd by my feet, (for
    'twas autumn,)
I mark'd at the foot of a tree the grave of a soldier;
Mortally wounded he and buried on the retreat, (easily all
    could I understand,)
The halt of a mid-day hour, when up! no time to lose—yet
    this sign left,
On a tablet scrawl'd and nail'd on the tree by the grave,
Bold, cautious, true, and my loving comrade.

Long, long I muse, then on my way go wandering,
Many a changeful season to follow, and many a scene of life,
Yet at times through changeful season and scene, abrupt, alone,
    or in the crowded street,
Comes before me the unknown soldier's grave, comes the
    inscription rude in Virginia's woods,
Bold, cautious, true, and my loving comrade.

A SIGHT IN CAMP IN THE DAYBREAK GRAY AND DIM

A sight in camp in the daybreak gray and dim,
As from my tent I emerge so early sleepless,
As slow I walk in the cool fresh air the path near by the
 hospital tent,
Three forms I see on stretchers lying, brought out there
 untended lying,
Over each the blanket spread, ample brownish woolen blanket,
Gray and heavy blanket, folding, covering all.

Curious I halt and silent stand,
Then with light fingers I from the face of the nearest the first
 just lift the blanket;
Who are you elderly man so gaunt and grim, with well-
 gray'd hair, and flesh all sunken about the eyes?
Who are you my dear comrade?

Then to the second I step—and who are you my child and
 darling?
Who are you sweet boy with cheeks yet blooming?

Then to the third—a face nor child nor old, very calm, as of
 beautiful yellow-white ivory;
Young man I think I know you—I think this face is the face of the
 Christ himself,
Dead and divine and brother of all, and here again he lies.

Here is the image of a funeral procession, conceived as a kind of democratic ritual of saying farewell to heroes of the community. If Whitman sometimes uses the expression "en masse," this is perhaps the essence of what he meant by that foreign term.

DIRGE FOR TWO VETERANS

    The last sunbeam
Lightly falls from the finish'd Sabbath,
On the pavement here, and there beyond it is looking,
    Down a new-made double grave.

    Lo, the moon ascending,
Up from the east the silvery round moon,
Beautiful over the house-tops, ghastly, phantom moon,
    Immense and silent moon.

    I see a sad procession,
And I hear the sound of coming full-key'd bugles,
All the channels of the city streets they're flooding,
    As with voices and with tears.

    I hear the great drums pounding,
And the small drums steady whirring,
And every blow of the great convulsive drums,
    Strikes me through and through.

    For the son is brought with the father,
(In the foremost ranks of the fierce assault they fell,
Two veterans son and father dropt together,
    And the double grave awaits them.)

    Now nearer blow the bugles,
And the drums strike more convulsive,
And the daylight o'er the pavement quite has faded,
    And the strong dead-march enwraps me.

In the eastern sky up-buoying,
The sorrowful vast phantom moves illumin'd,
('Tis some mother's large transparent face,
 In heaven brighter growing.)

 O strong dead-march you please me!
O moon immense with your silvery face you sooth me!
O my soldiers twain! O my veterans passing to burial!
 What I have I also give you.

 The moon gives you light,
And the bugles and the drums give you music,
And my heart, O my soldiers, my veterans,
 My heart gives you love.

It is true that William Carlos Williams revolutionized American poetry by intro-ducing his own form of current speech, based, presumably, on the rhythm of breathing. However, what is most important is his gift of living among people, the sympathy and empathy by which he is a sort of successor to Walt Whitman. Perhaps that is why he chose to be a physician, practicing general medicine in the town of Rutherford, New Jersey, where he was born. He looked, listened, observed, and tried to choose the simplest words for his notes on reality.

PROLETARIAN PORTRAIT

A big young bareheaded woman
in an apron

Her hair slicked back standing
on the street

One stockinged foot toeing
the sidewalk

Her shoe in her hand. Looking
intently into it

She pulls out the paper insole
to find the nail

That has been hurting her

TO A POOR OLD WOMAN

munching a plum on
the street a paper bag
of them in her hand

They taste good to her
They taste good
to her. They taste
good to her

You can see it by
the way she gives herself
to the one half
sucked out in her hand

Comforted
a solace of ripe plums
seeming to fill the air
They taste good to her

WANG CHIEN
768—830

If family is a microcosm of society, here we have a glimpse of old Chinese civilization. One can wonder at the stability of such relations as those between the daughter-in-law, the mother-in-law, and the husband's sister. The poem is very vivid and evocative, able to convey a complex relationship in a few lines.

THE NEW WIFE

On the third day she went down to the kitchen,
Washed her hands, prepared the broth.
Still unaware of her new mother's likings,
She asks his sister to taste.

Translated from the Chinese by J. P. Seaton

AL ZOLYNAS
1945—

Al Zolynas, a California poet of Lithuanian origin, teaches in San Diego. This poem is a good example of the bond between teacher and youngsters, though that bond is not always of such intensity.

LOVE IN THE CLASSROOM
—for my students

Afternoon. Across the garden, in Green Hall,
someone begins playing the old piano—
a spontaneous piece, amateurish and alive,
full of a simple, joyful melody.
The music floats among us in the classroom.

I stand in front of my students
telling them about sentence fragments.
I ask them to find the ten fragments
in the twenty-one-sentence paragraph on page forty-five.
They've come from all parts
of the world—Iran, Micronesia, Africa,
Japan, China, even Los Angeles—and they're still
eager to please me. It's less than half
way through the quarter.

They bend over their books and begin.
Hamid's lips move as he follows
the tortuous labyrinth of English syntax.
Yoshie sits erect, perfect in her pale make-up,
legs crossed, quick pulse minutely
jerking her right foot. Tony,
from an island in the South Pacific,
sprawls limp and relaxed in his desk.

The melody floats around and through us
in the room, broken here and there, fragmented,

re-started. It feels mideastern, but
it could be jazz, or the blues—it could be
anything from anywhere.
I sit down on my desk to wait,
and it hits me from nowhere—a sudden
sweet, almost painful love for my students.

"Never mind," I want to cry out.
"It doesn't matter about fragments.
Finding them or not. Everything's
a fragment and everything's not a fragment.
Listen to the music, how fragmented,
how whole, how we can't separate the music
from the sun falling on its knees on all the greenness,
from this movement, how this moment
contains all the fragments of yesterday
and everything we'll ever know of tomorrow!"

Instead, I keep a coward's silence.
the music stops abruptly;
they finish their work,
and we go through the right answers,
which is to say
we separate the fragments from the whole.

RAINER MARIA RILKE
1875–1926

This poem by Rilke narrates the increasing solitude of a person who feels separated from other human beings by her illness. She tries hard not to be left behind, but already her movements show that she is out of step with others. Yet at the same time a transformation is occurring, as if, through her growing blindness, she has moved into another realm.

GOING BLIND

She sat at tea just like the others. First
I merely had a notion that this guest
Held up her cup not quite like all the rest.
And once she gave a smile. It almost hurt.

When they arose at last, with talk and laughter,
And ambled slowly and as chance dictated
Through many rooms, their voices animated,
I saw her seek the noise and follow after,

Held in like one who in a little bit
Would have to sing where many people listened;
Her lighted eyes, which spoke of gladness, glistened
With outward luster, as a pond is lit.

She followed slowly, and it took much trying,
As though some obstacle still barred her stride;
And yet as if she on the farther side
Might not be walking any more, but flying.

Translated from the German by Walter Arndt

LEONARD NATHAN

1924—

Erotic imagination and disinterested care—how can we separate them? In any case, it is difficult to do so in this poem, the author of which is my colleague and co-translator Leonard Nathan, who lives in Berkeley.

TOAST

There was a woman in Ithaca
who cried softly all night
in the next room and helpless
I fell in love with her under the blanket
of snow that settled on all the roofs
of the town, filling up
every dark depression.

Next morning
in the motel coffee shop
I studied all the made-up faces
of women. Was it the middle-aged blonde
who kidded the waitress
or the young brunette lifting
her cup like a toast?

Love, whoever you are,
your courage was my companion
for many cold towns
after the betrayal of Ithaca,
and when I order coffee
in a strange place, still
I say, lifting, this is for you.

Is it appropriate or inappropriate? Perhaps it's appropriate, since the poet, Leonard Nathan, wrote and published it; and in spite of its joking form, this is a serious poem, sufficiently complex in its thought to discourage us from retelling it in our own words.

BLADDER SONG

On a piece of toilet paper
Afloat in the unflushed piss,
The fully printed lips of a woman.

Nathan, cheer up! The sewer
Sends you a big red kiss.
Ah, nothing's wasted, if it's human.

W. S. MERWIN

1927—

At any moment in our life we are entangled in all the past of humanity, and that past is primarily language, so we live as if upon a background of incessant chorus, and of course it is possible to imagine the presence of everything which has ever been spoken.

UTTERANCE

Sitting over words
very late I have heard a kind of whispered sighing
not far
like a night wind in pines or like the sea in the dark
the echo of everything that has ever
been spoken
still spinning its one syllable
between the earth and silence

STEVE KOWIT

1938—

What does it mean to realize that we are like all our fellow men, that closing ourselves off in our uniqueness, we are wrong, because whatever we feel, others feel too? It means to experience, be it for a moment, but in a truly sharp way, our common fate, the basic and inescapable fact of our mortality. Nothing is more obvious and yet rarely does a poet grasp it as the California poet Steve Kowit has in this joking-serious poem.

NOTICE

This evening, the sturdy Levis
I wore every day for over a year
& which seemed to the end in perfect condition,
suddenly tore.
How or why I don't know,
but there it was—a big rip at the crotch.
A month ago my friend Nick
walked off a racquetball court,
showered,
got into his street clothes,
& halfway home collapsed & died.
Take heed you who read this
& drop to your knees now & again
like the poet Christopher Smart
& kiss the earth & be joyful
& make much of your time
& be kindly to everyone,
even to those who do not deserve it.
For although you may not believe it will happen,
you too will one day be gone.
I, whose Levis ripped at the crotch
for no reason,
assure you that such is the case.
Pass it on.

ANNA SWIR
1909—1984

I have translated a number of poems by Anna Swir (in reality, Anna Swirsz-
czynska), because I value her for the intensity and warmth of her poetry, dictated
by eros, or by empathy and pity for suffering people. Her poems on war and the
Nazi occupation in Poland are among the best in their conciseness. She was also
a militant feminist and author of uninhibited love poems.

THE SAME INSIDE

Walking to your place for a love feast
I saw at a street corner
an old beggar woman.

I took her hand,
kissed her delicate cheek,
we talked, she was
the same inside as I am,
from the same kind,
I sensed this instantly
as a dog knows by scent
another dog.

I gave her money,
I could not part from her.
After all, one needs
someone who is close.

And then I no longer knew
why I was walking to your place.

Translated from the Polish by Czeslaw Milosz and Leonard Nathan

PHILIP LARKIN

1922—1985

This is a description of a Dutch painting; it doesn't matter whether as actually seen by the poet, or as a synthetic presentation of those tavern scenes so liked by Dutch painters. Philip Larkin is not a poet especially fond of people. And yet, perhaps, humor gives this poem its grace. It's just humor, not irony or sarcasm, and this is good.

THE CARD-PLAYERS

Jan van Hogspeuw staggers to the door
And pisses at the dark. Outside, the rain
Courses in cart-ruts down the deep mud lane.
Inside, Dirk Dogstoerd pours himself some more,
And holds a cinder to his clay with tongs,
Belching out smoke. Old Prijck snores with the gale,
His skull face firelit; someone behind drinks ale,
And opens mussels, and croaks scraps of songs
Towards the ham-hung rafters about love.
Dirk deals the cards. Wet century-wide trees
Clash in surrounding starlessness above
This lamplit cave, where Jan turns back and farts,
Gobs at the grate, and hits the queen of hearts.

Rain, wind and fire! The secret, bestial peace!

WALT WHITMAN
1819—1892

Some parts of the gigantic oeuvre of Walt Whitman remind me of the huge canvases of the masters of Renaissance painting. If, looking at those canvases, we direct our attention to a detail, we discover a multitude of carefully painted small scenes. The same is true in Whitman: there is something like a mosaic, composed of units that are autonomous.

FROM "THE SLEEPERS"

Now what my mother told me one day as we sat at dinner
    together,
Of when she was a nearly grown girl living home with her parents
    on the old homestead.

A red squaw came one breakfast-time to the old homestead,
On her back she carried a bundle of rushes for rush-bottoming
    chairs,
Her hair, straight, shiny, coarse, black, profuse, half-envelop'd her
    face,
Her step was free and elastic, and her voice sounded exquisitely as
    she spoke.

My mother look'd in delight and amazement at the stranger,
She look'd at the freshness of her tall-borne face and full and pliant
    limbs,
The more she look'd upon her she loved her,
Never before had she seen such wonderful beauty and purity,
She made her sit on a bench by the jamb of the fireplace, she
    cook'd food for her,
She had no work to give her, but she gave her remembrance and
    fondness.

The red squaw staid all the forenoon, and toward the middle of the
    afternoon she went away,
O my mother was loth to have her go away,
All the week she thought of her, she watch'd for her many a
    month,
She remember'd her many a winter and many a summer,
But the red squaw never came nor was heard of there again.

ANNA SWIR
1909–1984

*Anna Swir is the author of a moving cycle of poems about her father and mother,
of whom she speaks with attachment and gratitude, which seems to me striking in
view of a common tendency, particularly among young poets today, toward just the
opposite. It is not without importance to know her biography. She was the only
daughter of a painter who was abysmally poor. She grew up in his atelier in
Warsaw.*

I WASH THE SHIRT

For the last time I wash the shirt
of my father who died.
The shirt smells of sweat. I remember
that sweat from my childhood,
so many years
I washed his shirts and underwear,
I dried them
at an iron stove in the workshop,
he would put them on unironed.

From among all bodies in the world,
animal, human,
only one exuded that sweat.
I breathe it in
for the last time. Washing this shirt
I destroy it
forever.
Now
only paintings survive him
which smell of oils.

Translated from the Polish by Czeslaw Milosz and Leonard Nathan

SHARON OLDS

1943—

I decided to include this cruel poem for its expressiveness and passion. It appears to deal with a conflict of generations, but in reality it is a dirge for innocence. The daughter knows that her parents are doomed to suffer, but they do not and she looks at them with horror and pity.

I GO BACK TO MAY 1937

I see them standing at the formal gates of their colleges,
I see my father strolling out
under the ochre sandstone arch, the
red tiles glinting like bent
plates of blood behind his head, I
see my mother with a few light books at her hip
standing at the pillar made of tiny bricks with the
wrought-iron gates still open behind her, its
sword-tips black in the May air,
they are about to graduate, they are about to get married,
they are kids, they are dumb, all they know is they are
innocent, they would never hurt anybody.
I want to go up to them and say Stop,
don't do it—she's the wrong woman,
he's the wrong man, you are going to do things
you cannot imagine you would ever do,
you are going to do bad things to children,
you are going to suffer in ways you never heard of,
you are going to want to die. I want to go
up to them there in the late May sunlight and say it,
her hungry pretty blank face turning to me,
her pitiful beautiful untouched body,
his arrogant handsome blind face turning to me
his pitiful beautiful untouched body,
but I don't do it. I want to live. I

take them up like the male and female
paper dolls and bang them together
at the hips like chips of flint as if to
strike sparks from them, I say
Do what you are going to do, and I will tell you about it.

TADEUSZ ROZEWICZ
1921—

A Polish poet, Tadeusz Rozewicz, was marked in his early youth by the cruelties of war, in which he fought against the Nazis as a soldier of a guerilla unit. That experience influenced all his poetry, in which he is a desperate nihilist, but also a compassionate interpreter of the human condition.

A VOICE

They mutilate they torment each other
with silences with words
as if they had another
life to live

they do so
as if they had forgotten
that their bodies
are inclined to death
that the insides of men
easily break down

ruthless with each other
they are weaker
than plants and animals
they can be killed by a word
by a smile by a look

Tanslated from the Polish by Czeslaw Milosz

THOMAS MERTON

1915—1968

Thomas Merton, before he became a monk in a Trappist monastery, Gethsemane,
in Kentucky, had already been a writer, and obviously he respected writers
who shaped the style of his generation. In prose, the srongest influence was
exerted by Ernest Hemingway. When Hemingway killed himself, at the age of
sixty-three, a service for his soul was, for the monk Merton, also a farewell to
his own youth, to his adventurous "I," from which he looked for escape in the
monastery.

AN ELEGY FOR ERNEST HEMINGWAY

Now for the first time on the night of your death
your name is mentioned in convents, *ne cadas in*
obscurum.

Now with a true bell your story becomes final. Now
men in monasteries, men of requiems, familiar with
the dead, include you in their offices.

You stand anonymous among thousands, waiting in
the dark at great stations on the edge of countries
known to prayer alone, where fires are not merciless,
we hope, and not without end.

You pass briefly through our midst. Your books and
writing have not been consulted. Our prayers are
pro defuncto N.

Yet some look up, as though among a crowd of prisoners or displaced persons, they recognized a friend
once known in a far country. For these the sun also
rose after a forgotten war upon an idiom you made
great. They have not forgotten you. In their silence
you are still famous, no ritual shade.

How slowly this bell tolls in a monastery tower for a whole age, and for the quick death of an unready dynasty, and for that brave illusion: the adventurous self!

For with one shot the whole hunt is ended!

WALT WHITMAN
1819—1892

I end this chapter with, once again, Whitman. He spins out of himself a thread, both in his personal life and in his poems, looking for a response, an understanding, for friends, readers, the perfect opposite of an artist who turns away from people and the world.

A NOISELESS PATIENT SPIDER

A noiseless patient spider,
I mark'd where on a little promontory it stood isolated,
Mark'd how to explore the vacant vast surrounding,
It launch'd forth filament, filament, filament, out of itself,
Ever reeling them, ever tirelessly speeding them.

And you O my soul where you stand,
Surrounded, detached, in measureless oceans of space,
Ceaselessly musing, venturing, throwing, seeking the spheres
to connect them,
Till the bridge you will need be form'd, till the ductile
anchor hold,
Till the gossamer thread you fling catch somewhere, O my soul.

Woman's Skin

This is a short chapter, perhaps because it should be given to love poetry, and love poetry has always been abundant in any language, so there is no point in adding a few drops to the sea. Besides, it is not poetry written mostly by men that interests me, but something else, woman in her flesh, particularly as described by herself. In some epochs of history women took an active part in literary life and wrote court poetry (in China, in Japan, in France of the sixteenth century). Among them there were great poets, even if they didn't often succeed in breaking with convention and giving voice to their femininity. Today there is a plethora of poems written by women, but I do not find many corresponding to my very specific criteria.

STEVE KOWIT

1938—

Why is the most simple scene of a woman before a mirror a very sensuous poem?
Of course, it's because of a red lip, the tip of the tongue which licks it, and
because of the admiration with which she looks at her eyes.

IN THE MORNING

In the morning,
holding her mirror,
the young woman
touches
her tender
lip with
her finger &
then with
the tip of
her tongue
licks it &
smiles
& admires her
eyes.

> *after the Sanskrit*

CHU SHU CHEN

c. 1200

I nearly fell in love with this poet, Chu Shu Chen, about whom not much is known except that she lived some time around 1200, and one morning suffered because of her solitude. Reluctantly yet willingly she listened to her servant, who was ready to enhance her physical charm. The plum flower had a clearly erotic meaning in that civilization.

MORNING

I get up. I am sick of
Rouging my cheeks. My face in
The mirror disgusts me. My
Thin shoulders are bowed with
Hopelessness. Tears of loneliness
Well up in my eyes. Wearily
I open my toilet table.
I arch and paint my eyebrows
And steam my heavy braids.
My maid is so stupid that she
Offers me plum blossoms for my hair.

Translated from the Chinese by Kenneth Rexroth

STEVE KOWIT

1 9 3 8 —

The extreme frailty and transience of woman's beauty may give rise to one of those moments when authentic experience overcomes a convention, and this is why poems written about it sound true.

COSMETICS DO NO GOOD

Cosmetics do no good:
no shadow, rouge, mascara, lipstick—
nothing helps.
However artfully I comb my hair,
embellishing my throat & wrists with jewels,
it is no use—there is no
semblance of the beautiful young girl
I was
& long for still.
My loveliness is past.
& no one could be more aware than I am
that coquettishness at this age
only renders me ridiculous.
I know it. Nonetheless,
I primp myself before the glass
like an infatuated schoolgirl
fussing over every detail,
practicing whatever subtlety
may please him.
I cannot help myself.
The God of Passion has his will of me
& I am tossed about
between humiliation & desire,
rectitude & lust,
disintegration & renewal,
ruin & salvation.

after Vidyapati

LI CH'ING-CHAO

1084—1142

Li Ch'ing-chao was once as famous as Li Po and Tu Fu among men. I have read that often in her poems there is a fusion of convention (such as one sees in "the poems of an abandoned concubine") with real experience (the death of her husband).

HOPELESSNESS

When I look in the mirror
My face frightens me.
How horrible I have become!
When Spring comes back
Weakness overcomes me
Like a fatal sickness.
I am too slothful
To smell the new flowers
Or to powder my own face.
Everything exasperates me.
The sadness which tries me today
Adds itself to the accumulated
Sorrows of the days that are gone.
I am frightened by the weird cries
Of the nightjars that I cannot
Shut out from my ears.
I am filled with bitter embarrassment
When I see on the curtains
The shadows of two swallows making love.

Translated from the Chinese by Kenneth Rexroth

ANNA SWIR

1909—1984

Poems about an old woman are rare, as if there were a tendency to relegate her
to the realm of half-existence. But Polish poet Anna Swir returns to that subject
several times with love and compassion.

THE GREATEST LOVE

She is sixty. She lives
the greatest love of her life.

She walks arm-in-arm with her dear one,
her hair streams in the wind.
Her dear one says:
"You have hair like pearls."

Her children say:
"Old fool."

Translated from the Polish by Czeslaw Milosz and Leonard Nathan

William Blake was inclined to see human sins as phases through which humans pass and not as something substantial. In this poem by Anna Swir there is a similar empathy and forgiveness.

SHE DOES NOT REMEMBER

She was an evil stepmother.
In her old age she is slowly dying
in an empty hovel.

She shudders
like a clutch of burnt paper.
She does not remember that she was evil.
But she knows
that she feels cold.

Translated from the Polish by Czeslaw Milosz and Leonard Nathan

LINDA GREGG
1942—

I consider Linda Gregg one of the best American poets, and I value the neatness of design in her poems, as well as the energy of each line. Perhaps I am a bit biased, because Gregg comes from California and used to come to my classes at the university at Berkeley.

ADULT

I've come back to the country where I was happy
changed. Passion puts no terrible strain on me now.
I wonder what will take the place of desire.
I could be the ghost of my own life returning
to the places I lived best. Walking here and there,
nodding when I see something I cared for deeply.
Now I'm in my house listening to the owls calling
and wondering if slowly I will take on flesh again.

ANNA SWIR
1909—1984

Anna Swir wrote many poems about flesh. I wonder whether she was too brutal for her readers in Poland, or whether her feminism contributed to her being less valued than she should have been. Her love poems are somewhat strange in that they are not confessional.

THANK YOU, MY FATE

Great humility fills me,
great purity fills me,
I make love with my dear
as if I made love dying
as if I made love praying,
tears pour
over my arms and his arms.
I don't know whether this is joy
or sadness, I don't understand
what I feel, I'm crying,
I'm crying, it's humility
as if I were dead,
gratitude, I thank you, my fate,
I'm unworthy, how beautiful
my life.

Translated from the Polish by Czeslaw Milosz and Leonard Nathan

A similar neatness of the calligraphic line depicts lovemaking in the following poem by the same poet. Again, the lovemaking is not that of specific individuals with clearly portrayed faces.

THE SECOND MADRIGAL

A night of love
exquisite as a
concert from old Venice
played on exquisite instruments.
Healthy as a
buttock of a little angel.
Wise as an
anthill.
Garish as air
blown into a trumpet.
Abundant as the reign
of a royal Negro couple
seated on two thrones
cast in gold.

A night of love with you,
a big baroque battle
and two victories.

Translated from the Polish by Czeslaw Milosz and Leonard Nathan

STEVE KOWIT
1 9 3 8 —

In writing about love, there is always the difficulty of crossing a certain line in detailed description. Once, in French love novels, closeness between a man and a woman culminated in "les transports." And that was it, probably more effective than many blatant, detailed descriptions. In this poem, there is something of that discretion.

WHEN HE PRESSED HIS LIPS

When he pressed his lips to my mouth
the knot fell open of itself.
When he pressed them to my throat
the dress slipped to my feet.
So much I know—but
when his lips touched my breast
everything, I swear,
down to his very name,
became so much confused
that I am still,
dear friends,
unable to recount
(as much as I would care to)
what delights
were next bestowed upon me
& by whom.

after Vikatanitamba

JEAN FOLLAIN
1903—1971

Now, a few poems about women, but not written by women. From time immemorial, femininity was an attribute of nature. The mother earth received the dignity of a goddess in various religions, and was called Gaia by the Greeks; in grammar only the feminine gender fits nature, Ceres, Demeter, Cybele, or Rhea. A woman always was supposed to stand closer to the earth, to maintain permanent union with her, to be her delegate in the world of humans. This poem by a French poet is in that old tradition, which shows, additionally, the ambivalence in men's thinking about women.

A MIRROR

Having gone upstairs
on steps of dark oak
she finds herself before
a mirror with worm-eaten frame
she contemplates in it her virgin torso
all the countryside is ablaze
and gently arrives at her feet
a domestic beast
as if to remind her
of the animal life
which conceals in itself also
the body of a woman.

Translated from the French by Czeslaw Milosz and Robert Hass

EMPEROR CH'IEN-WEN OF LIANG

503—551

There was once an emperor who used to write poems. One day he woke up, opened one eye, and saw that his wife or concubine was getting up and going to make her morning toilet. And he wrote a poem about that, which expresses, let us assume, his wondering about the female species.

GETTING UP IN WINTER

Winter morning.
Pale sunlight strikes the ceiling.
She gets out of bed reluctantly.
Her nightgown has a bamboo sash.
She wipes the dew off her mirror.
At this hour there is no one to see her.
Why is she making up so early?

Translated from the Chinese by Kenneth Rexroth

STEVE KOWIT
1938—

At least one poem about being charmed by the nakedness of a woman should be included here.

WHAT CHORD DID SHE PLUCK

What chord did she pluck in my soul
that girl with the golden necklace
& ivory breasts
whose body ignited the river:
she who rose like the moon
from her bathing &
brushed back the ebony hair
that fell to her waist
& walked off
into the twilight dark—
O my soul,
what chord did she pluck
that I am still trembling.

after Chandidas

DENISE LEVERTOV

1923 —

Farewells to a body as it once was are like farewells to life. There is a feeling of the abyss of passing time in this poem.

A WOMAN MEETS AN OLD LOVER

'He with whom I ran hand in hand
kicking the leathery leaves down Oak Hill Path
thirty years ago

appeared before me with anxious face, pale,
almost unrecognized, hesitant,
lame.

He whom I cannot remember hearing laugh out loud
but see in mind's eye smiling, self-approving,
wept on my shoulder.

He who seemed always
to take and not give, who took me
so long to forget,

remembered everything I had so long forgotten.'

MAY SWENSON
1919–1989

In this song directed to her body, May Swenson writes about a peculiar relationship to it. She is not identical with it but is the owner of it. The body is her house, her horse, her hound, and death is like exposure and poverty.

QUESTION

Body my house
my horse my hound
what will I do
when you are fallen

Where will I sleep
How will I ride
What will I hunt

Where can I go
without my mount
all eager and quick
How will I know
in thicket ahead
is danger or treasure
when Body my good
bright dog is dead

How will it be
to lie in the sky
without roof or door
and wind for an eye
With cloud for shift
how will I hide?

ROBINSON JEFFERS
1887—1962

In this poem, a woman speaks, but what she says is related by a man. This is one of Robinson Jeffers' late poems, and even a cursory knowledge of his biography suffices to recognize the voice of Una Custer, Jeffers' wife, with whom he'd lived in Carmel since his youth.

CREMATION

It nearly cancels my fear of death, my dearest said,
When I think of cremation. To rot in the earth
Is a loathsome end, but to roar up in flame—besides, I
    am used to it,
I have flamed with love or fury so often in my life,
No wonder my body is tired, no wonder it is dying.
We had great joy of my body. Scatter the ashes.

TADEUSZ ROZEWICZ
1921—

This poem by Tadeusz Rozewicz is about absence, but just as in Samuel Beckett,
absence expresses something that is not attainable, yet nevertheless exists. And so
love, here, is defined only negatively.

A SKETCH FOR A MODERN LOVE POEM

And yet whiteness
can be best described by greyness
a bird by a stone
sunflowers
in december

love poems of old
used to be descriptions of flesh
they described this and that
for instance eyelashes

and yet redness
should be described
by greyness the sun by rain
the poppies in november
the lips at night

the most palpable
description of bread
is that of hunger
there is in it
a humid porous core
a warm inside
sunflowers at night
the breasts the belly the thighs of Cybele

a transparent
source-like description
of water is that of thirst

of ash
of desert
it provokes a mirage
clouds and trees enter
a mirror of water
lack hunger
absence
of flesh
is a description of love
in a modern love poem

Translated from the Polish by Czeslaw Milosz

ANNA SWIR
1909—1984

A few centuries ago European poetry counted a number of poems on the dialogue between the soul and the body. This genre still exists, and here, in "I Talk to My Body" by Anna Swir, it is modified into the tender-humorous conversation of a woman with her cherished possession.

I TALK TO MY BODY

My body, you are an animal
whose appropriate behavior
is concentration and discipline.
An effort
of an athlete, of a saint and of a yogi.

Well trained
you may become for me
a gate
through which I will leave myself
and a gate
through which I will enter myself.
A plumb line to the center of the earth
and a cosmic ship to Jupiter.

My body, you are an animal
for whom ambition
is right.
Splendid possibilities
are open to us.

Translated from the Polish by Czeslaw Milosz and Leonard Nathan

TROUBLES WITH THE SOUL
AT MORNING CALISTHENICS

Lying down I lift my legs,
my soul by mistake jumps into my legs.
This is not convenient for her,
besides, she must branch,
for the legs are two.

When I stand on my head
my soul sinks down to my head.
She is then in her place.

But how long can you stand on your head,
especially if you do not know
how to stand on your head.

Translated from the Polish by Czeslaw Milosz and Leonard Nathan

And yet, a humorous poem written by a man addressing his belly couldn't have been written. A woman's belly is something very different emotionally. In any case, it is a proper partner for conversation.

I STARVE MY BELLY FOR A SUBLIME PURPOSE

Three days
I starve my belly
so that it learns
to eat the sun.

I say to it: Belly,
I am ashamed of you. You must
spiritualize yourself. You must
eat the sun.

The belly keeps silent
for three days. It's not easy
to waken in it higher aspirations.

Yet I hope for the best.
This morning, tanning myself on the beach,
I noticed that, little by little,
it begins to shine.

Translated from the Polish by Czeslaw Milosz and Leonard Nathan

Situations

The diversity and multicolored richness of life come to a large extent from the innumerable situations in which we participate, being born at a given time, in a given country, into such and not other traditions and mores. And, above all, from our memory, and not only our own memory, for we are like a thread in a huge fabric of generations. That fabric today extends more and more, for knowledge of history and of the literature and art of other civilizations increases, and roads are open for travelling through centuries and millennia. In this chapter I place just some samples, though imagination suggests a multitude of "situational" poems.

TU FU
713—770

Divertissements from over a thousand years ago—so similar to ours that they provoke a feeling of solidarity, because they are, like ours, dependent on good weather, and we take pity on those girls whose makeup has been ruined.

DEJEUNER SUR L'HERBE

I

It's pleasant to board the ferry in the sunscape
As the late light slants into afternoon;
The faint wind ruffles the river, rimmed with foam.
We move through the aisles of bamboo
Towards the cool water-lilies.

The young dandies drop ice into the drinks,
While the girls slice the succulent lotus root.
Above us, a patch of cloud spreads, darkening
Like a water-stain on silk.

Write this down quickly, before the rain!

Don't sit there! The cushions were soaked by the shower.
Already the girls have drenched their crimson skirts.
Beauties, their powder streaked with mascara,
        lament their ruined faces.

The wind batters our boat, the mooring-line
Has rubbed a wound in the willow bark.
The edges of the curtains are embroidered by the river foam.
Like a knife in a melon, Autumn slices Summer.

It will be cold, going back.

Translated from the Chinese by Carolyn Kizer

JOANNE KYGER

1934—

I think that poems about situations could be drawn from a hat, relying upon chance, which would correspond to their nature, as they are somehow related to chance. Here we have Bolinas, a small town on the Pacific shore north of San Francisco, very quiet and once willingly chosen by hippies. Joanne Kyger, who lives there, practicing meditation, we learn, touches upon quite a problem. "Cessation of personality" is desirable but also dangerous.

AND WITH MARCH A DECADE IN BOLINAS

Just sitting around smoking, drinking and telling stories,
the news, making plans, analyzing, approaching the cessation
of personality, the single personality understands its demise.
Experience of the simultaneity of all human beings on this planet,
alive when you are alive. This seemingly inexhaustible
sophistication of awareness becomes relentless and horrible,
trapped. How am I ever going to learn enough to get out.

The beautiful soft and lingering props of the Pacific here.

                    The back door bangs
            So we've made a place to live
        here in the greened out 70's
                        Trying to talk in the Tremulous
                morality of the present
            Great Breath, I give you, Great Breath!

ALEKSANDER WAT
1900—1967

Hamlet exists in the consciousness of poets, otherwise such a poem as this one couldn't have been written. It is a text embroidering upon a text, upon the story of Hamlet, his mother, and Ophelia. Not by accident, this poem is dedicated to E. G. Craig, a great reformer of the theater in England. Craig had a long life. Wat met him in the south of France.

A JOKE

To Gordon Craig

Bunches of carnations in a tin pitcher.
Beyond the window, is that a faun playing a flute?
In a fusty room the semi-darkness of dawn.
The lovers sleep. On the sill

the cat purrs. In its dream a rabble of birds.
She wakens like a bird and, trembling,
opens her eye on the alabaster
shaded mournfully by her streaming hair.

She found in it her wreath fished up from a river
and searches for his hand, looking for protection.
Then plunges into sleep again—into a flow, a flow . . .

Suddenly the door creaked softly. Somebody enters. Surprised
Looks, hardly believes: My son—with a woman!
and retreats on tiptoe: O Hamlet! Hamlet!

VENCE, SEPTEMBER 1956

Translated from the Polish by Czeslaw Milosz and Leonard Nathan

PO CHÜ-I
772—846

Po Chü-I read and respected philosophers. Some people called him a Taoist. Nevertheless, he allowed himself malice in addressing a legendary sage, the creator of Taoism. Let us concede that it's a difficult problem, discovered by similar poets who announce the end of poetry, and yet continue writing.

THE PHILOSOPHERS:
LAO-TZU

"Those who speak know nothing:
Those who know are silent."
Those words, I am told,
Were spoken by Lao-tzu,
If we are to believe that Lao-tzu,
    Was himself one who knew,
How comes it that he wrote a book
    Of five thousand words?

Translated from the Chinese by Arthur Waley

This is Po Chü-I's poem about one of his troubles. Perhaps it doesn't concern us much, but let us only imagine: we make preparations for departure from the city, retiring to the house we had built in the mountains, and suddenly all this comes to nothing.

GOLDEN BELLS

When I was almost forty
I had a daughter whose name was Golden Bells.
Now it is just a year since she was born;
She is learning to sit and cannot yet talk.
Ashamed—to find that I have not a sage's heart;
I cannot resist vulgar thoughts and feelings.
Henceforward I am tied to things outside myself;
My only reward—the pleasure I am getting now.
If I am spared the grief of her dying young,
Then I shall have the trouble of getting her married.
My plan for retiring and going back to the hills
Must now be postponed for fifteen years!

Translated from the Chinese by Arthur Waley

A considerable number of Chinese poems in my collection can be explained as my attempt to jump over the barrier built by time between them and us. In this I behave like many of my contemporaries who discover that what had been, until recently, the trappings of exoticism has masked the eternal man.

AFTER GETTING DRUNK, BECOMING SOBER IN THE NIGHT

Our party scattered at yellow dusk and I came home to bed;
I woke at midnight and went for a walk, leaning heavily on a
    friend.
As I lay on my pillow my vinous complexion, soothed by sleep,
    grew sober:
In front of the tower the ocean moon, accompanying the tide, had
    risen.
The swallows, about to return to the beams, went back to roost
    again;
The candle at my window, just going out, suddenly revived its
    light.
All the time till dawn came, still my thoughts were muddled;
And in my ears something sounded like the music of flutes and
    strings.

Translated from the Chinese by Arthur Waley

WAYNE DODD

1930 —

Rural America persists in the consciousness of city inhabitants, for after all many of them have come from families with a rural background. Here, the news of a farmer's death brings members of the family from a distant city.

OF HIS LIFE

Beside the gravel pile, the lizard
warms himself in the dazzling greenness
of his life, watching us casually
through half-lidded eyes.
It is May.
Next week he would have been 57.
My daughter holds my hand, 3 years old
and ignorant, the airsickness forgotten,
and the hurried trip
and interrupted sleep.
Below the road
the whiteface cattle graze
in the morning peace.
The house is quiet.
Inside, his daughters stare unbelieving
into coffee cups, unable to imagine
the future.
My child throws some gravel
and the lizard fixes us
with both eyes, but does not
run, unwilling to leave
the warmth of the sun.
I can hear everything so clearly.
Years later she will ask
what he was like, her grandfather.
And I will try to remember
the greenness of this lizard,
he loved the sun so.

Raymond Carver was one of the best-known American short-story writers, but also an excellent poet. Death from cancer interrupted his work at a moment of full development, after he had overcome his alcoholism. I couldn't read this poem on Alexander the Great without thinking of his biography, to which, besides, he refers.

WINE

Reading a life of Alexander the Great, Alexander
whose rough father, Philip, hired Aristotle to tutor
the young scion and warrior, to put some polish
on his smooth shoulders. Alexander who, later
on the campaign trail into Persia, carried a copy of
The Iliad in a velvet-lined box, he loved that book so
much. He loved to fight and drink, too.
I came to that place in the life where Alexander, after
a long night of carousing, a wine-drunk (the worst kind of drunk—
hangovers you don't forget), threw the first brand
to start a fire that burned Persepolis, capital of the Persian Empire
(ancient even in Alexander's day).
Razed it right to the ground. Later, of course,
next morning—maybe even while the fire roared—he was
remorseful. But nothing like the remorse felt
the next evening when, during a disagreement that turned ugly
and, on Alexnder's part, overbearing, his face flushed
from too many bowls of uncut wine, Alexander rose drunkenly to
	his feet,
grabbed a spear and drove it through the breast
of his friend, Cletus, who'd saved his life at Granicus.
For three days Alexander mourned. Wept. Refused food. "Refused
to see to his bodily needs." He even promised
to give up wine forever.
(I've heard such promises and the lamentations that go with them.)
Needless to say, life for the army came to a full stop

as Alexander gave himself over to his grief.
But at the end of those three days, the fearsome heat
beginning to take its toll on the body of his dead friend,
Alexander was persuaded to take action. Pulling himself together
and leaving his tent, he took out his copy of Homer, untied it,
began to turn the pages. Finally he gave orders that the funeral
rites described for Patroklos be followed to the letter:
he wanted Cletus to have the biggest possible send-off.
And when the pyre was burning and the bowls of wine were
passed his way during the ceremony? Of course, what do you
think? Alexander drank his fill and passed
out. He had to be carried to his tent. He had to be lifted, to be put
into his bed.

FRANZ WRIGHT
1953—

This is a situation about which we read, and which presumably had been fixed in a painting by Picasso as well.

DEPICTION OF CHILDHOOD
After Picasso

It is the little girl
guiding the minotaur
with her free hand—
that devourer

and all the terror he's accustomed to
effortlessly emanating,
his ability to paralyze
merely by becoming present,

entranced somehow, and transformed
into a bewildered
and who knows, grateful
gentleness . . .

and with the other hand
lifting her lamp.

JAMES TATE

1943—

James Tate's poem is, to some extent, a satire on the profession of writing, and a connection between self-love and the urge to create.

TEACHING THE APE TO WRITE

They didn't have much trouble
teaching the ape to write poems:
first they strapped him into the chair
then tied his pencil around his hand
(the paper had already been nailed down).
Then Dr. Bluespire leaned over his shoulder
and whispered into his ear:
"You look like a god sitting there.
Why don't you try writing something?"

WISLAWA SZYMBORSKA
1923—

Writing is a vocation but many writers experience it also as a curse and a burden. In a way, they feel as if they are serving as instruments to a force alien to them. But writing, be it a blessing or a curse, may also be treated humorously by its practitioners, and in this amusing verse the word "poems" at the end of the lines serves to enhance the weirdness of that occupation.

IN PRAISE OF MY SISTER

My sister does not write poems
and it's unlikely she'll suddenly start writing poems.
She takes after her mother, who did not write poems,
and after her father, who also did not write poems.
Under my sister's roof I feel safe:
nothing would move my sister's husband to write poems.
And though it sounds like a poem by Adam Macedoński,
none of my relatives is engaged in the writing of poems.

In my sister's desk there are no old poems
nor any new ones in her handbag.
And when my sister invites me to dinner,
I know she has no intention of reading me poems.
She makes superb soups without half trying,
and her coffee does not spill on manuscripts.

In many families no one writes poems,
but when they do, it's seldom just one person.
Sometimes poetry flows in cascades of generations,
which sets up fearsome eddies in family relations.

My sister cultivates a decent spoken prose,
her entire literary output is on vacation postcards
that promise the same thing every year:
that when she returns,
she'll tell us, everything,
everything,
everything.

Translated from the Polish by Magnus J. Krynski and Robert A. Maguire

LAWRENCE RAAB
1946—

*The frailty of so-called civilized life, our awareness that it lasts merely by a
miracle, because at any moment it could disintegrate and reveal unmitigated horror,
as has happened more than once in our century—all this could contribute to the
writing of this poem. Its author lives in an idyllic New England, and has a window
with a view of an orchard.*

SUDDEN APPEARANCE OF A MONSTER AT A WINDOW

Yes, his face really is so terrible
you cannot turn away. And only
that thin sheet of glass between you,
clouding with his breath.
Behind him: the dark scribbles of trees
in the orchard, where you walked alone
just an hour ago, after the storm had passed,
watching water drip from the gnarled branches,
stepping carefully over the sodden fruit.
At any moment he could put his fist
right through that window. And on your side:
you could grab hold of this
letter opener, or even now try
very slowly to slide the revolver
out of the drawer of the desk in front of you.
But none of this will happen. And not because
you feel sorry for him, or detect
in his scarred face some helplessness
that shows in your own as compassion.
You will never know what he wanted,
what he might have done, since
this thing, of its own accord, turns away.
And because yours is a life in which

such a monster cannot figure for long,
you compose yourself, and return
to your letter about the storm, how it bent
the apple trees so low they dragged
on the ground, ruining the harvest.

TU FU

713—770

I have yet two Chinese poems, one of which is about meeting a monster, though not that dangerous, because it's only a tiger. It seems that in old China, at least in some provinces, such a meeting was not a rarity.

COMING HOME LATE AT NIGHT

At midnight, coming home, I passed a tiger.
The mountain's black, inside they're all asleep.
Far off the Dipper lowers toward the River.
Above, Bright Star grows great upon the sky.
With candle in the court I glower at two flames.
The apes are restive in the gorge, I hear one cry.
White head, old no more, I dance and sing.
Lean on my cane, unsleeping. And what else!

Translated from the Chinese by J. P. Seaton

The situation of amassed adversity—winter, evening, solitude, old age—can some-times so depress that even a poet sure of himself feels the uselessness of writing. Those of us who have experienced such evenings will recognize ourselves in that voice.

SNOW STORM

Tumult, weeping, many new ghosts.
Heartbroken, aging, alone, I sing
To myself. Ragged mist settles
In the spreading dusk. Snow scurries
In the coiling wind. The wineglass
Is spilled. The bottle is empty.
The fire has gone out in the stove.
Everywhere men speak in whispers.
I brood on the uselessness of letters.

Translated from the Chinese by Kenneth Rexroth

BRONISLAW MAJ

1953—

An unrepeatable situation. Only this, and not another man, so this and not another leaf. Which means that one can practice a philosophical poetry not using the dry terms of philosophy.

A LEAF

A leaf, one of the last, parts from a maple branch:
it is spinning in the transparent air of October, falls
on a heap of others, stops, fades. No one
admired its entrancing struggle with the wind,
followed its flight, no one will distinguish it now
as it lies among other leaves, no one saw
what I did. I am
the only one.

Translated from the Polish by Czeslaw Milosz and Robert Hass

ANNA SWIR
1909—1984

Poetry readings are not common in some countries. In others, among them Poland,
they draw an audience that doesn't treat poetry as an aesthetic experience only.
Rather, in one way or another, such audiences bring to the event their multiple
questions about life and death. This poem captures well the ignorance and help-
lessness of both the poet and her listeners.

POETRY READING

I'm curled into a ball
like a dog
that is cold.

Who will tell me
why I was born,
why this monstrosity
called life.

The telephone rings. I have to give
a poetry reading.

I enter.
A hundred people, a hundred pairs of eyes.
They look, they wait.
I know for what.

I am supposed to tell them
why they were born,
why there is
this monstrosity called life.

Translated from the Polish by Czeslaw Milosz and Leonard Nathan

Nonattachment

The futility of human endeavors, the fleetingness of human life, limited to a brief span of time, is a perennial subject of meditation in Babylonian poetry, in the Bible, in Greek tragedy, in Latin poets. The "vanity of vanities" of Ecclesiastes sets the tone for writings in Judeo-Christian civilization, otherwise so aggressive and grabbing. Nonattachment to the turmoil of daily strivings is advocated by prophets and saints. In the twentieth century, the meeting of civilizations, East and West, brings together biblical wisdom, Taoism, Buddhism, and Sufism in common praise of a detached attitude as a prerequisite for enlightenment.

Vita activa, an active life, or *vita contemplativa,* the contemplative life? Which to choose? That dilemma, formulated in medieval Europe and reflecting the polarity of the knight's and the monk's ways of life, is also present in old Chinese poetry. Poets were usually officials on various levels of the state bureaucracy, but they were perfectly aware of the merely relative value of riches and dignities. In many poems they hesitate between their desire to pursue a career and to retire to the country, far from the court and the market. Poetry was written by emperors as well. They had limited possibility of choice, except to peserve their nonattachment while occupying the throne.

This perennial theme is so essential for poetry that it has been molded into newer and newer forms.

RAYMOND CARVER

1938—1988

The most classical poem of nonattachment is that of a sudden realization, in a flash, of the shortness of the time one has left to live.

THE COBWEB

A few minutes ago, I stepped onto the deck
of the house. From there I could see and hear the water,
and everything that's happened to me all these years.
It was hot and still. The tide was out.
No birds sang. As I leaned against the railing
a cobweb touched my forehead.
It caught in my hair. No one can blame me that I turned
and went inside. There was no wind. The sea was
dead calm. I hung the cobweb from the lampshade.
Where I watch it shudder now and then when my breath
touches it. A fine thread. Intricate.
Before long, before anyone realizes,
I'll be gone from here.

DENISE LEVERTOV

1923—

A slow maturing, long awaited, probably identical with prayer, sometimes called by the mystics "the night of the soul" can, in modern poetry, take the lay form of a black eye mask.

EYE MASK

In this dark I rest,
unready for the light which dawns
day after day,
eager to be shared.
Black silk, shelter me.
I need
more of the night before I open
eyes and heart
to illumination. I must still
grow in the dark like a root
not ready, not ready at all.

PO CHÜ-I
771–846

One moment of nonattachment, of meditation, and, immediately following, the return of a high official, as we guess, to court intrigue and commercial transaction.

CLIMBING THE LING-YING TERRACE AND LOOKING NORTH

Mounting on high I begin to realize the smallness of Man's
    Domain;
Gazing into the distance I begin to know the vanity of the Carnal
    World.
I turn my head and hurry home—back to the Court and Market,
A single grain of rice falling—in the Great Barn.

Translated from the Chinese by Arthur Waley

ESKIMO (ANONYMOUS)

An Eskimo poet, who will forever remain anonymous, composed a song based on a legend of origins from the oral tradition.

MAGIC WORDS

In the very earliest time,
when both people and animals lived on earth,
a person could become an animal if he wanted to
and an animal could become a human being.
Sometimes they were people
and sometimes animals
and there was no difference.
All spoke the same language.
That was the time when words were like magic.
The human mind had mysterious powers.
A word spoken by chance
might have strange consequences.
It would suddenly come alive
and what people wanted to happen could
        happen—
all you had to do was say it.
Nobody could explain this:
That's the way it was.

Translated from the Inuit by Edward Field

And why after all does the world exist? That was the subject of a Hasid, Nachman of Bratzlav. And he tried, as did his predecessor of the sixteenth century, the master of the Kabbalah, Isaac Luria, to answer the question: How is it possible that the Highest, who fills everything that exists with Himself, could create the universe, which is not He?

FROM "THE TORAH OF THE VOID"

God,
for Mercy's sake,
created the world
to reveal Mercy.
If there were no world
on whom would Mercy take pity?

So—to show His Mercy
He created the worlds
from *Aziluth*'s peak
to this Earth's center.

But as He wished to create
there was not a *where?*
All was Infinitely He,
Be He Blessed!

The light He condensed
sideways
thus was *space* made
an empty void.

In *space* days and measures
came into being.
So the world was created.

This void was needed
for the world's sake,
so that it may be
put into place.

Don't strain to understand
this void!
It is a mystery—not to be realized
until the future
is the *now.*

       *

Once there was *light,*
much and powerful,
holy *light,*
and it was in vessels
—too much *light,*
too much power—
and the *vessels* burst!

When the *vessels* burst
the fragments
of Holiness
took form
becoming the *outered* sciences.

So, even of Holiness
there is offal:
Just as there is sweat
and hair and excrement,
so Holiness too
has its offal.

Translated from the Hebrew by Zalman Schachter

JELALUDDIN RUMI
1207—1273

We know as much about the beginning and the end, about the infinite complexity of the world, as does an embryo locked in its mother's womb. This parable by a Persian poet-mystic, making use of that metaphor, calls for our opening up to that whole dimension of existence which escapes our words.

Little by little, wean yourself.

This is the gist of what I have to say.

From an embryo, whose nourishment comes in the blood,
move to an infant drinking milk,
to a child on solid food,
to a searcher after wisdom,
to a hunter of more invisible game.

Think how it is to have a conversation with an embryo.
You might say, "The world outside is vast and intricate.
There are wheatfields and mountain passes, and orchards in bloom.

At night there are millions of galaxies, and in sunlight
the beauty of friends dancing at a wedding."

You ask the embryo why he, or she, stays cooped up
in the dark with eyes closed.

> Listen to the answer.
There is no "other world."
I only know what I've experienced.
You must be hallucinating.

Mathnawi, III, 49–6

Translated from the Persian by Coleman Barks

W. S. MERWIN

1927—

The following poem inspires us to reflect on what seldom crosses our minds. After all (literally after all), such an anniversary awaits every one of us.

FOR THE ANNIVERSARY OF MY DEATH

Every year without knowing it I have passed the day
When the last fires will wave to me
And the silence will set out
Tireless traveler
Like the beam of a lightless star

Then I will no longer
Find myself in life as in a strange garment
Surprised at the earth
And the love of one woman
And the shamelessness of men
As today writing after three days of rain
Hearing the wren sing and the falling cease
And boding not knowing to what

In African folklore, I have found a strange image of the Creator as a swarm of bees.

INVOCATION OF THE CREATOR

He is patient, he is not angry.
He sits in silence to pass judgment.
He sees you even when he is not looking.
He stays in a far place—but his eyes are on the town.

He stands by his children and lets them succeed.
He causes them to laugh—and they laugh.
Ohoho—the father of laughter.
His eye is full of joy.
He rests in the sky like a swarm of bees.

Obatala—who turns blood into children.

Translated by Ulli Beier

CHUANG TZU
3rd—4th century B.C.

Masters of nonattachment, the Chinese Taoists would give first of all practical advice—advice of the Way, for such is the literal meaning of the word Tao, *though it means much more and that is why it is untranslatable.*

MAN IS BORN IN TAO

Fishes are born in water
Man is born in Tao.
If fishes, born in water,
Seek the deep shadow
Of pond and pool,
All their needs
Are satisfied.
If man, born in Tao,
Sinks into the deep shadow
Of non-action
To forget aggression and concern,
He lacks nothing
His life is secure.

Moral: "All the fish needs
Is to get lost in water.
All man needs is to get lost
In Tao."

Translated from the Chinese by Thomas Merton

Nonacting is not the same as passivity. But energy alone is not everything, and sometimes, when we strive incessantly, we achieve an outcome just opposite to what was intended—we learn from the same Chuang Tzu.

THE NEED TO WIN

When an archer is shooting for nothing
He has all his skill.
If he shoots for a brass buckle
He is already nervous.
If he shoots for a prize of gold
He goes blind
Or sees two targets—
He is out of his mind!

His skill has not changed. But the prize
Divides him. He cares.
He thinks more of winning
Than of shooting—
And the need to win
Drains him of power.

Translated from the Chinese by Thomas Merton

JELALUDDIN RUMI
1207—1273

Because the question of good and evil has been tormenting us since the moment we plucked a fruit from the tree of knowledge, perhaps it's worthwhile to remind ourselves that there have been people who didn't take to heart that pair of opposite notions. For them, as for Jelaluddin Rumi, nonattachment meant simply that you could lie down in a meadow.

Out beyond ideas of wrongdoing and rightdoing,
there is a field. I'll meet you there.

When the soul lies down in that grass,
the world is too full to talk about.
Ideas, language, even the phrase *each other*
doesn't make any sense.

Translated by Coleman Barks and John Moyne

LI PO

701—762

Perhaps in this Chinese poem there is something similar to the poem by Rumi. Motionless sitting and meditating on a landscape leads to the disappearance of our separate existence, so we become the mountain we contemplate.

THE BIRDS HAVE VANISHED

The birds have vanished into the sky,
and now the last cloud drains away.

We sit together, the mountain and me,
until only the mountain remains.

Translated from the Chinese by Sam Hamill

DENISE LEVERTOV

1923—

Original sin doesn't leave us in peace, for it is enigmatic, if only because the distinction between good and evil is connected with the faculty of reason and with Satan's promise that "you will be like gods." Denise Levertov writes a poem of our repentance.

CONTRABAND

The tree of knowledge was the tree of reason.
That's why the taste of it
drove us from Eden. That fruit
was meant to be dried and milled to a fine powder
for use a pinch at a time, a condiment.
God had probably planned to tell us later
about this new pleasure.
                          We stuffed our mouths full of it,
gorged on *but* and *if* and *how* and again
but, knowing no better.
It's toxic in large quantities; fumes
swirled in our heads and around us
to form a dense cloud that hardened to steel,
a wall between us and God, Who was Paradise.
Not that God is unreasonable—but reason
in such excess was tyranny
and locked us into its own limits, a polished cell
reflecting our own faces. God lives
on the other side of that mirror,
but through the slit where the barrier doesn't
quite touch ground, manages still
to squeeze in—as filtered light,
splinters of fire, a strain of music heard
then lost, then heard again.

CH'ANG YU

c. 810

In poets of Asia, we often find the theme of liberation from "earthly ties," conceived as our participation in human society. Even emperors are not free from that strife.

A RINGING BELL

I lie in my bed,
Listening to the monastery bell.
In the still night
The sound re-echoes amongst the hills.
Frost gathers under the cold moon.
Under the overcast sky,
In the depths of the night,
The first tones are still reverberating
While the last tones are ringing clear and sharp.
I listen and I can still hear them both,
But I cannot tell when they fade away.
I know the bondage and vanity of the world.
But who can tell when we escape
From life and death?

Translated from the Chinese by Kenneth Rexroth

WANG WEI

701—761

Wang Wei was a poet and a painter but also an official, and many of his poems juxtapose contemplative life in the spirit of Taoism and Buddhism with active life and career from which it's not easy to be liberated. But in his old age he achieved a peculiar kind of nonattachment, when even poetry and painting seemed to him too close to earthly delusions.

LAZY ABOUT WRITING POEMS

With time I become lazy about writing poems.
Now my only company is old age.
In an earlier life I was a poet, a mistake,
and my former body belonged to a painter.
I can't abandon habits of that life
and sometimes am recognized by people of this world.
My name and pen name speak my former being
but about all this my heart is ignorant.

Translated from the Chinese by Tony and Willis Barnstone and Xu Haixin

If one lost the game, if one's political foes were effectively undermining one and at last triumphed, it was necessary to withdraw somewhere, to a house in the mountains, at least temporarily. Unfortunately, such a thing could hardly be done temporarily, and one had to accept that it would be forever. White clouds have the symbolic meaning of a world beyond and of the contemplation of things eternal.

A FAREWELL

I dismount from my horse and drink your wine.
I ask where you're going
You say you are a failure
and want to hibernate at the foot of Deep South Mountain.
Once you're gone no one will ask about you.
There are endless white clouds on the mountain.

Translated from the Chinese by Tony and Willis Barnstone and Xu Haixin

To be free, at least for a short time, to forget about the court and the market, as here, in a boat on the lake.

DRIFTING ON THE LAKE

Autumn is crisp and the firmament far,
especially far from where people live.
I look at cranes on the sand
and am immersed in joy when I see mountains beyond
      the clouds.
Dusk inks the crystal ripples.
Leisurely the white moon comes out.
Tonight I am with my oar, alone, and can do
      everything,
yet waver, not willing to return.

Translated from the Chinese by Tony and Willis Barnstone and Xu Haixin

TU FU

713—770

The bucolic theme seems to be present in practically all Chinese poets, and of course in the most famous, Tu Fu.

VISITORS

I have had asthma for a
Long time. It seems to improve
Here in this house by the river.
It is quiet too. No crowds
Bother me. I am brighter
And more rested. I am happy here.
When someone calls at my thatched hut
My son brings me my straw hat
And I go out and gather
A handful of fresh vegetables.
It isn't much to offer.
But it is given in friendship.

Translated from the Chinese by Kenneth Rexroth

PO CHÜ-I
772—846

Let us say, though, that there is a backstage to that praise of the healthy peasant
life. Poets belonged to the caste of the educated, and could sometimes idealize the
country and yokels who worked the soil, but it was not their milieu. Whether they
were building their villas among the vineyards, like Roman poets, houses in the
mountains, like the Chinese, or dachas, like the Russians, they were always aware
of a distance. And especially in China, where the literate had to pass numerous
and difficult state examinations.

LODGING WITH THE OLD MAN OF THE STREAM

Men's hearts love gold and jade;
Men's mouths covet wine and flesh.
Not so the old man of the stream;
He drinks from his gourd and asks nothing more.
South of the stream he cuts firewood and grass;
North of the stream he has built wall and roof.
Yearly he sows a single acre of land;
In spring he drives two yellow calves.
In these things he finds great repose;
Beyond these he has no wish or care.
By chance I met him walking by the water-side;
He took me home and lodged me in his thatched hut.
When I parted from him, to seek Market and Court,
This old man asked my rank and pay.
Doubting my tale, he laughed loud and long:
"Privy Counsellors do not sleep in barns."

Translated from the Chinese by Arthur Waley

MIRON BIALOSZEWSKI
1922—1983

*Miron Bialoszewski was a poet of Warsaw, rooted in the city's folklore and ex-
perimenting with street slang. He survived the complete ruin of his city, first in
the German action against the Jewish ghetto, then in the uprising of 1944. Not
similar in his writings to any of his contemporaries, he could have been the epitome
of the nonattachment achieved by some Taoists, although in him, it was spontaneous,
not programmatic. And he was a humorous poet, describing the most ordinary human
actions with an attention deserved by much greater events.*

A BALLAD OF GOING DOWN TO THE STORE

First I went down to the street
by means of the stairs,
just imagine it,
by means of the stairs.

Then people known to people unknown
passed me by and I passed them by.
Regret
that you did not see
how people walk,
regret!

I entered a complete store:
lamps of glass were glowing.
I saw somebody—he sat down—
and what did I hear? what did I hear?
rustling of bags and human talk.

And indeed,
indeed,
I returned.

Translated from the Polish by Czeslaw Milosz

MUSO SOSEKI

1275—1351

Nonattachment and liberation are, in poetry, often associated with old age because the years bring—in any case, they should bring—some wisdom, as in this poem by a Japanese poet.

OLD MAN AT LEISURE

Sacred or secular
    manners and conventions
        make no difference to him
Completely free
    leaving it all to heaven
        he seems a simpleton
No one catches
    a glimpse inside
        his mind
this old man
    all by himself
        between heaven and earth

Translated from the Japanese by W. S. Merwin

KENNETH REXROTH
1905—1982

Kenneth Rexroth, who used to live in Japan, wrote toward the end of his life a
parable on Buddha, a poem of far-reaching nonattachment.

FROM "THE CITY OF THE MOON"

Buddha took some Autumn leaves
In his hand and asked
Ananda if these were all
The red leaves there were.
Ananda answered that it
Was Autumn and leaves
Were falling all about them,
More than could ever
Be numbered. So Buddha said,
"I have given you
A handful of truths. Besides
These there are many
Thousands of other truths, more
Than can ever be numbered."

This poem may be considered as a last testament of Rexroth's.

A LONG LIFETIME

A long lifetime
Peoples and places
And the crisis of mankind—
What survives is the crystal—
Infinitely small—
Infinitely large—

In this Bushmen's song, there is a note of concern and lament, but probably it's more expressive of a serene acceptance of the immutable order of the world.

THE DAY WE DIE

The day we die
the wind comes down
to take away
our footprints.

The wind makes dust
to cover up
the marks we left
while walking.

For otherwise
the thing would seem
as if we were
still living.

Therefore the wind
is he who comes
to blow away
our footprints.

ANNA KAMIEŃSKA
[dates unknown]

Anna Kamieńska was a Christian deeply living both the Old Testament and the New Testament. In her old age she achieved much serenity and acceptance of the world created by God. I find this a very good poem.

A PRAYER THAT WILL BE ANSWERED

Lord let me suffer much
and then die

Let me walk through silence
and leave nothing behind not even fear

Make the world continue
let the ocean kiss the sand just as before

Let the grass stay green
so that the frogs can hide in it

so that someone can bury his face in it
and sob out his love

Make the day rise brightly
as if there were no more pain

And let my poem stand clear as a windowpane
bumped by a bumblebee's head

Translated from the Polish by Stanislaw Barańczak and Clare Cavanagh

History

This chapter is in reality an anti-chapter. For poets of the twentieth century, history has been all-pervading, and much as they would like to turn to the eternal subjects of love and death, they have been forced to be aware of wars, revolutions, and the changes of political systems. Poets have been internally divided, knowing that they should serve art, but at the same time feeling a moral compulsion to be politically committed. The number of good and bad poems on the events of the twentieth century runs into many volumes. Yet still we lack the criteria to distinguish what, in all that number, is durable as the art of the word and what has its place as a document. But let us leave an assessment of the relations between poetry and history to our successors of the twenty-first century.

My reticence in filling this chapter with poems has a very personal explanation. Throughout some periods of my life, I have been a committed poet, active both as an author of verse and as an editor of publications directed against mass crimes. Thinking of those times, I rejoice in being able to make an anthology such as this one, and it may be a source of optimism that in this cruel century such an anthology could be made. And that is why I decided to make this chapter short, limiting it to poems in which I notice a high degree of distillation. By distillation I mean that only the most essential elements are left. In this respect, poetry of the countries most severely tried by the calamities of the twentieth century seems to be privileged, because their poets have given shape to those experiences in a most concise way. In this chapter, the poems I have selected are intended just as examples of poets' struggle in transmuting too crude and too cruel a reality into words through an artistic distance.

LEOPOLD STAFF
1878—1957

This poem was written immediately after World War II, in Poland, among the ruins, of which those in the figurative sense were even more oppressive than the physical ones. There was literally nothing. How could a poet react to that situation? What was left was to do what a child does, who when trying to draw a house often starts with the smoke from the chimney, then draws a chimney, and then the rest. So this is a poem of naked faith.

FOUNDATIONS

I built on the sand
And it tumbled down,
I built on a rock
And it tumbled down.
Now when I build, I shall begin
With the smoke from the chimney.

Translated from the Polish by Czeslaw Milosz

ANNA SWIR
1909—1984

Fire consumed the city of Warsaw. First, the part where the Germans had made the ghetto, and then the rest of the city. A lonely woman running through streets that are on fire is enough as a metaphor of a "limit situation."

I'M AFRAID OF FIRE

Why am I so afraid
running along this street
that's on fire.

After all there's no one here
only the fire roaring up to the sky
and that rumble wasn't a bomb
but just three floors collapsing.

Set free, the naked flames dance,
wave their arms
through the gaps of the windows,
it's a sin to peep at
naked flames
a sin to eavesdrop on
free fire's speech.

I am fleeing from that speech,
which resounded here on earth
before the speech of man.

Translated from the Polish by Magnus J. Krynski and Robert A. Maguire

ALEKSANDER WAT
1900—1967

The scene is a river somewhere in Soviet Asia. The helmsman is obviously a Muslim. The narrator is a poet deported by the Soviet authorities to Asia. All this setup is perhaps useful in seeing how such basic data are transformed into a parable on history as a dangerous and ominous force.

FROM PERSIAN PARABLES

By great, swift waters
on a stony bank
a human skull lay shouting:
Allah la ilah.

And in that shout such horror
and such supplication
so great was its despair
that I asked the helmsman:

What is there left to cry for? Why is it still afraid?
What divine judgment could strike it again?

Suddenly a rising wave
took hold of the skull
and tossing it about
smashed it against the bank.

Nothing is ever over
—the helmsman's voice was hollow—
and there is no bottom to evil.

Translated from the Polish by Czeslaw Milosz and Leonard Nathan

JULIA HARTWIG
1921—

Expectation of an imminent calamity. Many people have lived through such a moment, but they haven't left poems about it. Yet those moments are an integral part of history, of many cities and countries.

ABOVE US

Boys kicking a ball on a vast square beneath an obelisk
and the apocalyptic sky at sunset to the rear
Why the sudden menace in this view
as if someone wished to turn it all to red dust
The sun already knows And the sky knows it too
And the water in the river knows
Music bursts from the loudspeakers like wild laughter
Only a star high above us
stands lost in thought with a finger to its lips

Translated from the Polish by Stanislaw Barańczak and Clare Cavanagh

SHU TING
1952—

This is a very ambiguous poem about something known to many people in this
century, an ideological commitment to a cause, to a party, to a movement. One has
had to cope not only with the inertia of the world but also with one's own doubt.
Is the voice in this poem speaking for moving forward in spite of one's doubt, or,
on the contrary, expressing the validity of doubt? We are not completely sure, either
way.

PERHAPS . . .
for the loneliness of an author

Perhaps these thoughts of ours
                will never find an audience
Perhaps the mistaken road
                will end in a mistake
Perhaps the lamps we light one at a time
                will be blown out, one at a time
Perhaps the candles of our lives will gutter out
                without lighting a fire to warm us.

Perhaps when all the tears have been shed
                the earth will be more fertile
Perhaps when we sing praises to the sun
                the sun will praise us in return
Perhaps these heavy burdens
                will strengthen our philosophy
Perhaps when we weep for those in misery
                we must be silent about miseries of our own

Perhaps
Because of our irresistible sense of mission
We have no choice

Translated from the Chinese by Carolyn Kizer

RYSZARD KRYNICKI

1943–

The history of the twentieth century has been largely a history of mass crimes. Yet it has also witnessed the heroism of idealistically motivated men and women who were ready to offer their lives for the causes they believed sacred. This poem compares that faith in ideas to the urge of a moth to fly toward a candle, toward its destruction. By an ironic twist, in reality the poet praises the constant striving of people toward a dangerous goal.

I CAN'T HELP YOU

Poor moth, I can't help you,
I can only turn out the light.

Translated from the Polish by Stanislaw Barańczak and Clare Cavanagh

ZBIGNIEW HERBERT

1924—

The Castle of Elsinore has epitomized a place where an entanglement of will and fate is violently resolved and history is seen as tragedy. In modern interpretation the stress is laid upon the political aspect of Hamlet's situation, as a man surrounded by spies and pretending madness for self-protection. But Hamlet loses his game and everybody loses. Instead of heroic clashes of will, a provisional, patched-up status quo rules. The poem doesn't pronounce a clear judgment.

ELEGY OF FORTINBRAS

for C.M.

Now that we're alone we can talk prince man to man
though you lie on the stairs and see no more than a dead ant
nothing but black sun with broken rays
I could never think of your hands without smiling
and now that they lie on the stone like fallen nests
they are as defenceless as before. The end is exactly this
The hands lie apart The sword lies apart The head apart
and the knight's feet in soft slippers

You will have a soldier's funeral without having been a soldier
the only ritual I am acquainted with a little
There will be no candles no singing only cannon-fuses and
      bursts
crepe dragged on the pavement helmets boots artillery horses
      drums drums I know nothing exquisite
those will be my manoeuvres before I start to rule
one has to take the city by the neck and shake it a bit

Anyhow you had to perish Hamlet you were not for life
you believed in crystal notions not in human clay
always twitching as if asleep you hunted chimeras
wolfishly you crunched the air only to vomit
you know no human thing you did not know even how to
      breathe

Now you have peace Hamlet you accomplished what you
       had to
and you have peace The rest is not silence but belongs to me
you chose the easier part an elegant thrust
but what is heroic death compared with eternal watching
with a cold apple in one's hand on a narrow chair
with a view of the anthill and the clock's dial

Adieu prince I have tasks a sewer project
and a decree on prostitutes and beggars
I must also elaborate a better system of prisons
since as you justly said Denmark is a prison
I go to my affairs This night is born
a star named Hamlet We shall never meet
what I shall leave will not be worth a tragedy

It is not for us to greet each other or bid farewell we live on
       archipelagos
and that water these words what can they do what can they
       do prince

Translated by Czeslaw Milosz and Peter Dale Scott

MOUSHEGH ISHKHAN
1913—

Armenians were the first to fall victim to genocide in the twentieth century.
Persecuted and dispersed, they have learned to live in exile in several countries and
on various continents. Since exile became the destiny of so many people in our
times, a poem on language is appropriate here. It extols an attachment to one's
mother tongue and a union through the language of all those who speak it.

THE ARMENIAN LANGUAGE
IS THE HOME OF THE ARMENIAN

The Armenian language is the home
and haven where the wanderer can own
roof and wall and nourishment.
He can enter to find love and pride,
locking the hyena and the storm outside.
For centuries its architects have toiled
to give its ceilings height.
How many peasants working
day and night have kept
its cupboards full, lamps lit, ovens hot.
Always rejuvenated, always old, it lasts
century to century on the path
where every Armenian can find it when he's lost
in the wilderness of his future, or his past.

Translated by Diana der Hovanessian

NAOMI LAZARD

1936—

Escapes over borders at the risk of one's life. Escapes on boats through dangerous seas. Long lines before consulates of happier countries. A dream of leaving behind oppression and misery. All this is a part of modern history, and for that reason this bitter poem acquires universal significance.

ORDINANCE ON ARRIVAL

Welcome to you
who have managed to get here.
It's been a terrible trip;
you should be happy you have survived it.
Statistics prove that not many do.
You would like a bath, a hot meal,
a good night's sleep. Some of you
need medical attention.
None of this is available.
These things have always been
in short supply; now
they are impossible to obtain.

       This is not
a temporary situation;
it is permanent.
Our condolences on your disappointment.
It is not our responsibility
everything you have heard about this place
is false. It is not our fault
you have been deceived,
ruined your health getting here.
For reasons beyond our control
there is no vehicle out.

CONSTANTINE CAVAFY
1863—1933

This poem has often been quoted, because it fits well the division of Europe, after World War II, by the Cold War. Nobody seems to have paid attention to the date of its writing, 1898. Cavafy, though he explored in his poems all the aspects of his Hellenistic world, including the Greek-speaking Byzantine empire, understood the word "barbarian" in its original Greek meaning, as applied to all those who are outside and have, instead of human speech, incoherent gibberish. His intuition allowed him to capture a centuries-old opposition between the inside and the outside of civilization.

WAITING FOR THE BARBARIANS

What are we waiting for, assembled in the forum?

> The barbarians are due here today.

Why isn't anything going on in the senate?
Why are the senators sitting there without legislating?

> Because the barbarians are coming today.
> What's the point of senators making laws now?
> Once the barbarians are here, they'll do the legislating.

Why did our emperor get up so early,
and why is he sitting enthroned at the city's main gate,
in state, wearing the crown?

> Because the barbarians are coming today
> and the emperor's waiting to receive their leader.
> He's even got a scroll to give him,
> loaded with titles, with imposing names.

Why have our two consuls and praetors come out today
wearing their embroidered, their scarlet togas?
Why have they put on bracelets with so many amethysts,

rings sparkling with magnificent emeralds?
Why are they carrying elegant canes
beautifully worked in silver and gold?

    Because the barbarians are coming today
    and things like that dazzle the barbarians

Why don't our distinguished orators turn up as usual
to make their speeches, say what they have to say?

    Because the barbarians are coming today
    and they're bored by rhetoric and public speaking.

Why this sudden bewilderment, this confusion?
(How serious people's faces have become.)
Why are the streets and squares emptying so rapidly,
everyone going home lost in thought?

    Because night has fallen and the barbarians haven't come.
    And some of our men just in from the border say
    there are no barbarians any longer.

Now what's going to happen to us without barbarians?
Those people were a kind of solution.

Translated from the Greek by Edmund Keeley and Philip Sherrard

PERMISSIONS

Every effort has been made to obtain permission from the appropriate parties to include these works, but if any errors have been made we will be happy to correct them. We gratefully acknowledge the following permissions:

CH'ANG YU. "A Ringing Bell," tr. Kenneth Rexroth, from *Flower Wreath Hill* by Kenneth Rexroth. © 1979 by Kenneth Rexroth. Reprinted by permission of New Directions Publishing Corp.

CHUANG TZU. "Man Is Born in Tao" and "The Need to Win," tr. Thomas Merton from *The Collected Poems of Thomas Merton.* © 1963 by The Abbey of Gethsemani, Inc., 1977 by The Trustees of the Merton Legacy Trust. Reprinted by permission of New Directions Publishing Corp.

EMPEROR CH'IEN-WEN OF LIANG. "Getting Up in Winter," tr. Kenneth Rexroth, from *Flower Wreath Hill* by Kenneth Rexroth, © 1979 by Kenneth Rexroth. Reprinted by permission of New Directions Publishing Corp.

CHU SHU CHEN. "Morning," tr. Kenneth Rexroth, from *Flower Wreath Hill* by Kenneth Rexroth. © 1979 by Kenneth Rexroth. Reprinted by permission of New Directions Publishing Corp.

ROBERT CREELEY. "Like They Say" from *Collected Poems of Robert Creeley, 1945–1975.* © 1983 by The Regents of the University of California. Reprinted by permission.

WAYNE DODD. "Of Rain and Air" from *Sometimes Music Rises.* © 1986 by Wayne Dodd. Reprinted by permission of the University of Georgia Press. "Of His Life" from *The Names You Gave It.* © 1980 by Wayne Dodd. Reprinted by permission of Louisiana State University Press.

CARLOS DRUMMOND DE ANDRADE. "In the Middle of the Road" ("No meio do caminho"), tr. Elizabeth Bishop, from *The Complete Poems: 1927–1979* by Elizabeth Bishop. © 1996 by the heirs of Carlos Drummond de Andrade. Translation © 1979, 1983 by Alice Helen Methfessel. Reprinted by permission of Farrar, Straus & Giroux, Inc.

GUNNER EKÉLOF. "Greece," tr. Larson and Nathan, from *Songs of Something Else.* © 1982 by Princeton University Press. Reprinted by permission of Princeton University Press.

EDWARD FIELD. "The Journey" from *Counting Myself Lucky: Selected Poems 1963–1992.* © 1992 by Edward Field. Reprinted with the permission of Black Sparrow Press. "Magic Words" reprinted by permission of Edward Field.

JEAN FOLLAIN. "Face the Animal" (1961), tr. Heather McHugh, from *Poems by Jean Follain.* © 1961 by Editions Gallimard, Paris. Translation © 1981 by Princeton University Press. Reprinted by permission of Princeton University Press. "Black Meat" (1964) and "School of Nature" (1947) from *Transference of the World.* © 1964, 1947 Editions Gallimard, Paris. Translations © 1968, 1969 by W. S. Merwin. Reprinted by permission of W. S. Merwin. "Music of Spheres" and "Taxidermist," trs. Czeslaw Milosz and Robert Hass. All poems reprinted by permission of Editions Gallimard, Paris.

ROBERT FRANCIS. "Waxwings" from *The Orb Weaver.* © 1960 by Robert Francis, Weslyan University Press. Reprinted by permission of University Press of New England.

ROBERT FROST. "The Most of It" from *The Poetry of Robert Frost,* Edward Connery Lathem, ed. © 1942 by Robert Frost. © 1969 by Henry Holt and Co., Inc. and 1970 by Lesley Frost Ballantine. Reprinted by permission of Henry Holt and Co., Inc. and Jonathan Cape, an imprint of Random House UK Ltd.

ALLEN GINSBERG. "A Strange New Cottage in Berkeley" from *Collected Poems 1947–1980.* © 1955 by Allen Ginsberg. Copyright renewed. Reprinted by permission of HarperCollins Publishers, Inc. and Penguin UK Ltd.

LINDA GREGG. "Adult" from *Alma.* © 1985 by Linda Gregg. Reprinted by permission of Random House, Inc. "A Dark Thing Inside the Day" and "Night Music" from *The Sacraments of Desire.* © 1991 by Linda Gregg. Reprinted with the permission of Graywolf Press, Saint Paul, MN.

EAMON GRENNAN. "Woman at a Lit Window" from *As If It Matters.* © 1991 by Eamon Grennan. Reprinted with the permission of Graywolf Press, Saint Paul, MN.

JORGE GUILLÉN. "Flight," tr. A. L. Geist, from *Guillen on Guillen: The Poetry and the Poet,* Jorge Guillen and Reginald Gibbons, eds. © 1979 by Princeton University Press. Reprinted by permission of Princeton University Press.

JOHN HAINES. "The Train Stops at Healy Fork" and "On the Mountain" from *News from the Glacier.* © 1982 by John Haines, Weslyan University Press. Reprinted by permission of University Press of New England.

JULIA HARTWIG. "Above Us," tr. Stanislaw Baranczak and Clare Cavanagh, from *Polish Poetry of the Last Two Decades of Communist Rule.* © 1991 by Northwestern University Press. Reprinted by permission of Northwestern University Press.

ROBERT HASS. "The Image" from *Praise.* © 1974–1979 by Robert Hass. First published by The Ecco Press in 1979. Reprinted by permission. "Late Spring" from *Human Wishes.* © 1989 by Robert Hass. First published by The Ecco Press in 1989. Reprinted by permission.

SEAMUS HEANEY. Excerpt from "Clearances" from *The Haw Lantern.* © 1987 by Seamus Heaney. Reprinted by permission of Farrar, Straus & Giroux, Inc. and Faber & Faber Ltd.

ZBIGNIEW HERBERT. "Elegy of Fortinbras" from *Postwar Polish Poetry,* Czeslaw Milosz, ed. Reprinted by permission of Bantam Doubleday Dell Publishing Group.

JANE HIRSHFIELD. "A Story" from *Of Gravity and Angels.* © 1988 by Jane Hirshfield, Weslyan University Press. Reprinted by permission of University Press of New England.

MOUSHEGH ISHKHAN. "The Armenian Language Is the Home of the Armenian," tr. Diana der Hovanessian. Reprinted by permission of Diana der Hovanessian.

ISSA. Haiku, trs. Lucien Stryk and Takashi Ikemoto, from *The Penguin Book of Zen Poetry.* Reprinted with the permission of Northern Illinois University Foundation.

ROLF JACOBSEN. "Cobalt," "Express Train," "Rubber," and "The Catacombs in San Callisto," tr. R. Greenwald, from *The Silence Afterwards: Selected Poems of Rolf Jacobsen.* © 1985 by Princeton University Press. Reprinted by permission of Princeton University Press.

ROBINSON JEFFERS. "Boats in Fog," "Carmel Point," "Cremation," and "Evening Ebb" from *Rock and Hawk.* © 1929 and renewed 1957 by Robinson Jeffers. Reprinted by permission of Random House, Inc.

ANNA KAMIEŃSKA. "A Prayer That Will Be Answered," tr. Stanislaw Baranczak and Clare Cavanagh, from *Polish Poetry of the Last Two Decades of Communist Rule.* © 1991

by Northwestern University Press. Reprinted by permission of Northwestern University Press.

JAAN KAPLINSKI. "My Wife and Children" and "We Started Home, My Son and I" from *The Wandering Border.* © 1987 by Jaan Kaplinski. English translation © by Jaan Kaplinski with Sam Hamill and Riina Tamm. Reprinted by permission of Copper Canyon Press, P. O. Box 271, Port Townsend, WA 98368.

KIKAKU. Haiku, trs. Lucien Stryk and Takashi Ikemoto, from *The Penguin Book of Zen Poetry.* Reprinted with the permission of Northern Illinois University Foundation.

GALWAY KINNELL. "Daybreak" from *Mortal Acts, Mortal Words.* © 1980 by Galway Kinnell. Reprinted by permission of Houghton Mifflin Co. All rights reserved.

DAVID KIRBY. "To a French Structuralist." Reprinted by permission of the author.

TED KOOSER. "Late Lights in Minnesota" from *Sure Signs: New and Selected Poems.* © 1980. Reprinted by permission of the University of Pittsburgh Press.

STEVE KOWIT. "Notice" from *Mysteries of the Body.* © 1994 by Steve Kowit. Reprinted by permission. "Cosmetics Do No Good," "When He Pressed His Lips," and "In the Morning" from *Passionate Journey.* © by Steve Kowit. First published by City Miner Books, P.O. Box 176, Berkeley, CA 94701. Reprinted by permission.

RYSZARD KRYNICKI. "I Can't Help You," trs. Stanislaw Baranczak and Clare Cavanagh, from *Polish Poetry of the Last Two Decades of Communist Rule.* © 1991 by Northwestern University Press. Reprinted by permission of Northwestern University Press.

JOANNE ELIZABETH KYGER. "And with March a Decade in Bolinas" and "Destruction." Reprinted by permission of the author.

VALERY LARBAUD. "Images," tr. William Jay Smith, from *Collected Translations.* Reprinted by permission of New Rivers Press.

PHILIP LARKIN. "The Card-Players" from *Collected Poems.* © 1988, 1989 by the Estate of Philip Larkin. Reprinted by permission of Farrar, Straus & Giroux, Inc. and Faber & Faber Ltd.

D. H. LAWRENCE. "Butterfly," "Maximus," and "Mystic" from *The Complete Poems of D. H. Lawrence,* V. de Sola Pinto and F. W. Roberts, eds. © 1964, 1971 by Angelo Ravagli and C. M. Weekley, Executors of the Estate of Frieda Lawrence Ravagli. Used by permission of Viking Penguin, a division of Penguin Books USA, Inc. and the Estate of Frieda Lawrence Ravagli.

NAOMI LAZARD. "Ordinance on Arrival" was first published in *The Ontario Review* and appeared in *Ordinances,* Owl Creek Press, 1984. Reprinted by permission of the author.

LI-YOUNG LEE. "Irises" from *Rose.* © 1986 by Li-Young Lee. Reprinted with the permission of BOA Editions, Ltd., 92 Park Avenue, Brockport, NY 14420.

DENISE LEVERTOV. "Contraband," "Eye Mask," and "Witness" from *Evening Train.* © 1992 by Denise Levertov. "A Woman Meets an Old Lover" from *Life in the Forest.* © 1978 by Denise Levertov. "Living" from *Poems 1960–1967.* © 1966 by Denise Levertov. Reprinted by permission of New Directions Publishing Corp. and the author.

PHILIP LEVINE. "A Sleepless Night" from *New Selected Poems.* © 1991 by Philip Levine. Reprinted by permission of Alfred A. Knopf, Inc.

LI CH'ING-CHAO. "Hopelessness," tr. Kenneth Rexroth, from *Flower Wreath Hill* by Kenneth Rexroth. © 1979 by Kenneth Rexroth. Reprinted by permission of New Directions Publishing Corp.

LI PO. "Ancient Air," tr. J. P. Seaton, from *Chinese Poetic Writing.* © by J. P. Seaton. Reprinted by permission of J. P. Seaton.

LIU TSUNG-YUAN. "Old Fisherman," tr. J. P. Seaton, from *Chinese Poetic Writing.* © by J. P. Seaton. Reprinted by permission of J. P. Seaton.

ANTONIO MACHADO. "Rainbow at Night," tr. Robert Bly. English translation © by Robert Bly. Reprinted by permission. "Summer Night," tr. Willis Barnstone. English translation © by Willis Barnstone. Reprinted by permission.

ZBIGNIEW MACHEJ. "Orchards in July" trs. Czeslaw Milosz and Robert Hass. Translation © 1996 by Czeslaw Milosz. Reprinted by permission.

BRONISLAW MAJ. "Seen Fleetingly, from a Train," "An August Afternoon," and "A Leaf," trs. Czeslaw Milosz and Robert Hass. Translation © 1996 by Czeslaw Milosz.

MEI YAO CH'EN. "A Dream at Night," tr. Kenneth Rexroth, from *One Hundred Poems from the Chinese.* © 1971 by Kenneth Rexroth. Reprinted by permission of New Directions Publishing Corp.

THOMAS MERTON. "An Elegy for Ernest Hemingway" from *The Collected Poems of Thomas Merton.* © 1963 by The Abbey of Gethsemani, Inc., 1977 by The Trustees of the Merton Legacy Trust. Reprinted by permission of New Directions Publishing Corp.

W. S. MERWIN. "Utterance" from *The Rain in the Trees.* © 1988 by W. S. Merwin. Reprinted by permission of Alfred A. Knopf, Inc. "Dusk in Winter" and "For the Anniversary of My Death" from *The Lice.* © 1963, 1964, 1965, 1966, 1967 by W. S. Merwin. Reprinted by permission of the author.

OSCAR V. DE L. MILOSZ. "The Bridge," trs. Czeslaw Milosz and Robert Hass. Translation © 1996 by Czeslaw Milosz.

ROBERT MORGAN. "Bellrope" and "Buffalo Trace" from *At the Edge of Orchard Country.* © 1987 by Robert Morgan, Weslyan University Press. Reprinted by permission of University Press of New England. "Honey." Reprinted by permission of the author.

NACHMAN OF BRATZLAV. "The Torah of the Void" from *Exiled in the Word,* Jerome Rothenberg and Harris Lenowitz, eds. © 1989 by Jerome Rothenberg and Harris Lenowitz. Reprinted by permission of Copper Canyon Press, P.O. Box 271, Port Townsend, WA 98368.

LEONARD NATHAN. "Bladder Song" and "Toast" from *Carrying On: New and Selected Poems.* © 1985. Reprinted by permission of the University of Pittsburgh Press.

OU YANG HSIU. "Fisherman," tr. Kenneth Rexroth, from *One Hundred Poems from the Chinese.* © 1971 by Kenneth Rexroth. Reprinted by permission of New Directions Publishing Corp.

SHARON OLDS. "I Go Back to May 1937" from *The Gold Cell.* © 1987 by Sharon Olds. Reprinted by permission of Alfred A. Knopf, Inc.

MUSO SOSEKI. "Magnificent Peak" and "Old Man at Leisure," tr. W. S. Merwin and Soiku Shigematsu, from *Sun at Midnight* by Muso Soseki. Reprinted by permission of W. S. Merwin and Soiku Shigematsu.

SOUTHERN BUSHMEN. "The Day We Die," tr. Arthur Markowitz.

LEOPOLD STAFF. "Foundations" from *Postwar Polish Poetry*, Czeslaw Milosz, ed. Reprinted by permission of Bantam Doubleday Dell Publishing Group.

WILLIAM STAFFORD. "Vacation" from *Stories That Could Be True*. © 1977 by William Stafford. Reprinted by permission of the Estate of William Stafford.

WALLACE STEVENS. "Study of Two Pears" from *Collected Poems*. © 1942 by Wallace Stevens and renewed 1970 by Holly Stevens. Reprinted by permission of Random House, Inc. and Faber & Faber Ltd.

SU MAN SHU. "Exile in Japan," tr. Kenneth Rexroth, from *Flower Wreath Hill*. © 1979 by Kenneth Rexroth. Reprinted by permission of New Directions Publishing Corp.

SU TUNG P'O. "On a painting by Wang the Clerk," tr. Kenneth Rexroth, from *Flower Wreath Hill*. © 1979 by Kenneth Rexroth. Reprinted by permission of New Directions Publishing Corp.

MAY SWENSON. "Question" from *The Complete Poems to Solve*. © 1993 by The Literary Estate of May Swenson. Reprinted with permission of Simon & Schuster Books for Young Readers, an imprint of Simon & Schuster Children's Publishing Division.

ANNA SWIR. "The Greatest Love," "I Starve My Belly for a Sublime Purpose," "I Talk to My Body," "I Wash the Shirt," "Poetry Reading," "The Same Inside," "The Sea and the Man," "She Does Not Remember," "The Second Madigral," and "Troubles with the Soul at Morning Calisthentics," trs. Czeslaw Milosz and Leonard Nathan, from *Talking to My Body*. © 1996 by Anna Swir. "I'm Afraid of Fire" tr. Czeslaw Milosz. Reprinted by permission of Copper Canyon Press, P.O. Box 271, Port Townsend, WA 98368.

WISLAWA SZYMBORSKA. "In Praise of Self-Deprecation," "Four in the Morning," "Seen from Above," and "In Praise of My Sister," tr. Magnus J. Krynski and Robert A. Macguire, from *Sounds, Feelings, Thoughts: Seventy Poems*. © 1981 by Princeton University Press. Reprinted by permission of Princeton University Press. "View with a Grain of Sand," tr. Stanislaw Baranczak and Clare Cavanagh, from *Polish Poetry of the Last Two Decades of Communist Rule*. © 1991 by Northwestern University Press. Reprinted by permission of Northwestern University Press.

JAMES TATE. "Teaching the Ape to Write Poems" from *Absences: New Poems*. © 1970, 1971, 1972 by James Tate. By permission of Little, Brown and Company.

TOMAS TRANSTRÖMER. "Outskirts" and "Tracks" from *Selected Poems 1954−1986*. © 1985 by John F. Deane and Tomas Tranströmer; © 1975 by Robert Bly and Tomas Tranströmer. First published by The Ecco Press in 1987. Reprinted by permission. "Syros," trs. May Swenson and Leif Sjöberg. © 1972. Reprinted by permission of the University of Pittsburgh Press.

TU FU. "Travelling Northward," "Sunset," "Winter Dawn," "South Wind," "Clear After Rain," "To Pi Ssu Yao," and "Snow Storm," tr. Kenneth Rexroth, from *Collected Shorter Poems* by Kenneth Rexroth. © 1956, 1944, 1963 by Kenneth Rexroth. Reprinted by permission of New Directions Publishing Corp. "Coming Home Late

INDEX OF AUTHORS

INDEX OF TITLES OR FIRST LINES

808.81   A book of luminous
B   things.

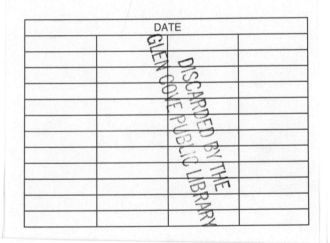

DATE			

A NOTE ON THE TYPE

The text of this book is set in Bembo. This type was first used in 1495 by the Venetian printer Aldus Manutius for Cardinal Bembo's *De Aetna*, and was cut for Manutius by Francesco Griffo. It was one of the types used by Claude Garamond (1480–1561) as a model for his Romain de L'Université, and so it was the forerunner of what became standard European type for the following two centuries. Its modern form follows the original types and was designed for Monotype in 1929.

CONTENTS

ACKNOWLEDGMENTS

I wish to express my gratitude to persons who helped me in compiling this anthology. My friend and co-translator of my poetry, Robert Hass, encouraged me and worked with me on the English versions of some poems. At his suggestion, we jointly taught a graduate seminar in the English Department of the University of California at Berkeley in 1993 using the poems of this anthology as material for our sessions. The enthusiastic reactions of students gave me a new assurance as to the value of my judgments. Another Berkeley poet and friend, Leonard Nathan, closely followed my endeavors and drew my attention to several poems fitting my purpose.

Work on the anthology, from its beginning, received warm support from my wife, Carol, who also offered advice, helped type the early manuscript draft, and organized the many details necessary to complete this project. Kimball Fenn, a graduate student in the English Department at Berkeley, brought her intelligent assistance, competence, and diligence to typing, editing, and compiling the permissions' citations for the manuscript.

Requests for permission to make copies of any part
of the work should be mailed to:
Permissions Department, Harcourt Brace & Company,
6277 Sea Harbor Drive, Orlando, Florida 32887-6777.
Permissions acknowledgments appear on pp. 307–314.

Library of Congress Cataloging-in-Publication Data
A Book of luminous things: an international anthology of poetry/edited
and with an introduction by Czeslaw Milosz.
p.   cm.
Includes index.
ISBN 0-15-100169-3
1. Poetry—Collections.   I. Miłosz, Czesław.
PN6101.B585   1996   95-38060
808.81—dc20

Designed by Lori J. McThomas
Printed in the United States of America
First edition
A B C D E

A Book of
Luminous Things

AN INTERNATIONAL ANTHOLOGY

OF POETRY

Edited and with an introduction by

Czeslaw Milosz

HARCOURT BRACE & COMPANY

New York   San Diego   London

A Book of
Luminous Things

FOREWORD

D. WILLIAM JOLLEY
Director
Confections Market Information Group
Nestlé

Communications conglomerates, computer industry giants, and global consumer products companies are rushing to get "wired." On-line services are giving away membership software; Web sites grow by the hour; the television and the computer are on a collision course for consumers' living rooms.

In corporate offices, hotel conference rooms, and university classrooms marketers are trying to understand the implications of interactive communication technology for their businesses and their brands. The early innovators have learned by doing, but many have been disappointed. The size of the interactive audience is nearing 6 million, and according to some estimates, will reach 30 million by the year 2000.

But while many are clicking, few are buying. Sales through the Internet are estimated to be only $300 million in 1995. The promise of instant global distribution that costs almost nothing is attracting a tidal wave of "cyberpreneurs" to the Internet. However, many pundits tell us it's just Internet hype, and the prognostications of the Information Superhighway will follow the way of the telephone when it first entered the mainstream of American life: most predictions never came true. For many on the sidelines however, the debate between zealot and skeptic has created a perception of confusion and controversy, fear and caution.

Electronic interactive communication, though, is unlike previous technological change. The expertise to extract value won't take as long as it did with previous innovations. Accessibility is more immediate, and there are fewer barriers to experimentation. But probably the most significant factor in its growth will be the nature of the relationship between the user and the technology—one that is symbiotic and self-optimizing. Michael Spalter expresses it this way: ". . . content attracts users, users create more content, new content enhances the value of the site and more users are drawn to the marketplace." Consumers will be active participants in the evolution of the interactive marketplace.

Early interactive marketers have approached the Internet as an electronic extension of direct marketing, 800 numbers, and relationship advertising. Correspondingly, the two most prevalent marketing strategies used on the Internet today are cybermalls and home pages. Both of these approaches however have come under attack for not addressing the concerns of the interactive consumer.

Rosalind Resnick, in her recent article "Business is Good, Not" (*Internet World,* June 1995), cited five reasons why Web sites can get up to 30,000 hits a day, but produce a mere 200 orders. Resnick says, "Despite its cool hyperlinks and flashy graphics the Internet is not a comfortable place to browse." Furthermore:

- It's not easy to find the shops: It's a lot easier to pick up the phone and order a pizza.

- It's hard to comparison shop: There is a hesitation among Internet merchants to take off their gloves and compete on price.

- Security is lax: Secure payment systems such as digital cash are still in their infancy.

- There aren't enough shoppers: Except for AOL, Prodigy and Compuserve, Internet users tend to be less likely to plunk down their money for goods and services.

- It's not much fun: You won't find the benches, fountains, ice cream shops or espresso bars.

If cybermalls and home pages are the Internet's equivalent of unwelcome catalogs, junk mail, and newspaper coupon ads, then which marketing strategy will most effectively exploit the impact that inter-active communication technology will have on consumers' decision processes?

Representing a wide range of professional perspectives, the authors of *Interactive Marketing: The Future Present* offer hard facts about the present conditions of the interactive marketplace and insightful speculation into the future of interactive marketing. Provocative implications for the traditional elements of the marketing mix are convincingly spelled out.

From a marketing perspective, retail scanners are perhaps the closest parallel to a recent innovation in information technology that has influenced how marketing is conducted. Scanners revolutionized marketing and research practices by providing point-of-sale information in overwhelming detail and speed. It wasn't until 10 years after its first use that the technology became a mainstay in the marketing community. The latest restructuring of competitive advantage is being led by ECR (Efficient Consumer Response), where scanner technology provides the information link between consumer, retailer, and manufacturer necessary to manage supply chain alliances.

Just as foresighted marketers discovered how to harness the power of scanner data to gain a competitive advantage, so too will the more innovative of the early adopters of interactive communication technology devise strategies to exploit the marketing potential of the Internet. The leading indicators point to content selection and product feedback by consumers based on the satisfaction of their needs as the strategic drivers of interactive marketing.

As consumers interact with the Web, they will self-segment themselves through membership in user forums, news groups, and specialty clubs to form common interest "virtual communities." The strength of an enterprise's prior association in consumers' minds with these interest areas will influence their choices of where to purchase the products and services related to their needs. Competing manufacturers will hesitate to form alliances among themselves to serve these "need markets." Instead, this critically strategic role will be filled by Interactive Marketing Organizations (IMOs)—intermediary firms representing coalitions of manufacturers whose produce lines meet the needs of particular interest groups.

This example will help to explain how this new strategy will work:

> John wants to purchase a pair of hiking boots. He is interested in the outdoors, so he has been a member of the Sierra Club and subscribes to *Backpacker* magazine. John also regularly visits their sites on the Internet to get information and exchange ideas and places to go. John signs on, goes to *Backpacker* and requests information on hiking boots. *Backpacker* presents John with a checklist of intended uses and optional features. He selects his desired features and their relative importance to him. *Backpacker* provides three recommendations that fit John's needs with manufacturer's prices (John could ask to see the entire list of boots "carried" if he wishes). John clicks on the boots he wants to bring up the manufacturer's home page advertisement, giving him the opportunity to enter into a dialog with the manufacturer. John decides to select the boot, his credit card is debited, an order is sent directly to the manufacturer, or local distribution center, and the boots arrive at his house the next day.

Once the technology is able to make such an experience fun, easy, quick and secure, IMOs will influence the choices of millions of consumers. By controlling cyber shelf space, IMOs will be able to control the purchase options of consumers. Cybermalls and home pages will become less effective modes of interactive marketing because their content will not provide the full spectrum of the need environment to satisfy consumers, their product range will be limited to the manufacturer's own lines, and consumers will not have developed the same affinity with a cybermall or an advertiser's home page that they already have developed from previous experience with the IMO interest-area provider, such as *Backpacker*.

Because IMOs furnish credible and relevant information about a wide range to products and services intended to satisfy particular needs, consumers will become loyal to the IMOs that allow them to:

- Make comparisons of features and prices more quickly.
- Acquire relevant product knowledge more easily.

- More efficiently compare a wider range of choices.
- Interact with other users with similar interests.
- Obtain information and entertainment related to the area of interest.

And because IMOs will possess efficient access to a self-qualified market and vast databases on individual consumers and their brand choices, manufacturers will seek fiduciary relationships with IMOs for cyber shelf space and user information. The strategic value of this relationship to manufacturers is enormous. Benefits of a strategic alliance with IMOs will enable manufacturers to:

- Maintain a presence in critical "need markets"
- More quickly respond to consumer's needs
- Customize features to better fit buyer groups' preferences
- Identify gaps in existing product lines for new product opportunities
- Develop relationships with individual customers
- Tailor more effective brand strategies to particular market segments.

How will IMOs influence the marketing process? Among others, it seems likely that three important shifts will occur:

1. Innovation will speed up, requiring business processes—supply chain and product development—to keep up.

2. Direct selling to consumers via electronic marketing will reduce consumers' dependence on traditional retail distribution channels and will motive express delivery companies to expand their services to individual homes.

3. Marketing spending will be directed at and through IMOs to influence consumers' options and choices in cyber shelf space.

In summary, a marketer's strategic perspective should not be driven by the attitude of, "Can I justify advertising in this new medium?" but, rather, from the point of view of, "How quickly can I begin learning how to use this new technology for competitive advantage?" The core competency of faster learning and faster innovation to satisfy the educated needs of more sophisticated consumers will be the key drivers of competitive advantage in the interactive marketplace.

At Nestlé, experimentation in the interactive marketplace is being managed as a worldwide corporate initiative. Company divisions are taking the lead in this learning process as their product lines, marketing strategies, and consumer franchises coincide with the marketing advantage of the Internet.

If manufacturers' call to action in the 1990s is ECR, by the end of the decade it will be replaced by ICR: Interactive Consumer Response!

INTRODUCTION

The purpose of this book is to examine the nature and scope of impact that interactive communication technologies are (and will be) having on the world of marketing and marketing communications. We recognize, at the outset, the impossibility of doing much more than scratching the surface. The dizzying speed of change dates "futuristic" predictions virtually as they are made. That limitation, however, helps explain why we have included the articles presented here. For while the authors describe and discuss many of the new and truly amazing technologies and applications being used today and being anticipated tomorrow, they focus on how we need to think about them. In some cases this new world of interactivity means doing things in totally new ways. In others, it doesn't. But in all instances, it means rethinking approaches and strategies and melding the best of the traditional with the new.

We are living in one of those rare and unique periods of history when we are able to witness the emergence of an entirely new mode of communication, just as if we were living in the 15th century and witnessed the invention of the printing press, or were present earlier in this century and heard the first radio broadcasts or watched the first television programs. Today, we are witnessing the dawn and development of computer-mediated interactive technologies, from interactive kiosks, CD-ROM catalogs, personal digital assistants and on-line services to fully interactive television systems with electronic coupons, virtual malls and movies-on-demand, and of course the mother of all interactive technologies—the Internet and the World Wide Web.

Like Gutenberg's printing press, these emerging interactive technologies are revolutionizing the way we store, distribute, retrieve and present information. In its time, the printing press proved to be a catalytic technology that helped bring about the Reformation and Renaissance. The parallel is drawn by the former CEO of Apple Computer, John Sculley, who observed that, "We are, today, in need of a second Renaissance, which like the first also can be galvanized by technology" and that interactive multimedia represents a "tool of a near tomorrow" that, "like the printing press, will empower individuals, unlock worlds of knowledge, and forge a new community of ideas." However, the impact of the emerging interactive technologies will not take one hundred years to make itself felt, as was true for Gutenberg's printing press. Sculley also observed: "The changes are already happening. They started with the widespread acceptance of the microcomputer and continue as we move toward videocomputers, interactive television, and electronic books. Three industries—computers, television, and publishing—that were quite separate during the sixties started to overlap in the seventies and eighties." By the nineties these three industries have become inextricably intertwined.

The need for this text is premised on the fact that within the next decade interactive multimedia will emerge as the predominant mode of information storage and retrieval. As the new digital-interactive-information technologies begin to supplement and inevitably supplant the established media of print and broadcast as our primary means of data storage and information dissemination, marketing researchers and marketing communication specialists will need to acquire an entirely new sensibility in order to use the emerging technologies to their fullest potential.

The catalyst of this revolution and inter-industry fusion can be directly attributed to *digitalization*. For:

> With digitalization all the media become translatable into each other—computer bits migrate merrily—and they escape from their traditional means of transmission. A movie, phone call, letter, or magazine article may be sent digitally via phone line, coaxial cable, fiberoptic cable, microwave, satellite, the broadcast air, or a physical storage medium such as tape or disk. If that's not revolution enough, with digitalization the content becomes totally plastic—any message, sound, or image may be edited from anything into anything else (Brand, 1987).

Like the limitless energy that can be generated by nuclear fusion, the communication power which can be generated by media fusion is formidable. The ability to digitally mix all media on a common palette provides one with the ability to present and simultaneously illustrate any idea or concept with multiple windows of audio and visual, text and graphics.

The INFO-NOMICS of Interactive Multimedia

Beyond the power and beauty proffered by the digital palette, the sheer magnitude of information that can be cost effectively assembled and disseminated by interactive technologies ensures its preeminence. Interactive multimedia remain unsurpassed in the amount of information which can be accessed. Whether on-line or on-disk, no other medium can match the sheer volume of personally selected and instantly accessed information. Indeed, by whatever attribute—qualitative or quantitative—one evaluates the character and impact of a medium, interactive multimedia communication has a decided edge over all preceding print-based, broadcast and analog media. On the now common 5" (650 "meg") compact disk you can store up to 250,000 pages of text, "the equivalent of 500 books—a truckload—instantly computer searchable and publishable at one-fiftieth the cost of printing on paper" (Brand, 1987). But, as remarkable as the current capacity of compact-disk technology is, it is nothing compared to what will be coming on the market in the near future. To wit:

> IBM has already demonstrated a rewritable optical disk based on the blue laser, and it offers five times the density of any disk that is read by infrared lasers. . . . If you're not impressed by a mere five-fold increase in storage density, what does 50 times do for you? That capacity is possible today with new multilevel disks being developed by IBM . . . combine a Baby Blue Laser and one of these multilevel disks and you'd have a rewritable DVD [digital videodisk] that holds 50 times the data of today's music CD. That's enough room for 33 hours of laserdisk-quality video (Heald, 1995).

Blue laser technology is also being applied to the development of 3-D TV. The U.S. Navy is already using a red, green and yellow laser system to track aircraft. By replacing the yellow laser with blue laser, "the Navy's system will be able to recreate real-time 3-D images of any subject in any color" (Heald, 1995). Needless to say, with 3-D TV one's product demonstrations can take on a whole new dimension. If an on-screen 3-D presentation of your product is not enough, perhaps having the ability to set up your "demo" right in the middle of the consumer's living room is more intriguing. For the next step beyond 3-D TV is already being perfected:

> . . . holovision, or, as the researchers at MIT prefer to call it, holovideo . . . [is] a real-time 3-D holographic display that projects images into dimensional space. You don't need special glasses or a helmet to view its true-to-life images; it's reality without substance—you can reach out to touch the image, but when you do nothing's there (Heald, 1995).

The MIT team expects to have a "salable" holovision system as early as 2005. While we are waiting for our home version of the Starship Enterprise's "Holodeck," engineers at Bell Labs, IBM and Stanford University are working on a three-dimensional data storage system known as "holostors:"

> To create a holostor . . . [one uses] traditional holographic techniques to record "pages" of digital information at different angles on a piece of polymer film that's about the size and thickness of a dime. . . . A charge-coupled device . . . reads the digital data projected by the holostor. Each page can be accessed just by changing the angle of view, and each dime-sized volume can hold more than 100 pages. . . . Eventually, IBM expects to shrink the dime-size down to the size of a pin head, providing 100 times more capacity. You could slip one of these babies into your holographic VCR and record 6 hours a day for a year before you filled it up. (Heald, 1995).

Truly, these advances in information storage and presentation are mind-boggling and fantastic. But the more immediate challenges to traditional marketing practices are already in play with the advances in information distribution and retrieval. What can be more revolutionary than the World Wide Web. Here, marketers are given a FREE information distribution system that is global in reach with tens and eventually hundreds of millions of consumers with instantaneous, interactive, up-close and personal access to one's every marketing message. With on-going enhancements, such as Xing Technology Corporation's server software, Streamworks, every marketer will have the ability to run the equivalent of their own personal radio and TV networks. As recently reported by *Interactive Age*:

Coming: Web TV
Xing readies software that enables real-time audio, video

> Streamworks . . . delivers audio and video on demand, rather than requiring a user to download a file off the Web and play it back from a local drive. The system can be used to deliver stored files and can broadcast live programs, as well. "The big picture is that this eally turns the Web into a radio network, and a little further out, a TV network. . . . And it does it by the existing (Internet) infrastructure. That's a powerful concept (*Interactive Age*, July 31, 1995).

Every domain of marketing communication is being profoundly affected by these pronounced advances in interactive communication technologies. Accordingly, there is a pronounced need for marketing practitioners to acquire a new sensibility and skills to how best blend these new technologies into the marketing mix. To this end it was the editors' intention to invite a wide range of authors with academic as well as professional perspectives on interactive technology's ramifications on marketing.

Ergo, the power and promise of the interactive technologies awaits. By the turn of this century interactive multimedia communication will have emerged as a full-fledged, if not dominant form of communication. To dismiss its inevitable impact on marketing strategy and technique is to prematurely evaluate its potential simply on the bases of its current level of adoption. One need only be reminded of the following story:

> In the city of Mainz, Master Johanne Gutenberg has just developed a machine that can reproduce manuscript-like pages in many copies. News of his work has reached the local ruler, the Elector of the Rhineland Palatinate. In the spirit of Renaissance inquiry, the Elector asks a group of scholars and businessmen to assess the machine's impact on the local economy and culture. Since bureaucracy is just beginning to assert itself as an organizational force, the group is designated The Select Committee to Evaluate Multiple Manuscript Production:
>
> The committee visits Gutenberg's workshop . . . the inventor demonstrates his machine . . . the committee is impressed, but skeptical. After considerable debate, the group submits its report to the Elector. The machine is undoubtedly a technological advance, the report concludes, but it has only limited application to the Palatinate's needs. The committee recommends that the government not invest research and development funds in the project. Its reasons are direct and cogent: (1) a large workforce of monks copying manuscripts would lose their jobs if the Gutenberg machine were encouraged; (2) there is no heavy demand for multiple copies of manuscripts; and (3) the long-term market for printed books is doubtful due to the low literacy rate.(Dizard, 1989).

It's easy for us today, with the benefit of more than four centuries' perspective, to feel superior to the Elector's Select Committee. However, despite all the optimism and ebullience about the "wired-in future," many long-time observers express a sense of *déjà vu* about all the excitement. Their feelings aren't simply reactionary responses to "newfangled" inventions. As the following review of past developments shows, the interactive future is fraught with peril for the unwary and uncautious.

The Past as Prologue: Surviving and Prospering in the Interactive Future

As advertising and marketing scholars and practitioners evaluate the array of interactive technologies that are discussed in this book, it should be kept in mind that we have—in a way—been through this before. Twenty years ago, Warner Amex Cable debuted QUBE, a cable system promising interactive television, electronic town halls and utility monitoring. This service led to the creation of MTV and Nickelodeon and other cable networks. It did not prove to be a profitable venture and, ultimately, eerily reminiscent of today's hype, plunged Warner Communications into a financial crisis. The interactive cable television system made many promises about home shopping, banking and education. After 20 years, only some of these "futuristic" options are viable such as the home shopping industry which combines broadcast programming with 800 telephone numbers and education with an offering like Mind Extension University. For every new interactive service being touted, there are countless others being quietly dismantled. But we can learn much from the failures as well as the successes.

In the early 1980s, videotext experimenters hooked up telephone lines to TV's so viewers could shop, bank and schedule travel from their living rooms. The ideas developed in this old narrowband videotext platform are being transferred to today's broadband interactive platform reports Gary Arlen of Arlen Communications in *Advertising Age,* 1994. Companies such as Time Warner, J.C. Penney, Cox Cable Communications that failed in videotext are some of the biggest players in the current interactive marketplace. Perhaps the lessons learned from the ill-fated videotext industry can serve as a guide on how to navigate the broadband expansion of interactive services.

Knight-Ridder Newspapers, Inc., rolled out Viewtron Interactive Cable Videotex Service on October 31, 1983, offering more than two million frames of text and graphics to its users (Iles, 1987). Yet, this service never caught on even though a prior three-year market test predicted consumer acceptance. Robert Iles (1987) presents a number of reasons why Viewtron failed:

1. Incorrect choice of a target market, and a strategy aimed at sign-up rather than a long-term relationship.

2. Failure to determine customers' needs and respond with compelling solutions.

3. Failure to recognize the coming competition from PC-based platforms.

4. Errors in developing technology that produced over-priced terminals which limited penetration and presented too much information without a sensible way to review and organize it for rapid understanding.

5. Corporate impatience on developing market acceptance.

6. Weak to nonexistent corporate and brand identities (pp. 130–131).

The companies now trying to build the successful interactive future should pay attention to what happened in the videotext industry because the same issues are still being addressed.

The driving force behind the hype of a multimedia connected consumer home is the regulatory struggles between cable and telephone companies, as each seeks to define their place in the interactive future (Higgins, 1993). Mark Stahlman, president of New Media Associates, a New York City-based research and investment firm, predicts that, "As the monopolies crumble, from a regulatory standpoint it is to each of their advantages to proclaim that the other guy is a serious threat, as it's in both their interest to proclaim that they are a serious threat to the other guy" (Higgins, 1993, p. 130). This need affects public policy which leads to claims of interactive offerings that may still be years down the road. Cable franchise wars of the 1970s also employed the same tactics of promising services not yet developed to win a local franchise. The analogy to vaporware in the software industry is also obvious. All these promises lead to unrealistic expectations from public policy makers and their constituents. Unfulfilled expectations breed regulation and deplete equity.

Unrealistic expectations gloss over the reality of technological limitations, unproven business models and nonexistent consumer demand for services. Alessandro Piol, director of an AT&T division investing in multimedia startups, notes that, "People underestimate the amount of new technology and amount of work that needs to be done. Not only do you have all these technologies, also you're dealing with products and business models that have no track record" (Higgins, 1993, p. 130). Yet, there is a fear that if one remains on the sidelines, the potential interactive cash cow will pass you by. There is little beyond relatively primitive clickstream market research to substantiate a demand for interactive services. The systems necessary to offer these services are years away from being built and are expensive to create today.

Adding computer power and processes to television is about to radically change its functions and expectations. The power will shift to the viewers who gain control over what and when programming is shown. Eventually, viewers will be able to manipulate the actual content of the programming, such as determining camera angles on sporting events to choosing an alternative ending on their favorite shows. This fact of converging computers and television legitimizes the amount of capital flowing into new strategic partnerships. What is unknowable is how this new world will look, act and empower its users. George Gilder writes that with the help of interactive television, "the human spirit—emancipated and thus allowed to reach its rarest talents and aspirations—will continue to amaze the world with heroic surprises" (*The Economist*, 1994).

Digitalization of content is how this brave new world will come about. In a digital medium, information is represented by 1s and 0s. This represents a fundamental shift away from the analog model where analog is continuous and mimics its source. Digital information is discrete and describes its source. This enables television to move from a passive, dumb terminal displaying someone else's viewpoint to an information appliance where information can be manipulated and custom tailored by the user.

The strategic alliances being formed in the interactive industry center on the distribution of this new digital information stream to a computer or television. There are speculations of how these two platforms will merge or combine. No one is sure what hybrid system may result. As *The Economist* states, "Bandwidth for its own sake is pretty useless. But connect it to powerful computer "servers" containing huge amounts of digital data; add switching technology so that everyone is connected to everyone else; and now you have a telephone network that can transport pictures, text, and voices—an information highway. Connected to it, the TV set becomes an information appliance, letting viewers choose programming, games, video-phone services or anything else on the network" (1994). Whoever finds the "right" ratio of content, distribution, and price-value will become one of the winners of this high stake gamble.

There are two implications of the movement of information in a digital world. The first is a public policy issue concerning the nature and organization of the information infrastructure. Questions arise over who has access, who is liable for the content and who controls the flow. The second is that 1s and 0s are 1s and 0s regardless of the medium. There will be less of a difference between radio, newspapers, TV, movies, magazines and so forth. Nicholas Negroponte, director of MIT's Media Laboratory, states, "In a digital world, the medium is no longer the message—the message is the message" (*The Economist*, 1994). James Clark, former founder of Silicon Graphics and now chairman and CEO of Netscape Communications, observes, "Computer technology is moving so fast that each generation of equipment is obsolete every two years. The television can't keep up" (Dawson, 1994, p. 31). Gary Bolles (1995) does a quick summary of the best and worst each platform brings to the interactive future:

> At its best, the computer industry is a model of speed and innovation . . . And at its best, television entertainment can challenge, stimulate and educate.
>
>   . . . the computer industry doesn't have a great record when it comes to stability. . . . But applications do break. . . This is software . . . Bugs happen . . . Worse, those software pieces will continue to change rapidly.
>
>   As for television . . .How much TV have you watched lately? . . . If your perception is that TV obstinately remains devoted toward satisfying the needs of the lowest common denominator, join the rest of America. (p. 21)

Distribution systems become more like commodities because 1s and 0s can be delivered over any digital network whether wired or wireless. Its content becomes the value-added component. Content must be compelling in order to snare the attention of the users since they will have the control and power to determine what to watch and when. Time

Warner, Viacom, US West, Bell Atlantic, GTE and others are all trying to determine the services and programs users will pay for. Each system has developed a navigation system so that all these bewildering choices do not alienate the users. Service offerings tend to fall into five broad categories:

1. Video options: video on demand with VCR-like capabilities and the ability to assemble video content such as all the news reports of the Chicago deaths attributed to the heat wave of 1995.
2. Home shopping options.
3. Interactive programming options: video and computer games played solo or with another connected user regardless of geography.
4. Multimedia enhanced reference and education databases.
5. Communication services options: video-phoning to tele-conferencing to electronic messaging.

Telephone companies from the regional Bell operating companies and the leading independents such as GTE, Southern New England Telephone, and Rochester Telephone are all racing to build video platforms that are capable of utilizing existing infrastructure and setting the stage for eventual replacement of voice-only platforms. Examples cover Ameritech's 15-year "grand plan" to create a broadband network; Bell Atlantic's test of different video delivery systems in the mid-Atlantic; Bell South's and Southwestern Bell's purchases of cable companies; Nynex's experience as the largest cable/telephony operator in the United Kingdom and its investment in Viacom; Pacific Telesis's seven-year plan to provide broadband services; US West's investment in Time Warner and its commitment to building a broadband network; GTE's MainStreet experiment in Cerritos, CA; Rochester Telephone's and Southern New England's Telephone's video on demand experiments. Tom Kerver (1994) reports the strengths and weaknesses that telephone companies bring to the video platform:

- Strengths
  - Money: announced plans for such upgrades already anticipate expenditures in excess of $50 billion
  - Reputation in products and reliable service
  - Political clout

- Weaknesses
  - Video-related experience is sorely lacking
  - Slow to react to change; highly bureaucratic
  - Very heavily regulated and more closely monitored by consumer groups (p. 72)

Yet, despite the regulatory and public policy considerations, the lure of such broadband services is too much to forgo. The digital world blurs the distinctions between the media industries, which accelerates the competitive forces resulting in the trend to converge.

Two fears become apparent that are driving companies toward merging and exploring the multimedia landscape. As mentioned above, there is industry encroaching among established industry markets—telephone, computers, cable, broadcast, publishing, and so forth. E-mail traveling across the Internet, which sometimes uses the same telephone network, costs the same whether the receiver is next door or in the next country. The other fear, as mentioned before, is the fact that profit potential is too large to let go by. From these fears, two assumptions have arisen:

1. The losers will be those who stood still and watched.
2. The myth that the synergies between the traditional markets are the starting points for the multimedia riches and yet the reality may be that old skills count for very little (*The Economist,* 1995).

The destination is mostly unknown and that drives the companies to experiment with new marketing and advertising strategies and tactics, unexplored internet options, and unproven data collections and research strategies.

Asking potential users how much they will pay for interactive programming is a lot like asking users how much they will pay for a car that flies. As is typical of most high-tech products, the consumer has little or no idea of what the interactive future is or how much it is worth to them. They do know how to participate and ask for some of the interactive programming that is available in stand-alone pieces: mail-order and home shopping is worth a combined $80 billion; video rentals are worth $15 billion; and online services are worth $35 billion (*The Economist,* 1994). If a company can deliver an integrated and compelling network that offers these services, then it has the potential of tapping into a combined industry revenue flow of $130 billion. These are very enticing numbers that lure industry giants to grab a share of the riches. Until that can happen, issues involving cost, user-friendliness and, most important, consumer interest must be resolved (Egol, 1993).

About This Book

Shortly before publication of this book we did a simple search of the Internet for sources of marketing information. The search, which used just a single key phrase, yielded nearly 500 entries. In light of that search and the brief discussion of the history of various companies in the brave new world of interactive media, the opening sentence of this Introduction—that its purpose is to examine the nature and scope of impact that the new interactive technologies will have on marketing research, strategies, and marketing communications techniques and tactics—feels a bit overly ambitious, if not downright unrealistic. Recent history shows that incorrect action can be disastrous; yet, as this brief search indicates, inaction can be just as costly.

That qualification aside, *Interactive Marketing: The Future Present* is organized to be a guidebook to the interactive future:

1. Section I—Marketing Strategies and Tactics—presents articles by leading thinkers and practitioners who discuss the various ways to think about interactive media and how to apply them to one's existing marketing programs. More than just theorizing, the authors analyze approaches being used today and examine their strengths, weaknesses, and implications for the future.

2. Section II—Media Tactics and Techniques—surveys the possibilities of all the new media choices available today and those coming in the near future. Again, authors discuss how marketers should think about these options and how they have been and can be applied, both individually and in conjunction with other media, to produce more effective programs.

3. In Section III—Data Collection Analysis and Research Strategies—the authors explore the ways that marketers can find out more about their markets and apply that knowledge in practical ways.

No single publication, no book or article, can provide all the information needed to compete in the new era that is upon us. But *Interactive Marketing: The Future Present* does provide a tool for strategizing and implementing successful, productive marketing programs in the new interactive age.

References

Bolles, Gary A. (1995, July 10). ITV: The worst of both worlds. *Inter@ctive Week*, p. 21

Brand, S. (1987), *The Media Lab* (Viking Press: New York) pp.18, 20.

Dawson, Fred. (1994, June 20). "Unrealistic" interactive services called years away. *Multichannel News*, p. 31.

Dizard, W.P. Jr. (1989), *The Coming Information Age: An Overview of Technology, Economics, and Politics* (Longman: New York & London) pp. 45–46.

Egol, Len. (1993, December). Potholes on the data highway? New technology may not blossom as fully as some expect. *Direct*, pp. 11, 26.

Full Service Network. (1994, August). Press release, *Time Warner Cable*.

Heald, T. *Future Intense*, (June, 1995) pp.19–22.

Higgins, John M. (1993, November 29). Sorting through the hype of interactive multimedia. *Multichannel News*, pp. 3, 130–131.

Iles, Robert Alan. (1987). *Death of a system: An historical analysis of the marketing of Viewtron Cable and the implications of that venture on current and future interactive videotex.* Master's thesis, The Florida State University, Tallahassee.

Interactive Age, July 31, 1995, p. 1.

Kerver, Tom. (1994, May 23). Telephone companies: Overbuilding and underbuilding. *Cablevision*, pp. 72, 76, 80.

Lang, Curtis. (1994, May 2). Arlen's angle on interactive. *Advertising Age*, pp. 20, 23.

Multimedia's no-man's land. (1995, July 22) *The Economist*, pp. 57–58.

Sculley, J. (1988), as quoted in his introduction to: *Interactive Multimedia Visions for Multimedia Developers, Educators and Information Providers,* Edited by Sueann Ambron and Kristina Hooper (Microsoft Press: Redmond, Washington, 1988).

Television: What if they're right? (1994, February 12) *The Economist*.

SECTION I

Marketing Strategies and Tactics

This first section provides a broad cross-section of marketer experiences and expectations about interactive technology. From traditional retailing to business-to-business marketing, the following chapters review how the interactive revolution is quickly changing how marketers are reinventing the exchange of goods and services.

Richard Cross and Janet Smith of Cross•Rapp•Associates, a strategic database marketing company, begin this section with "Customer-Focused Strategies and Tactics: Interactive Marketing Weighs in for Customers," analyses of several very different companies that have developed solid frameworks for thinking about and developing interactive marketing strategies. These companies have developed their own mix of interactive tools to strengthen their relationships with their customers, using a range of approaches that are generating long-term loyalty and brand equity. Each company profile provides in-depth information about how the firm reviewed its environment and responded with interactive marketing. These analyses, which include both end-consumer and business-to-business examples and identify both the promises and the pitfalls, set the agenda discussed in the articles that follow.

In "Interactive Retailing: More Choices, More Chances, More Growth," Lisa Reinecke Flynn discusses the challenges faced by retailers who will see the traditional importance of location quickly fade away. Instead, those retailers who can develop strong brand equity will have the best opportunity to effectively use the tools of interactive, particularly the Internet. She outlines how interactive technology will enable retailers to profitably reach ultra-niche segments and buying circles. This chapter also begins to address the major question of how to make decisions balancing what is possible with what is too far off by giving insight into the threats and opportunities facing retailers in the future.

In "Interactive Kiosks in the Retail Environment: What Do Customers Really Want?" Tom Hutchison provides a unique insight into the appreciation of application of interactive kiosks in retailing. Hutchison's experience as a musician, researcher and consultant with the music industry gives the reader an expert view of what would appear to be a natural application of interactive technology—the interactive music kiosk. As with the history of all technology, this application has had mixed success. The lessons learned will help readers better gauge the kiosk's potential for generating inexpensive sales and improved customer experience.

High-tech/high-touch will be as important to the direct sale as ever, as the next articles show. In "Marketing and Selling High-Tech Products," John V. Crosby, President of Micrometrics, explains and demonstrates how marketers of complex, high-tech products aren't following their own advice to customers and are missing an important opportunity to increase sales productivity and effectiveness. He analyzes, specifically, the concept of the "complex sale," and how astute firms can use the Account Development Cycle to effectively organize the processing of information and communication to better expedite this process. From prospecting to ultimate presentations, Crosby reviews the hardware, software, and tactics that can be used.

Vic Cherubini follows with some powerful case studies that show how smart marketers are using disk-based media—electronic catalogs and presentations—to give added power to all their customer contacts. Exploring both the practical, operational as well as the strategic implications of interactive tools, Cherubini includes step-by-step guidelines for developing electronic tools and checklists for evaluating their cost-effectiveness and implementation.

In "Extending the Sales Reach," Kenneth Henderson and Robert Greene demonstrate how partnerships with clients are a natural outgrowth of successful interactive marketing—and that the traditional "three-foot distance" between buyer and seller is taking on totally different dimensions. Because of the anonymity afforded by interactive techniques, the "Davids" will be able to effectively compete with the "Goliaths" of business. This will have an enormous influence on sales contact, relationships, and on the nature of services provided by salespersons.

Everyone is talking about the importance of knowing and being known by your customers. What could be more central to public relations—or a better definition of its role? In "Public Relations and the Interactive Media: The Practice Is Outpacing Predictions," Jay Rayburn explores some of the current technological advances as they relate to public relations, as well as some of the coming trends and what they mean for the profession. In the coming world of "seamless communication," the most noteworthy development is the clear indication that predictions can hardly keep pace with actual developments.

In many ways, direct marketing has served as a precursor to the full interactive revolution. The excitement generated by the 1970s classic Ginsu knife ads with early use of phone response and easy payment reflects the core of involvement that interactive marketing offers. Richard S. Hodgson, president of the direct marketing consulting and catalog development service company, Sargeant House, discusses how the trends in both direct marketing and interactive strengthen the direct marketing industry. In "Considerations for 21st Century Direct Marketers: Focusing on the Basics in New Environments," he attempts to answer what happens when consumer participation in the Internet takes time away from previous activities with case studies of firms that have successfully positioned themselves for this future. And he provides important direct-marketing counsel to all those who would plunge into the world of interactivity: keep your eye on the numbers.

1

Customer-Focused Strategies and Tactics

Interactive Marketing Weighs in for Customers

Richard Cross
Janet Smith

Richard Cross is president of Cross•Rapp•Associates, a strategic database marketing company co-founded with Stan Rapp. Cross•Rapp•Associates' clients include *Fortune* 100 companies from consumer, business-to-business, nonprofit, and governmental fields.

Janet Smith is a veteran marketing communications consultant and an associate of Cross•Rapp•Associates. A former marketing manager with Digital Equipment Corporation, she is broadly versed in marketing technologies.

Cross and Smith are co-authors of numerous articles and of *Customer Bonding: Pathway to Lasting Customer Loyalty* (NTC Business Books, 1995).

The year is 1996. Jack P., 33, is an architect who lives on the outskirts of Seattle with his working wife and two children. Their lives are chock-o'-block full of technology-facilitated interactions with marketers. These interactions often add new value to old relationships, giving Jack and his family more choices and more control than ever over their lives.

- Jack starts his day with a breakfast cereal the local supermarket has learned to promote to his family from prior purchase history and quickly scans the news summaries faxed to him during the night by his personalized news service.

- Jack's wife, a telecommuter, settles in to a day at her home office. After checking her e-mail and voice mail boxes, she tackles her day's work of evaluating new software programs. She saves time whenever she can by using fax-on-demand or on-line bulletin board systems provided by software vendors to get instant product literature and technical support.

- En route to work, Jack drops their three-year-old off at a day care center discovered through their county's on-line parenting resource, and uses his car phone to reserve a family pass for the visiting circus from a local radio station's automated entertainment hotline. Stopping at his favorite coffee chain, Jack runs his loyal customer card through a card reader and, with the help of the chain's database, is instantly served his latté exactly the way he likes it, in the members-only express lane.

- At work, Jack spends much of the day in on-line conferencing and messaging, exchanging drawings and specifications for a new theater under negotiation with civic contracting authorities in Miami.

- He stops on his way home at the dry cleaners, where he pays for his items with a debit card linked to his bank's buyers' club, which earns him rewards for his purchases.

- At home, he spends time helping his seven-year-old read "My Daily," the new national kids' newspaper that Jack helped to develop by participating in the publisher's Parent Circle. After supper, the family enjoys a Disney movie rented from Blockbuster delivered that afternoon with the groceries (ordered via the community interactive TV channel). Blockbuster thoughtfully checks Jack's profile and throws in his favorite type of low-fat popcorn.

- After the kids go to sleep, Jack and his wife finish the day paying some bills through their on-line banking service. Before turning in, Jack uses his local newspaper's on-line bulletin board to check the weather in Miami, where he is due by late afternoon the next day.

Jack P. is getting to be an average consumer[1] these days. His life is busy and full, and he is increasingly involved with marketers who save him time and effort by offering him what they already know he is most likely to want. Jack and his family get what they want from marketers who care enough to record and fulfill their preferences, anticipate their needs, and reward their loyalty. They are actively engaged in the consuming side of the interactive marketing equation. Interactive technologies have fundamentally altered their relationships with the companies they do business with.

In this chapter, we show how interactive marketing technologies are used to transform and redefine relationships with the Jacks of your customer world. We look at five specific examples—each using a different technology to add value to the buyer-seller equation. In some cases, the added value is inherent in the technology itself. In others, the creative application of the technology provides added value. But in all cases, the marketers have figured out a way to fit the technology into a marketing strategy that focuses on customer benefits. The facilitating technologies in our discussion are magnetic card readers, interactive voice response systems, electronic bulletin boards, fax-on-demand, and the Internet's growing information access capabilities.

Our perspective is customer-oriented. It stems from our view that any marketing technique, technology or process will fail unless the marketer steps into the shoes of the customer and understands the customer bonding process. By understanding how each customer interaction creates and strengthens customer bonds, marketers can develop a *customer- and information-based* framework for defining and executing interactive marketing strategies.[2] Such an orientation, we believe, is crucial to any attempt to create lasting success in interactive marketing. Because, for all the activity and interest engendered by new, technology-aided communications channels—on-line systems, telemedia, kiosks, CD-ROMs, and the like—the success of interactive marketing techniques and processes will depend entirely on their success in building lasting customer relationships.

Direct Marketing at Warp Speed—With a Twist

Interactive marketing balances the benefits scales in the marketer-customer relationship (see Exhibit 1.1). For example, an on-line purchase transaction can look deceptively like the traditional direct marketing process speeded up thousands of times. All the fundamentals of direct marketing are involved, but the interactive technology adds new benefits:

1. **Speed, access, and information.** Direct marketing and interactive marketing both use two-way communications channels for dialogue and information capture. Customer interaction provides marketers with the customer information needed to do market segmentation and targeting. Interactive marketing speeds the information capture and expands the marketer's bounce-back options. The consumer also benefits from the increased speed of the interaction and often gains access to broader information sources as well. In fact, on-line shopping permits consumers to seek information directly from a seller *and* from tens of thousands of the seller's customers who are accessible through discussion forums and e-mail.

2. **Measurable value over time.** Marketers who use databases to track performance over time are used to thinking about "customer lifetime value" (CLV). But interactive marketing gives *consumers* unprecedented opportunity to track the value of their transactions as well. In the new technology-assisted equation, buyers know exactly how much they are spending with a particular business and how much reward and recognition they are due. The buyer can measure new opportunities brought on by interactive marketing in terms of "Lifetime Savings and Rewards Opportunity" (LSRO). If you're accumulating points or miles for your purchases, for example, you can easily quantify which airline gets most of your business. In fact, since most airlines have reward programs, you can readily quantify the value of your loyalty. You also know whose mileage rewards are most valuable to you.

In the new interactive marketing equation, both parties value and measure loyalty: the marketer in terms of each customer's lifetime purchases and the customer in terms of the relative long-term value of the various buying sources at his or her disposal.

3. **Precision demand and relevance.** The traditional direct marketer's ability to deliver the right product to the right customer at

EXHIBIT 1.1 The Changing Market Balance

A. The Traditional Marketing Balance

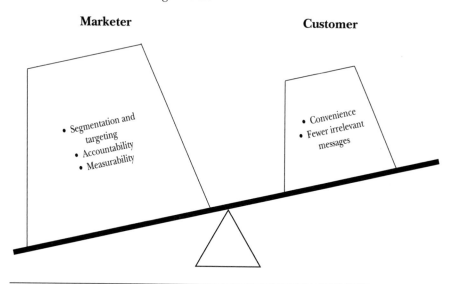

B. The New Interactive Marketing Balance

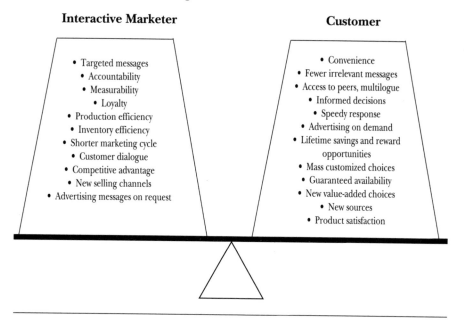

Interactive Marketing balances the benefits scale in the marketer-customer relationship.

the right time is a much sought-after ideal. The potential efficiency of the direct marketing system is a major factor in the decision by more and more marketers to shift resources to database-driven marketing programs. But, while marketers drive that trend, customers derive as much benefit from it—if not more. Personalization, individual treatment, mass customization, and freedom from extraneous advertising messages will soon be expected by every customer. What today constitutes the highest levels of customer satisfaction will be substandard tomorrow, when customers will expect suppliers to fully anticipate their needs and do their shopping for them. In the interactive age, the ability of a marketer to deliver only relevant information will become a key selection criteria in the customer's shopping process.

Let's look now at some examples of actual programs that demonstrate how the buyer-seller relationship changes. Each of the stories that follow uses a different facilitating technology to create new benefits for buyers and sellers. As you read these examples, pay attention to these benefits. At the end of the chapter, we will return to look at the key success factors for creating such results yourself.

Creating Relevancy with Telemedia at U S West

Telecommunications provider U S West stresses *relevance* as a key benefit consumers gain from its interactive marketing programs. In fact, the impact goes far beyond just relevance. We studied one of several programs underway and were struck by how a relatively simple concept, aided by an equally basic interactive technology, allows the company to dramatically alter its relationships with two entirely different sets of customers—business and consumers. U S West achieved this by creating a means for those customer groups to interact with each other and for each to *measure* the value of their relationship in hard dollars.

The program, called *Your Value Card*, is a turnkey relationship marketing service that U S West launched in Omaha, Denver, and Phoenix. The program matches area merchants with consumers, building traffic for the former and delivering savings opportunities for the latter. At no charge, U S West provides each interested consumer household with two plastic cards, magnetically encoded with a unique household identification number. They also provide a thick, indexed guide to participating merchants, each of whom lists specific savings offers for Your Value Card users.

Consumers present their cards to these merchants at the time of purchase along with their cash, check, or credit-card payment to receive the promised benefit. The merchant swipes the card through a magnetic stripe card reader that records the date, dollar amount, and location of the transaction. U S West records the transaction in its cardholder database, which also contains a wealth of demographic and lifestyle data appended from third-party sources. As transaction history builds, U S West analyzes it to determine the customer profiles for each merchant, makes recommendations for specific programs each merchant could undertake to acquire or retain customers, and even executes the communications for those programs.

What's happening here is a total change in the relationship U S West has with its customers. The consumer is getting savings, broader access to information about available shopping sources and, over time, increasingly relevant information from merchants in categories of interest. The merchant builds traffic while obtaining a means for profiling and segmenting its customer base for more targeted marketing in the future. And U S West is building a significant base of information on different segments of its own customer base while acting as a paid mediator between buyer and seller. Wow!

David Downes, U S West's Vice President and General Manager of the Marketing Information Products Groups, says that:

> This kind of service enables businesses that don't have their own database marketing resources to do a better job of delivering relevant communications to consumers. It helps them reduce the marketing cycle time, the time it takes to get to market with a promotion, analyze the results, and get back in the market with a more targeted and efficient approach.
>
> The real opportunity with interactive technologies is to provide both businesses and consumers with opportunities to be more relevant: Consumers are saying, "We want to hear from the businesses we already do business with, and from companies that offer similar services." To respond to this, marketers have to be able to deliver what consumers want, when and how they want it.

How does the program change the consumer's experience? We asked a couple of Your Value Card users in Denver this question. One family of four took to the card instantly, using it for everything from veterinary services and new tire purchases to dining entertainment. "It isn't a credit card. It's a *savings* card," explains Mrs. Eunice Bergen of the

Denver suburb of Thornton. "In the first full week we had the card, we saved $80." The Bergens also feel that the card changes the family's relationship with participating merchants. "Yes, you do start to change the relationship," Mrs. Bergen says. "We took our dog to the vet and discovered that our vet honors the card even though he already knows us. That means a lot. We've also discovered merchants through the program that we wouldn't have known about otherwise. We don't mind these merchants using the program to collect information about us if it means better information and savings on the items we care about."

Bruce Jensen, an assistant school principal in Denver, says that he hasn't been using the program long enough to see targeted offers based upon his purchases. But, he noted, the Your Value Card is now the first place the family looks when shopping for a new service. And he notices that he is frequenting certain merchants more often now that they participate in the program.

Aside from the database and related analysis tools that U S West provides, the key facilitating technology for Your Value Card is the card reader, which is installed in every participating merchant location and is used to capture the transaction data that creates a city-wide consumer

EXHIBIT 1.2 U S West Your Value Card

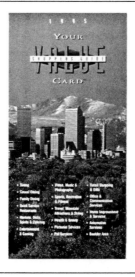

U S West is building a data-rich customer information base while acting as a paid mediator between segments of that base.

database. In the program's first three months of operation in Denver, 530 participating vendors had installed the readers in 1200 sites.[3] The card readers are pre-programmed by U S West to recognize each merchant's current Your Value Card transaction offer, and to capture the appropriate data. The units also have the capacity to prompt the merchant's staff by asking questions about the transaction; this capability may ultimately be used in expanding the relationship marketing effort.

In Omaha, Nebraska, where Your Value Card was first launched, about *half* of all consumer households now carry and use the card. In Denver, where U S West launched the program in February of 1995, about three-quarters of households had received a card by May.

While U S West is the first of the so-called "Baby Bells" to initiate this type of program, other media companies in the U S are experimenting with them as well. From community-based efforts like that of the *Greensboro Daily News* in Greensboro, North Carolina to Time Inc.'s Pathfinder shopping mall[4], examples of experimentation with new ways to serve and relate to customers are coming along as fast as new technologies permit. The best efforts will be those that, like U S West, affect the equation between seller and buyer by continually improving the consumer's access to relevant information and savings.

Consumers Have a Voice at KMPS Country[5]

Radio has been called the most personal of the mass media. It reaches into the most private activities you do while at home, at work, at play, and on the road. But it is a one-way, non-interactive, broadcast medium. To reap the advantages of interactivity, many radio stations are installing interactive voice response (IVR) systems, sometimes accompanied by fax-request lines and on-line bulletin boards. Callers who dial into these systems are offered a host of information and interactive options, such as signing up for frequent listener membership benefits, offering feedback or requests to the station or its on-air personalities, getting information about community events, weather, or financial markets, or even shopping electronically with the station's advertisers. In some cases, members are granted access to private portions of the IVR system after keying in their membership number on their touch-tone telephone keypad. Stations typically issue machine-readable membership cards, which are used to record member transactions or other member-supplied information at participating merchant locations or station-sponsored events.

These technology-based relationship enhancements give listeners a way to get more of their individual needs filled from a medium that is not typically customizable. At the same time, they receive access to information and to measurable rewards for their loyalty. The new interactive technologies combine to turn passive listeners into active customers.

A ground-breaking station using *all* of these capabilities is country station KMPS in Seattle, Washington. In mid-1995, the station had 185,000 members in 140,000 households for its *Loyal Listener Club*. Through the benefits of the club—an IVR-based member information line, a monthly glossy magazine, special access to events, discounts on advertiser services, and an Internet site—KMPS enhances the benefits listeners enjoy while expanding revenue-producing advertiser options as well. In fact, the station is the first we are aware of that has been able to completely abandon the Arbitron ratings system.[6]

Fred Schumacher, vice president for KMPS and its sister station, KZOK, began the KMPS *Loyal Listener Club* as a database-building effort in 1991, initially using only an interactive voice response system to facilitate listener communication. He describes the transformative power of technology tools in enacting a customer-focused marketing strategy:

> The IVR system allows us to relate to our customers as individuals and to satisfy at least some of their individual needs. And, by moving some information programming off the air and onto the IVR system, our air time is less cluttered and we can play more music.

Listeners have clearly welcomed the opportunity to access station information and to guide "product" direction by voicing their preferences about on-air personalities, programming options, and ancillary services. They log over 40,000 calls per month (see samples from a single day's input in "KMPS Listeners Talk," Exhibit 1.3). The station uses this listener interaction to guide programming. Each call is transcribed and distributed daily to station management. Listener electronic mail messages from *KMPS Online* are likewise distributed immediately. And, when appropriate, integrated marketing manager Dean Sakai responds directly to individual callers or writers.

According to Sakai, the interactivity of the IVR and on-line communications channels has strengthened the station's brand identity and its bonds with listeners and advertisers. He believes club members have a high degree of trust in the station, too, noting that they have been very willing to bring friends into the club.[7]

Customer information obtained via these listener interaction channels is added to a detailed base of demographic, psychographic, and purchase intention information provided by listeners at sign-up and at kiosks located at station events. This base of data enables the station to direct programming more effectively at different audience segments and, likewise, to build customized advertiser programs for different segments.

Thanks to the falling cost of database and IVR technologies and the increasing accessibility of on-line communications channels, even the smallest stations have options for conducting more real-time interactive marketing. According to Rob Sisco, vice president of marketing services at IVR vendor Fairwest Direct, radio stations are using IVR for survey gathering, audience profiling, music research, and for rewarding and recognizing frequent listeners. Stations wishing to develop at-work listening audiences have integrated the systems with enhanced fax technology, he notes. For example, they may broadcast fax messages to consenting workplace club members to announce programs (such as daily workplace listening contests). Some stations also offer fax-on-demand services, so listeners can request information they hear about on-air or on the IVR system.

EXHIBIT 1.3 KMPS Listeners Talk by IVR and E-Mail

KMPS in Seattle has built a database of 185,000 Loyal Listener Club members, and now offers advertisers an integrated system of marketing options including broadcast radio, interactive voice response, IVR, events, a monthly magazine, direct mail, and online. The interactivity has changed the way listeners relate and enabled the station to abandon the Arbitron ratings system.

"We have so much contact with our listeners through direct mail, the phone line, the Internet, and our community events," explains Dean Sakai, integrated marketing manager. "We've created stronger bonds with our listeners than most stations, and grabbed a share of the

EXHIBIT 1.3 (Continued)

most loyal listeners in the market. And we have the capacity to track what's happening with our loyal listeners, to know exactly what they're responding to and how." He shared a sampling of one day's listener input:

- "You are awesome. The best country music station in Seattle. I started to listen to country music six months ago. You guys make it easy to keep listening. You play all my favorite songs, the DJs are really great to chat with, and the Loyal Listener Club is the greatest! I got my card and I am so excited; I am official! I even have a KMPS sticker on my car, so keep doing what you are doing; love you guys!!"

- "I love your station. And I like your Loyal Listener Line. I can call anytime and find out things that I want to know for the weekend and the week."

- "This is my loyalty to KMPS. . . . When the other radio station called me and asked what my favorite radio station was, I lost $1,000 because I said, 'KMPS!' You guys are awesome, keep it up."

- "I went to the concert last night and thanks for providing such good entertainment. Every D.J. I met was really nice. I had a problem with my Loyal Listener Card and they took every effort to get the card working, and then provided me with another way to enter in the contest for the trip to California."

- "I am one of your loyal listeners. I have a problem with your new format during the day. It doesn't let me make dedications. In fact, the format is very inflexible. You can't do anything for customers or anything that involves your listeners much at all during the day. I would really like to see that change."

- "I think you guys like, rock, you know? I just signed up for the club and I think it's pretty cool 'cause you have lots of discounts and stuff. I 've like already used it four times and I just got it like two days ago. So, you guys are doing really good . . . Rock on."

Radio consultant Peggy Miles of D.C.-based Miles Marketing notes that interactive technology is changing relationship structures for stations that are using them to create loyalty programs. "You develop a relationship with your listeners and then extend that relationship to include your advertising customers. Your brand then becomes something like a good housekeeping seal of approval."

Creating a Private On-Line Community: ETEC Delivers Instant Access

New York-based Entertainment Technology Communications Corporation (ETEC), the primary trade publisher, trade show organizer, and de facto trade association for the entertainment event supply industry,[8] is one of a small, but growing number of organizations that are creating private on-line services dedicated to the needs of a specialized professional community. We predict that there will be an explosion of such communities, each open only to subscribers, but accessible from the public byways of the Internet.

The service, called *Entertainment Technology Online Direct (ETEC Direct)*, is a subscription service that provides access to information and interaction opportunities not otherwise available in the industry. It also serves as a wide area network for companies with multiple locations, enabling employees or associates in different offices to link up and communicate instantly, around the clock, about important projects. Operations director Scott Iverson explained that the network does the same for far-flung networks of freelancers and individual consultants, architects, design, sound, and visual professionals. In its first months of existence, it rapidly became the industry's hottest way to get news and to work out business negotiations, project management, creative development, and production issues. In discussing the benefits to users, Iverson says:

> A local service like ETEC puts you in a community of professionals with similar needs and wants. . . . You have a captured audience. The public highway of the Internet is like a no-man's land. You have to find your niche, which can take a long time. And there's no sense of community except in the places you find that you like to go.

ETEC users are greeted with a graphical menu of options relating specifically to the entertainment industry (see Exhibit 1.4). The system is optimized for the transmission of sophisticated graphics, photographs, moving video images, music, and various interactive tools. Menu options offer everything from job-matching services to *Live Design,* an interactive design tool that lets entertainment professionals collaborate on design or architectural drawings on-line. Users can also access Entertainment's magazines, *Lighting Design* or *Theater Crafts International,* locate and rent equipment, hire talent, exchange ideas by electronic mail, or participate in one of many discussion forums. About 100 companies signed up as charter advertisers when the system was launched in 1995, and subscribers are signing up at the rate of about 1,000 per month. An Internet gateway also permits ETEC subscribers to send messages and information to Internet users, or to enter the service from an Internet location. And ETEC creates home pages on its World Wide Web (WWW) server for companies wanting to have a commercial presence on the Internet.

The private on-line service model offers several key advantages over traditional information delivery mechanisms or the public and commercial on-line services:

1. Users get increased access at greater speeds to more relevant information and more flexibility in how they do business. As a print publisher, ETEC could never provide such instant access to up-to-the-minute information. And Internet marketing options, while improving, are still limited by transmission speed, security problems and the difficulties many users have with access and navigation.

2. The sponsoring company becomes an intermediary among its various customer groups, facilitating their interactions. In return, it increases its value to them and creates new revenue sources.

3. A private network gives all parties maximum flexibility and control over the way information is presented and used.

Such services are naturals for any environment in which the audience shares definable common lifestyle or workstyle interests, including business-to-business, association, civic, and non-profit communities. For example, the city of Alexandria is creating *Electronic Alexandria,* which, when fully operational, will provide area residents and merchants with on-line access to information on city government, local sports, recreation, and cultural activities, and to dining and tourism

EXHIBIT 1.4 ETEC Main Menu Screen

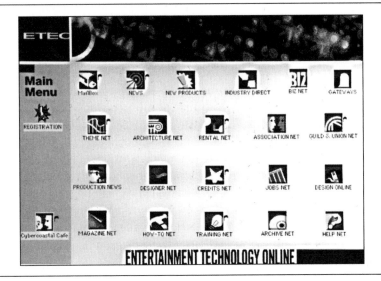

*Entertainment Technology Online (ETEC) has launched a cybermarket for the
entertainment industry.*

features. It will also permit citizens and businesses to communicate
directly via e-mail and discussion forums, and to post useful information or sponsored advertising on the community network. In the process, the relationship between the City and its many constituencies will
shift dramatically as *Electronic Alexandria* becomes a source through
which constituents can find resources, information, customers, and
services.

When Customers Won't Wait: Instant Information
Delivery with Fax-on-Demand

The rise of interactive marketing is creating a new era of customer
service. Increasingly, consumers expect and demand on-a-dime delivery of information and service. If you make them wait, you may lose
them to a competitor who comes through faster. They also appreciate
having choices about how they access information. Surveys have shown
that many people are still more comfortable getting information by
phone or fax than via computer. Fax penetration is still far greater than

that of on-line services. This makes fax-on-demand (FOD) an interactive telemedia workhorse that gives marketers a way of instantly accommodating the precision demands of today's customers.

Long before we became active on-line users in our own office, for example, we were avid users of fax-on-demand options offered by office products catalogers, publishers, and others. The ability to get detailed product information from a supplier or to retrieve an article from a trade publication with the push of a button has saved us time, money, and frustration on many occasions. The combined benefits of increased service (information) and decreased costs (time) make us appreciate those service providers who give us the option of retrieving information this way. We even conducted some of our research for this book using a daily news digest service, *iNews,* that is delivered to us by fax. When we find a news item of interest to us, we pick up the telephone, enter a request code, and the entire article is faxed to us in a matter of minutes. It's a convenient, easy, and inexpensive way to access a broad set of information resources.

As marketers ourselves, we also use fax-on-demand to distribute information about our articles and books to interested readers. For this, we use a service called MarketFax, based in Irvington, New York, which has even developed the capability to match requesters' fax numbers with names and addresses so that we can follow up on an inquiry.[9] MarketFax works with publishers like *The Wall Street Journal, Golf* magazine, and *Success,* developing custom applications such as interactive reader inquiry services and reader surveys that save time and money for readers and advertisers. MarketFax president Ed Liss also works with associations to develop value-added services for its members. One of these, the National Association of Realtors (NAR), uses fax-on-demand to provide advance information for its annual conferences. It also uses an electronic reader response program in its monthly magazine that pulls about 2,000 responses per issue. Liss explains:

> Every week, MarketFax automatically follows up all incoming information requests with a targeted fax broadcast. Using this combination of fax-on-demand and follow-up fax broadcasting, advertisers are experiencing sales closings in the 50 percent range.

This is increasing advertising revenue for NAR, Liss continued, and is attracting more advertisers to the publication: "Advertisers are placing more of their budget dollars in the magazines," he says, "because it pulls for them and the results can be easily measured."

Today, travel-service providers, telecommunications equipment sellers, publishers, financial services, radio stations, pharmaceutical manufacturers, realtors, and the Federal government are among the many organizations that use fax-on-demand. For some, it is a profit center, used to sell information. Others use it to add value to their relationships with customers. Business-to-business marketers are discovering its appeal as a selling tool for salespeople, dealers, and customers. One telecommunications firm we spoke with plans to put in a reporter's line to keep the media informed.

Fax-on-demand adds benefits to both sides of the marketer-consumer equation. These benefits are similar to those available in an on-line environment:

- Prospects and customers can enter and re-enter the sales cycle at will and get detailed information at the precise moment they want it.

- In some cases, customers can choose to complete the sales cycle while browsing through the system. Because callers are self-qualifying, the sales cycle is shortened and does not intrude on the customer or prospect.

- The technology permits maximum information relevance and accuracy.

- The marketer gets instant measurement capability to determine how well a marketing program is performing.

San Jose, California cataloger Hello Direct launched an FOD service for its customers in 1994. The privately held company, which markets telecommunications products such as telephone systems, headsets, cellular accessories, fax/modem switches, and even an FOD system, mails four catalogs per year to over 18 million consumer and business catalog buyers. Product developer Ron Becht says that the new system augments the 30 "customer care" representatives in the firm's telemarketing center, providing round-the-clock information access to prospects and customers around the world. Callers use it to get detailed sales and technical information about the company's products. He believes that consumers appreciate having the option of doing some of their buying research this way.

"We average about 1,500 fax-on-demand contacts per month," explains Becht. "The system opens up a variety of opportunities. It lets prospects and customers get more detailed information on products in our catalog. It frees up our service representatives to be on the phone with customers by off-loading from them the time-consuming job of sending technical information to callers. Our new system also lets individuals request a catalog by simply entering a voice-mail message with their name, address, and fax number. It's a seamless, back-end information delivery solution," he continued. "And a nice added benefit to our customer base."

Internet: Attracting Interest over the Ultimate Public Medium

In the rush to create a commercial presence on the Internet, the crazy-quilt network of gateways and connections, many companies are simply transposing traditional advertising and selling paradigms onto this new, most interactive of mediums. Instead of taking advantage of the incredible interactive potential of the portion of the net that supports hypertext links,[10] they spend the consumer's time and patience on image-building text and graphics telling consumers about their products or services, or they alienate whole groups of individuals by being overly commercial in an on-line chat forum.

The Internet is uniquely suited to developing higher levels of relationships, to establishing dynamic customer communities, and to allowing satisfied customers to become your champions by telling others in the Internet community about your service. Here, the power balance shifts most visibly to the consumer—commercial participants are newcomers in a world that still consists largely of computer-advantaged young men who are justifiably proud and protective of the vast Net community they populate. As access improves and more mainstream consumers come on line, we expect to see a rapid shakeout of the marketers who don't understand that the highest use of the Internet is as a "listening" medium.

One company that clearly understands this is Hanover, New Jersey-based PrePRESS Solutions, a $50 million company that manufactures and sells image-setting equipment, software, training, and services to designers and publishers around the world. The company's new Internet site, *PrePRESS Main Street,* is not your standard amalgamation of company product information. Rather, it feels like a small town community, one that offers you a lot of resources. Among the choices are:

- *Main Street Gazette,* on-screen newspaper updated daily with news stories from around the industry.

- Café Moiré,[11] where mannequin Cynthia invites you inside to participate in news groups and chat sessions.

- The Convention Center, where PrePress presents full reports, complete with digital still images, of products, speakers, and events from major trade shows around the world.

- Classified Advertising, where anybody can place free ads for services or equipment wanted to buy or sell.

- *PrePRESS DIRECT! SuperSTORE,* the Internet version of the company's well-known catalog, redesigned with links to pricing and purchase options.[12]

- A library, with downloadable reference material on a host of prepress issues and PrePRESS products.

- The Print Shop, where browsers can get tips and tools, including free downloadable software utilities to enhance prepress performance.

Company president Robert Trenkamp says that he has wanted to do something like this since the late 1980s. He makes no bones that he wants to sell product through this effort, but he has larger objectives as well. By creating a "gathering place" for the industry, the company hopes to expand awareness, interaction, and credibility. "Our objective is to participate in just about every transaction somebody in the prepress community engages in for the acquisition of goods and services," he explains. "To do that, we need a flow of the entire prepress community through our site."

Trenkamp has a penchant for breaking new, interactive ground in the industry. In 1991, he launched a catalog operation that has become a major part of the company's business and created broad awareness for the firm worldwide. Trenkamp told us that the Internet site is likewise having an immediate, positive impact on catalog sales, as Internet browsers find products of interest and contact the company's catalog operation. The impact is global, too. Translated pages of the catalog are available on the site in four languages to aid overseas viewers.

"We are beginning to accumulate an understanding of what our customers' needs and wishes are," explains Trenkamp. "We're trying to

EXHIBIT 1.5 PrePRESS Main Street Screen

By creating an Internet "gathering place" for prepress production professionals,
PrePRESS Solutions hopes to expand industry awareness, interaction, and credibility.

segment our marketing approach down to an audience of one, so that we don't present people with things they don't want to hear." Ultimately, Trenkamp believes that consumers will expect their suppliers to remove the shopping burden from them. "I see a huge change coming in business-to-business marketing, picking up on what's happening in consumer marketing with mass customization," he says. "You're going to see personal shopper relationships, where customers will say, 'You know what I need and what's going on in the industry; keep me supplied with ideas.' We'd love to be the go-fetch person for everybody in our target audience."

The Internet, and other interactive technologies that can monitor and measure every interest of the customer, afford the means for companies to become the "go-fetch" resources for their customers. The ability to "listen," to capture hard data on customer interests and preferences, and to do so with up-to-the-hour timeliness, gives marketers such opportunities. If database marketing is the wave of the future, then this kind of dialogue between consumers and marketers is the water itself. And the Internet, and subsequent generations of interactive network, offer the ideal medium for creating and sustaining true customer dialogues. Consumers will voice their preferences for marketers who empower them with such access, flexibility, relevance, and time and cost savings.

Conclusion: Working at the Interactive Nexus

The interactive race is on. Companies that fail to get in shape quickly will soon be left in the dust. Marketers are gaining ground when they grasp the subtleties of the changing buyer-seller relationships and are willing to deliver greater power to their customers:

- U S West's *Your Value Card* builds a major information base for a supplier of local telephone services, while delivering savings and new information to customers.

- KMPS radio gains detailed information for its advertisers while its listeners benefit directly with access to events, savings, and an easy means for giving feedback on what they like and don't like.

- ETEC becomes the center for a whole new way of doing business in the entertainment industry, gaining new revenue sources for its creator while its customers get new flexibility and instant information access.

- Hello Direct improves its customer service productivity by giving consumers new information options in the sales cycle for technical products.

- *PrePRESS Solutions* creates an Internet gathering place for an industry and gets the opportunity to learn how to become the trusted information provider for each and every customer and prospect.

For every forward-thinking marketer, of course, there are many more who simply want to be where the action is and don't understand that their role must change. For some, fascination with the technology overpowers common sense and good business judgment. Others seem to have a superficial, product-focused mentality that leads to off-putting programs that quickly collapse from consumer disinterest or disdain.

Here are three simple rules that can help you keep sight of the relationship impact of your interactive technology initiatives:

1. Fit interactive marketing into a larger strategy that continuously creates new benefits for being your company's customer.

2. Strive for a balance between the company's marketing objectives and the consumer's shopping needs and objectives.

EXHIBIT 1.6 Interactive Marketing Technologies Weigh in for Customers

---

From Marketers' Strategies	To Consumers' Benefits
Lifetime Customer Value	Lifetime Savings and Reward Opportunity
Improved Product Quality	Mass Customization
Targeted Messages	Fewer Extraneous Messages
Loyalty	Rewards and Recognition
Production Efficiency	Lower Prices
Inventory Efficiency	Guaranteed Availability
Distribution Efficiency	Wider Availability
Zero Defects	Product Satisfaction
Information Dissemination	Informed Decisions
Electronic Customer Communities	Access to Peers, Multilogue
Customer Dialogue	Seller Responsiveness
Reduced Marketing Cycle	Speedy Response, Time Savings
Competitive Advantage	New Value-Added Choices
New Selling Channels	New Supply Channels
Advertising Messages on Request	Advertising Messages on Demand

3. Find ways to make each technology-based program provide multiple benefits to both parties.

Interactive marketing is about changing the ability of both marketers and consumers to affect the "relationship" in relationship marketing. Exhibit 1.6 demonstrates how emerging market strategies actually give consumers more power in the marketing equation. Consumers' abilities to choose the relationships they want grow greater as the shopping process is extended and adapted to more interactive channels. Marketers who understand this are using every tool available to give their customers every reason to be their relationship choice.

In short, consumers are no longer the direct marketer's archer's targets in the new interactive marketing paradigm. Instead, they are constantly on the move, like surfers who delight in finding and riding the information waves that interest or amuse them. Marketers who give up their bows and arrows and focus on creating worthwhile waves are the ones who will find them returning again and again.

References

1. We use the word "consumer" loosely; our discussion applies also to buyers of business goods and services.

2. These bonds and the marketing discipline that works with them are described by Richard Cross and Janet Smith in *Customer Bonding: Pathway to Lasting Customer Loyalty* (Lincolnwood, IL: NTC Business Books, 1995).

3. Card readers are valuable tools for building databases. Some offer direct interaction options; they can be programmed to pose specific questions at the time of transaction, for example, or to issue coupons based upon the transaction occurring.

4. Available on the Internet and the major commercial on-line services: America Online, CompuServe, and Prodigy.

5. Some of this material is based upon an article by Richard Cross, "Broadcast Radio Tunes In To Listeners," *Direct Marketing,* June 1995.

6. Arbitron is a media measurement system that estimates audience size and makeup, which effectively determines station advertising revenue potentials.

7. Sakai estimates that one member-get-member promotion alone grew the club membership by a full 20 percent.

8. This industry is made up of companies providing equipment and services to theaters, arts companies, concert organizers, movie producers, and other entertainment companies. Players include lighting and stage designers, costume makers, tour organizers, promoters, publicists, etc.

9. MarketFax recently added the follow-up capability, which it can provide within 24 hours.

10. Hypertext is a special markup language that allows a text element to become a pointer to another information location. Consumers shopping in a hypertext catalog, for example, might click on the word "alligator" to find out more about the use of alligators in the manufacture of clothing accessories. A growing subset of the computer sites that make up the Internet support this hypertext capability: that subset is commonly referred to as the World Wide Web, or simply as "the Web."

11. "Moiré" is a graphic arts term referring to a repeating pattern in a poorly reproduced color photograph.

12. Because security remains a concern on the Internet, users have multiple choices for ordering, including printing out an order form and faxing it, calling the company's 800 number, or dialing into a secure site.

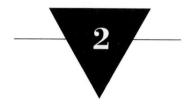

C H A P T E R

2

Interactive Retailing

More Choices, More Chances, More Growth

Leisa Reinecke Flynn

Leisa Reinecke Flynn is Associate Professor of Marketing at Florida State University. Her research, which appears in *The Journal of Business Research, Marketing Letters*, and many other journals, is primarily in the area of psychometrics and consumer behavior.

Imagine getting ready to take your family to your sister's wedding in another city. After the last-minute rush to get everyone out the door and on the way, you breathe a sigh of relief when everyone and everything is finally in the car and you are on your way. About ten miles out of town your teenage daughter asks what you finally picked out for the wedding gift. Aha! You knew you had forgotten something. No problem. You use the on-board computer and cellular phone connection to dial into your favorite interactive shopping service. Using voice commands, you ask the service to look for bridal registries that contain your sister's gift choices. The service finds two. You choose the store nearest your destination and give the computer your price range. The service suggests the fine china and lets you know that your sister has not received much of her pattern yet. You tell the computer to order two place settings of the fine china and that you will pick up at a store about fifty miles from your destination in two hours: "Oh, and don't forget to wrap it for a wedding." The service knows your credit card number and automatically bills your account.

This scenario points out two of the major dichotomies that face interactive retailers. The first is the balance between what is really possible today, given existing technology, and what is somewhere off in the future. The second issue asks, "What is the place of direct or non-store marketing and how much room will that leave for the traditional, store-based retailer?" In this brief look at interactive retailing I will try to sort out the real from the planned and/or imagined and look at the threats and opportunities for traditional retailers in a more interactive, direct marketing world.

Interactive Retailing Today

Anyone who tells you that interactive retailing is taking over has jumped the gun. Estimates are that electronic shopping now accounts for less than one half of one percent of retail sales and that in ten years it will make up 5 to 25 percent of the total (Belsie 1994; *The Economist* 1994; Kehoe 1994; Tompkins 1994; Reda 1995). The leaders in interactive retailing today are the on-line services such as CompuServe, America On-line and Prodigy. Each of these offers subscribers various shopping opportunities. Other popular sources for electronic marketing are the television shopping channels such as QVC and The Home Shopping Network. While there is no doubt that the on-line services are offering true interactive retailing, it is an exaggeration to say the same for the television channels. The customer does not really *interact* with QVC and HSN. She merely watches a linear parade of products on the screen and waits for the goods she is interested in to appear.

A more futuristic system being tested in Orlando, Florida, in 1995 is Shopper Vision. This service, being developed by Time-Warner, allows the user to enter a store (currently Winn-Dixie Stores and Eckerd Drugs are taking part), and with their television remote and a set top box, travel down "aisles" in a store. The screen shows what is essentially a planogram of the store's shelves with prices under pictures of the products. The shopper is even able to read label information. This innovation leapfrogs over the videotext lists that were the hallmark of interactive television shopping in its infancy. The shopper then selects items from the "shelves" and places them in a "shopping cart." The consumer can pay either by credit card or be billed on the monthly cable bill (Aho 1994; Robichaux, Trachten, and Naik 1994).

Two other forms of interactive retailing are in existence today. One is made up by the mostly small retailers on the World Wide Web. The products offered are mostly esoteric ones like one pet supplier's "organic cat ticklers." Even the few larger retailers that have made their way onto the web, like Spiegel, are offering only a few products on-line. One of the *eight* items that Spiegel offers in its on-line home furnishings catalogue is a lava lamp. One of the biggest problems with Web retailing is payment. Credit card numbers are not yet fully secure on the Internet, although new encryption technology should move toward overcoming this impediment in the near future.

The other form, which is lower tech and therefore more widely usable, is the CD-ROM catalogue. Some of the larger catalogue companies have jumped into this format. In what is emerging as the typical format, several catalogue companies produce a co-op disk. One such joint disk features Lillian Vernon, Spiegel, Lands' End, and Wireless (Gattuso, 1994). Catalogue shoppers can see video clips and hear music samples. Cataloguers have a clear advantage in this new format because they already have the images and the order fulfillment systems. A huge advantage that this form of catalogue retailing has over the paper version is the cost of reproduction and mailing. CDs cost less than $2 to produce and little more than a letter to mail; and one CD takes the place of up to 40 paper catalogues. This is a major advance for catalogue marketers who see mailing and reproduction costs (in particular, paper) as their biggest single threat.

The Future

There are many amazing predictions of what the future will bring to and take from retailers and customers. In the near future we will see more computer interactivity within traditional stores. Kiosks in stores will help us find merchandise and then match it with other coordinating items in home decorating and clothing stores. Computer video systems will take our measurements and allow us to "try on" clothes without piling them up in a dressing room (Reda 1995). In grocery stores "smart buggies" or checkout conveyers will add up our purchases and accept payment without the help of a clerk. These systems are in the works or, in some cases, already in the stores. One of the earliest uses of computers in stores has been in bridal registries. This process has been traditionally carried out by the sales clerk but now is becoming self-service. It is likely to be one of the first traditional services to become highly in-store interactive. The bridal registry is a likely use of the interactive kiosk.

Looking even further into the future, the experts predict that a customer will be able to order nearly anything from a home terminal for either overnight or even faster delivery. Included in this service would be information on the customer's sizes, color preferences, and existing wardrobe for clothing and color schemes, and floor plan for home furnishings. The service would also keep track of the home inventory of goods and preferences for grocery items. The system might even be able to tell you which items others have recently purchased so you will be able to avoid duplicating a gift (Tompkins 1994). Imagine a "Friends and Family" buying circle where all of your extended family's recent purchases are available for consideration before you choose a gift.

Perhaps the future development with the most potential to shake up retailing is when access to the Internet becomes nearly universal. While this state is fairly far off, it doesn't take much imagination to foresee new and different competition on the horizon for the traditional retailer. When setting up a store front is as easy as designing a hypertext page the only thing that will differentiate retailers is their ability to manage and control their sources of supply. Location will be meaningless for any good that is not highly convenience oriented (Schneider 1994). The atmospherics in the "store" are reduced to keystrokes and scanned images put together by a page designer. Anyone with a supply of some good or service, a computer, and a link to the Internet can be in business overnight.

These cyber-retailers will be lean and mean with no money tied up in bricks and mortar, no commercial district rent to pay, no windows to dress, no rest rooms to clean, and no hours to keep. Shrinkage due to shoplifting will be eliminated (although inside theft will remain a problem). All of the expertise will be in buying. An extra and valuable part of the deal will be improved consumer reconnaissance. On-line transactions will allow the electronic retailer to learn more and more about that consumer and provide a much more individualized offering to the consumer (Peppers and Rogers 1995).

Further yet into the future, some are predicting that many more goods will be produced on demand. As automation allows for goods to be produced more and more quickly, the shorts you want will be made to your electronic measurements and delivered to your door. Machines calibrated for each individual order will take information from your buying service and manufacture one of a kind items to suit your personal specifications. There will be virtually no need for inventory; and because there will be no showroom, there will be no floor models.

The futurists predict a computer-based wonderland where consumers, shopping from home, can buy not only everything they need but nearly whatever they can imagine. The future of retailing, they say, goes way past the Jetsons.

Reality—and What it Means for Today's Retailers

What effect all these changes will have on today's retailers is hard to say. It seems pretty certain that some part of the market will shift to electronic retailing of some form. Chances are that a fair percent of busy, technologically savvy consumers will purchase a fair percentage of their staple goods via an interactive service (*The Economist* 1994). Chances are also good that these same consumers will buy some shopping goods in the same manner (Schneider 1994). Shopping for books, recordings, and small electronic devices, or any product with a fairly strong brand recognition could easily be accomplished on-line (Peppers and Rogers 1995). As economically successful people get busier, as factors like traffic and crime make staying home look better and better, as computers become more pervasive, and as access to the Internet is available to many homes, the trend toward electronic retailing will pick up speed.

What, then, is the bottom line for traditional retailers? The most likely scenario is that this change will bring about the same sort of successes and fallout as other retailing revolutions. Some capital-heavy retailers will wait too long and be left behind. They have been jaded by promises going back as far as twenty years predicting the end of retailing as we know it. Their businesses will be hurt. Others, venturing into interactive realms that the consumer will reject, will suffer. Still others will aggressively pursue innovation—and succeed.

It seems to me that the likely winners are those retailers who already do a fair amount of direct business. Already, traditional catalogue retailers such as Spiegel, Lands' End, J.C. Penney, and Service Merchandise have their toes in the water (Robichaux, Trachten, and Naik 1994). Others with reputations for being pro-technology are also dabbling. WalMart has a Web site, for instance. Still other winners will be found among the esoteric bunch of small retailers who have sprung up and continue to spring up daily on the Web. Anyone with a supply of anything can create a hypertext data file and load it onto the Net and reach a potentially huge market. When advertising postings are a free good, barriers to entry into the retail market are extremely low. These smaller players will open up new ultra-niche segments that were previously too small to be served by a traditional retailer.

Another effect of the computerization of retailing might be a shift of the balance of power back to the national manufacturers and away from the retailers. If the importance of location fades away, so might the prominence of the retailer. On the other hand, the value of regional distribution centers already owned by the large retailers could form the cornerstone for the interactive revolution based on speedy direct sales.

The biggest casualties might be the traditional department stores. The department store is heavily capital intensive and aims at a broad segment of the market. With labor costs climbing, many of these upscale retailers have become more and more self-service. At the same time they have become more alike, carrying the same merchandise assortments as each other. They aim at the markets that are most likely to own and use home computers. They carry many items that might be easily sold via computer and thus are vulnerable to competitors offering more novel merchandise. Finally, the margins that department stores need to cover expenses could likely cover the expenses of an interactive retailer. Thus, on-line prices that include delivery would likely be no more than department store prices.

One inescapable factor that will balance out the losses of the department store is shopping as a form of entertainment. Home shopping systems are likely to add to the alienation that modern consumers already feel. Shopping has always provided a scene for social exchange. Stores and shopping centers that are able to play up their value as a meeting and entertainment place will be more able to protect their share of the market. The Mall of America in Minnesota and the West Edmonton Mall in Western Canada are successful examples of shopping as entertainment.

As to who will succeed as an interactive retailer, I believe that the established stores have a good chance. While their brick and mortar infrastructure may be overkill for direct, on-line marketing, they have the brand equity and the consumer's trust. Being trusted by the consumer will be a key in the consumer's willingness to take the risks associated with shopping in a new way. In other words, the consumer is more likely to buy from a trusted name on-line than from a new name on-line.

The keys to success for all retailers in the future will be the same as they are today. If a retailer can provide the assortment of goods that the consumer wants with superior convenience and prices that are the same or only marginally more than competitors, they stand to succeed. Given the right market they stand to put a real dent in the business of traditional retailers.

Conclusion

The interactive age holds both opportunity and threat for traditional retailers. Those who sell highly standardized "convenience" products stand to suffer as consumers find easier ways to replenish staple items. At the same time, consumers will continue to rely on retail stores for human interaction, and for products that they want to experience before they buy. Astute retailers will be able to expand their own brand name equities into on-line services as they gain from highly automated and efficient retail processes (Bradshaw 1994). When consumers order on line in real time from computers at home that offer versions of the store's own planogram, the stores can automate the distribution process more completely.

For consumers and entrepreneurs the new age will bring more choices than ever. More and different types of convenience will be available for consumers with the technical ability and the money. Interactivity promises so much more information about the consumer and so much increased efficiency that any retailer will be able to greatly increase the personalization and, therefore, the meaningfulness of its services to its customers. The retailer will also be able to carry less inventory and buy much more accurately and efficiently. Whether the consumer buys in-store or from home, the successful retailers that exist today have the advantages of consumer trust, existing sources of supply, knowledge of customer base, and the financial position to keep up with trends in interactivity. New ways of carrying out the exchange process will present opportunities for entrepreneurs with vision. Overall, the growth phase of interactive retailing will be turbulent and be littered with the remains of services that did not fit the market. Despite the pooh-poohs of the big retailers with their feet stuck in the mud, this is an innovation (or set of innovations) that is entering the growth phase.

References

Aho, Debra (1994), "Winn-Dixie, Eckerd go Interactive," *Advertising Age* (April 18) p. 16.

Belsie, Laurent (1994), "Retailing 2005: Electronic Malls, Virtual Shopping Carts," *The Christian Science Monitor* (December 15), pp. 1–16.

Bradshaw, Della (1994), The End of the Queue," *The Financial Times* (June 16), p. 18.

The Economist (1994), "The Interactive Bazaar Opens," (August 20), pp. 49–51.

Gattuso, Greg (1994), "Lillian Vernon Looks to the Future," *Direct Marketing* (August), pp. 33–35.

Kehoe, Louise (1994), "On-line for a Speedy Sale," *The Financial Times* (June 23), p. 16.

Peppers, Don and Martha Rogers, (1995), "The End of Mass Marketing," *Marketing Tools* (March/April), pp. 42–52.

Reda, Susan (1995), "Will Consumers Catch Up with Interactive Shopping," *Stores* (March), pp. 20–24.

Robichaux, Mark, Jeffrey A.Trachten, and Gautam Naik (1994), "Interactive Home Shopping Channel Slated by U.S. West, Nordstrom, Penney," *The Wall Street Journal* (May 18), p. A4.

Schneider, Fred (1994), "Get Ready for Virtual Retailing," *Supermarket Business* 49 (December), pp. 46–49.

Tompkins, Richard (1994), "Shop-till-you-drop at the Touch of a Button," *The Financial Times* (June 9), p. 20.

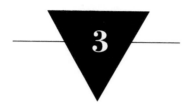

Interactive Kiosks in the Retail Environment

What Do Customers Really Need?

Thomas W. Hutchison

Thomas W. Hutchison is currently a faculty member in the Department of Recording Industry in the College of Mass Communication at Middle Tennessee State University. His research and consulting efforts include consumer analyses for Geffen Records, including projects on the artists White Zombie, Peter Case, Billy Walker, Jr., Sonic Youth, Weezer, Hole, and many other acts. He has also conducted bounceback card and focus group research for Polydor/Nashville Records and Sony Music/ Nashville.

The latest rage in automated retailing is the interactive information kiosk, strategically placed in high-traffic areas of retail stores and accessible to consumers. This information "vending machine" is technology's answer to the ultimate salesperson, armed with a depth of product knowledge and information that overshadows even the most knowledgeable of sales clerks. Multimedia kiosks are designed to offer an increased level of customer service, replacing sales clerks for some tasks and thus reducing overhead. Additionally, kiosks have shown some success in generating incremental sales which would not be achieved through traditional marketing efforts. The kiosks must provide one or both of these services to be cost effective and meet with success in the marketplace.

Instrumental to the success of these systems is whether the presence of the machines will save enough money on sales help or generate enough incremental sales to offset the cost of the machines. Achieving this goal has been made easier by the reduction of initial costs for installation as the price of the technology falls.

Additionally, acceptance of the machines by consumers provides the vital link in determining ultimate success. Early pilot projects met with mixed success as lack of attractiveness and complexity of the machines discouraged all but the most technologically inclined customers: response times were too slow, touchscreens broke, the kiosks were not maintained and updated, and the graphics were lacking. Kiosks were also misapplied in situations which were not suitable for the service, such as placing travel information kiosks in hotels after the travelers had completed their travel itineraries. There were other problems as well. A real estate kiosk called "HomeSight" was tested and abandoned in 1986 due to high costs of entry and lack of customer interest (Wiesendanger, 1991). In 1989, Sears tested and scrapped a project involving 10 "Gift Sender" kiosks in its Chicago-area stores. That same year, Proctor and Gamble tested and then abandoned computerized information kiosks in supermarkets. The success or lack of success is tied to return on investment. The cost of installing the kiosks must be offset by cost savings or incremental sales (Bredin, 1993). Current costs of kiosks are estimated at about $10,000 apiece (Bredin, 1993), however, some estimates put the costs from several thousand dollars to $100,000 or more (Wiesendanger, 1991). Other estimates range from $4,000 to $16,000 each (Muldoon, 1985).

The early failures have prompted firms to re-evaluate the role of kiosks in the retail environment. The acceptance of automated teller machines and personal computers lowers the barriers and predisposes consumers to rely on computer-operated machines for business information and transactions. "To be successful, in-store media must develop new technologies designed to make the shopping trip easier and more enjoyable" (DeNitto, 1993). Reduction in development costs and vastly improved technologies make the kiosks once again attractive to retailers. As competition increases, "retail will likely be one of the most technologically leading industries of the next decade as it becomes increasingly information-intense" (Bob Martin, Executive VP/Information Systems, Wal-Mart).

In-store Interactive Kiosks

Kiosks are simply electronic information centers (Muldoon, 1985). Each has a television screen which displays graphics and menus. Kiosks have either a self-contained computer with multimedia capabilities, or may be online with a mainframe computer. The stand-alone kiosks, which are the most abundant, are personal computers (PCs) with videodisc or CD-ROM disc systems providing the graphics and database information (*Chain Store Age Executive,* 1992). A one-videodisc system can hold the equivalent of a 108,000-page catalog (Muldoon, 1985). In most cases, the user interacts with the system via touch-screen technology that IBM and other companies have been refining since 1980 (Hume, 1992). The cost of the touch screen has decreased to about $1000 (as of 1992), down several thousand dollars from just a few years ago. The overall decrease in computing costs and increase in multimedia capabilities have transformed the once-mundane black-and-white text kiosks into a pleasant interactive entertainment experience.

As the problems have been addressed, acceptance of these user-friendly kiosks by shoppers has increased. Schwartz (1992) remarks: "Americans are ready to retrieve information and order products via computer kiosks" (p. 122).

The goal of such kiosks is to provide an increase in level of service at a reduced cost to the retailer. Reilly (1993) states that the biggest complaint of consumers buying in a traditional in-store environment is a lack of knowledgeable sales help. "Kiosks are very often much more helpful than salespeople" (Muldoon, 1985, p. 23). The sheer volume of product categories and brands has made it difficult for salespeople to keep abreast of all product information, as workers can only memorize a limited amount of product and pricing information (Hume, 1992; Schwartz, 1992). In today's market, consumers are more sophisticated and informed. "They want as much information as possible before making a buying decision" (Wiesendanger, 1991, p. 42). Since the kiosk, with its enormous database, has all the answers, the customer's frustration level is reduced (Muldoon, 1985). Imperative in developing the kiosks is the need to anticipate the realm of possible consumer questions and requests for information and to provide that information in an easily accessible manner.

Diffusion Level of Interactive Kiosks

In 1985, Muldoon (1985) estimated that 4,500 electronic kiosks were then in use by retailers. Muldoon forecasted an installed base of 113,000 by 1990. More recent estimates of the diffusion level figure 62,000 kiosks operating at the end of 1992, with 40,000 new units being installed in 1993. By 1996, it has been estimated that 2 million systems will be in use, making them more common than gasoline pumps (*Business Week*, 1992). The latest estimates, however, predict a more realistic installed base of 358,000 by 1997 (Weiss, 1995).

Two-thirds of the interactive kiosks are in retail locations, with the other 33 percent serving tourists in hotels, airports and convention centers. Retailers have been some of the first major users of multimedia projects (Chandler, 1992). Exposure to automated teller machines (ATMs) in the 1980s has predisposed customers to accept the use of the systems (Muldoon, ibid, Weiss, 1995). Research conducted on the users of one kiosk system reveals that more than 80 percent of the users said they would recommend the systems to others (Chandler, 1992).

Examples of the use of such systems include Sears, which is spending $7 million for 6,000 kiosks to handle customer catalog orders and inquire about credit. K-Mart is testing interactive "Information Centers" for home electronics and automotive departments (*Chain Store Age Executive*, 1992). Minnesota Twins baseball fans are lured to a kiosk showing game highlights on a video screen. Once drawn in, the fan can use the screen to order tickets to the games, even previewing the view of the field from the selected seats before purchasing the tickets, all of which is handled at the kiosk (Higgins, 1993). The BrowseStation™ allows video rental customers to preview clips from 700 videotapes before making a selection from the automated vending dispenser

(Higgins, 1993). MusicSource™ operates a database kiosk loaded with sheet music data for 23,000 songs (Greenleaf, 1993). The "Instant Sheet Music Kiosks" print sheet music on demand, saving inventory and shipping costs.

Kiosks in Retail Record Stores

Interactive kiosks serve several functions, from product information, to media previewing, to actual ordering and delivery of the product. In retail record stores and record departments in discount stores, interactive kiosks are projected to serve some of the information functions of:

1. Song or artist identification
2. References to other works by the same artists
3. Music previewing opportunities.

The market share of recorded music sales by retailers has been diminishing in recent years (Silverman, 1993), dropping from nearly 89 percent of the market share in 1988, to 84.9 percent in 1992 (RIAA report, 1993). Meanwhile, direct market sales account for 14.6 percent of the market share, up from 10.3 percent in 1988. In an effort to regain market share and lure customers back to retail stores, the record retailers "have moved aggressively to entertain customers by installing live deejays, or listening booths and kiosks" (Silverman, 1993, p. 116).

EXHIBIT 3.1 Record Store Kiosks

Name	Text reference	Music sampling
MUZE™	Yes	No *
Source™	Yes	No *
K-Mart	No	Yes
Robot Music Store	Yes	Yes
Telescan™	Yes	Yes
i-Station™	Yes	Yes

* Some newer models contain the sampling function.

Several competing interactive kiosk systems currently are in testing and use in retail record stores. Some retail chains (such as Wherehouse and Tower) have been testing more than one type of system to determine which system best suits their needs. Exhibit 3.1 illustrates the types of kiosks currently available.

The MUZE™ System

One such interactive information system is the MUZE™ system, developed by Paul Zullo and Trev Huxley (Leinfuss, 1993). The MUZE™ system is a database of music information that includes identification of songs (or recognition) by "title, a keyword in the title, or an alphabetical list of a performer's songs" (Leinfuss, 1993, p. S-13). MUZE™ will identify which album the song appears on, who the artist is, and other information about the album, such as additional musicians and reviews. The system also displays a graphic of the album cover artwork for many of the selections.

Access to the information is made possible through an IBM "customer membrane keyboard" and a touch-screen monitor. The hardware for the system includes an IBM 386-40 CPU (central processing unit) with four megabytes of RAM (rapid access memory), a videocard with one megabyte of memory, a 212 megabyte hard drive and an IBM CD-ROM (compact disc-read only memory) drive. The hardware system costs $6,000 and monthly software updates run about $1,150 per year (Jaffe, 1993). As of September 1993, there were 135 systems in operation in major retail stores such as Tower Records, Musicland, Virgin, and others, and another 135 back-ordered systems (Jaffee, 1993; Leinfuss, 1993). More recent estimates (source: MUZE™ marketing department, March 1994) place the installed base at about one thousand units.

Research (unspecified source in Leinfuss, 1993) indicates an average of 700 to 800 "lookups" per day with about one-fourth of those resulting in printouts of the information. The survey showed that 34 percent of the users made incremental purchases as a result of using the system and that 81 percent agreed "that the presence of the system encourages them to return to the store" (Leinfuss, 1993, p. S-13).

Elements that are absent from the MUZE™system include: (1) the ability to search using keywords from the lyrics, and (2) the ability to audibly sample the music. MUZE™ is experimenting with a limited number of audio samples, but developer Huxley is opposed to converting the system into a "free jukebox" for fear of overuse by users not intending to purchase recordings.

Phonolog's SOURCE™ System

In competition with the MUZE™ system is the "Source," an interactive CD-ROM-based reference kiosk from Trade Services Corporation, publishers of *Phonolog*™ reference books found in record stores (McGowan, 1993). The Source, which is an electronic version of the *Phonolog* book, lists more than one million song titles and 80,000 albums on the CD-ROM discs which are updated monthly. The system costs about $3,000 and is available through leasing plans.

K-Mart's Video and Music Kiosks

K-Mart discount chain has been testing a music preview kiosk containing the top 50 songs accompanied by video clips whenever possible. The kiosks are located in a newly designed Music and Movies department, aimed at attracting the teenage market (Crump, 1992; *Discount Store News*, 1993a, 1993b). In addition to attracting customers into the store, the kiosks are intended to help the customers make the correct music selections, to encourage add-on sales and to curtail returns. The first prototypes used laser disc technology (Pemberton, 1993), but have recently been updated to CD-ROM systems, thus reducing the costs (*Business Wire*, 1993). Designed by PICS Previews, the new systems had been installed in 600 locations across the country as of June 1993.

The Robot Music Store

In 1989, The Robot Aided Manufacturing Center (RAM) developed a prototype Robot Music Store. The computerized self-contained automat provides retail services for music customers through the use of interactive kiosks and robotics. The 140 square-foot cylinder kiosk is designed to be located in the open court shopping areas of malls (*Washington Times*, 1989). The circular glass enclosure houses 5,400 compact discs, about 36 discs per square foot, compared to a traditional record store which carries 10 CDs per square foot (Murray, 1990). Loss of product (shrinkage) due to employee theft and shoplifting is virtually nonexistent as the kiosks are serviced by just one person (*Chain Store Executive Age*, 1990).

Customers are serviced through four interactive listening stations (Fox, 1989), which play 30 second samples of the most popular song on each album (*Washington Times*, 1989b), take orders, accept payment by cash or credit card, return change and receipts, and through the use of a large mechanical robotic arm, dispense the product to the customer through a drop bin (Murray, 1990). The listening station at each quadrant contains an ATM-style keypad and screen at chest level and speakers overhead—after the company scrapped plans for including headphones at the unmanned booths (*Chain Store Executive Age*, 1990).

The entire system costs $130,000, much less than the cost of setting up a conventional retail outlet (Murray, 1990). A prototype system was placed in a Minneapolis shopping mall (*The Washington Times*, 1989a). The company expected to have 150 stores in place by 1991, yet has met resistance from malls that already contain a conventional music store (Murray, ibid).

The limitations of the system include the fact that the kiosk only stocks 2,000 of the top selling titles, far less than a conventional store. And a customer who is "unsure of a title cannot, for example, whistle a tune and get help in finding what he wants" (Murray, ibid).

Telescan™ Listening Posts

In 1992, Telescan, Inc., developed an in-store listening post designed to boost music sales and reduce returns of unwanted merchandise (Russell, 1992). The interactive kiosk listening stations contain selections from 150 albums—the 100 top-selling pop titles and a few top titles in various specialty categories—in 20 to 30 second "snippets," with up to three songs per album. All major record labels are participating in the system.

The hardware features a CD-ROM drive, a telephone style keypad and headphones, and costs $1,495 per unit. Monthly updates cost $25 per month for the disc, which includes accompanying artwork and liner notes. In July of 1993, Telescan, Inc. announced an arrangement made with *Billboard Magazine* to build a database of the publication to include in its instore kiosk (*Editor and Publisher Magazine*, 1993). The enhanced version will enable users to compare sales data for particular artists.

The i-Station™

Perhaps the most technically (but not mechanically) advanced interactive music kiosk system is the i-Station™, developed by Intouch Group,

Inc. The i-Station can store music, graphics, text and video for over 30,000 albums on its multi-disc CD-ROM system (Ross, 1992). The system uses a UPC code scanner to allow customers to approach the machine with a disc in hand, scan the UPC code from the disc, and preview up to five songs from the album. The system also includes reviews of the album, concert information, cross-reference to other albums by the same artist and similar albums in the same music genre, and allows dispensing of coupons for other products (Miller, 1992). In addition, the customer is asked to rate the songs on a one-to-five scale.

In late 1992, the company placed test machines in three Wherehouse (retail) outlets in San Diego, three in Streetside (St. Louis) and in Tower Records in New York City (Miller, 1992). In addition to serving as a previewing station for record customers, the dual-purpose design of the machine also enables record companies and retailers to compile data on usage of the system and correlate that data with scanner data collected on sales at the cash register (Ross, 1992). Customers are required to obtain a customer identification card, at no charge, before using the system. The card application includes demographic and product interest information and enables the system to build customer profiles based on the kinds of selections a user makes. During the test period, the company compiled a database of nearly 100,000 households from the seven systems. Intouch plans a massive roll-out of the machines to retailers in 1994 (Emerson, 1993). Under the financial plan devised by Intouch, both the store and the record companies fund the system. The retail store rents the kiosks for approximately $300 per month. The record companies must pay $28 annually per store for the inclusion of one new title and twenty catalog (older, previously released) titles (Keel, 1992). For each new album released by a record company during the year, the cost of adding the new title to the system is $28 per store, but includes the addition of twenty more catalog titles.

Limitations of the system include the fact that the product must be identified and located in the store by the consumer before accessing the machine. In the case of out-of-stock albums, the store clerks possess a catalog with the bar codes of most titles, and this UPC code for the particular product can be scanned in from the catalog. While the system does allow cross-referencing by artist, song or title identification based upon lyrics or the artist is restricted to speculation. Confirmation by sampling the music may confirm or deny the customer's assumption. To enhance the song identification capabilities of the system, Intouch arranged with *Billboard Magazine* to include the *Billboard* weekly charts for display on screen (Miller, 1992). The user can browse the charts and listen to samples of the top albums from each chart.

Survey of Record Store Customers

Goals of the Research

The present study was designed to measure kiosk and record listening booth usage by record customers and how information needs are being served through kiosk use and use of store personnel. The study involves retail record stores and measures attitudes toward sales personnel, use of these personnel, and ties these needs to music preferences. Kiosk use is related to information need, demographic characteristics of the consumer, music preferences, product involvement and the desire to preview new music before purchase.

Sample

For the present study, six retail record stores were selected and surveys were conducted on a total of 374 consumers. The study was limited only to stores which contain one of three types of interactive kiosks, the Telescan Source™, the i-Station™ or the MUZE™ system. Four of the stores are located near the West Coast and the other two in the Southeast. The age groups for the sample closely correlate with the known age distribution of record consumers according to the RIAA statistics. Also, consistent with RIAA figures, the gender ratio for the sample was 61 percent male, 39 percent female. The following are some of the more significant findings:

- **Use of (Reliance On) Store Clerks for Assistance in Identifying Recorded Music:**

  More than 44 percent of the respondents rely on sales help to identify a song title on at least a sometimes basis, compared to the less than 30 percent who indicated that they rely on the clerks to identify songs based upon a piece of the lyric. More than 42 percent indicated that they rely on sales clerks for artist identification at least sometimes.

- **Use of Clerks and Perception of Clerks:**

  Significant correlations were consistently found between the measures of knowledgeability of store clerks and use of these clerks for identifying (1) artists, (2) song titles, and (3) songs based upon some of the lyrics. Significance for the relationship of rating store clerks as friendly and use of these clerks for assistance was found only for the measurement of assistance with *song titles.*

- **Kiosk Usage:**

  Thirty-eight percent of the sample have used a record store kiosk. Kiosk use varies by both kiosk type and by store, indicating that there are factors other than type of kiosk which determine popularity and contribute to the rate of kiosk use.

- **Use of Kiosk and Purchase Rate:**

  Kiosk users purchase significantly more CDs and make more visits to the store than non-kiosk users.

- **Kiosk Use and Listening Booth (Station) Use:**

  Listening booth users are more likely to also be kiosk users than are non-users of the booth. Among stores which contain an interactive kiosk, use of the kiosk is more widespread among customers than use of the listening stations.

- **Music Preferences and Use of the Listening Booth and Kiosk:**

  Fans of alternative, rap, club/techno/house and world music are more likely to use a listening booth than fans of other music genres. Also, fans of alternative and rap are more likely to use the kiosk, and fans of country music are less likely to use the kiosk.

- **The Need to Preview New Music Before Purchase:**

  The group of respondents who use the listening booth, and the group of respondents who use the kiosk, rate the importance of "being familiar with most of a new album before buying" higher than do non-users. Therefore, kiosk developers should incorporate music previewing capabilities into kiosk applications.

- **Use of New Technology:**

  People who are more familiar and comfortable with personal computers are more likely to use the kiosk for a greater number of tasks than noncomputer users.

- **Kiosk Use and Demographics:**

  Kiosk users are generally younger than non-users. Significant differences were found for gender: a higher proportion of males use the kiosk than females.

- **Reasons for Using the Kiosk for the First Time:**

  Usage of the kiosk at the present time is based much more upon curiosity than actual need or by recommendation from a store clerk.

- **Services Provided by the Kiosk:**

  Nearly 72 percent rated the kiosk as informative and helpful. For ease of use, more than 79 percent agreed with the statement that the kiosk was very easy to use.

The Bottom Line

Customers report that they are first attracted to the kiosk system out of curiosity, not by the sales clerk recommendation. More efforts should be made to encourage kiosk recommendation by retail sales personnel.

Kiosk companies should cross reference songs by hook, not just title—especially for new music and commonly mistitled songs. Who can tell you what those songs might be? Sales clerks. In other words, know your potential customer's needs down at the store level.

References

Anonymous. 1993. "Telescan, BPI deal." *Editor and Publisher Magazine* (July 31): p. 19.

Anonymous. 1993. "Teen consumers are music to K-Mart's ears: K-Mart Corp's Auburn Hills, Michigan prototype store's Music and Movies department." *Discount Store News* 32/3 (February 1): p. 49.

Anonymous. 1993. "Latest K-Mart prototype pushes limit of discount retailing: K-Mart Corp's prototype store, Auburn Hills, Michigan." *Discount Store News* 32/3 (February 1): p. 29.

Anonymous. 1989a. "Robot on the job in music store." *The Washington Times* (November 22): Section B, p. 8.

Anonymous. 1989b. "Robot store fetches customers' selections." *The Washington Times* (December 8): Section B, p. 7.

Anonymous. 1993. "Digital video technology helps customers preview products on in-store kiosks." *Business Wire* (June 28).

Anonymous. 1990. "CD kiosk tests retail appeal of robotics: robot music store brings factory technology to shopping mall." *Chain Store Age Executive* (April): pp. 60–62.

Anonymous. 1992. "Nontraditional POS." *Chain Store Age Executive* (July): pp. 14–15.

Bredin, Alice. 1993. "Touch-screen technology handles credit functions: Mervyn's tests kiosks." *Stores* (March): p. 36.

Chandler, B. 1992. "Multimedia" multifaceted retail tool." *Discount Merchandiser*, 32(10): p. 40.

Crump, Constance. 1993. "K-Mart kiosks help, welcome shoppers." *Crains Detroit Business* 8/46 (November 16): Section 1, p. 28.

DeNitto, E. 1993. "Brave new world for in-store media," *Advertising Age* (November 1): p. 52.

Emerson, Jim. 1993. "Intouch groups complete testing of interactive multimedia kiosk." *DM News* 15/19: p. 6.

Fox, William. 1989. "Robot sells compact discs." United Press International (November 20).

Greenleaf, Vicki D. 1993a. "MusicSource U.S.A., Inc., in final stages to complete joint venture agreement to provide 100 kiosks and services to China." *Business Wire* (December 3).

———. 1993b. "MusicSource U.S.A., Inc., holds annual shareholders' meeting, announces extensive catalog database updates." (Company press release).

Higgins, S. 1993. "Executive update: computers and automation." *Investor's Business Daily* (September 29): p. 3.

Hume, Scott. 1992. "Retailers go interactive: Blockbuster kiosks hype films, gather data." *Advertising Age* (February 24): p. 29.

Jaffe, Larry. 1993. "Record store kiosk helps in customer service and tracking." *Direct Marketing News* (October 25): p. 2.

Keel, Beverly. 1992. "Computer could hike disc sales." *Nashville Banner:* Section D, p. 1.

Leinfuss, Emily. 1993. "Music-loving duo creates inquiry kiosk that's selling albums in record stores." *MUZE, Inc. Computer Pictures* 11/5 (September): Section S, p. 13.

McGowan, Chris. 1993. "'VideoHound' bow-wows on CD-ROM: potential seen for resource, promo use." *Billboard* (September 25): p. 75.

Miller, Trudi. 1992. "Intouch i.stations to use Billboard charts." *Billboard* (October 31): p. 8.

Muldoon, Katie. 1985. "The brave new world of interactive kiosks." *Direct Marketing News* (March 15): pp. 22–24.

Murray, Chuck. 1990. "Roboclerk in tune with service industry." *Chicago Tribune* (May 28): Business, p. 1.

Pemberton, H. 1993. "Retail kiosk favors CD-ROM, PICS: Preview contract with Horizons Technology, Inc., kiosks for previewing audio and video products." *Laserdisk Professional* 6/6 (November): p. 212.

Reilly, Patrick M. 1993. "Music stores grow larger and livelier, adding previewing posts, apparel, pizza." *The Wall Street Journal* (June 18): Section B, p. 1.

Recording Industry Association of America. "Industry yearly sales statistics, 1993."

Ross, David M. 1992. "Try before you buy—in-store music preview system." *Music Row* (December 23): p. 1.

Schwartz, Evan I. 1992. "The kiosks are coming, the kiosks are coming." *Business Week* (June 22): p. 122.

Silverman, David. 1989. "Name that tune: campaign to back-announce songs hopes for some record success." *Chicago Tribune* (March 4): p. 2.

Weiss. 1995. "Multimedia hits the streets." *New Media* (February).

Wiesendanger, Betsy. 1991. "Kiosks: automated wonder or lead balloon?" *Sales and Marketing Management* (August): pp. 40–43.

Marketing and Selling High-Tech Products

The Cobbler's Children

John V. Crosby

John V. Crosby is publisher of *Turning Points*, a monthly forecast of the U.S. economy. The publication, now in its twenty-seventh year, is one of the fifty primary contributors to The Blue Chip Economic Indicators. His thirty-year career as a senior executive in the semiconductor and micro-electronics industries included responsibility for design engineering, product management, operations, software development, and sales/marketing management at both the domestic and international levels. He is author of the forthcoming *Managing the Big Sale: A Relational Approach to Marketing Strategy, Tactics and Selling* (NTC Business Books).

Today, about forty thousand companies in the United States manufacture or develop a mind-boggling array of ingenious and sophisticated high-technology products ranging from air-to-air missiles to metal oxide semiconductors to Z-marker beacons. Most of these companies have invested heavily in the technologies needed to produce their products. Ironically, however, their decision to purchase a new PC is often driven by a more mundane need, such as the hiring of a single, new employee or the need for one specific capability, such as e-mail, spreadsheet or word processing. Like the cobbler's children, these high-tech companies tend not to use their own technologies to better serve the needs of their internal corporate "family."

Few companies, for example, have a vision of how current information technology can be applied to improve their internal business practices and operations. It's true that many companies are purchasing notebook and laptop computers for their salespeople and that some companies are even using EDI (electronic data interchange) to reduce paperwork, lower inventories, and shorten the order entry cycle. Few, however, are looking to see how their various business processes can be tied together electronically to increase the quality and speed of information flow between strategic marketing, tactical marketing, and sales. While these statements apply to the entire range of products and businesses, I will focus on products and services requiring a complex sale, where the need is indisputable and the payback can be enormous.

The Complex Sale

The complex sale differs from other types of sales in several respects. It often involves technologies and concepts that are new to the customer and invariably involves several decision makers and multiple groups of people in the buying decision. These different decision makers and groups often have differing needs and wants and often go about decision making in very different ways; e.g., sales vs. accounting; engineering vs. customer service. Because of these differences, a complex sale usually requires several different sales presentations to different levels of the organization before the sale is closed. The aftersale service of such products also differs from the aftersale service of products for which there is a single decision maker. Preparing for, supporting, and following up the complex sale requires a lot of interaction between and among the strategic marketing, tactical marketing, and salespeople.

Marketing and Sales as a Relational Process

The terms *marketing* and *sales* are often used interchangeably, but they are not the same. Marketing involves the identification, planning, and development of served markets, definition of major product lines, analysis of major competitors and positioning of product lines in their respective markets. Sales, on the other hand, involves direct customer contact—calling on and qualifying the target accounts, developing the accounts, closing the many sales opportunities and taking the lead in aftersales service.

Success in defining markets, developing the products, identifying and qualifying the prospective accounts, and closing each of the many sales opportunities emerging within targeted accounts requires extensive collaboration between marketing and sales. We think that the functions of strategic marketing, tactical marketing and sales are much more powerful and more readily understood when approached relationally and conducted within the context of the account development cycle (discussed later). The account development cycle provides a useful macrostructure for discussions about the different roles and responsibilities of marketing and sales and the flow of information in, between, and among them.

Both marketing and sales interact with and get information about customers, whose needs and requirements define the ability to "do business" and make sales. Marketing (both strategic and tactical) tends to get its information on an aggregate, or "big picture," level. This parallels marketing's primary responsibility for delivering overall market share and profitability.

Sales, on the other hand, tends to be more "here and now." The primary role of sales is to sell existing products and services at a level of price, quality, and performance acceptable to customers. Information generated by the sales force tends to be oriented to these immediate needs.

Each of these operations contains part of the total "customer picture," and how they relate (and "interact") is critical. When each of these roles is symmetrical—is "independent" and generates information only for its own needs—the chances for customer dissatisfaction are high. This symmetry or independence also amplifies confusion and conflict within the organization. When players operate relationally—sharing information that they generate with others and assimilating information generated by others receive into their operations—a broader perspective of organization needs, and success, and customer satisfac-tion results.

When viewed relationally, the question of what constitutes a satis-fied customer or a successful marketing and sales organization shifts away from looking at one or the other function and, instead, focuses on the patterns of interaction that take place between the customers, sales, and marketing. Exhibit 4.1 illustrates this relational nature.

Implicit in a relational diagram is the notion of relationships. They are the building blocks of success. When strong and effective relation-ships are in place, ideas and differences of opinion that might other-wise be viewed as competitive and divisive are transformed into advan-tages and opportunities through dialogue and understanding. Mem-bers of organizations that take the time to create a climate wherein effective relationships can be constructed and nurtured are much more likely to weather adversity and change than those who do not. Success-ful interdependence occurs when marketing is dependent on sales and the customer; sales is dependent on marketing and the customer; and the customer is dependent on both marketing and sales. Each function acts upon and is, in turn, acted upon by the others in recursive patterns of "interaction." Effective communications are key.

EXHIBIT 4.1 Relational Diagram of Marketing and Sales

The Account Development Cycle

If we expand the conceptual diagram in Exhibit 4.1 to encompass the wider context of business development, we come up with the *account development cycle* (Exhibit 4.2) The cycle moves from strategic planning to market development to target account development to target account service and expansion and back to strategic planning. Each of the steps in the cycle has its own respective pattern with feedforward and feedback loops to the other steps in the cycle. The focus here is to illustrate how these various functions can be tied together electronically in a manner that some people are calling *interactive marketing.*

Seminars, Trade Shows, Print Media—and the Cobbler's Children

The tale of the cobbler and his shoeless children serves as an interesting metaphor for describing the tools and technologies used in the marketing and sale of high-technology products and services. Most marketing people in high-tech companies tend to be trained as engi-

EXHIBIT 4.2 The Account Development Cycle

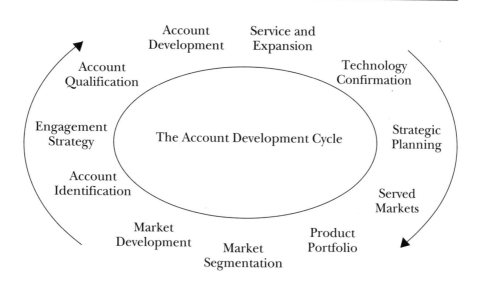

neers first and as marketers second. As engineers, they spend most of their time developing and refining technically sophisticated products and less time developing the processes by which their products are marketed, sold, and serviced. For the most part, they believe that the buying decision is a rational process and that the customer will make the "right" decision if the features of their products are presented clearly. Most high-tech companies interact with their marketplace with a "lead-generation" model they've been using for years.

To get the word out about their products and services, high-tech companies host technical seminars, participate in trade shows, and advertise in specific trade magazines. These media are oriented to emphasizing the technical features of the company's latest products. The purpose of this type of advertising is to generate sales leads, which are then followed up by the sales force.

The vehicle used most commonly for these sales leads is the "bingo" card. These *reader service cards* are post-card-size requests for more information. In the case of seminars and trade shows, they are distributed to the attendees. In the case of magazines, they are included in the issue. They are used to request a reprint of an article or to request additional information about your company, your products, and your services. It's scary, but this is the primary interface between many high-tech companies and their prospective customers!

The bingo cards contain some qualifying information that the reader (or requester) fills out at the time of the request. Information is usually limited to the type of business in which the company is engaged, organization function, number of employees, and buying plans for the future. These reader cards are usually routed to a third-party literature fulfillment house where, several weeks later, the requested information is sent to the requester. The literature fulfillment house may also qualify the leads further and forward them to the company's sales organization. Qualification at this level usually consists of a telemarketing call to the requester with additional questions about their title, job responsibility, decision-making authority, budget level, planned application, and projected timeline. All good information but starting to get a little cold by now.

The qualified leads are then delivered by U.S. mail to the company's sales department. It's not uncommon for these leads (which are already several weeks old) to languish in someone's in-basket until they determine that a large enough number has accumulated to warrant packing them up and shipping them, once again, via U.S. mail to the responsible sales manager. The sales manager is then expected to distribute the leads to the appropriate sales person for them to act upon. What's wrong with this picture?

To begin with, the sales manager usually doesn't know, in advance, that the leads are coming and, when they arrive, often has no idea of what ad or show generated them or when they were generated. Besides that, anywhere from several weeks to several months may have elapsed since the original request was made and no self-respecting sales person is going to walk into that buzzsaw. As a consequence, they are usually not acted upon! Now, let's speculate how the process could be improved using the account development cycle as a model and current information technology.

Marketing and Sales On-Line

First, you have to have some basic hardware and software capability. If you have yet to purchase any computers, we recommend that you provide your marketing and sales people with notebook or laptop computers equipped with high-speed modems (28.8 Kbps minimum) and loaded with standard software packages such as Microsoft Office or Lotus SmartSuite. Include a software product like LapLink to enable people to synchronize their desktop files with their notebook files as well as to provide simple remote file-sharing resources. Simple contact management capability exists within Office and SmartSuite or, as we recommend, you can move initially to something like Lotus Notes. Notes is a powerful groupware product that is very flexible and will grow with you as your company grows.

Strategic Marketing

Using the relational model mentioned previously, strategic marketing can take the lead in overall business planning and define the markets to be served and the products for each. This means reviewing each of the markets served, analyzing the product portfolio, and understanding the buying decisions. Review your marketing communications or positioning strategy and verify that the information channels selected are still valid. This includes conducting any marketing research that may be required. Make this information available to sales people on your network. Pattern the structure of your information after some of the better Web Pages on the Internet.

Strategic marketing should then prepare and publish a long-term forecast. This forecast is based on certain projected share-of-market goals being realized, which then becomes the initial forecast by market segment and product line that tactical marketing (i.e., marketing communications) and operations can use for planning. This should be posted and maintained on the internal network and accessed freely by tactical marketing as they take on the task of market development. Tactical marketing then prepares a short-term operating forecast which then becomes the basis for the monthly, quarterly, and annual revenue forecast. Typically, the short-term forecast is updated monthly and the long-term forecast is updated semi-annually. These marketing forecasts serve as the planning basis for the business. The mere fact that the forecast is posted to the network eliminates costly time delays and unnecessary work when updated.

Tactical Marketing

While strategic marketing is responsible for the definition of served markets and the definition of broad product lines, tactical marketing is responsible for market development and the development of specific products. When tactical marketing is responsible for specific product development, they are the ones most qualified to identify prospective buyers. Tactical marketing can utilize the many electronic databases available to identify prospective target accounts. The variety of commercial databases accessed on-line or from local CD-ROM's generally provide a rich source of information about the target accounts. With tactical marketing screening the tens of thousands of companies to produce a short list of prospective accounts by sales territory, an incredible amount of time and money is saved. Tactical marketing also can use their knowledge of the prospective accounts, as well as the probability of certain product applications emerging within the accounts, to construct a sales kit and an engagement strategy for use by the sales force.

The sales kit contains all the necessary information for the sales person to use when calling on, qualifying, and developing the account. The sales kit is all electronic and is also distributed electronically. Using standard presentation software in Office or SmartSuite, multiple slide presentations can be crafted and assembled to support different types of sales presentations. Sample spreadsheets can be embedded and actual photographs scanned in if desired. For example, when presenting to senior management, you want your sales people to emphasize those factors that are important to management which are typically not the same factors that are important to their engineers. However, the messages are otherwise consistent at all levels of the organization.

Marketing can also use the same materials in their training of the sales force. The sales kit contains copies of related articles, white papers, product data sheets, testimonials, and competitive profiles. The sales kits are posted to the network and are downloaded by the sales people as needed. With prospective customers defined, sales kits constructed and engagement strategies defined, the shotgun approach to advertising can be replaced with narrowly focused efforts. All information can be distributed electronically in a very short period of time.

If you don't want to adopt the account development model and find that you still want to continue to use trade shows and print advertising, then shop for a literature fulfillment house that will work with you to post the bingo cards electronically to your network. From there, the cards can be routed directly to the sales person's notebook computer including a copy of the ad and a reference to the source and date. A copy can also be forwarded to the responsible marketing person. This alone shaves weeks off the lead time and eliminates unnecessary handling.

Sales

Sales people are highly skilled individuals with limited time and resources. They are expert in calling on customers, developing relationships, and using those relationships to help them identify, qualify, and develop each of the many specific opportunities emerging at the account. Unfortunately, they are often given tasks that decrease their face-to-face selling time and contribute nonproductively to their workload. To help lighten their load and increase available selling time, please don't ask them to prospect or to forecast unconstrained demand for their territory. It's a waste of their time.

What is important, within the account development model, is for the sales people to use the short list of prospective accounts to identify and track each of the emerging opportunities through their respective selling cycles. These efforts produce the rich data required by marketing for them to gauge the success of their strategy. With the data available electronically and on the network, different users can structure and review the information in any manner they desire. For example, strategic marketing might be interested in a top-down analysis by market segment and major product line. Tactical marketing, on the other hand, might be interested in a bottom-up analysis of individual products by specific customer. Both types of analyses are appropriate. With the basic data available electronically, the sales person doesn't have to spend extra time putting different analyses together. Each user can access the data and generate analyses specific to his or her needs. As each sales person tracks opportunities, using suitable software, he or she can develop a complete account history that can then be accessed for regularly scheduled account reviews.

The purpose of the account review is to conduct a business won/ business lost analysis to verify that your strategic assumptions and tactical plans are still on track. Detailed account reviews can be held quarterly and attended by strategic marketing, tactical marketing, and sales. Sales chairs the reviews, and each salesperson is asked to review each of the accounts. These reviews can be used to validate the assumptions and effectiveness of the sales kits, training, and engagement strategy. Are we on-track or off-track? Do we know why we're winning or why we're losing the business? Each sales person uses the notebook computers to step through each account. Hard copies are not made. The process uses an overhead projector that projects directly from the computer.

The Present and Future

Most companies active in business-to-business marketing and sales are almost certain to have computers and the ability to go on-line. For a modest investment, you can experiment with fax-on-demand, bulletin board systems, and the Internet. The Internet offers a host (pun intended) of options. One commercial access provider, for example, offers—for less than $20 per month—e-mail, World Wide Web (WWW), File Transfer Protocol (FTP), Telnet, Gopher, Usenet News, and Internet Relay Chat (IRC). What's amazing is even the information on how to use the Net is on the Internet and it's free!

The e-mail capability permits you to communicate with your customers even if you don't have an e-mail server. If you don't like the regular e-mail, you can establish a subscribed list (moderated or unmoderated) using Listserv or Majordomo. E-mail is great for sending out new product announcements, alerts, or for conducting electronic focus groups. With subscribed lists, subscribers can be pre-screened or qualified, so the potential fit between topic and subscriber is maximized.

The WWW is one of the hottest new areas and provides you the opportunity to experiment with ways in which you can merchandise your company. The Web can also provide pointers to more specific information. It's really advertising using interactive electronic media and is being touted as a replacement for CD-ROM's.

FTP enables you to transfer files to and from remote computers. Security is established by the host computer and the scope of your privileges is defined by your authorization level. FTP opens up all sorts of possibilities in communicating with customers. For example, simple electronic forms can be constructed to capture critical information like inventories and orders. This can be done without the high cost and rigid structure of EDI (electronic data interchange).

Gopher is an Internet navigation tool. It allows you to find and retrieve information using a structured hierarchy of menus and files. The Gopher client (your computer) connects to a Gopher Server somewhere in the world depending on the topic of interest. Gopher uses Telnet to connect to other remote applications.

Usenet News is great! It's the electronic equivalent of a news clipping service and a great way to keep track of what's happening in your industry and in the world. You can select the type of news in which you are interested from a wide variety of choices. Throughout the day, news items are posted to the news categories you selected and made available to you when you log in. You can read, copy, and print the articles as you wish.

The last resource, IRC, is still a little "clunky," but it allows you to carry on an interactive conversation between two or more users. While not a secure means of communicating, it does offer some interesting possibilities for future discussion groups or on-line marketing research. The downside is that it's slow and open to inquiring eyes.

When we move to the account development model, we generate even more options. When tactical marketing takes responsibility for the identification of prospective accounts, your company automatically picks up a 15 to 20 percent increase in available selling time because you no longer require your field sales people to prospect. Add to that the advantage of knowing who the account is and what's being targeted and you will probably pick up another 5 to 10 percent.

With nothing more than notebook computers and access to the Internet, sales kits can be constructed and distributed electronically, thereby standardizing sales presentations and eliminating the need for the sales people to prepare their own presentations. Ahh! No more all-nighters for the sales people.

Product data sheets can be posted to the Net with each customer downloading and printing as many copies as needed. With this concept, the huge inventories of outdated data sheets that often lie around for months, is eliminated as is the cost of printing them to begin with. With all the recent hype about CD-ROM's, we think the better way to go is to put your product catalog and data sheets on the Net and let interested parties access them directly. This also prevents your customers' inadvertent use of an outdated version of the CD.

Lastly, when you eliminate the monthly chore of the salesperson generating a detailed forecast by part number by customer by month for the next six or twelve months, you've made a friend for life. Sales people hate to generate forecasts. When you track each opportunity through its selling cycle, you generate the forecast automatically!

5

The New Disk-Based Marketing Communications Tools

Guidelines for Creating Powerful Electronic Catalogs and Presentations

Vic Cherubini

Vic Cherubini is founder and president of the E.P.I.C. Software Group, Inc., a specialized advertising agency that develops computer-generated sales presentations for its clients. Mr. Cherubini has spent over 15 years in industrial sales and marketing.

Sales and marketing professionals are now exploring the use of the computer as a new sales medium. It is estimated that well over 100 million computers are being used worldwide. The application of computer technology continues to spread into areas not traditionally thought of as computer territory. Marketing professionals are using the interactive nature of computers to involve prospects in their message. If used intelligently, the computer can demonstrate product information in ways never before possible with traditional media like print or video.

Why have sales and marketing lagged behind other fields when it comes to utilizing high-tech tools? Because using the computer as an air-cooled calculator for automating spreadsheets is far more intuitive than using it to sell your products or services.

The idea of using the computer as a sales tool is new to most people. For many companies, the sales department represents the last major business area to be given computer support. But why? Consider for a minute that no other department has such a strong potential to affect a company's bottom line. Although increasing productivity in other areas may result in reduce costs, an increase in sales productivity will translate to an increase in revenues.

When sales and marketing managers are asked, "How do you intend to integrate electronic media into your direct marketing strategy for the next one to five years?", the response is often silence. Most managers feel that they should be doing something, but are unsure about how to effectively incorporate new media technologies into their marketing plans.

The question is particularly relevant to those in database marketing. Today, market is experiencing a revolution. Mass marketing is dead, and to be successful, a company must tailor its message to a select target audience. Database marketing provides a support structure for direct marketing campaigns centered around computer powered demonstrations.

While many new media technologies are available to sales and marketing people, this chapter will focus on three that are widely used by industries to call attention to their products and services. They are:

- Disk-Based Ads
- Electronic Catalogs
- Fax-on-Demand

It should be noted that the following observations are presented from the viewpoint of a practitioner, not as a scientific approach to the subject.

Disk-based Ads

When faced with communicating a message, most sales and marketing professionals will turn to traditional mediums such as print, television and direct mail. With the explosive growth of personal computers, a powerful new medium can now be considered, *disk-based advertising*.

What is a disk-based ad? Imagine for a moment that you are the marketing manager of a company manufacturing industrial valves. You have a great new product with a unique design and your mission is to get your target market—piping engineers—to notice, specify, and buy your product. You must find the most direct route through the scores of competitors' ads to reach your target audience.

You consider running a print ad in the trade publications, but the ad will most likely get lost in the crowd. Even a full page ad wouldn't be enough to thoroughly explain the benefits of your new "pressure release port." The ad would need to be broad because you have no way of focusing on the specific need of an individual customer.

You might consider producing a video tape of the valve in action. Although video tape players are simple to use, unlike a computer, they may not be sitting, readily available, on your prospect's desk. Additionally, the video does not involve the viewer in the presentation, and cannot print what it displays. It is "static" in that the prospect watches it passively in a linear fashion. No interaction is required, and it assumes that everyone learns at the same rate.

Contrast those traditional methods with a disk-based ad. A single floppy disk can hold the equivalent of several hundred pages of information. The program can include graphics and sound to illustrate how the valve works. The disk-based ad will be designed so the prospect can "open" the valve (using the up arrow key). The prospect watches as water enters the valve. The sound of water is added to enhance the effect.

To really add value, an intelligent selection guide may be built into the program that allows an engineer to pick the best valve configuration for a given application. With one keystroke the valve spec can be transferred electronically to their CAD program and be used in a specific project design. Another keystroke prints the valve along with detailed technical specifications. Disk-based advertising saves the company printing and distribution costs while providing the client with specific information needed to make an informed decision.

When should a company consider using a disk-based ad? Ask yourself these questions. If you answer yes to all, a disk-based ad should be on your list.

- Does your sales information change frequently?

- Does your sales pitch need to be customized for each prospect?

- Does your target market have easy access to computers?

- Do you need a way to differentiate yourself from the competition?

Interactive Electronic Catalogs

Since the days of Gutenberg, anyone faced with producing a printed catalog knows the problem. No sooner than the ink dries, something changes. The information in your new catalog is outdated even before you have a chance to put it in the mail. Reprinting is out of the question, so you learn to live with the limitations. Every company has a horror story about a misprinted catalog or brochure. Just think of the last catalog you printed. Wouldn't you love the flexibility to be able to go back and make "just one more change"? In the world of database marketing, static information is the exception and change is the rule. Keeping a printed catalog up-to-date is an ongoing battle. Consider a high-tech alternative . . . the interactive electronic catalog.

Imagine placing your entire printed catalogue on a single floppy disk. Specification sheets, photographs, order forms, reference materials, and many of the items you have in that 3-ring binder will fit on a diskette. Using the latest advances in compression technology, an amount of information can fit on a 3.5" high density disk. Now, when something in your catalog changes, it is simply a matter of overwriting the old information with the new. From that point on, your catalog is current. Does this mean that every time you update the information on your interactive electronic catalog you have to send out a new disk? No. Because your new catalog is in a digital format, you can send it by modem anywhere in the world for the price of a phone call.

If you had your digital catalog on an electronic Bulletin Board System (BBS), any of your customers could call in and "download" the latest catalog information whenever they want. Although it may sound like a page out of Flash Gordon, many companies are taking advantage of this technology to boost sales.

If you're looking for a way to provide high-quality information and reduce production and distribution costs, an electronic catalog might be the answer. The good news is that the prices of electronic catalogs have dropped over the past two years. Nowadays, an interactive electronic catalog may cost less than its printed predecessor and will definitely reduce expenditures when it comes time to update catalog information.

Common Applications of Interactive Electronic Catalogs

- *Product Guide*—Help your customers determine which products or services are best suited for their specific needs. By linking in an Expert System (a software program that acts like an "expert") you can help a customer select the best product for a specific application.

- *Diagnostic Guide*—The electronic catalog can help your customers determine the cause of a problem, then recommend a solution.

- *Configuration Guide*—Let the catalog help your customer place an order that is complete. When one item is ordered, the program will automatically remind the customer about companion items.

- *Resource Tool*—Provide your customer with a glossary of industry terms, a conversion calculator, or any other useful tools that will help them with their work. Every time they refer to the program, your company's name will be prominently displayed on the screen.

Much of the sales and technical literature an engineer receives is quickly discarded. The environmental and economic impact over time, can be significant. Few people will throw away a diskette, since it can be immediately and easily recycled.

The Evolution of Electronic Catalogs and Disk-based Presentations

In the beginning . . .

For many years disk-based presentations have been used by software companies to market and sell their programs. A demo disk allows a potential customer to experience a software program prior to making a purchase. These software companies used the computer as a natural platform on which to demonstrate their offerings.

With the introduction and widespread acceptance of the IBM PC in the early 1980s, computers began appearing on the desks of professionals outside of data processing departments. It is estimated that over 100 million computers are now in use and that more than two-thirds of all white-collar professionals use them in their work.

Computing power became more affordable to large market segments. This trend continued to increase as computers became easier to use and costs dropped. It was not long before business executives realized the power of this device for sales and marketing applications. Using a floppy disk to communicate information is now a powerful tool for those businesses with customers that have access to personal computers. A disk can hold hundreds of pages of sales and technical information. Unlike printed sales technical literature, which may quickly become dated, digital information can be easily updated or completely overwritten. Sound, animation, and attractive graphics can be used to entertain while informing. Interaction involves the viewer in the presentation, creating a lasting impression. The advantages of disk-based catalogs and sales tools have become too important to ignore.

For companies with very large volumes of sales and technical data, the CD-ROM disk (Compact Disk-Read Only Memory) is proving to be a viable alternative. A single compact disk can contain the equivalent of 250,000 printed pages.

Once a CD-ROM disk is pressed (mastered), the information on it cannot be changed. Even so, the cost of creating, duplicating and distributing a master disk makes CD-ROMs a feasible alternative to traditional methods. It is estimated that only 4 to 7 percent of computers in the current marketplace have CD-ROM drives installed. As more computers come equipped with CD-ROM drives, the proliferation of electronic catalogs and disk-based ads will increase.

Computers will increase in power and functionality as will interactive disk-based sales and technical presentations. Multimedia catalogs that integrate text, graphics, video and audio components in one system will become a highly effective way to sell. The use of interactive electronic catalogs will move from being interesting curiosities to mainstream sales and marketing tools by the turn of the century.

Case Study—Shell Chemical Company

Shell Chemical Company produces a wide variety of Kraton Polymer products used by chemists to manufacture pressure sensitive tapes, sealants and adhesives. In 1993, Shell was faced with finding a way to provide hundreds of pages of sales and technical data to the adhesive chemists it serves.

Shell's marketing department, led by Bruce Toig, was looking for an alternative to traditional printed sales literature. They needed an effective way to distribute the large amounts of sales and technical data that comprised the line. Toig said: "The computer turned out to be the perfect medium to bring together elements of our printed sales literature, video, and presentation graphics." Packaged in an attractive mailer, the single floppy disk contains an interactive computer program designed to promote the company's line of elastomers.

The program, called SAGE (Shell Adhesive Guide for Everyone), works by simply loading the disk into an IBM-compatible computer and typing the word SAGE. Colorful graphics, animation, and sound are used to inform and entertain a chemist seeking information. All technical documents can be quickly printed if a hard copy of the information is needed.

The main advantage of the program is that it contains a lot more than just technical information. One part of the program contains a powerful Adhesive Design Guide. The user can simply enter the design parameters they'd like the adhesive to have, and the computer immediately calculates the results. Lab experiments that may take weeks to perform can now be accomplished in seconds.

Other sections of the program contain video animation of KRATON

Polymer molecules in action pulled directly from a Shell educational video. Incorporating this video segment in the program enables a new user to step through the production process at the molecular level. Shell also included an entertaining, information packed game in the program. The game, the SAGE Challenge, pits the skill of the user against the computer on industry specific questions.

The SAGE program was developed to provide Shell with an alternative to printed sales literature. "When you print the traditional catalog and the information changes, you can be stuck with reprinting and disposing of the old catalog," said Toig. With electronic sales literature, you simply copy over the old file with the new information. Another key advantage of Electronic Catalogs is that they can be sent anywhere in the world via modem for the price of a phone call.

Shell Chemical Company distributes the program to its key customers by direct mail and leaves a copy for prospects to review after a sales call. The Shell sales reps also have the SAGE program loaded on their notebook computers and use it to give interactive sales presentations and demonstrations at trade shows. "We have included a survey in the program for users to complete and return to Shell," states Toig. "This will help us determine what new features we may wish to add to the next version of the SAGE electronic catalog ."

A Summary of Features and Benefits

Why are vendors turning to the computer to sell? The estimated cost of a business-to-business field sales call now exceeds $275. The average technical person receives over 90 pounds of direct mail each year. With these figures, sales and marketing managers are challenged to find alternative, innovative methods of delivering their message and increasing customer awareness.

Economical

While the cost of a four-color printed catalog in a three-ring binder may exceed $50, the same information can be placed on a floppy disk for a much lower cost. Mailing the disk is also considerably more economical than the expense of sending a printed catalog.

EXHIBIT 5.1 Seven Steps to Creating a Disk-Based Presentation

Step	Action Required	Time
1 Project Definition	Identify and quantify goals and objectives. Determine users' needs, including customers.	Week 1
2 Prototype Design/ Development	Create project team to determine how to maximize company image. Create a flow chart based on needs. Produce storyboard showing design and action. Present to management for approval.	Week 3
3 Produce Rapid Prototype	Create a skeletal structure for review. The most difficult and intensive part of program.	Week 5
4 Produce an Alpha Version	At this stage the program has been thoroughly tested and debugged. Only minor changes should be needed. Production of collateral materials should begin.	Week 12
5 Presentation of Master	Master presented for sign-off. The disk should be scanned for viruses and put through a series of quality control tests prior to sign-off.	Week 14
6 Duplication/ Distribution	Disks are duplicated and distributed. Follow-up on user response begins immediately.	Week 16
7 Maintenance/ Updates	Changes made on ongoing basis	Ongoing

EXHIBIT 5.2 Additional Costs Associated with Disk-Based Presentations

Budget Item	Description
Media Style	Disks can be provided in a number of formats, from black and white to color or silk-screened or with photography.
Packaging	Options range from a plain package to an elaborate mailing package that includes sales literature.
Software Support/ Fulfillment	This can be handled internally or outsourced.
Program Maintenance	Well-designed programs include the ability to update information easily.
Training	Materials are—or should be—designed to be used by novices. Since the program will go unused if the salesperson fears being embarrassed in front of a client, training should be easy to implement and complete.

Easy to Update

If information on a printed piece of sales literature changes or is incorrect, in most cases the only practical option is to reprint the entire piece. For product lines that are rapidly evolving, having the information in an electronic format allows for immediate changes. With an interactive disk-based catalog there is never any reason to distribute obsolete information.

Interaction

Printed sales literature is static and involves no interaction on the part of the reader. Computerized sales presentations require the user to become involved in the demonstration.

Calculations

The promotion of a product that requires calculations can be enhanced by including a number-crunching feature in the program. Error checking can also be included to ensure that correct values are entered.

Animation/Sound

Colorful animation and sound can also be included to increase the impact of the demonstration.

Unique Format

Distributing a presentation on a floppy disk enables a vendor to differentiate their company from the competition. Imagine getting a floppy disk at a trade show. Although you may return from the show with a large amount of printed material, the disk will surely get more post show consideration than most of the printed literature.

Corporate Image

A skillfully created disk-based catalog gives vendors a high-tech image while providing its sales people with a powerful tool. It also builds loyalty by satisfying customers' needs for accurate, easy-to-find information.

Consistent

The computer can help even the best salesperson improve the quality of a sales call. After demonstrating a product or service on the computer, the sales professional can leave the disk behind for further review. Sharing knowledge and expertise enables customers to feel more confident in their buying decisions and leads to repeat purchases.

Reusable

Floppy disks are the ultimate recyclable resource. Unlike printed information which requires the use and eventual disposal of valuable resources, new information can be repeatedly written over old data.

Increased Retention

Studies show that people retain 20 percent of the information they hear, 40 percent of what they see, and 60 to 70 percent of the information they interact with. Since individuals learn at different rates, computerized sales presentations make excellent training tools. Psychologists have determined that the more senses you involve in a learning experience, the greater the levels of retention.

Electronic Transfer

By using a modem, an electronic catalog can be transferred over the telephone lines for the price of a phone call. For companies with overseas operations, this can represent large savings in courier costs. Linking your firm electronically to the companies you serve may create a strategic advantage that will be difficult for your competitors to overcome.

The age of computerized sales literature is upon us. While we are flooded with information, the computer can be used as a filter to collect only the information we need. Using tools like expert systems, animation, and sound will not only ensure a more informed purchase, but will make the product selection process more enjoyable.

Fax-On-Demand

Virtually unheard of ten years ago, the fax machine has taken the business world by storm. While even in the smallest companies, the fax has become the de facto standard of instant communications, it's about to become even more important with the introduction of a new technology called, "Fax-on-Demand."

Fax-on-Demand provides a customer with the information needed to make a buying decision, 24 hours a day, 7 days a week. It will have a profound effect on the way sales and technical information is communicated by database marketers. Let's contrast the way business is conducted today versus the possibilities with Fax-on-Demand.

Advertising appearing in trade journals usually includes a "reader response number" at the bottom of the ad. If you want additional information about a product, you circle that ad's number on the bingo card. The card is sent back to the magazine, combined with other responses for the same information and returned to the manufacturer for follow-up. Unfortunately, it may be weeks before the requested information gets back to the customer.

In contrast, Fax-on-Demand, provides an immediate response to a customer's information request. The magazine ad now contains a phone number to call and a product information number. Your knowledge-hungry customers call your Fax-on-Demand system, enter the number in the ad, and the information is immediately delivered.

Implementing Fax-on-Demand

There are two ways to implement Fax-on-Demand:

1. **Use a Fax-on-Demand service bureau.** A host of companies are providing Fax-on-Demand services, and most applications can be installed in less than a day. Most services charge an initial set-up fee and bill by the minute for access to the system. Set-up charges vary with the size of the application, but typically range from $500 to $3,000. The cost to access the system ranges from $.30 to $.35/minute. A page of text with a simple graphic on it will take 45 seconds to transmit and a three page document with a cover sheet will cost the sender about $1.00 to transmit.

2. **Set up your own Fax-on-Demand System.** An in-house Fax-on-Demand system is recommended for those companies that have information that changes often or must remain confidential. Although Fax-on-Demand is an exciting technology, it has a way to go before it becomes "plug and play." Even small systems can be daunting to those who are new to the technology.

A popular way to ensure success is to work with a Fax-on-Demand VAR (Value Added Reseller). VARs specializing in these systems can install the system, load your data, record the voice prompts, and train your people in less than a week. Simple systems can be set up for less than $5,000.

What are some recommended applications for Fax-on-Demand?

- Specification Sheets

- Sales Literature

- Newsletters

- Material Safety Data Sheets
- Article Reprints
- Pricing & Inventory Information
- Media Packets

Suggestions and Conclusions

With over 100 million computers now in use, database marketers may be missing some excellent opportunities if they are not exploring alternative media such as computer powered sales tools. Although it takes time for people to accept and adapt to new technologies, we will soon see the proliferation of CD-ROM catalogs with full-motion video, high-fidelity sound, and software that is transparent to the user. While other advanced technologies like artificial intelligence and virtual reality are on the horizon, marketers need to focus on developing applications that utilize existing technologies.

Extending the Sales Reach

Interactive Technology and Personal Selling

Kenneth V. Henderson, Jr.
Robert C. Greene, Jr.

Kenneth V. Henderson, Jr., is an adjunct Professor of Marketing in the College of Business of Florida State University. He previously served in senior marketing management positions in both the financial and consumer packaged goods industries.

Robert C. Greene, Jr., is an Associate Professor in the University of New Brunswick School of Business. He joined academia after a thirteen-year international marketing career in the computer industry. Bob is also the co-owner of A.E.C. Chadwick, Ltd., a marketing consulting company specializing in business development and strategic alliances in the high-technology, interactive field.

Since when was Nova Scotia a worldwide center of financial information? Since the daily operations of EMX, a Nova Scotia stock brokerage firm, which are based on interactive technology in the form of satellite transmissions, went into effect. Its sales brokers receive signals which contain stock quotations from virtually all the typical sources: the NYSE, NASDAQ, Chicago, Hong Kong, London, and other exchanges worldwide. The firm uses its propriety software to sort through this wealth of information, in real time, and send the relevant numbers to their clients located all over the world. Individual clients are able to base their purchase and sale decisions on up-to-the-minute information. Stock brokers at EMX are practicing the new interactive rules that apply to personal selling.

During the past half century personal selling practices have undergone very positive developments. Personal selling has evolved from an era that emphasized "pushing products" to an era that emphasizes "partnering." Salespeople have grown from "peddlers" to "diagnosticians" who provide solutions to customers' needs and problems. Emerging interactive technology provides salespeople with the tools to build quality partnerships with buyers that are as important as the products they sell.

Marshall Field once said, "The distance between the salesperson and the potential buyer is the most important three feet in business." But interactive technology in use today has stretched that distance to three continents! However, the principle remains the same. Every employee should emphasize customer satisfaction. Salespeople should think of everything they say or do in the context of their long-term, high quality partnership with individual customers. Sales force automation provides specific customer information, identifies potential needs, and suggests possible solutions.

Personal Selling—A Definition

Personal selling is the process of informing customers and persuading them to purchase through direct person-to-person communication in an exchange situation. The key phrase in this definition is "direct person-to-person." Personal selling enables the marketer to personalize and adjust messages according to the immediate feedback of customers.

The New Rules of Selling

Interactive technology is leveling the competitive field, changing customer expectations, and modifying the rules of personal selling. Here are five new rules of personal selling.

1. Customers are better informed about products and options.

Salespeople walk into a new arena when they call on customers. Purchasing managers no longer refer to printed price lists and manuals. They retrieve current information—from their desktop personal computers—to access Internet, Web, and electronic bulletin boards. Further, many companies have turned to a team-buying-center approach where people from different functional areas of the company are involved in the purchase decision. Today salespeople must be able to access a great deal of information quickly and accurately. Laptop computers, modems, faxes, and cellular telephone are commonplace sales tools.

2. Better-qualified prospects are more likely to buy.

Companies can compile databases using sales histories, credit ratings, and other sources to develop ideal customer profiles. Calls on these prospects provide a higher chance of sales success.

3. Salespeople can spend more time selling.

Sales reports, forecasts, prospecting, and many follow-up activities can be automated. Some companies already practice computer-to-computer ordering where a customer can place an order directly through a dedicated telephone line link to a supplier's computer. When salespeople spend more time calling on qualified prospects, they should make more sales.

4. Companies seek partnerships.

Increasingly, companies are seeking long-term relationships with their suppliers. This practice builds a team spirit while it also produces greater efficiencies and cost savings. The relationship is built on service, prompt responses to customer needs, and trust.

5. Interactive technology permits sales Davids to compete with the Goliaths.

One of the major suppliers of Apple computers and software is a thirteen year old who sells through the Internet. Interactive technology brings anonymity where reputation is built entirely on service rather than company size.

When Personal Selling Is a Major Part of the Promotion Mix

When are circumstances appropriate for marketers to emphasize personal selling rather than advertising, sales promotion, or publicity efforts? The answer rests in the fundamental 4Ps elements of the marketing mix, namely, the product, promotion, place, and price.

Personal selling is appropriate when the product is complex, represents a major purchase, or requires a demonstration. Armed with interactive technologies, salespeople have answers to difficult questions at their fingertips and can involve technical people at their home facilities in real-time problem solving activities to satisfy buyers' needs. Perhaps the next major leap in the application of interactive personal selling is represented by virtual reality. Imagine an engineer inspecting machinery in a virtual factory or a buyer test driving a virtual automobile that changes options and models with the touch of a button! Interactive technology can simplify the complex and demonstrate any product the salesperson can imagine.

Personal selling is often needed to "push" a product through the distribution channel. It is especially valuable when channel intermediaries need training. Distance learning techniques can bring the expertise of the supplier company into the classroom of the buyer's company.

Personal selling is also a preferred promotional method when price must be negotiated. With up-to-the-minute information available from interactive sources salespeople can provide adequate margins while remaining competitive.

Finally, personal selling is appropriate when the limited number of buyers do not warrant advertising or mass media promotions. Sales managers find it difficult, if not impossible, to monitor how salespeople deliver their message. Interactive technology overcomes this limitation of personal selling. "Canned" presentations can be personalized automatically.

The Basic Steps Remain

Prior to the advent of interactive technology, the sales cycle was largely personal in terms of a great deal of "face time." The process passed through seven stages: prospecting, preapproach, approach, presentation, handling objections, closing, and follow-up-after-the-sale. Prospecting could involve driving down the highway and checking out the factories with the big smoke stacks. The preapproach might have included asking the receptionist some questions before actually approaching the plant manager. The approach, that magical 90 seconds, might have taken place on the plant floor with the sales representative tracking down the production supervisor. Presentations often took place on the fly. Closing occurred after objections were overcome. If the salespeople were smart, they followed up frequently and regularly.

In this world of interactive technology, the personal touch and the steps in the sales cycle remain unchanged. Note *touch*. It is a good word to describe selling in the 1990s. Touching is personal. "Reach out and touch someone." How can sales representatives utilize "personal touches" through electronic media and interactive technology?

The process begins with prospecting. Companies supplementing their personal selling efforts with interactive database marketing are gathering mountains of information about prospects, crunching it to identify ideal customers, then "drilling" through these layers of data to assemble those characteristics that represent qualified potential customers. Database marketing purifies the prospecting step that will always consist of three components. First, the potential customer must have a need the supplier's product satisfies. Second, the potential buyer must have the resources to acquire the product or service. Third, the potential customer must possess the willingness to buy the product or service. In complex selling environments, salespeople constantly reinforce these three components—the need, resources, and willingness. They telephone voice mail messages, e-mail correspondence, fax information, and use the Internet to "keep in touch" with buyers.

Having the right information at the right place at the right time enables salespeople to react to immediate feedback and respond with proper decisions. The slim laptop has replaced the bulging briefcase.

The salesperson who is prepared to promptly solve problems, quote prices, and schedule deliveries provides good service to buyers. Good service saves time and time is money. Salespeople who are best prepared with up-to-date information required to make the sale usually *do* make the sale. Interactive technology enables salespeople to ensure their preapproach is based on current information and their approach targets the appropriate subjects during the fertile moments when first impressions are formed.

Whether tailored specifically for the individual prospect or straight from the can, presentations are probably the most confusing component of selling. The best presentations simply review agreements previously made. Salespeople who e-mail information to potential buyers, fax possible solutions to their needs, and arrange conference telephone calls between technical personnel in buyer and supplier companies have begun successful presentations before they even plug in their laptops with projector setups.

A sales axiom is that a smooth presentation reflects a disinterested prospect. Frequently an objection is a request for additional information. Consider two salespeople handling the same objection from a potential client. The first salesperson returns to his office, determines the answer, then mails a response to the client. The second salesperson accesses her laptop while she sits in the prospect's office. Within minutes her company e-mails the requested information to the potential buyer. With whom do you think the potential buyer will want to form a partnership? Obviously salespeople who do not remain on the cutting edge of technology will lose in the increasingly competitive marketplace. Closing the sale is not difficult if everything is handled properly throughout the presentation. When the presentation is well organized and delivered well the results are often a successful sale. But the closing of a single sale does not end the process. Servicing the account after the sale is a major determinant of whether long term partnering will develop. Conscientious follow-up is critical to successful personal selling.

Here—and Now

This chapter has addressed how salespeople are assimilating various interactive technologies into their daily lives. How they use e-mail, voice mail, faxes, modems, and laptop computers to enhance their communication efforts with buyers. However, the future of interactive personal selling is bright beyond traditional areas. For example, many companies are turning to sites on Web. They are creating searchable databases that guide customers through the process of selecting products and services. Customers are actually selling products and services to themselves on behalf of host companies!

The future will indivisibly link personal selling to interactive technology. Successful salespeople will actively use these communication advances to develop the strongest relationships with customers by providing the best service.

Public Relations and the Interactive Media

The Practice Is Outpacing Predictions

J. D. Rayburn, II

J. D. (Jay) Rayburn is Associate Professor and Director of Graduate Studies in the School of Communication of Florida State University. His teaching and research interests include public relations, media uses and gratifications, and media effects.

The new media of communication—on-line services, the Internet, CD-ROMs and CD-i, e-mail, interactive multi-media—are creating powerful new distribution channels to reach and influence audiences. This chapter examines these new media and how they will influence the practice of public relations, and how they will be influenced by the public relations professional. In today's environment discussions about integrated communication and seamless communication are commonplace. While the specific application is often debated, the fact of integrated (or at least supported) communication is a reality. And, perhaps, no innovation has fostered this movement more than the new media and the capabilities of information delivery. This chapter outlines how public relations uses the new media to support the overall communication function of an organization.

Public Relations Applications of the New Media

Elsewhere in this book appear various lists of what the authors define as "new media." Rather than repeating this list, what follows are descriptions of how these various media are used by public relations practitioners to reach both internal and external audiences. The primary job of public relations is to build *relationships* between an organization and its publics. In a for-profit organization, these relationships must be in place if marketing efforts are to be successful. In an integrated marketing paradigm, the lines often blur between where public relations ends and marketing begins. What is important, however, is how these two functions support the overall mission of the organization. For public relations, the question becomes one of how best to use the new media to build these necessary relationships.

The Coming of Communicopia

A 1993 article in the *New York Times* heralded the coming of "Communicopia"—an explosion of electronic communications options that will let people not only watch 500 cable channels and browse in electronic shopping malls, but also let the viewer choose camera angles in sporting events, make video phone calls, and even play along with game shows. Each day brings new evidence that Communicopia is not far off. The options mentioned above are already available in some cities in the United States. Construction of what Vice President Al Gore calls the "information superhighway" is well under way. Millions of miles of fiber-optic cable have been laid. An estimated 40 million people are connected to the Internet. That number grows by 1 million monthly. The three largest on-line services—CompuServe, America OnLine, and Prodigy—have over 5 million subscribers, and Microsoft is introducing its own on-line service. And Congress has passed a recent bill allowing cable companies and phone companies to enter into each other's business. With all these and many more changes, the question becomes: How will these changes affect public relations?

Technology and the Workplace

A recent (1994) survey by Forbush and Toon listed a series of predictions by public relations professionals and journalist, including:

- Virtually all newsrooms and news sources (colleges, universities, businesses, and government agencies) will connect to the Internet or some other global network.

- Public relations officers will routinely transmit news material directly into news organizations' computer systems.

- The darkroom will give way to an "imaging center" from which staff photographers will transmit photographs, video, and other graphics directly to the news media.

- Electronic mail and other electronic delivery systems will render the paper-based news releases obsolete.

- Public information officers will routinely use desktop computers to edit and send video files to reporters.

These predictions, compiled in 1993, were supposed to be about what would happen by the year 2000. Yet most of them have come true by mid-decade. A quick phone call to any daily newspaper would find the capability of most to receive information via the Internet, or a local Freenet. Even relatively small-market publications publish reporters' Internet address. Many already have Home Pages; those that don't are building them.

Technology and the Media

Other predictions from Forbush and Toon centered on how changes in technology will affect the media, and the ability of the public relations practitioner to communicate with the media. Among these predictions are:

- The traditional news media will continue to exert great influence or even expand their influence because either the new technologies will have less impact than is being predicted, or the media will exploit the technology to their own benefit,

- An expanding array of new digital and cable forms will sharply erode the power of the traditional media,

- The explosion in cable channels will bring with it a greater reliance on academic institutions for content, and

- The distinction between news and entertainment will become further blurred.

A main concern expressed by respondents in the survey was how to get through the "noise" of competing communication channels to get to reporters. They conclude, however, that the technology, while offering no magic solutions, will provide more options for reaching the media.

If the reporter becomes too difficult to reach, or is just uncooperative, the Internet does offer an alternative means of communication. According to Marilyn Waters (1995), CEO of Watermark Public Relations and Marketing: "The Internet offers what PR practitioners say they crave: a forum for unfiltered, direct two-way communications" (p.25). Claudia Gaines, (1995) president of The Headline Group echoes the idea: "Any vehicle that delivers information directly to the consumer, can accommodate an educational, long-form message that reaches highly targeted audiences, is going to be embraced as a new and valuable media environment." And Higginbotham (1994) reported the use of a local interactive connection by a candidate for a county commissioner's campaign.

Other predictions expressed in the Forbush and Toon survey include:

- Reporters will use technology to cast a wider net for sources,

- E-mail will change our work patterns,

- Computer bulletin boards and databases will change the way we interact,

- Transmitting pictures electronically will become commonplace, and

- Multimedia and virtual reality will be part of the public information toolbox.

Evidence of these predictions already abounds. According to Plummer (1995b),

> Every culture has its hangouts and cyber space is no exception. Journalists congregate on Internet mailing lists and newsgroups, and in forums on commercial on-line services. These are exceptional locations for PR pros to schmooze, network and learn more about the inner-workings of their targets' industry. Hard-core pitching is practically taboo, though, so be a fly on the wall until you understand the subculture of the group. (p.18)

Electronic mail use has become commonplace. As Horton (1994) notes: "Every day, employees zap thousands of e-mail messages back and forth. Some messages travel through a single department, some resemble one-on-one telephone conversations, others come straight from the top and reach every employee. The management at IBM, for example, recently sent an e-mail memo to its 110,000 US. employees. The message urged employees to contact lawmakers to suggest the defeat of health-care bills proposed by two Democratic leaders" (p.10).

Databases are used more and more frequently by public relations professionals, according to Shell (1995a). He reports that Rochelle Knoller, manager of the Public Relations Society of America's Information Center, spends more time daily keying in search words than she does using print directories. "The power of an on-line search is its timeliness and its ability to produce large volumes of information in a short period of time. . . . Everyone is in a hurry. Nobody wants to say, 'I'll go to the library. I'll look it up.' There's no question that the bulk of information is now coming from on-line sources" (p. 26). Nexis, Dialog, DataTimes and NewsNet, Shell notes, are the databases most frequently used by public relations practitioners.

The Case in Point

While an exhaustive list of all the public relations applications of interactive media is beyond the scope of this chapter, what follows is a representative cross-section of how some practitioners have incorporated interactive media into the practice. Roche (1995) describes three tools available for media relations work: electronic directories of media outlets on CD-ROM, media contact management software, and media relations systems. While these certainly have "glitz appeal," Roche warns that problems such as up-to-date accuracy do exist.

Elasser (1995) reports a joining of forces between MediaMap, PR Newswire and OneLink. OneLink is an electronic connection that combines MediaMap's existing Media Manager databases software with PR Newswire's distribution network which permits the practitioner to retrieve a media list, electronically attach a press release, and transmit the document to editors in the form they want—e-mail, fax, or mail.

Although many firms are either on or getting on the World Wide Web, Edelman Public Relations Worldwide was the first to build a Home Page. Hoechster (1995) offers the following advice for others who think they may want to be on the Web. "It's important for an agency to develop an Internet-based service for the benefit of its clients as well as the journalists and analysts who cover them. . . . Build a Home Page only if you have a strategic reason. . . . The trick to a successful Home Page is making it interesting so people will come back for frequent visits" (p. 13).

Technology now exists that permits two individuals to work on a press release in "real time." Silicon Graphics, for example, has a computer system equipped with a small video camera on top of the monitor. On the screen practitioner A sees practitioner B's face on half of the screen (and vice versa), and the release on the other half. The two individuals can communicate via voice and video while each has the capability to modify the text. A recent AT&T television campaign also demonstrated similar technology.

But if the computer isn't handy, Hewlett-Packard has announced HP OmniShare, a new interactive document conferencing system which allows both parties to view, revise, send, receive and discuss the same document at the same time. The system features a thin writing tablet and a cordless pen. The system downloads documents by FAX, personal computer, or handwriting. And it operates through the phone system!

There is now an Internet service that alerts public relations professionals to breaking news the second it hits the wires. Internet News Alert is an interactive real-time news service that tracks wire services such as Knight-Ridder, Standard & Poor's, Tribune Wire, Business Wire, and PR Newswire. News Alert, unlike other clipping and retrieval services, provides real-time news keyed to pre-determined topics from hundreds of sources. Each time the user logs on to the service, the file is up-dated with the most recent information.

Interactive multimedia now provide the practitioner with the ability to produce news releases, newsletters, brochures, and annual reports on CD-i and CD-ROM. The huge storage capacity of these discs permit an organization to provide audio, video, text and graphics for media and consumers. The user merely highlights a key word within the text and receives available background information on that subject.

Presentation software has made handwritten presentations, chalkboard demonstrations and acetate overheads a thing of the past. Clients now expect their public relations personnel to be on the cutting edge of presentation and image enhancement applications. Although there are several software packages currently available, Powerpoint, Persuasion and Quick Time are three most commonly used. And IBM will soon release a notebook computer whose screen can be placed directly on an overhead projector thus eliminating the need for a separate LCD unit.

Not to be outdone, NASA put "outer space" into cyberspace. Borenstein (1995) reported that the March 2 launch of Endeavour was equipped to receive transmissions via the Internet. "The new service allows you to take a virtual reality tour of NASA's newest orbiter, pinpoint the shuttle's position above the Earth, see where Endeavour's telescopes are pointing, watch its astronauts at work, and sign the visitors' log." (p. 3A)

And the profession itself has "wired up." Shell (1995b) reports, "When asked his top goal for 1995. . ., PRSA president John Beardsley said he wanted to increase the Society's presence in cyberspace. Five months later he got his wish: PRSA's very own Home Page on the World Wide Web" (p.29). Information available here includes a membership directory, information on chapters, information about seminars and the national conference, a section on leadership, a section for the Public Relations Student Society, and a section concerning professional accreditation. And this isn't just a national phenomenon. Many state and regional associations, for example, the Florida PRSA, are on local versions of the Net.

Finally, CompuServe and America On-Line have bulletin boards where professionals can pose questions and share information. A recent discussion on CompuServe, for example, dealt with the value of professional accreditation.

Some Cautions about the New Media

Larry Weber (1995), president of The Weber Group in Cambridge, MA, issues a strong warning to the public relations practitioner:

> Don't embrace technology for technology's sake. Use common sense to determine when to use new media and when to use more traditional methods. It's great to have electronic relationships, but we will always need old-fashioned human contact. We still need to meet some editors in person. We still need to put on special events. We still need to talk to people on the phone. . . . Yes, there are new media and there are new rules. But these are new rules for an old game. The basic game of public relations has not changed and it won't. The tools, media and rules are different, but the principles are the same (p. 11).

Weber's warning, while certainly on point, is only part of the admonition for PR practitioners. The rest is this: new media "form" without substance to back it up is just as dangerous as a glitzy publication, great graphics, or great audio and video with no substantive message behind the gloss. For example, in discussing Home Pages on the Internet, Weber says, "The problem is most Home Pages are boring. They don't offer useful and interesting information. They don't include powerful graphics or hyperlinks to other information. They don't get updated frequently. They're not giving Internet surfers a reason to wander to their site. . . . To put it bluntly: If we use technology to bore people, we gain nothing. We won't impress anyone just because we selected a high-tech vehicle" (p.11).

A further caution for the PR professional concerns dealing with the reporter. The axiom of "find out *how* the reporter wants the information" is just as true with the new media as with the more traditional media. While John Dvorak, a writer for *MacUser* and an influential columnist in the computer industry wrote a letter to public relations people saying he would no longer read news releases on paper, Bovet (1995) summarizes a survey of 725 writers, editors and reporters that found that 51% still preferred to receive press releases through regular mail. Thirty-seven % said they preferred e-mail, while 12% preferred FAX.

Plummer (1995a) conducted an e-mail poll of 300 journalists about their feelings toward on-line media relations. About half who answered the survey preferred receiving "pitches" via e-mail, while the other half liked mail, faxes and overnight mail, in that order. Plummer also reported the results of a study by Ross and Middleberg that predicted in five years half of all managing editors of magazines and newspapers would prefer receiving information via on-line, about one-fourth would prefer paper, 15% would prefer disk, and about 10% CD-ROM.

Another finding in Plummer's study concerned on-line pet peeves as they related to public relations people. Among these pet peeves were:

- Trouble screening the messages,

- Difficulty in getting off mailing lists,

- Having in-baskets clogged with releases about obscure products or services that have no local interest,

- Multiple notices from the same individual,

- Calling several times after the reporter received the release to see if he or she wanted to do a story about the release,

- Not investigating exactly who should receive information before sending it,

- Annoying junk mail and on-line surveys.

Although some of these are new, most ring familiar from times gone by.

To correct these peeves, Plummer offers the following suggestions.

1. Ask permission before e-mailing. If a reporter prefers another source, use it.

2. Publicize your e-mail address on business cards and stationery. Offer to send information via e-mail on the standard paper release.

3. Be concise. Be brief in both the e-mail header and in the message within.

4. Don't send junk mail (called "spamming" on-line). Be even more sensitive when sending information on-line.

5. Pick up the bill. Make sure the e-mail service of the recipient does not charge the recipient for in-coming mail.

And in Conclusion . . .

The interactive media are making an impact on the public relations profession. Most practitioners agree that public relations will continue to do what it has traditionally done—press releases, special events, media relations, investor relations, publications, etc. It will, however, certainly conduct business in a much different way because of these new technologies.

References

Binkley, Christina (1995). "As Florida's Computer Networks Spread, Businesses Seek to Log On," *Wall Street Journal.* February 15.

Borenstein, Seth (1995). "Internet Access Is your Ticket to Ride Shuttle," *Tallahassee Democrat.* March 5.

Bovet, Susan F. (1995). "Hi-tech Editors Lead Charge into Cyberspace," *Public Relations Journal.* May.

Elasser, John (1995). "Trendwatch," *Public Relations Tactics,* June.

Forbush, Dan and John Toon (1994). "PR in the 21st Century," *CASE Currents.* Spring.

Higginbotham, Mickey (1994). "Candidate bytes into Free-Net Debate," *Tallahassee Democrat.* October 15.

Hoechster, Steve (1995). "Building a Home Page on the World Wide Web," *Public Relations Tactics,* June.

Horton, APR, James L. (1994). "E-mail Delivers Internal News in Real Time," *Public Relations Tactics.* October.

Gaines, Claudia (1995). "Will the Internet be the Next Great PR Tool," *Public Relations Tactics.* June.

Plummer, Amy W. (1995a). "Managing Media Relations in Cyberspace," *Public Relations Tactics.* June.

Plummer, Amy W. (1995b). "Where Journalists Hang out Online," *Public Relations Tactics.* June.

Roche, Peter (1995). "High-Tech Tools for Media Relations," *Public Relations Tactics,* August.

Shell, Adam (1995a). "Information Center Finds Answers Quick with Help of Databases," *Public Relations Tactics.* June.

Shell, Adam (1995b). "PRSA Now Calls the Internet Home," *Public Relations Tactics.* July.

Varian, Bill (1995). "Grown-up Free-Net Is Ready to Head out on its Own," *Tallahassee Democrat.* August 13.

Waters, Marilyn J. (1995). "Will the Internet be the Next Great PR Tool," *Public Relations Tactics.* June.

Weber, Larry (1995). "Why Getting Wired Makes Sense," *Public Relations Tactics.* June.

CHAPTER

8

Considerations for 21st Century Direct Marketers

Focusing on the Basics in New Environments

Richard S. Hodgson

Richard S. Hodgson is President of Sargeant House, a Westtown, Pennsylvania, company that provides direct marketing consulting and catalog development services to companies throughout the world. He is also author of more than a dozen books, including the classic *Direct Mail and Mail Order Handbook,* and hundreds of magazine articles on direct marketing. Dick is a member of the Board of Directors of Foster & Gallagher, Inc., a leading U.S. direct marketing firm, and was formerly a charter member of the Board of Directors of QVC Network, Inc.

As we rapidly approach year 2000, everyone seems to be anticipating dramatic changes in lifestyles and the ways business will be conducted throughout the world. While it's natural to focus on exciting new developments, there's a danger for direct marketers who spend too much time and money on emerging technology, assuming the gadgets and gimmicks of the future will mean replacing most of the techniques spelling success for today's direct marketers.

This rush toward the 21st Century seems to have begun in earnest in the early 1980s. At a direct marketing conference, futurist Alvin Toffler predicted everyone would soon be working at home in their "electronic cottages." A top executive of American Express told us we's better lose no time in molding new technology to suit our own purposes since everyone was going to be sitting in front of their interactive TV sets, doing most of their business transactions by merely pushing a few buttons.

What happened to those confident predictions of a brave new world where everything was going to change, where all of us would sit in front of our television sets or computers to do all of our home and business shopping, where our mailboxes would gather dust as printed media disappeared from the scene?

It seems the direct marketing futurists overlooked one important thing. They forgot to ask consumers if they wanted new ways of doing things. Throughout the world, billions have been spent trying to get consumers to fall in love with the latest in electronic gadgetry and abandon their printed catalogs, direct mail, newspapers, magazines. But consumers keep coming back with the same answer: "Why change?"

This leads to the important issue of "critical mass." While I see this as a major problem today, it could easily become an even larger problem in the future, particularly for companies that already have well-established marketing methods against which the success or failure of interactivity must be measured.

You don't have to look any further than cable home shopping to understand the importance of this factor. Over 100 companies—including many of the biggest marketers in America—have spent many millions trying to get involved in this single interactive medium. Yet, only two—HSN and QVC home shopping networks—have been successful in developing profitable national businesses.

The major problem has been critical mass—getting carriage by enough cable systems so they could reach sufficient homes to develop a profitable business. Not only do direct marketers need to be concerned about total critical mass, but also the number of people likely to be accessing the medium during any given time frame. For example, as the number of marketers participating on the Internet continues to grow, the percentage of consumers willing to devote the time and effort during any given time frame to seek out and "listen" to each marketer's sales message tends to diminish.

Even if every household in the U.S. had Internet-accessing capabilities, the competition for each message offered might be so large there may not be critical mass large enough to serve the requirements of many marketers. And when you add the competition from on-line services, newly developed interactive cable programs, et al, this problem becomes even more complicated. Of course, the critical mass necessary to constitute a viable business varies greatly. But, at the present time and for the near future at least, the numbers just aren't there for the majority of businesses.

In his marvelous book, *Megatrends*, John Naisbitt observed,

> The gee-whiz futurists are always wrong because they believe techno-
> logical innovation travels in a straight line. It doesn't. It weaves and
> bobs and lurches and sputters.

And today's electronic technology is weaving, bobbing, lurching and sputtering. But that doesn't stop the direct marketing futurists from predicting straight line adoption of what is now being called the "Information Superhighway."

One of the hottest subjects at direct marketing meetings and in the trade press has been the imminent arrival of an interactive Information Superhighway, with cable systems offering 500 channels of programming. With the trend toward demassification in direct marketing, multiple cable channels would appear to offer an efficient way to reach specialized audiences. And if it were possible to eliminate the rising costs of paper, printing and postage plus large staffs of human order operators, think of all the increased profit potential! Sound too good to be true? It is. And it is likely to be so for many years to come.

What has stirred up all this interest is a process called "digital compression." The basic technology has been developed. But practical implementation is still in the experimental stage, with many different variations being tested. Digital compression can be compared to instant coffee. Coffee processors remove the water, ship only the solids, and the consumer adds back the water before drinking. With digital compression, redundant information in a digital television signal is removed before transmission, then added back on the home television screen before viewing. By this process, as many as 10 channels can be transmitted within the same band-width required for only one channel today.

But 500 is not a magic number. With digital compression, there could be room for 300, 600 or 1,000 channels or more. But will consumers really want that many channels? And will they pay for them? Thus far, every study I've seen indicates there's no overwhelming demand on the part of consumers for more channels. Consumers' main complaint is not the lack of choices, but the cost of service. And additional channels will mean substantially added costs.

And what about interactivity? A limited audience may not be willing to pay for the devices which will make it possible to interact with a television set and again, it is likely to be many years before homes equipped with interactive TV sets provide the critical mass for direct marketers to consider it a viable market.

Meanwhile, there are a number of services which permit interactive electronic direct marketing via personal computers. However, all of them combined haven't come close to the sales success of QVC, which racks-up annual sales well over $1 billion and keeps growing. QVC founder, Joe Segel, points out:

> Text and non-moving pictures won't satisfy the public. Moving images are more appealing than still images, and listening is more appealing than reading. Those are two powerful reasons why every text-based and still-picture-based interactive television experiment in the past has failed. That's also why no computer-terminal-based service has ever generated anywhere near the volume of retail merchandise orders that the televised shopping channels have achieved. To gain maximum acceptance, the visual appearance of interactive services needs to be more television-like than computer-like.

There's also the matter of what John Naisbitt called, "High Tech/High Touch." With so many parts of our lives involving "high tech," there comes a time when the majority of consumers want the "high touch" of less complicated things. When they get home from technology-loaded jobs and turn on their TV sets, they just want to become passive viewers. Perhaps this partially explains the success of today's "low tech" home video shopping.

As a charter member of the Board of Directors of QVC Network, I had a first-hand opportunity to observe the vast difference between what direct marketing futurists predict and what the public really wants. Sure, QVC took advantage of the new electronic technology. But QVC founder Joe Segel was astute enough to recognize there were two important elements needed to make home video shopping appeal to the marketplace: it had to be *simple* and *common*. Consumers didn't have to learn anything new. Just turn on a TV set and dial a telephone. No complicated keypads, no special buttons to push, no computer or modem to install.

"The appropriate response to technology," Naisbitt said, "is not to stop it, but to accommodate it, respond to it, and shape it." And that's what Joe Segel did at QVC. By taking the basic principles of direct marketing that he had learned in developing The Franklin Mint, and combining them with today's new technology, he captured the fancy and pocketbooks of millions of American consumers, building QVC into a billion dollar direct marketing business.

QVC programming is simple. Each hour, 24 hours a day, a separate category of merchandise is presented. A friendly show host describes each item of merchandise and often has live conversations with viewers, who have an opportunity to ask questions about the items being presented and to tell why they like it. To purchase, viewers simply pick up their phones, dial a toll-free phone number, and talk to a friendly order taker. Everything is simple and common.

This approach reaps great rewards. QVC logs-in thousands of orders in a single hour. When clothing from upscale retailer Saks was presented, QVC sold the entire $570,000 available inventory in a single hour.

Often celebrities join the QVC show hosts to present merchandise which carries their names. TV personality Joan Rivers sold $10 million of costume jewelry in five weekend presentations, and actress Morgan Fairchild sold some $1 million of jewelry in just three hours.

While celebrity presentations add a little extra oomph to presentations, the vast majority of sales are made without them. And QVC doesn't make the mistake of many would-be home shopping programs which put the emphasis on entertainment, rather than on selling. Viewers are never allowed to forget the reason for the programming is to sell merchandise.

This format has been so successful that QVC adds 100,000 new customers each month and well over 50 percent of them become repeat buyers. Amazingly, thousands actually purchase as many as 100 times a year.

This all happened in less than a decade, and certainly represents one of direct marketing's greatest success stories of the 20th Century. There's a lesson to be learned from QVC's success and other things which have been happening in today's world of direct marketing. During the past 50 years, I've seen direct marketing evolve from simple Multigraphed letters and black-and-white catalogs into a potent multimedia powerhouse destined to become increasingly important in the 21st Century.

There are three key direct marketing developments of the 20th Century which I'm convinced are part of the groundwork critical to the continuing success of direct marketing's future. I feel it's important to understand these cornerstones and how they evolved as we rush toward the 21st Century.

The Trend toward Demassification

Cataloging has become a highly specialized business. Today there are over 10,000 consumer mail order specialty catalogs in the U.S., plus thousands more carrying all types of business products. What distinguishes these catalogs of today is how specialized they have become. No matter what personal interests you may have, there's a catalog to serve your wants and desires. Consider just one field—food. There are mail order catalogs specializing in meats, fruit, cheese, nuts, candy, gourmet specialties, cooking utensils, popcorn, caviar, fruitcakes, wine, etc...

Catalogs have gone through a process which American sociologists call "demassification." There was a time when all telephones were black, all refrigerators were white, and teenagers wore the same outfit all day long. Today, however, people everywhere demand choices. Instead of wanting the same things everyone else wants, they want to express their individuality.

Interactivity

Whenever that Information Superhighway is mentioned, the subject of interactivity is almost always included. It is as if interactivity is something new. Actually, interactivity has long been an important element of successful direct marketing, although direct marketers usually call it "involvement."

Long ago, direct marketers discovered that you could get better repsonse by encouraging the customer to become actively involved in a promotion. We adopted techniques like sweepstakes, contests, paste-on stamps, tokens, rub-offs and other involvement devices to make our mailings more interesting and to encourage response.

We created order and inquiry devices which make it easy to respond. And when toll-free telephone service became available, direct marketers were quick to take advantage of this interactive device. For some reason, the proponents of advanced electronic interactive devices seem to have adopted the idea that there's something magic about being able to push a few buttons on a gadget hooked up to a television set or on a home computer in order to respond to an offer. But listen to what Joe Segel of QVC had to say at last fall's Direct Marketing Association Convention in Toronto:

> Everyone knows how to dial a phone and place an order. So, present-day systems are about as simple as they can be. If a new system requires more steps to do esentially the same things, consumers may resist it. It would be to the peril of creative geniuses to forget that people always gravitate towards doing things in the easiest possible way. Recognize that you ahve a secret weapon. The direct marketing industry as it now exists has a unique kind of interactive system utilizing voice recognition software that is infinetely superior to anything that the most talented software engineers or computer manufacturers can produce. It's called the human order entry operator.

Integrated Marketing

"Integrated Marketing" is another of the buzz words we hear so much today—and for some reason the futurists think it's something new. But it's something successful direct marketers discovered years ago. It's just the term that's new. We call it "multimedia promotions." Probably no direct marketer has been more successful in utilizing multimedia than American cataloger Foster & Gallagher. At one time, all of Foster & Gallagher's direct marketing was done through catalogs. But businesses like Breck's Dutch Bulbs and Spring Hill Nurseries were highly seasonal. Off-season catalogs were uneconomical.

So, Foster & Gallagher pioneered in the use of solo mailings and statement and package inserts to build a year-round business. More recently, they've added an extensive outbound telemarketing program. And their Michigan Bulb business makes extensive use of newspaper and magazine advertising. No medium goes unexplored. While the Breck's Spring Hill and other Foster & Gallagher catalogs continue to prosper, the company's on-going growth can be attributed to a well-balanced blend of different media.

Also pioneering multi-media for direct marketing was Omaha Steaks International, another highly seasonal business selling gourmet meat products which in the U.S. are primarily purchased for Christmastime gifts. But Omaha Steaks was turned into a 12-month success with solo mailings and a highly-effective year-around telemarketing program to supplement Christmas season catalogs.

Of all of the 20th Century media to impact direct marketing, the use of the telephone—both inbound and outbound—has had the greatest impact. But for the majority of direct marketers, telemarketing is not a stand-alone marketing medium. Instead, from the very beginning, it had been most often carefully integrated into a multi-media program.

In conclusion, I see three major hurdles to the full adoption of new media technologies in direct marketing, time, management and critical mass.

Time

Time and again, I hear that the amount of time it takes to initiate a search for information and complete a transaction is the main objection to the use of most electronic interactive marketing techniques. While this may be perfectly acceptable to those who approach interactive media as a "hobby," it is definently a stumbling block for those who are content with present methods.

Management

Most people in top management grew up in a "non-interactive" era, and/or are likely to have heard more about interactive failures than about successes. They may have personally watched funds previously budgeted for interactive ventures go down the drain. Therefore, getting managment approval—and consequently adequate budgeting—to embark on interactive marketing, and being able to continue to secure budgeting through sometimes lengthy trial and error periods, can be very difficult.

I'm constantly seeing examples of companies that have decided to put their toe in the interactive marketing waters, only to abandon their projects when great things don't happen immediately. I suspect one of the main reasons for such actions is that many top managements aren't willing to devote personal time to things whose ultimate pay-off is likely to be far down the road.

There are only so many things that can be given "thinking time" in a busy business environment. Just getting top managment in many companies to spend "thinking time" on the company's overall marketing is often difficult enough without getting interactive on management's "thinking" agenda.

Critical Mass

As I stated in the introduction, I see this as the greatest problem that interactive marketers must face. With more and more companies developing a presence on the Internet and through other interactive mediums, the critical mass needed to ensure a profitable return on investment diminishes greatly. Again, the critical mass necessary to constitute a viable business varies. At the present time, the numbers just aren't there for the vast majority of businesses.

SECTION II

Media Tactics and Techniques in the Interactive Age

The new media offer a whole new range of possibilities for communication with customers, both actual and potential. This section explores how interactivity is creating and will create improved customer relationships. On one hand the tried-and-true basics—know your customer's needs and wants—not only will still apply; it will rule because new means of "meeting" customers and measuring the effectiveness of communications with them will change the rules of the game.

Mass marketers are given their final wake-up call by Don Peppers and Martha Rogers in "One-to-One Media in the Interactive Future: Building Dialogues and Learning Relationships with Individual Customers." As the "dawn of the Information Age" breaks all around them, Peppers and Rogers lament the fact that "the mass marketers will be holding their aching heads, trying to figure out what happened to their credentials. . . . We are passing through a technological discontinuity of epic proportions, and most are not even remotely prepared." In order "to take full advantage of the new media and information technologies now becoming available," Peppers and Rogers maintain that the marketer will need a wholesale shift in their world-view, for "The old paradigm, a system of mass production, mass media, and mass marketing, is being replaced by a totally new paradigm, a one-to-one (1:1) economic system. . . . It is the fractionalization of mass media and the rise of one-to-one (1:1) media that mandate 1:1 marketing." Next, in "The Impact of Interactive Communication on Advertising and Marketing And Now a Word from Our Consumer" by Edward Forrest, Lance Kinney and Michael Chamberlain, the changing role and scope of activities of the advertising agency in an interactive world is examined.

This paradigm shift from mass media and marketing to interactive media and 1:1 marketing described by Peppers and Rogers is elaborated on by Cheri Anderson. In "Computer as Audience: Mediated Interactive Messages," Anderson addresses the total spectrum of implications on advertising as we move from traditional passive-analog media to active-digital media. Accordingly, Anderson observes that "Current practices in advertising, ranging from creative strategy to research methods, will need to be rethought as technological advances in digitalization, computer intelligence and interactivity continue to permeate media. In the active media configuration, advertisers need to address the question: "What constitutes an audience?" Accordingly, in her most perceptive conceptualization, Anderson suggests that "because of the computer's role in the active media configuration," it should be included as "a component of the interactive audience."

Next, Michael Spalter provides additional conceptual assistance for those traditional mass marketing practitioners contemplating Peppers and Rogers' challenge to upgrade their credentials and shift to the new 1:1 paradigm. In "The Seven I's to Success: Maintaining a Customer Focus in an Interactive Age," Spalter observes that as "consumers and companies continue to migrate from the physical marketplace to the electronic marketspace, maintaining customer focus will require new management constructs and reengineering of existing structures. . . . Unfortunately, the vast majority of businesses currently online have neglected or failed to ask several fundamental marketing questions." Spalter poses the questions and in the process of delineating the answers, utilizes what he terms the Seven I's—Interconnection, Interface, Interactivity, Involvement, Information, Individualism, and Integrity. For the marketer in transition from the mass to interactive modus operandi, Spalter's Seven I's are a timely supplement to the classic 4 P's (product, place, promotion and price) of the classic marketing mix.

"God is in the details" is a long-established truism. And in "The New World of Marketing on the Internet: Some Practical Implications of the New Tools and New Rules of Interactive Marketing," Charles F. Hofacker surveys some of those details, specifically the nuts and bolts (nodes and links) of the Internet. The different types of services available on the Net are delineated, as are the important protocols and their implications. He describes what this operationally different world will mean for the new marketer. Current marketing resources are described, as is the contemporary practice of marketing on the network. In addition, Hofacker describes what this operationally different world will mean for the marketers in the not-too-distant future.

In "Media and Marketing Strategies for the Internet: A Step-by-Step Guide," Tracy Emerick predicts that: "The Internet will revolutionize marketing as it is known today . . . [and] . . . Any person or business not getting involved with the Internet today will be left on the sidelines within five years." For those who take his prognostications seriously, he outlines a three-step process and strategy for developing Internet marketing programs, using the basics that are in productive operation today. And, of particular concern to marketers and marketing management, he delineates five primary cost areas and gives guidelines for managing them effectively.

The next two chapters—"Creative Strategy for Interactive Marketing," by Carol Nelson and Rocky James, and "Copywriting for Interactive Media," by Herschell Gordon Lewis—literally write the rule-book on Internet advertising strategy.

Nelson and James maintain that "the Internet implicitly has superimposed its own set of rules onto the world of advertising strategy," and consequently there are "absolute rules for adapting conventional advertising to Internet advertising." To date, the problem as Nelson and James see it, has been that "much Internet advertising is prepared not by marketers but by programmers and technicians. This parallels having ads written by typesetters. Technical proficiency supplants communications skills, and the result may be a technological triumph and a motivational flop." For those creative strategists who find themselves interactively challenged, Nelson and James provide a ten-step program which, if followed "may not result in a brilliant campaign, but it should result in a competitively professional campaign."

Having observed that, "as the twentieth century draws to an end, a new challenge to advertising creative teams defies previous rules of communication," Herschell Gordon Lewis also lays down some new rules and guidelines—and even a commandment or two—for communicating and selling effectively in the interactive future. However, he counsels, in "Copywriting for Interactive Media," the basics still apply, perhaps more than ever. And what are those basics? Know the specific characteristics and protocols of the medium, play or write to its strengths, and motivate the receiver of your message—give the receiver of your message a reason to respond or buy.

Theories, rules, and guidelines are meant to translate into productive activity, the ultimate being a successful campaign. Charles Marrelli provides it in "Anatomy of a Web Advertisement: A Case Study of Zima.com." In this in-depth, step-by-step analysis of a successful campaign—"the first national consumer packaged good to have a dedicated Web server"—Marrelli "breaks down the original Web site into its component parts" and "illustrates the strategy and the mechanics behind building a massive advertising presence in cyberspace." This stage-by-stage construction of the Zima Website provides concrete examples demonstrating the importance of the home page; the use of e-mail; the provision of timely company and product information; the role of on-line sampling, contests and giveaways; navigation strategies; icon design; techniques to encourage dialogue, handle feedback and build camaraderie and brand identity.

In the final article in this section, John Nardone addresses the two basic questions that stymie enthusiasts and skeptics alike: "Does it *work?*" and "How do we *know*—i.e., How do we measure it?" In a masterful linkage of the "traditional" media concepts of reach and frequency to application to the new interactive media, Nardone explores the "interesting new dynamics raised by the nature of self-selected advertising and the navigational structure of the Web." He introduces, explains and illustrates such concepts as "surface area", "distributed content," "depth of immersion," and "I.R.I.S." (the Internet Reach and Involvement Scale) as a tool for measuring effectiveness of communications on the Web.

9

One-to-One Media in the Interactive Future

Building Dialogues and Learning Relationships with Individual Customers

Don Peppers
Martha Rogers

Don Peppers is founder and President of Marketing 1:1, Inc., a marketing consultancy specializing in relationship management business development, and marketing technology issues.

Martha Rogers is Professor of Telecommunications at Bowling Green State University and a founding partner of Marketing 1:1, Inc.

Peppers and Rogers are co-authors of *The One-to-One Future: Building Relationships One Customer at a Time*, called by *Inc.* Magazine "one of the two or three most important business books ever written."

In late 1991 the telegraph industry's life was taken, suddenly and brutally, by the facsimile machine. For more than 150 years, the telegram stood for immediacy and importance. It was an icon for urgency. But now, Western Union has closed down its telegraph service around the world. The fax was a new technology the telegram could not survive.[1]

The shift from teletype and telegram to facsimile transmission represents one aspect of what some business consultants term a paradigm shift—a "discontinuity" in the otherwise steady march of business progress.

The automobile was another discontinuity, one that radically transformed both the economy and society. When the automobile first appeared, it seemed to be merely a horseless version of the well-known carriage. Predicting the consequences of the automobile's introduction would have been nearly impossible. Who could have imagined that a noisy, smelly, unreliable machine would eventually be responsible for the creation of suburbs; the fractionalization of families; and the growth of supermarkets, malls, and the Interstate Highway System?

It is as difficult to see beyond such a discontinuity as it would be for a nine-year-old boy to imagine being fifteen. He can easily visualize being ten, and he may dream about twelve, but it is virtually impossible for him to plan on what his life will be like when his hormones kick in. Hormones are a discontinuity.

Today we are passing through a technological discontinuity of epic proportions, and most are not even remotely prepared. The old paradigm, a system of mass production, mass media, and mass marketing, is being replaced by a totally new paradigm, a one-to-one (1:1) economic system.

The 1:1 future will be characterized by customized production, individually addressable media, and 1:1 marketing, totally changing the rules of business competition and growth. Instead of share of *market*, the goal of most business competition will be share of *customer*—one customer at a time.

Economies of scale will never again be as important as they are today. Having the size necessary to produce, advertise, and distribute vast quantities of standardized products won't be a precondition for success. Instead, products will be increasingly tailored to individual tastes, electronic media will be inexpensively addressed to individual consumers, and many products ordered over the phone will be delivered to the home in eight hours or less.

In the 1:1 future businesses will focus less on short-term profits derived from quarterly or annual transaction volumes and more on the kinds of profits that can be realized from long-term customer retention and lifetime values.

The discontinuity we are now living through will be every bit as disruptive to our lives, and as beneficial, as the Industrial Revolution was to the lives of our great-grandparents. The way we compete will change dramatically enough over just the next few years to alter the very structure of our society, empowering some and disenfranchising others.

The 1:1 future holds immense implications for individual privacy, social cohesiveness, and the alienation and fractionalization that could come from the breakdown of mass media. It will change forever how we seek our information, education, and entertainment, and how we pursue our happiness. In addition to the "haves" and "have nots," new class distinctions will be created between the "theres" and "there nots." Some people will have jobs that require them to be there—somewhere—while others will be able to work mostly from their homes, without having to be anywhere.

At the early Daimler-Benz Company, the Mercedes planning department was asked to forecast the ultimate size of the automobile market. Unable to visualize the profound changes the automobile would provoke, they planned forward from their own present, in which only the wealthy owned cars, and predicted an eventual total of one million automobiles worldwide. Today, of course, there are more than 500 million cars on the world's roads. Mercedes underestimated the car's potential because the planners correctly guessed the population could never support more than about one million *chauffeurs*. They didn't plan backward from a future in which people would drive their own automobiles and mass production would make millions of cars affordable to the middle class.[2]

In the same way that Mercedes' planners had difficulty seeing beyond the technological discontinuity represented by assembly line automobile production, it is difficult for most of us now to imagine life after mass marketing.

It will disrupt everything, but ultimately 1:1 technology will create an entrepreneurial froth of opportunities. When the dust has settled, a plethora of new businesses—millions of them—most not even conceived today, will have sprung up across the economic landscape as naturally and randomly as wild flowers after a severe winter.

In a world in which communication and information are practically free, ideas will be the new medium of exchange.

New Media for a New Future

Mass media are as bland as hospital food, or anything else that has to be served the same way to everybody.

The only reason "awareness" advertising plays much of a part at all in marketing today is that the mass media available for promoting a product electronically and inexpensively are not very good at doing anything else. Mass media carry a rising cacophony of competing messages, each one being shouted by a marketer intent on being heard above the surrounding noise of his competitors.

But just having one's shout heard above the clamor is clearly inferior to the ultimate goal as a business—the final purpose of all marketing activity—which is to generate sales and loyal customers.

Using the new media of the 1:1 future, a marketer will be able to communicate directly with customers, individually, rather than shouting at them in groups. Current and future 1:1 media are different from today's mass media in three important ways:

1. *1:1 media are individually addressable.* An addressable medium can deliver a single, separate message to a particular individual. Until very recently, virtually the only addressable medium of any significance was a slow, cumbersome, expensive postal system. Not any more. New 1:1 media allows a marketer to send information to individual consumers without using the mail at all.

2. *1:1 media are two-way, not one-way.* Today's mass media only convey one-way messages from the marketer to the customer. But new media are already available that allow customers to talk back to a business, and more are being invented literally every month. What will they say?

3. *1:1 media are inexpensive.* Imagine a business as small as a house painter, or an accountant, or a babysitter, reaching customers and prospective customers individually, in quantities small enough to be affordable. Businesses that today have little alternative but to send out printed flyers in the mail, or post 3 x 5

cards on supermarket bulletin boards, will be able to use individually addressable electronic media to reach new customers and to keep the ones they have.[3]

Many new media with 1:1 capabilities are already in place, and more are being proposed, invented, and deployed every year. We are already halfway through the discontinuity. But it is still difficult for most of us to see beyond it.

Paying Customers for Dialogue Opportunities

Marketers will be able to create dialogue opportunities with customers by providing them first with valuable information (such as investment counseling) or mass-customized news for free, and then paying for these services out of the revenue benefits of increased loyalty and product sales made possible by the dialogue. This "explicit" bargain, struck with individual consumers, resembles the "implicit" bargain that has driven mass media economics for decades. If commercial messages make up the difference between the $1.25 a reader pays for a Sunday *New York Times* and the $12.00 it actually costs to produce, why couldn't commercial messages pay for more individualized information?

And why not make the bargain even more explicit? Why not simply *pay* customers (or prospective customers) to generate dialogue opportunities?[4]

Creating Markets: Bringing Buyers and Sellers Together

Because a fax bulletin board resides on a computer and can be instantly updated or altered by computer input, it can be as flexible as necessary to convey very tailored information. A number of companies have recently gone into the business of creating markets for various products and commodities, using computers to convey information by interactive fax. If a jeweler in Topeka is looking for prices on a two-carat ice blue, she could call RapNet, a diamond exchange, and use her phone's touch tones to get the computer to fax back to her a list of prices from as far away as Antwerp.

If someone is looking for art, one new clearinghouse has a computer hooked up to answer inquiries by fax-response. Just step through Art Co-op's touch-tone menu, dial in a code number for the artist being looked for, and the computer will download to his fax machine a complete list of recent prices for the artist's work. Some of these information-dispensing firms charge subscription fees, while others give out information for one-time charges collected over 900 numbers.[5]

Fax-response can also be used to feed immense computerized databases directly to fax machines on request. One Rockford, Illinois company, Government Access & Information Network, Inc. (GAIN), offers a fax-response service that allows anyone with a fax machine to be able to tap into one of several extensive government databases. For $3.50 per document, anyone can call GAIN, use the touch tones on their fax machine to navigate around the system and retrieve, with relative ease, a document on, say, federal grants or assistance available under programs such as Women's Business Ownership Assistance, or Veterans Entrepreneurial Training and Counseling.[6]

When the video dial tone finally arrives, anyone with a phone and a camera will be able to go into the television "broadcasting" business. The video dial tone will spur the growth of an assortment of video service bureaus—companies that collect all sorts of video programming from all over the world, store it digitally in their own computers, and load it selectively into the video mailboxes of various consumer subscribers, according to the individual subscriber's preferences and needs.

Because anyone will be able to send a video signal to anyone else, the video service bureau business is likely to be highly competitive. Most such bureaus will offer not only a variety of video-on-demand but also access to sophisticated computing, gaming, and other interactive information and entertainment products.

And how will customers pay for this kind of video storing, sorting, and forwarding service custom-tailored to their own tastes?

They *could* simply pay for the service. They could elect to watch every program, news show, sporting event, beauty contest or movie on a pay-per-view basis. Since 25 cents worth of advertising enters each home every time someone watches a half-hour prime-time television show today, that's what a programming provider would have to collect to make it an economic proposition. Or maybe consumers may choose to pay a flat fee for a wide variety of choices, similar to the way cable services are sold today.

The alternative to paying for these services is to make deals with advertisers, through service bureaus, who will be only too happy to pay for it for a customer, provided that customer will agree to see their ads in the process. What does a customer have that's valuable enough to marketers to pay for services customers want? Information about themselves. Is a customer a cheap date if he or she trades information to a marketer in exchange for free media use? Everybody buys *something*. The information-for-media deal is, after all, foreplay to a transaction and, if all goes well, the precursor to a long-term relationship.

In the past, mass marketers have bought huge segments of audience—male 25-44, income $30,000 up, homeowners, white-collar, employed. In the 1:1 future, marketers have the wherewithal to use information about individuals—and to make deals with individuals to get that information. In the 1:1 future, running "commercials" will be practically free. What will be costly will be the time, attention, and information of individual customers.

Customers with Long Nails and Hair on Their Hands

When a marketer begins to engage in a dialogue with each customer individually, through whatever means, the customer he talks with is very unlikely to be totally satisfied, and will let him know. If every complaint is an opportunity to collaborate, once a marketer begins to facilitate genuine dialogue, he will be faced with many such opportunities.

Prodigy, a joint venture by Sears and IBM, has served as a good model of an interactive, dialogue-intensive marketing environment. The company provides a wide variety of interactive services to anyone with a personal computer and modem, but unlike most on-line computer operations, Prodigy's services are aimed primarily at home consumers, and many of the services are subsidized by commercial sponsors.

Prodigy has about 200 different advertisers operating on its network, and a good proportion of them sell their products on-line. Advertisers and merchants are free to engage any of the one million or so individual Prodigy subscribers in an e-mail dialogue designed to increase interest in their product and, eventually, to make a sale. Or a subscriber can interact with a Prodigy advertisement, within a limited framework.

For instance, an advertiser might have a questionnaire available and, if the consumer answers it, he or she will be sent a premium or discount of some kind.

Chevrolet offered a $500 rebate to Prodigy users who requested it, applicable to the purchase of a GEO. The subscribers who called up the Chevy ad offering the rebate, after being alerted by an "awareness" ad at the bottom of their screen, were mailed the rebate. Then, a few weeks later they were mailed a postcard from the local GEO dealer encouraging them to come in and test-drive the car.

Prodigy has a lot of problems. For one thing, subscribers find it to be friendly but extremely slow—so slow that relatively more computer-literate people turn their noses up at it. But the biggest problem with Prodigy, as an interactive medium, is not the engineering of its response time, but the engineering of its marketing structure. Believe it or not, even though Prodigy allows consumers to respond directly to messages from marketers, on the front end the system operates as if it were a totally non-addressable mass medium. The same "awareness" ads go to *every* subscriber, and because of the enormous time and expense required to program, produce, and manage the advertising, the company prefers to work mostly with national advertisers. Prodigy wants national advertisers despite the fact that for any service to be genuinely interactive it should be a low-barrier tool for local marketers. Nevertheless, the Prodigy system can still serve as a model for some kinds of consumer-to-marketer-to-consumer dialogue. This is the kind of interactive dialogue that will develop as genuinely 1:1 electronic media begin to proliferate. And it's not always a pretty picture.

Advertisers using the system and interacting with customers on an individual basis have found themselves forced to be extremely straightforward and, above all, responsive. Advertising rhetoric, and PR language, are not going to be sufficient to carry on a conversation.

PC Flowers is a company launched on Prodigy. William Tobin, its president, says that when consumers go on-line with a marketer their expectations of service increase exponentially. They

> grow long nails and hair on their hands . . .
> They tell you when you really didn't do a good job, and they want your firstborn back for it.[7]

One of the most important features of a 1:1 medium is that it will facilitate customer-initiated dialogue, and customer-initiated dialogue is going to be heavily weighted toward complaints—about product quality, about service, about pricing, about attitude. The perceived quality of a company's product or service will be the ruthless, brutal, and absolutely final arbiter of that firm's success. Today quality may be king, but tomorrow it will be somewhere between ayatollah and demi-god.

What is important to recognize, of course, is that all these individual customer complaints existed in the past. They were always there, but they weren't voiced directly to the marketer. The more dialogue a marketer can encourage from customers, the more complaints he has a right to expect. With any genuine mechanism in place for engaging in dialogues with customers, the marketer will have more opportunities than ever before to solve individual consumer problems. The marketer will have more opportunities to resolve difficulties, to create *customer*ized products to address individual needs, to collaborate *individually* with each customer—and to gain a much greater share of each one's business.

Before a marketer begins to get all worried about the amount of time being consumed by having dialogues with customers, keep in mind that most of this dialogue is totally automated. Most customer "conversations" will consist of touch-tone interactions. Most actual text-based (keyboard) or audio (voice) communication from a customer will be "mailboxed" to the marketer, if his system has been organized the right way.

The key here is to ensure that the marketer uses automated, computer-intensive systems to absorb the vast, "middle" bulk of his dialogue cost burden. This will allow him to pay closer, more labor-intensive attention to conducting more specialized dialogues on either end of this middle. The marketer will need to allocate most of the firm's customer service labor costs to high-value customers on one end of the spectrum, and to complainers on the other—complainers who can be converted to ultra-loyal collaborators, but only through careful, personal attention.

The Future of Dialogue: Direct Response in Reverse

Soon electronic bulletin boards and mailboxes of various kinds will be common, on computer e-mail systems, "host" messaging systems like HomeFax, voice-mail audiotex, and, in a few years, video mail systems.

The real future of 1:1 media may be a form of direct-response marketing in reverse. Consumers will direct messages and offers to audiences of marketers, who will respond. Remember that most bulletin boards are based on low-cost, low-barrier technologies. So consumers will soon have their own bulletin boards that are scanned by marketers looking to sell them things.

Suppose a consumer could "post" a message for all interested retail electronics stores in his area saying that he was looking for a new 27-inch or bigger television with some digital capability. No reason to limit the offer to retailers. He could send his offer to the major electronics-by-mail companies too. Anyone interested in having his business? Absolute reliability in warranty service is a must, and any store wanting to sell him television should be prepared to give him two satisfied customer references.

This kind of shopping is done personally by many people now, but it is done in a series of phone calls or visits to different establishments. The criteria for a purchase could vary considerably, of course, from the hypothetical example above, depending on who the customer is and what her preferences are. She might just be looking for the lowest price on a particular model of new car. Or she might want a very low price, but not necessarily rock bottom, from a dealer with a good reputation in the service department. Or maybe she needs a bank to handle her IRA account. Or a grocery store willing to provide special help for the physically disabled.

What we're talking about is the fact that, eventually, an individual consumer will be able to send his or her own message to a collective group of marketers—sort of an upside-down "target audience" application.

Because there are few organized media for bulletin boards and mailboxing at present, this kind of message is rarely sent today, although it could blossom next year—or next week. The most direct way for it to occur would be for a host system to go into business, making money by imposing a charge, either explicitly or implicitly, to the consumer (an implicit charge might be in the form of a commission or transaction fee from marketers selling goods through this service).

The host company would have to provide several services to assure an orderly information market. First, it would need to provide the hardware and software to run the system. The system could be voice-mail audiotex, or fax-response, or computer e-mail. Audiotex, although awkward in some respects, would be the most easily accessible to the largest number of consumers today. Second, the host would have to guarantee the integrity of the system. For the consumer, this would mean not divulging the name and address to marketers. The host would know the consumer's identity, but a marketer would only be able to find it out when the consumer responded positively to one of his offers.

To attract marketers, the host would have to ensure that the users of the system were legitimate consumers, shopping for goods and services for their own use, and not competitors, suppliers, or others trying to test the bottom of each marketer's bargaining capability. The host could do this by charging consumer participants a transaction fee to cut down on frivolous "shopping." Also, the host could require statements of good faith from consumer participants and carefully track which items each consumer shops for (presumably, only a competitive car dealer would shop for cars more than once every few months, for instance).

Ultimately, of course, the only genuine insurance for a marketer that he is not quoting his lowest prices to a competitor is to know his customers and most likely prospects from previous exchanges. Providing any kind of dialogue tool to current customers and prospects will enable him to secure a deeper, more profitable, and less competitively vulnerable relationship with each of them. But the deeper each relationship is and the more it is based on dialogue, the less regimented that relationship will be. If it's real dialogue, the marketer won't be controlling it all by himself any more. The customer will be just as much in charge as the marketer is.

The ultimate implication of 1:1 media, using electronic mailboxes and bulletin boards in any form, is that the traditional marketing structure—we make, you take; we speak, you listen—will be turned completely upside-down.

The customer will speak, and the marketer will listen. The customer will ask, and the customer and the marketer will both make, together.

The Support Structure for the 1:1 Future

The technological support structure for the 1:1 future is half in place, and the other half is coming sooner than we realize. By the end of the decade, many major magazines will offer subscribers not only personalized advertising, but personalized editorial content as well. Some newspapers may also offer personalization. Fax machines, already found in 30 percent of Japanese homes, will be found in more than 50 percent of US households (and many of these will actually be fax-modems attached to personal computers).

Already, airplane seat backs come not just with telephones, but with interactive video screens as well, connected by satellite to programming providers and catalog merchandisers. Microwave ovens will soon respond to the spoken instructions. Nintendo sets will be used for homework, connecting televisions by phone to databases that provide encyclopedias, textbooks, and news. Consumers driving their cars will be able to choose from hundreds of customized pay-radio programs delivered over the cellular bandwidth.

Interactive televisions will also be with us before the end of the decade—whether such service is brought to consumers' homes by a cable TV company also offering phone service, or by a phone company also offering TV service, or brought to the home computer via Internet and Worldwide Web services that transmit video as well as text and graphics. Once a true "video dial tone" capability is available, anyone with a phone and a television camera will be able to go into the business of TV "broadcasting" for fun or profit.[8]

These new technologies may sound inaccessible to individuals and small businesses, but in fact just the opposite is true. They are accessible in a way that mass media have never been. In a future of video mailboxes and electronic bulletin boards, of computer sorting and storing and forwarding to individualized communications, the old economics of scale that gave an overwhelming advantage to gigantic marketers will evaporate.

What many of us don't realize is just how close the 1:1 future already is.

If fax machines in people's homes and appliances we can talk to sound too far-fetched, then think back on a world without automatic teller machines, or cellular phones. That was 1980. In 1980 the number of televisions with remote control devices was statistically insignificant. There were no compact disks, almost no videocassette recorders, and no video rental stores. Only restaurants had microwave ovens. Facsimile machines cost several thousand dollars each, took five minutes or more to transmit a single page, and were found only at very large companies. No one had a personal computer.

Every twenty years since 1900 the amount of computational power— machine brainpower—that could be purchased with one dollar has increased by a factor of a thousand. That's more than a million-fold increase just since 1950! If the real cost of manufacturing automobiles had declined since 1950 at the same rate as the real cost of processing information, it would be cheaper today to abandon a Rolls Royce and buy a new one rather than put a dime into a parking meter. Today there is more computational power in a new Chevrolet than there was in the Apollo spacecraft that went to the moon.[9]

Put another way, for what it cost a 1950 marketer to keep track of all the individual purchases and transactions of a single customer, today's marketer can track the individual purchases and transactions of several million individual customers, one at a time.

One Customer at a Time

The mass marketer visualizes his task in terms of selling a single product to as many consumers as possible. This process involves advertising, sales promotion, publicity, and frequently a brand management system for organizing the efforts of the company's marketing department. The marketer's task has always been to make the product unique in a way that would appeal to the largest possible number of consumers and then to publicize that uniqueness with one-way mass-media messages that are interesting, informative, and persuasive to the "audience" for the product.

A 1:1 marketer, however, will not be trying to sell a single product to as many customers as possible. Instead, the task will be to sell a single customer as many products as possible—over a long period of time, and across different product lines. To do this, a marketer will need to concentrate on building unique relationships with individual customers, on a 1:1 basis. Some relationships will be more valuable than others. The best relationships, and the most profitable business, will define a marketer's best customers.

Imagine a florist in a small town, for example, The florist's task can be visualized in two different ways.

A traditional marketing approach would be to calculate market share by counting up a shop's total sales of flowers for any given year. Divide that by the grand total of flower purchases in the town, and the florist discovers she has, say, 10 percent of the total flower business. Using the traditional, mass marketing approach—which inevitably follows from market-share thinking—this florist could run some specials for Mother's Day and Valentine's Day, when a lot of people buy flowers. This might increase her traffic and maybe even her share of the market, providing her competitors don't lower their prices too. But it will cost her some of her profitability. So will the newspaper ads and radio spots necessary to publicize the sale.

Any extra business she gets will be from customers who only come in because she's offering a discount, or running a sale, or giving away a premium, or doing more advertising. All of these customers will defect to competitors the moment those competitors offer similar inducements.

Now imagine a different approach to business. Last year a professional on the East Coast called a local, independent florist in a small Midwest city where his mother lived to have flowers sent to her on her birthday. Three weeks before her birthday this year, he received a note from the same florist, reminding him (1) that his mother's birthday was coming up, (2) that he had sent spider lilies and freesias last year for a certain price, and (3) a phone call to the specified number would put another beautiful bouquet on his mother's doorstep on her birthday this year.

This small, independent florist is working hard to improve her share of her customer's business. Instead of spending just to publicize her products to an entire market, using non-addressable mass media to make the same offer to everyone as if no one had ever bought flowers from her before, she is taking a share-of-customer approach. This florist is engaged in a 1:1 communication with an individual customer, *to get more of that one individual's business.* The information she has about *this* customer—Mom's birthdate—cannot help her get more business from any other customer, but with *this* customer, it gives her a distinct and bankable advantage.[10]

She is performing a service—reminding our friend of his mother's upcoming birthday—and is making her flower shop indispensable and easy to do business with. This doesn't mean the florist isn't also working on acquiring new customers. She just makes sure that she gets every possible bit of patronage from those customers she already has. Her tools? Nothing more than a PC and a lot of common sense.

The company which takes a share-of-customer perspective will build relationships with customers which will transcend the comings and goings of the individual employees in the marketing or sales departments. With a thousand-fold decrease every twenty years in the cost of information processing, today a company can follow, and follow up on, the individual purchases and transactions of millions of individual customers simultaneously, one at a time, for the same cost required to track a few hundred customers in 1970. And every year it gets less and less expensive to track all those customers. This means the possibility of an *electronic* relationship that allows every employee in the company to *remember* the entire relationship and allocate resources wisely to the most valuable customers.

The information tools required to manage millions of such individualized relationships are already available. However, understanding the capabilities of these tools—and knowing when and how to use them—are not trivial skills. For instance, instead of doing research in the comfortable old way—conducting surveys and projecting the results to a broad, undifferentiated target audience—marketers will conduct research by conducting "experiments" with individual customers. In the 1:1 future a marketer might conduct hundreds or thousands of different experiments at once.

The most indispensable element of a relationship with each customer in the 1:1 future will be dialogue and feedback. What do customers really want? What does *this customer* really want?

Clearly, product and service quality will be paramount—to say that quality has always been king sounds trite. But it has never before been possible for most large marketing companies, or even very many smaller ones, to identify and capitalize on individual customer satisfaction, or to detect and prevent individual dissatisfaction and defection. Soon the push for product and service quality will come directly and explicitly from a company's *individual* customers, talking one-to-one with that *company*.

Without a satisfactory product and an acceptable level of service, no customer will be willing to continue a relationship with a marketer for long. But customers do not all experience the quality of a product in the same way. One customer's convenience is another's hassle. Since every customer's quality experience is a subjective event, a 1:1 marketer will be dealing not just with product quality but with *relationship* quality.

The nature of the relationship with each customer in this new environment will be collaborative. Instead of having to be "sold to," customers increasingly will "sell themselves," stepping hand in hand with the marketer through the complicated information exchanges that will, more and more, accompany individual product sales.

As customers, we can already see this beginning to happen. Marketing companies are asking us to collaborate with them in the selling process—whether it's the long-distance company asking us to specify the twenty phone numbers we'd most like to receive discounts on; or a bank asking us to complete money transfers at the ATM machine, or via touch-tone phone, or an automobile company asking us to complete a survey and rate their dealer's service department, or to make a wish list of the options we'd like on our next car.

The more individualized this kind of collaborative interaction is with regard to a particular customer, the more the marketer and that customer will develop a joint interest in the success of the marketer's own marketing effort—as it applies to that customer.

Instead of measuring the success of a marketing program by how many sales transactions occur across the entire market during a particular period, a 1:1 marketer will gauge success by the projected increase or decrease in a customer's expected future value to a company. The true measure of success, one customer at a time, will not be market share, but share of customer.

Interactivity *Requires* 1:1 Marketing

Before being able to take full advantage of the new media and information technologies now becoming available, a marketer has to have a practical set of principles for applying these capabilities. Today's mass marketing paradigm has no *need* for interactive media and computers that track individual customer transactions, linked over time. Tracking customers and conversing with them individually are not tasks that fit into a market-share approach to competition.

But the instant a marketer begins thinking in terms of share of customer, rather than overall market share, new vistas of competitive opportunities will open up. Suddenly, we will see all sorts of ways to employ interactive, addressable media technology, and sophisticated computers. Instead of being overwhelmed by these new tools, we will want more and better tools, *more* interactivity, *more* computer memory and processing power.

The key share-of-customer requirement is to *know* each customer, 1:1. A marketer must know which consumers will never purchase the product at all, so she can stop spending money and effort trying to get them to do something they never will. And she must know who her loyal customers are, so she can take steps to make sure that hers is the brand they choose even more often.

Most companies today are not prepared at all for the kind of cataclysmic change in business competition that is just around the corner. Many, however, are already beginning to apply the principles of the 1:1 future to engage in a totally new and dramatically different form of competition.

Thinking about marketing and communication turned upside-down can be a challenge. Marketers have gotten comfortable with the methods they've been using for the past four decades. Market share. Segmentation. CPMs, GRPs, ratings and shares. Psychographic and geodemographic analysis. These have become the shrines of a religion to the mass marketer. Some say the game is changing. Wrong. The game is *over*, and when we all wake up (tomorrow morning) in the dawn of the Information Age, the mass marketers will be holding their aching heads, trying to figure out what happened to their credentials.

Nearly a hundred years ago, mass production made mass marketing possible. But it was the rise of mass *media*, in the form of radio and national magazines, that *mandated* mass marketing. Likewise, new developments in technology make mass customized production possible, but it is the fractionalization of mass media and the rise of one-to-one (1:1) media that *mandate* 1:1 marketing.[11]

The heart of 1:1 marketing will be a focus on winning a greater share of each customer's business precisely because marketers now have the computational power to remember every detail about a customer's transaction history, and that includes communication. (It's about time. After all, customers have always been able to remember their interactions with companies.) Instead of trying to sell as many packages of product this quarter as possible, marketers will be able to use this new-found memory to satisfy each individual customer's needs. Instead of assigning a product manager the task of trying to sell as many packages of bologna this month as possible, Hormel will task a customer manager with getting Hormel products into Johnny Smith's lunchbox. Instead of trying to sell as many Windows packages as possible to whomever will buy them, Microsoft will instead focus on winning share of disk for many different applications and programs—for each customer, 1:1.

It's obvious that growing *each customer's* business has dramatic implications for the rules of engagement:

- A new emphasis on long-term relationships with consumers (building Lifetime Value, or LTV).

- High-quality product and service, since repeat customers won't happen any other way.

- Differentiating customers, and spending more resources on those who are more valuable.

- Initiating and maintaining dialogues in order to build learning relationships with consumers, and abandoning the old-fashioned advertising monologues of the mass marketer.[12]

Advertising and Dialogue in the 1:1 Future

In the old-fashioned mass-media paradigm, the way advertising has worked has been simple: Figure out the likely prospects and aim standardized messages at that target market using mass media for delivery. If the marketer can win awards in the process for her cleverness and wit, great. But the primary goal has been media efficiency against a specified audience who is likely to see the media vehicle chosen. While they're there, they just might get a glimpse of the ad. The marketer's goal is to penetrate the cerebellum with the message that his gum has longer-lasting flavor or his hotel provides a better stay for the money.

That worked fine when we could make reasonable predictions about where people's attention would be directed. But with a cosmic explosion in media choice, as well as the ability of the interactive customer to *talk back*, future advertisers will have to completely rethink the way they talk with consumers. When marketers talk to customers through interactive radio (cell phones), fax response, electronic mail, interactive TV with 500-channel capability, and other new media, what new rules will govern play?

The nature of "advertising" and promotions face major changes. In the 1:1 future, advertising's role will shift from building awareness and affective response to serving as a broker between marketers and customers, providing an explicit bargain for dialogue participation, and finding new ways to be considered part of the entertainment milieu.

Several new media already offer the technological capability that will characterize interactive television and can serve as an analogy for the video dial tone. Specifically, the Internet offers the host computer necessary to serve as information intermediation that will protect consumer privacy while providing explicit bargains between marketers and individual consumers.

In the past, copywriters and others responsible for marketing communications have based their success on unique selling propositions, positioning, and other creative strategies designed to direct a broad appeal to a defined but mass audience. In the future, copywriters will face the challenge of personalized message delivery as well as the profound implications of dealing with individual feedback made possible through currently available interactive media.

In the 1:1 future, advertising will be *invited, solicited*, and *integral.*

- Invited: Successful advertisers will have to stop their frenetic shouting at customers, and will instead engage in the polite invitation. "We will credit $4.00 to your phone bill if you watch our infomercial and call our toll-free number with the PIN code we've recorded in the middle." The bargain is explicit: Listen to our pitch and we'll give you something you want — a pay-per-view, maybe, or a few minutes of cell-phone time.

- Solicited: Customers will keep marketers honest when they can initiate the dialogue. A customer goes on-line, identity protected by an information intermediator, and sends the following ad: "I want to buy a 15-75mm camera with point-and-shoot capability that also allows manual control. Need auto-rewind-before-shooting feature, and carrying case. Willing to spend $100-$300. Who wants my business?" Responses could appear in the customer's coded video or fax mailbox from local retailers, national electronic mail order shops, manufacturers, and individuals looking to resell a used camera.

- Integral: As customers opt out of advertising per se *because they can*, the advertising will become more and more a part of entertainment and information. Already product placement in movies is big business, with clear distinctions in placement fees for background use vs. handling by the hero. In the future, we will see a greater fusion of publicity, advertising, and careful product placement in nearly every media outlet.

Does this mean mass media, and old-fashioned mass media advertising, will disappear? Is this truly the end of all mass marketing? No—no more than farming disappeared when America left the Agricultural era for the Industrial age. It just meant that fewer people were needed for farming, and more people were needed instead to work in factories in the city. As a minor side effect, all of society changed, but we still eat. So we will still see Michael Somebody advertising Nikes and Pepsi (after all, it's no fun to pay over $100 for shoes if your friends haven't heard of the brand), but we will also see a lot less mass media advertising.

What this means for marketers is a greater challenge to get their messages to individual consumers. What this means for consumers is more messages that we might truly find useful, and fewer messages that we classify as "junk." New media mandates a new strategy, or we will simply send "junk mail at light speed."

The question is not how we can use the Internet to make products more profitable. The question is how we can use new tools, and old tools, to make *each customer* more profitable, one customer at a time.

References

1. The telegram was discontinued by Western Union in December 1991. See Levin, Gary, "Western Union Not Fading into Sunset: New Services are Added as Telegram Drops," *Advertising Age,* April 27, 1992, p. 54.

2. Daimler story details were discussed with Bernd Harling, manager of corporate communications for Mercedes-Benz of North America, Inc. Telephone interview, December 16, 1992.

   The number of cars on the world's roads is a conservative estimate based on 424,365,795 cars in 1989, with annual net growth of approximately 12 million. Motor Vehicle Manufacturers Association of the United States, *Motor Vehicle Facts and Figures,* 1991, p. 37.

3. Peppers, Don and Rogers, Martha, *The One to One Future, Building Relationships One Customer at a Time,* New York: Doubleday/Currency, 1993, Ch. 7.

4. Peppers, Don and Rogers, Martha, "Let's Make a Deal", *Wired,* February 1994, p. 74.

5. Using the fax machine to bring buyers and sellers together was reported by William M. Bulkeley, "Faxes Prove to Be a Powerful Tool for Setting up Electronic Markets," *Wall Street Journal,* July 28, 1992, p. B3.

6. We spoke to Marcia Linley, V.P. and Director of Technical Operations for GAIN, by telephone, March 3, 1993.

7. Prodigy's William Tobin is quoted from *Direct,* August 1992, p. 36.

8. Paragraphs about the support structure for the 1:1 paradigm are based on current developments, reported widely. For an overview, see:

Personalized ads and editorial: Albert Scardino, "Donnelley Develops a Way for Magazines to Get Personal," *New York Times*, November 20, 1989, p. D8.

Fax machines: *Newspapers and Voice*, "Hot Off the Fax," April 1992, pp. 20-25; Takami, Hirohiko, "Facsimile Diffuses to Home Users," *Business Japan*, November 1989, pp. 73, 79, 81; Judith Waldrop, "Strong Fax Sales will Challenge Postal Service," *American Demographics*, June 1991, p. 12.

Airplane video screens: Larry Riggs, "Catalogues Contacted for a New In-flight Program," *DM News*, June 8, 1992, pp. 1, 2.

Microwave ovens respond to speech: John J. Keller, "Computers Get Powerful 'Hearing' Aids: Improved Methods of Voice Recognition," *Wall Street Journal*, April 7, 1992, p. B1.

VCRs respond to speech: Richard Zoglin, "Can Anybody Work This Thing? New Gadgets Keep Aiming to Cure VCR Illiteracy. The Latest Lets People Simply Talk to Their Machines," *Time*, November 23, 1992, p. 67.

Extended Nintendo: Eben Shapiro, "Nintendo and Minnesota Set a Living Room Lottery Test," *New York Times*, September 27, 1991, p. A1.

Cellular radio: Howard Schlossberg, "Like your Ballgames on TV? Get Ready to Pay for Them," *Marketing News*, April 13, 1992, p. 14.

150 channel to 500-channel capacity: Mary Lu Carnevale, "Ring In the New: Telephone Service Seems on the Brink of Huge Innovations; Baby Bells, and Cable Firms Vie to Win Video Market and Add a Host of Services," *Wall Street Journal*, February 10, 1993, pp. A1, A7; John Markoff, "A System to Speed Computer Data: Compressing Images May Lead to a Variety of New Products," *New York Times*, January 30, 1991.

Interactive TV: Alice B. Cuneo, "The Fine Points of Interactive TV," *Advertising Age*, May 11, 1992, p. 60.

9. Information about fiber optic lines abounds, but we drew from George Gilder, "Into the Telecosm," *Harvard Business Review*, March-April 1991, pp. 150-61, and John J. Keller, "Pacific Bell Tests Fiber-Optic Lines for Home Phones," *Wall Street Journal*, August 27, 1991, p. B4. Of course, many marketers do realize just how close the 1:1 future really is. See Betsy Spethman, "Marketers Tap Into Tech," *Advertising Age*, January 25, 1993, pp. 30. Also see George Gilder (*Microcosm: The Quantum Era of Economics and Technology*. New York: Simon & Schuster, 1989), who suggests that, throughout most of this century, the amount of computational power that can be bought for one dollar has increased by a factor of 1,000 every twenty years since 1900. He suggests that the rate is speeding up and is now probably every ten years. Or less.

10. Peppers, Don and Rogers, Martha, *The One to One Future, Building Relationships One Customer at a Time,* New York: Doubleday/Currency, 1993, Ch. 2.

11. B. Joseph Pine II, Don Peppers, and Martha Rogers, "Do You Want to Keep Your Customers Forever?", *Harvard Business Review,* March–April 1995, p. 103.

12. Learning relationships are introduced in Pine, Peppers, and Rogers, *Harvard Business Review,* March–April 1995.

CHAPTER

10

The Impact of Interactive Communication on Advertising and Marketing

And Now a Word from Our Consumer

Edward Forrest
Lance Kinney
Michael Chamberlain

Edward Forrest is Director of the Interactive Communications graduate program at Florida State University. His ongoing projects include multiplatform CD-ROM and CD-I disc production, and World Wide Web page-site development.

Lance Kinney has worked on both the agency and client sides, including research in affective response and attitude measurement.

Michael Chamberlain is Director, New Media Activities, of United News & Media, plc, London, England. He is also Chairman of OIT Limited, a subsidiary company specializing in the creation of electronic online sites.

What impact will interactive communication have on:

- The role and scope of activities of the advertising agency?
- The form, style and substance of the advertising message?
- Target market segmentation, definition, and strategy?
- Media planning?

Are you ready for:

- The communication concept?
- Interactive advertising-pods?
- Partipulation?
- Technographics?

This chapter will use as an organizing scheme Harold D. Lasswell's (1948) classic communication paradigm:

Who

Says what

To whom

In what channel

With what effect

As an organizing scheme, Lasswell's paradigm allows us to independently address each core component of a mediated communication system. Wherein: *Who* concerns the agent that conceives and controls any given communication. *Says What* refers to the message—its contents and aesthetics. *To Whom* refers to the audience for which the message was produced. *In* What Channel refers to the medium through which the message is transmitted. And, *With What Effect* concerns the nature and magnitude of impact that the message has on the audience's attitudes, beliefs and behavior.

Specifically, we will be contemplating the range of effects that can be expected as the commercial communication industry moves from a mass-mediated to a computer-mediated system.

The Advertising Agency/"Who"

Like so many other instituions born and bred in the industrial age of mass production, mass media and mass consumption, the advertising agency has, in the main, approached the new media with hesitation and skepticism. Advertising has always been an industry that was quick to exploit (if not create) new trends. But, unlike the trends of the past, the new communication technologies have not been readily embraced according to the initial reports by industry observers:

> . . . traditional agencies are woefully behind in mastering technology and getting their clients involved in interactive projects. An August, 1994, *Advertising Age* ranking of the top 29 agencies as to interactive technology use awarded high marks only to Ogilvy & Mather. . . . "The majority of large agencies are doing everything they can to frustrate the interactive movement," asserts Alan Brody, program director of Createch, a Scarsdale, N.Y. company that sponsors interactive advertising conferences.

Interactive advertising means reengineering the way suppliers, producers, and consumers interact. And, as every technology manager knows, reengineering frequently engenders resistance (Wilder, 1994).

It is suggested that the emerging interactive technologies will reengineer the way suppliers, producers, and consumers interact in at least three critical ways.

1. *The agency will evolve: From carnival barker to communication clearinghouse.* With respect to reengineering the the nature of the relationship between the agency and consumer, we will witness the essential character of the advertising agency evolve *from* that of a *barker* on the mass-media midway—of simple slogans and "unique selling points," *to* that of an on-line *mediator* of comparative and compelling information that will assist the consumer at every stage of the consumption cycle. To date, advertising's most basic charge has been to provide the consumer with a few bits of information in the most direct and entertaining manner possible. For the most part, all that was needed was a catchy headline and/or visual to grab attention, some body copy to describe the products comparative benefits and a logo and slogan to promote memorability. However, we are experiencing an ever increasing array of products and services from which to choose, and coupled with the

increasing pace of modern life, we have less time for comparison shopping than ever before. Moreover, it has always been the case that when it came to "high-ticket" items (such as appliances, automobiles, homes, etc.) and specialty products (such as audio and video components, consumer electronics, etc.) the gap between advertising and sufficient information was filled by the "salesman." It remains that on both fronts—for salesman as well as for commercials—there is room for improvement in the quantity and credibility of information provided consumers. Thus, "instead of cramming the world's airwaves with eye-catching images, clever jingles, and celebrity hucksters," advertising now has the ability to "evolve into a two-way medium in which consumers with PCs and a modem can choose the information they want to access." To wit:

> A PC-based diskette produced by automaker Ford is an example of what sets interactive advertising apart. Called the Ford simulator, the program lets potential buyers compare colors, engine sizes, options, and payment plans for Ford's entire consumer line of 25 cars and light trucks. Information not hucksterism, is the goal, says Larry Dale, a Ford marketing specialist in Dearborn, Mich. "The more information they have," he says about high-tech shoppers, "the better vehicle they will have in mind when they go to a dealership." (Wilder, 1994)

2. *The agency will evolve: From working* for *the media and advertisers . . . to working* with *the consumer.* A second function that interactive technology will reengineer will be the nature of the relationship between the agency and the media. Historically, an "adman" was the middleman who bought wholesale chunks of space in magazines and newspapers and then resold parcels to individual advertisers. In turn, the adman received a 15 percent commission ("kick-back") from the medium for his efforts. The advertising agency evolved by adding on the copywriting and design functions to the media placement services of these original "space brokers." In recent years the traditional 15 percent commission has been squeezed by sponsors who want to pay agencies directly for their labor, and not indirectly for the amount of media space or time they consume. Many agencies now place advertising for commissions of 10–12 percent or less. Moreover, the media buying services that were once the sole province of a full-service agency are today provided by specialized media services serving many accounts. And, copywriting, along with print and broadcast production, have moved to so-called

"boutiques." Other agencies have moved into specialty areas and niche services such as promotion and direct marketing. A predictable consequence of this trend of agency specialization is the emergence of the "interactive advertising agency." As opposed to the advertiser of the past, the interactive advertiser sees his task *less as a pitchman* for sponsors *than as a consultant* for consumers. To quote one leading interactive pioneer:

> We see interactivity as enabling brands to create better relationships with their customers, said Gerald O'Connell, Modem Media's founding general partner. . . . Modem Media, Westport, Conn., specializes in designing, advertising and promotional campaigns on Interactive platforms, ranging from CD-ROM to the Internet. . . .
>
> One campaign Modem Media designed . . . involved a college football poll conducted on Prodigy Services Inc. The objective, O'Connell said was to "create an affinity between college football and Coors Light." Consumers were able to vote for their favorite teams using Prodigy's on-line service, or by phoning to an "800" toll-free number, and win such prizes as a trip to the Super Bowl game. The campaign generated 10,000 responses in a week. (*Interactive advertising pioneers*, 1994)

At its best, the interactive agency will serve as a facilitator of an ongoing, on-line conversation between the advertiser and consumer, providing the customer not only with exactly what information they need—when they need it (on demand advertising), but also additional venues though which to interact with the sponsor.

3. *The agency will evolve: From the marketing concept to the communication concept.* The fundamental principle on which the advertising and marketing industries have operated throughout the past decades has been the *marketing concept* (defined as profit through consumer satisfaction based on the ability of the product or service to deliver the attributes promised by advertising). While the marketing concept will continue to be important, the ad agency will increasingly need to pay hom-age to (what we define as) **the communication concept:** *The process wherein the ad agency enables, engages, facilitates, sustains and rewards interaction between consumers and advertisers throughout the entire consumption cycle.*

Future advertising success will be found in giving the consumer the easiest, most rewarding access to relevant information before, during and after the purchase. Interactive technology enables the advertiser to personalize his approach to every customer and exchange relevant information that will prove mutually beneficial. For example,

> ... when the French edition of *Vogue* wanted to spice up print ads in a perfume supplement, it put a lip-sticked kiosk in the cosmetics area of a Paris department store. The interactive kiosk. . . . didn't dispense fragrance but offered personalized advice. . . . it asked shoppers about the personality of the woman who would use the perfume. . . . Kiosk users could pick up a phone receiver in the kiosk to hear the questions whispered by a female voice. At the end, the kiosk program printed recommendations for the aromas that best matched the woman's lifestyle. . . . (The customer response as described by the sales manager) "it was amazing . . . there was a line from 10am to late at night" (Clark, 1994).

In the future, the bottom line will not only be a matter of marke*t share* (measured by a company's percentage of sales relative to the total sales in a product category) but also *info-share,* measured by the number of clients active in a database that is developed and maintained via interactive technology.

Perhaps the compensation pattern of future advertising will have less to do with the amount of advertising placed or produced, than with the number of inquires any given interactive ad generates. Already this is the system in which direct marketers operate, as do "fulfillment houses" that channel information on consumers back to advertisers via "kickback" cards in magazines and telephone contacts. However, the leads that are passed back for follow-up are often weeks and sometimes months old. Interactive technology simutaneously offers the consumer advertising on demand and the advertiser the opportunity to follow-up any inquiry with additional "just-in-time" promotional materials and purchasing information.

The Commercial Message/"Says what"

The nature and contours of the advertising message itself will undergo drastic change. As we move *from* the mass- *to -* the multi-mediated world of interactive communication at least four predictions can be made regarding its impact on the character and contours of the commercial message itself.

1. The commercial message will become multi-dimensional and transactional. We will move from one-way, truncated 30 second spots, 1/2 page spreads and 7-word billboard blurbs to interactive advertising-pods of product information that can be peeled back like an onion with "tell-me-more" and "show-me-more" buttons, while the consumer provides the advertiser with key facts and data:

2. The commercial message will be move *from intrusive* commercial messages that intermittently interrupt the on-going media experience of the consumer *to invited conversation,* wherein the consumer actively seeks out and requests advertising and promotional materials—defined by Don Peppers and Martha Rogers as *invitational advertising.* The reader might note that this and other original insights into advertising's "one-to-one" future with individual customers were elaborated on by Don Peppers and Martha Rogers in the previous chapter:

> Successful advertisers will have to stop their frenetic shouting at customers, and will instead offer polite invitations designed to initiate or continue individual customer dialogues. Starting a dialogue, either with a current customer or with a potential new customer, will be the primary goal of any marketer hoping eventually to sell products or services. Advertisers will no longer find it beneficial to irritate viewers into remembering their brands. Not only is this a bad way to begin a dialogue, but it is very likely that in the interactive future a consumer who feels irritated with a certain ad or brand will be capable of forbidding that brand from appearing on his own set again. (Schrage, Peppers, Rogers and Shapiro, 1994)

3. The commercial message will be *less ephemeral* (zapped in a matter of nanoseconds; skipped with a flip of the page; driven past at 65 mph) and *more embedded* with information being part and parcel of the program with which the individual is interacting. Indeed, the evolution of corporate web sites (such as the one produced by Modem Media for Zima Clearmalt—described in chapter 17 of this book) is reminiscent of the early days of broadcasting, when programs were wholly produced and controlled by a single sponsor and its advertising agency.

4. Finally, in terms of style and substance, the "commercial" message will move from *glib* and superficial titillation with intangible rewards *to substantive* value-added "infotainment" with immediate and

tangible rewards. No longer will the simple play-on words, funny innu-
endo or double entendre—with a slice of cheese or beefcake thrown
in—be the consumer's only reward for paying attention. The interactive ads of the future will necessarily offer consumers something real
and something tangible for their time and attention:

> . . . in the age of interactivity, this formerly implicit bargain between
> advertiser and consumer is likely to become decidedly explicit. . . .
> We're talking about deal city, here. Imagine getting offers like these
> when you turn on your television:
>
> - Watch this two-minute video on the new Ford Taurus, and we'll
>   pay for the pay-per-view movie of your choice.
> - Answer this brief survey from Kellogg and we'll pay for the next
>   three episodes of "Murphy Brown."
> - Push the Tell-Me-More button on your remote at any time during
>   this ten-minute infomercial, and you might win a Caribbean cruise.
>   (Schrage, et. al., 1994)

The very nature of the advertising business has been to inform consumers about "new and/or improved" products in an entertaining way. The
expanded frontiers and contours of the new media allow the advertiser
to expand the commercial message with much *more "info"* and enables
the consumer to *participate in the "entertainment":*

> Interactive ads can evolve into compelling direct-response environ-
> ments—informative, intimate, and immediate . . . . It's easy to
> imagine McDonald's producing an educational video game called,
> say, Burger Hunt, for its kiddie customers. Ronald McDonald gives the
> player a random quantity of 'McDollars' and the child has to maneu-
> ver, Mario-like, through mazes of Hamburglars and other McDonald-
> Land obstacles to buy and bring back just the right number of burgers,
> fries, shakes, and McNuggets—plus change—to win. . . . The point
> is simple: Games are dual purpose—they create compelling experi-
> ences and get customers even more involved with the product. Coca-
> Cola, Toys R Us, PepsiCo, and Nabisco may all ultimately design
> games to imprint their products onto the neurons of their younger
> customers. . . . Similarly, Chrysler or Toyota might develop VR driving
> games for adolescents and adults to promote their cars. (Schrage,
> et. al., 1994)

In the 1960s, a prominent political advertising practitioner, Tony Schwartz, spoke of a phenomenon he called *partipulation:Wherein, you could heighten the involvement an individual had with any given commercial if you got them to "participate in their own manipulation."* Certainly, these new interactive ad-games—which in the act of playing consumers will get their neurons imprinted—takes that psycho-behavorial process to heights Tony Schwartz never dreamed of.

The Audience and Consumer/"To whom"

To date, the audience to whom advertising has been directed has been defined in bulk terms—i.e. adults, teens, households, women 18 to 49, men 25 to 34. When dealing with the mass media the mass audience was packaged and sold by the "cost-per-thousand" and by "gross rating points." However, as noted by Paula George Tompkins, president of the SoftAd Group (an interactive ad agency in Mill Valley, CA., with such clients as Ford and Abbott Labs):

> You can't use traditional measurements like cost-per-thousand and cost per response. . . measuring interactive is a lot more involved and detailed. . . . (Wilder, 1994)

Interactive technology will generate a virtually endless stream of consumer information. Instantly a marketer will know what individuals are interested in his product. Within seconds of any inquiry the advertiser can respond to each and every consumer's unique set of questions and needs. The sale can be closed before the consumer ever even encounters a competitor's product on the shelf.

> Of course, that means big piles of new data for marketing experts to sort through and analyze. But this is not the traditional number-crunching variety of marketing information. Detailed buyer profiles present a different information technology challenge than that produced by massaging reams of transaction records from supermarket checkout scanners or telemarketing centers. (Wilder, 1994)

Perhaps the standard demographic descriptors of the audience will need to be supplemented with something like technographics: *combined index of general demographic measures (i.e. age, sex, income, education, etc.) and specfic measurements of an individual's ownership and use patterns of interactive technologies.* Thus, traditional demographic market segments, like women 18 to 49, can be further defined by their access to and amount of time spent with any given interactive technology. Instead of cost-per-thousand we may need to calculate "hits-per-pod" or maybe "mouse-clicks-per-sale."

The Communication Medium/"In What Channel"

> The real problem with advertising is that there's going to be so much of it. (David Abbott, Chairman and Creative Director, Abott Mead Vickers, one of Britain's top five advertising agencies, quoted in the *Financial Times Weekend,* Apr. 30–May 1, 1994.)

The Internet and World Wide Web, America Online, Prodigy . . . are just some of the on-line services that we can add to the list. Other new media advertising vehicles include an alpha-spaghetti of acronym platforms likes CD-ROM, CD-I, CD-ROM-XA, VIS, DVD, 3DO, etc. Its all on-line, on demand and brought to you by cable, satellite, fiber optic, optical discs, cellular and wireless technologies. In the emerging interactive media world, mass media will refer more to the number of channels than to the nature of the audience. Tomorrow's audience will order à la carte. In addition to all the various on-line services and optical disc options, tomorrow's media consumer may have five hundred-plus TV channels from which to choose. It has been estimated it could take up to 14 minutes to survey (zap through) all the channels, lest it be for the intelligent agents ("KnowBots") pre-trained to their master's or mistress's voice that will screen out the excess, and deliver only a limited "menu" of program choices . . . tailored to taste. You like sports? Your "KnowBot" may locate 30 events for your review. Movies? fashions? News? Sitcoms? All there in abundance, and again that is not including any entertainment alternatives like movies-on-demand or CD-ROM games. And, how about advertising?

> Imagine a television channel devoted entirely to commercials . . . no programming . . . no chatty spots from a shopping network. Only ads. Most people would agree that the station's audience would be a small, eclectic slice of the demographic pie: insomniacs and masochists. Yet,

by year's end (1994), 10,000 PC users in four U.S. cities will test an interactive online service that some may regard as the cyberspace equivalant of this imaginary advertising channel. The service called ProductView Interactive, will carry pitches for cars, vacations, stereos, financial services, and sporting equipment. Consumers will be able to comparison shop by clicking icons and hypertext to obtain detailed information about an advertised product. (Wilder, 1994)

With What Effect

Is the ad agency ready for all of this? Are traditional advertising techniques facing imminent extinction? Is an entire industrial age species in danger of becoming "road-kill" on tomorrow's information superhighway? It is becoming ever more apparent that the heady days of the "go-go" 1970's and 1980's are over. Yesterday's advertising campaigns were all about targeting the masses—using mass media to get your (client's) message across. Reach and frequency was the name of the game. One 'good' TV commercial made for up to $ 1-1/2 million—the British Airways "Manhattan" commercial cost that much—could be used time and again to reach the target market with advertisers willing to pay over five times that amount to reach the right audience, such as Budweiser at the "Superbowl." And that's for just one spot. Few and far between are the mass advertising campaigns today wherein a few media purchases generate lots of (easy) commission.

The full-service ad agencies of yesteryear promising global brands, and global marketing strategies to match, have been pummeled by recession, culminating in reduced fees and commissions, and correspondingly dismal levels of earnings. Staffs are smaller, expected to accomplish more with less. The only "innovation" of note has been the growth of specialist media buying "shops" which cudgel media owners into lower-than-rate-card deals. Program sponsorship, product placement and airtime "barter" deals have also grown in popularity. But they are small beer. Clients have become increasingly demanding regarding measurement of performance, with many now coupling agency compensation with market share gain or other performance measures. Large and small agencies alike have been buffeted by the winds of change. They have been forced to reach new accommodations with their clients, and work in much reduced circumstances.

As a result, the agencies claim they are being squeezed so badly on margins that there is little room for maintaining existing services never mind creating or developing new interactive ones. As Martin Nisenholtz, former VP of interactive marketing at Ogilvy & Mather Direct, observed:

> A lot of big consumer product companies had people dedicated to new technologies. . . . but budgets were cut. . . . You have to justify everything you do in terms of short-term value. That's tough to do with interactive technololgy. (Wilder, 1994)

Meanwhile, the tick of high-technology marches on. The necessity to prepare for its impacts is not entirely lost on the advertising community. By the end of 1994, "the industry's two major trade groups, the Association of National Advertisers and the American Association of Advertising Agencies (also known as the Four A's), formed a joint task force to study the new media" (Maddox, 1994). Advertising executives like Betsy Frank, executive vice president and director of strategic media resources, Saatchi & Saatchi, admits that: "Most of our clients recognize they are going to have to make some pretty significant changes in how they communicate with and motivate their customers" (Maddox, 1994). And, no louder wake-up call could be given than that of Edwin Artzt, chairman and CEO of Procter & Gamble Co., who in a May '94 keynote speech at the Four A's annual convention "exhorted advertising representatives to wake up to the reality of new media technologies" (Wilder, 1994).

Just what exactly that "reality" will be, nobody really knows. There remains a gaping void between the ultimate promise and present performance of interactive technology. Because of this state of affairs advertising practitioners "have shifted from what's possible to what's real." (Maddox, 1994). Until the hardware manufacturers, software programmers and distribution companies narrow the gap, some observers are putting out the "do not disturb" sign for folks like Procter & Gamble's Edwin Artzt. In his petition to "Give Ad Agencies A Break," Al Perlman makes the case to "debunk one of the myths on the state of the interactive market:

> . . . The myth: Advertising agencies aren't doing their share to make interactivity happen. The reality. Bull. . . . Where's the infrastructure? . . . the bandwidth's just not there yet for the video, imaging and audio

> that will enable the type of creative execution clients are expecting
> . . . . The business paradigm for most interactive business is undefined
> . . . . How is fulfillment handled? Billing? Security? Customer Service?
> Advertising comes with many of its own built-in questions. Whom does
> it reach, how many respond, how is the impact of the ad measured?
> Add interactivity to the equation and all of the questions multiply
> (Perelman, 1994).

Indeed, determining the ultimate impact that new interactive technologies will have on the advertising industry is difficult. Moreover, early speculation on the probable applications and initial impact of new media technologies is often off the mark. There is no reason to believe that the prognosticators of grand nature and scope of interactive advertising are any more immune to *media-myopia* than their predecessors; (*with media-myopia defined as a* unique combination of shortsightedness *when it comes to estimating the public's desire for any given technological advance* AND rearsightedness *when it comes to ascertaining its ultimate utility*).

Albeit, the "potential" impacts that new interactive technologies may have on the advertising industry have been recognized. The emerging spectrum of communication technologies will offer the consumer a wide range of options from which to receive information on consumer goods and services. To be sure, the new interactive technologies will allow the consumer greater control and a more central role in how and how much product/service information is accessed. Whether or not the consumer wants to assume a new role and excercise greater control remains to be seen. As Schrage, et. al., observed:

> The fashionable, faux futurism predicts that this time will be different,
> that this time new media technology will guarantee the individual the
> upper hand over the advertiser. Maybe; maybe not. More likely, we'll
> see these new media renegotiate the power relationships between
> individuals and advertisers. Yesterday, we changed the channel; today
> we hit the remote; tomorrow, we'll reprogram our agents/filters.
> We'll interact with advertising where once we only watched; we'll seek
> out advertising where once we avoided it. Advertising will not go away;
> it will be rejuvenated. (Schrage, et. al., 1994)

References

Clark, T. (1994). From Pfeiffer to Perfume: Real Interactive Ads, *Interactive Week*, October 10, 1994, p. 32.

Interactive Age, (1994). Interactive advertising pioneers, September 26, 1994, p. 55.

Financial Times Weekend (1994). Quote of David Abbott, Chairman and Creative Director, Abott Mead Vickers, one of Britain's top five advertising agencies, Apr. 30–May 1, 1994.

Lasswell, H. D. (1948). The Structure and Function of Communication in Society. In L. Bryson (Ed.) *The Communication of Ideas* (pp. 37–51) New York: Harper and Brothers.

Maddox, K. (1994). Advertisers seek interactive info, *Interactive Age*, September 26, 1994, p. 45, 55.

McLuhan, H. M. (1964). *Understanding Media: The Extensions of Man.* Toronto: University of Toronto Press.

Perlman, A. (1994). Give Ad Agencies A Break, *Interactive Week*, October 10, 1994, p.23.

Schrage, M. (1994, Feb.). Is Advertising Finally Dead?—part 1 and, Is Advertising Really dead—part 2, AdViruses, digimercials, and memgraphics: The future of advertising is the future of media, with Don Peppers, Martha Rogers, and Robert D. Shapiro, *Wired* magazine, Issue 2.02, Transmitted 94-04-18 to, and cited from, America On-line).

Wilder C. (1994). Interactive Ads, *Information Week*, October 3, 1994, pp. 25–29.

11

Computer as Audience

Mediated Interactive Messages

Cheri Anderson

Cheri Anderson is a doctoral candidate in the School of Journalism and Mass Communication at the University of Minnesota. Currently, she is a research assistant for the Raymond O. Mithun Land Grant Professor. Her research has concentrated on projects relating to interactive technology.

Today children still play with Dixie cups connected by a string to simulate telephone communication. Thirty years ago this primitive device accurately modeled mediated communication. Like the Dixie cups and string, hardware and wires were passive conduits that connected senders and receivers. Advertising research focused on the Dixie cups (senders and receivers), what should go into the cups (content) and receivers' reactions in a fixed environment.

That Dixie cup "model" has become increasingly inaccurate given the recent technological developments in digitalization, computer intelligence and interactivity. Traditional passive and analogue media are changing to active and digital media.

EXHIBIT 11.1 Passive Media

DIXIE CUP – – – – – string – – – – – string – – – – – – – – – DIXIE CUP
(Sender)   (message—analogue transmission)   (Receiver)

EXHIBIT 11.2 Active Media

DIXIE CUP – – string – – **C O M P U T E R** – – – string – – – DIXIE CUP
(Participant) (message - digital transmission) (Participant)

The configuration in Exhibit 11.2 is active because the computer recognizes and manipulates content independent from direct human intervention. The computer functions as an intelligent mediator between participants. Unlike the TV set, which is a passive conduit for content, the computer is an active agent that processes and renders content based on users' preferences. Because of the computer's role in the active media configuration, it is a component of interactive audiences. This does not imply that the consumer is no longer the primary audience component, but rather suggests that the consumer works in tandem with the computer to form an integrated "audience." The challenge of bringing together active consumers and computers is in the interfacing of the two. The communication environment needs to be predictable enough for computers to participate yet flexible enough for consumers to find the advertising experience satisfying.

Universe of Bits

The process of digitization breaks down and converges distinct media such as letters, slides, text, audio, video, photographs, phone calls and animation into a digital "stew," or set of information bits. The digital bits are transmitted along the information infrastructure (the string) in two layers—content and descriptive—to consumer hardware such as personal computers or set-top boxes. Content bits are any form of content broken down into digital bits. Descriptive bits provide information about the arrangement and nature of content bits (Lippman, 1994). These bits are largely invisible to end users but necessary for the computer to process users' requests. Below are examples of how consumers can request bits. Consumers can:

- request the bits to be rendered on the screen such that frames of a movie appear in a different order.

- set up detector chips to censor or retrieve specific content bits.

- have the stock quotes and sports scores spoken aloud.

- select different geographic locations on a map and automatically receive top news from these areas in audio, video, text or a combination of the three.

- request full motion video of homes for sale and then take a "virtual" tour of the neighborhood.

In these examples, the computer is a component of the advertiser's audience because it plays a role in manipulating and rendering content.

Consumers' ability to navigate through massive amounts of content bits, at this level, makes their relationship with advertisers more symmetrical. For example, advertisers and programmers no longer call the shots in terms of creating a schedule because consumers can convert time into space (Lippman, 1994). Consumers can break down a traditional broadcast schedule into customized packages of bits they are interested in and have them rendered on their screen. This is similar to database searching, where librarians enter a search query and instantly retrieve all the relevant information from the database. Searchers do not have to spend hours viewing all the text. They simply define the parameters for a universe of information (the material they're interested in) and it appears on the screen. Media hardware in consumer homes are no longer mere distribution boxes with buttons for tint and chrome, but intelligent media that enable the processing of content (in terms of consumer preferences) in ways advertisers may not currently imagine.

Computer-Mediated Advertising

A brief and general understanding of computer-mediated communication (CMC) is needed to understand how the active media configuration will impact advertising. CMC has multiple definitions used in different contexts. For this paper CMC is defined as interactive (defined in detail below) communication mediated by computer intelligence. The term computer-mediated advertising (CMA) is used to indicate advertising in the context of an active media configuration.

A low-level example of CMA was exemplified in a JVC promotion. JVC, a stereo manufacturer, prompted listeners of a telecast of the JVC Newport Jazz Festival to call an 800 phone number. The phone was answered by an automated attendant who requested that the caller provide certain information by pressing buttons on the phone keypad. The caller's information triggered responses from the central computer and the automated attendant issued a prize number and the addresses of nearby JVC dealers. In short, the mediating computer took consumer input, independently processed and routed the information, and responded with an individualized message.

More sophisticated CMA joins consumers and computers in a real-time, interactive dialogue mediated by computer intelligence. The computer not only retrieves an individualized message from the central database but is able to suggest several unique avenues of action based on consumer input. Michael Schrage (1994) illustrates the idea of CMA:

> Imagine interactive ads built around expert systems that offer custom-calibrated investment advice. A potential customer might answer a series of questions, or be confronted with a set of investment options, and the responses would lead to a digital description of the investor's risk-profile. Based on that profile, the appropriate financial vehicles would be put on display. This can be translated into travel planning or finding the perfect wedding present (p. 124).

Interactivity

In this section, general and specific interactivity will be defined. Neuman (1991) defines interactivity as "the quality of electronically mediated communication characterized by increased control over the communication process by both the sender and the receiver, either can be a microprocessor" (p. 104). My set of sub-definitions unravels the complexity of interactivity by focusing on a set of dimensions and attributes that emerged from a grounded theory coding process (Corbin and Strauss, 1990). The five dimensions are: (1) Information Flow, (2) Message Availability, (3) Immediacy of Feedback, (4) Type of Perception and (5) Customizer of Content. Listed below is a brief description of each dimension of interactivity with the attributes of each dimension in italics:

1. Information Flow is defined by the transfer of information from one point to another. Interactive messages consist of *multiple information flows* between participants. Non-interactive messages consist of *one-way flow* of information between a sender and receiver.

2. Message Availability is defined by when a message is available. Who determines at what point in time the message is seen or heard? Interactive messages are available when users want to access them—*availability on-demand*. Non-interactive messages have *fixed availability*; they are only available when the sender makes them available.

3. Immediacy of Feedback is defined by the time it takes feedback to return to the original sender (maybe a microprocessor) of a message. Interactive messages support *real-time feedback* using the same medium the message was sent in. Non-interactive messages have *severely delayed feedback*. For example, feedback such as a letter to an editor is severely delayed in time.

4. Type of Perception refers to how users should perceive their experiences with messages. Interactive messages should be perceived as *intelligent and responsive interaction* because the microprocessor behind the screen can perform a variety of functions (refer to the introduction). Non-interactive messages are perceived as *exposure* as opposed to transaction or interaction.

5. Customizer of Content refers to who formats, arranges or manipulates the content. *Users customize* the content (with the aid

of a microprocessor) of interactive messages by arranging or modifying content bits in different ways. Non-interactive messages are *customized by senders.*

General Shift in Activeness

Digitalization, computer intelligence and interactivity, as described above, enables a shift in "activeness" or control from the advertiser toward the consumer/computer. This is not a total shift in control, but rather an opportunity for consumers to use computers to (1) efficiently sort through large amounts of content and (2) elicit individualized and intelligent advertising. In short, consumers are making the relationship between advertisers and consumers more symmetrical.

The three column chart in Exhibit 11.3 illustrates a shift in "activeness" from the advertiser toward the consumer-computer relationship. The first column lists the ways traditional advertisers have been active. The second and third columns list the ways that consumers and computers, under the conditions of active media (computer intelligence and interactivity), are and will be active. This chart is not meant to be exhaustive, but rather to provide a broad overview of the general shift in "activeness."

Interfacing the Consumer and Computer

Once advertisers deposit their digital bits on a network, they no longer control how or what bits will be rendered. After deposit, consumers and computers work with the digital bits to create their advertising experiences—a multiplicity of content renderings. Dance's helix model of communication (1967) is one way to think about interactivity and the multiplicity of communication:

> If you take a helically coiled spring, such as the child's toy that tumbles down staircases by coiling in upon itself, and pull it full out in the vertical position, you can call to your imagination an entirely different kind of communication than that represented by compressing the spring as close as possible upon itself. If you extend the spring halfway and then compress just one side of the helix, you can envision a communicative process open in one dimension but closed in another.

EXHIBIT 11.3 Shift in "Activeness"

FROM THE	TO THE	
Traditional Advertiser	**Active Consumer**	**Computer**
decides message content	selects and customizes content bits	works with descriptive bits
	Σ browses/filters through content bits	Σ interprets descriptive bits in order to configure content bits
	Σ customizes content bits to be rendered	Σ processes consumer requests independent of direct human intervention
	Σ recontextualizes imagery	
	Σ sets preferences and defaults	Σ renders the individualized bits
decides media for distribution	decides how bits are rendered	digitization–convergence of media
	Σ audio, full motion video, text or multimedia	
	Σ temporal and spatial dimensions (conversion of time into screen space)	
decides audience/ target based on research	decides advertiser based on specific interests, consumers are the targeters	enables the search for content
	Σ downloads/renders content of choice	Σ infobots, knowbots or smart agents search content
decides schedule	decides schedule	asynchronous information retrieval
	Σ content bits on-demand	
	Σ convert time into space (condensing and expanding content)	

> At any and all times, the helix gives geometrical testimony to the concept that communication while moving forward is at the same moment coming back upon itself and being affected by its past behavior, for the coming curve of the helix is fundamentally affected by the curve from which it emerges (p. 296).

Termination of the helix is dependent upon the consumers' level of interest. If consumers are particularly interested in a topic or product, they may continue communication and request several different renderings of content. In accordance with the helix model, each rendering will influence the structure and content of subsequent renderings. If there is little interest, they may choose to terminate communication in the early stages of a dialogue. Termination can also occur if consumers request information that the computer cannot render due to missing content bits, or when descriptive bits do not allow the computer to recognize content in a specified way.

Emerging Issues and Areas of Research

What do active media (computer intelligence and interactivity) mean for advertising? Below is a list of issues and research questions that address advertising implications.

Exposure and Response

P1. The time gap between advertising exposure and brand response will be closed. CMA enables consumers to select ads and instantly respond by purchasing products or inquiring about product attributes. The removal of the time gap radically alters the current role of memory and recall in advertising testing. Memory will be relevant insofar as consumers can recall whether the transaction or service encounter experience was positive or negative. Furthermore, creating memorable advertisements will not be as important as developing interactive dialogues that retain the attention of consumers until the point of purchase.

Research Questions:

How will copy testing change in light of active media? What interactive techniques can be used to keep the attention of consumers long enough to make purchasing decisions? What will be the role of brand equity in responding to CMA? How will the content of commercials change to reflect the bridging of exposure and response?

Likeability

P2. Advertisers will establish likeability by measuring the number of consumers accessing the ad and the time spent with different renderings of content as opposed to measuring the overall likeability with a few interview or survey items. The multiple ways of operationalizing likeability in the active media configuration will allow advertisers to adjust specific components of an advertising campaign very rapidly.

Research Question:

In the active media configuration, there is an increase in the number of factors that go into determining likeability such as downloading time, quality of video and the flexibility consumers have to manipulate content, etc. What implications does this increase have for measuring the construct of likeability?

Affect Advertising

P3. Affect advertising will be produced differently in CMA. Instead of using human characters to provoke an emotional response, advertisers will use computers that generate impersonal files of bits. These bits can be rendered through an interactive dialogue that simulates a human-like presence and elicits an emotional response. For example, Apple's "Welcome to Macintosh" greeting, although just a file of text, provokes a far more comfortable and positive feeling than does a DOS prompt

Research Questions:

What is the range of emotions and feelings that computer bits can generate? Do computer-induced emotions endure over time as do human-induced emotions? What role will aesthetics play in creating different types of CMA? Depending on the situation, how will people respond to these affect strategies?

Messages in a CMA Context

P4. The dialogue and narrative structure of advertisements will change. CMA will be non-linear. Continual shifts and narrative strands will hinder the suggestion of chronology. Sequential explanations and cause-and-effect relationships between products (cause) and positive benefits (effect) will be harder to convey because consumers will view different renderings of content in a non-linear way. New ways to strategically place products and use humor, etc., will need to be created to accomodate CMA. For example, an advertiser may create an ad that culminates with a humorous punchline; however, the active consumer may decide to bypass that narrative.

Research Questions:

How can advertisers structure their messages in a computer-mediated context that maximizes the ability of consumers to retrieve interesting and needed information? Can advertisers successfully borrow ideas from other non-linear media such as video games, dictionaries or hypertext applications? What are the differences in enthusiasm toward the product or service between watching an ad and jointly creating an ad? If it's hard to establish causation, can other "meaning-yielding" relationships (i.e., metonym, metaphor or index) be used effectively in CMA?

Media Strategy

P5. Digitization eliminates the distinctions among media. Therefore, traditional media strategy concerns such as finding the optimal medium to place product demonstrations (which used to be TV) or detailed information (which used to be print magazines) will be replaced with finding the optimal way to arrange bits to communicate particular ideas. Media planners should no longer think in terms of separate hardware (i.e., TV or radio) but in terms of different arrangements of content bits.

Research Question:

How do different combination of bits affect the feel, communicative power and connotative meanings of advertisements?

Aperture

P6. Advertisers will need to create apertures (ideal openings) within the digital environment instead of waiting for other content producers to create an environment conducive to advertising. This can be done by starting Internet listserves or creating web sites on the World Wide Web and FTP (File Transfer Protocol) sites.

Research Question:

Since advertisements will not be embedded in programs, how will the orientation of ads change to attract an audience without the "pull" of a broadcast TV program or other non-advertising content?

Communication Models

P7. CMA resembles interpersonal communication more than it resembles mass communication. Advertising in an interpersonal context will raise new questions concerning the credibility and trustworthiness of advertising sources.

Research Questions:

How will trust and credibility be established in CMA? What formats or messages will subvert credibility?

Targeting

P8. Consumers will target advertisers as opposed to advertisers targeting consumers. One reason for this role reversal is the structure of information in an active media configuration. Instead of advertisers deciding what content will be seen and when, consumers will be making the choices concerning selection and manipulation of content. In addition, advertisers can no longer predict where large audiences will be at particular times. The fixed structure of broadcast media, which once retained the majority of viewers across 3 channels, is being replaced with the request for customized packages of bits in real-time.

Research Questions:

How will advertisements be positioned in the active media configuration such that interested consumers can find them? What types of incentives will work in terms of directing potential consumers to an advertising site? What should be considered an act of targeting by a consumer? For example, if a consumer requests information on boating conditions twice a week, should the local boating company treat that individual as a serious prospect?

Consumer Involvement

P9. CMA will consist of multiple levels of information ranging from product features to information on safety issues and warranties, etc. Interested consumers can spend 30 seconds to several minutes browsing, absorbing and playing with the information. Furthermore, consumers can be information producers. They can post original information on the network relating to consumer experiences that can (theoretically) be retrieved by anyone in the world with access to the network.

Research Questions:

How will the ability to access multiple layers of information, as opposed to simply seeing and hearing one-way advertisements, affect information processing and decision making? How will consumers navigate through information? What impact will consumer testimony (postings on the network), independent from advertising efforts, have on other consumers' purchasing decisions?

Media Buying

P10. Traditionally, the common unit for media buying was 30- or 60-second spots for TV or quarter, half or full page for print media. A new common unit will need to be created to purchase time or space in a digital and active media environment. Perhaps advertisers will be charged by the amount or types of bits or per contact.

Advertisers can have permanent sites (servers on networks) that can download information at any time. Advertisers can update their sites with multiple layers of information such as sales and specials. They can create direct hypertext links to on-line service agents who can answer questions. In this sense, technology is expanding the boundaries of advertising space.

Research Questions:

How will advertising time or space be priced? Who will do the charging? Who will do the purchasing?

Privacy

P11. CMA will enable continual data-gathering. Computers can track what information is requested and connect this information to real consumers. This is similar to computers that track catalog requests or coupon returns to learn more about consumers' interests. In some cases, consumers input information (fill out a warranty card or make selections from a computer screen) and this information is later assembled in ways unknown to consumers. These organizations can draw false conclusions from the way they assemble different bits of information. The problem is not limited to false conclusions. Accurate conclusions could also be used in ways that are contrary to consumers' best interests. For instance, what if information could be assembled to indicate that the consumer was probably a user of illegal drugs or had more income than reported to the Internal Revenue Service? In the active media environment where information can be gathered, processed and acted on with great speed, either false or true conclusions about consumers can become a major problem.

Research Questions:

How can advertisers manage the use of consumer information in ways that will reduce potential threats to consumer privacy? What are acceptable ways of contacting prospects who are found indirectly? How might companies within relevant industries work together to self-regulate the use of private information (perhaps some type of shared database with different classes of information, i.e. restricted, open to the public, etc.). What government agencies should be responsible for regulation and how should these agencies be regulated?

Conclusion

Current practices in advertising, ranging from creative strategy to research methods, will need to be rethought as technological advances in digitalization, computer intelligence and interactivity continue to permeate media. In the active media configuration, advertisers need to address the question: "What constitutes an audience?" The computer is an intelligent part of the audience, reading and interpreting descriptive bits in order to manipulate and render content bits. While users' ability to customize the rendering of content bits may signify a loss of control for advertisers, the technology can also be used to expand the boundaries of advertising space. With the advent of CMA, all advertisers will need to open their minds to methods that embrace the integrated audience of computer and consumer.

References

Corbin, Juliet and Strauss, Anselm. (1990). *Basics of Qualitative Research, Grounded Theory, Procedures and Techniques.* Newbury Park: Sage Publications.

Dance, Frank. (1967). *Human Communication Theory.* New York: Holt, Rinehart and Winston, Inc.

Lippman, Andrew. (October, 1994). *The Future of Digital Media.* Presentation at the Electronic Transformation of Image and Text Conference. Minneapolis: University of Minnesota Continuing Education.

Neuman, Russell. (1991). *The Future of the Mass Audience.* Cambridge: Cambridge University Press.

Schrage, Michael. (February, 1994). "Is Advertising Finally Dead?" *Wired.*

CHAPTER

12

Maintaining a Customer Focus in an Interactive Age

The Seven I's to Success

Michael Spalter

Michael Spalter's work in interactive marketing has been covered in a range of publications including *Business Week,* the *New York Times,* the *New York Daily News, Women's Wear Daily, Ad Week,* and the *Journal of Commerce.* Spalter created one of the first interactive multimedia marketspaces, hailed as a "new concept in retailing," for Bloomingdale's. His clients include a number of Fortune 500 companies that he advises on interactive marketing.

©1995 Michael Spalter

As many consumers and companies continue to migrate from the physical marketplace to the electronic marketspace,[1] maintaining customer focus will require new management constructs and reengineering of existing structures. This means a whole range of opportunities and threats will emerge. Unfortunately, the vast majority of businesses currently online have neglected or failed to ask several fundamental marketing questions:

- Why would a consumer want to do business in a marketspace?

- What are the key success factors to creating an outstanding marketspace?

- What new competencies will organizations need to successfully compete and involve customers in their marketspace?

- What can marketers do to individualize and personalize customers' experiences?

- What must be done to demonstrate a company's integrity and insure that consumers' privacy and security are safeguarded?

Many forward-looking businesses understand that new electronic distribution channels provide opportunities to expand market reach while enabling consumers to make transactions faster and more convenient. Consumers empowered to control, choose, and help create their own commercial experiences will wreak havoc on rigid, inflexible organizations unwilling or unable to adapt to the marketspace. In a classic domino effect, many marketing practices are falling as networks and interactivity cause a series of systemic changes. This realization has caused many executives to ask, "What makes a company thrive in the marketspace?"

The answer is: *maintaining customer focus.* To do this one must understand two key principles about how and why interactive marketing differs from traditional marketing practices. First, networks and the ability to communicate over them from **anywhere** in the globe at **anytime** remove the constraints of space and time associated with physical marketplaces. Maintaining customer focus will require businesses to adjust to the staggering changes brought about by the marketspace.

Second, traditional mass marketing media have consisted of monologues presented to the consumer through print, audio, and visual media such as newspapers, magazines, direct mail, radio, or television. The advent of commercial online services and the far reach of the Internet have, for the first time in mass marketing history, created the potential for a mass interactive **dialogue**. This shift is redefining marketing practices and the businesses that depend upon them. Interactive marketing is rapidly destroying and blurring the traditional distinction between push (as in sales workers) and pull (as in advertisers). How this one issue alone is handled will make or break entire companies and industries. The historic distinctions and professions built around this old paradigm are becoming eclipsed by new modes of conducting business, giving birth to the Age of Interactive Marketing.

Business people are just beginning to understand that some of the most sacred concepts in marketing are being challenged and made obsolete:

- Market research is evolving into market **usership.**

- Database marketing is evolving into database **consuming**.

- The marketing mix is evolving.

- Traditional distinctions between mass media advertisers and salespeople are blurring.

This article offers a construct to aid individuals charged with maintaining a customer focus in an interactive age. Utilizing what I call the Seven **I**'s, marketers can better analyze and prepare for their transition from the marketplace to the marketspace. The Seven **I**'s are:

1. Interconnection

2. Interface

3. Interactivity

4. Involvement

5. Information

6. Individualism

7. Integrity

Interconnection

New marketing approaches made possible by the evolution of large and complex interconnected networks, often referred to as **"information highways" (I)**, and the creation of marketspaces are destroying many sacred cows and forcing dramatic changes in organizations small and large, domestic and foreign. Just as the introduction of railways, highways, telephone lines, and broadcasting of radio and television signals have changed businesses and lifestyles, the rapidly growing information highways will leave no one untouched. Interconnected information highways represent an entirely new distribution channel with as much potential to redefine business and society as the introduction of any technological innovation in history.

Millions of individuals throughout the world are becoming interconnected because of networks—the most famous, of course, being the Internet. Navigating on the networks, individuals can guide themselves to areas that contain information ranging from news services to commercial malls. Once within an area of interest, known as a **forum (I)** or discussion group, they can begin to participate in a **"virtual community (I)."** Inside a virtual community one can communicate with other individuals from around the world. As people travel, or **"surf" (I)** the information highway, many would say they are now in **cyberspace (I)**.[2] The "information" speeding down the highway is anything that can be digitized and transmitted—images, text, audio or graphics, ranging from real-time news feeds such as Reuters to entire inventories of product lines such as the L.L. Bean catalog. Virtual communities formed around special interests, ranging from occupational to social to religious, are uniting millions of individuals as barriers of space and time are lifted.

The era is not far off when networks will interconnect hundreds of millions of people around the globe who will be able to use such features as real-time, interactive, full color-video to explore myriad informational resources and entertainment offerings as well as conduct commerce. The private commercial online services and the World Wide Web, commonly referred to as the "Web," on the Internet are filled with examples of businesses that have taken their content and put them into a digital format. These early examples, while primitive, enable students of interactive marketing to see specifically how many old notions about marketing and communications are threatened. As the allure of attracting denizens to these virtual communities grows, businesses increasingly are beginning to move from the traditional brick and mortar marketplace into the electronic marketspace. A business wishing to maximize its profits in the marketspace will want to be located in areas with the maximum accessibility to the largest number of potential customers. Businesses must decide what kind of network to establish a presence on to optimize market reach:

- Should a business be on a commercial service such as America Online, Microsoft Network or CompuServe, or is a site on the World Wide Web on the Internet more appropriate?

- What about creating a marketspace on all the commercial services that serve as a gateway to a larger Web site?

Where a corporation chooses to establish a presence in the marketspace is as important as in which city and on what street corner a retailer decides to open its doors. Interconnectivity will require many marketers to adopt an international perspective and will accelerate the trend towards globalization. A traditional market segmentation should be conducted to gain a thorough understanding about which networks and sites are attracting target customers.

A key strategic marketing factor is the ease with which individuals from around the world can access one's sites. On the Internet, for example, geographic barriers hold almost no meaning in the marketspace. A thorough analysis of where target market members are deciding to spend their time online will help determine whether a presence should be maintained on one or more networks. A highly focused and targeted network or site might already be attracting and maintaining the very customer groups you are interested in reaching.

Analyzing other sites on a network and their proximity to your "icon" will help pinpoint where establishing a marketspace makes sense for a specific organization. On America Online's main menu, for example, there are fourteen categories of explorable member areas ranging from personal finance to education. Ideally, organizations want to be in an area that serves as an interconnection and focal point for those with desirable buying patterns. Once a business has selected a network on which to establish a presence, the challenge becomes getting users to "click" onto their site—one that may compete with hundreds if not thousands of other areas.

Interface

The interface of a marketspace can make or break a business online. Corporations are just beginning to acknowledge the profound commercial impact and challenge of repurposing their businesses to create digital assets that can be electronically displayed and purchased. Marketing organizations must adopt a new core competence of market-oriented interface development if they hope to capitalize on the interactive age. If a marketer is successful in inducing trial, the consumer will enter the marketspace.

Recent history is filled with examples of how a superior interface can catapult a product from relative obscurity to a position of market leadership. Apple Computer's Macintosh, with its intuitive graphical user interface, helped Apple become the leader of the personal computer revolution in the 1980s. The Mosaic browser, another intuitive graphical user interface, helped fuel the explosive growth of the World Wide Web and Internet in the mid 1990s. America OnLine emerged as the leading commercial service from out of nowhere to eclipse Prodigy and CompuServe; AOL's interface is regularly cited as one of the primary reasons for its success.

The importance of creating a "user friendly" intuitive interface cannot be overstated. As networks proliferate and the importance of marketspaces grows, traditional marketing techniques will be fully utilized and exploited to induce trial in order to get an individual to "click" into a site. Building brand awareness in the form of icons online will be a challenge for businesses. When surfing, for example, through a marketspace, would one be more interested in clicking on an icon that represents the Apple logo or on a word that states, Apple? As consumers are induced to try a marketspace, the comfort and security of clicking onto a visual icon that represents a known brand will be of increasing strategic importance.

The interface can determine whether an individual wishes to explore the marketspace or move on to another site of interest. Careful construction of a market-oriented interface will assist consumers in passing through the buying process. An intelligent interface will incorporate the "stage models" of the buying process:[3]

- Problem Recognition
- Information Search

- Evaluation of Alternatives
- Purchase Decision
- Postpurchase Behavior

As the traditional distinctions between advertising and sales blur, it will be the interface that increasingly is charged with communicating a company's products and value to the target customers. Assuring that the interface successfully captures the attention of potential customers will require a coordinated multidisciplinary effort that involves the following disciplines:

- Marketing
- Sales
- Advertising
- Psychology
- Design
- Computer programming
- Operations
- Market research

Marketers need to understand how interfaces influence customers. Perhaps the single most important component of successful interface design is an iterative design process that is driven by customer feedback. Thanks to the ability to precisely monitor the "click streams" of users online, it is possible to conduct extensive testing of a proposed interface (more discussion on this will follow in the Individualism section). As a result of database technology, unprecedented measurements are at the disposal of marketers, enabling the desired response to an interface design to be continually improved.

Finally, careful attention must be paid in the interface design to language and cultural differences. Subtle social and cultural differences will have to be incorporated into the various interfaces created to meet customer needs throughout the world. Few examples exist of interfaces that respect linguistic and cultural differences. Unfortunately, this disregard for many consumers reinforces the general lack of customer focus online. The day is not far off when marketers will address this situation and empower users with the ability to explore the marketspace using their native language.

A quick tour of the Treasures of the Louvre on the World Wide Web illustrates how easy it is to translate one or more languages in an interactive setting. English speakers visiting the Louvre online and unable to speak French have the option of reading descriptions in English. By offering this simple language option in the interface, descriptions of the Louvre's holdings are now accessible to tens of millions of additional visitors. The interface, if planned successfully, will induce trial. It is the degree of interactivity of the marketspace, however, that will determine whether a customer's interest is piqued.

Interactivity

Marketers continue to rush like lemmings into the online world, pumping millions of dollars into dozens of ventures. Yet few commercial organizations are attempting to provide new modes for the viewing, listening to, and testing of their products and services. In order to do this, one must understand interactivity: What will and will not work in an interactive medium.[4] Publishing houses, movie studios and others have tried to conquer the interactive market but no clear front-runner has emerged. Many of these marketers encounter frustrations when customers do not respond to their sites as they wish. This new medium seems to offer opportunities to manipulate and navigate through content in innovative and exciting ways, yet many executives who grasp the growing importance of interconnectivity quickly grow disillusioned.

Why?

Many marketers are not maintaining a customer focus. They are not asking what **customers (I)** value in an interactive age. They are unwilling or unable to fully explore a key principle of the new medium—interactivity. Thanks to interactivity, for the first time in history mass media has moved from a monologue to a dialogue. Now customers can interact with content and other human beings, steering their own experience and opening up a new era in business history.

Interactivity includes letting customers:

- control and choose the content they are viewing.

- "chat" or communicate in real-time with one or more individuals.

- e-mail one or more individuals.

- post and respond to posts on bulletin boards.

For those of you completely unfamiliar with interactive services and marketspaces, let's assume that you are interested in buying a magazine for pleasure reading, but have been unable, due to time constraints, to get to a newsstand. Instead, you can visit an area on the Web hosted by Time Warner called "Pathfinder" that enables you to actually interact with the magazine content being shown. In this site, you will view a screen in which the logos of magazines are displayed, ranging from *Money* **(I)** to *Time* **(I)**.

With the click of a mouse, you can decide which magazine you wish to "tour." By clicking on a logo, say *Time* **(I)**, you can begin **interacting (I)** with images, sounds, graphics and text areas. Within the virtual version of *Time* **(I)** it will soon be possible to interact with advertisements.

This simple yet awesome capability instantly alters the field of marketing in much the same way that Automatic Teller Machines forever altered the banking industry. The ability for the marketer to interact with a consumer viewing a product or service through a medium similar to TV is revolutionary. This simple step will be as important in the history of marketing and customer service as were the expansion of railroads and the U.S. Postal System. The magnitude and scope of this simple yet profound ability is changing the business world.

Thanks to recent and ongoing technological achievements, products reaching the customer over the information highway offer much more seductive interactive graphics capabilities than an ATM. These souped-up **multimedia(I)** elements (multimedia is the integration of video, sound, music, graphics and text) can make the virtual experience far more fun and stimulating than many have previously thought possible. A key difference between ATMs and Interactive Marketing on the information highway is the ability to communicate and express oneself. Tackling this difference will make or break many businesses hoping to compete in the marketspace. Understanding and then leveraging the ability to communicate with customers online will determine the successful marketspaces from the also-rans. The age-old adage that understanding your customer is the cornerstone to business success will have greater meaning than ever before in the marketspace.

Voilá. With the press of a button in an online magazine ad, you can tour the inside of a car, get information, go for a visual test ride, and review a bulletin board of customer feedback. After you tour the car, you can then return to the magazine or arrange with the click of a button to be put into contact with a dealership. Soon customers will be able to ask any number of additional questions and even make a purchase—including details of optional service contracts and dealer financing. Depending upon the sophistication of the interactive experience, you may be able to order the car without ever speaking to anyone, or the marketer may wish to "pull" you to "push" an icon on your screen. This new ability to interact with media will redefine entire industries.

Many adept marketers and sales executives fail to see that for the first time their customers have a media outlet to express their **emotions (I)**. To some, the idea of a person sitting alone in front of a television typing away as the ABC Evening News or a Honda commercial airs may seem absurd. Yet more and more people are communicating and interacting with each other at their computer terminals. Whether at a TV or a computer terminal, users must be involved in the interaction; by failing to engage customers in dialogue and account for their responses, many businesses are losing and will continue to lose precious opportunities to maintain their customers' patronage.

We are still in the early days of **new media (I)** usage (also known as **multimedia (I)**) and people are amazed at the ability to integrate text, audio, video, graphics and animation. Less well understood or contemplated is the **interactivity (I)** of the new media work. The maturation of the interactive multimedia format must be addressed as the market explodes if the marketspace is to reach its potential. The key to an interactive marketing site is whether this new environment dramatically enhances the customer's experience. Many marketers are jumping to the wrong conclusions about this new medium, assuming that traditional media (text, audio, video, photography, animation) will naturally provide an interactive experience when digitized and made into a marketspace. This is a waste of precious marketing budgets.

Most existing content (whatever medium it was created in) was **not (I)** designed to be interactive. An excited marketer tells a techie, "Here is the company's sales catalog, get us online. . . ." The techie says, "Of course," but then the challenge begins: How to take traditional media content and make it interesting and stimulating in an **interactive (I)** format. Note that the CD-ROM market has not been driven by the titans of industry but by individuals like the Miller brothers, creators of MYST, who, through their unique understanding of the interactive environment, engage and involve thousands of customers.

Trip Hawkins, founder of multimedia companies Electronic Arts and 3D0, summarizes the importance of interactive multimedia: "In the sense that audio is the medium of hearing, and video is the medium of viewing, multimedia is the medium of 'doing'."[5] Getting customers to interact with a marketspace is not the same thing as getting them involved. Active customer involvement leads to customer loyalty.

Involvement

Businesses can profoundly influence the success of their sites by paying careful attention to crafting an atmosphere that encourages customer involvement. A key success factor is to decide how one creates new, original customer experiences for an interactive setting, or transfers traditional works into new and potentially enhanced materials that actively involve users by engaging them in forums, bulletin boards, and customer clubs. Ongoing research should integrate traditional products and services in innovative, powerful ways. As with traditional marketing, the answers to what works reside with your customers.

Initially, there are several ways to attract individuals to a particular site. These include:

- Creating an inviting, intuitive interface for content.

- Linking your site to a popular area or site that will serve as a gateway to your site.

- Leveraging brand equity.

- Integrating traditional marketing communication materials such as advertising, correspondence, bills and promotional materials with information on how to access your site.

Like window shopping in the physical marketplace, it will take more than a well-known brand name and compelling interface to engage potential marketspace customers. On America Online with its over 500 databases, content alone does not dictate success at sites such as Military City, Motley Fool (a financial area) and American Express' ExpressNet. It is the ability to express one's emotions and react to content by interacting and communicating through bulletin boards, chat features and email that make these sites so successful. Communicating empowers individuals to become **involved** in their community of interest. Preparing a marketspace that will involve users is a critical strategic task.

As users interact with the content within a marketspace, a cycle of success can be created wherein content attracts users, users create more content, new content enhances the value of the site and more users are drawn to the marketspace. The cycle of success is broken if the subject matter and ensuing dialogue lacks flair. Unless customers have a compelling hook that engages and involves them in a site, the peril of losing potential business is high. Involving consumers can be done in a number ways including:

- Continually updating and refreshing content.

- Sponsoring and moderating interesting and stimulating chats with guest experts and/or interesting topics.

- Creating direct links with content for customers to voice their opinions through bulletin boards.

- Reviewing and commenting on customer messages or posts contained in bulletin boards.

- Acquiring or aligning with other content providers who might serve as a hook within your site (e.g., Amdahl, a site on the Web, has a number of hypertext links to interesting sites ranging from *HotWired* (**I**) to the White House Server).

- Offering sophisticated search mechanisms that help consumers pinpoint information. (e.g., Time Warner's Pathfinder has a built in search feature for topics covered within magazine articles. The search enables a reader who is reading an article on the Supreme Court, for example, to search *Time's* (**I**) extensive databases for articles on a particular Justice).

The thousands of marketers establishing their businesses in the marketspace must understand the importance of interactively involving customers to maintain their interest and involvement. Marketing organizations must grapple with how digital assets can be enhanced and made interesting, stimulating, and easy to navigate if put into an interactive format.

Interactive marketers capable of producing experiences that appeal to wide audiences will understand that the key to interactivity rests in involving and capturing users' attention by enabling them to control their own experience and communications. Interactive marketers will:

- Like a Ray Kroc, make their sites synonymous with quality and value

- Like a Ralph Lauren, make one want to see their latest offering

- Or, like a David Ogilvy, make the viewer cry, laugh, or smile.

One of the first challenges for traditional businesses in the marketspace is to get people who understand how to transform content to involve users. The best way to do this is to take a product or service and ask why and how its content would work in an interactive format. The most common answer is that it is a more convenient channel of distribution, one that penetrates directly into the home. Many products, however, do not work in this medium, which should not be surprising since many goods rely for their marketing upon consumer reaction to physical sensations such as touch, smell and taste. As these traditional businesses begin to explore what content they wish to market with interactive new media, it would be helpful to include creative, multimedia specialists in the process of selecting products and services. Rather than have a seasoned marketing guru dictate that his or her top-drawing product line be the first interactive project because everyone knows and loves the brand, have a creative multimedia specialist detail for you the ways in which the product can become interactive.

The new paradigm is most apparent in the World Wide Web where individuals can utilize hypertext. The WWW interconnects tens of thousands of Internet servers containing digitized information in a range of formats including text, graphics, video, and sound. Hypertext enables users to control how they view the information presented. This ability transforms the user's traditional linear experience into a non-linear one. A customer, for example, can be reading an article about a company in *Money* **(I)** Magazine and then "click" on the company's name and through a hypertext link move to another database sponsored by the Reference Press **(I)** that provides a detailed background on the company.

The Marketing Mix is Evolving

Traditional mass marketing media, as discussed earlier, have been essentially monologues presented to consumers through print — newspapers, magazines and direct mail, radio—one-way audio, or TV—one-way audio and video. The potential for an interactive dialogue forever **(I)** changes promotion, and therefore customer focus. The distinctions and professions built around traditional notions of marketing are now in the process of becoming eclipsed by new modes of conducting business, giving birth to the age of Interactive Marketing. It is now possible to read online a newspaper or magazine article about an interesting product or service, then click on the name of the company offering the service and immediately be linked to a marketspace. Once in the marketspace, consumers can order the product or service that caught their interest.

Many business people use the marketing mix popularized by E. Jerome McCarthy (consisting of the Four Ps: Product, Price, Place and Promotion) to develop a marketing campaign.[6] Interactive Marketing stirs this mix. Promotion is undergoing a radical change which has not been thoroughly explored, much less documented.

Promotion within the marketing mix has encompassed the two distinct and often complementary sales tools of advertising and personal selling historically known as Pull and Push. The advertiser attempts to **pull (I)** you to a product, showcasing it in a **nonpersonal** way that will draw you into the place where the product is sold, while the salesperson attempts to **push** you to the product in a **personal (I)** pitch by bringing product information (and possibly the product itself) to you directly. Think about the difference between a Coca-Cola commercial on TV and the Avon person knocking on your front door.

With the birth of Interactive Marketing, we now see the demise of this dichotomy. Indeed, the distinction between pull and push is becoming increasingly blurred. The blurring of the roles of salespeople and advertisers in the marketing mix means that we must reassess:

- The very nature of advertising and a sales force

- The entire idea of a distribution channel (i.e., what happens to traditional distribution channels when the needs they now fulfill can be met in front of a PC?)

- The ways in which some traditional business processes can be adapted to take advantage of the revolutionary impact of new media.

The dramatic changes underway in the marketing mix will affect all the Ps, forcing marketers and businesses to address one of the greatest changes in the history of modern business. As an example, the information highway enables customers to deal directly with manufacturers, thereby potentially cutting out a number of intermediaries such as salespeople and retail outlets. Cutting out these segments (known as disintermediation) of the distribution channel lowers expenses.[7] Savings are usually passed on to consumers resulting in lower prices. The recent interest in Barry Diller's QVC is an early and primitive example of the future.

Not only will Interactive Marketing change advertising and salespeople's roles, but it will force many industries to reconsider the other components of the marketing mix.

- If a business can cut out sales commissions, how does this affect the Pricing strategy of a product?

- If a one-person business can reach the entire globe through the Internet what constitutes a geographic market and what does this mean for Place strategies?

Understanding how the marketing mix is affected by interactive marketing can help business people prepare for the imminent changes in their organizations. Those able to grasp these structural changes will be of unique value to their organization by helping it successfully adapt to the interactive age.

Let's turn to the blurring of the salespeople and mass advertisers' roles and examine what this may mean for the advertising industry (which relies heavily upon pull strategies) and then turn to those industries (such as real estate, retailing, and financial services) that depend heavily upon salespeople and push strategies.

Advertising Age **(I)** reports that over $139 billion was spent on advertising in the United States in 1992. Interactive marketing could become one of the best-funded efforts in our society to use interactive information technologies. Marketers **must** address the impact that this new era will have upon their profession, when individuals can control and choose when they want to initiate being pushed in real time. With traditional television and radio advertising, the majority of ads leave an impression upon the individual that attempts to **pull (I)** them into a store at some future time period to purchase a product or service—this is about to change.

We have already seen the evolution towards real-time interaction in its most primitive form with ads like those for the Ginsu knife that ask the viewer to telephone for a direct order during a 30 second spot (one-way video—television, and two-way audio—the telephone). QVC and its home shopping network, as well as the introduction of infomercials, are evolutionary steps in this process of getting people to be pulled and pushed in real time. Online services shatter old notions of personal sales and mass media advertising by offering both in real time! Consumers watching an advertisement now can not only control what they are viewing, but if moved to make an impulse purchase can do so.

What is the significance of all this?

In marketing there is a model known as the "hierarchy of effects continuum"[8] which attempts to persuade a customer to purchase an item.

EXHIBIT 12.1 Hierarchy of Effects Model: (I)

Cognitive (B)   **Affective (B)**   **Behavior (B)**

Awareness—> Knowledge—> Liking stage —>Preference—> Conviction—>Purchase

---

Until recently, most mass media advertising attempted to build awareness of a product. The less complex the product or message, the more an organization would depend upon advertising to pull customers to purchase a product or create an image. Procter and Gamble, for example, spends over a billion dollars a year to spread its simple messages.

Financial services, real estate, and insurance, on the other hand, offer more complex products with many variations and do not rely on pull-type methods as heavily as consumer product companies. It is not surprising that there are 1,932,000 salespeople in the finance, insurance and real estate industries or that there are 6,281,000 salespeople in retail and personnel services (US BLS Current Population Survey Annual Average Data 1993).

It has been far more difficult and expensive for these salespeople to use mass media to advertise a specific financial instrument, home furnishing, shoe, or house on Main Street. National chains often attempt to differentiate themselves through mass media by promoting their level of service or the overall quality of their corporation—and, by association, their salespeople. The goal is to pull consumers to their salespeople and then push them into an interactive dialogue to purchase a specific product.

As mentioned earlier, QVC is helping to break the mold. So are Richard Simmons and other infomercial tycoons. These entrepreneurs took a gamble on buying 30 or 60 minutes of commercial time that would enable them to move slowly through the entire hierarchy of effects model, reaching millions of viewers with the hope that there would be a payback. Both QVC and Simmons have successfully coupled one-way video with two-way audio to make the transaction an interactive experience. Unlike the lone traveling sales person who knocks on your door or cold-calls you (capable in the most wildly successful day of reaching perhaps fifty prospective customers), QVC or Simmons reach millions! And those millions can initiate contact by picking up a phone and talking to a salesperson.

Yet, Home Shopping Network is becoming quaint when compared to marketspaces on online computer services and interactive television. The integration of two-way video and audio is now being realized in a primitive fashion through the use of CD-ROM and interactive multimedia. It is only a matter of time before consumers will be able to determine to what extent they wish to learn about products or services. Today, when you are watching a television program, you have little choice but to sit through a commercial message during an intermission. The rise of online services and interactivity completely changes this paradigm. Mass media no longer has meaning when any individual can interact and control contact with the marketer. Messages delivered through mass media and electronic lines have been exclusively delivered in a linear fashion. It may seem absurd to think that an individual could ask over his television set what a particular knob on an appliance actually did. Equally absurd to some is the notion that one could specify during a commercial message desired product comparisons or image reviews. That is all changing. Now marketer and consumer not only transact but must interact. Those marketers who avoid interaction will undoubtedly lose sales, and even their very companies.

Information

As interactive marketing evolves, the entire paradigm of database marketing is being turned on its head because database **consuming (I)** is being born.[9] Database consuming is the result of customers' using database technology to target products just as marketers have been using databases to target customers. Database "shopping engines" will give consumers access to the same technologies marketers have been using for decades. Database consumers, as a result of the advances in information technology, have access to unprecedented tools that enable them to search out almost instantly vast amounts of information on products and services offered throughout the globe. Imagine having the ability to enter a product name and price in a database and then find every business that carries the particular product and the price at which they are selling it. Database consuming will strengthen the individual's control, choice and empowerment and will heighten the importance of providing useful information to consumers. Database consuming will also increase the importance of advertising in informing, persuading and reminding. Assuming a marketspace is successful in creating an intelligent interface that interactively involves customers, it will be the freshness and variety of infomation offered that will keep customers coming back time and time again.

An example of database consuming is illustrated with a revolutionary new tool of the marketspace—the **key cost (I)**. Thanks to the key cost marketers will better appreciate the critical role of advertising in nurturing and maintaining their brands. The key cost will become the first cousin to the "key word" found in many popular word processing programs and will enable consumers to search out the lowest price for a product. The key cost will make the difference between quality, service and price more distinct in the minds of consumers during the purchasing decision.

Millions of people are familiar with the key word search function in word processing programs that enables the user to scan thousands of entries or pages of text to locate a particular string of letters or numbers. The key word has made finding a needle in a haystack as simple as typing the word "needle." A process that in the past might have taken days, weeks, or even months is reduced to seconds. The key cost search will become one of several powerful functions a customer might use while database consuming.

The adage that "knowledge is power" will have a new significance for those consumers using the key cost function when database consuming. Immediately, they will have the ability, from the comfort of their homes, to comparison shop based upon price anywhere in the world at any particular time. Consumer awareness of what an item costs, coupled with the ability to have it delivered overnight, could potentially force entire industries to change.

CUC International's Shoppers Advantage offers a glimpse of the potential of database consuming. CUC's members can access online, from their homes, over 250,000 brand-name products, enter a series of parameters (e.g., cost, features, etc.) and read about the different products that match their interests. When CUC customers make a purchase through Shoppers Advantage they also receive a low price guarantee and extended warranty. CUC is currently working with Time-Warner in Orlando and Viacom in Northern California to launch two different interactive TV home shopping ventures. America Online's much publicized CD-ROM, 2 Market, also shows the potential of database consuming. It enables consumers to view scores of catalogs while searching for, requesting information about, and viewing over 39,000 products from some of the top retailers in the world including Tiffany & Co., L.L. Bean, Williams-Sonoma and many more. One can enter a product type such as "linen" and immediately see which of the numerous companies on the CD-ROM carry such products. Instead of wasting time price shopping from store to store, consumers will sit at a desk in front of their personal computer, type in the particular product they want, and limit the search to the lowest five prices. Within seconds they might find the same product offered at a store across the street for, say, $180, and also find it on sale by a reputable business in a different state or even country for only $70. Database consumers will cut their costs by searching out the best prices on items ranging from underwear to kitchenware.

Marketspaces that wish to avoid becoming casualties of key cost searches must explore innovative ways to add tangible value to consumers by integrating desirable information into their marketspaces. The World Wide Web, for example, hosts a relatively unknown stock brokerage, Security APL (SECAPL), that illustrates an intelligent use of interactive media. SECAPL offers visitors to its site free stock quotes. The quotes attract users who wish to receive minute-by-minute updated information updates (there is a fifteen minute delay). After a symbol is entered, SECAPL then offers a hypertext link to an experimental site that utilizes the EDGAR Dissemination project, a site for Security and

Exchange Commission's filings.[10] EDGAR provides a whole array of information required by the SEC pertaining to publicly traded companies.

Another powerful example of intelligent bundling of information is found in Time-Warner's marketspace, Pathfinder, on the Web. Time-Warner has made an agreement with the Reference Press, publisher of *Hoover's Guide to Corporate America*. A reader of *Money* **(I)** magazine online could read, for example, an article about General Motors, and within the article click on the words "General Motors" to receive a detailed profile with information offered by Reference Press. Both of these examples illustrate a way to differentiate a marketspace by offering consumers additional value. Note that each of these examples provide utility by offering a link to a third-party information source.

Businesses will change prices on products with much greater frequency, in a manner similar to the ever-changing prices we see in the airline industry. Markets will be forced to become more efficient as businesses respond to educated consumers. Distribution systems, in the process, will continue to evolve as delivery times increasingly become a source of competitive advantage. Consumers will not only expect a price in the range of the best key cost price, but also speedy and reliable delivery of their item. Outstanding service guarantees will become commonplace for many organizations hoping to conduct business online. We might even see entirely new forms of distribution arise because of database consuming.

Individualism

As interactive online networks begin to proliferate, market **research (I)** will give birth to market **usership (I)**.[11] Market usership makes it possible for online marketers to pinpoint who is using their marketspaces and what features those customers are using. Market usership builds on the previous **I**'s of Interconnection, Interface, Interactivity and Involvement by helping to individualize the customer's experience. What does market usership mean for the advertiser, the market researcher, and the marketer?

Advertisers should be able to create more effective campaigns because for the first time in history marketers can receive real-time feedback about viewers' choices and reactions. Just as an ATM records every transaction you make while using a system, online services will be able to record and create reports based on your interaction and feedback. It will soon be possible for businesses in the marketspace to statistically record exact usership of their various offerings. Jim Birschbach, TCI's corporate director of advertising sales, observes, "Nielsen can tell us about viewership, but we can tell you about usership."

Because advertising has been based on one-way communication, there is no opportunity to exchange ideas between advertiser and consumer, no feedback from consumer to marketer. The old role of market research—to supply feedback from the marketplace to the marketer—has constituted a method of converting advertising from a one-way to a two-way communication process.

Never before have marketers been able to precisely measure the impact of media in advertising. Instead, estimations and polls such as the famed Nielsen ratings have been used to determine the effectiveness of marketing campaigns. Armed with new, exact knowledge and precise measurement tools, advertisers can determine with unprecedented accuracy market reach and frequency, customers preferences and dislikes. Not only will marketing organizations be able to communicate in real-time through their advertising, but, of equal importance, they will be able to know by whom, when and for how long their product or service was being viewed.

The potential for interactive marketers to better serve and individualize customers' needs thanks to market usership will help to maintain customer focus by giving marketers the ability to:

- Mass customize products and services

- Craft more effective advertising

- Better measure the effectiveness of advertising media

- Improve the measurement of the effectiveness of the advertising message

- Make improved decisions in such areas as product development, channels of distribution, media selection, and resource allocation.

Market usership could play as important a role in mass customization as that of the assembly line in the era of mass production. Market usership should enable savvy marketers to individualize their products and services adding greater value and utility to products and services being offered. B. Joseph Pine II, a pioneer of the mass customization movement, describes in his book the range of companies that can transform information through mass customization:

> Customized services that can be performed on standard information include personalizing, categorizing, generalizing, analyzing, integrating, repackaging, facilitating, monitoring, filtering, locating, and matching, not to mention making the information convenient and readily accessible whenever and wherever a customer wants.[12]

Market usership will force marketers to be more accountable to their clients and provide better customer focus and targeted messages. Marketing and market research will become far more of a science, drawing upon the ability to precisely quantify aspects of a marketing program. When a marketer can sit at a desk and view in real-time the success or failure of a campaign, a new hybrid of marketing, advertising and accounting will be created. Just as the accounting profession has introduced activity-based cost accounting, thanks to market usership we may see the beginning of a new measurement form to be known as activity-based advertising. A campaign's success could hinge upon how much measured activity or interaction consumers have with the ads.

Imagine as a marketer having the ability to know exactly how many people were viewing your ads, or if you could know immediately what products or services were capturing the interest of your target markets. What would these options mean to your business?

Integrity

The final "**I**" that is critical to developing a succesful marketspace is maintaining its *integrity*. This includes issues relating to privacy, security and confidentiality. No matter how adept a marketer is at crafting the other Is of the mix, if a marketspace does not provide the customer with peace of mind that their privacy, security and confidentiality are inviolate, all efforts at creating a compelling marketspace are in vain. Many humanists and business ethicists are justifiably concerned about privacy issues in the digital age. The birth of market usership suggests that unprecedented amounts of personal information can be stored and compiled by the proprietors of marketspaces.

Because of the nature of electronic marketspaces and market usership, every "click" that an individual makes online can be recorded. Detailed and precise personal histories might potentially be created about online users in various marketspaces. The thought of an unscrupulous or unethical marketer gaining such personal information should send chills down consumers' backs. Adding to potential problems will be the lack of regulations currently in place to monitor electronic commerce. What might be considered standard practice in one country might be grounds for suits in another. Some countries, for example, forbid pornography of any type being purchased, but on the Internet there are several areas where such material is sold indiscriminately.

Another area where marketers must be vigilant is in insuring that intrusive email messages are not generated from a marketspace. A key differentiator between traditional marketing and interactive marketing, as suggested earlier, is the consumer's ability to choose and control his or her experiences. When marketers begin to flood electronic mail boxes with unsolicited offers and promotions, consumers are stripped of the empowering aspects of interactive marketing. Marketers who dare to take this risk will find newly empowered consumers who will not think twice about publicly "flaming" the offending company or expressing their displeasure at such blatant and unwelcomed solicitations.

Any electronic dialogue online can be stored indefinitely. What if a customer is having a sensitive conversation about an important personal issue and, to his surprise and horror, a business chronicles the entire conversation online by simply saving the text as a file? Customers also need to be concerned about the level of security afforded their personal information.

There are some individuals who would use interactivity to prey upon unsuspecting people. Insidious electronic practices range from financial frauds to horrific tales of pedophiles frequenting cyberspace to seduce innocents. Those sponsoring marketspaces must consider the full consequences and responsibilities of creating an online meeting place. America Online, for example, offers a parental chat control that limits children's access to areas that might be inappropriate. Careful attention must be paid by marketers to insure that malcontents and potential criminals do not use their areas as a vehicle for illicit activities. Tight editorial controls, coupled with persistent and consistent monitoring of bulletin boards and chat rooms, can help detect and prevent potential problems. Marketers wishing to maintain customer focus should give careful thought to guaranteeing the security of users' information.

While some people may be scared, even outraged that a digital environment allows for easy and infinite duplication of communication, other ethical and socially responsible marketers as well as concerned consumers might have reason to be ecstatic over this capability. It will be much easier to determine when deceptive or misleading sales practices are being used: at the end of any sales presentation in which claims are made about a product or service, the consumer can simply press the save function, thereby documenting who said what and when. Conversely, the marketer can also document consumer misrepresentation of important information such as employment history on a mortgage or job application. Needless to say, there will have to be a mechanism that prevents tampering with saved files.

A basic rule of thumb among business ethicists is that if your actions were reprinted on the front page of a newspaper you should still feel comfortable with what you did. Now the ethicists' words can be taken to heart by all marketing organizations who sell online. The ability to use the "save" function at the end of a sales presentation will guard against those wishing to sell snake oil packaged as perfume.

Conclusion

The Seven **I**'s presented here attempt to provide guidance to marketers in the emerging age of the marketspace. The tectonic shifts underway in the world of marketing will be sure to change the way we buy, what we buy and eventually the very foundations of commerce. If, as Joseph Schumpeter suggests, "The defining characteristic (of the entrepreneur and his function) is simply the doing of new things, and doing things that are already done, in a new way (innovation),"[13] then interactive marketers will help to define business in the twentieth first century. As businesses begin to establish themselves in the electronic marketspace, a critical and fundamental marketing lesson must not be overlooked—meeting and exceeding human beings' needs and wants. Some executives may focus upon one of the I's more than others, but to overlook any of them completely is risky. In the final analysis, the marketspace will continually change and reinvent itself as adventurous souls attempt to make their interactive impact.

References

1. A term recently coined by Jeffrey Rayport and John Sviokla of Harvard Business School in their article: "Managing In the Marketspace" *Harvard Business Review* **(I),** November–December 1994, p. 141.

2. A term coined by science fiction writer William Gibson to describe a virtual spatial representation of digital information and information structures.

3. Philip Kotler, *Marketing Management* **(I)** 6th ed., (Prentice Hall, Englewood, NJ) 1988, p. 194

4. Michael Spalter, "Desperately Seeking Artist," *MediaWeek* **(I)**, July 18, 1994, p. 12.

5. Trip Hawkins, "State of The Media," *CYBERARTS*, Edited by Linda Jacobson (Miller Freeman: San Francisco) 1992, p. 13.

6. E. Jerome McCarthy, *Basic Marketing: A Managerial Approach* **(U)** (Homewood, Ill.: Richard D. Irwin, 1981)

7. Michael Spalter "Here Come The CyberYuppies," *The Futurist* **(I)**, May/ June 1995, p. 20.

8. Robert J. Lavidge and Gary A. Steiner, "A Model for Predictive Measurements of Advertising Effectiveness," *Journal of Marketing* **(I)**, October 1961, p. 61.

9. Michael Spalter, "Keyed Up: As Technology Changes the Face of Retailing Advertising Figures to Play an Important Role," *AdWeek* **(I)**, October 10, 1994, p. 30.

10. This site is not affiliated with the SEC.

11. Michael Spalter, "Interactive Age Will Transform Market Research Into 'Usership,'" *Advertising Age* **(I)**, May 5, 1994, p. 26.

12. B. Joseph Pine II, *Mass Customization: The New Frontier in Business Competition* **(U),** (Cambridge, MA: Harvard Business School Press, 1993)

13. Joseph A. Schumpeter, "The Creative Response in Economic History," *Journal of Economic History* **(I)**, Vol. VII (May, 1947), p. 151.

The New World of Marketing on the Internet

Some Practical Implications of the New Tools and New Rules of Interactive Marketing

Charles F. Hofacker

Charles F. Hofacker is an associate professor of marketing in the School of Business at the Florida State University and is president of New South Network Services, an Internet business services company. Hofacker has conducted research on interactive media and other aspects of computer-mediated marketing.

It is 1950. A new medium called television has appeared. You have been asked to prognosticate how marketing will work on this new medium. Could you have been able to predict the 15-second spot? The appearance of the infomercial? Shopping channels? MTV?

Discussing marketing on the Internet and other online systems is a pretty tall order at this time. Realistically, we have about as much chance of predicting what will happen to as I would have had predicting the "Mighty Morphin Power Rangers" phenomenon from watching "Lassie."

In contrast, it is fairly easy to understand the properties of a personal computer. We know that these machines run at certain speeds, that they can create or show text, audio, or video. Yet when we combine hundreds of millions of these devices together in an open network, what will result? Surely we will experience emergent properties we would not have dreamed of. The complexity of the coming global computer architecture will radically exceed anything that humankind has done so far to entertain or inform itself. Thus I must confess at the outset that any specific details on how the Internet will impact marketing will necessarily not appear in this article.

Instead, I would like to provide an overview of what the Internet currently is, to discuss some of the marketing resources available on the Internet, and then review some of the types of marketing activity currently being engaged on the Net. Finally, I provide some general hand waves in the direction that I think things are going to go. I invite the reader to videomail me in 10 years to review this article!

What is the Internet?

An *internetwork* or an Internet is a network of networks. *The* Internet, or simply, the Net, is the sum of all the interconnected TCP/IP networks. The acronym TCP/IP stands for Transmission Control Protocol/Internet Protocol. Just as there are protocols for having a business lunch—one should use one's left-most fork for the salad—there are protocols for how computers and computer networks talk to each other. TCP/IP is an open standard in that it is not owned or controlled by any particular company or agency. The Internet itself is open in the sense that anyone can pay to connect a device to it as long as the technical TCP/IP specifications are met.

The TCP/IP specifications were originally designed to withstand the chaotic conditions that might occur during a nuclear war. It is neither centrally managed, controlled nor coordinated. In fact, no one knows in any real sense how many computers are attached to it or how many people use it. Since it spans all seven continents, no government can exercise legal authority over it. In reality, there is no "it" to exercise legal authority over.

The Current Range

At this time the basic services available on the Net include e-mail, e-mail lists, Usenet News, Interactive Relay Chat, and the World Wide Web. The most basic is electronic mail. Electronic mail consists of a message that is forwarded and stored for a recipient or a set of recipients. At this time e-mail messages tend to be primarily text.

Often lists of individuals are mapped to a single e-mail address. The mapping allows one to reach all of the individuals on the list through the single address. Often these lists are organized around topical areas. The following is a sample from a recent search of the Internet using the key words "email lists marketing":

- Inet-Marketing Mailing List Archive by Thread
- Join Our Press List
- Other Useful Resources
- Janal Communications Home Page
- Mailing List Registration
- Forman Interactive Corp. Vendor List
- Lincoln University World Wide Web Server
- The AMA Marketing Mix

The above are just a few samples of entries—in no particular order—of more than 450 responses. Listings represented every level of detail and description.

Usenet, also called "network news," consists of a hierarchical collection of topics. Each topic contains messages or postings from participants. Postings on each topic, or newsgroup, propagate through the network from one "news" server to another via a special protocol called, logically enough, *network news transmission protocol*. With e-mail, the message goes to the reader's mailbox, and remains there unless explicitly deleted. The reader must connect to the news server to read Usenet, and messages will be deleted unless the reader explicitly saves them.

Interactive Relay Chat is a way to engage in real time conversation. For the most part, at this time conversation is executed in text. A related service is a Multi-User Dungeon (MUD), which allows a number of people to interact in a fantasy or virtual world.

The World Wide Web is a client/server application allowing information providers to provide information using server software to information seekers using client software. Popular clients can handle text, audio, graphical images, or video. The Web is based on a hypertext format in which the viewer can click on highlighted information to pursue certain topics further.

All documents on the World Wide Web can be referred to by their Uniform Resource Locator, or URL. A web document might have an address like

    http://cob.fsu.edu/

which is the actual URL for the College of Business at Florida State University. Generally, the part after the double slash consists of a domain name, or the name of an Internet computer. Often, specific file information is provided after the last slash so that if I wanted to refer to a specific page belonging to the FSU marketing department, I would use the URL

    http://cob.fsu.edu/mar/index.html

Web documents, or pages, are created using the hypertext markup language, HTML. Markups are commands inserted in the text which are then interpreted by the client. As an example, the paragraph markup is <p>. When the client sees this command, rather than showing it to the viewer, it creates a paragraph break in the text. A hypertext link is created with the <a> markup. Suppose I wanted the phrase "Marketing on the Internet" to be highlighted for the viewer, and that if the viewer clicked on the phrase they would be able to browse the WWW2000 page at Vanderbilt University. I would use this construction:

    <a> href="http://www2000.ogsm.vanderbilt.edu/">Marketing on the
    Internet</a>

Everything between the <a> and the </a> would be highlighted. The URL for the WWW2000 page at Vanderbilt is included as the HREF (hyptertext reference).

Another World Wide Web page covering marketing on the Internet is called /MouseTracks/. Its URL is

http://nsns.com/MouseTracks/.

Marketing Activities on the Net

At this time the focus of marketing activity on the Internet is the World Wide Web. The Web is being used both as a marketing communications medium and as a way to perform direct marketing or selling. For the former activity, we have, in effect, the possibility of a complex online pamphlet available to any would-be customer wishing to find more information about the product. Of course, various types of sales promotions are possible, and are being explored already, including contests and deals. Traditional advertising support for content is present as well, as sellers place clickable icons on frequently visited sites. One advantage of the Web in this respect is that the efficacy of a placement can be easily assessed. When someone clicks on an advertiser's icon, a digital record is retained. Consequently, calculating reach and frequency of the ad is straightforward. Some hypothetical log records are shown below:

clients.net.address — [26/Jul/1995:18:00:00] "GET /directory/ file.html"

clients.net.address — [26/Jul/1995:18:01:00] "GET /directory/ file.number2.html"

otherclients.net.address — [26/Jul/1995:18:02:00] "GET /directory/ file.html"

Here an Internet visitor from site "clients.net.address" visited our server on July 26th at 18:00. That individual started at a certain file (/directory/file.html), then clicked on another page to retrieve a second file (/directory/file.number2.html). A second visitor arrived another minute later. These logs can be treated much the way consumer goods manufacturers and others treat retail scanner data. Reports and statistical analyses can be formulated which focus on who accessed the pages, what pages were accessed and in what sequences, and when the pages are visited. It is also possible to randomly change the format seen by any one viewer thus allowing for experimental research on optimal page design.

Online selling is being facilitated through the development of secure (or at least more secure) credit card transactions or virtual cash substitutes. The essence of moving bits instead of things is that the marginal cost of a transaction tends towards zero. System software will enable small purchases of less than $1 (US) to be easily executed. Vendors are beginning to use the Web as an interactive catalog with images or, in the case of music, sound samples of the product . Ordering occurs in real time in much the same way as it might on a toll-free phone line.

In addition to its use of the Web, business is using e-mail to engage in one-on-one conversation with customers. However, generally speaking, e-mail is not well suited for use as a mass medium. The same consumer who calmly tosses aside junk postal mail without a hint of anger might decide to retaliate to junk e-mail with a 10 megabyte "e-mail bomb" directed back to the sender. An example mail bomb might be a file containing a very large image of the words "NO THANK YOU." Even if only 1/10th of 1 percent of the recipients of an unsolicited e-mail campaign choose to exercise this option, it could drive a marketer's computer system to its virtual knees, making it impractical to communicate with genuine prospects. Unsolicited e-mail is not a good idea.

A Look into the Future

Extrapolating forward a few years, it seems clear that the number of companies participating in the Web will increase worldwide by two or more orders of magnitude. This raises the issue of clutter and attracting attention. No doubt the Internet will move in a familiar direction; capital requirements will increase, possibilities for synergy across media will emerge, and the economic scale of both the players and the messages will increase. There will be a limit, however, to the similarity between the Internet and other media.

Unique to the Internet will be the manner in which consumers or browsers traverse from page to page. Specific enhancements to Web software will prove critical. One could draw an historical analogy and consider what the remote control device has done to television advertising as well as to editing and cutting style prevalent in programming. This precedent, however, provides a mild preview of the kind of change that the Internet will engender.

The Web relies on an open and simple protocol, the hypertext transmission protocol (HTTP). In addition, there is a standard (known as the Common Gateway Interface, or CGI) that allows Web pages to interact with *any* computer program. Thus, anything you can do with a computer you can do on the Web, and inventing things you can do with Web pages is as easy as writing a program. In light of this, the system software associated with the World Wide Web can be expected to rapidly change and to have important and, from our current perspective, unpredictable results on Web viewing. The essence of computing is the flexibility and adaptability afforded by software. TV, radio and magazines contain hardwired messages. Even CD-ROM is limited to a finite number of presentation combinations. The viewer is limited in the manner in which information can be accessed. The driving force behind the Internet is software in all of its flexibility.

At this time, we are already seeing a growing number of Web sites which provide searching, sorting, editing and filtering services to users looking for other Web sites. Achieving retailing revenue or communications reach on the network will depend on the technical capabilities of these services and how people use these capabilities in their browsing behavior.

There is another sense in which the Internet will provide a radically different marketing environment from the worlds of magazines, television, or radio. Those media form communications channels which are hierarchical in nature. One-way communication from the publisher to the consumer predominates. But just as television was not radio with pictures, the Internet will not be TV with a mouse. The analogy with TV breaks down due to the amount of computational and telecommunications power sitting at the periphery of the network. The notion of "interaction" means something quite different when used to describe the Internet as compared to when it is used to describe a fixed CD-ROM, for example, or a stand-alone desktop computer. Interaction means that the customer is going to be able to communicate with you as easily as you can communicate with them. Consequently we might expect the network to exhibit far more direct marketing, or even personal selling, than today's mass media. The network will enable, and indeed require, relationship marketing.

There is a further implication of the empowering potential of the technology of the Internet. The Net exhibits an historically unparalleled efficiency in storing, manipulating and transporting content. Today's Internet allows users to cheaply publish text, and ISDN telephone lines and cable modems will allow users of tomorrow's Internet to cheaply publish CD-quality sound or video. It is safe to predict that there will be a massive increase in the competition for consumer attention. Each new magazine splinters the print audience into smaller and smaller segments. Each new cable TV network splinters the television audience into smaller and smaller segments. The one thing that is not growing is the amount of free time available to the consumer to look at all this stuff. Now throw mom-and-pop TV stations, radio stations, Web sites, and recording studios into this mix! The Internet will make our current audiences look like the era of *Life* magazine and the "Ed Sullivan show." And the fact that the Internet is transnational will make for even more competition.

The transnational characteristic of the Net will also make regulation of the online market problematic. A lack of regulation and the lack of barriers to entry might conceivably generate a high level of perceived risk on the part of the consumer. This perceived risk might slow the growth of the medium. In addition, there is a shortage of qualified technical computer specialists. When you couple the shortage with the openness of the network, it seems likely that there will be many incidents involving computer security and the network. These incidents could freeze the consumer even more. In general terms, however, there are some spectacular opportunities for marketing in the online realm. This is one area that marketers in all companies should be watching carefully.

14

Media and Marketing Strategies for the Internet

A Step-by-Step Guide

Tracy Emerick

Tracy Emerick is president of Taurus Direct Marketing, a direct marketing agency and consultancy and president of Receptive Marketing, an electronic mall on the Internet. He is past chairman of the Business-to-Business Council of the Direct Marketing Association and is a director for the Direct Marketing to Business Conference and Business Database Marketing Conference of Dun & Bradstreet. He is co-author of *Business-to-Business Direct Marketing* and *Desktop Marketing*.

The Internet allows for a wealth of interactive marketing opportunities. The opportunities are even more expansive than its interactive predecessor, the telephone. While the use of the telephone as a marketing tool is still active, the Internet's multi-media presentation abilities combined with its inexpensive cost structure provide the ideal tool for direct and channel marketing of goods and services.

The Internet is a method of communication utilizing networked computers as the medium. A variety of different information transfer applications (protocols) are used to facilitate the finding, viewing, and transfer of information. Marketing on the Internet can incorporate a number of different applications.

Electronic Mail

The most widespread use of the network is the exchanging of electronic mail. This application provides a direct electronic communication link between companies and customers or prospects. E-mail employs standardized transfer of text-based messages. In addition, other files of any type (text, graphics, applications etc.) can be attached to an e-mail message, although better methods exist to transfer large files.

A method of sending a single message to a large group of people all at once is referred to as a mailing list. Such a list can be private, limited by mailing list administrator, or public, where any interested party can join the list by requesting the administrator to be added. Lists are best used for a select group with the same interests:

- Professional people
- Customers
- Sales people
- Distributors/Dealers
- Retailers

An e-mail request for information can trigger an automated mail delivery of a file or an e-mail response. This process is called, quite appropriately, an automated response and is analogous to a modern fax-back system.

World Wide Web

Though the Internet's network of computer networks has been in existence for more than 20 years, it is the recent adoption of the World Wide Web that has fueled the rapid growth and expansion of the commercial use of the network. This new application provides a graphical user interface (GUI) between the end-user and server computer being accessed on the Internet. Initially designed as an information delivery method, the Web's graphical and text delivery interface provides the same appearance as traditional printed materials. Along these lines, material on the Web is published on individual, inter-linked pages.

The World Wide Web interface has done for the Internet what the Windows operating system did for the PC in the late 1980s, making the Internet easy to use and navigate by the common untrained person using point and click skills. The World Wide Web provides colorful presentations and the ability to download any digital information to the viewer. Since any information including text, images, sound and video can be converted to a digital format, the presentation opportunities on the Web are limitless. The web employs a hypertext system, which allows designated text and pictures (and portions of them) to be linked to other documents.

Browsers that translate web pages for the end-user can also serve as the interface for less advanced Internet information applications. Though these information and communication mediums are less desirable for marketing efforts, there are appropriate uses for them.

Internet Gopher was the premier information display on access interface before the recent growth of the WWW. Gopher sites provide collections of information in fully indexed databases and are structured by directories/folders and files stored in hierarchical menus. The application provides a document search and retrieval system. Gopher sites can serve in situations where text-only presentations are employed. Gopher's replacement by the WWW as the primary Internet application is inevitable as the interface is available only in black and white.

Usenet and Newsgroups are structured groups compiled over the Internet for discussion of a particular theme. Anyone can post and read a particular newsgroup, which produces near-anarchy. The system works on threads of discussion. An initial posting starts a thread and others comment in a forum atmosphere. Newsgroups can be started among current or prospective customers of a marketing operation to provide user input, profiling, and research. Newsgroups cannot be controlled however, creating challenges for the Internet marketer.

Internet Marketing Strategies

Internet Marketing Strategies can be described, planned, and executed in three steps.

Phase 1: Internet Presence—Advertising and Public Relations

World Wide Web Home Page: Developing a presence that serves as the basis for a corporation, division, product group or other entity for worldwide electronic review. The home page can serve several functions:

1. Advertising/PR presentation for channel and end users.
2. Messages to encourage browsers to take further action via phone or fax.

Phase 2: Involvement from the Home Page—Promotion

Promotional use of the Internet delivers the information currently delivered using other media ranging from the sales representative to broadcast media. The advantage of the Internet is that complete explanations can be delivered and downloaded locally for use by the customer and prospect.

1. Product/Service offerings—corporate, division, product group.
    A. Electronic pages that can serve the same function(s) as
        (1) Sell sheets
        (2) Specification sheets
        (3) Presentation brochures
        (4) Technical explanations
        (5) Press releases
        (6) Organization messages
        (7) Executive letters
        (8) Utilization suggestions

2. Dealer/Retailer Locator—where to purchase products and services

    A. Linear listings by state, country or other hierarchy, or

    B. Search engine supported by relational database.

3. Presentations for browser review or sales to administer.

Phase 3: On-line transaction—Interaction

The most developed use of the Internet allows for interaction with individual customers and prospects. Interaction can include everything from answers to specific questions to on-line ordering at the wholesale and retail levels.

1. Dialogue—Real-time discussions with all levels of the channel.

    A. Secure or non-secure channels news group.

    B. End user news group.

2. Research—Decision making information gathering.

    A. Channel information gathering

    B. End user information gathering.

3. Service—Product/service information dissemination and discussions.

    A. Product/service utilization service.

    B. End user and channel service.

4. Support—Product/service explanation and problem solving.

    A. Product/service utilization support.

    B. End user and channel support.

    C. Sales support

5. Lead acquisition—New business opportunities.

    A. Leads for channel sales.

    B. End user leads.

6. Ordering—Sales to channel and/or end users.
   A. Wholesale
   B. Retail

Internet Marketing Costs

Internet marketing costs can be divided into five areas:

1. Equipment
2. Connection Fees
3. Development Costs
4. Employee Management Costs
5. Communications Costs

Equipment costs will vary depending on how extensively a company wants to use the Internet in its marketing communications:

- Basic: Desktop computer and modem—$4,000

- Extensive: Server with direct connect equipment—$75,000

Connection fees can include:

- Basic: Dial-up to local Internet Service Provider—$12–$20 per month

- Extensive: Dedicated T1 line direct to Internet—$1,000–$5,000 per month

Development costs generally include:

- Basic: Home Page and three informational pages $1,500 - $4,500

- Extensive: $100,000 +

Additional development is also necessary as the site changes and improves. Employee management involve:

- Basic: Incidental and random use of Internet

- Extensive: Dedicated systems administrator(s), dedicated communicators, manager

Worldwide communications costs—a key benefit of the Internet—are no more than the cost of the connection fees, no matter how basic or extensive the site.

Internet Audience

The Internet audience can be divided into seven segments (an eighth segment is market participants who do not use the Internet) at present:

- Market: Customers, current and past. Prospects, those people who might become customers. Surfers or browsers who are not and will never become customers but still browse your Internet site(s) for entertainment.

- Decision Responsibility: Power to make decisions. Authority is based on job assignment/description. Influence has neither power or authority.

- Internet Involvement: Active uses the Internet as a part of daily activity. Passive has access but seldom or never uses the Internet.

- Off-Line: does not have access.

EXHIBIT 14.1 Reaching Internet Audiences

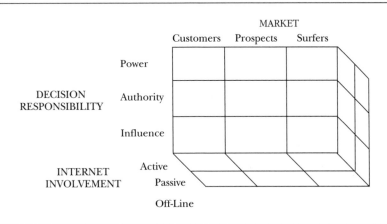

Database and Internet Marketing

The Internet is a communications option that can be used to present database information to users and to capture information for inclusion into a database.

A marketer can maintain a database of simple products/services, descriptions and prices. This database can be put on-line for customers, prospects, company employees, distributors, dealers, retailers and anyone else who might benefit from the information. A user requests information from the database and it is presented to the user from the database.

This process is accomplished using Gopher for text based information. For the WWW, the information is passed through an on-the-fly HTML generator, which converts the text for transmission and calls up the graphics already in GIF format. If you keep the database current, the user receives the latest information available, in real time.

The Internet can also be used to gather information from a market. The same information you gather using any other media (mail, phone, personal visit) can be gathered over the Internet. The information you gather can be for research, lead generation, selling products/services or any other type of feedback, including customer satisfaction surveys.

Your ability to organize a database is enhanced when the user is doing the data entry. This can also pose a problem, however, if you want information to be consistent. Information gathering over the Internet may use a few basic principles:

1. Limit information requests to a form which can be completed in three to five minutes. It is too easy to exit a site if the user's involvement lessens.

2. Don't ask for information that requires the user to leave their workstation, they will probably not come back. Exceptions to this are if you are registering serial numbers or some other transaction which will benefit the user in some way.

3. Limit response options per question or you will not be able to analyze the results.

4. Use open-ended questions when quantitative response measurement is not necessary.

5. Build in questions which separate surfers from customers and prospects.

Employee Management in Internet Marketing

Logistics of employee management for supporting an Internet site are similar to the logistics of managing a telemarketing or telesales site with one exception, the communicators do not need to be in any particular physical location.

Communicators must be trained in the facets of your business and of customer expectations and demands as they relate to your products and services. Since the Internet allows all users (unless you require a password for entry into all or part of your site) communicators must be schooled in how to determine cranks from legitimate contacts.

The best type of individual for the position of communicator is a person with low aggressiveness and high emotion, often referred to as amiable or affiliator. This type of individual enjoys working with a group and has the ability to deal with various markets with equal ease.

Full consumption of a person's time is always a consideration when staffing any position. An Internet communicator should be monitored the same as all employees. Measurement criteria for this position are yet to be determined. Measurement could be based on number of email messages handled in a day and/or it could be measured in customer satisfaction (seen in re-orders from existing customers). Internet communication may not be a full time position in your company. However, someone should be assigned the responsibility of responding to email and other Internet inquiries.

You can control the flow of messages to answer based on the programs you put on line. If you do not want inquiries, do not provide a way for people to respond to your site.

One way to reduce the need for response is to set up automatic responses for certain types of inquiries. These responses are delivered automatically when an inquiry is received. This can be programmed as an auto function.

You can also set up a FAQ (frequently asked questions) location to answer the repetitive questions, thus reducing the need for increased staffing due to increased inquiries.

One person with some level of understanding of your business and with some pre-written information resources can handle 35 - 45 inquiries an hour. This number is estimated based on the number of inquiries handled in a full workday. A communicator will probably only be online four to five hours per day because of the need to research certain inquiries.

Keeping a site current and interesting also requires an Internet marketing manager. It is easy to put up a site, but keeping it current is more challenging. This function is not defined in most companies since just getting on the Internet is the task at hand. Once active, however, the site needs to be constantly reviewed and updated. Sites that become too big and lack navigation or entertainment value can be cluttered and exhausting for a user. Ease of use and clarity of navigation aids is essential for a site to keep user involved.

Using the Internet as a method of customer and channel contact assumes that customers and channel partners are able and interested in embracing this communications medium. The logistics of working with the market require that you support many skill levels. Until the Internet is more widely used, a great deal of time will be consumed by education and skill development. Skill development can be a strategic tool for you to work with your channel partners. If you provide training and applications which make working with you more convenient and cost-effective, you can leverage this in terms of profits through longer lifetime value of customers.

Promotion on the Internet

Promoting your site can be accomplished in a variety of ways both on and outside the Internet. The options available are:

1. Publishing your Internet address in your printed materials and advertising. Like your phone number, your Internet address will be recorded for use by customers and prospects. Surfers may pick up your address from print advertising, but will be excluded when you use targeted media like direct mail to reach your desired audience.

2. Using publicity to reach your marketplace. Getting your address out in this fashion is a hit-or-miss proposition since PR is uncontrollable and may or may not reach your marketplace in a timely fashion.

3. Inside the Internet using announcement locations and search engines.

4. Links from other Internet sites in exchange for links from your site.

As in all communications, involvement, both physically and mentally is a key guideline. If a person is not involved with your message, they are not involved with your promotion. If there is not involvement, there will be no behavior modification-action to take the next step in buying from you. Internet promotion can take on three characters:

1. Information only, a site which only gives information is a dialogue—you to the reader.

2. Custom information, a site where users can gain information specific to their needs.

3. Feedback, a site where users gain and give information.

The custom and feedback Internet sites can build a database for future contact. Each visitor's email address can be captured and used for future contact. It is important that this be done with caution. The culture of the Internet is self-governing and can create problems if a marketer is too aggressive in promoting products and services.

The Internet is governed by general agreement of use called netiquette. This unwritten set of rules allows information to be sought but never delivered unsolicited. Unwanted solicitation of information can result in angry complaints to your e-mail box, called "flaming" or overloading of your server by bombarding it with automated messages from an upset individual, called "spamming."

To avoid getting flaming and spamming, out-bound promotional activities should be in the form of announcements. The announcement provides opportunities for users to visit your site for something that benefits them. Promotional information can include all materials currently available in printed form or in text form used for press releases.

The key to active Internet promotion is to offer something of value to the user you want to visit your site. People are never annoyed with a topic of interest to themselves. Offer development is covered in another section.

Developing Internet Offers

The use of any media to communicate requires a series of steps from the time of contact until the time of closure. A simple model is Attention—Interest—Desire—Action (AIDA). Your Internet promotion will follow these steps, or some steps along these lines, as you reach out into cyberspace to attract people to you and then to do what you want them to do—from simple feedback to on-line buying. Each one of the steps in the relationship moves a person from a surfer to a customer. Surfers can move through each step more easily if there is something in it for them. You need to develop these "somethings" by developing offers which people will respond to.

Offers can be general or specific. General offers might be taken advantage of by anyone on the Internet regardless of their specific areas of interest. These offers might be information on the standings of professional sports or weather reports in various parts of the country. A general offer is designed to attract a broad audience.

A specific offer is one which is focused on the needs of a specific person. An example might be monitoring and reporting on the migration habits of the North American horned owl. This type of information is of interest only to people interested in horned owl or bird migration. A site where telemetry engineers can discuss the effects of temperatures on wing vibration at super-sonic speeds will certainly only be of interest to this type of engineer.

Offers can be used to move people through three basic steps of relationship building:

1. Attract visitors

2. Involve prospects

3. Sell/support customers

Attracting visitors is the biggest challenge of the Internet. It requires you to have something of interest and that you be known. Using promotion you can deliver your offer. Your offer should be easy to understand. An example might be: Review and download the ten keys to success, URL http://yoursite.com. This offer is such that any person who wants success might drop in for a visit, just to see what you've got. With promotion, this offer could generate thousands of visitors per day.

If you want a specific market you could offer the Five Engineering Tests for Professional Publishing, URL http:yoursite.com. This offer will attract a specific type of visitor.

When a visitor has arrived to take advantage of your attracting offer you have gained their Attention. Now you must involve the visitor in order to create Interest and Desire. If the visitor arrives, copies or downloads your free guide and leaves quickly, you have not taken advantage of the visit. You must engage the visitor in some way to gain the physical and mental involvement. One approach might be to ask for certain information from the visitor, before you provide the download file. As you are asking the information, you could be providing additional information, along the same lines as the attracting offer.

You can embed another offer inside the fulfillment of the first offer. Once a visitor is on-site you can make another, more attractive offer. One that will enhance the life of the visitor in some way. You should ask for feedback at this point and provide enhancements to the offer which will keep the prospect involved. In the case of the success keys, you might have a questionnaire the visitor completes in order to receive a success quotient. This custom report is provided as an additional service, just for taking the time. When the custom report is delivered, you have the opportunity to move to the profitable portion of the relationship.

Action is the step in the process when you receive money for what you are or might deliver. In the example you could have a complete success guidebook for a person for $48.49 which can be billed to their credit card or paid at a later time. The same approach can be used for our engineers, who might receive a special report on wing stress if they will answer a few questions which lead to the $850 desktop calculation software package (billed or charged to a credit card).

Your Action step can also be to gather sufficient information about each other to move to a non-Internet environment—a sales visit or a phone contact. Test the approach of selling on-line, you might be surprised with the result.

The Internet Mall

Participating in a mall can be a great way to promote and sell products and services to business and consumers. The advantages to participating in a mall are very similar to the advantages of a merchant participating in a retail mall.

1. The mall owner is responsible for the construction of the mall. Design and layout of the Internet mall and merchant participation are costs incurred by the mall owner. This means the cost of entering a mall can be less for the merchant than setting up a site.

2. The mall owner is responsible for bringing traffic to the mall. Promotion of the mall and merchants fall with the mall owner. This reduces the promotional effort necessary by the merchant. Which in turn reduces the need to learn all about Internet marketing so time can be devoted to merchandise and not marketing issues.

3. The mall which has critical mass can be more fun than a visit to a stand alone site. Visiting a mall is a leading form of entertainment in the United States. Visiting Internet malls can also be entertaining if the mall is well laid out and has a variety of merchandise and services.

4. On-line ordering is a difficult and expensive process to develop. Mall owners not only provide space; they can also provide on-line ordering capabilities for the merchant so the merchant does not have to do this themselves.

There are disadvantages to participating in a mall:

1. You may be restricted in how you are presented on the Internet.

2. You may lose some flexibility in how your products and services are presented.

3. If a mall does not do a good job of promotion, you might have less traffic.

4. Mall entertainment can create a lot of visitors with few sales.

5. You may not have direct access from surfers, prospects and customers. They may be forced to come to you by way of the mall home page and not directly into your location.

Mall participation should be one avenue you use to create a presence on the Internet. It is a low maintenance way to gain presence and link to other pages you have in the Internet.

Combining Internet with Integrated Marketing Strategy

As discussed, the Internet is a communications media. Like all media it should be used in concert with other media. The combined effects of multiple media reaching into a market at the same time is generally higher overall than the results of each media added together.

The advantage of the Internet is the relative low cost of the media for worldwide communications. The disadvantage is that not all people in your market are on-line.

The Internet is generally not coordinated with other media because the medium is so new it does not have a formal link to the marketing communications plan. The Internet is used as a general catch-all for information without regard as to how it ties in with current non-Internet promotion.

An example of using the Internet in concert with other media was the release of "Batman Forever" in the summer of 1995. The producer promoted the movie on TV, print media and on-line. Supposedly the movie opened with one of the highest grossing first week-ends in history.

Combining media can take several approaches as seen in this matrix. The numbers indicate an option and are an index of difficulty in managing multi-media programs.

Option 1

This is the simplest form of multi-media. All media being used have the same message and request the same action. An example is an insurance promotion which asks you to call an 800 number or to respond over the Internet. The same message will be delivered on the Internet and in print advertising.

EXHIBIT 14.2 Multi-Media Options

	Same Message/ Offer	Different Message/ Offer
Same Action	1	2
Different Action	3	4

Option 2

The use of one medium to drive people toward a certain action. The promotion of the Batman movie in all media was designed for the same action, to get you to go to see the movie. The media messages were different, each geared toward the medium being used. In this case the Internet promotion was more involved and expensive than any other media used in the program.

Option 3

Using the same message and/or offer to move different people to different actions is relatively easy to promote. The difficulty is trying to determine the results if people can take separate actions. The same message/offer has several methods of action. A manufacturer can offer a set of guidelines for caring for a printer. The action is to secure the guidelines which might be accomplished by contacting the manufacturer or by contacting a dealer. These two options create difficulty for understanding the outcomes.

Option 4

Different messages with different actions is the general state of affairs in most companies. One example of a controlled multi-media approach with different actions is used by Publisher's Clearing House when you are instructed to go to your mail box in order to mail in your contest entry. This use of different message with different actions must prove profitable since it is repeated year after year. The next option will be to put this entire program on the Internet and let users subscribe and enter on-line.

Using the Internet with Channels

The Internet is a low cost, immediate way to communicate with channels. An example of a shoe manufacturer will serve to illustrate:

- Ace Shoe Manufacturer develops a series of pages showing its current shoe styles and general pricing. Each shoe style is given a complete work-up from construction through tips on when to wear the style.

- The distributor can review styles and place orders for stock. The orders can be placed via a privately accessed order form using assigned passwords and account codes.

- The dealer/retailer can accomplish the same as the dealer placing orders with the distributor or with the manufacturer as is the store's method.

- Sales people at all levels can access the Internet presentation for personal education and for presentation to customers. The latest styles and codes are always current so the sales people are not selling old inventory.

- End users/customers can review the manufacturers' styles and general pricing along with all other available information. The site also has a listing of dealers/retailers so the end user/customer can purchase the style or styles they desire—perhaps even order on-line, a real challenge for the channel.

Manufacturers can provide for end user feedback which can be shared with distributors and dealers in a secure location. This information can provide strategic information for all participants in the channel. The Internet can also be used to complement or supplement existing communication programs ranging from sales people to printed materials and order forms. You can also establish new channels domestically and worldwide using the Internet because of its low cost and immediate information transfer.

Predictions on the Internet

The Internet will revolutionize marketing as it is known today. The revolution will confound marketers, customers and governments trying to regulate and tax unprecedented global commerce. As the tools used on the Internet expand and the speed of data transmission accelerates, the Internet will become a one-to-one marketing medium offering customized interchange between seller and buyer.

Use of the Internet is currently experimental. Surrounded by excessive hype and hyperbola the actual utility of the medium has yet to reach senior executives. Once the utility is known traditional methods of print and broadcast advertising, printed materials and even sales calls will be minimized as part of the media mix. The Internet's capacity for color graphics, sound, text and eventually video will provide the basis for on-demand marketing and sales.

The Internet will also bring about the end of distribution as it is structured today. Combined with rapid delivery systems for goods, the Internet will negate the need for stocking distributors, globally. The roles of distributors and resellers will be replaced with on-line demonstrations, service and support provided directly by the manufacturer. Only value-added distributors will survive the next decade.

Distribution channels will be streamlined and the remaining companies in the channel will use the Internet as a user-friendly electronic data interchange (EDI). The Internet will be used to support perpetual sales meetings, on-line trade shows, end user research and feedback vehicle as well as product review, updates and ordering, both wholesale and retail.

Eventually the computer, telephone, and television will become a single unit which multi-tasks between the various information resources for entertainment, business, finances and news. The Internet will flourish as the tools and access become simplified. Cable companies will offer Internet through the cable connection giving the home user every day transmission speed enjoyed only by expensive dedicated lines today.

Any person or business not getting involved with the Internet today will be left on the sidelines within five years. Tomorrow, school children will be using the Internet instead of going to the library. The next generation of business, where employees work from the home, will use the Internet instead of the telephone.

Creative Strategy for Interactive Marketing

10 Rules for Adapting and Winning in the New Marketplace

Carol Nelson
Rocky James

Carol Nelson is Executive Vice President, Communicomp, a full-service direct response agency based in Plantation, Florida. In addition to speaking on marketing and advertising subjects at conferences all over the world, her articles appear regularly in the business press. She also is author of several books on marketing and advertising, including *Women's Marketing Handbook*, which received a 1994 *Choice* award, and *The World's Greatest Direct Mail Sales Letters*, with Herschell Gordon Lewis.

Rocky James is Executive Director, Electronic Media Development and Production for Communicomp. Previously, he was Special Projects Producer for NBC Network News in Burbank and Segment Producer for NBC. James has produced numerous infomercials, including the "Carlton Sheets No Money Down" segment for AMS. His articles on infomercials and TV direct response appear regularly in the business press.

Sure, everyone's jumping on the interactive advertising bandwagon. It's new, it's novel, it's exciting. But it won't ever be a viable advertising vehicle.

We hear that argument—or something very much like it—almost every day. And yet, that's what the newspaper die-hards said when radio surfaced in the early 1920s. It's what radio die-hards said about television back in the 1950s.

Advertising will never fly on the Internet. Why would *anyone* pay to look at advertising?

Sound familiar? That's exactly the argument we heard from the network television die-hards about cable TV back in the 1980s. Yet people not only watch infomercials, they actually pick up the phone and order product.

If you advertise on the Internet, how will anyone see it?

That's one of the first questions detractors ask when they begin to think about interactive advertising on the net or online services. As they exist, they're more like broadcast media (as people "channel surf" from site to site) or Yellow Pages directories (as people search sites by classification) or outdoor billboards (as people speed right past your "billboard" on the info superhighway) than direct response media.

The World's Biggest, Most Confusing Circus

First-time browsers—and they're fewer and fewer, as about 50,000 people each week join the fingertip parade into the netherworld—are stunned by the variety and breadth of offerings.

Who cares if Barnum was right when he said, There's a sucker born every minute? On the Internet, it's as difficult to find Barnum as it is to find the suckers. But Barnum had a virtue along with his vices: He was a spellbinder, and he'd be a strategy-hero on the Internet. Barnum knew that the moment he lapsed into high-flown language, the group in front of his tent would evaporate. He knew that the slightest tinge of unclarity would create confusion as an unhappy replacement for artificial enthusiasm.

Barnum knew how to sell. He wasn't a technician. He didn't use technical talk. He didn't throw terminology around as a meat-cleaving weapon.

To Internet advertisers looking for maximized response, the clarion call would be, "Go thou and do likewise."

But the Internet and online interactive services have terrific poten-tial for direct response advertising, precisely because they *are* interac-tive . . . if you know how to use that interactivity to its best advantage.

And the advantages are unique, just as the disadvantages are unique.

Staged Events

The speed with which Internet advertising is sophisticating itself is—well, it can be frightening. Today's brilliant innovation is tomorrow's old hat; and even the most jaded television viewer, who has seen trends come and go in a flash, has to be bewildered when terminology and procedures he has just heard for the first time are already obsolete.

One strategy that does work, although the word w*ork* has another implication here, is the Online Conference. The huge competitive advantage is that a conference is *interactive*, and interactivity is the key to loyalty—or as much loyalty as the electronically-charged consumer of the late 1990s can muster.

Along with conferences are meeting halls, in which an Internet advertiser ostensibly asks individuals to participate with ideas and sug-gestions. Here again, implementation demands gradual accretion of a user database to enable the advertiser to contact—whether by e-mail or by mail or by phone—the people who have entered the advertiser's lair and left their names and contact addresses. Careful structuring of what the meeting is about will result in a positive public relations event.

Now, a heavyweight Internet concept: *customer loyalty programs.*

Such programs make more sense on the Internet than in any other medium, not only because—as we've pointed out—the customer comes looking for you instead of your having to prospect randomly for him or her. But also because the Internet isn't free. Oh, yes, it's *virtually* free because the cost-per-hit is insignificant; but it isn't free. This compares to a cold-list name calling you and asking for a copy of your catalog. Treasure that person!

Customer loyalty programs can be as basic as points, such as the frequent flyer programs that have been in place for a generation. But the Internet has an edge over the airlines: The huge, ponderous, and expensive machinery involved in monthly or quarterly contact with members doesn't exist. Members can check their points with a click of the mouse-button. If the advertiser, in an act of supreme benevolence, contacts members by mail (or even e-mail), that's frosting on the cake of a constantly improving relationship.

Technical aside: Those who subscribe to online services such as Compuserve and America Online are instantly accessible because their addresses don't change even if they move across the country. No change of address bookkeeping here!

Surveys aren't quite staged events, because each survey is one-on-one. The advantage to the advertiser is that surveys are structured, while conference halls are unstructured. This gives the advertiser an edge—provided the advertiser knows how to use that edge: Structuring questions to be most beneficial. The best consultants for this type of survey might well be political consultants, who know how to generate questions that cloud the mind and distort actuality.

Like the conference, the survey is apparently 100 percent interactive. If the advertiser follows the survey with a report to participants, score another point for Internet strategy.

The key to staged events is *enthusiastic participation*. Keep the pot boiling. Keep excitement high. Don't lapse into bored sameness, because bored sameness is just about the most contagious disease carried by the Internet.

A New Tool for the Marketing Toolbox

Marketing principles are the same across all media. Only the "toolbox" changes. (Would that more advertising agencies, who exploit one medium because that's the one with which they feel most comfortable, embraced this truism.)

Therein lies a strategic challenge—no, a warning:

> Much Internet advertising is prepared not by marketers but by programmers and technicians. This parallels having ads written by typesetters. Technical proficiency supplants communications skills, and the result may be a technological triumph and a motivational flop.

What's the difference between creating a direct response advertising message for interactive media and traditional media such as mail, television, and print ads? Very little. (A "But . . . " disclaimer is coming up.) Interactive media are the perfect vehicles for your direct response messages. But the interactive age has ushered in a new way to communicate. And as we pick our way carefully through the differences that do exist, we find the communications differences are great enough to warrant an entire chapter in this book.

How to Integrate Your Interactive Advertising into Your Existing Advertising Campaign

The Internet implicitly has superimposed its own set of rules onto the world of advertising strategy. Recognition of these rules may not result in a brilliant campaign, but it should result in a competitively professional campaign.

These are the absolute rules for adapting conventional advertising to Internet advertising in today's volatile marketplace:

1. Passive messages are out. Absolutely. No exceptions. We're fanatical about this because, of all the rules we might impose, violating this one will drive browsers out of your site as though you have the plague. And you do—the plague of dullness.

We put this rule at the top of the list because nearly every one of the nine rules that follow stem from this first rule.

2. Grab and shake the reader instantly. Whoever said television is the medium that generates an instant reaction hasn't hit the Internet. Television is slow-motion compared to a nervous mouse-hand, hovering in limbo and ready to flee at the slightest indication of irrelevance or tedium.

3. Your cover page and the first page of text have to be not only "killers" . . . but have to download *fast*. Slow downloading has destroyed many a bright promotional idea. The "killer" mandate is true of many media, but the fast-to-load mandate is peculiar to this medium because the whole concept had never existed until the Internet existed. That may not seem so difficult, but of all the rules and principles and suggestions in this chapter, it's the one most likely to bite you if you don't follow it. Try it just once and you'll see: This is where many a veteran communicator stumbles.

4. Ask for response—*any* type of response that makes even a little sense—immediately. As the medium slowly matures, another avenue of *intensification* exists. It's one even sophisticated Internet advertisers overlook, perhaps because they are blinded by the glamour of the

medium: e-mail to responders. When you get a response from them, make sure you're equipped to send a response right *back* to them—and *right now!* As one veteran interactive fund-raiser (yes, you can successfully generate response for a fund raising campaign, too), Stacey Switzer says, "Never underestimate the short attention span of your audience. People expect instantaneous response, not a day or a week later!"

Technically, this is easy to do. It also is in keeping, from a strategic point of view, with the state of mind of those who respond to Internet advertising. Certainly, recognizing *who* the recipient of the message is, receptivity will be greater than it would be to a mailed newsletter. You're in the most competitive bazaar ever created, and response is the key to lengthening the browser's gnat-like attention span. Fast, *fast,* FAST have a contest, give away something free, issue an invitation, have a "Today Only!" special. Alertness will pay off. And that leads directly to. . . .

5. Change your message often. Yes, you can run a campaign on television for thirteen weeks and "build" a reaction. You can't do that on the Internet. A browser sees your message, or even your first page . . . says, "Oh, it's one I've seen before" . . . and quickly mouses over to a fresh message by a more astute competitor. Changing your message even every day isn't too often, because your best browsers will hit your surf every time they lurch onto the electronic superhighway. Only once need they say, "I've seen that before." Then they're gone—and it very well could be forever. (If your type of business doesn't lend itself to daily updates, start with a "Chuckle of the Day" or a cartoon or a wise saying. But don't think sameness will sink through layers of apathy, the way it does with a radio campaign. This medium is high-powered. (Exhibit 15.1 shows how one online fund raising foundation has set up its home page to be flexible . . . and easily modified.)

6. Advertise your site in other media (see Exhibit 15.2). If they never see you, they won't buy from you. If they don't know you're there, they'll never see you. (Is this cheating? Certainly not. It's the 21st century application of an integrated campaign.)

To make Internet advertising "visible" within the gigantic morass of information smashed loosely together in this electronic jungle, reminder advertising in other media is necessary. This is the Internet version of *The Reader's Digest* and Publishers' Clearing House mailings, reinforced by short-term saturation television reminder-advertising.

EXHIBIT 15.1 The Nature Conservancy Page on America Online

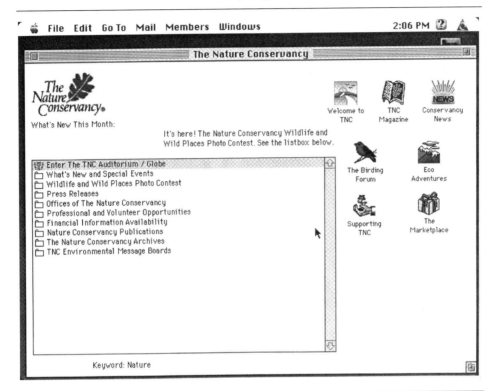

Make it easy, they will come! Make it entertaining and informative, they will come back! says Stacey Switzer. The Nature Conservancy page on America Online makes change . . . and response . . . easy.

7. Establish "links" with like-minded companies. This is what the "Shopping Mall" concept is all about. A financial institution established a Mall, all of whose tenants are linked by a common thread—the bank—as the mall's center. The bank promotes the mall; the tenants benefit from the patronage, just as smaller stores in a conventional mall benefit from the advertising and traffic generated by the mall's anchor store (Exhibits 15.3, 15.4, 15.5). An Internet Solutions company shows off its work by establishing a link to its clients (Exhibit 15.6).

"Member-get-a-member." This venerable technique, as old as book clubs, has found a marvelous home on the Internet. This medium is almost custom-designed for member-get-a-member, not only because

EXHIBIT 15.2 Ad in *Wired*

DO YOU HAVE THE FIBER TO ENTER THE 21ST CENTURY?

FIND OUT ON THE INTERNET.

Stop at the Developers Lab and begin a challenging journey into the future. Along the way, test your knowledge of information technology to make sure you're ready to hit the highway. While you're at it, test those business applications to find out if they have the right stuff.

networkMCI
DEVELOPERS LAB

http://www.mci.com/developerslab/

Space ads in targeted magazines point readers to the advertiser's Internet page. Because this ad appeared in Wired *magazine, the advertiser can assume the reader will already have Internet access.*

referrals don't require any postage nor phone calls nor information beyond an e-mail address, but also because the capability of issuing rewards for referrals is so easy.

9. When you get an order or an inquiry, handle it with lightning speed. That means the same day if possible . . . certainly no longer than one business day. If you don't have this capability, stay off the Internet until you do, because you'll be getting returned merchandise, flame messages, and damaging word-of-mouth (or word-of-mouse).

10. Test. Test. Test again.

How many genuine experts exist . . . gurus who can make (and prove) proclamations about Internet strategy?

As an educated guess: None.

This is because we lack a solid base of testing. Testing has been not just the cornerstone of other media, but their salvation. Testing showed newspapers how emphasis on "Lifestyle" sections and local news could

EXHIBIT 15.3 First Union Corporation Mall Ad

This ad shows how this bank uses interactivity, as well as the shopping mall anchor concept, to its best advantage. Prospects can apply for a credit card online and even leap to sister merchants with the click of a mouse.

EXHIBIT 15.4

7.9 % APR

Introductory Rate
Exceptional rate after 6 months: only 5.9 percentage points over Prime*
No annual fee -- ever!

Get the Gold MasterCard value you've been seeking.
Apply online for *fast* response.
*See terms and conditions screen.

Credit Card Application Form

To apply for a Credit Card from **First Union Nation Bank of Georgia**, please fill in the following **4** categories of information: *Applicant Information, Credit Reference, Review Information, Terms and Conditions*. When all of the boxes are checked below, you may **Submit** your application. The information you enter will be kept in strictest confidence.

1. Applicant Information

2. Credit Reference

3. Review Information

4. Terms and Conditions

[Submit] [Cancel]

Copyright ©1995, First Union Corporation

bring survival in a television-glutted information arena. Testing shows direct marketers which prices, which approaches. which letter length, which motivators, which colors, and which enclosures will turn so-so-results into winners. Testing shows television advertisers which markets are most responsive and which approaches bring customers into stores and automobile showrooms.

EXHIBIT 15.5

CommunityCommerce

Your First Stop on the Information Highway

Community Commerce(sm) is First Union National Bank's vision of the future for community banking. First Union is creating a marketplace on the Internet's World Wide Web. A marketplace designed to offer merchants an opportunity to offer their products and services for sale to a new world market. It is a virtual community that consumers will want to visit again and again to access information, products and services in a feature rich environment.

For the next few weeks, First Union will be presenting merchants with unique products and services. A variety of different payment systems and interfaces will be presented to evaluate efficient mechanisms for encouraging commerce on the web. Please help us evaluate our system by giving feedback on your experiences with each of these merchants.

First Merchants

New merchants will be added to CommunityCommerce during the coming weeks. The first merchants introduced under the trial system include:

- **PC**Travel™ - PC Travel - the only real-time airline reservation and ticketing service on the Internet! PCTravel allows reservations and ticketing at travel agent prices with no fees for using the system. Tickets are delivered next-day in the U.S.
- Fountainhead Water Company - Deep artesian wells in the Blue Ridge Mountains release pure, clean water with nothing added, just as nature intended. Fountainhead brings you this taste by bottling it at the source.
- CBO - Community Business Online's AutoNetwork® - For those of you shopping for a car, there's no better place to start your search. Go visit a live up-to-date database of dealer inventories all over the country.

How can your organization be a Member of CommunityCommerce?

CommunityCommerce is the perfect site for creating your companies own virtual storefront on the Internet.

EXHIBIT 15.6 Internet Solutions

WELCOME!

Choose one of the links below to find out more about Maxperts, Inc.

| **Networks** | **Client/Server** | **Messaging**

CAL OnLine!. Check out Maxperts client, an adult service that utilizes the latest and greatest in multimedia delivery !

Now featuring full service WWW design and publishing services

THANKS FOR VISITING the Maxperts Home Page! If you have any questions, just drop us a line at info@maxperts.com

Return to the Maxperts home page

If you're a service company, the Internet makes it simple to show what you've done for your clients, just by linking their pages to yours.

The Internet, as of this writing, is itself a test. Results are all over the lot because the medium hasn't settled down, nor have its browsers identified themselves into segmentable groups. The challenge of Internet testing may not be met to a degree at which it becomes useful ammunition on a textbook level, until well into the 21st century. This is because change piles upon change, and fishing for the best approach to any one marketing project puts an advertiser in the position of a football referee trying to dig into a pile of 22 bodies to see who has recovered a fumble.

As the first generation of Internet advertising matures, an imperative to those who read these words and front the second generation:

- Test. Test. Test.

- Experiment.

- Test your messages. Test your sites. Test your techniques.

Then, for the love of heaven, analyze what you've discovered. If you're especially kind, share the results of your testing with those who will follow—the third generation of Internet advertisers, who will assume as a matter of course what we have learned with such painstaking experimentation.

When you have results, analyze them and learn from them. If you're a marketer and not just a researcher—and that's the point of all this— use them for your ongoing promotions until further testing shows you the marketplace . . . or *your* marketplace . . . has changed.

Why might your marketplace change when others remain static? For the same reason singular marketing changes have occurred throughout history. Technology and human desires don't alter themselves in a lump. Fashion might change while breakfast cereals don't. A hot new competitor arises in a single field, and suddenly that industry requires retooling while others sail smoothly across calm marketing seas. Alertness calls for recognition of which factors affect *your* business.

Be on the lookout for changes. Believe us, they'll be there.

The Internet is the wildest, most exciting, and most challenging advertising medium we've ever had the good/bad fortune to encounter. The strategist finds it both exhilarating and exasperating . . . and that's what keeps us alert.

Copywriting for Interactive Media

New Rules for the New Medium

Herschell Gordon Lewis

Herschell Gordon Lewis is regarded as the world's leading authority on writing copy that sells. He has written more than a dozen books on the subject, including *Sales Letters That Sizzle* and *The World's Greatest Direct Mail Sales Letters*, with Carol Nelson. He is a regular columnist for such publications as *Direct Marketing Magazine, Direct, Catalog Age,* and *SELL-ING.* He is President of Communicomp, a full-service direct response agency based in Plantation, Florida.

As the twentieth century draws to an end, a new challenge to advertising creative teams defies previous rules of communication.

Advertising on the Internet is a mutant. It combines the targeting specificity of classified advertising . . . the need for aggressive seeking-out of Yellow Pages . . . the instant visual excitement of television . . . the quick-change potential of radio . . . the taut copy discipline of catalogs . . . and the romance of space advertising.

Correction: It combines those elements if it's done properly. If it isn't, advertising on the Internet combines the arrogance of an egomaniac . . . the dryness of an unwanted sermon . . . the frustration of pay-TV when you realize the movie is dull or one you've seen before . . . and the hard-to-find whereabouts of a master spy.

I'll explain that last reference: Reaching an advertiser through one of the on-line services marketplaces isn't difficult. Reaching an advertiser who has a "home page" can be a test of determination and skill. For example, the Internet address of one printer is:

http://www.ais.net/dppc

Not quite as mnemonic as 1-800-FLOWERS, is it?

The point, and the reason the Internet at this point is closer to the Yellow Pages than to television: To reach an advertiser, the prospective customer has to:

1. Pay a monthly time-limited Internet access fee.
2. Have at least a passing familiarity with computer use.
3. Keep at hand a strange, arcane combination of letters representing the specific Internet address.

If you conclude that the copywriter also should be adept at creating a *referral* message (to familiarize prospects with the Internet address) in other media, you're right. If you conclude that the very nature of a referral in a newspaper or magazine ad or on a CD-ROM or even a refrigerator magnet means we have a "two-step" conversion instead of a simple transaction, you're right.

An additional flusterer: The image of the Internet walks the tightwire between wild "hype" in publications dedicated to the supremacy of electronic media and total disdain in publications dedicated to their own self-preservation. In fact, the medium deserves neither.

Logical Limitations, Logical Expectations

The Internet sprang upon public consciousness so suddenly that some advertisers replaced their usual dour skepticism with awestruck idol-worship. They fell victim to the self-devouring *"That which is different equals that which is better "* cult. Because it was new, they felt *any* message would shake the cosmos. They were wrong on three counts:

1. Their cosmos was too small.
2. Their browsers weren't valid buyers, but "groupies."
3. They didn't know how to combine medium and message.

The copywriter who assumes what works in other media will work on the Internet *may* be right. Chances are, if it's a classified ad that pulled and pulled and pulled, it will work on the Internet. Chances are, if it's a rewrite of a four-page direct mail letter, it won't pull on the Internet. I'll tell you why.

The Cardinal Rule of Internet Copywriting

One of the venerable rules of force-communication becomes the primary litany of a copywriter who wants his or her message to accomplish the three sequential goals that cause the cash register to ring:

1. The reader has to find the message.
2. The reader has to comprehend the message.
3. The reader has to respond to the message.

The three goals are simple, you say? Obvious, you say? Truisms, you say? Wonderful.

Explain, then, the deadness of this copy—the first that meets the eye—when a browser fights his way (and that's what he has to do, with the delays in graphics and staggering multiplicity of sites) to an advertiser's nest:

Welcome to The Sony Electronics Consumer products. We are pleased to present over three hundred of our products to you, and provide a comprehensive listing of features which you can use to familiarize yourself with our products. We plan to expand upon our offerings in the near future to make your visit even more enjoyable, as well as to provide you with additional information. In the meantime please feel free to browse our digital catalog.

This copy exemplifies the difference between a salesperson and a clerk. Copywriters who know what motivates readers are salespeople. Describers who say, "Here it is . . . you decide whether you're interested or not," are clerks.

So we have The Cardinal Rule of Internet Copywriting:

Specifics outsell generalizations.

If we bother to analyze why the message—*the very first message we get from this advertiser*—is flat, colorless, and with a zero impact-quotient, we have lots of ammunition. The first sentence marches in place. "We are pleased to present over three hundred of our products to you" suggests work on our part, sorting through a pile. " . . . Provide a comprehensive listing of features which you can use to familiarize yourself with our products" is slide-rule writing, analytical instead of inspirational, without a single motivator in its multisyllabic innards.

You may think "We plan to expand upon our offerings in the near future to make your visit even more enjoyable, as well as to provide you with additional information" isn't execrable copywriting. If that's what you think, I hope you're my competitor. In fact, the copy is worse than execrable, because it suggests that whatever we see now, we ll have better pickings later on.

And this leads us to. . .

The Second Rule of Internet Copywriting

Second only to The Cardinal Rule is this one, just as logical, just as profound, just as significant, and just as easy to implement if you're a salesperson and not just a clerk:

Offer fast, clear, right-now benefits.

Obvious? Not to this marketer, who apparently doesn't even know a far more primitive rule of communications . . . one so old it goes back to the abacus, let alone computers:

Present tense outsells future tense.

The Second Rule of Internet Copywriting and the ancient Present Tense rule are congruent, because dealing in the future is Micawber-like—good things are going to happen tomorrow. Prospective buyers have had their cynicism hardened by generations of wild claims by television advertisers and politicians and by "once-you're-out-of-the-store-it's-out-of-date" obsolescence of computers and software. They don't want to wait until tomorrow. Why should they? Tomorrow they may not be here. Tomorrow *you* may not be here. Tomorrow a competitor might make a better offer.

(This is another reason why the promise of fast delivery increases response and the disclaimer "Allow 4-6 weeks for delivery," however valid, depresses response.)

The Third Rule of Internet Copywriting

The Third Rule of Internet Copywriting, like the first two, separates salespeople from clerks.

Salespeople know how to generate and stimulate the buying impulse. A key generator/stimulator is:

> Knock their socks off . . . immediately.

Direct marketing copywriters know that subtlety doesn't work. They know that sneaking up on the reader doesn't work. Multiply that by ten times and you have the Internet ambience, where the combination of an impatience-potential and unrelieved co-existence of competitors will have that mouse popping away in another direction before you get to your much-delayed point. Fire a big gun to start the battle and you might score a hit. Waiting until you see the whites of their eyes might have your own eyes rolled back in your bloodied head.

What might be a proper heading?

So a proper heading for an Internet advertisement might be one of these:

- Today only: $50 off our best-seller!
- Price slashed for browsers only: 28.8 modem, $119!

- Call this private number for Internet customers only and get our current issue free!

- *Today's closeout superbargains*—first *come, first served.*

- 5% discount for each mispelled word you find in this message.

That last one misspells *Misspelled* deliberately, to get them started. Remember, the reader wants benefits now. She's already seen and recognized one, so how difficult can it be to find the others. While she's finding them, she's not only reading your message, but she's actually enjoying herself because you ve transformed a hard-boiled sales pitch into an interactive game.

What do all those samples have in common? No, it isn't that so many of them use final exclamation points, although many "Benefit right now" headings are (and should be) exclamatory.

(A parenthetical point: One exclamation point at a time, please. Two exclamation points are not only sophomoric; they actually weaken each other, because the reader becomes aware that they're a device and penetrates our ploy.)

What these headings—and the hundreds you'll discover as you fight for position on the Internet have in common is immediate gratification, the "Open Me Now!" cry that gets an answer when mild pleas or quietly dignified logic goes not just unrequited but unnoticed.

If They Can't Set the VCR Timer, Can They Surf with Us?

A 1995 survey points up two problems marketers face when establishing a presence on the Internet. First, 80 percent of respondents answered "No" when asked if they want to surf the Internet. Second, among women 88 percent answered "No." This makes the medium questionable as a logical target for many, many items that find comfortable homes in traditional media.

As this book is published, we still can generate an excuse: The medium is new, and those who use it for shopping are computer superliterate. As a few years roll past us, the level will drop to the computer literate . . . then the semi-literate . . . then everybody.

Except: It hasn't happened with videocassette recorders. And whether the density of 28,800-baud modem-equipped computers will ever equal the market penetration of VCRs is a question it's simply too soon to answer.

The astute copywriter gears his copy for clarity, no matter who the target is. That way, more people might be tempted to dip a toe in the surf. The "digit-head" approach to copy, loaded with arcane and unexplained initials and jargon, will kill off the timid, the less-than-enthusiastic critics, and the first-timers whose own uncertainty doesn't need reinforcing.

The Communicator Arrogance *Syndrome and Its Conqueror:* The Clarity Commandment:

Even in its infancy the Internet has spawned an unpleasant cadre of copywriters—totally computer-literate and contemptuous of those who aren't. They succumb to The Communicator Arrogance Syndrome: "If you don't understand what I'm saying and how to respond, the hell with you."

A caution: If you're tempted to aim your message in a narrow direction, first ask yourself whether your ideal target matches that direction. A successful commercial message *of any type* conforms to this Great Law:

> Effective force-communication reaches, at the lowest possible cost, the most people who can and will buy what you have to sell.

(The "lowest possible cost" inclusion isn't a suggestion to underproduce a message; rather, it's the suggestion to avoid *over*producing a message.)

So if what you're selling is computer-related—as so many early Internet offers are—you're on reasonably safe ground assuming that most people who can and will buy what you have to sell are your confrères. If you're selling flowers for Mother's Day and ignore that great law, you're costing yourself some orders you otherwise would have had.

The move to a point at which Internet advertising can be, to hybridize a computer term, reader-friendly is a logical anticipation. More exciting is the Internet as the best and easiest way to establish an international marketplace. And an international marketplace means the writer has to pay extraordinary attention to The Clarity Commandment:

When you choose words and phrases for force-communication, clarity is paramount. Don't let any other component of the communications mix interfere with it.

The moment your message has the opportunity of reaching beyond the bounds of your own country, take the vow: No jargon. No argot. No slang.

Some of the phrases I've seen on the Internet—obviously attempts to project a casual, reader-friendly image: "You'll be a happy camper if . . ."; "Yes, Virginia, there is a Santa Claus"; "Don't be jerked around by. . ."; "A Grand Slam Home Run!" To browsers in other countries, these can be as indecipherable as "Yes, we have no bananas."

Closer to Classifieds than to Catalogs

Catalog companies are prime Internet advertisers, and with good reason. Not only must they be aware of what their competitors are doing, but they also logically embrace a medium that allows them to make copy and price changes in an instant.

Traditional printed catalogs generate orders from two sources:

1. Those who chance upon the catalog, see something they like, and order;

2. Those who, while ordering one item, page through the catalog and decide to order a second item totally unrelated to the first.

Both these advantages are "iffy" in the Internet because the Internet more closely parallels classified or Yellow Pages advertising than catalogs. The browser has to enter a key word. It parallels looking for homes for sale or classic cars or office equipment in the classified pages. If I'm looking for a loft to rent and you're offering a terrific bargain on Jeep Grand Cherokees, we'll never see each other.

That's why headings and greetings are crucial not only to the success of Internet catalogs but to their basic visibility.

How does Internet catalog copywriting differ?

In theory—and, usually, in practice—Internet catalog copy doesn't differ at all from its paper cousins.

But this might be a mistake based on the oversimplified rationalization that a catalog is a catalog, in whatever medium it appears. It isn't, and I'll start a major argument with the "Different = better" cult by telling you why.

Let's suppose you're browsing or surfing or for that matter gawking. Are you truly in a buying mood? . . . Or are you enjoying the novelty of the medium, the way new television owners watched wrestling and Frankie Darro movies in the 1950s because the medium was the message?

The gap between browsers and customers is ocean-wide in the world of printed catalogs and planet-wide in the universe of electronic catalogs. To convert an Internet browser to a customer, shock treatment is in order, for two reasons:

1. Photographs, at this point, in no way parallel in clarity even a coarse 85-line screen.

2. Orders, except for "pay when you're satisfied" offers, demand a credit card. No checks. No company purchase orders. Because abuses can be rampant, often a call-back to verify the order gives the customer's creeping case of Buyer's Remorse the opportunity to cancel.

Enthusiasm and the electronic edge

So enthusiasm has to permeate the copy. Here s the copy for an attaché case, offered by a well-known cataloger. I wasn't able to check it against the printed catalog, but I assume it's identical because it typifies copy in the printed catalog:

Lighthouse Attache

The Lighthouse Attache is our lightest and sportiest, yet it's still plenty tough. Made of rugged vinyl-backed nylon cloth, it weighs just 10 oz. We sew it with bound and welted seams that won't give out on you, and the fabric gives, unlike hard-sided attaches. Whatever your line of work, its 10 almost infinitely adaptable interior pockets are sure to provide a place for most all your portable office needs. Its roomy exterior pocket has space for important last-minute files. Useful umbrella and key holders; carrying strap, luggage tag included. Made in USA. 17 _" x 13 _" x 3 _".

Colors: Dark Burgundy, Black, Charcoal, Hunter, Classic Navy, Olive Khaki, Regal Navy.

SKU #2869-9M99

$42.50

For a holiday (Father's Day) promotion, the company changed the pitch entirely, four weeks before the holiday to introduce and play up personalization that gives cachet to a gift:

> FREE MONOGRAMMING on the [NAME OF COMPANY] Original Attaché.
>
> A great gift for Dads and new Graduates!
>
> Our Attache is made of rugged 18 oz. cotton canvas that ll handle all the rough stuff you put it through. For extra durability we bind the inner seams. Inside are a bunch of pockets for stashing your essentials—files, books, calculator, pens, you name it!
>
> It's made in our own Midwest shops. But lately it seems, we've been making them a little faster than we're moving them . . .
>
> Have we got a deal for you! For a limited time, we'll monogram our attaché with your name (maximum of 10 letters) or initials (maximum of 3 letters) free of charge. Made in USA. 17-1/2" × 13" × 3-1/2".
>
> Monogram styles available: Script initials, Side Block Initials, Diamond Initials, Block Name or Initials, Circle Initials, Greek Letters, Double Diamond.
>
> Colors available: Charcoal, Hunter, Dark Burgundy, Stone Brown, Classic Navy, Black, Olive Drab
>
> SKU #2915-3M9x
>
> $42.50

See the difference? And while you're at it, see the edge an electronic catalog has over a printed catalog? No printed catalog can change copy "on a dime" to fit a short-period selling opportunity. While they were at it, this creative team also eliminated that blah phrase "all your portable office needs." They can't decide whether *attaché* and *initials* should be capitalized or not. And why they keep "you," as they should, but abandon "Dad" and "the Graduate" as possible targets for a gift-buy is a mystery, but they adapted their copy to the four-week period before Father's Day, adding a factor that injects logic to a gift-buying decision.

The category heading became more salesworthy, too. Instead of "Attache Case," it was "FREE MONOGRAMMING on Attache." (No accent marks or fractions yet in this marketplace.)

A coffee company faced a different problem. This was one of their Internet product descriptions:

> THE BETTER BLADE GRINDER
>
> Our exclusive blade grinder grinds evenly with its unique sloped chamber that spins beans throughout the chamber, resulting in a uniform grind.
>
> Applicable sales tax will automatically be added to your order.
>
> SKU #111186
>
> *$19.95*

What was the problem, aside from using variations of the word "grind" three times in one sentence? One of being able to show the item properly. The "sloped chamber" remains a mystery. So does the size of the item. So does the whole concept of "blade grinder," which might have a science-fiction overtone to those who don't know the terminology.

Pros, Cons, and a Not-Too-Cloudy Crystal Ball

Because an Internet browser has to use a "mouse" to reveal copy longer than a handful of lines, and because illustrations aren't as yet remotely comparable to those in conventional printing processes, the Internet marketer is best off promoting items that lean on (a) timeliness; (b) huge bargain; (c) quick availability; (d) closeouts. Every one of these—especially in a gigantic marketplace with many thousands of addresses—demands copy that shouts, not whispers.

A more profound reason to shout is the time-factor. Most Internet access sources charge a flat monthly fee against a specific number of hours. If the first impression doesn't generate a "Wow!" response, your offer—no matter how attractive you think it is—encounters the danger of browser-abandonment. (As advertisers develop ways to circumvent the cost factor—the way a furniture store will pay taxicab fare to its premises—this problem will diminish.)

The best service a copywriter can provide for the entire medium is to help the Internet develop an image of hot deals . . . right-at-the-moment offers that have just come up and will disappear before they could make their way to other media.

This opinion may distress writers whose view of their profession is more exalted than realistic. It may annoy Internet-hypers who believe the entire world shares their spirit of adventure. It may outrage disciples of the "That which is different equals that which is better" cult.

But—again, in my opinion—it will please advertisers who keep score not by their personal ego-satisfaction but by the number of times the cash register rings.

And getting the cash register to ring is what effective copywriting is supposed to do, isn't it?

Anatomy of a Web Advertisement

A Case Study of Zima.com

Charles Marrelli

Charles Marrelli, a senior copywriter at Modem Media, was one of the key strategists in the conceptualization and development of the Zima.com World Wide Web site. The father of the serialized character, ì Duncan, î Marrelli is a member of the Modem Media creative team.

One of the first advertisers to venture into cyberspace was the alcohol beverage, Zima Clearmalt. The reasons for reaching out so strongly to the online consumer were obvious. Zima was targeting consumers 21-34, opinion leaders, relatively upscale, and skewing heavily male. Sound like the Internet audience? Absolutely.

It all started with an e-mail address cryptically printed on the inside label of the bottle, "youcan@zima.com." From that channel, the brand received thousands of e-mail messages from curious consumers around the country. Shortly after that, the advertiser set up shop on the burgeoning World Wide Web (http://www.zima.com), where it became the first national consumer packaged good to have a dedicated Web server. The following article breaks down the original Web site into its component parts in an effort to illustrate the strategy and the mechanics behind building a massive advertising presence in cyberspace.

The Home Page: Priority One

Probably the most important aspect of any Web site is the first thing that users see upon entering. It's analogous to the cover being the most important feature of an entire magazine. Let's examine the reasons. With online surfers visiting anywhere between ten and one thousand sites in a given Web experience, a site's graphic statement becomes a tremendous factor in the decision to stay or leave. Within seconds, the consumer should get an idea of what the site is all about and where to go within the site. If the opportunity is missed, the surfer may never return, given the wide array of choices at his/her disposal.

Another truism of Web usage behaviors is that many consumers only see the front page regardless of how compelling the internal content may be. These folks are more interested in the breadth of content on the Web versus the depth. An advertiser's best wish in this scenario is that the consumer says, "Zima.com . . . cool!" and bookmarks the site for future reference.

In the case of Zima, the design team created a banner graphic that leveraged imagery directly from the television commercials. It's a good example of integrated marketing communications, where high familiarity with the television spots was used to the brand's advantage in cyberspace.

Ideally, the graphic element(s) on a home page should be as small as possible (in kilobytes) without compromising the visual strategy. A

EXHIBIT 17.1 Zima Banner Graphic

handy rule of thumb is to keep individual graphic elements less than 50 K and not to exceed 150 K for the entire front page. The majority of consumers surf the Web at a 14.4 baud rate. This is certainly adequate. However, tremendously large graphics can be time consuming and troublesome for these individuals. Many will stop the process and abandon the page once they begin to feel impatient. At the risk of sounding Zen, graphics are only useful if they can be viewed.

Product Information—Re:Zima

One of the most obvious uses of the World Wide Web or any online service is the attainment of information. Despite my previous section, imagery and fluff only get you so far with the wired audience. Whether surfing for the population of Bolivia, the minority opinion in *Brown v. Board of Education,* or the number of home runs Wade Boggs had in 1987, the online consumer is constantly on a quest for information.

A popular convention on the Internet is the FAQ (Frequently Asked Questions), where an authority compiles a listing of the most common questions, along with their answers, on a given topic.

For Zima, a key requirement of the marketing team was to publish accurate product information. Zima Clearmalt was introduced nationwide in 1994 and completely defined an entire category of alcoholic beverages. By default and by design, there were a number of questions in the marketplace (". . . what is this stuff, anyway?).

The Zima.com Q&A, known as "Re:Zima" (Exhibit 17.2) was developed to address the most common consumer questions. Consumers received answers to questions like "How many calories are in Zima?"

EXHIBIT 17.2 Zima Q&A

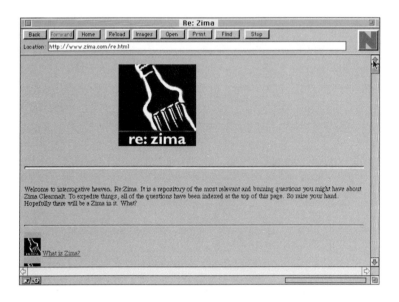

and "What are the ingredients in Zima?" Through traditional advertising, there was no cost-effective way for consumers to delve into so much information. The Web enabled consumers to satisfy their curiosity about an ambiguous product.

The copy strategy behind Re:Zima was to take the brand team's stock answers to questions and "jazz 'em up," making the responses more palatable and entertaining for the online audience.

The E-mail Feedback Loop: Write to Us

The most basic, yet crucial aspect of online advertising is the e-mail component. The wired consumer is intelligent, inquisitive, and more often than not, has something interesting to say.

Any online site, commercial or not, should give its audience the opportunity to interact. To a large extent, the comments are innocuous (". . . . love your product. Keep up the good work!"). In other cases, the comments may reveal a problem that the brand management needs to know ("I've had a difficult time finding Zima on the shelves in my area."). In any event, it becomes incumbent upon the advertiser to reply in some way to all e-mail correspondence.

EXHIBIT 17.3 The E-mail Feedback Loop

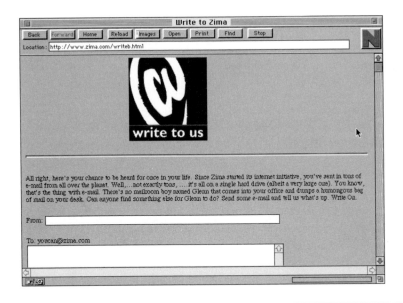

With Zima, the sheer volume of incoming e-mail necessitates a program that automatically sends a message back to the consumer. Such a program is commonly referred to as a mailbot, or an infobot, which acknowledges the message and thanks the consumer for the feedback. Next, every message is individually scanned by the brand's customer service department. If a second level of response is necessary (". . . sorry you've had trouble finding Zima," for example), a more personal correspondence is sent out, sometimes directly from the brand management. It's this one-to-one dialogue that underscores the essence of truly interactive marketing.

For the purpose of consumer research, all e-mail is bundled monthly and delivered to key members of the brand team. By scanning the collective consumer feedback, the team can qualitatively assess the performance of the brand, the effectiveness of the Web site, and the psychographics of the consumer.

A final component to the e-mail feedback loop is a proactive Zima e-mail strategy that broadcasts messages to the "Tribe Z" affinity club on roughly a monthly basis. Once a consumer has voluntarily placed himself/herself on the list, he/she can expect things like "Zima Holiday Facts," an informative and slightly irreverent report on the history of certain holidays. Holiday mailings arrive the day before the holiday, St. Patrick's Day, for example. Along with the entertaining message, late-breaking product news and site enhancements are also listed. Through this channel, Zima maintains consistent contact with the online audience, whether they have visited the site recently or not.

Online Product Usage Scenarios: Interactive Gold Sipping

Online environments allow software marketers the opportunity to make samples of their product available online. But, how does a beverage marketer do the same? After all, Zima is not a digital product. Or is it?

When the brand introduced a new product, Zima Gold, to the marketplace in the spring of 1995, there was a clear need to drive consumers to sample it. Hence, the Zima Gold virtual sipping demonstration.

Here, we see the creative use of copy and visuals to simulate a consumer trying Zima Gold for the first time. Each time the viewer clicks on the Zima Gold bottle, less beverage appears in the bottle. The copy walks the viewer through the thought processes of a first time Zima Gold drinker. Such an execution, although possible in traditional print or broadcast media, would be very expensive (print) and not nearly as interactive (print or broadcast) as the interactive version.

EXHBIT 17.4 A, B, C Zima Gold Virtual Demonstrations

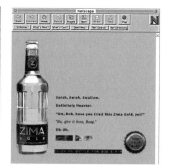

Navigation Structure: The Fridge

Any Web site needs some way to get at the information on the server—
a method for internally surfing the site. This is known as a navigation
structure. Some sites have a text-based clickable table of contents.
Other sites employ various kinds of graphical buttons. Still other sites
use more complex, visually rich image maps. An image map is a single
graphic which has multiple hotspots programmed into it. These hotspots
can hyperlink internally to the site or elsewhere on the Web.

For Zima, the decided navigation structure was a combination of
buttons and an image map. The various buttons were clearly evident on
the top of the home page The image map utilized in Zima.com was
branded "The Fridge." It points to ten discrete areas (other pages)
within Zima.com.

The reason for utilizing a virtual refrigerator as a navigation structure should be obvious. A refrigerator is an excellent real world metaphor for a virtual beverage to be located. Where can one get real Zima?
In a refrigerator, of course. Where does one access Zima digital content? Naturally, in "The Fridge."

EXHIBIT 17.5 The Zima Fridge

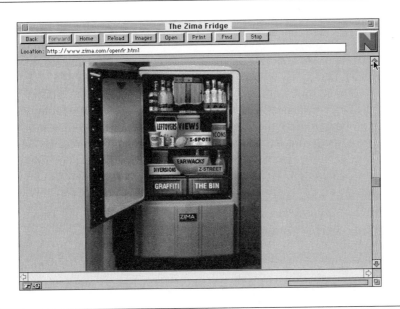

The "Duncan" Installments: An Exercise in Frequently Updated Content.

A Web page is analogous to a diner. It may have its burgers, fries, and milkshakes on a daily basis. Indeed, it is even open 24 hours. However, in order to keep the "regulars" coming back for more, it must frequently change the menu. A site that is unchanging is ofttimes left for dead by the Web audience. In order to provide a degree of freshness to the Zima site, a character named *Duncan* was developed to deliver a bi-weekly journal that kept the site fresh for the online audience.

Duncan was created as the typical Zima drinker. The strategy was to give the character a number of different occasions for drinking or purchasing the product. Duncan was also built to convey a sense of "coolness" and "regular guy" appeal for the Zima product.

Duncan is never seen by the online audience. His journal writings appear every two weeks without fail on the Zima.com site. Duncan journal installments range from things like mountain biking to paying taxes to dating his virtual girlfriend, Alexandria.

Multimedia elements are woven into the copy in order to exploit the potential of the Web as a medium. In addition to the copy, each

EXHIBIT 17.6 Duncan

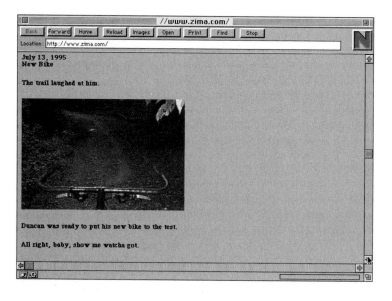

Duncan installment features an image, an icon, a sound, and a pointer to an external site on the Web. Of course, each installment also features a reference to Zima.

For example, when Duncan bought a new bicycle, the image was a bike trail, the icon was a bicycle helmet, the sound was the character sighing as he began his journey, and the pointer went to a bicycle manufacturer on the Web. Every time the installment changes, the multimedia elements are also changed to fit into the story. By providing fresh content at Zima.com through Duncan, the site is always timely and relevant for Web surfers who frequent it often.

Consumer Research: Web Questionnaires

The online environment is well suited for the collection of consumer demographics. In keeping with the tradition and culture of the Internet, survey respondents should always be self-selected. To exemplify the relative ease of collecting consumer data on the Internet, let's examine two other direct marketing channels of research: direct mail and 800/900 automated telephone systems.

In the direct mail environment, it is incumbent upon the consumer to fill out the survey, insert it in an envelope, and mail the survey back to the advertiser. This is not impossible; it is simply a great amount of work. It is not surprising that a *successful* direct mail campaign generates a one or two percent response rate. Additionally, the advertiser usually foots the bill for each response. Thus, a direct mail program can become a victim of its own success via the relatively high cost of postal service.

In the Telephone Voice Response (TVR) arena, data collection has another set of complications. Like direct mail, the advertiser is often handed the bill for each interaction. With a phone survey, the advertiser is paying for minutes, so the longer the interaction, the more costly the phone call. Additionally, the medium itself is cumbersome at best for administering surveys. A multiple choice question that might be answered in five seconds on a printed or online survey can take over a minute on the phone, because *each choice* must be read until the respondent answers the question.

Form-driven online surveys offer significant advantages over traditional methods. A recent e-mail survey given to "Tribe Z" members generated a phenomenal forty-five percent response rate. The online demographic is much more willing to respond to surveys due to:

EXHIBIT 17.7 Web Survey

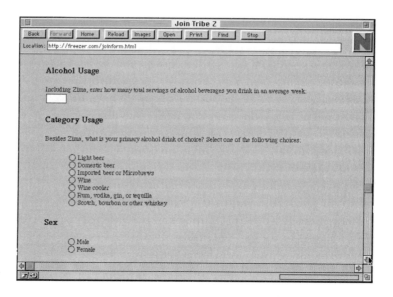

1. The relative ease of response—consumers merely select "reply"

2. There is nearly instantaneous feedback from the advertiser by using an automated mailbot.

In the Web environment, survey research is incredibly simple. Consumers need only to click on the appropriate radio button to register a selection. Thus, the process becomes incredibly expedient and easy for the consumer to participate in. A word of warning. Even on the Web, long and obtuse surveys become tiresome unless there is some compelling incentive for the consumer to fill out the questionnaire.

Affinity Clubs: Tribe Z and The Freezer

Online advertisers are enabled with an environment that makes it incredibly easy to create affinity clubs for self-selected consumers. There is a tremendous allure for the online user to be included in special or secret areas of the Web that only he or she can access. Web advertisers can utilize secured servers to create exclusive environments for high affinity groups.

Early in the Zima online initiative, "Tribe Z," an online affinity group was originated to develop a better communication channel between the Zima brand and self-selected Zima drinkers. Members of Tribe Z filled out an online survey and gained access to an exclusive area of Zima.com, known as "The Freezer." All Tribe Z members were enabled with their own passwords to access this area.

The purpose of The Freezer was twofold. It gave high affinity consumers a sense of exclusivity in their own *private* online environment. For the advertiser, it provided an extra level of data collection. Since each consumer was given a unique password, unobtrusively tracking the consumer within the environment was possible.

From the content perspective, The Freezer is an experiment in *participatory design.* The Freezer's visual metaphor is an unfurnished loft. Every few weeks, the members of Tribe Z are enabled with a set of decisions upon what elements go into the loft environment. The purpose is for consumers to derive a sense of ownership and involvement in the site based upon the decisions they collectively make.

The long term strategy for The Freezer is to allow consumers to eventually "move-in" and place their own home pages within The Freezer. In this sense, the brand becomes a haven for the Tribe Z

EXHIBIT 17.8 An Affinity Club

EXHIBIT 17.9 The Tribe Z Table Vote

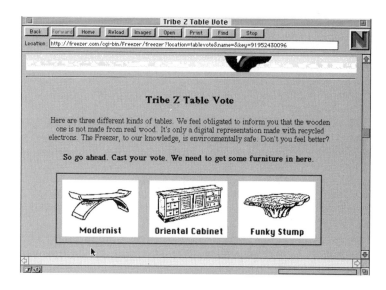

member to personally inhabit. The Tribe Z member then becomes a cohort with the brand, a contributor of content, in the online advertising campaign.

Pointers to Other Web Sites: Z-Spots

One of the most fascinating things about Zima.com is that you get to *leave* it. Huh? Now why would an advertiser ever want a consumer to leave? Stay, stay, stay, right? Well, not exactly.

The entire World Wide Web is built largely upon the notion of *hyperlinking*, whereby a Web surfer jumps from one site to the next like digital hopscotch. One minute the consumer may be on a server in Dallas, with a single "click" he/she may be on a server in Brussels, another click may take the consumer to a server right around the block. It is the notion of an interlinked community that makes the World Wide Web such a dynamic and thriving environment. Hyperlinking is what the Web is all about. At the risk of being trite, no site is an island.

Strategically, a major component of the Zima site was to point to other Web sites that offered interesting and relevant content for the

EXHIBIT 17.10 Z-Spots

Zima target market. Labeled "Z-Spots," the purpose of the page was to give consumers an index to other compelling sites on the Web.

The showpiece of "Z-Spots" is the Zima Bar and Restaurant Guide, which serves as a "directory of directories" for consumers looking for local nightspots across the country. The guide segments into four separate geographic regions: Northeast, South, Midwest, and West. From this listing, consumers can find places of interest all over the country.

Z-Spots is an excellent example of an advertiser as a gatekeeper of content. Instead of driving consumers *away* from the site, it actually draws consumers *to* the site, since the guide is actually a useful tool for finding other sites around the Web. The advertiser becomes an "arbiter of coolness" for the online audience.

Downloadable Multimedia Files: Views, Earwacks, Icons, and Diversions

In this article, much has been said about "the online consumer." So, exactly what is it that this individual *consumes*? Certainly, information.

EXHIBIT 17.11 Zima Views

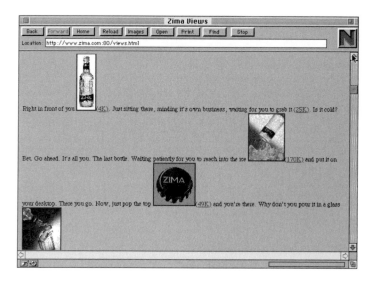

That has already been discussed in large part. Another thing which this individual wants is *digital stuff*, for lack of a better expression. Images, sounds, icons, games. In other words, the online advertiser, particularly an advertiser like Zima, has to offer the digital equivalent to T-shirts, caps, buttons in cyberspace. This *stuff* might be more commonly referred to as "downloadable multimedia files."

Within Zima.com, there are four areas that primarily offer these files, all accessible through "The Fridge." They are labeled "Views" (digital imagery), "Earwacks" (small sound files), "Icons" (desktop icons for Mac and Windows), and "Diversions" (shareware video games).

Let's investigate the Views section. Within Views, consumers have the opportunity to preview and potentially download a number of different Zima images. Once the consumer clicks on an image, it is downloaded to the user's hard drive through the ftp site. The size of each file is given in parenthesis next to the image. This way, the individual knows what to expect in terms of download time for a particular image.

A residual benefit to offering these items online is that they can become a part of the consumer's daily computing experience. Many consumers within the Zima demographic like to use images on their desktop as backgrounds or they like to customize their icons. By making such "refrigerator magnets" available, Zima is given the chance to be on thousands of computer monitors every day, whether or not the consumer is online.

Advertising for Advertising

A subject that has yet to be discussed is promoting an advertiser's web site. It's perfectly fine to invest the time and resources to build an online presence, but if nobody sees it, the entire exercise has been futile. For a Web site, user traffic is the equivalent to television ratings. It validates that Web surfers are indeed visiting the site, and thus being exposed to the marketing communication.

There are typically four ways to publicize a Web site. They are:

1. Paid pointers
2. Reciprocal/voluntary pointers
3. Web directory registration
4. Traditional media channels.

For the purpose of this article, I'll give a detailed description of each tactic.

Zima was an early pioneer in sponsoring other Web publishers in exchange for a premium banner links. A premium banner link is ideally a large graphic at the top or the bottom of a Web page that links back to the advertiser's site. The basic criteria that Zima employed to evaluate media purchase was:

1. Content relevance to the Zima demographic
2. Verifiable traffic that the sponsorable site generated
3. Zima's banner size and positioning within the sponsorable site.

Content Relevance

Like traditional media, Zima sought to advertise within sites that interested people in the target market. Sites like Hotwired (http://

www.Hotwired.com), Word (http://www.word.com) and Virtual Radio (http://www.microserve.net:80/vradio/) fit the bill by delivering Zima a demographic and psychographic profile of its users that was consistent with the brand's targeting objectives.

Verifiable Traffic

Quite simply, a Web site has to demonstrate a large amount of traffic. One of the most compelling features of Web publishing is that traffic volume and server accesses are quantifiable. Sites like Hotwired actually require readers to presubscribe to the service, thus guaranteeing an addressable readership for the purpose of selling ad space.

Banner Size and Positioning

Another important factor in paying for pointers is actual size and positioning within the sponsored site. In Web advertising, size and positioning are everything. Obviously, the more real estate a banner occupies, the more likely the chance that it will be accessed. With regard to positioning, ad space is more valuable relative to its closeness to the home page. A banner placed on the main home page will receive more impressions than the same banner placed a couple levels deep. Placement within a page is also a significant variable. For example, a banner placed on the top of a page typically generates more clicks than a banner on the bottom of the page.

Unpaid and reciprocal pointers are also very important. For example, citation of Zima as "Cool Site of the Day" generated the single largest amount of one-day traffic the site has ever seen. In many instances, Zima receives pointers from other sites merely because they like the Zima site. This can be a highly cost effective way of generating traffic to the site. Reciprocal pointers ("I'll scratch your back . . .") can be incredibly beneficial as well, particularly from highly trafficked sites.

Directory listings can make a tremendous impact collectively. Many web surfers employ directories like yahoo (http://www.yahoo.com) to search for content on the ever-expanding Web. In most cases, registration with these directories is free. By registering Zima with all the major directories and search engines, Zima was able to maximize its reach and guarantee that it would be "discovered" by Web surfers that had employed these various research tools. Another strong grassroots tactic for publicizing a Web site like Zima was to post the site's address to all the relevant usenet newsgroups.

A final method for publicizing a Web site is to utilize traditional vehicles like television ads, magazine ads, outdoor placements, and T-shirts. Any marketer that has made an investment in online advertising should make the additional effort to publicize the site in *every* other piece of marketing communication. Although the message may go unnoticed with non-wired consumers, it will be picked up and appreciated by consumers that do have Internet access.

Alcohol Issues: 21 Means 21

The final issue that must be discussed with regard to an alcoholic beverage advertiser like Zima is responsible marketing.

To be certain, online demographics tend to match up tremendously with the brand's target market. However, the truth is that there are some members of the online audience that are below the legal age limit to consume the product. Although Zima can never police its site to be 100% sure of a 21 plus audience, certain tactics can be employed to combat the occasional attendance of minors at the site.

EXHIBIT 17.12 Controlling Club Membership

A message directly accessible by clicking on the main banner advises consumers that Zima is for "Adult Humanz Only," and that "21 Means 21." By placing the message directly on the banner, Zima is making a statement to younger members of the audience that the site (and more importantly, the beverage) is not for them.

On the same accord, Tribe Z membership is limited to individuals 21 and over. Age disclosure is a necessary component of the Tribe Z survey and any individuals citing their age as younger than 21 are forbidden membership in the affinity club. To be certain, the brand only wants to communicate with consumers who can legally purchase the product.

The Future of Zima.com

The Zima brand has made a clear investment in cyberspace and Web advertising. The site will continue to be maintained, with major interface overhauls occurring on an annual basis. Zima's future uses of the World Wide Web include increasing participation from the ranks of Tribe Z, an ongoing investment in the latest Web multimedia technologies, and a more intelligent e-mail system that automatically reads consumer mail and attaches the appropriate feedback. Since Zima arrived to the party early, so to speak, the brand can enjoy the advantages of experience. However, with a medium like the Web being constantly in development, the only way to maintain an advantage is to continue to stay on the edge of the technology curve.

CHAPTER

18

Measuring the Effectiveness of Interactive Media

Internet Media Evaluation and Buying Strategy

John C. Nardone

John C. Nardone is the Account Director for Consumer Products at Modem Media. In that role, he manages the overall strategic direction for all consumer-oriented business. He has been responsible for the development of IRIS, the first pricing model that can be used to evaluate media properties on the Internet. Prior to joining Modem Media, Nardone was a product marketing strategist at such leading consumer product companies as Procter & Gamble and PepsiCo.

In a traditional media model, the usual objective is to get your message in front of as many targeted consumers as possible, at an effective frequency, for as low a cost as possible. In the world of the Internet, this is still partly true; however, some interesting new dynamics are raised by the nature of self-selected advertising and the navigational structure of the Web.

Media for Reach, Media for Association

There are two general objectives for media planning on the Web. The first, as in traditional media, is to get your message to as much of your target audience as possible. The second is to associate your advertiser's Web content with related and complementary content, in order to enhance the impact and value of your marketing message. The ideal media plan effectively accomplishes both, creating maximum "surface area" for the advertising and multiple points of access for consumers.

Media Reach

Obviously, advertising on the Internet is self-selected by the consumer. This makes it imperative that the advertiser provide cues for the consumer that encourage him to access the ad. Thus, the typical set up for an advertisement on the Internet has two parts. First, the advertiser places a billboard within a content provider domain. This billboard provides an advertising message on its own, but also leads the consumer in some way to the content behind it. The billboard is then "linked" to the "home page" of the advertiser's own Web site. The consumer sees the billboard—and if he chooses to "click" on it, he is immersed in the graphics, information, and utilities of the advertiser's home area. In effect, the advertiser makes use of the traffic flow of the content to herd consumers into the advertising. The more enticing the banner (from a creative standpoint) and the more traffic that sees it, the more consumers that will likely be delivered to the advertiser's site.

Content Association and Integration

Media placements in outside content provide links to the advertiser site. But the nature of hyperlinking also allows an advertiser to "point to" content outside his own site that supports the marketing message and is relevant to the user. Done correctly, the advertiser takes assumptive ownership of the outside content because he has provided access to it. This allows him to inexpensively build a more substantial well of content and information, and create more power and value for the consumer.

In an ideal situation, the outside content is seamlessly integrated into the advertiser's site, but the advertiser's site is also integrated into the outside site. We refer to this idea as "distributed content," meaning that the advertising content is distributed into other sites on the Web. This distribution is accomplished by soliciting contribution and cooperation from content providers. The objective of this cooperation is to create "shared content" that meets the needs of the advertiser, but also fits snugly in the content environment. The beauty of the Web is that it does not matter whose server the content resides on. It can be seamlessly accessed from either the advertiser or content site—it simultaneously exists in both.

Distributed content does two important things for the advertiser. First, it blurs the line between "editorial" and advertising. This allows the consumer to be gently led into the advertising content without raising his natural skepticism and resistance to the ad message. Second, it is a powerful contributor to creating "surface area" for the advertising.

In the world of traditional media, this sort of content integration is nearly impossible to achieve. At best, it takes the form of "advertorial," but is usually clearly segregated from the true editorial. This is because publications have historically maintained a strict "church and state" separation between advertising and editorial content. But the Internet allows for much more flexibility in format and structure, and content providers are beginning to learn how to use that flexibility to maximize revenues. They are becoming more and more willing to work with advertisers to create new kinds of win-win relationships.

Media Valuation

Heretofore, discussions of reach, frequency and efficiency have not been part of the Internet media discussion. However, some quantifiable method of valuation must be incorporated into our thinking if we are to give new media fair consideration as part of the overall media mix.

In order to value the typical ad placement, we must place values on the reach and frequency of the billboard, and the "depth" of immersion into the advertiser's Web site. To do this, we use a conceptual model dubbed I.R.I.S., for Internet Reach and Involvement Scale.

The Modem Media Internet Reach and Involvement Scale (IRIS)

We can consider the reach value of an ad impression within a Web site to be similar to the cost per thousand reached by a similarly targeted print publication. For the sake of demonstration, we can use a young techno-savvy audience, similar to the CPM of Wired or MacWorld magazines: about $70 per thousand. And while one might argue that a billboard impression is not equivalent to a print page impression, we would point out that on the Web, an impression is a confirmable impression. There is no leap of faith, unlike in print, where an impression is only assumed for each ad in each copy of the print run.

Because of the navigational complexity of moving around within a Web site, a well-placed billboard is likely to be viewed several times within a session. Thus these frequency impressions occur within a relatively short period of time, so we believe they should be discounted to one third the value of the initial reach impression—about $23 per thousand.

Finally, the depth impression is valued according to a direct mail model. For comparison's sake, assume that seeing the billboard is like receiving a direct mail piece. Clicking on the billboard is like opening the envelope. The value of clicking on the billboard is then equal to the cost per unit of a direct mailing, divided by the percentage of people who are likely to open it. For this example, we will use some standards provided by the Direct Marketing Association: a simple glossy brochure, delivered to a targeted list, would cost about $.75 per unit, including list, printing, and postage. But the DMA also estimates that only 68 percent of the mailing will actually be opened by the intended target. The value is $1.11 per impression ($.75/68 % = $1.11).

To apply this model, we will assume that 10,000 people view a billboard on a page in an on-line or Web-based publication. The reach value is $700 (10,000 × $70 per thousand). Next, we assume four links in and out of that page, so the consumer is likely to return to that page four more times in the session—4 × 700/3 = $930. Finally, we assume that 10 percent of the people actually click on the billboard and enter the advertiser's web site—1000 × $1.11 = $1110. The total value of the ad placement is $700 + $930 + $1110 = $2740.

As you evaluate this model for your own business, you should adjust the "rule of thumb" values for the print and direct mail comparisons, based on your own industry and experience. And since the model is heavily weighted toward the direct mail component, it makes sense that businesses that lend themselves to direct type communication are likely to highly value Internet advertising.

Measuring Traffic

Of course, in order to actually apply the I.R.I.S. model, you need an accurate measure of the reach, frequency and depth components. Several companies, including Nielsen and Arbitron, have launched third-party services to track and authenticate Internet traffic. At this time, however, none of the competing services have been adopted on a wide-scale basis, and only a few Websites have implemented a system to explicitly track these measures themselves. Most properties only quote the number of "hits" to their area, and brag about the astronomical numbers they think they are generating.

BEWARE: hits are not a measure of reach or frequency—and worse, many of the content providers do not understand this fact themselves.

When doing preliminary media evaluations, there is a way to extract a good estimate of reach and frequency from that "hit" measurement. The entire explanation is rather arcane, but the short answer is that real traffic (reach) is approximately equal to the number of hits to the page with the billboard on it, divided by two times the number of graphical interfaces on the page (hits/(2 × GI)). This is a conservative rule of thumb, and should be checked in each individual case.

The complete step by step pricing procedure is outlined below:

1. Log into the Web page in question and, as you do, watch the lower left corner of your screen. You should be able to count the number of times the "host server" clicks before the page is fully downloaded on to your screen. Each of these clicks is a "hit."

2. Navigate the site, and take note of how many times you return to the home page during your session. Each time you do, another hit is logged to that page.

3. Add these two counts together.

4. From the owner of the Web property, request the average number of hits per month to the page you are interested in advertising on. Get a copy of the server log as back up.

5. Divide the average hits per month by your line three total for your reach number.

6. Multiply reach on line five by line two for your frequency measurement.

7. Estimate the percentage of the reach that will access your site— 10 percent is a good rule of thumb. (You can then confirm that estimate once you are up and running for post analysis. To facilitate this, make sure you Web designer can trace the traffic to your homepage from each of your ad placements. This will allow you to trace the source of your traffic from your own server log, and match it back to numbers provided by the media properties)

8. Multiply your reach estimate by your assigned CPM value.

9. Multiply your frequency estimate by one third of the CPM value.

10. Multiply your depth estimate by the assigned depth value.

11. Add lines 8, 9, and 10 for your value estimate.

Planning and evaluating media placement opportunities on the Internet can be a fairly straightforward process. Just recognize the similarities and differences from traditional media planning, and be sure to consider the need to herd traffic to your advertiser's site as well as the opportunity to associate the advertising with related content on the Web.

Without too much extrapolation, you can compare the Web to your other media options and make an educated cost/benefit/efficiency decision about its place in your media mix based on familiar print and direct mail benchmarks. Of course, your success in advertising on the Internet will ultimately be determined by the specifics of your business, the target audience fit and the quality of your creative. So be sure your Internet initiative is managed by someone who understands both the creative and the media dynamics of operating in this exciting new advertising vehicle.

SECTION III

Data Collection and Analysis and Research Strategies

The final section addresses the research challenges and opportunities afforded by interactive technology. The interactive "event" allows for the rapid collection of consumer opinions and self-reported preferences. However, it also can collect a wide range of unobtrusive or covert measures of behavior that can go beyond the ambiguous counting of "hits" or number of downloadings from consumers at a Web site. For example, the net user's clickstream provides an objective profile of a set of the consumer's decisions. The schemes that an individual uses may help with future segmentation of a market. The length of time between choices, or how long the user dwells on a choice, will provide some measures of latency. These have previously been associated with level of interest and attitude toward a choice.

Sampling issues may be made more complex as bias from self-selection is a significant issue with interactive media. Other issues concern the potential generalizability of a sample, particularly with the rapid growth of the population using interactive procedures.

In chapter 8, Richard Hodgson raised the question of how interactive participation may influence and displace the time devoted to other activities. Interaction pioneers Wotring, Kayany and Forrest tackle this challenge in the first chapter of this section, "Consuming Technologies at Home." They discuss how studying "what people do" with these new media, the uses and gratifications, will become more important in future research. The authors predict a move toward more use of qualitative techniques and naturalistic observations. One particular approach, the "new domestic paradigm," has been developed in Australia and the U.K. This perspective investigates how families incorporate the increasingly complex domestic communications technology into the fabric of family life, rules and relationships. Most media consumption takes place in the home. Will the new Internet options bring families together, like early TV? Or will this new technology foster an isolation begun with the multiple-set TV household? The authors conclude the chapter with a comprehensive discussion of the upcoming questions concerning how the family of the future will evolve with the new interactive technology.

In "Customer Service and Interactivity: The Ongoing Conversation," Lucia Fishburne and Daniel Montgomery provide a view of how the consumer's active involvement with interactive media will cause, facilitate or possibly impede developments in service. They discuss how personal buying profiles, compiled by store-level scanner and card purchases (credit and debit), will allow companies to better understand what consumers want now and in the future. The ability to purchase customized Levis is only the beginning of what the authors call "superserve," a way companies will differentiate themselves by a new form of relationship marketing. Appropriately, they note how privacy issues will become more acute as when any relationship gets close.

A coverage of the more quantitative aspects of interactive marketing begins with Mickey Bennett of Nielsen NorthAmerica. Bennett's experience in "analytics," the movement toward modeling behaviorial data, is particularly relevant for the digital age and its streams of interactive choices. In "A Blueprint for Successful Syndicated On-Line Research," he first outlines the types of insights to consumer decision making that will be available. For example, where buyers of my brand come from, and why triers did or did not stay? While the present use of site audits is providing useful data, he argues that their interpretation is not always clear or as ultimately useful as a longitudinal panel approach. He explains what the interactive platforms of the future will be, and how on-line advertising, promotion and purchase activity can be viewed by a market researcher. His review provides a good roadmap for how the Internet will be used, who the players will be, and how the research function will be organized.

Martin Block, who has done extensive research with scanner data, continues the discussion of quantitative analysis from the interactive media with a discussion of neural networks and the new software available for analysis. In many ways, the researcher of the future will be challenged with having too much data. The question of how to identify patterns will be one of what Block refers to as "Marketing Communications Engineering." Block notes that these techniques assume that the phenomena being examined are dynamic and the relationships are often non-linear, the apparent norm in interactive marketing. These assumptions challenge traditional techniques. After many years of hearing about artificial intelligence, he notes that its application appears increasingly appropriate for the pre-processing of the very large data files generated by interactive events. His easily understood examples provide insights into the use of this new application of neural networks and the interpretation of its output. He discusses how this same technology can also be used to identify and connect individuals in a complex marketing data base like those being compiled for the Internet.

Rob Jackson, Vice President of Marketing at Donnelley Marketing, Inc., and Paul Wang from Northwestern University's Medill School, provide a careful review of the potential when database marketing and interactive networks such as Prodigy, CompuServe and America On-Line converge. With children as young as four years old taking basic computer classes in preschool, the linkup of technology can't be stifled because today's older generation is only slowly embracing this new technology. These authors review how communications and database marketing are evolving through stages. These two areas will ultimately lead to full interactive communications between buyer and seller with an information network as a critical active partner in the process. Finally, they tell how to develop an interactive database by going through five progressive stages ending in its final rollout and application.

CHAPTER

19

Consuming Technologies at Home

New Consumer Research Techniques

C. Edward Wotring
Joseph M. Kayany
Edward J. Forrest

C. Edward Wotring is currently an Associate Professor in the Department of Communication at Florida State University. His research, which includes study of the uses and effects of interactive communication technologies and mass media, has been published in such journals as *Interact, Journal of Advertising Research,* and *Journal of Broadcasting and Electronic Media.*

Joseph M. Kayany is an assistant professor in the Department of Communication at Western Michigan University. He is the author of numerous journal articles and convention papers.

Edward J. Forrest is Director of the Interactive Communications graduate program at Florida State University. His ongoing projects include multiplatform CD-ROM and CD-I disk production, and World Wide Web page-site development.

The impact of communication technologies on the knowledge, attitudes and behaviors of consumers has been one of the most important concerns throughout the history of communication, advertising and marketing research. Even today the effects question is still very much at the heart of research efforts as we seek new tools, research designs and approaches to affirm effects that seem so self-evident to common sense yet too complex to measure.

Perhaps because mass communication-oriented researchers particularly in the U.S. have the predilection for quantifiable, measurable outcomes gained through controlled empirical research designs, effects research has almost exclusively dealt with measurable changes in the individual consumer.

The importance of the study of psychological and behavioral effects notwithstanding, the various social, cultural and familial environments of media use have largely been ignored by researchers. Most media consumption, however, occurs in the "domestic space" of the home and within the context of familial relations. The domestic context in which media is consumed affects patterns of media use which in turn affects not only the individual members of the family unit but also the domestic system of interrelationships and family decision making on issues relating to product purchase and consumption. This approach opens new directions for media research.

Linear Models and the Passive Consumer

The majority of the effects research has been from the perspective framed by the question "what does the media do to people?" This question has been central to all mainstream research studying effects of comic books, war time propaganda, radio, television (particularly violence, even today), pornography, movies, and advertising (copy-testing, test marketing, tracking, and effects of political ads on voting behavior).

The typical model-driving-effects research is epitomized by Harold Lasswell's (1948) *who* (a source) says *what* (a message) to *whom* (a receiver) via which *channel* (TV, print, radio, etc.) with what *effect* (purpose of message—usually persuasion). Even with the addition of a feedback loop from the receiver back to the source, the model is quite linear, directional and assumes a more or less passive audience. Of course more current models (e.g., theory of reasoned action, expectancy value theory, elaboration likelihood model) have added additional variables, increasing their complexity and predictive power; but the emphasis remains persuasive in purpose and directional in nature. The focus is how to get the attention of a relatively passive audience and deliver to them a message which attempts to reinforce or change their level of knowledge, attitudes, behavioral intentions, and/or behaviors. *Reach and frequency* and *impressions* are the important buzzwords in the advertising vocabulary.

Finally, the effectiveness of these models is determined primarily with quantitative research methodologies—measurable outcomes from survey or experimental research designs where subjects are studied under controlled conditions. Other than the reliance on focus groups for concept and copy testing, and the use of diaries for some in-home monitoring, more qualitative techniques such as ethnographies and field studies are seldom employed. While these so-called "alternative" methods provide a rich source of data, they are time-consuming to do, expensive, and difficult to interpret.

New Interactive Technologies and the Active Consumer

The development of interactive technologies—CD-ROM, CD-I, modems, e-mail, the Internet and interactive television (the information super-highway)—is forcing a change in the theories and methodologies traditionally used to study mass media effects. As these new technologies diffuse into the public and private sectors, research is needed to determine the uses, cost-effectiveness, and other effects of these new technologies. Scholars are pointing out that traditional linear mass media effects models are inappropriate with interactive multimedia technologies. New models are currently being developed and alternative research methodologies are being used to understand how users interact with these new media and the effects of these media on communication processes (see e.g., Rogers, 1986; Williams, et al., 1988; James, et al., 1995; Kayany, et al., 1995).

The fundamental principle underlying all interactive technologies is, of course, interactivity itself. And interactivity entails an active, as opposed to passive, consumer. This suggests that the traditional media effects models should be reversed with a "receiver" actively seeking information of various types including products and services from "sources" using the interactive technology as the "channel" or conduit for information flow. Stuart Brand (1988) coined the term *broadcatch* to describe this process where the consumer "browses, grazes or hunts" for information on the Internet or from optical disks often with computer-aided searches.

While the effects of these new media on consumers are arguably an important issue, the idea of an active consumer seeking information raises additional questions for researchers. For example, rather than only asking, "What does the media do to people?" it seems appropriate to also ask, "What do people do with these new media?" This latter perspective, called "Uses and Gratifications," investigates the gratifications individuals seek from various media. Benefit segmentation in marketing/advertising is very similar, as is functionalism.

The so-called "critical" or Marxist paradigm asks other important questions, e.g.:

- Who controls/owns these new media and the accessible information on them, and for what purposes?

- Are the new media creating a new class structure of the information "rich" and "poor"?

- How will individual privacy be protected? Who is reading our e-mail and monitoring our credit card purchases and for what purposes?

The *domestic paradigm* analyzes the family/household as a whole from a systems perspective; e.g.:

- How does the family use the technological system to develop and maintain the family culture and relate to wider cultures of school, community, society, etc.?

- How do technologies impact on family consumption decisions and behaviors?

While all approaches to studying the new media are important, including traditional effects research, determining when, how and why consumers use these technologies is of central importance to advertisers, marketers and media scholars.

New Media and New Research Methods

The ways in which research is carried out appears to be changing as well.

First, traditional mass media effects research has generally been theory driven: hypotheses are tested based on some theory. For example, the effects of advertising on brand loyalty are studied based on various persuasion theories. Another approach to studying media is exploratory in nature and is used to develop theory.

This latter approach, sometimes referred to as "grounded theory" seems appropriate to the initial studies of new technologies. Since interactive multimedia are very new and quite different from previous forms of mass media, exploratory studies to "test the waters" should be done rather than using current theory more appropriate to traditional mass media studies.

Second, the kinds of research designs used to collect observations/ data are also changing from *quantitative* approaches used to study media effects to more *qualitative, naturalistic* observations appropriate to exploratory research. For example, standard interviews could be combined with participant or other unobtrusive observation to monitor consumers' uses of new technologies.

Media Consumption and the Domestic Paradigm

Developed by media scholars in Australia and England, the "domestic paradigm" offers a unique perspective on how families use new technologies. This research has examined how families incorporate the increasingly complex domestic communication technological system into the fabric of family life, rules and interrelationships. While previous studies focused primarily on television, this paradigm applies to other technologies as well. The example we will use here focuses specifically on computer-mediated communication (CMC), a fairly new entrant to the domestic technological system and suggests how families adapt and incorporate the computer as a medium of communication into the domestic system of relationships, roles, goals, and purchasing decisions, as well as into the existing system of communication technologies in the household. Modem-based communication is the precursor to the information superhighway, so studying CMC may have implications for it as well.

Most media consumption occurs in the domestic space, within the context of familial relations. However, this domestic context has largely been ignored by researchers, except perhaps as an intervening variable (Goodman, 1983). The focus, for instance, of television research has traditionally been on individual effects. Second, television has most often been represented as an agent of values and behavior. There is another dimension to the presence of television in households—as an artifact or a tool that is actively used by members of the family. Television becomes a thread in the family tapestry of relationships and interactions, not only as a subject of meaning but an object in the domestic relational system as well. Each family interprets the television content in its own terms and interprets the use of television through its own screen of family rules (Goodman, 1983) and uses television as an artifact to interact and relate with the other elements in the family space.

Although television occupies a central position in the domestic technological system, it should not be seen in isolation. An increasing number of communication technologies—multiple television sets, radios, telephones, fax machines, computers, cellular phones, CD-I, etc.—are finding a place in households and form what is termed the *domestic technological system*. These technologies may be used by family members as individuals or as a family, but the use is defined and constrained by the domestic environment of familial interrelationships and goals. Households are located at the "intersection of the public and the private" (Sinclair, 1993, p. 8), and they "construct their technologies in different ways, creating private meanings (redefining public ones) in their positioning, pattern of use and display" (Morley & Silverstone, 1990, p. 35). Examining how "relations to communication technologies are organized in and through the context of domestic social relations" (Morley & Silverstone, 1990, p. 33) may indicate a paradigmatic shift as the focus shifts from a study of media "texts" towards the interactive relationship in which domestically contextualized media consumers derive meaning from media texts. It was John Sinclair who first termed this perspective the domestic paradigm (Sinclair, 1993, p. 1).

Some of the research questions raised by these researchers are:

- How are communication technologies incorporated into the relationships of gender and generation?

- How are communication technologies related to the organization of domestic space, to the temporal routines and social rituals and relations in the household?

- How do family members use communication technologies to assert their collective and individual status and identities through their style of consumption and social use of communication technologies?

- How do families use communication technologies in the process of purchasing decisions and behaviors?

- How does the family use communication technologies to link the micro family system to other macro systems of institutions, community, nation and world (Sinclair, 1993, p. 2)?

The computer adds a unique dimension to the "domestic socio-technical system" because it is a medium of both *communication and consumption*. During the last decade, computer-mediated communication (CMC) has extensively been studied but almost exclusively from the institutional and organizational (task-intensive, but relationally leaner) contexts. However, computers and modems are no more just office equipment. The rate at which Americans are buying home computers and going on-line is staggering. Approximately one in three households in the U.S. (32 million) have computers. The number of people connected to the Internet is projected to be 20 million and another 4.55 million are connected to other commercial services such as Compuserve and Prodigy (Miyasato, 1994). With the increasing number of home computers that are connected to public and commercial networks, technologies of media consumption are supplemented by avenues for interactive communication from the domestic space—from the private space of the family to the public sphere of the global village.

Domestic Redefinitions

Individual consumers are often assumed to define their use of a communication technology in terms of their own personal needs and gratifications. However, when consumption occurs in a bonded group, as in a family, the needs of others affect one's own consumption. In addition, families as integrated relational units have their own goals, often established by the parents. Rules are arguably concrete expressions of such definitions of technology use that accommodate needs of individual family members, goals of family as a unit and to an extent of those with whom they communicate from the domestic space. These domestic rules on technology use are often affected by already existing family functions, boundaries and relations.

On-line usage in the domestic space

On-line use in a family can be a collective activity, where family members support, encourage, guide and motivate each other. Further, on-line activity can be engaged in not only to meet one's own needs but also of other members. On-line communication may be directed not only to one's personal friends and those around the globe who share similar interests but also to friends of the family, neighbors, members of the community, etc. Friends made in cyberspace can become family friends as they are introduced to other family members. Thus beyond the private, personal use of on-line communication, there may be a collective aspect of on-line usage when it occurs within a family, that affects the style and targets of one's CMC activity.

Effects of on-line usage in the domestic space

The effects of on-line usage from homes can be at two levels: personal or domestic. At the personal level, configuring one's CMC use to the domestic system may constrain it. On the other hand, the presence and support of family members may enhance one's on-line activity. As a family, CMC may bring the family closer; on the other hand, it may become a very private activity that creates greater distance among family members. CMC activity may enhance or constrain one's social life. More time may be spent with "virtual" friends across the globe and less time devoted to classmates, co-workers, neighbors, etc. Or CMC can establish or strengthen community ties.

CMC use may affect one's consumption patterns of other media. For instance, heavy users of CMC may find themselves watching fewer hours of television or making fewer phone calls.

An artifact in the domestic space

As an artifact within the familial system, the computer becomes an object of interactions among family members. These in turn may affect, either positively or negatively, the existing relationships and roles. For instance, the teenager may become the CMC guru for the parents, a change in the usual familial roles.

Location of technologies in the domestic space

It may be very interesting to look at how families organize communication technologies in the domestic space. By mapping the location of these technologies, perhaps we can gain an insight into which technologies are central or peripheral to the homeostasis of the domestic system or which are visible (centrally located in the familial consciousness) or invisible (integrated to the extent of being moved to the familial subconscious).

Advertising and Marketing Implications

Some purchasing decisions will be made by individual family members and others by parents and/or the family as a whole. To make those decisions, family members will seek information, and such information is available through CMC. How such information is presented and how it is sought and used by families in the purchase decision-making process are important issues. On-line advertising certainly takes a different form from traditional television, radio and print commercials, but the most effective means of presenting such information needs to be determined. On-line shopping and purchasing is another issue. Most likely the family will establish rules concerning these activities as to who can do this and when, and for what kinds of products. How such on-line information seeking and shopping affect traditional means of product information seeking and shopping such as going to the mall, catalog purchases, television shopping network use, etc. are interesting implications. While mall shopping is a form of socializing, the use of on-line bulletin boards may well perform the same socializing function.

Alternative research methodologies

Proponents of the domestic paradigm have used ethnographic and qualitative designs with mixed results. The research group in England that pioneered this line of research used a "raft" of qualitative measures (Silverstone, Hirsch, & Morley, 1991) such as time-use diary, interviews, participant observation, household maps, network diagrams and family albums. John Sinclair (1993) attempted a more quantitative design and conducted a survey among suburban families in Melbourne, Australia. We recognize the necessity of a "raft" of qualitative and quantitative research designs to investigate such systemic effects. However, at this exploratory stage of studying CMC in households, a survey design is considered satisfactory to generate basic models of domestic CMC use. Results from such a survey could identify families of varying characteristics for follow-up interviews and in-depth qualitative observations. These findings also provide baseline data of technology use prior to the introduction of interactive television.

Research Questions

Listed below are several issues and related questions developed from the domestic paradigm. Hopefully they can guide research efforts designed to better understand uses and effects of new communication technologies.

1. Family relational contexts of communication technology use: New directions and alternate perspectives.

Research Question: How significant is the family relational context in understanding technology use and predicting its effects? How have communication researchers grappled with the relational dimension of interactive technology use?

2. Multiple technologies amidst a web of interrelated persons; a systemic approach to viewing technology use.

Research Question: What are the implications of research on an individual's use of single technologies vs. a study of a technological system integrated into the spatial boundaries and interrelationships of a family? What new research directions are suggested by the domestic paradigm?

3. Familial integrity and definitions of technology use.

Research Question: How do families incorporate different technologies into their common space? How do they define technology use with family rules? Who makes the rules? And what kind of families have guidelines for communication technology use? Are family rules on technology use a predictor of family integrity? Do different styles of making rules (authoritarian vs. participatory) affect family integrity?

4. Centripetal and centrifugal modes of communication from households: Gender, age and role differences.

Research Question: Can technologies be classified according to the way some of them tend to bring a family together whereas others encourage family members to move into their own private spaces? What are the gender and generational differences in such a use of domestic technologies—either to "come home" or to "fly away"?

5. Modes of domestic computer mediated communication.

Research Question: How has computer mediated communication created a niche in the domestic socio-technical system? How do the patterns of CMC use and definitions affect perceived outcomes of computer mediated communication?

6. Mapping technologies in the domestic space: Linking spatial significance and consumption patterns.

Research Question: Are there discernible patterns in the way technologies are organized in homes? Can the spatial organization of technologies in homes tell us anything about how these are central/peripheral, or visible/invisible to family integration and interaction?

7. Domestic technologies and community networks.

Research Question: How do technologies link the household to the community? Can we distinguish between technologies that promote domestic privacy and those that nurture extension of contacts beyond the domestic walls? Are there gender and generational differences that affect the way technologies are similarly used?

8. Domestic uses and familial gratifications in households.

Research Question: Uses and gratification research traditionally has focused almost exclusively on the individual. How does the domestic context affect gratifications obtained and restrained?

9. Consumption Decisions and product information-seeking.

Research Question: How are decisions concerning product purchases made by the family, and what role do communication technologies play in the decision-making process? Do family members access on-line information sources to aid in such decisions? To what extent is shopping done on-line, and by whom? Does the family have rules concerning such on-line purchasing? How does such on-line information seeking and shopping affect traditional means of product information seeking and shopping (going to the mall, catalog purchases, television shopping network use, etc.)? What is the best way of presenting advertising and product information on-line or on optical disks to effectively communicate with consumers?

10. Pseudo-communities, para-social interaction and domestic alliances.

Research Question: How different is the para-social interaction by a single individual in front of TV from that of a family watching TV while interacting with each other. How does the domestic context impact on technology use as well as the development and participation in pseudo communities? Further, how does technology use create and sustain domestic alliances, perhaps across gender and generational differences?

11. Home education through home entertainment systems.

Research Question: Educational institutions are increasingly turning to communication technologies to deliver education to people's homes. Distance education research has focused primarily on delivery systems and programs from the point of view of the institutions. How are these educational programs incorporated within the predominantly entertainment oriented technological system?

References

Brand, S. (1988). *The media lab: Inventing the future at M.I.T.* New York: Penguin Books.

Goodman, I. F. (1983). Television's role in family interaction: A family systems perspective. *Journal of Family Issues*, 4(2), 405–424.

James, M. L., Wotring, C. E. & Forrest, E. J. (1995). An exploratory study of the perceived benefits of electronic bulletin board use and their impact on other communication activities. *Journal of broadcasting and electronic media.* In Press.

Kayany, J. M., Wotring, C. E. & Forrest, E. J. (1995). Relational control and interactive media choice in technology mediated communication situations. *Human communication research.* In Press.

Lasswell, H. L. (1948). The structure and function of communication in society. In L. Bryson (Ed.), *The Communication of Ideas* (pp. 37–51). New York: Harper and Brothers.

Miyasato, L. (1994, July/August). Reality Check. *Aldus Magazine,* p. 47.

Morley, D., & Silverstone, R. (1990). Domestic communication-technologies and meanings. *Media, Culture and Society*, 12(1), 31–55.

Rogers, E. M. (1986). *Communication technology: The new media in society.* New York: The Free Press.

Silverstone, R., Hirsch, E., & Morley, D. (1991). Listening to a long conversation: An ethnographic approach to the study of information and communication technologies in the home. *Cultural Studies*, 5(2), 204–227.

Sinclair, J. (1993). "The domestic paradigm: Researching the use of communication and information technologies in the home. *EJC/REC*, 3(3&4), 1–13.

Williams, F., Rice, R. E., & Rogers, E. M. (1988). *Research methods and the new media.* New York: The Free Press.

CHAPTER

20

Customer Service and Interactivity

The Ongoing Conversation

Lucia Fishburne
Daniel Montgomery

Lucia M. Fishburne is a doctoral candidate in in the School of Communication at Florida State University. Her primary research interests are consumer behavior and new media uses, with an emphasis on music used in a marketing communication context.

Daniel Montgomery is an Associate Professor and Director of the Organizational and Business Communication Program in the School of Communication at Florida State University. He is widely published in the area of organizational change and professional ethics.

There is a revolution going on right now. It swells from the convergence of a multitude of factors that are redefining the relationship between the consumer (the buyer) and the corporation (the seller). The phenomenon of interactivity, both in the technological and managerial sense, is at the heart of this revolution. Interactivity promises to not only redefine what we mean by the term *customer service* but to revolutionize the service delivery system. The gurus of interactive technologies foresee a bright future in customer service. They envision numerous possibilities. Some are evident today; others are just over the horizon.

Examples of current applications that quickly come to mind are the highly segmented personalized data bases used by retailers. These allow companies to develop idiosyncratic profiles of their customers that in turn allow them not only to target their promotions, marketing and advertisements but also to help provide "superservice," e.g., reminding the customer that he or she gave the same present to their spouse two years ago or that a new musical artist, similar in style to a favorite artist, has a new CD available.

Personal buying profiles can be compiled via scanner and credit card purchases. These profiles allow companies to get to know their customers' preferences and lifestyles via purchasing behavior. Such information facilitates target and niche marketing, which allow the company to go where the consumer is and offer products geared to their lifestyles and needs rather than requiring the consumer to hunt through the multitude of offerings to find what they are looking for.

Future developments in interactive technologies will expand the delivery of such highly personalized services. They will, for example, enable producers to monitor consumer demand, track minor variations, individualize market strategies, and ultimately permit the customer to become an active participant in the product development cycle. Consumers will no longer be the end target of the production or service delivery process. They will play an integral role from start to finish. Whether it is tailoring their own jeans to fit their specific measurements and tastes, designing their homes and interiors, or engaging in mate selection via interactive dating services, consumers will become partners in the cycle. The "virtual reality" provided by interactive technologies may not allow us to take a new car around the block for a test drive, but it will provide us with the next best thing.

Nascent in these examples are trends that we believe will reshape the definition of customer service in the age of interactivity. These include: the changing lifestyles and subsequent needs of customers; the increasing role and power of the consumer in all areas of the production and delivery cycle; the necessity for producers and others to offer highly customized products in addition to generic offerings; and the reorganization of companies to anticipate and adapt to these developments.

In this chapter, we will examine each of these developments and discuss how interactivity may either drive, facilitate or, in some instances, impede these developments. We will discuss the evolution of customer service: its past, present and future. We will look specifically at the role the new interactive technologies can play in rethinking as well as delivering customer service. We will look at how interactive technologies affect this evolution both with internal and external customers. And in conclusion, we will consider the question of whether the promise of interactivity for customer service constitutes little more than "snake oil" or whether it will provide us with the tools necessary to offer "real time" super service.

Customer Service: The Changing Landscape

To gain a better understanding of where customer service is headed in the future, the first step is to look at where it has come from. How has customer service as well as the buyer/seller relationship evolved?

The Past: Buyer Beware

The battle cry of caveat emptor emerged from a market culture freshly intoxicated with the technological advances embedded in the Industrial Revolution. Production quantity rather than quality was the goal. There were no customer service departments, consumer protection agencies, or watch-dog groups looking out for the buyer. On a retail level the focus was more times than not the sale at the moment—not cultivating loyal customers for a future purchase. The strategy was oriented to a short-term relationship between the seller and the buyer. It did not take long, however, for customer satisfaction to be recognized as a valuable asset for developing repeat buying behavior and soon companies began to offer customer service.

Customer service still had a long way to go. At this point it was basically a conduit for handling customer complaints. The usual outcome was a refund or an exchange or a disgruntled customer who vowed to never buy from that company again. The interaction between the company via the customer service employee and the customer was based on an assumption of mutual distrust. The customer generally believed that they had been wronged and the customer service employee generally felt that the customer was a problem to be dealt with.

The Recent Past: The Customer as a Necessary Nuisance

Enter the age of the lawsuit! Customers began to wage a legal battle against negligent companies. Consumer protection groups organized and the battle cries of the Ralph Naders of the land were not merely heard, they were listened to. Consumer rights became a household word. Consumers began to realize that they could have a voice in the marketplace through the money they spent. Companies began to acknowledge consumer power as their bottom lines were affected. Customer satisfaction and service as well as quality began to be recognized as strategic concerns.

The Present: The Quality Revolution and the Emergence of the Internal Customer

The 1980s signaled the beginning of the quality revolution in the United States. The craftsmanship and pride that had long been a part of manufacturing traditions in Europe, and more recently in Japan, finally reached our shores. With it came a redefinition of the customer to include not just the external customer—the recipient of the final product or service—but also the internal customer—anyone who contributes directly or indirectly to the final product. Quality begins with recognition of customer desires or needs and then permeates every aspect of the production or service delivery process. It encompasses everyone from bookkeepers to custodians, to receptionists. With the quality revolution, employees had a new job description—one that is best summarized by Scandinavian Airlines' companywide job description: "If you aren't serving the customer, your job is to be serving someone who is." Or, as Dunn & Bradstreet commands, ask yourself two questions: "Where does my work go? Who is my work important to?" (Anderson and Zemke 1991, p. 33)

The change in how companies viewed "the customer" was instrumental in the quality revolution. The time-honored tradition of checking products at the end of the assembly line (the famous Claire Johnson test depicted in the Honda lawn mower commercials) was replaced. Quality control is now a process. It begins with the suppliers and comes full circle when market reactions to the product or service are fed back into the development cycle. The results have been dramatic. As Tom Peters, management visionary, observes, quality is now considered the standard in many U.S. industries. Acts of customer service that were so rare two decades ago that they made headlines (e.g., the L.L. Bean story of a man who was given a no-questions-asked refund on a jacket purchased during World War II) are now commonplace. Today quality products and services are the norm. They are "the necessary but not sufficient conditions" for economic and organizational survival.

Beyond Quality Control

Customer service has evolved into a valuable marketing strategy tool. Superior customer service is viewed as a differentiating factor that results in greater competitive advantage. Such an advantage is needed within the context of a mature marketplace that must look beyond quality or price strategies to maintain a competitive edge.

At the heart of superior customer service is a positive buyer/seller relationship. The buyer-seller relationship is now acknowledged as the outcome of a complex, dynamic, two-way communication rather than a simple stimulus-response situation. All aspects of buyer-seller communication can be considered part of customer service. Even satisfying pre-purchase customer needs for information is now viewed as an integral part of a company's customer service. The quality revolution accounts for much of the redefinition of the relationship between the buyer and the seller. The new interactive technologies provide powerful tools for developing and maintaining this relationship.

The Future: Creating an Ongoing Conversation with your Customers

In the decade ahead, superservice will be the watch word. Producers and service providers will need to offer "just in time" products, at desired levels of quality and guarantee customer satisfaction. By offering superservice, providers can differentiate themselves in the market place, build a competitive advantage and establish long-term relationships. The new imperative is: Don't just serve your customers. "Dazzle" your customers! (Peters, 1994)

For many companies, the first opportunity to dazzle the customer occurs in the form of the customer service hotline. When a customer contacts customer service, he has expectations about how he will be treated. Timeliness, helpfulness, courtesy, respect—all of these attributes of customer service—can reflect a corporate image. Based on their past experience with this company or another, the customer's expectations may include positive or negative assessments of these attributes. Reinforcing a customer's expectations via superior or inferior customer service has far-reaching implications.

In addition to customer expectations, the customer's perception of a company is another element involved in the customer service experience. Because customers communicate their experiences with your company to other people, customer perception has the potential to assist or hinder your attempt to develop new customers. How do the new interactive technologies help you to meet your customer's expectations and improve their perceptions of your company? By putting information at their fingertips either directly or through your customer service employees.

Superior customer service goes beyond courteous and helpful employees. Employees who deliver customer services are in the information business. They need immediate access to up to date product information as well as information on the customer. Technologies that facilitate quick and complete access to product as well as customer information empower employees to superserve consumers. Providing the consumer direct access to product information through user-friendly interfaces such as interactive kiosks or on line services is another route to superserving customers.

Outsourcing Customer Service

As companies continue to downsize, they increasingly contract out (outsource) their support work. Peter Drucker (1995) projects that "In ten or fifteen years, organizations may be outsourcing all work that is "support" rather than revenue-producing, and all activities that do not offer career opportunities into senior management." Customer service may well satisfy these criteria.

Similarly, the idea of the freestanding "independent consumer-information company (I.C.I.C.)" has already been proposed (Snider & Ziporyn, 1992). Such an organization would "sell information about products without selling the products themselves and without having any ties to the companies that make and sell the products" (p. 206). Interactive technologies will play a major role in both of these scenarios as tools to achieve optimal convenience, connectedness, choice, and creativity—elements of success for both businesses and consumers.

The Four C's: The Elements of Superservice

Remember the four P's in the classic marketing mix—product, price, promotion, and place? The idea is to consider all of these elements in developing a successful marketing plan. We suggest a similar tool when developing superior customer service—the four C's: convenience, connectedness, choice, and creativity. Like the four P's of the marketing mix, there is a lot of overlap among the four C's of the customer service mix.

Convenience

Customer service starts by taking a good look at your customers' needs and lifestyles. For example, probably the most significant trend of the past (and future) decade is what Faith Popcorn (1992), a trend analyst, terms "cocooning." Cocooning refers to the "full scale retreat into the last controllable (or sort of controllable) environment—your own digs"(p. 27). Couple this trend with the prevalence of the two-income household and the result is that the amount of time your customers have for pre-purchase activities (i.e.,investigating product differences, price variations, etc.) is shrinking.

Meanwhile, new products are proliferating with very few differentiating features the consumer can use for comparisons. Buying has become more complicated. Even shopping based on price is confusing. Discount pricing strategies have resulted in many products becoming "commoditized" to the point where, from the buyer's point of view, one product is as good (or as bad) as another. How can a company stand out in this kind of environment? By addressing two of the most basic needs consumers have—the need for quick access to product information coupled with a mechanism to filter such a vast amount of information. This is convenience.

The music industry is moving quickly into this type of customer service. In a keynote speech to music industry professionals, Frank Biondi, Jr., CEO of Viacom International, Inc., said "interactivity will be embraced because choice and convenience are desirable." He further acknowledged that "new technology will help you to superserve your audience as music formats continue to splinter."

There are several options using interactive technologies that can be provided to address the need for convenience. Probably the most convenient option is to access complete, up to date information using a home computer with a modem. More and more companies are offering home pages on the Internet for this purpose. More common are 1-800 numbers that the consumer can call and speak to a real person who has access to the same information via computer—in essence, connectedness once removed. A little less convenient and dependent on the time constraints of retail business hours is accessing product information via an in-store kiosk with or without help from a salesperson.

Connectedness

Simply speaking, the new interactive technologies are valuable tools which enable corporations to connect to their customers and future customers. This connection allows companies to detect and respond quickly to the changing relationship between the buyer and the seller. By tracking current trends and predicting future trends in consumer lifestyles, purchasing, and expectations, companies get a needed headstart in developing new products in today's congested market-place. Using interactive technologies in this kind of consumer research is not only cost efficient, it also enhances accuracy—i.e., by getting your information from the source.

Connectedness also pertains to networking the internal customers in a company—i.e. the employees. The better-networked employees are within a company, the quicker they can respond to the customers' needs. Personalized service can be provided by any employee who can access a customer's personal profile or purchasing history file. Connectedness basically addresses the need to be well informed in order to superserve the customer.

Choice

The greatest strength of interactive technologies with regard to customer service lies in the element of consumer choice. Specifically, an interactive interface allows the pre-purchase or post-purchase consumer to control the breadth and depth of information being sought.

Buying a new appliance serves as a good example. Jane has decided to purchase a new range. She currently uses natural gas and thinks she wants to stay with this energy choice but is also interested in electric options depending on the features. How can interactive technologies meet her needs in this pre-purchase consumer service situation? She can log onto an interactive source of information via an in-store kiosk or her computer at home. This will eliminate some of the bias associated with commission-supported salespeople. She can choose to review all ranges based on price, size, energy source, configurations, and/or other features. She can choose to see a picture of any range she is interested in. Locations of stores selling specific ranges in her area can be obtained. All of this can be done quickly without the help (or hindrance) of a salesperson. Jane may decide that she wants to talk to someone who can interpret some of the technical specifications offered. This could be done by e-mail, a 1-800 number, or an actual salesperson at the store. It is Jane's *choice* as to how much information she gets and how she is going to get it.

Creativity

The fourth C is creativity. Creativity, we believe, represents the culmination of the trend toward consumer empowerment. We have come a long way since the days of "buyer beware," but in our estimation "you ain't seen nothin' yet." Creativity will become the new frontier in customer service, and it is here that interactive technologies can reach their full potential.

Leonard Barry's research suggests that we can gauge the quality of customer service by asking: is the service reliable? Is it responsive? Does it provide assurance; i.e., does your service lead to customer confidence and trust in you, your product or organization? Does it convey individual attention and empathy? And do the tangibles, your office, building, employee dress, project the desired appearance? No doubt these are some of the mainstays of customer service. But new technologies will lead us into a new dimension—the dimension of customer as the creator or co-creator of products.

For years, customer-oriented companies have attempted to get to know their customers. They have relied on the traditional modalities of focus groups, surveys, complaint boxes and the like. As helpful as these methods are, they neglect an important consideration: the customers don't always know what they want. There are numerous examples of companies that patiently and painstakingly assessed consumer wants only to find that when they delivered the products or services the customer didn't want them or they were outdated by the time they arrived in the marketplace. Perhaps the most noteworthy example is Big Blue—a company renowned for customer service.

Moreover, marketing strategies based on surveys and focus groups discount the importance of creativity. They focus on the world as it is now; not on the world as it could be. They ignore such great success stories as 3M's Post-it Notes, which evolved not from marketing savvy but from the serendipitous genius of a 3M chemist.

In our rapidly changing world, we need to do more than survey our customers. By all means collect data but realize its limitations. First and foremost, it is only a partial snap shot and generally by the time you have analyzed and synthesized the results, it is dated. In some areas consumer interests are changing so rapidly organizations have abandoned the formal planning process. They don't have time (Peters, 1994). Moreover, survey and focus groups results reflect current knowledge: what the customer knows or wants now. They don't educate the customer about what is possible. Focus groups and surveys are not the ideal vehicle for giving customers a glimpse of the future and assessing their reactions.

According to Peters (1994), Heil, Parker, and Tate (1995), and others we need new vehicles for involving the customer in the product development cycle. We need to find ways of developing a "symbiotic" relationship: a mutually beneficial relationship that will allow producers and consumers to learn and grow together (Peters, 1994). Merely asking customers if they like what they have (e.g., "Are you satisfied with your main frame?") will not give you the information you need to meet your customers' rapidly changing world. Yogi Berra captured it when he was asked the time and he responded, "Do you mean now?"

As a producer, you need to know what is possible. Your job is to educate your customers to the point where they can make an intelligent and informed product decision—even if this means losing their business in the short-run. Take, for example, the software company that takes the time to educate prospective customers. The company must ascertain and predict consumers' needs, show them the options, explain how or if the product will meet their needs, and if necessary, refer them to a competitor. Stupid? Perhaps, but this and a good deal more will be expected. According to Heil, Parker and Tate (1995), tomorrow's leader in the customer revolution will be a "change agent, visionary, values-driven, persistent, participative, and *creative*" (p. 261).

Interactive technologies can assist tomorrow's leaders who can, for example, use these technologies to create what Senge (1990) terms "micro-worlds" where purchasers or product developers can peruse the potential options. They can review options by price, quality, color, and other relevant characteristics. They can balance price vs. quality vs. durability vs. appearance. They can, in effect, mix and match until they find the right combination. And, through the "virtual reality" of interactivity, they with the consumer "test drive" the possible choices.

Does this sound too futuristic? The future is now for more and more companies that have already put new technologies to work for them. In Tokyo, one company is using a virtual showroom to allow kitchen renovation customers to "walk through" different kitchen prototypes. Of course, there are many shortcomings to this approach still to be worked out, most of which are a function of technological limitations—improvements in graphics quality, extensive time needed to prepare individualized designs, inability to change details on the spot, etc.

Going a step further with interactive, customers may help build the product. Our example of the software that will allow individuals to tailor their own jeans is just one example of what will become commonplace in the future. The companies that can foresee such possibilities and recognize when and where such applications are desirable will have a definite step-up on their competitors. Notice we said when and where. In many instances, interactivity will allow you to customize a service or product, but this begs another question: do your customers want a customized product or would they prefer the ease of buying generic. For years, Detroit offered a myriad of options to its customers, only to find that many consumers did not want to choose. They wanted the simplicity of standard features. By the same token, some individuals may prefer anonymity and ease of purchase provided by generic offerings, e.g., some people may not want the dimensions of their leg, thigh and buttocks stored in a nationwide database!

There is a flipside to consider in using new technologies to establish on going dialog for getting to know your customers better. It has to do with the customers' perceptions of your company. Remember that this is a two-way communication scenario. We've talked about communicating product information which enables the customer to make better purchase decisions. We have also discussed the need for convenient and quickly accessible technical support for some products. There is something else equally important that is communicated to the customer—the values, beliefs, and personality of the company—as Faith Popcorn (1992) puts it, the corporate soul.

Corporate soul is an important marketing element today, and it will most likely be even more so in the future. Consumers are making purchases that reflect their own values and beliefs. They expect companies to be responsible and accountable. Interactive technologies offer another channel to promote not just the product but to communicate the company's image. There are many important issues in the world today—the environment, human rights, animal testing, to name a few—that affect a growing number of consumers' choices in what they buy. An excellent example of an innovative form of customer service which also communicates corporate soul is that of Working Assets, a long-distance service company. Working Assets donates ten percent of its billings to a variety of nonprofit groups. Although the older interactive technologies of telephones and credit cards are the tools for this service, it is clearly a fresh approach that goes far in communicating a positive, responsible company image. If this trend continues to grow as expected by some, interactive communication technologies used as vehicles for transmitting the corporate image will play an even greater role in customer service.

New Interactive Technologies: Savior or Snake Oil?

Throughout this chapter, we have provided you with a glimpse of how interactive technologies can be used to provide superservice to customers. In our closing comments we would like to offer some caveats. Interactive technologies are tools and, like any tool, can be used for a variety of purposes. Whether or not companies and producers will use them to offer superservice remains to be seen. Certainly they have tremendous potential, but potential does not guarantee success. For years, organizations have had access to the ultimate in interactive capacity and many have not only ignored it but have actually used it to thwart their customer service. We are speaking of human beings. Surveys have repeatedly shown what customers want, and yet many companies and organizations have failed to provide it. Even in areas where high tech is readily available, such as in the computer and computer software business, it is not uncommon to be put on hold for fifteen minutes, or have to talk to recorded messages, or to be sold a product that does not fit your needs and then be told it cannot be returned. As Stall, author of *Snake Oil on the Silicon Highway* notes, if you want an introduction to rudeness get out on the Internet! Whether the advances in interactive will become the vehicle for superservice or "the ultimate revenge of the nerds" is open to debate (*Tech Nation*, June 2, 1995).

From the authors' perspective, the answer rests somewhere in between. Among unreconstructed executives, interactivity will be used primarily as a means of cost cutting, e.g., computerized ordering and complaint handling. In this format, it will become one more way of keeping the consumer at arm's length and amassing short-term profits at the expense of long-term organizational survival.

Well-meaning but uninformed executives will use it to bludgeon their consumers with too much information, leaving them only more confused. As Moiré Gunn observes, many of us faced with the information glut provided by new technologies would gladly "pay" for less information (*Tech Nation*, June 2, 1995). Still, other companies will launch themselves into an interactive abyss. Several years ago a *Wall Street Journal* headline quipped "What if we give an interactive party and nobody comes?" Unlikely, the article asked? When one considers the number of highly visible failures in interactive ventures, it is clear that interactive is, at best, going to lurch into our lives. A smooth technological evolution into the future is unlikely. Along with the successes there will be numerous failures—many of which may actually detract from current standards of customer service. But, this is part of the competitive process and one that we are likely to accelerate in the decade ahead (Rothschild, 1992).

Ultimately, forces other than interactivity will drive the customer revolution. Competitive trends in the world economy, in particular, will determine the role of interactivity. Intense world-wide competition will require organizations to downsize, reengineer and even cannibalize themselves in order to survive (Peters, 1994; Rothschild, 1992). Time and flexibility will be essential. Companies will have to see and exploit market opportunities as they occur. They will not have time to play "catch-up." In some sectors, one can envision companies operating by the now famous dictum of one outdoor recreation equipment company: "Don't compete; obsolete." In other words, by the time you start to worry about price wars, exploiting the demand curve and the like, it is too late. The successful companies of the future will spend less time worrying about their competitors and more time searching out new opportunities and developing new products to exploit those opportunities. "Epochal shifts in the global economy have given them a sultan's power to command exactly what they want, the way they want it, when they want it, at a price they want it, at a price that will make you weep. You'll either provide it or vaporize." (*Fortune*, Autumn/Winter, 1993 p. 8).

In this environment, managers must create a new view of customer service. Just as they will have to give up notions of what constitutes "work station" or acceptable employee performance, they may have to develop a new concept of customer service—one that will allow them to not only detect problems or needs and desires but to predict and educate consumers to the possibilities. They will have to find ways of having an on-going "cradle-to-grave" dialog with their customers.

Interactive technologies offer this possibility. Why not involve the customer from the beginning? Put customers on design teams; include them in employee suggestion programs—ones that are tied to meaningful incentives; and create electronic bulletin boards where they can voice their complaints.

Nystrom's, L.L. Bean, and other service exemplars have done "low-tech" versions of dialoging for years. They have made it easy for customers to have an on-going conversation with their companies primarily by removing the hassle. They do this by offering a "subjective guarantee" of complete customer satisfaction. They, in effect, wed their customers "for better or for worse." They will commit themselves to the customers' long-term, subjective satisfaction not short-term profit provided by a quick sale or the refusal to provide a refund or a replacement.

Companies following this strategy recognize that they are not selling a product but a service. The product may change, but the service delivery system must stay in tact. As Swatch and Nike have demonstrated, they are not in the watch or the shoe business but the lifestyle business. As lifestyles change, so will their products. In this scenario, all a producer has is the on-going relationship with the customer.

Companies that learn this lesson will find remarkable ways of making interactive technology a vehicle for enhancing customer satisfaction. They will recognize it as a tool: a vehicle for doing their job better. But they will not assume that new technologies necessarily lead to customer satisfaction. They know from experience that serving the customer is work. In most instances people do not want to communicate with a computer. Unless there is an issue of desired anonymity involved (e.g., did you bounce a check) or the need for after-hour services, most people prefer human communication.

Unfortunately one-to-one customer service for most employees is not a rewarding activity. We do not like dealing with difficult people; we do not like taking the extra time required; and we don't like the distraction—especially when other tasks are waiting. If companies are to make the full use of interactive technologies, they must embed them in a larger context: mainly a company philosophy that values and rewards customer service. Customer service must be seen as an integral part of the job, not as a nuisance. Employees must be rewarded for the performance of service in tangible and meaningful ways. They must be rewarded for going out of their way to satisfy, delight, and "dazzle."

Moreover, companies must give employees the authority to provide exemplary service. They must trust them to make decisions on the spot without consultations with superiors. Take for example, Nordstrom's dictum: "Use your good judgment in all situations. There will be no additional rules" (Anderson and Zemke, 1991, p.49). Embedded in this rule are two important concepts: first, employees can be trusted; and second, as Peters (1994) notes, the only way to trust someone is to trust them. Companies that follow these are taking important steps toward creating a working environment where employees know they are valued and respected. And, in turn, employees are more likely to convey the same qualities to the outside world.

New technologies in and of themselves are not the answer but they do provide a new means of communication with customers. Companies that use technologies to operationalize a real and sincere commitment to customer service will continue on the road to excellence. Companies and organizations, on the other hand, that continue to focus on short term gains, view employees as untrustworthy and incapable of making independent decisions will use these new technologies to make our lives miserable—but in new and more maddening ways.

Summary

A quick response to the customer's unmet needs or dissatisfaction with a product affects the bottom line. Customer service can be considered as a way to initiate/continue an on-going dialog with consumers in an effort to learn what they want and need. It opens the door for establishing an interpersonal relationship between the company and the customer. And, in view of that, all of the dynamics of interpersonal communication will come to play in the company/customer relationship. Customer service is becoming an integral feedback loop to research and development of new products through providing an on-going conversation with the consumer.

The new electronic interactive communication technologies are unsurpassed as tools to facilitate such a relationship with one exception: actual face to face communication with all your customers—an impossibility in this day and age. Establishing a presence on the Internet is one example of how a company can utilize new technologies to interact with customers. Such a presence in cyberspace is available to any company regardless of budget limitations—it's a level playing field. This presence can be as low key as an e-mail address or as elaborate as a full multimedia homepage. The mere use of this type of new technology communicates that your company is innovative and wants to be connected to its customers. In other words, it provides another channel for expressing the corporate soul.

Getting to know the customer and his or her lifestyle is the name of the game these days. Traditional telephone customer service can be enhanced through the use of customer profiles developed on a computer database. Employees can enter useful information about customers as they converse with them via a customer service call. Other employees can access that information during a future interaction in an effort to personalize service.

There is a dark side to personalized service—privacy issues. Fidelity Investments, Inc., has used technology to replicate the intimacy of being a small town bank by building comprehensive backgrounds on their clients. This information, financial as well as personal, is quickly accessible by any client representative. A client might mention that they will be going to Hawaii in June on vacation; the representative inputs it into the client's background information; and, in a future call, a different representative could ask the client, "How was Hawaii?" Some people simply do not want companies to be collecting such personal information. This is a growing problem that will need to be addressed by companies attempting to superserve their customers. Progressive companies will view the problem of customer privacy as an opportunity to develop a responsive solution which will improve their service to the customer at the same time improving their corporate image.

To summarize, a new vision of customer service is emerging from innovative strategic management techniques involving the qualitative elements of the relationship between the seller and the buyer. Customer service is being cradled in the broader concept of customer satisfaction. And concepts like customized service and products, convenience, choice, connectedness, as well as creativity are part of the whole bundle. Progressive companies seeking greater competitive advantage in a highly competitive and commoditized marketplace are looking at customer service as the last frontier for differentiating themselves from the competition.

References

Anderson, K. & Zemke, R. (1991). *Delivering knock your socks off service.* New York: AMACOM.

Drucker, P., (1995, March 29). The network society. *The Wall Street Journal.*

Heil,G., Parker, T. & Tate, R. (1995). *Leadership and the customer revolution.* New York: Van Nostrand Reinhold.

Hwang, S., (1992, April 6). Getting personal: Fidelity Investments, computers are designed to make the company seem more human. *The Wall Street Journal,* p. R19.

Meet the new customer. *Fortune,* Autumn/Winter 1993, p. 8.

Peters, T (1994). *The Tom Peters seminar.* New York: Vintage Books.

Popcorn, F.,(1992). *The Popcorn report.* New York: HarperCollins.

Rothschild, M. (1992). Bionomics: Economy as ecosystem, New York: Henry Holt.

Snider, J. & Ziporyn, T. (1992). *Future Shop.* New York: St. Martin's Press.

Yamada, K., (1992, April 6). Almost like being there: Virtual technology is finally moving out of the lab. *The Wall Street Journal.*

Note: quote from Frank Biondi, Jr. came from his keynote address at the 15th annual Music Video Conference, as cited in a *Billboard* magazine article (Nov. 1993).

21

A Blueprint for Successful Syndicated On-Line Research

Consumer Panel Research Methods Applied to the On-Line Economy

Mickey Bennett

Mickey Bennett is Director of Marketing for Nielsen NorthAmerica's Consumer Information Services Group, which uses personal scanning technology to report purchasing of nondurable consumer goods. He has directed the development of consumer analytic systems, which are used to gain strategic insights from consumer transactional data.

Analyzing consumer activity captured over time from the same consumers yields some of the most insightful behavioral information a marketer could want. As a marketer, I want more than a report card of market share and total sales. I would love to know:

- Where do the buyers of my brand shop?

- How frequently do they shop?

- Who are my heavy buyers?

- What else are my buyers buying in my category?

- Where do buyers of my new brand come from?

- When I lose buyers, what brands do they buy?

- Am I getting good trial purchasing? From Whom?

- Who is the trier of my brand who didn't come back?

- Who is the trier who is coming back a lot?

- How can I get more of them into my brands franchise?

Anyone responsible for growing a business has asked questions like these to help set marketing strategy and tactics. Imagine the competitive value of identifying a new segment of consumer interest before your competition, or having better knowledge of consumer behavior in your market. Marketers of all consumer goods and services are better armed for competition when they understand consumption patterns and trends of consumers in their respective markets or categories.

Since the late 1950s, consumer packaged goods marketers have had the benefit of consumer panel information to help them set competitive strategy. This type of consumer activity measurement is reported from the same set of households over time and is broadly classified as a longitudinal methodology. Tracking the same set of households over time yields insights from a view of the total consumption activity for each household. Proper sampling and recruiting techniques allow a relatively small sample to statistically represent a larger population. Every on-line marketer should be demanding the consumer behavior insights which only consumer panels can deliver.

Capturing this type of longitudinal consumer information is a complex research challenge. Consumer panel research demands the researcher strike and maintain a delicate balance of capturing a robust activity database and keeping the data collection process as passive as possible. The data gain marketing value when a representative set of consumers consistently and accurately report on their consumption.

Consider the question of tracking PC on-line consumer activity. Why do I say a consumer panel is the best methodology to capture consumer on-line activity? Today's technology, which has enabled PC on-line activity, should obviously be able to capture consumer on-line activity to allow marketers the insights noted above without the need for expensive and sophisticated consumer panel data capture. After all, the on-line services know who their users are and what their users' activity is while they are in the on-line service! Why can't marketers gain access to the consumer activity information which on-line service providers will easily be able to capture?

It is a fair question, but the fact is on-line marketers will not be able to acquire actionable marketing information from the services themselves. It is true that third-party researchers doing independent site audits will help business-to-business advertisers and agencies as well as marketers of space on less popular or niche sites. But the competitive situation and revenue pressures of the on-line services will prevent them from allowing their information to be used to deliver the consumer insights needed by on-line marketers to compete. The sophisticated insights packaged goods marketers enjoy can only be delivered by longitudinal consumer panel research.

In this chapter, I will compare the measurement of consumer activity from an on-going consumer panel versus measurement from an on-line service provider. I have 13 years experience with in-home scanner consumer panels as large as forty thousand households. I also have experience with third-party consumer information captured when retailers sell their sales data to third-party research firms for processing. In this chapter, I will analyze the dynamics of these two methodologies. Each methodology has its unique issues of quality, utility and cost. As advertisers and marketers in a consumer on-line economy, I believe you will see that only the consumer panel methodology delivers the marketing insights required to succesfully compete in the emerging PC based on-line economy.

It is difficult to exist today in a media business without any measurement of the audience. Looking at the importance of advertising to the cable and magazine industries, it is clear that accurate consumer activity measurement is a critical component of an economy fueled by advertising. As we consider the case for consumer panel measurement of the PC on-line economy, we will also examine the development of the advertising industry and its capacity to support the PC on-line medium because of its revenue importance to the on-line economy; advertisers, agencies, Value Added Networks, on-line content providers and of course researchers.

The PC: Today's Interactive Medium

As the recent media hyperbole surrounding the "Information Highway" subsides, we are seeing real, albeit immature, Personal Computer Based Interactive technology available today as well as television-based interactive technology being field-tested. Interactive television tests are underway with several big name backers. These tests have shown one consistent finding for all involved; Interactive Television (ITTV) is expensive to implement without vast industry expenditures to upgrade current signal delivery infrastructure. Everyone also agrees that standards for signal delivery and in-home signal processing will be very slow to arrive, given the attractive market size, potential payouts to winners and the long-term revenue stream afforded to the owners of the appliance technology which will eventually earn a place in most people's homes. Given the technological challenges and industry realignments required to develop and fund this gargantuan effort to bring television-based shopping, entertainment and communication to the majority of U.S. homes, it is unlikely that this nascent industry will achieve significant economic mass in the next five years.

Only recently featured in the public media, the Internet has been gaining notoriety at an astounding rate, driving awareness deeply across the population. The Internet's rate of growth is itself newsworthy, as is the daily number of new Internet home pages and e-mail addresses mentioned in newspaper and magazine articles, print advertisements and direct mail announcements. The Internet has become such a de facto standard for interuser connectivity, that even the established commercial on-line networks (Prodigy, America On-Line, CompuServe)[1] have rushed new software releases to market which feature access to the Internet via their commercial service. Established software publishers (such as Microsoft, IBM, Adobe and Netscape)[2] as well as new aggressive firms (Spry with Internet-In-A-Box, or private networks like Business MCI, Mecklermedia, Commerce 2000, Ziffnet and others) are being attracted to the Internet environment bringing new capabilities, competition, cost efficiencies and innovation to those engaging in commerce in the emerging on-line economy.

Given the cost issues associated with a materially significant implementation of Interactive Television, the PC, not the television, will be the interactive medium used by the most people for the foreseeable future. Forrester Research (Cambridge, MA) took the position in December of 1994, that "The PC will be the only viable interactive device in the next 2-5 years." [3] I am personally convinced it will be around in the next twenty years as well, although it will be more PDA[4] like in form factor and cheap wireless broadband will be commonplace. The PC has proven to be a sustainable medium as evidenced by the rapidly growing popularity of On-Line Services and the increased penetration of PC's with modems across commercially important consumer segments of the United States.

Consumer PC Ownership Reaches Critical Mass

The penetration of PC's into American homes has increased by 30% in the last two years. In 1995 about 40% of all households with televisions also have PC's.[5] Half of those PC's have modems. Fifteen percent of the total PC population in homes are connected to an on-line service. The competitive economic forces at work have driven down prices and consumers are showing that this market is very elastic.

As seen below, the absolute numbers are not only impressive, but the rate of growth is increasing and expected to sustain that high growth rate through the next three years. Falling PC prices, intense competition for PC's in the home market, new generations of pre-installed, ready to switch on , CD-ROM, multimedia, on-line service ready PC's are all keeping the consumer market hot. Loads of new CD-ROM software and constantly improving on-line service offerings are also supporting the PC becoming a ubiquitous household appliance. *The Wall Street Journal* recently reported that in 1994 more households purchased PC's than color televisions.

Today's Consumer of On-Line Services

A recent study by AST Computers of two-thousand United States computer buyers confirmed the likelihood that the PC is truly a new consumer medium. The study revealed that nearly 34% of these PC

EXHIBIT 21.1 U. S. Household Penetration of PCs Modems and On-line Service Access

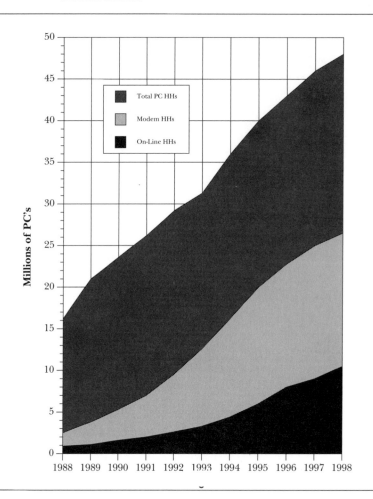

Source: Forbes ASAP, p. 72, April 10, 1995 [6]

owners were connected to an on-line service. The total user base reported spending an average of 13 hours per week on the PC. The average person only spends 9 hours per week watching Prime Time Television! America On-Line (AOL) alone is accessed by about 1/25 of the audience of a single television network on a given day, but ABC and NBC were both working hard to "brand" areas on the AOL service until NBC jumped to the Microsoft Network to produce programming content.[7] My interpretation of this network interest is that that we will have a very broad, heterogeneous universe of users with a mix of on-line behavior. This emerging consumer behavior dynamic can only be understood through the thorough tracking and analysis of consumer activity by the various user segments. Consumer panel research is the best methodology for capturing a full range of analytic measures of consumer activity.

Dependable information about actual users is very vague at this point, since research services are only beginning to explore and learn about this market themselves. It is generally recognized that the profile of those using on-line services is a very desirable advertising target: male, upscale, affluent and well educated.[8] Current estimates of 1995 Consumer On-Line Service access is about 4 to 4.4 million consumers. These consumers bought $200 million worth of goods and services through on-line vendors in 1994. By 1998, 19.5 million consumers are expected to purchase about $4.8 billion in goods and services.[9] While these estimates predict an optimistic five-fold increase in business per household, the fact is that commerce is rapidly adapting to the PC on-line environment. As industry quickly fills the gaps in required technology, such as enabling on-line banking and shopping by providing secure transactions and enabling better, faster graphics by providing increased bandwidth, competitive pressures will make access cheaper and improve services and innovation. The best advertising method of all, "word of mouth" from friends and co-workers, becomes more commonplace everyday, so we can be sure the PC based use of interactive on-line services will continue to grow at its rapid pace. Consumer panel research will provide the means to understand the trends and changing dynamic of the consumer marketplace as the on-line economy evolves.

On-Line Advertising Activity Parallels Postwar TV Growth

In the Spring Special Edition of *Advertising Age*, the focus was a retrospective into the last 50 years of television advertising. Scott Donaton, the respected *Ad Age* columnist, brilliantly related today's interactive challenge for advertising agencies to a nearly identical challenge when television was the upstart technology, much as interactive, on-line media are perceived today. Back then, radio and print media were so entrenched, that advertisers were reluctant to "test the waters." At that time (late 1940s), Leo Burnett urged the industry to experiment: " The courage of Agencies to change long-established habits and procedures and to get wet all over . . . is, in my opinion, the index to the strength of the advertising agency business of the future."[10] That message seems remarkable when considered with a more recent message from Ed Artzt, then Chairman of Procter & Gamble, delivered last May to the American Association of Advertising Agencies (4A's) annual convention at the Greenbrier Resort. Artzt said: "Our most important ad medium, television is about to change big-time. . . ." He asked the 4A's to get together to "understand how consumer viewing habits will change as a result of these new technologies." Jay Chiat (Chiat/Day Agency) described the agency reaction as, "Hey, my agency doesn't know anything about interactive media, we'd better do something about it."[11]

They did do something about it. In the nine months since Artzt's call to action, ad agencies have added Interactive or New Media Units which are aggressively fighting for recognition as "Interactive Agency of Record" for their clients. On April 2, 1995, the country's eighteenth largest advertiser, AT&T, announced that Modem Media, of Norwalk, Conn. would be their Interactive Agency of Record. Modem Media also lists Coors, Zima and CBS as clients. Other advertisers are also reviewing agencies' interactive capabilities. To ensure it had the right on-line advertising skill sets on hand, America On-Line purchased Ted Leonsis's interactive media agency, Redgate, last year.

On-line Advertising—A Description

The creative requirements of on-line advertising will also tax the old school agency way of thinking. Obviously the interactive model of message delivery changes from the broadcast environment, since people will have to be shopping for information on a product, in the process of buying the product, or interested in the editorial or entertainment value of an advertiser's on-line message to reach your message. The ad agencies that are already working in the interactive area will deliver value to their clients by drawing the customer's interest to the message effectively, and delivering a positive experience to the consumer, whether the experience is making a purchase, getting information or being entertained.

Scott Kurnit (now of Network MCI, prior he was the SVP Business Manager of Prodigy) describes a scenario where advertisers can place

"Activerts" on any on-line service for a fee. The consumer can press on the button (example: Colgate has a new article on their site which describes "Five ways to get a toddler to brush his teeth without a fight.") to transparently get to the Colgate area, where, just like a magazine, the consumer can browse, place a bookmark, print an article (unlike a magazine) or scan the content to learn about toddlers and tooth care.

Consider the tone of this approach. The advertiser delivers a real interactive message which the consumer values. The on-line service gets paid as a deliverer of the interested consumer, plus some base fee similar to a slotting allowance for the activert on their system. The agency can be compensated its percentage for the slotting fee, the responses, and with the ratings produced by the proposed enterprise, the demographics of the buy and the demographics of the responders will all be reported in GRP terms, which can be rolled up in a total delivery number as the agency does today.

Follow The Money: An On-Line Economy Needs a Common Currency

The audience of this new PC-based media is a new audience, which has yet to be identified and measured to support advertising sales. The measures must be expressed in terms that traditional advertising media planners and buyers can understand and use. Media buyers require audience measurement including demographics of individuals exposed to the advertising and a measure of the exposure frequency to develop Gross Rating Point equivalent measures.[12]

To ensure the industry gains acceptable metrics to use as a common currency, a new group, CASIE (The Coalition for Advertising Supported Information and Entertainment) was formed in early 1995 to establish on-line and interactive research standards. As David Marans, SVP, Director of Media Research at J. Walter Thompson said of CASIE, "The goal is to have some kind of common currency." The coalition represents the American Associate of Advertising Agencies, the Association of National Advertisers and the Advertising Research Foundation. This organization has already developed preliminary recommendations for research of on-line and interactive media. The group is trying to balance current industry measurements with the capabilities of the new media.

CASIE recommends that a universal standard be developed to calculate a user's "clickstream" or path through the on-line service.

They would also like to see "second-by-second" measurements of usage as opposed to several second interval of today's TV measurement systems. They also recommended that passive people meters be tested for on-line and interactive TV services. The most relevant recommendation was for a "sample to be formed for interactive and on-line measurement and monetary incentives offered to participants, as with Nielsen's People meter sample."[13]

Delivering required advertising metrics such as GRP's and demographic information to advertisers, agencies, on-line service providers,Value Added Networks (VAN's) will enable a growth in advertising placements on these on-line media by quantifying the audience delivered at a given cost. Dollars available for this media will grow as on-line services penetration reaches the majority of the US population, because budgets for advertisers could then be drawn from larger national advertising budgets. Until recently, most on-line advertising was

EXHIBIT 21.2 Tracking On-Line Advertising "Clickstream" Links

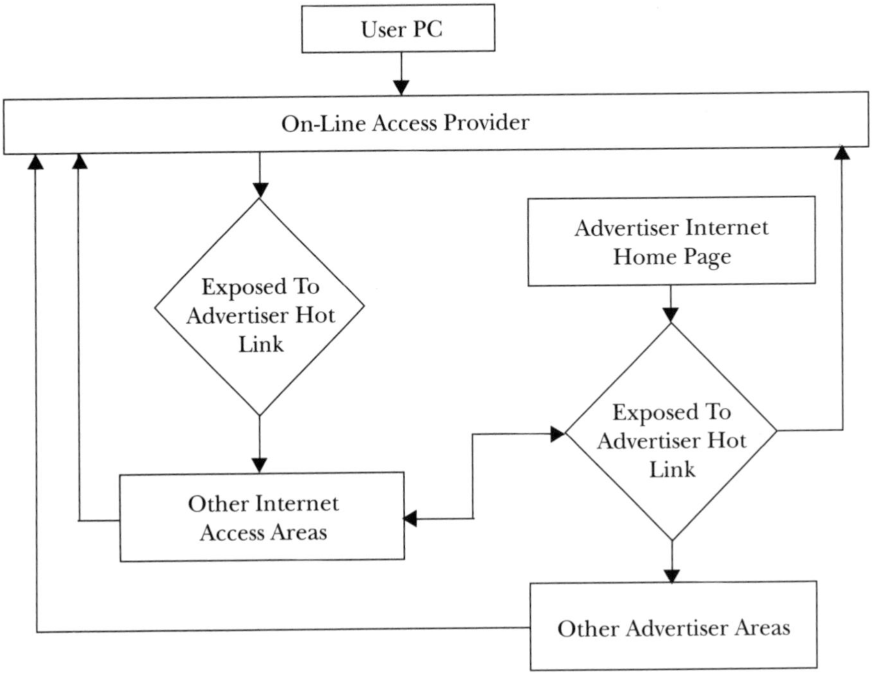

considered a learning experience and was funded from ad-hoc advertiser budgets. With high quality metrics available to report on the reach and frequency of the advertising delivery, the advertisers and agencies will know what they are buying and it can be included as part of a typical media buy.

Are the Big Agencies Ready for Interactive?

As Exhibit 21.3 indicates, even back in August of 1994, major agencies have made their interactive capabilities a very visible part of their strategic offerings. If this table were updated today, not only would we see more agencies, like Ogilvy and Mather Interactive, but we would also see the inclusion of some aggressive upstarts in this area, such as Modem Media, CKS,[14] and others who meld technological understanding with the new marketing communications demands.

EXHIBIT 21.3 Advertising Agencies With Dedicated Interactive Groups

Agency	Advertising Agency Interactive Media Group Activity					
	Internet	Commercial On-Line	PC Software & CD-ROM	Kiosks	Interactive TV	Electronic Retailing
Ayer	•	•	•	•	•	
Bates USA					•	
Bozell		•	•		•	
Leo Burnett		•	•		•	
Chiat/Day	•	•			•	•
Earle Palmer Brown						
Fallon McElligot	•	•				
Foote, Cone & Belding		•	•	•	•	
Grey Advertising	•		•	•	•	
Martin Agency			•			
Ross Roy Communications	•	•	•		•	
Wells, Rich Greene/ BDDP		•				

Source: Mike Garvey, *Advertisng Age;* August 15, 1994

Interactive Advertising Industry Economics

The consumer panel will report detailed activity on popular business-to-consumer advertising sites (Internet or VAN). For the business-to-business, specialized and niche industrials, the custom audit service of the Network Cooperation Model would usually be the best methodology for measuring business-to-business advertising effectiveness.

It is important to recognize the culture and power at work today concerning how advertising is bought and sold. All advertising purchased by media planners, and funded from the general advertising budget of the advertiser, must be measured in terms of GRP's. The most valuable GRP's are those targeted and delivered to the right buyer demographic group. Most advertising which cannot be quantified as part of the general advertising activities will fall under other specialty budgets which are not always administered by the agency, hence removing any interest on the part of the agency to recommend this specialty type of advertising. Typically, the media buys are placed by agencies and paid for by advertisers. The majority of these buys will be national, so that the funding will come from a general advertising budget. Many advertising efforts to date have come from ad-hoc advertising budgets, which are much smaller than the general funds. The larger, nationally represented access providers will capture the lion's share of the advertising dollars available, much as today's broadcast networks capture the lions share of total television advertising dollars. These national access providers will be likely to use an in-house sales team to sell ad placements. Local and regional providers will probably see their advertising revenue develop more slowly.

Compensation based on pay-for-performance methods will not be readily embraced by ad agencies. Pay for performance neglects the fact that good ad work cannot salvage an inferior product, a bad offer or a poor service. Today, agencies need to be compensated for more than just the creative fees. Agencies will want to place buys and perform planning functions within this media just as they do today for traditional media, but a commision or other compensation plan will have to evolve. The ratings metrics, which could be drawn from a consumer panel, will mirror the statistics used today by agencies to measure delivery effectiveness; and it would be a key part of that agency compensation infrastructure. Additional sources on-line related revenue for agencies will be advertising client Internet areas via traditional media such as television, radio, direct mail or print ads.

Will Businesses Pay for On-Line Advertising?

Internet usage has increased an average of 8% per month, roughly doubling in size every year. As Clinton Wilder notes in his recent article[15] on business and the Internet, "If you haven't already added a '.com' electronic mail address to your business card, you will soon." He cites recent improvements in Internet access, such as the World Wide Web (WWW) and graphical browsers like Mosaic as driving the explosive growth of businesses using the Internet and WWW for communication and commerce. Mary Cronin, author of *Doing Business on the Internet*,[16] feels that "Critical mass has arrived." With secure financial transactions coming on-line this year for some networks, Cronin expects this to advance Internet commerce viability even more in 1995.

Businesses detailed in the *Information Week* Special Report included: JP Morgan, Hyatt Hotels, Schlumberger and GE Plastics. These companies all cited valid and quantifiable reasons to justify Internet and WWW access. Wilder points to Ford's interactive CD-ROM disks, Fidelity Investments (Boston) with on-line ads on Prodigy, and Hyatt's Internet Web page of vacation and resort information as examples of good business sense. He summarizes ". . . for big ticket items, it makes good business sense to give buyers as much interactive information as possible."

Gateway and Oracle both signed on as advertisers on Ziff-Davis Web sites. Hot Buttons and point and click icons will appear on the home pages of ZD Net to "lure"[17] users to ads and additional product or usage information about the sponsors' products and services. The cost per advertiser for a full rotation across ZD magazine home pages will total $25,000 per quarter. David Schnaider, V.P. General Manager of ZD Interactive said that rotating the ads will ensure a broader exposure for the advertisers' messages. This network in total has one million pages viewed per month, with 250,000 "accesses" and users spend an average of 5–7 minutes per site.

Almost singlehandedly making a case for on-line consumer panel tracking, General Motors announced it would buy 2–3 million dollars in on-line advertising, provided the "commercial on-line services (VANs) and Internet Web Sites must be accountable for their users by hiring a third party service to certify their subscriber bases." In the same article from *Inside Media*, Wayne Friedman reported that GM planned to "buy a number of hyperlinks" and messages on a mix of online areas.[18]

VAN and On-Line Service Provider Advertising Revenue

Another reason to support on-line consumer panel research is to measure the audience and consumer activity such as shopping and game use across different services. They can also report on the relative audience delivery of larger "hyperlink" areas. On-line service providers act as "directories" capable of delivering users to areas (via hyperlinks), such as commercially sponsored areas in the service or commercially sponsored areas on the Internet where advertiser messages and advertiser/consumer interaction can occur. These services will always present a "Home Page" or a Welcome Page which presents what's new or lists available directories, such as shopping or advertiser directories. Each of these areas will attract a different audience based on their mix of content or services.

This directory capability is like a "Link" from one cyberspace area to another. The user just sees the information requested. Advertisers will buy schedules of links much as with Cable interconnects or Local TV Stations, or TV networks sell today to advertisers. Jeffrey Dearth, presi-

EXHIBIT 21.4 On-line Advertising Delivery Model

Consumer	User PC Session			
Access Method	On-Line Access Provider			
Content Mix	Editorial	Entertainment	Reference	Retail
Exposure Methods	Activerts	Hypertext Links	Static Ads/Notices	
Exposure Types	Active Exposures		Passive	
	Advertiser Controlled Areas			
Advertiser Areas	Internet Home Page	Private BBS	Sponsored Areas/Forums	

dent of *New Republic* magazine points out the "explosion of Web Pages" will make links between pages the key, calling them "the new currency on the Web." Advertisers will buy "schedules" of these links. He further proposed that as the Web grows and moves toward more vertical markets, there will be Web sites relating to "particular special interests" linking together forming the equivalent of special interest "cable" channels.[19] In the figure above, the *Active* exposures include activerts and hypertext links. These active methods of advertising take a consumer to the message, or advertiser controlled area, such as an advertiser's home page.

The service providers will make money from advertisers for the posting of the directory notice or ad, and more from the "pay-for-performance" aspects of delivering consumers to advertisers areas (through these electronically linked addresses). Of course, they also receive the revenue stream for providing the dial-in connectivity to their service or a gateway to the Internet. However, these revenues will not increase and in fact have actually dropped by over 30% from several service providers as competitive pressures to rapidly acquire on-line subscribers continue to mount. This pressure to hold the line on subscriber connectivity costs and the pressure to upgrade infrastructure and services to compete will increase the importance of advertising revenues for these service providers. The advertising-related compensation will clearly drive these service's revenues as advertisers respond to the increased penetration of on-line services. Other infrastructure services to enable this advertising growth include ratings measurement availability (one service provided by the proposed enterprise) and standardized advertising placements[20] and rate cards from on-line services.

Research Methodologies for Advertisers, Agencies, VAN's and On-Line Service Providers

Data will be captured in two forms: audit and longitudinal consumer panel. The first methodology, site-specific audits, would be proprietary studies sponsored by an advertiser or its agency. These would be best suited for business-to-business sites or smaller niche consumer sites which may not be reported in syndicated studies. The audit data will be provided via a purchase of site activity tapes from the specific on-line service. These tapes could be enhanced with site visitor demographic information provided by the on-line service to aid "audience" analysis. The permissible uses of the data will be dependent on the cooperation of the specific on-line service for all data. Wayne Friedman in *Inside Media* reported[21] the on-line services do not want "third party concerns revealing imperfections in their service" and "they want to resell their own user information data because they perceive it to be of tremendous value." Taking a lesson from the consumer packaged goods industry, where retailers resell their own store data tapes to market research companies such as IRI and Nielsen, the on-line services selling their data will ensure that the data is very costly to purchase and that the services will be very restrictive in the allowable uses of the data they provide.

The second methodology, using a longitudinal consumer panel, yields a much more robust and actionable database of media and marketing information. The consumer activity will be captured via a consumer panel research methodology using very passive proprietary data capture techniques. Unlike the site-specific audits mentioned above, where the data are owned by the on-line service, the panel data collected is owned by the enterprise and is fully syndicatable. The most fundamental measure, and the most valued in the next few years, will be GRP types of ratings: measures of audience reach and frequency of exposure to an advertising message. Later, shopping and other "pay-per-use" features (such as on-line games) can be measured to help the players in the on-line economy value their services and set competitive strategy.

The consumer panel methodology will also allow reporting on total on-line activity by consumers which will deliver advertisers, advertising agencies, content providers and on-line services a common measure of consumer advertising impact of PC activity and trends. This type of syndicated information has never before been available for use by on-line services themselves. On-line services will find the cross-service, independently gathered consumer panel information, very useful for strategic decisions such as where to place on-line advertising, evaluation of service performance relative to other services. This information will also lend input to the services strategy: to acquire new visitors or enhance repeat visits by current visitors.

Using the consumer panel methodology, a syndicated panel operator skilled in this type of research could also provide high-end, value-added strategic analytics. These strategic analyses were developed over many years of consumer packaged goods data capture. Dr. Al Kean of Management Science Associates created and refined many of these approaches using longitudinal consumer panel information. Having started their careers at MSA, Tod Johnson and Andy Tarshis join other eminent analysts of these panel data, including Greg Starzynski of the NPD Group, Bernie Ryan of MSA and Todd Hale, Greg Ellis, Rich Maturo, Meredith Spector and Robert Tomei from A.C. Nielsen. Traditional longitudinal consumer panel data enables analysis of a specific site or VAN for Visitor Demographics, Site or VAN Trial & Repeat, Cross-Site Visitation, VAN Loyalty (Share of On-Line Requirements), Activity Group based analytics (such as profiles of frequent visitors) and many others.

Several years ago, while working with Andy Tarshis on "Single-Source" consumer panels, Rich Maturo and I produced some very exciting analyses where consumer panel purchasing was tied to the households actual television viewing. We gained unique experience analyzing commercial viewing and consumer purchase activity from a panel of 6,000 households in New York, Chicago and Los Angeles. This experience is directly applicable to tracking consumer on-line advertising exposure and on-line purchase activity.

For an example of these analytics, picture a report covering on-line shopping area visitors. The report would list demographic groups, and for each group the report would list the on-line shopping areas. Shoppers visiting multiple "virtual malls" in the report period would be tracked and an interaction index could be generated revealing cross shopping patterns.

Another useful analysis would be a conversion measure which would be the ratio of buying visitors at a site to the total site visitors for the same time period. Using a consumer panel methodology, buyer demographics could be reported, as well as repeat visitation frequency and information on items purchased.

Another report could detail sites visited by heavy on-line game players, and detail the interactions of those heavy players with other sites. This would highlight the best areas on which to place advertising to reach heavy on-line game players. The same analysis could be done for sites on gardening information, sports information, fashion, automobiles, travel and other sites. Since we are considering a longitudinal consumer panel, we can track consumer exposure and flow not only on the Internet and Web sites, but also on Value Added Networks.

PC Media Market Segments

Besides the customer segments listed in Exhibit 21.5, other major purchasers of these data will be Financial Analysts; Telco/Cable/Television Strategic Planners, Banks and Credit Card issuers and advertising sales brokers (like today's Local Television Station Sales Rep Firm) who will sell advertising space for regional Internet access providers who won't have an internal advertising sales force like the larger network providers will.

On-Line Services Face Increased Competition

This potentially huge advertising market has attracted the attention of some very well-funded competitors who have already started, or are starting, new Value Added Networks (VAN's) and other on-line access services.

EXHIBIT 21.5 The Market for On-Line Research By Type of Data

Market Segment	Consumer On-Line Usage		Consumer Off-Line PC Usage		Consumer/Business Custom Audits	
	Basic Syndicated Analytics	Value Added Analytics	Basic Syndicated Analytics	Value Added Analytics	AD-Hoc Custom Audits	On-Going Custom Audits
Ad Agency Media Buyers	✓		✓			
Advertiser Strategic Planners	✓	✓	✓	✓	✓	✓
Software Publishing Planners		✓	✓	✓		
Value Added Networks–Consumer	✓	✓		✓		
VAN Content Providers–Consumer	✓	✓	✓			
Internet Site Producers–Consumer	✓	✓			✓	✓
Internet Site Producers–Business					✓	✓
Private Network Producers–Business					✓	✓

Microsoft and IBM have each established their own on-line networks and will bill users monthly for access through their networks.[22] Leveraging their broadly installed user base for their operating systems, both firms will have the phone numbers for their respective networks included as defaults in their new operating system releases. Microsoft is including "one-button" access to the Internet in its new release of Windows 95, slated to ship in August. IBM announced similar access in its new release of OS/2 Warp, which has already shipped.

AT&T is expected to release their on-line service any day, Pacific Bell (California) is aggressively signing up their installed telephone customers to Pacific Bell's access network. Netcom, and other Internet access providers are also marketing their firms, although more through niche media. These smaller Internet providers are typically regional, drawing business and advertising opportunities from their respective regions. These larger access providers will have the ability to deliver and sell national "advertising" in an on-line format, and that will enable agencies to allocate funds from a larger general advertising fund, moving away from current ad-hoc budgets.

Times-Mirror Co., Tribune Co., *The Washington Post*, Knight-Ridder and the Newhouse Family's *Advance Publications* have all purchased a $20 million equity stake (about 15%) of NETSCAPE, which is the most popular (estimates at 90%) Web browser in use today. The Bozell business to business unit handling Netscape advertising says ". . . the home page of the upgraded Netscape navigator will have ads from AT&T, EDS, General Motors, MasterCard, Adobe and Netcom.[23] These advertisers paid a $40,000 fee to appear on the Netscape home page.

The newspapers mentioned above were motivated to pursue their own on-line service access because of the unattractive financial terms offered them by the other established on-line services. As content providers and advertisers negotiate the best placement and "distribution" channels for their content, longitudinal viewer research will be critical to support this industry's marketing information needs as the technology and industry competition continues its evolution.

The Competitive Environment for On-Line Research

One of the first Interactive research services, Pathfinder, was announced from ASI/Arbitron/Next Century Media, and it validated the advertising industry's interest in this information. General Motors announced an agreement with this research entity for $200,000 worth of information. Others, including Bell South, were announced as expected to sign deals soon. The consortium (CASIE), formed under the auspices of the Association of National Advertisers , American Association of Advertising Agencies and the Advertising Research Foundation, has validated their approach using what is being referred to as "clickstreams." The panel approach uses this same "approved" clickstream methodology, expanding it to track unique consumer activity across services. Within weeks, ASI dropped out of the earlier alignment and joined a new entity with Nielsen Media and Yankelovich called ANYwhere research. While this new group was announced in the *Wall Street Journal* in early June, there were no products or services announced, only that the entity would look into research on the Internet.

Several companies have reportedly talked with on-line services to discuss subscriber demographic and activity information which the services should be capturing. These services expect to purchase data directly from the on-line services to act as "third party validators," reporting user visitation frequency and length of stay. These competitors will be limited to reporting only through cooperating services probably for an increasing percentage of revenue, and will be forced to use inaccurate household level demographic overlays for user information since detailed personal information is not likely to be readily available from service users given current privacy concerns. At the least the information will be of limited marketing value at an individual user level. The information captured from each service, and the quality of that information is also likely to vary for each on-line service.

These third-party audit-type research services would deliver more commodity-like information when compared to the information available from a consumer panel. A consumer panel would be the industry's sole resource for interaction and trial and repeat types of information across services and sites. The consumer panel operator would be in a competitive position which would not be dependent on service provider data cooperation or payments to those services. In the long term, costs for data will be a marked advantage of the consumer panels, since there will be an incentive for the services to sell their usage information at an increasing cost to the "third party validators." I would draw comparisons between packaged goods research suppliers like Nielsen and IRI who purchase data tapes from retailers for a price and they are dependent on broad industry participation by the retailers for their data "raw materials." A panel service, which collects data directly from the consumer, is usually a syndicated service with the freedom to compare effectiveness and audience across services and competing sites. This panel service would not require without requiring on-line service cooperation, restrictive covenants regarding the permissible uses of the data or onerous payments for data access.

The audit approach will provide more accurate accounting of less popular or niche consumer on-line sites and a means to measure business-to-business site visitation. Each methodology of capturing consumer behavior has its advantages, and there is a place for both in the market. In any case, we can be sure that a consumer panel service will provide unquestionably superior insights into on-line user behavior, trends and attitudes.

Alternative Consumer PC Media Research Methodologies

Traditional "Recall-Based" Ad-Hoc Consumer Research

Methodology description. This broadly described set of traditional non-longitudinal research methods for conducting direct consumer research is the most typical type of research currently being conducted on today's consumer PC media usage. Telephone, mail, and even some On-Line Survey methods are all being employed by a variety of firms to serve their respective interests.

These sample sizes have ranged from several hundred to several thousand, although none have been conducted on a longitudinal sample. Arbitron had announced a periodic survey to be conducted named PATHFINDER. This survey was recall-based and asked a broad range of questions on on-line media usage. It earned the firm publicity in *Ad Age, Inside Media, The Wall Street Journal* and other publications. Next Century Media of Woodstock New York and ASI of Glendale, California, also cooperated with some of the Pathfinder project.

Odyssey Research conducted a frequently cited study which clustered users into technology receptive groups, and providing demographics for the groups. This was a one-time study not likely to be repeated. Specialty consultant firms such as Frank Magid Associates, Arlen Communications, and a handful of others, including management consulting firms like Andersen Consulting and Coopers and

Lybrand[23]have conducted studies which are frequently intended to provide public relations exposure for the firms within their area of recognized expertise, such as retailing, catalogs, direct marketing or technology management.

Dr. Sunil Gupta[25] is conducting a business panel survey to attempt to assess business uses on the World Wide Web, and it will probably be the most definitive work in this area. Dr. Gupta had completed a similar survey of consumer use last year and the results will be forthcoming shortly.

Methodology Strengths and Weaknesses. All of the ad-hoc approaches mentioned above are designed to provide early indications of the attitudes and opinions of users, self-reported users and recalled usage of on-line services. The shortcomings of any recall-based methodology are readily known. Plus the ad-hoc approach cannot deliver actionable marketing insights into usage patterns and the user graphics important for setting accurate ratings information.

One clear advantage of these traditional random sample research methodologies is that a sample can be asked questions which may be inappropriate for an on-going consumer tracking panel, such as personal questions on religious affiliation or political opinions. They may also allow fast reads of specific questions via phone studies. A disadvantage of this technique is respondent representation within a small "random" sample.

Important Trends. These traditional researchers mentioned above will find it increasingly difficult to attract quality random samples given increased unlisted numbers, privacy concerns, the recurring threat of increased government legislation and the increase of unscrupulous firms selling under the guise of research. Consenting participants in longitudinal panels typically exhibit a response rate of 75% or more to monthly attitude and opinion surveys.

Specialized ad-hoc research will always be an important research tool, and firms will continue to provide this type of research to the PC media industry through a mix of field methods and with varying degrees of quality.

Valuable Custom Ad -Hoc Survey capabilities is another service that can be sold in the form of custom monthly surveys which are distributed electronically to the PC consumer panel. These survey data, including attitude and opinion information can be linked to actual PC usage for unique marketing insights. For example, a survey of user's print media reading habits might be compared to on-line magazine access areas for the purposes of cross media promotion. Heavy game users on-line may exhibit very specific attitudes about certain other recreational interests off-line, which could lead to special Internet links being promoted on those game areas home pages.

On-Line Network Cooperation Model

Network Cooperation Methodology Description.

This area is the most popular area of research being focused on by Arbitron, Nielsen, possibly Audits and Surveys[26] and other research suppliers. Under this model, a third-party "Auditor" such as Nielsen or Arbitron, could be contracted by the on-line service provider such as America On-Line or by an advertiser, such as Colgate to perform an audit of the number of "hits" or on-line users exposed to that area. The networks are logging household data by account ID and they are thus able to provide information on which users went where and for how long on their service.

The key point for the on-line services is that the processing of this information is required to help sell and value the consumer traffic and exposures in those areas. The services cannot do this themselves because of credibility reasons. However, to adopt a census approach, such as reporting on all users' activity for each minute of every day would not be very cost effective. Some summarization of the data will be likely.

Comparing these data to Supermarket data tapes Nielsen and IRI currently get from their retail panel,[27] the amount of data will typically have a time value for the service and they will summarize the records. Supermarkets report on unit sales by UPC each week, and what the price was. To store every transaction and every product for an average of 15,000 trips per week, and an average of about $125 per week of UPCs would be very expensive for each retail store to capture, log and transmit. With several million users logging in to an ever broadening mix of areas and services, the costs to maintain transactional data for each user will force some level of summarization to balance costs with the minimum information required to sell advertising.

Methodology Strengths and Weaknesses. The major strength of this methodology is that a "census" approach is expected. All users of the service will have all actions tracked and logged at all times. This is not a realistic expectation because of two reasons: (1) the cost of storing and accessing these detailed data transactions for all users, and

EXHIBIT 21.6 Service Provider Cooperation Data Collection Model

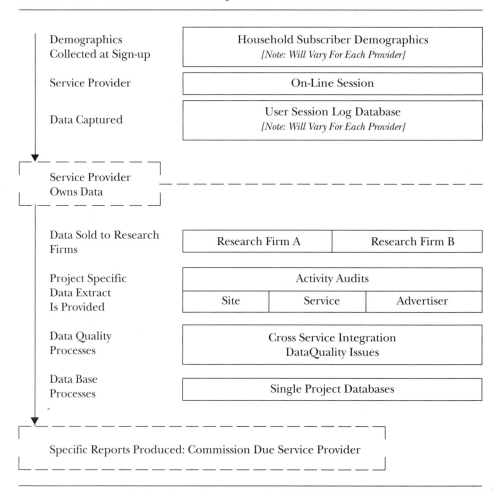

(2) The difficulty and expense of capturing and maintaining user demographic, attitude and opinion and purchasing transactions. As supermarkets have learned, these services will also learn which records are relevant for them to store and resell to third party auditors. There will be a clear marginal expense at some point which will not justify logging all data for all customers. These services will be in the business of selling advertising access. Technology offers the hope of total information, but the fiscal realities do not.

Third-Party Auditors' Costs. The major cost a third-party auditor will bear is the cost for data access. Since these data are acquired and "owned" by the on-line service provider, there will always be the need to "pay the piper." Supermarket chains learned within a few years that reselling their already captured sales (front-end scanning) information would yield a new profit center. Nielsen and IRI both bid up the value of these tapes, and without any replacement goods, they are still forced to pay onerous fees to the retailers for the retailers' tapes of store-scanned sales. Neither vendor could deliver on its contracts without the weekly retailer tapes. A similar model applies to third-party auditors seeking "tapes" of on-line user activity. Costs will only rise as the on-line services realize their monopolistic pricing and attempt to maximize value for their firm through increased cooperator costs for data tapes. Therefore, each sale will already be burdened with a commission fee due to the on-line service provider which could be 10%-25% of the project cost to the client,[28] usually the advertiser.

Additionally, the data will be delivered in disparate media and formats. The actual detail and accuracy of the data collected will vary for each separate service. Most services will also place restrictions and covenants on the legal use of the data sold to the third party vendor. For instance, the data may not be released for publication without prior clauses and will almost definitely not be approved for release or comparison to other on-line services. The differences in data collected mentioned above will likely contribute to a confusion under this multi-supplier scenario as well.

Measuring Unique Site Visitors—An Issue of Data Quality. Advertisers are interested in the effective exposures of their message to the targeted audience in the method and frequency which will deliver the desired result and lead to a purchase decision of the advertiser's product or service. Most methods used today to capture information on-site visitors have several shortcomings. They only measure "hits," which is generally a gross count of the number of times a site is accessed. This does not allow the capture of repeat visitation, key indicator of most sites' long-term success or delivery on the promised benefit.

A new service from Internet Profiles Corp., named I/Count[29] assigns a unique ID code to the IP address coming into a site. This helps with repeat read, but many users have multiple Internet accounts, like one at work and another from America On-Line, each will have a different IP address. The next question important to a marketer is "Who are these people accessing my site?" Internet Profiles president will introduce I/Code in the third quarter which will be a standard software registration form that will give users an incentive to provide demographic data voluntarily. Because of privacy concerns mentioned earlier, and the obvious annoyance factor associated with entering personal information to just about every home page, users will get tired of logging onto those sites and many sites will sacrifice key data for less valuable information on its site attendees.

On-Line Service Competitor Cooperation. It is extremely unlikely that any on-line service will allow release of its ratings data to any other service. It is even more unlikely that the larger VAN services would actually provide data consistently over time for ratings purposes. These proposed service reported data, being supplied by the service themselves, would also be suspect to most savvy advertisers and agencies.

As an early example of industry cooperation, Prodigy conducted an independent audit by the print industry auditor, Audit Bureau of Circulation. Other on-line providers did not follow suit and thus Prodigy gave its competitors an unfair advantage, forcing Prodigy to cancel its audience measurement attempt.

In this period of increasing competition with new services competing for the hotly growing pool of potential subscribers, it is extraordinarily unlikely that on-line service providers would release or make public in a cooperative mode, what they will consider to be proprietary marketing information. This reinforces the need for the independently operated, statistically supported consumer based panel methodology for measuring ad performance and "audience" for this and other PC based media.

Consumer Panel Research Model

Consumer Panel Methodology Description. Consumers have agreed to join and cooperate on panels since the 1950s in the United States. They will typically be selected via acceptable market research standards in order to represent an appropriately geographic and demographic population. The most recent U.S. Census projections are typical targets. Since these individuals volunteer to participate, lifestage and demographic information is more readily captured at a convenient time only once per year at their choice of time to complete. The information captured is generally more accurate and complete than ad-hoc phone or mail surveys. This person based information is then analyzed together with logged activity information captured from the person's PC

EXHIBIT 21.7 Consumer Panel Data Collection Model

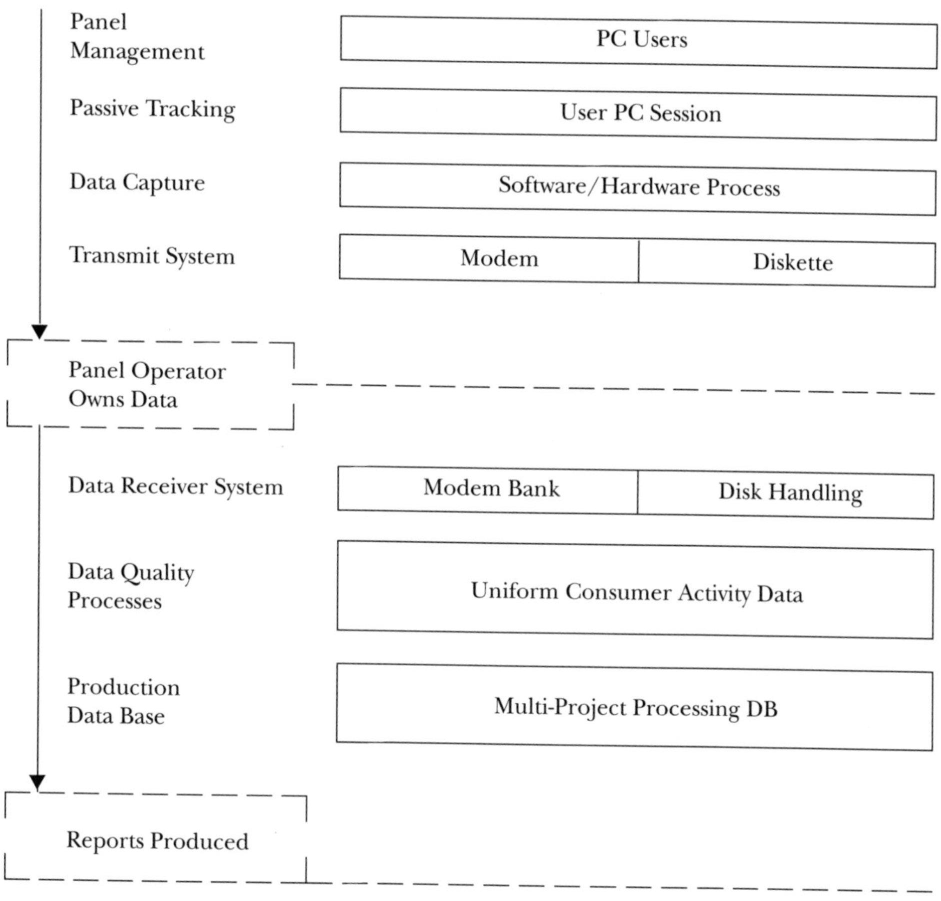

Panel Management	**PC Users**
Passive Tracking	User PC Session
Data Capture	Software/Hardware Process
Transmit System	Modem / Diskette

Panel Operator Owns Data

Data Receiver System	Modem Bank / Disk Handling
Data Quality Processes	Uniform Consumer Activity Data
Production Data Base	Multi-Project Processing DB

Reports Produced

Media habits, such as site visit time, length of visit, repeat visitation, responses, interactivity, and GRP Rating, and share of voice equivalent for that individual's demographic group. Specialized reference resources are also created to understand the types of programs, services and activity users are accessing through their PC media. Highly customized proprietary analysis and basic syndicated analytics would be deliverables.

Consumer PC Panel. The sample will be controlled to balance PC ownership across major census age, income, education and other demographics such as to present a projectable sample to the total U.S., in terms of PC ownership and usage. The panel will also be balanced to represent modem ownership as well as CD-ROM ownership, among the home PC population.

Methodology Strengths and Weaknesses. Consumer participate in Consumer Panels for surprisingly similar reasons each time they have been surveyed and for whatever type of data collection methodology is used, even diaries or questionnaires. The reason cited most frequently for participation is "To have my opinions heard". Other factors noted to drive participation have included feeling special by participating, being interested in the methodology (such as when technology is involved in the data capture) and getting the gifts. Actual gift values per year are typically in the range of forty to seventy dollars per panelist per year.

Since panelists volunteer, and with effectively managed continuity programs, they continue to participate for multiple years.[30] They also willingly release their activity information to you for their time on the panel. This information is owned by the venture, and constitutes an asset, although there is a limited value for old inventory, referred to as "back data" and usually being more than six months old. The privacy of the participating individuals is respected, but since they represent a sample of representative demographics, their individual behavior will be projected to represent the estimated universe of PC-using consumers. The data will always be reported on at a reasonable level of aggregation for analytical or market targeting purposes.

Shopping On-Line. Even without the secure transaction capability, shopping services are making money on-line. There are eighty merchants in CompuServe's electronic mall. Shopping 2000, the internet shopping mall from Contentware carries J.C. Penney, Spiegel, and a dozen other high-profile marketers. The two major CD-ROM catalog "malls" are Magellan's "The Merchant" with 39 catalogers and Redgate's 2Market with 28 catalogers. These catalogers pay between $20,000-$40,000 per release to include their products in the CD-ROM.

ProductView is an advertiser supported service which seeks to be paid by advertisers for only the "hits" it delivers, including the names and addresses it hopes to capture from information seeking on-line shoppers.

Financial services, leisure and travel, and automotive marketers have been very active on-line and with interactive disks or CD-ROM interactive advertising efforts.

Security is cited as a real concern among businesses and consumers when asked about actually selling on an on-line service. Wilder reports that dozens of security software suppliers are working to solve the security problem.[31] Two noteworthy partnerships in this area are Microsoft-VISA International and CommerceNet-RSA Data Security. Although expected soon, adequate security for financial transactions does not currently exist. When it does, expect consumer on-line shopping to increase. On-line ordering capability would enable households with one phone line to order and interact with customer service while active in the shopping area. Today, an on-line shopper (usually) must exit the on-line area and then phone an 800 number and order as via a catalog.

A consumer panel should include tracking of the various PC-based shopping applications and the on-line shopping applications. As connectivity bandwith becomes both cheaper and widely available, this area will explode. Catalog marketers continue to face sharply rising paper costs and continual postal rate increases. Bandwidth and security will enable On-Line Shopping to be the next "killer app" of PC Media.

Marketing Issues Best Answered Through Consumer Panel Information

Since these panelists will be reporting unique activity within the household and by each active member of the household, our mix of marketing information services will be quite robust. The unique mix of marketing information available will address issues for on-line marketers, advertisers and service providers as well as software publishers and distributors.

Issues addressed will include: Which services provided the highest access period in prime time? What was the demographic profile of the frequent visitor to an advertiser's Internet home page? How many repeat visitors are there per month? How many accessed each of the advertisers who had "links"[32] from my site? Am I charging enough for my effective spots as a network service? Am I paying a reasonable fee and am I reaching the right target audience if I am an advertiser? Who is advertising where? How frequently? How successful is it for them? Which services and which times are the best for me to reach my audience? Who's shopping, and how many come back to buy? What software publisher's software is losing ground, and which need a re-stage? What software retail channel (on-line, catalog, DM, retail) is doing better with what types of software? Who is buying and what are they paying? Who are my heavy users and what else do they do with their PC time? Do I have copromotion opportunities? As an on-line service, are there PC applications for which I should be selling or renting access time? How else can I reach other people like my heavy users, to attract new site visitors?

Key Trends Supporting Consumer Panel Research

Misuse of personal information gathered under the guise of research (Selling-Under-Guise) is a problem already impacting the research industry. Powerful headlines pressure government to focus on privacy, such as through Vice President Gore's Privacy Working Group. They were presented guidelines for on-line service privacy by the Interactive Service Association[33] which allowed the services to sell subscriber names by notifying the subscriber at sign up time and there will be an easy "opt-out" method to allow users to say no to disclosure of their names. Most relevant to this proposal is the following reported stipulation "Only names, addresses and *broad usage patterns may be exchanged or rented; no list may include data on individual session activities.*" In that same article Editor John Featherman of *The Privacy Newsletter*, called the ISA's self-regulation a farce noting that the profit-minded will ignore no-penalty guidelines.

A few very public abusers of privacy, some of whom may try and capture lists under the guise of research will cause laws to be passed limiting the value of the demographic and activity based reporting of the Service Network Cooperation model, and will support the voluntary consumer panel method. Even when collected, the marketing value and useability of the information collected will limit its research value.

Privacy issues on-line are hot topics, and it is likely the government may pass privacy laws which would restrict release of information passively captured from the on-line services without the permission of users.

More likely, users will be very wary of releasing their demographic information on-line when asked on-line. As Iang Jeon, Director of electronic marketing at Fidelity Investments noted "Just because of technology, we can't lose sight of the customer. We wouldn't ask a customer walking into an investment center to fill out a questionnaire.

People will accept commercialization of the Web, but you have to do it the right way."

The panel allows information to be collected once per year, and the panel operators credibility must be established with the panelist for those first contacts. This could be addressed by judicious use of selected direct mail contact, the use of unique ID numbers when on-line, and on-going panel participation compensation/incentive plans.

People will always respond to certain human wants and needs. Based on historical levels of cooperation, we can always expect people to participate in research, provided it is real and they feel they are being heard and making a contribution to how we live. The consumer panel is the only viable methodology for on-line marketers to measure switching behavior between networks, and to report on comparative shares and marketplace strengths. It will be the best way to measure on-line advertising, on-line sales of consumer goods and services and the sources of on-line links. On-line marketers will then have the powerful consumer insights that have been used for years by sophisticated packaged goods marketers.

References

1. These large Value Added Networks (Commercial On-Line Services: CompuServe, AOL, Prodigy) as well as new Internet Connection Services recently announced by Pacific Bell (focused on California market) and MCI (national focus) provide a "directory" type of service to users and advertisers since these services represent a Users Point-of-Entry into the on-line environment. They can sell space to promote other product or service commercial areas in other parts of the Internet. This function of funneling or directing users to certain areas will make these Value added networks valuable "Virtual Real Estate", much as Supermarkets control product placement on their shelves, and thus directly aid a given products sales by placing it on an end-aisle display.

2. Adobe announced a pending commercial release of a version of Adobe's ACROBAT graphical design and layout software. This release, which has been in beta test for four months, is expected to be released this April. It was co-developed with Netscape, and will be distributed via the Internet. The new ACROBAT graphical software will allow easy creation of Internet Home Pages without forcing a user to learn HTML (Hypertext Markup Language). This will facilitate Internet use for business and consumers. *InformationWeek,* March 24, 1995.

3. Jeffrey Dearth, President of *New Republic* magazine; *Electronic Marketplace Sourcebook*, January 1995, Thompson Publishing Group, p. 4.

4. Personal Digital Assistant—PDA's are essentially PC's designed for maximum portability with very small form factors, typically with touch screens, stylus pointing devices and wireless communications capability.

5. *Forbes ASAP*, April 10,1995, p.72; Additional reference is given to information from Veronis, Suhler & Associates, Jupiter Communications, Electronic Industries and Wilkofski, Gruen Associates.

6. Ibid

7. Tom Noglows & Tom Steinert-Threlkeld, *Interactive Week*, May 22, 1995, p. 15.

8. Katy M. Bachman, American Demographics, Marketing Tools publication, March/April 1995, p. 59.

9. Forrester Research, as quoted in *Forbes ASAP*, April 10, 1995, p. 69.

10. Scott Donaton, *Advertising Age*, Spring 1995 Special Edition , p. 54.

11. Richard Rappaport, *Forbes ASAP*, April 10, 1995, p. 66.

12. Nielsen Media provides these surrogate GRP ratings and demographic services for several types of alternative media such as Airport News Channels and other place based media. Having these ratings available enables buying and selling of advertising on these media within existing agency/client relationships.

13. Wayne Friedman and Jane Weaver, "Calculating Cyberspace: Tracking 'Clickstreams'", *Inside Media*, February 15–28, 1995, pps. 1, 44.

14. Founded in 1987, clients include United Airlines, Motorola, TV Guide On-Screen, Pacific Bell and Apple Computers.

15. Clinton Wilder; "The Internet Pioneers", Information Week, January 9, 1995, pps. 38–48.

16. Doing Business on the Internet, Mary Cronin, published by Van Nostrand Reinhold, 1994.

17. Martin O'loughlin, "Home-Page Positioning"; *Inside Media*, p. 13.

18. Wayne Friedman, "GM Dangling Cyberspace Dollars"; Inside Media, p. 8.

19. Jeffrey Dearth, President of *New Republic* magazine; *Electronic Marketplace Sourcebook*, January 1995, Thompson Publishing Group, p. 4.

20. An Advertisers Internet site, created using HTML, follows the de facto standard available now. These sites can be found using a Mosaic type "Browser". The site can also be transparently accessed from network areas where "featured" or regular service listings in the major Value Added Services.

21. Wayne Friedman, "GM Dangling Cyberspace Dollars", *Inside Media,* May 24, 1995, p. 8.

22. Christine Hudgins-Bonafield; "How will the Internet Grow?", *Network Computing,* Mar 1, 1995, p. 84.

23. John Motavalli, *Inside Media,* March 29, 1995, pp. 4 and 45.

24. Emerging Retail Formats Conference, May 26–27, NYC, Sponsored by International Business Communications.

25. Research Project on the Commercial Uses of the World Wide Web, University of Michigan Business School, Ann Arbor. Conducted 4/95–6/95.

26. Audits and Surveys presented an Audit based approach for analysis of on-line service usage at the ARF conference in March 1994, although their PR since has been minimal.

27. Nielsen and IRI acquire data from approx. 3500 supermarkets nationally each. They are beginning to capture "census" or all data, each transaction, all stores, but it is expensive to maintain because the data are voluminous.

28. While this fee is clearly negotiable, the percentages mentioned are typical cooperation fees seen with retailer data sales for test projects in the Consumer Packaged Goods industry.

29. Clinton Wilder, "Know Your Net Surfers", *Information Week,* April 17, 1995, p. 30.

30. To avoid panelist bias, whether perceived or real, some panels are rotated (panelists are regularly removed from the panel and new panelists are added. This approach does have operations expenses which may or may not be justified in designing the panel methodology.

31. Wilder, p. 39.

32. Hotlinks between internet sites activated by clicking on a logo or an ad space in one area which automatically takes you to the next "linked" space.

33. Jeffrey O'Brien, "Just A Slight Omission", *DIRECT* magazine, May 1995, pps. 1, 43.

22

Marketing Communications Engineering

Using Self-Organizing Neural Networks

Martin Block

Martin Block is Professor of Integrated Marketing Communications in the Medill School of Journalism of Northwestern University. His research, which focuses on analytical tools and marketing communications technology, has appeared in academic journals and in the business press all over the world. He is author of *Business-to-Business Marketing Research* and (with John Totten) of *Analyzing Sales Promotion*. Block was involved in the early development of QUBE and in National Science Foundation-sponsored research involving two-way cable.

Marketing communications professionals in the past have had to rely primarily on their accumulated knowledge of industry lore and their own intuition to manage their activity. While empirical research commonly plays a role in the marketing communications process, it is often inconsistent in its quality and application, and often seen by the marketing communications professional as having limited value. Typical responses to the question "Why isn't research used more?" are that it costs too much, isn't relevant, or stifles creative thinking.

Computer technology, however, is about to remove these objections and radically change the way marketing communications is managed. Computer technology dramatically lowers the cost of data collection and storage so that, unlike in the past, data is both plentiful *and* accessible. Scanner data, marketing databases, and syndicated data have all become part of the marketing communications lexicon. A major problem for many of today's researchers is that they must shift from collecting data and designing research to making sense out of these relatively new and large quantities of already existing data. The market research task is increasingly becoming an analytical one.

Computer technology is likely to influence analytical methods as well. Today's analytical tools should eliminate, or at least diminish, problems with data relevance in order to allow virtually any kind of data or group comparison for managers at all levels of analytical sophistication. These tools should support and *encourage* creative thinking and informed decision making regarding key strategic marketing problems.

The term *marketing communications engineering* refers to a collection of analytical tools and procedures that require both extensive data and computerization. The underlying computational procedures are typically recursive or iterative and wouldn't be possible in practical terms without reasonably powerful computers. Examples of these analytical tools include artificial neural networks and non-linear dynamics.

While the tools and procedures themselves are interesting, the true test is in their application to marketing communications problems. Characterizing these tools as "engineering" science is meant to suggest the application of analytical techniques that previously have not been applied to marketing communications, or that have been abandoned but will solve a number of previously intractable marketing communications problems. The term *engineering* also fits because of the underlying mathematical sophistication and dependence on data. Engineering also distinguishes the tools and techniques from the traditional linear statistical approaches that most market researchers have been trained to use. For instance, artificial neural networks are a good example of a technique that previously has not been used in the context of marketing communications. Computer simulation and expert systems are examples of techniques that have been abandoned, but that hold great potential for managing communications today.

What follows is a brief description of some of the tools and techniques and the marketing communications problems that they help solve.

Traditional Analytical Approaches

Most marketing communications professionals have been well trained in using the general linear statistical model. They know how to run regression analyses and can compute and interpret chi-squares. Market research courses across the country have taught these techniques for years and continue to do so.

These traditional analytical tools were developed in an environment where data was expensive and difficult to collect and computational procedures were viewed as difficult and time-consuming. Data collection techniques and survey research methods occupy the content of most traditional market research courses. The presumption, of course, has always been that data is not available. Analytical techniques, referred to as "statistics," have consisted of turgid computational procedures accomplished with desk-top calculators for many years. In fact, most of the traditional analytical tools, such as multiple regression, have been adapted to computers from hand procedures. Computers in this case have served only to make the computational process much faster and easier. Furthermore, the underlying assumptions with traditional procedures, particularly in the use of a static linear model to describe relationships among variables, still apply—the technique has simply been automated.

These traditional analyses were not developed with the full capability of the computer in mind, such as the ability to iterate. And while supermarket checkout data, or "scanner data" as it is commonly labeled, was always potentially available, it was never practical to collect until a bar-code reader was attached to a micro-computer and placed in the checkout aisle. Computerization has made it much easier to collect and store data so that now marketing "databases" abound. The environment today is extraordinarily data rich, not data poor, as traditionally assumed.

The Marketing Communications Engineering Approach

Marketing communications engineering is the application of analytical techniques and procedures that require computerization. The techniques assume from the start that the phenomena being modeled are dynamic, that the relationships among variables are often non-linear, and that there is more than sufficient descriptive data available.

The beginnings of the notion of marketing communications engineering can be found in Claude Shannon and Warren Weaver's, *The Mathematical Theory of Communication*, first published in 1949. This ground-breaking book describes communication as a process that can be modeled mathematically. Other developments contributing to this idea include: the pursuit of artificial intelligence, better communication measurement, the advent of widespread syndicated marketing data, and the birth of chaos science. All of these developments share strong common threads of a mathematical nature and reliance on computer technology.

Artificial Intelligence and Neural Networks

The pursuit of artificial intelligence—that is, getting a computer to think like a human being—has yet to reach its promised goal. Out of the effort, though, has grown rule-based expert systems and simulations which have application in marketing communications planning. Expert systems today, for example, provide the interface between the analyst and the market data provided by both Information Resources Incorporated (IRI) and Nielsen Marketing Research. The rule-based expert system still doesn't play a very good game of chess but is efficient at pre-processing very large data files.

Artificial neural networks have arisen from the notion of artificial intelligence. Sometimes referred to as "connectionists," artificial neural network developers have been able to solve a number of practical problems, thereby generating some publicity. While neural network theory will be discussed in more detail later, it is important to note that there are two main types of networks: those which are supervised and those which are unsupervised (or self-organizing).

Supervised artificial neural networks consist of a system of neurons or "nodes" and connections among them where some of the neurons can be designated as input neurons and some as output neurons. The state of the input and output neurons are known, so the problem becomes one of establishing the appropriate connections between the input and output neurons, along with hidden neurons that may exist between them. These connections are established through an interactive training process. The resulting network model can then receive new input and predict the appropriate output.

A supervised artificial neural network is very similar to multiple regression, with dependent output variables and independent input variables. Actually, most problems that lend themselves to regression also lend themselves to supervised artificial neural networks. It is debatable as to which performs better. Analysts who work with both techniques generally say that regression, in the hands of a very skilled analyst, can outperform the artificial neural network. In the hands of a much less skilled analyst, however, the neural network will win. To date at least, supervised artificial neural networks have not revolutionized marketing analysis.

The self-organizing, or unsupervised, artificial neural network is a different story. These networks do not have inputs or outputs, but rather only patterns of connections. The self-organizing neural network must determine the connections in ways other than training. The self-organizing network is a logical extension of a perceptual map and provides a powerful tool for developing and evaluating marketing communications messages. This will be discussed in some detail later. For more information about artificial neural networks, the Rumelhart and McClelland book, *Parallel Distributed Processing: Explorations in the Microstructure of Cognition*, is an excellent source.

Better Measurement

Better communication measurement has been available for many years, but has not seen widespread acceptance in the marketing community. Metric multidimensional scaling (MMDS) has been around for over thirty years. The necessary computer programs were developed at Bell Labs before divestiture. Newer algorithms have found their way into today's popular statistical packages and are readily available. Still MMDS marketing applications are not used in proportion to the utility of the technique. Part of the reason for this lack of use has been the lack of understanding of the method and the past difficulty in accessing the software.

One of the most innovative metric MDS approaches is the Galileo^{tm} system described by Woelfel and Fink in *The Measurement of Communication Processes: Galileo Theory and Method.* The Galileo method works from metric similarity or distance data among a set of concepts, providing a perceptual "map" that visually shows the closeness, or relationships, among the concepts. In addition, Galileo will geometrically derive potential message strategies to move one concept toward another target concept in the perceptual space based on these relationships. The message strategy capability of the Galileo system is now more than twenty years old.

The problem that Galileo has experienced is that it originated as a mainframe program with a somewhat awkward user interface; this limited its availability. Galileo has since been released in a microcomputer version that is very easy to use (Windows95^{tm} and Unix versions) distributed through Terra Research & Computing.

Artificial neural networks logically extend the use of perceptual maps to generate message strategies. It is Joseph Woelfel, the developer of the Galileo system itself, who saw this connection and has since added the neural network components to the system. The neural network component is one of the few self-organizing software systems available today and actually has application far beyond the analysis of perceptual maps and communication message strategies. The self-organizing neural network computer tool can be applied to the analysis of syndicated marketing data, including the rather difficult problem of combining databases.

Syndicated Marketing Data

Data is now available to the marketing communications strategist in quantities and quality never before imagined. Data describing characteristics of buyers and prospects, purchase behavior, and media consumption are readily available for most product categories. The user, however, must select the critical data from the vast oceans of available data and apply the appropriate analysis to that data in order to answer the managerial questions at hand.

Syndicated data is almost always dynamic, requiring time series analysis. This is especially true for sales data. Traditional time series analyses require a highly skilled analyst to tease out the critical relationships. Issues such as seasonal factors, autocorrelation, non-linear relationships, and variable interactions all require special attention. A good description of the state-of-the-art of marketing-related time series analysis can be found in the Hanssens, Parsons and Schultz book, *Market Response Models: Econometric and Time Series Analysis.* This type of analysis uses the computer mainly for its computational speed, depending upon the special skill and insight of the analyst.

Managing and understanding tactical marketing interventions such as advertising and sales promotion has evolved to a practice often labeled "fact-based" marketing. This requires an analyst to identify a historical sales baseline from the time series data and then predict the division of sales into base versus incremental volume. Presumably incremental volume is attributable to the marketing tactic. The ability to predict incremental sales attributable to a marketing effort depends upon the establishment of an accurate baseline.

Experience has shown that computation of the baseline using traditional methods is more difficult than it might first appear to be. Baselining is today one of the most controversial methodological issues surrounding the analysis of syndicated market sales data. For a more detailed discussion of baselining and fact-based marketing, see Totten and Block, *Analyzing Sales Promotion.*

Chaos Science

A very important potential element in marketing communications engineering is the development of the new chaos science. Chaos theory has been applied mainly in other fields, such as quantum physics and fluid dynamics. Application of the theory to marketing communications has received only slight attention.

Some very preliminary attempts have been made to apply chaos theory to the understanding of marketing sales data. In this case, a method referred to as "rescaled range analysis," used to understand the water level of the Nile River, was borrowed. The sales data clearly exhibit "chaos," and the analysis provides a theoretical reason why baselining is so difficult and controversial. There is little question that chaos science will ultimately provide an important contribution. More important for now is the acknowledgement of a different way of thinking and the dependence of computers. For more discussion of chaos science, the Shroeder book *Fractals, Chaos, Power Laws: Minutes from an Infinite Paradise,* is an excellent source.

Marketing Communications Engineering Tools

The key requirement for a tool to be included in the communication engineering kit is that it (1) is computer-dependent and (2) assumes the underlying phenomena to be both non-linear and dynamic. The tools must also have the capability of being applied to typical marketing communications problems, such as building marketing databases, segmenting markets, acquiring and retaining customers, and developing and delivering message strategies.

To date, the best-developed of the tools is the self-organizing neural network which is the subject of the rest of this chapter.

Perceptual Mapping

Multidimensional scaling (MDS) quantifies the perceptions and images that people have about a market, a brand, or any concept by assessing how similar or dissimilar people perceive them to be from various other related concepts. MDS is often called perceptual mapping because, in addition to deriving the perceptual "distances" among brands or concepts, the procedure will plot these concepts as points in a geometric space so that they are visually shown as a picture or a "perceptual map." From this map, the mental picture people have of a particular market or topic area can be easily seen. By interpreting how near or far different points in the map are from one another, insight can be gained into how different brands or concepts are positioned in the audience's mind, and what are the perceived relationships among these concepts.

Designing the most effective messages for an audience in order to strengthen or change their mental image is an important use of MDS. If maps are created and compared for two different audiences, for example loyal customers and the non-loyal or non-customers, it is often possible to find even very subtle differences in their perceptions that explain the differences in their buying behavior, just by the way the points appear to shift within the space from one group to the other. This then leads to the development of a communication strategy that targets differentiated messages towards different perceptual segments.

The creation of a map that lays out the position of one brand relative to another brand or descriptive concept shows the perceptual structure of a market and the positioning of brands within that market. Key competitors would be revealed as those brands which cluster near the brand in question. Marketing communicationss are developed, then, in an attempt to change people's perceptions in the hope that buyer behavior will also change in the desired way. Unfortunately, communication tactics frequently go awry. And when they do, it is often because the marketing strategist did not fully understand how the audience perceived the brand in the first place or how the communication would be perceived by the targeted audience. A marketer has an advantage whenever he or she can visualize—or make a mental picture—of what the audience perceptions actually are and develop message strategies based upon what would drive those attitudes and beliefs about the brand in a positive direction.

To use MDS, the concepts must be selected, and data on how similar the concepts are to one another needs to be gathered in order to construct the map. These data are usually referred to as *similarities* or *proximities data*. Such distance measures are needed for every concept relative to every other concept in a complete pairwise fashion in order to derive more stable coordinates for each in the map.

Developing Message Strategies

It is possible to use perceptual mapping to identify key concepts that might be used in creating alternative message strategies with the purpose of changing the market's perceptions in a desirable way. Galileo can identify the best concept or combination of concepts which, if associated with your brand, should have the impact of moving it closer to the respondent's position. The system can also take advantage of the established connections among concepts as an artificial neural network.

Self-Organizing Artificial Neural Networks

The brain is actually a network of interconnected "neurons." Information is processed through the interactions of large numbers of these neurons, which store and retrieve patterns of information. When a neuron is stimulated, it becomes "active," and sends signals to all the other neurons to which it is connected. Neural networks store information as patterns in the same way that a TV screen or electronic scoreboard does; by activating some of the dots or light bulbs and leaving others off, any pattern can be displayed. Because the neurons in a neural network are connected to each other, the neural network can do more than simply display patterns of information. It can store and retrieve those patterns, and recognize patterns it has stored even if they have been distorted or are incomplete.

In an artificial neural network, products, attributes and people are represented as neurons. Each of these products, attributes and people may be more or less tightly connected to each other. Products that are similar may be tightly connected, so that, for example, activating "airline" in the network would probably activate "United," "American" or "Delta" as well. People can also be represented as neurons—connected to both attributes and products. "People neurons" are connected to attributes that are important to them, and they are more tightly connected to products and services that they buy and use than to those that they don't buy or use. All product development, communication and marketing strategies are essentially efforts to connect a product or service more tightly to people.

In a Galileo system, neurons aren't simply connected or not connected to each other, but instead the strength of each neuron connection is stored. Therefore, if the attribute "comfortable" is connected to an airline such as United, *how* comfortable United is perceived to be is known. A product, service or object does not just belong to a category, it belongs to that category to a certain degree. In a natural neural network, neurons that are tightly connected are typically located close to one another. Hence, it is possible to diagram the connections among neurons or concepts such as people, objects, or attributes, in the form of a map which can portray a picture of the structure of the network.

Using Qualitative Research

Qualitative research, such as in-depth focus group interviews, have long been popular in communications research. However, the interview transcripts could, in the past, only be subjectively analyzed and summarized. Recently, software has been developed that will computer-analyze the interview transcripts and, by content analyzing the words and word sequences used repeatedly within the interview, quantify the strength of word associations in order to create a map of those conversations. The software, CATPAC™ is based on the principal of a self-organizing neural network and patterned after the way the brain works and is now part of the Galileo System.

The program works by designating each word in the text as a neuron (automatically eliminating words such as "the," "and," "but," etc.) and then scanning systematically through the text, blocks of words at a time, looking for word associations. For any two words appearing together in the same block, the connections between those "neurons" are strengthened. Therefore, words that occur in proximity to one another repeatedly become associated in the program's memory. Any words that appear at least twice are identified as key concepts.

Because this is an artificial neural network, the activation of any neuron travels along the connections to all other neurons, and other neurons whose associated words may not be in the window can also be activated. These neurons can, in turn, activate still other neurons, and so on. The program "cycles" through the text, usually more than once, in order to identify the key associations and calculate the strength of each word association. These weights can then be used in the same manner that similarity data is used to create a perceptual map.

One of the benefits of this kind of text analysis is that the program will pick up on words and word associations that even an experienced listener may not be aware of. Whereas in the perceptual mapping procedure described before, the concepts for the space must be derived in advance. In this procedure, the program identifies the key concepts based on what is actually said by respondents.

An example of how CATPAC works using some "pizza data" follows. Exhibit 22.1 shows a text derived from some in-depth interviews where people were asked to describe the difference between a select set of pizza restaurants. Asking people to describe *the difference* between products is usually a good method, since they then usually report attributes which make a difference, instead of attributes which all the products might share.

To analyze these interviews, CATPAC was set to cycle only once, identify no more than 20 unique words, and use a window size of 5 words. Exhibit 22.2 shows the most basic output of CATPAC. It consists of a summary of the parameters selected and a frequency count of the main words found in the text. It shows that there were 115 total words in the text, and that 17 unique words were found. There were 138 windows in the analysis, and 21 lines of text.

The left-most columns in Exhibit 22.2 present the major words in descending order of frequency of occurrence. They show that "Little" was the most frequently occurring word, that it occurred 13 times, which was 11.3% of all occurrences. "Little" appeared in 58 or 42.0% of the scanned windows. This last figure is referred to in the output as a "CASE FREQ" and indicates the number of times a given word appears

---

EXHIBIT 22.1 Pizza In-depth Interview Transcript

I like pizza, hot and fresh. I like quick delivery, like Domino's gives, but I need quality like Pizzahut. Little Caesar's is inexpensive, but I guess Pizzahut has quality. Domino's delivers, but Domino's is expensive. Little Caesar's is inexpensive, and you get two at Little Caesar's. Little Caesar's two for one deal is inexpensive. I like good flavor, like Pizzahut, but I guess Domino's is faster. Sometimes you want it faster, and Domino's is faster. If you want good flavor, Pizzahut is for you, but if you want it inexpensive, Little Caesar's is the best. It's good, Little Caesar's is good, but Pizzahut is good too. Domino's is not as good, but fast. Domino's is fast. I think Domino's has fast delivery, and Domino's fast delivery means a lot to me. Pizzahut's quality is important, but it's not worth it; Little Caesar's two for one is really good. Two for one? Little Caesar's is the two for one place. Pizzahut quality sets it apart, but Little Caesar's is inexpensive. Pizzahut is expensive. But of course Domino's fast delivery can be important. When you want fast delivery, Domino's is the fast delivery place. For inexpensive pizza, Little Caesar's is most inexpensive of all. Inexpensive Little Caesar's is the place for two for one. Little Caesar's two for one. Little Caesar's is inexpensive.

---

in a case. The words "pizza," "faster," and "place" occurred least often, 3 times each. CATPAC didn't consider any words that occurred fewer than 3 times, since that would have resulted in the identification of more than the 20 unique words requested.

Exhibit 22.3 shows the output from a hierarchical cluster analysis. This analysis reflects the information contained in the text quite well. The words "Little" and "Caesar" cluster very sharply together as might be expected. "Domino" and "Fast" cluster very closely, and the word "Delivery" joins this cluster at a slightly lower level (Domino's specializes in fast delivery). Similarly, "Pizzahut," "quality," and "like" form a third cluster. As one moves downward through the diagram, each of the clusters grows larger, including more and more terms. Eventually, the first cluster includes "Domino," "fast," "delivery," "you," along with the subcluster "you," "want," and "faster." Little Caesar ends up in a cluster which includes "little" "Caesar," "inexpensive," and "place" with the subcluster "two" and "one." (Little Caesar offers two pizzas for the price of one).

EXHIBIT 22.2 CATPAC Outputs

Total Words	115	Threshold	.000
Total Unique Words	17	Restoring Force	.100
Total Windows	138	Cycles	1
Total Lines	21	Function	Sigmoid (–1 - +1)
Window Size	5	Clamping	Yes
Slide Size	1		

Descending Frequency List

Word	Frequency	Percent	Case Frequency	Case Percent
Little	13	11.3	58	42.0
Caesar	13	11.3	57	41.3
Domino	11	9.6	46	33.3
Inexpensive	9	7.8	37	26.8
Pizza Hut	7	6.1	35	25.4
Two	7	6.1	32	23.2
Good	7	6.1	28	20.3
Fast	7	6.1	26	18.8
Like	6	5.2	21	15.2
Delivery	6	5.2	26	18.8
You	6	5.2	26	18.8
One	6	5.2	27	19.6
Quality	4	3.5	20	14.5
Want	4	3.5	20	14.5
Pizza	3	2.6	12	8.7
Faster	3	2.6	11	8.0
Place	3	2.6	15	10.9

As in the human brain, the connections between simultaneously active neurons are strengthened following the law of classical conditioning. The pattern of weights or connections among neurons forms a representation within CATPAC of the associations among the words in the text. This pattern of weights represents complete information about the similarities among all the words in the text. Technically, the pattern

EXHIBIT 22.3 Pizza Cluster Dendrogram

```
G   P   D   F   D   Y   W   F   L   P   Q   T   O   L   C   I   P
O   I   O   A   E   O   A   A   I   I   U   W   N   I   A   N   L
O   Z   M   S   L   U   N   S   K   Z   A   O   E   T   E   E   A
D   Z   I   T   I   .   T   T   E   Z   L   .   .   T   S   X   C
.   A   N   .   V   .   .   E   .   A   I   .   .   L   A   P   E
.   .   O   .   E   .   .   R   .   H   T   .   .   E   R   E   .
.   .   .   .   R   .   .   .   .   U   Y   .   .   .   .   N   .
.   .   .   .   Y   .   .   .   .   T   .   .   .   .   .   S   .
.   .   .   .   .   .   .   .   .   .   .   .   .   .   .   I   .
.   .   .   .   .   .   .   .   .   .   .   .   .   .   .   V   .
.   .   .   .   .   .   .   .   .   .   .   .   .   .   .   E   .
.   .   .   .   .   .   .   .   .   .   .   .   .   .   .   .   .
.   .   .   .   .   .   .   .   .   .   .   .   .   .   .   .   .
.   .   .   .   .   .   .   .   .   .   .   .   .   .   .   .   .
.   .   .   .   .   .   .   .   .   .   .   .   .   ^ ^ ^   .   .
.   .   ^ ^ ^   .   .   .   .   .   .   .   ^ ^ ^   .   .
.   .   ^ ^ ^   .   .   .   .   .   .   .   ^ ^ ^ ^ ^   .
.   .   ^ ^ ^   .   .   .   .   .   ^ ^ ^   ^ ^ ^ ^ ^   .
.   .   ^ ^ ^ ^ ^   .   .   .   .   ^ ^ ^   ^ ^ ^ ^ ^   .
.   .   ^ ^ ^ ^ ^   ^ ^ ^   .   .   ^ ^ ^   ^ ^ ^ ^ ^   .
.   .   ^ ^ ^ ^ ^   ^ ^ ^   .   ^ ^ ^   ^ ^ ^   ^ ^ ^ ^ ^   .
.   .   ^ ^ ^ ^ ^   ^ ^ ^ ^ ^   .   ^ ^ ^   ^ ^ ^   ^ ^ ^ ^ ^   .
^ ^ ^   ^ ^ ^ ^ ^   ^ ^ ^ ^ ^   .   ^ ^ ^   ^ ^ ^   ^ ^ ^ ^ ^   .
^ ^ ^   ^ ^ ^ ^ ^   ^ ^ ^ ^ ^   .   ^ ^ ^   ^ ^ ^   ^ ^ ^ ^ ^ ^ ^
^ ^ ^   ^ ^ ^ ^ ^   ^ ^ ^ ^ ^   ^ ^ ^ ^ ^   ^ ^ ^   ^ ^ ^ ^ ^ ^ ^
^ ^ ^   ^ ^ ^ ^ ^   ^ ^ ^ ^ ^   ^ ^ ^ ^ ^   ^ ^ ^ ^ ^ ^ ^ ^ ^ ^
^ ^ ^   ^ ^ ^ ^ ^ ^ ^ ^ ^ ^   ^ ^ ^ ^ ^   ^ ^ ^ ^ ^ ^ ^ ^ ^ ^
^ ^ ^   ^ ^ ^ ^ ^ ^ ^ ^ ^ ^ ^ ^ ^   ^ ^ ^ ^ ^ ^ ^ ^ ^ ^ ^ ^ ^ ^ ^
^ ^ ^ ^ ^ ^ ^ ^ ^ ^ ^ ^ ^ ^ ^ ^   ^ ^ ^ ^ ^ ^ ^ ^ ^ ^ ^ ^ ^ ^ ^ ^
^ ^ ^ ^ ^ ^ ^ ^ ^ ^ ^ ^ ^ ^ ^ ^ ^ ^ ^ ^ ^ ^ ^ ^ ^ ^ ^ ^ ^ ^ ^ ^
```

of connections among neurons is a complete paired comparison similarities matrix, and so lends itself to statistical analyses such as cluster analysis and perceptual mapping.

How the Network Works

Any time a word is in the window, the neuron representing this word becomes active. Connections among active neurons are strengthened so that words occurring close to each other in the text tend to become associated.

When words are present in the scanning window, the neurons assigned to those words are active, and the connection among all active neurons is strengthened. But the activation of any neuron travels along the pathways or connections among neurons, and can in turn activate still other neurons whose associated words may not be in the window. These neurons can, in turn, activate still other neurons, and so on.

Controlling how the network operates involves setting a number of parameters. When a word is found in the window, its neuron is activated, but it can become de-activated again as the network goes through its normal processes—just as an individual sees things, becomes aware of them, and then forgets them. If people never forgot, their minds would become so cluttered with images in only a few minutes that they could not go on with life. When a node is clamped, it is prevented from turning off again. It's like writing a reminder note that the network must always pay attention toward.

CATPAC can simulate four different kinds of neuron functional forms and other parameters: threshold levels, decay rate, and learning rate.

To briefly explain, each neuron is either turned on by being in the moving window or else receives inputs from other neurons to which it is connected. These inputs are transformed by a transfer function. After the inputs to any neuron have been transformed by the transfer function, they are summed, and, if they exceed a given threshold, that neuron is activated; otherwise they remain inactive. Different threshold levels can be set making a neuron more or less likely to become activated.

When an object is seen, neurons that represent that object are activated. When the object is gone, the neurons turn off again. The decay rate specifies how quickly the neurons return to their rest condition after being activated. Raising the rate makes them turn off faster; lowering the rate means they are likely to stay on longer.

When neurons behave similarly, the strength of the connection between them is strengthened. The learning rate is how much they are strengthened in each cycle. Increasing this rate makes the network learn faster.

Self-Organizing Neural Network Simulations

Although the actual functioning of a neural network, like the human brain, can be extremely complicated, in principle the way a neural network works is very simple and easy to understand. A neural network learns by connecting together the neurons that represent any particular pattern. Since they are connected together, when some of them are activated they spread their activation to the others connected to them, which turns on the rest of the pattern. The neurons in the pattern may also be negatively connected to neurons not in the pattern, so that when the neurons in the pattern are active, they tend to turn off all those neurons not in the pattern. Thus, when a network sees part of a pattern, it can recall the rest of the pattern, even in spite of incomplete or erroneous information, as long as enough of the pattern is there to activate the rest.

Exhibit 22.4 shows a network consisting of six nodes representing the words "Cat," "Dog," "Barks," "Howls," "Meows," and "Purrs." Each of the nodes may take on the value "0" (off), or "1" (on).

The nodes are connected to each other by weights that represent their relative "closeness" in the network. They communicate with each other by a simple linear threshold rule. The way a node responds to the set of signals it receives is determined by its activation function.

Following this rule, we assume the network receives the input "Meows" from its environment (i.e., the node which represents "Meows" has been activated). This sets the activation value of "Meows" at +1, and the activation values of the other nodes at 0. Multiplying the weights in each column by the activation values of the corresponding rows, then summing within each column shows that the activation of the node "Meows" will "spread" to the nodes "Cat" and "Purrs", setting their activations to 1, but will leave the nodes "Dog," "Barks," and "Howls" off. Exhibit 22.5 shows that activating the node "Howls", will also activate the nodes "Cat," "Dog," and "Barks". Exhibit 22.6 shows that activating both the nodes "Barks" and "Howls" will also activate "Dog," but will leave "Cat," "Meows," and "Purrs" off.

This example shows clearly that communication among the nodes of the network produces an apparently qualitative change in the pattern recognition and storage capabilities of the network. When the nodes do not communicate, the network can represent a pattern of virtually any complexity when activated directly by the environment, but the complete input is required to produce the complete pattern.

EXHIBIT 22.4 Dog and Cat Network with Meow Input

		Cat	Dog	Input = "Meows"			
				Barks	**Howls**	**Meows**	**Purrs**
	Cat		−.8	−.9	.2	.8	.9
	Dog	−.8		.9	.3	−.8	−.7
	Barks	−.9	.9		.5	−.3	−.9
	Howls	.2	.3	.5		−.2	−.1
+1	Meows	.8	−.8	−.3	−.2		.8
	Purrs	.9	−.7	−.9	−.1	.8	
		on	off	off	off	on	off

When the nodes communicate, however, the complete pattern can be produced with only a partial input. When a sufficient subset of the nodes in a stored pattern is activated, the activation of those nodes will spread through the links and in turn activate the rest of the nodes in the pattern.

It is worth emphasizing the fundamental role communication, as it has been defined here, plays in this process. A pattern is stored by "connecting" its elements together. Things that "go together" are "close." Nodes or elements in turn communicate their activation values to other nodes in proportion to their closeness in the communication network. If a node is "on," it will tend to transmit that "on-ness" to other nodes through the links between them, so that the "on-ness" will spread to other nodes which represent the other elements in the pattern. Similarly, if a node is "off," it will tend to communicate its "off-ness" to other nodes through the links between them. The entire pattern is encoded in the pattern of communication among the nodes as connections or weights, and can be recovered by the activation of any suitable subset of nodes.

All of a network's "memory" is stored in the weights or connections among the neurons. A network learns by setting these weights. One way self-organizing neural networks learn patterns is by a simple Pavlovian conditioning rule: When two or more neurons are simultaneously active, the connection among them is strengthened. This means, quite

EXHIBIT 22.5 Dog and Cat Network with Howls Input

		Cat	Dog	Input = "Howls" Barks	Howls	Meows	Purrs
	Cat		−.8	−.9	.2	.8	.9
	Dog	−.8		.9	.3	−.8	−.7
	Barks	−.9	.9		.5	−.3	−.9
+1	Howls	.2	.3	.5		−.2	−.1
	Meows	.8	−.8	−.3	−.2		.8
	Purrs	.9	−.7	−.9	−.1	.8	
		on	on	on	on	off	off

EXHIBIT 22.6 Activated Nodes

		Cat	Dog	Input = "Howls" and "Barks" Barks	Howls	Meows	Purrs
	Cat		−.8	−.9	.2	.8	.9
	Dog	−.8		.9	.3	−.8	−.7
+1	Barks	−.9	.9		.5	−.3	−.9
+1	Howls	.2	.3	.5		−.2	−.1
	Meows	.8	−.8	−.3	−.2		.8
	Purrs	.9	−.7	−.9	−.1	.8	
		off	on	on	on	off	off

simply, that neurons that have behaved similarly in the past are likely to behave similarly in the future. They receive information in the form of patterns, which they learn to recognize, and which they can recall later. Self-organizing networks develop an internal representation of the information to which they have been exposed. They are useful because one can enter fragments of a pattern the network has learned, even in somewhat distorted form, and the network can recover the original pattern.

Mentioning one or more of these objects (as one would in an advertisement) activates the neurons that represent those objects. These activated neurons in turn activate those other neurons to which they are closely connected, while turning off those neurons to which they are negatively connected. This interactive activation and competition network thus simulates the process by which one or more ideas stimulates still other ideas.

Using the rather simple pizza data analysis discussed previously and shown in Exhibits 22.1 through 22.4, the network simulator shows some interesting results. When the neurons which represent "fast" and "delivery" are activated, the simulator responds "Domino you want faster." When "Pizzahut" is activated, the network responds with "quality," and when "Little Caesar" is activated, the network responds with "two," and "inexpensive place."

Self-Organizing Neural Network Application

Self-organizing neural networks are one example of marketing communications engineering. The rather simple example shows how messages can be developed and evaluated. Not only can better messages be selected, but also wrong messages can be eliminated. Messages can be evaluated over time and/or over multiple exposures and in their true competitive environment—things that traditional methods have been unable to do.

The same technology can also be used to identify and connect individuals described in a marketing database. This kind of application is currently in the experimental stage, but shows great promise. If one is using only the traditional analytical tools at hand, being able to connect the varied media usage data, product purchase data, and other data with the hope of being able to systematically develop marketing communications tactics seems like an impossible dream. With self-organizing neural networks and the related tools not only can the tactics be developed, but they can be developed for an individual customer or prospect in real time. The scheme would be very similar to the simple "Dog and Cat" networks described previously.

It is a short leap to an automated interactive marketing system if the computer can also have the ability to directly communicate with the individual consumer. Whether this will be the Internet or some other communications system remains to be seen, but certainly the application of self-organizing neural networks and marketing communications engineering will make true interactive marketing a reality.

References

Hubert L. Dreyfus, *What Computers Still Can't Do: A Critique of Artificial Reason.* Massachusetts Institute of Technology, 1992.

Galileo User Manual. Terra Research & Computing, Birmingham, Michigan, 1990.

Dominique M. Hanssens, Leonard J. Parsons and Randall L. Schultz. *Market Response Models: Econometric and Time Series Analysis.* Kluwer Academic Publishers, 1990.

David E. Rumelhart and James L. McClelland (eds.). *Parallel Distributed Processing: Explorations in the Microstructure of Cognition, Volume 1: Foundations,* Massachusetts Institute of Technology, 1986.

Manfred Schroeder. *Fractals, Chaos, Power Laws: Minutes from an Infinite Paradise.* W. H. Freeman and Company, 1991.

Claude E. Shannon and Warren Weaver. *The Mathematical Theory of Communications.* University of Illinois, 1949.

John C. Totten and Martin P. Block. *Analyzing Sales Promotion: How to Profit from the New Power of Promotion Marketing.* Second Edition. The Dartnell Corporation, 1994.

Joseph Woelfel and Edward L. Fink. *The Measurement of Communication Processes: Galileo Theory and Method.* Academic Press, Inc., 1980.

CHAPTER 23

The Convergence of Database Marketing and Interactive Media Networks

New Sources, New Uses, New Benefits

Rob Jackson
Paul Wang

Rob Jackson is Vice President of Marketing and Information Services at Donnelley Marketing, Inc., and is President of the Chicago Direct Marketing Association. A frequent speaker, he also writes on database marketing and database enhancement for *DM News* and other industry publications.

Paul Wang is Associate Professor in the Graduate Direct Marketing Program at the Medill School of Journalism, Northwestern University. He also is Technical Editor of the *Journal of Direct Marketing*.

Jackson and Wang are co-authors of *Strategic Database Marketing* (NTC Business Books).

We are witnessing a marketing evolution and revolution. It is an evolution for the consumer and revolution for media and communications. As the two come together in the interactive communications world, database marketing applications move to the center stage in the battle for share of mind, time and the attention of consumers.

The Power of Information Networks

You cannot help but be aware of interactive media in general, and interactive information networks, in particular. In an average month, there are over 3,000 news stories about the Internet, information networks and marketers venturing out into cyberspace. PC owners are accessing on-line services by the millions. By conservative estimates there are more than 5 million individuals accessing interactive media via their computer. Our best example is a nurse we talked to. She purchased a computer and accessed America On-Line because she was tired of dating services and print ads she used to attempt to find "Mr. Right." On AOL, in the chat areas, she met many new friends, including her current boyfriend. Being wired was, for her, a social experience— proof positive, that it is not just computer jocks, but nurses, teachers, children and housewives who are using the new media. Many come and look around, but the question is. . . how many stay and for what motivations? The $64,000 question is, What will it take to get and keep Everywoman and Everyman wired and tuned-in on a ongoing basis? And, once they are on and stay on, what level of commerce can and will be conducted on-line?

The vision and today's reality are still far apart. Many visionaries see the electronic world becoming the center of commerce in the future as retail is today. Some do not agree. Microsoft is determined to position itself as the conduit for all electronic commerce of the future via the Microsoft Network and links to the Internet. The answer lies in understanding very complex dynamics of communications, media, distribution, acceptance of technology and change itself.

Dramatic Changes in Consumers and Media

We must first look at the changes in the consumer and the media that have helped create the dynamic growth in interactive communications. From this change and our observations, we can start to develop models of how to market effectively to the consumer in the electronic world.

Mostly by accident, the traditional mass media has helped create the demand for the interactive world. Nowhere has change been more pronounced than in the communications media. This convergence of media and consumer behavior is best illustrated by today's best mass media successes. For example, one of the top-rated television shows, "Home Improvement", is watched by about 18 million households per episode. But many marketers communicate more effectively via targeted (non-mass) media to 25 or 30 or more million households. For example, Donnelley's Carol Wright Co-op mailings reach 30 million households each month. The envelope-opening rate per thousand household exceeds viewership of the top-rated show. With longer exposure time and more information per advertisement, direct mail in this case can provide better sales punch than mass communication.

Traditional network television is losing its vise grip on the consumer as alternatives become available. Media represents content. Consumers watch because the media has content that they are interested in. Changes in technology have brought changes in control. It was not so many years ago that if you wanted to watch the news, you had to be sure to be home by 5:30, and if you missed it, you were out of luck until 10:00. Then came the VCR which enabled you to tape your favorite program for viewing at your leisure. Content did not change, just the ability of the consumer to exert control on how and when he/she interacts with it. Enter the world of cable and 50 to 100 or more channels, providing the consumer with a significant increase of programming that appeals to almost any special interest and is available at almost any time.

There is, however, only so much news and weather and each must repeat the same thing over and over. The interested viewer comes in and out based upon need, interest, and time. This communications process, however, is only one way. It allows for no interaction between viewer and content provider.

Now, multiply this by the 50 or more stations available to the average wired household. Thus, the media has driven two changes in the consumer. First, it has created a consumer who is overloaded with options and little control which leads to frustration. Second, in the process, we have created an information-aware, almost information junkie consumer who is now conditioned to many options for information and entertainment in the media. There is specialty programming to interest almost any consumer, but no easily available road map to chart, access and control content. The consumer has little control over the content, timing and programming that he/she must choose from and no hope to interact with the content or content providers in a meaningful way. It is no wonder that when presented with the ability to choose content, timing and access that the consumer gravitates toward interactive media applications.

Just as the dynamics of media communications have changed, so has the consumer. With exception of some commodity products, most consumers base their purchases on information. We all search for information before we make purchases. Many products require more information search than others. Consumers expect today's communications to be information based, to help expedite the information search process. If a piece of communication does not provide useful information, consumers will go to other sources to gain the information they require to make an informed decision.

The purchase of an automobile is an example. Until recently, consumers relied on the manufacturer as their primary source of information. This was delivered in 60 second spots, print ads and visits to the showroom. Many consumers no longer accept the credibility of those communications without verification—and they have many sources to turn to other than the manufacturer. From *Consumer Reports*, auto magazines, on-line services and networking to services that provide cost-plus pricing to negotiate the best deal, massive amounts of information are available from third parties. This same process is true for any considered purchase from PC software to a hair dryer and the books and magazines we buy and read. The bottom line is that the consumer has raised the bar on the information required in order to make purchases.

Fundamental Change in Acceptance of Technology

In addition to the convergence of media and consumer change and information delivery level, we are seeing a fundamental change in the average consumer's lifestyle delivered by acceptance of technology. This change has been driven first by the technologically enabled, then the early adoptors and gradually by the consuming public. Cellular phones are a great example. Ten years ago, most cellular phones were limited to CEOs or super sales reps. Today, most are not sold to businesspeople, but to family members. Proliferation of cellular phones has become so great that many areas are being forced to add additional area codes to handle the volume of numbers and activity. Fax machines are another example. As little as five years ago, fax machines were primarily found in offices. Now the fastest growing segment is for home use. Similarly, PC sales have now overtaken TV's in dollars sold each year. It is estimated that by the end of 1995, there will be more than 50 million multimedia PC's in use. We as a society, are gradually becoming more technically enabled and less phobic of new technology.

The Proof is with the Children

The most telling example, though, is our children. Four-year-olds are taking computer classes in pre-school and eleven-year-olds take class notes on laptops and e-mail them to classmates. High school students turn in their papers via e-mail, and most college students are active on the Internet. It matters only a little whether we as today's older generation embrace technology and electronic media; it is already the present for our children. They have embraced technology and on-line communications. The move to full electronic commerce and on-line content usage will be as common and easy as flipping on the TV remote is today.

Characteristics of Information Networks

To learn how to master electronic media, we first must understand how it serves the needs of the consumers who are using it and the dynamics that make it a powerful medium. The information networks have three important characteristics. They are:

- Information networks are a highly effective communications medium.

- Information networks are a significant distribution channel for a wide range of products and services.

- Information networks are sophisticated marketing databases.

Information networks such as Prodigy, America On-Line, CompuServe, and The Microsoft Network effect communications in three important ways. First, they communicate information and entertainment content similar to existing mass media communications channels. You can view news, weather, sports and entertainment of all types: both original content designed and produced for electronic media and content duplicated from existing mass media. Several networks are experimenting with audio and video transmission. Limitations today are down load time for the information to reach the consumer's PC based upon data delivery restrictions. It is inevitable that data compression technology will eliminate this problem and full video/audio will become as common on the information networks as text and graphics are today.

The biggest difference between information networks and traditional media is its fully interactive capabilities. Individuals can customize the information they want from the massive volumes of information available. They can also interact to ask questions, gain in-depth information or target just plain entertainment value. Interaction can be with other consumers, content providers or personalities such as politicians, entertainers, authors and individuals with other specialty expertise— none of which is possible with traditional media channels.

Exhibit 23.1 is a model relating interactive capabilities with capability to deliver compelling content to consumers. The delivery of content is described technically by the term *bandwidth,* which represents the size of the pipeline required to deliver data to the consumer's PC or television. The richer the content (i.e., video and audio data), the wider the bandwidth required. Today the bandwidth available for delivery of interactive data to PCs is limited. In order to provide richer content via PCs, compression technology must advance to deliver richer content, or the pipeline capability must increase to accomplish the same result.

Today, on-line services have great content and strong interactive communications capability with the data. However, given the narrow bandwidth restrictions, there is limited distribution of rich content defined by video and audio transmission that are received in traditional broadcast media. CD-ROMS, on the other hand, have strong video/audio content, but are limited in their interactive capability relative to the amount of data that is captured on the CD-ROM. Interactive broadcast that will come of age in the later 1990's, will have rich capabilities for audio and video transmission, but less interactivity and content than the interactive networks.

The second important aspect of communications is targeted directional communications. The information networks can watch patterns develop in consumer on-line behavior and direct the consumer, on-line, to similar content or related areas of communications value. This

EXHIBIT 23.1 Comparison of Information Density and Delivery Capability

```
 I
 N      H         *
 T      I      On-line
 E      G
 R      H                              Interactive TV
 A                                            *
 C
 T
 I      L
 O      O              *
 N      W           CD ROM

         NARROW ◄─────────────────► WIDE

            BANDWIDTH OR DELIVERY CAPABILITY
```

(INTERACTION)

has important implications for advertisers and marketers. Not only can marketers develop a communications and content center on an information network, but they can also build targeting models that will identify on-line subscribers with propensity for their products/services/information and direct them to their locations on the services.

The third important area of communications is one-on-one message delivery. Via e-mail or network generated communications or advertising communications, marketers can talk to individual consumers in a cost-effective manner. Since each subscriber that entering an information network is tracked by a unique ID code while on-line , custom and targeted messages can be delivered to any subscriber who directs them to content-, interaction- or marketer-sponsored areas. This delivers on the ability to truly implement one-on-one marketing activities.

The information networks are also significant distribution channels. Traditional media have limited ability to directly effect the distribution of products and services. In fact, they are limited to direct response offers and TV shopping activity such as the Home Shopping Network. To purchase a product or service, the consumer must go to another intervening distribution channel, such as Retail, to actually purchase the product or service. Electronic networks offer the opportunity to bypass this process. With detailed information on any marketed product or service, including video and audio, the consumer can gain all the information required to make an informed purchase. Consumers can even purchase their groceries and specify delivery time in some areas of the country. The day is coming when you will be able to enter your on-line department store, stroll down the aisles, stop and browse merchandise, pick it up and examine it in detail, and choose to put it in your electronic shopping cart—or not. The experience will duplicate the traditional retail experience down to the noise in the store. . .except that you will never leave your chair and PC in your home. Information networks and electronic media delivery offer dramatic potential for major change in how we view and implement distribution of products and services.

Information networks are also sophisticated marketing databases. Each on-line consumer is tracked by his/her behavior on the network. Thus, each network knows what content the subscriber accesses, how long he/she stays there and what products/services he/she is interested in or purchase. Marketers who sponsor areas or sell merchandise/services on-line , also know who stops in their area as well as who purchases or inquires. The database allows for significant interaction with a marketer's customers in an on-line environment. This facilitates information search, targeted marketing and relationship marketing, providing customers with a fast way to get help if they have a problem with the product or service they have purchased.

Six Requirements for Developing Successful Applications

There are six characteristics required to develop successful communications and marketing applications on information networks.

- The content must be compelling and take advantage of multimedia presentation capabilities.

- The content must be dynamic in nature.

- The content must be information-rich. It must provide the necessary information and "deliverables" to satisfy the consumer's purchase requirements.

- The content must have high entertainment value. With a high level of competing programming and advertising, a successful application must stand out from the competition.

- The content must be personalized to the needs of the user and his/her interests. It must look like the application was developed just for them, not for thousands or millions of viewers.

- The content must be interactive in nature and delivery.

With these six requirements in mind and a detailed understanding of how to maximize the marketing value of the three key characteristics of information networks, marketers can proceed to develop on-line applications.

Database Marketing Is the Key

Do not start electronic media marketing communications without understanding the power and function of database marketing. Maximizing the value of on-line marketing applications requires a detailed knowledge of the subscriber and that subscriber's propensity towards the purchase of a product or service. Product propensity can be determined by past purchase behavior or by modeling common characteristics between and among consumers and individuals who have exhibited the particular purchase propensity in the past. A marketing database makes the bridge from subscriber to customer.

A marketing database is a collection of data about customers and prospects that effects what and how you sell them. At its simplest, it can be a list. At its most complex, it links together all the information needed to manage a complex business. The process of database marketing communications can be represented by a model that has three phases (Exhibit 23.2).

Identification involves accessing the database to target appropriate customers or prospects. The next step is to develop the appropriate communications effort based upon the requirements of the business and the targeting program. Once the communications program has been completed, the results (consumer response) are recaptured in the database for analysis that will modify the process of selection of customers or prospects for the next communications effort.

EXHIBIT 23.2 Database Communications Model

IDENTIFICATION ——> COMMUNICATION ——> CAPTURE

As explained in detail in our book, *Strategic Database Marketing*, most database applications can be classified into one of three points of entry:

- Capturing and managing historical data—Marketing databases are used primarily to track data captured from tactical marketing programs. Data in the database is usually limited in scope. Applications from the database are limited to tactical programs.

- Marketing intelligence—Marketing intelligence databases build on the data captured in a historical application. The major difference is that customer data is enhanced with other overlay data, and sophisticated modeling techniques are used to provide analysis for detailed decision making capabilities.

- Integrated business resource—This type of database serves as an information resource for the entire business. This is accomplished by integrating all key business information sources or functions in the organization. Examples might include finance, customer service, distribution, inventory, manufacturing, research and marketing.

No matter which database marketing model is correct for a business and its data-driven marketing applications, each requires a combination of three key building blocks. With the three key building blocks, a marketer can build databases as sophisticated or simple as the needs dictate. These building blocks are also the key to the link between database marketing applications and information networks. For a detailed discussion of the three building blocks and how they vary in combination by the three points of entry into database marketing, see *Strategic Database Marketing*.

The three key building blocks are:

- Data—A marketing database is only as powerful as the data it houses. To accomplish effective database marketing applications, the marketer must develop a source data strategy to maximize the collection of the right data for their applications.

- Technology represents the ability to manage customer data and access that data for decision making capabilities. The marketer must learn to harness technology to provide a platform to access the information you collect about customers and prospects.

- Research techniques—Segmentation and modeling techniques complete the final building block. Via research, marketers unlock the power of the data they capture and store.

Each marketing database application will require a different combination of data, research and technology for successful application. First, you must determine the appropriate applications for database marketing for your business. Then, you can determine the data, research and technology required to explain, house and access your customers.

Once you have developed a database application, you can develop ongoing communications programs that maximize the value of your customers or develop new customers. Traditionally this has been accomplished via the communications media of direct mail or telemarketing. Both are highly targeted, one-on-one mediums that can deliver unique messages to a customer or targeted prospect. It is this aspect of database marketing that allows for a perfect match with electronic media applications on information networks.

Linking Database Marketing and Information Networks

A marketing database provides the perfect resource to maximize information network applications. In fact, you can draw many parallel comparisons between the key aspects of data driven marketing and information networks. As with information networks, except in a more limited context, marketing databases allow for control and management of communications with customers. In a database, communications are based upon the relationship that the consumer has with the company. Normally, this is based upon the purchase of a product or service or an inquiry about the same.

The communications effort is delivered via direct mail or telemarketing or some other targeted medium. A marketing database allows for distribution of products and services via mail or other channels instead of or supplementing traditional products distribution. A marketing database can also support other distribution channel efforts. Similar to information networks, a marketing database is the repository for customer information. This includes information collected as a part of the interaction with the customer, or added to enhance the existing information collected about the customer.

Current communications programs are passive based efforts. The standard model of communications is shown in Exhibit 23.3. The seller communicates to the buyer via a medium such as television, print, radio, newspaper or magazines or direct mail and the buyer (consumer) must purchase via an intervening distribution channel such as a retail store. In the electronic network environment, the medium and distribution portions collapse into the medium itself. The network is the communications medium and controls the distribution process for the product or service.

The first level (Exhibit 23.6) represents the current state of the bridge between information networks and a marketing database application. In this model, there is no direct bridge or link between the information network and its subscriber database and a marketer's database. Neither can communicate directly to the other, and neither share data or customers with the other. The best that a marketer can do is to ask customers for their e-mail address if they have one or develop an on-line presence and capture subscriber names and match those to the existing marketing database. The link is used to provide persuasion on the seller's behalf to create interest by a current or potential buyer.

Three Models Bridging Databases and Networks

Three models of the convergence of marketing database and information network for customer communications applications represent three levels of sophistication of the communications and targeting process and the bridge between the information network and the marketing database.

The second level (Exhibit 23.7) represents data sharing and interaction between the information network database and the marketing database. However, this is accomplished in an off-line environment.

In this model, an information network and a marketing database compare files at a third-party location. Each can then determine the overlap between the two. The marketer can then target communications directly to its customers who subscribe to the on-line service, either by on-line communication or by direct mail. The information

---

EXHIBIT 23.3 Passive Communications Model

SELLER<———>MEDIUM<———>DISTRIBUTION<———>BUYER

EXHIBIT 23.4 Electronic Network Communications Model

SELLER<——————>INTERACTIVE<——————>BUYER
NETWORK

**EXHIBIT 23.5 Bridge between Electronic Networks and a Marketing
Database**

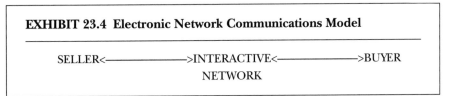

INTERACTIVE   MARKETING
NETWORK   DATABASE

Communications <————————————————> Customers'
Distribution   Purchase Behavior
Database

EXHIBIT 23.6 Level-One Model

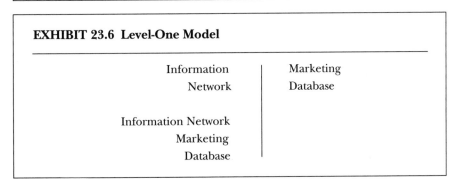

Information | Marketing
Network | Database

Information Network |
Marketing |
Database |

EXHIBIT 23.7 Level-Two Model

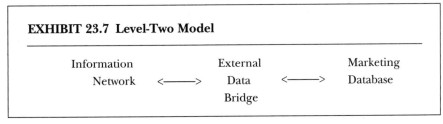

Information   External   Marketing
Network   <———>   Data   <———>   Database
                     Bridge

network can deliver targeted directional messages to the marketer's customers via e-mail and opening screen messages sponsored by the network or jointly with the marketer. Thus level two communications represent targeted dialog between the buyer and seller via the information network.

The third level (Exhibit 23.8) represents a integrated bridge between the information network and the marketing database. Here, the two are electronically linked, matching customers and prospects for individual or joint marketing communications programs. This offers the marketer and the information network the opportunity to provide fully integrated, targeted communications linking the past behavior managed by the marketer and the power of on-line communications delivered by the information network. The process represents full interactive communications based upon dialog and feedback between buyer and seller with the information network as an active partner in the process.

Characteristics of Successful Bridge Efforts

Successful applications bridging database marketing applications and electronic networks must all have several common characteristics:

- They must start with an existing customer base that allows for targeting and tracking opportunities between the marketer's database and the information network.

- They must create an environment that makes commerce and communications more effective for the consumer. They must present an interesting and value-driven alternative to the consumer.

- They must facilitate the coming together of buyers and sellers.

- The communications between buyer and seller must be easily accessible and easily reachable.

- There must be clear benefits that clearly drive the consumer to the electronic network commerce opportunity as compared to current options.

- They must facilitate the sale by making it easy to buy.

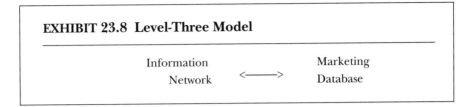

EXHIBIT 23.8 Level-Three Model

Marketing programs developed for this new world of media, distribution and tracking are still basically the same as traditional database marketing applications. They are designed to make and keep customers. If you target your offer correctly, you will make the sale. If you reinforce the sale and keep customers happy, they will buy again over time.

Database-driven programs are customer driven . . . not sales driven. Information networks are and will be powerful facilitators of commerce- and customer-based marketing. We have identified 15 specific applications that can be developed by bridging a marketing database effort with an information network. Each can be implemented by accessing one of the three levels of interaction between a marketer's database and an information network (Exhibit 23.9).

Starting Your Own Database Driven Information Network Marketing Effort

Once you have determined the appropriate database driven information network applications for your business, you must next figure out where to start. We suggest that you start by reviewing, again, the characteristics that we feel are required for a successful effort. First, you must develop and manage a marketing database. It will form the basis for tracking customers and their relationship to your business both inside and outside the electronic media world. Then, based upon the applications of electronic customer marketing that you feel are appropriate, you need to test, test and re-test again. Once you have gained experience with selling/prospecting and communicating with customers and potential customers in the on-line world, you can effectively develop financial and communications models that will facilitate a successful effort.

The model in Exhibit 23.10 represents an example of a test to roll-out grid for entry into database-driven information network marketing.

EXHIBIT 23.9 15 Marketing Opportunities Linking Marketing Database and Information Networks

1. Communications efforts targeted to customers—The most important aspect to database marketing is targeting and reaching customers. By identifying the overlap between a marketer's database and an information network, this can maximize the strength of commerce in this new environment.

2. Prospecting for new customers—By effectively developing information and selling presence in the information network environment, prospecting can be extended to electronic media

3. Delivering communications based upon prior purchase behavior—By capturing and managing prior purchase behavior in your marketing database, a marketer can communicate in the on-line world based upon the consumers prior purchase behavior.

4. Reinforce customer purchase behavior—By communicating with the customer after the sale, the on-line e-mail communications environment allows for cost effective and efficient means to keep customers happy

5. Cross-sell/up-sell and complementary sell—By capturing and tracking a customer's prior purchase behavior, the marketer can sell other products and services to the same customer.

6. Communicate with prospects/customers based upon purchase potential—Communications can be implemented based upon customer potential models. This controls the costs involved with selling a customer and maximizes sales potential

7. Targeted delivery of sales promotion—Delivery of sales promotion based upon customer purchase behavior with no waste due to one-on-one targeting.

8. Increase the effectiveness of multichannel products and services distribution—Tracking provides detailed information on customers and products and equalizes the power of traditional distribution channels over products and goods delivery to consumers.

9. Understand customer/product dynamics via customer interaction By communicating with customers and tracking purchases, the marketer gains invite into the marketing process.

10. Eliminate communications waste and deliver highly targeted communications—By reaching customers with targeted messages based upon information needs and purchase behavior, sales are maximized. Targeted communications represent traditional savings over mass communications efforts in the electronic media environment.

11. Conduct market research—Electronic information networks represent captive audiences for product, customer, media, distribution and communications reach.

12. Provide immediate and personalized customer service—E-mail offers the ability to keep in contact with customers to maximize their experience with the product and service. It identifies problems that will keep the customer from making future purchases.

13. Create integrated communications programs—Information network based programs can provide consistent messages with other customer directed communications and marketing activities. The nature of the medium allows for reinforcement of brand equity and delivery of greater levels of information and reinforcement leading to the sale.

14. Manage customer communications and sales potential—By tracking customers in a marketing database, the marketer can practice customer communications management. In this process, customers that wish to be contacted primarily via electronic networks can be pulled from other communications efforts. In the future, entire customer segments may be managed via different communications alternatives.

15. Reach new customer segments not available with traditional media—Certain customer segments, such as younger consumers, will be more reachable via electronic media than traditional media.

EXHIBIT 23.10 Bridge Testing Model

	FUNCTION					
	ID Customers	ID Prospects	Info. Delivery	Lead Gen.	Sale	Customer Service
MODE						
Test						
Stage 1	X	X				
Stage 2				X		
Stage 3			X			
Stage 4					X	X
Roll-Out	X	X	X	X	X	X

The model represents several stages of testing. First, the marketer tests the ability to identify customers and prospects who are in the marketing database and can be reached by marketing on an information network. At this stage, information can be analyzed to identify characteristics of each group and the overlap. The next step is to use a network to develop leads, communicate with customers and facilitate the information search by consumers. Finally, customers can be moved from other distribution channels to on-line sales and customer service if appropriate. If successful at any testing level, depending upon the nature of the applications you have chosen, the effort can be rolled out to one or more information network environments.

Ultimately, the success of the effort will based on an economic value to customer-based communications for either facilitating the sales process or by selling and delivering via the electronic network. By linking the information network effort to a marketing database, you can match current and new customer behavior patterns and develop payback analysis for your applications. To some degree, getting involved will require a leap of faith. In truth, you may not be able to figure out the payback until you "get there" with your applications, and it may take some time to determine where and when the payback occurs.

Summary

Information networks represent an exciting new world of communications possibilities. However, it is important to remember that all marketing communications are about customers: Creating, keeping and managing customers. If you manage customers effectively, you will create sales. And the key to managing customers is a marketing database. It allows a marketer to cost effectively understand customer behavior and maximize customer value. With this knowledge, the database becomes the bridge to the world of electronic media via information networks. A marketing database facilitates all the key aspects of information network marketing—communications, distribution and data capture. By bridging these, the marketer creates a powerful resource.

The convergence of database marketing and information networks is both an evolution and revolution. It is also an opportunity that is unparalleled in communications and targeting history. The emergence of consumer interest and information networks has created the opportunity for database marketing to play a powerful role in the future of electronic communications.

About the Authors

Cheri Anderson is a doctoral candidate in the School of Journalism and Mass Communication at the University of Minnesota. Currently, she is a research assistant for the Raymond O. Mithun Land Grant Professor. Her research has concentrated on projects relating to interactive technology.

Mickey Bennett is Director of Marketing for Nielsen NorthAmerica's Consumer Information Services Group, which uses personal scanning technology to report purchasing of nondurable consumer goods. He has directed the development of consumer analytic systems, which are used to gain strategic insights from consumer transactional data.

Martin Block is Professor of Integrated Marketing Communications in the Medill School of Journalism of Northwestern University. His research, which focuses on analytical tools and marketing communications technology, has appeared in academic journals and in the business press all over the world. He is author of *Business-to-Business Marketing Research* and (with John Totten) of *Analyzing Sales Promotion.* Block was involved in the early development of QUBE and in National Science Foundation-sponsored research involving two-way cable.

Michael Chamberlain is Director, New Media Activities, of United News & Media, plc, London. He also is Chairman of OIT Limited, a subsidiary company specializing in the creation of electronic on-line sites, including the Internet, fax on demand, and audiotex services.

Vic Cherubini is founder and president of the E.P.I.C. Software Group, Inc., a specialized advertising agency that develops computer-generated sales presentations for its clients. Mr. Cherubini has spent over 15 years in industrial sales and marketing.

William Coble is a doctoral candidate in the School of Communication of Florida State University. His research is concentrated on communication research in interactive communication. Coble was in entertainment marketing and sales for more than seven years, including home video experience with RCA/Columbia Pictures Home Video; interactive television experience with TV Answer (now EON); and cable experience with the Cable Television Administration and Marketing Society (CTAM). Coble contributed information on the historical development of interactive media to the Introduction to this book.

John V. Crosby is publisher of *Turning Points,* a monthly forecast of the U.S. economy. The publication, now in its twenty-seventh year, is one of the fifty primary contributors to the Blue Chip Economic Indicators. His thirty-year career in the semiconductor and microelectronics industries included responsibility for design engineering, product management, operations, software development, and sales/marketing management at both the domestic and international levels. He is author of the forthcoming *Managing the Big Sale: A Relational Approach to Marketing Strategy, Tactics and Selling.* (NTC Business Books).

Richard Cross is President of Cross Rapp Associates, a strategic database marketing company co-founded with Stan Rapp. Cross Rapp Associates' clients include Fortune 100 companies from consumer, business-to-business, nonprofit, and governmental fields. Cross is co-author, with Janet Smith, of *Customer Bonding: Pathway to Lasting Customer Loyalty.*

Tracy Emerick is President of Taurus Direct Marketing, a direct marketing agency and consultancy and President of Receptive Marketing, an electronic mall on the Internet. He is past chairman of the Business-to-Business Council of the Direct Marketing Association and is a director for the Direct Marketing to Business Conference and Business Database Marketing Conference of Dun & Bradstreet. He is co-author of *Business Direct Marketing* and *Desktop Marketing.*

Lucia Fishburne is a doctoral candidate in the School of Communication at Florida State University. Her primary research interests are consumer behavior and new media uses, with an emphasis on music used in a marketing communications context.

Leisa Reinecke Flynn is Associate Professor of Marketing in the College of Business of Florida State University. Her research, which appears in *The Journal of Business Research, Marketing Letters,* and many other journals, is primarily in the area of psychometrics and consumer behavior.

Edward Forrest is Associate Professor and founder and director of the Interactive Communication graduate degree curriculum at the Florida State University. His ongoing projects include multiplatform CD-ROM and CD-I disk production, World Wide Web page-site development, and interactive advertising and multimedia strategy research.

Robert C. Greene, Jr., is Associate Professor in the University of New Brunswick School of Business. He joined academia after a thirteen-year international marketing career. Bob is also the co-owner of A.E.C Chadwick, Ltd., a marketing consulting firm specializing in business development and strategic alliances in the high-technology, interactive field.

Kenneth V. Henderson, Jr., is an adjunct professor of marketing at Florida State University. He previously served in senior marketing management positions in both the financial and consumer packaged goods industries.

Richard S. Hodgson is President of Sargeant House, a Westtown, PA, company that provides direct marketing consulting and catalog development services to companies throughout the world. He also is author of more than a dozen books, including the classic *Direct Mail and Mail Order Handbook*, and hundreds of magazine articles on direct marketing. Dick is a member of the Board of Directors of Foster & Gallagher, Inc., a leading U.S. direct marketing firm, and was formerly a charter member of the Board of Directors of QVC Network, Inc.

Charles F. Hofacker is Associate Professor of Marketing in the School of Business of Florida State University and is President of New South Network Services, an Internet business services company. Hofacker has conducted research on interactive media and other aspects of computer-mediated marketing.

Rocky James is Executive Director, Electronic Media Development and Production, for Communicomp, a full-service direct response agency based in Plantation, Florida. Previously, he was Special Projects Producer for NBC Network News in Burbank and Segment Producer for NBC. James has produced numerous infomercials, including the "Carlton Sheets No Money Down" segment for AMS. His articles on infomercials and TV direct response appear regularly in the business press.

Rob Jackson is Vice President of Marketing and Information Services at Donnelley Marketing, Inc., and is President of the Chicago Direct Marketing Association. A frequent speaker, he also writes on database marketing and database enhancement for DM News and other industry publications. He is co-author, with Paul Wang, of *Strategic Database Marketing* (NTC Business Books).

Joseph M Kayany is Assistant Professor in the Department of Communication at Western Michigan University. He is author of numerous journal articles and convention papers.

Lance Kinney has been in advertising on both the agency and client sides. His primary research interests are in the areas of emerging advertising vehicles and in affective response and attitude measurement.

Thomas W. Hutchison is currently a faculty member in the Department of Recording Industry in the College of Mass Communications at Middle Tennessee State University. His research and consulting efforts include consumer analyses for Geffen Records, including projects on the artists White Zombie, Peter Case, Billy Walker, Jr., Sonic Youth, Weezer, Hole, and many other acts. He has also conducted bounceback card and focus group research for Polydor/Nashville Records and Sony Music/Nashville.

Herschell Gordon Lewis is regarded as the world's leading authority on writing copy that sells. He has written more than a dozen books on the subjects, including *Sales Letters That Sizzle* and, with Carol Nelson, *The World's Greatest Direct Mail Sales Letters.* He is a regular columnist for such publications as *Direct, Direct Marketing Magazine, Catalog Age,* and *SELLING.* He is President of Communicomp, a full-service direct response agency based in Plantation, Florida.

Charles Marrelli is senior copywriter at Modem Media. He was one of the key strategists in the conceptualization and development of Zima.com World Wide Web site. The father of the serialized character, Duncan, Marrelli is a member of the Modem Media creative team.

Daniel Montgomery is Associate Professor and Director of the organizational and Business Communication Program in the School of Communication at Florida State University. He is widely published in the area of organizational change and professional ethics.

John C. Nardone is Account Director for Consumer Products at Modem Media. In that role he manages the overall strategic direction for all consumer-oriented business. He has been responsible for the development of IRIS, the first pricing model that can be used to evaluate media properties on the Internet. Prior to joining Modem Media, Nardone was a product marketing strategist at such leading consumer product companies as Procter & Gamble and PepsiCo. He was responsible for the launch of several new products, including Priviet Vodka, and Stolichnaya Oranj Vodka. He also managed the "New Cola Concepts" group at PepsiCo.

Carol Nelson is Executive Vice President, Communicomp, a full-service direct response agency based in Plantation, Florida. In addition to speaking on marketing and advertising subjects at conferences all over the world, her articles appear regularly in the business press. She also is author of several books on marketing and advertising, including *Women's Marketing Handbook*, which received a 1994 *Choice* award, and *The World's Greatest Direct Mail Sales Letters*, with Herschell Gordon Lewis.

Don Peppers is founder and President of Marketing 1:1, Inc., a firm specializing in relationship management and marketing technology issues. He is author (with Martha Rogers) of *The One-to-One Future: Building Relationships One Customer at a Time*. His and Rogers's' articles about marketing and interactive have appeared in publications around the world, including *Wired, Harvard Business Review, Direct*, and *AdWeek*.

J. D. Rayburn, II is Associate Professor and Director of Graduate Studies in the School of Communication of Florida State University.

Martha Rogers is Professor of Telecommunications at Bowling Green State University and a founding partner of Marketing 1:1, Inc., a marketing consultancy specializing in relationship management, business development, and marketing technology. She is author (with Don Peppers) of *The One-to-One Future: Building Relationships One Customer at a Time*. Rogers's work has been accepted for publication by *Harvard Business Review, Electronic Marketplace, Wired*, and other leading academic and business media.

Janet Smith is a veteran marketing communications consultant and an associate of Cross Rapp Associates. A former marketing manager with Digital Equipment Corporation, she is broadly versed in marketing technologies. Smith is co-author, with Richard Cross, of *Customer Bonding: Pathway to Lasting Customer Loyalty*.

Michael Spalter is an interactive marketing consultant. His work in interactive marketing has been covered in a range of publications including *Business Week, The New York Times, Women's Wear Daily, AdWeek,* and *The Journal of Commerce*. He created one of the first interactive multimedia "marketspaces," hailed as a "new concept in retailing." His clients includes a number of Fortune 500 companies that he advises on interactive marketing.

Paul Wang is Associate Professor in the Graduate Direct Marketing Program in the Medill School of Journalism of Northwestern University. He also is Technical Editor of the Journal of Direct Marketing and, with Rob Jackson, co-author of *Strategic Database Marketing* (NTC Business Books).

C. Edward Wotring is currently Associate Professor in the School of Communication at Florida State University. His research, which includes study of the uses and effects of interactive communication technologies and mass media effects, has been published in such journals as *Interact, Human Communication Research, Journal of Advertising Research, Journalism Quarterly, Journal of Broadcasting and Electronic Media, Communication Research,* and *Journal of Communication*.

INDEX

American Marketing Association

The American Marketing Association, the world's largest and most comprehensive professional association of marketers, has over 40,000 members worldwide and over 500 chapters throughout North America. It sponsors 25 major conferences per year, covering topics ranging from the latest trends in customer satisfaction measurement to business-to-business and services marketing, to attitude research and sales promotion. The AMA publishes 9 major marketing publications, including *Marketing Management*, a quarterly magazine aimed at marketing managers, and dozens of books addressing special issues, such as relationship marketing, marketing research, and entrepreneurial marketing for small and home-based businesses. Let the AMA be your strategy for success.

For further information on the American Marketing Association, call TOLL FREE at 1-800-AMA-1150.

Or write to
American Marketing Association
250 S. Wacker Drive, Suite 200
Chicago, Illinois 60606
(312) 648-0536
(312) 993-7542 FAX

TITLES OF INTEREST IN MARKETING

For further information or a current catalog, write:
NTC Business Books
a division of *NTC Publishing Group*
4255 West Touhy Avenue
Lincolnwood, Illinois 60646–1975 U.S.A.